The Greek and Roman Critics

The Greek and Roman Critics

G. M. A. GRUBE

Professor of Classics at Trinity College
University of Toronto

TORONTO

UNIVERSITY OF TORONTO PRESS

First published in Canada 1965
by University of Toronto Press
This edition 1968
© G. M. A. Grube 1965
Printed in Great Britain by
Robert Cunningham and Sons Ltd
Alva, Clackmannanshire

Contents

Abbreviations used in the Notes and Bibliography

AJP   American Journal of Philology
CP   Classical Philology
CQ   Classical Quarterly
CR   Classical Review
HSCP   Harvard Studies in Classical Philology
JRS   Journal of Roman Studies
LSJ   Liddell and Scott, Greek-English Lexicon, revised
         by Stuart Jones and Roderick Mackenzie
RE   Pauly-Wissowa, *Realenzyklopädie der klassischen
         Altertumwissenschaft*
REG   Revue des études grecques
REL   Revue des études latines
Rh.M.   Rheiniches Museum
TAPA   Transactions and Proceedings of the American
         Philological Association

Preface

The purpose of this book is to provide a clear and reliable account of what the Greeks and the Romans said about literature, and of the development of literary, critical and stylistic theories during the thousand years or so from Homer to the third century A.D. The words criticism and literary theory must be understood in this broad sense, and this saves us from conforming to, or examining, any modern definition of either term. The book is addressed to all those who are interested in the history of criticism; it does not require any knowledge of Greek or Latin; any Greek or Latin word used in the text will by that time be perfectly familiar to the reader or else immediately translated, the only exception being an occasional footnote where the ancient words themselves are in question – if indeed these are exceptions. I hope, however, that the book may be equally useful to classical students and scholars, since this is a field which many of them have neglected.

The Greeks invented most of our literary genres, and their reflections on literary subjects should therefore be, as they indeed are, of considerable interest. In criticism as in most fields of artistic endeavour, the Greeks were the originators while the Romans, whose originality lay in other fields, adopted, adapted and passed on to the Western world the theories of the Greeks. Yet the Roman contribution should not be underrated; they not only transmitted the Greek heritage but made it their own in the process just as their literature, in its period of greatness, was Greek in its forms but essentially Roman in spirit as in language. When we come to Roman times the Greek and Roman critics are contemporaries and should not be studied in isolation from each other.

In this study I have put the main emphasis upon the critical texts which we possess; my aim is to make clear what these critics said and what they meant when they said it. Even this, of course, involves matters in controversy, sometimes of date, frequently of interpretation. When dealing with such matters I have tried to state my own views clearly, and briefly the reasons for them, but I have also attempted to state the nature of other views, and referred the reader in the notes to the works where he will find such other views fully argued and discussed. More than this was not possible if the ancient texts themselves were to receive the attention they deserve.

Where texts are not available I thought it sufficient to indicate the known
general lines of development, and to pay less attention to specialized
particular problems or the elaborate conjectures of modern scholars which
are not infrequently elaborated on very little, and very doubtful evidence.
The less we know, the more we like to guess. I have here also tried,
wherever relevant, to state what the guesses are, and given the necessary
references in the notes. By and large, however, the more doubtful reconstructions of modern scholars are of interest only to those who have
already acquired the knowledge of ancient theories of literature and style
which this book is intended to provide.

Our subject is not clearly defined, nor are its boundaries clearly established. It overlaps with literature, rhetoric and education. This is not a
history of literature, and a general knowledge of the Greek and Latin
literatures must to some extent be taken for granted. It is not the style of
our authors, but their theories of style, which is our concern, though the
two cannot always be divorced and some statements made here no doubt
more properly belong to a history of literature. As for rhetoric, I have
repeatedly emphasized that the term 'rhetoric', to the ancients, included
the whole art of expression at least in prose, so that a good deal of rhetorical
theory applied to all prose literature, and indeed to some extent to poetry
as well. Nevertheless, some rhetorical works – the *Rhetorica ad Alexandrum*
in the fourth century B.C., the more technical works of Cicero, in the
first, those of Hermogenes in the second century A.D., for example – are
concerned with the techniques of the craft of public speaking and of
argumentation in the courtroom. These belong rather to the history of
rhetoric in the narrower modern sense, and will be dealt with briefly, if
at all. As for education, wherever poetry is as essential a part of education
as it was in Greece, or wherever, as in imperial Rome, the art of speaking
and writing *is* the curriculum of higher education, it is clearly impossible
to divorce theories of education from theories of literature, as we shall
find particularly in dealing with Cicero and Quintilian. However, I have
tried not to get too deeply involved in the technical subtleties of the
rhetoricians' workshops, the *officinae rhetorum* as Cicero contemptuously
called them. We must steer our course along the main stream of literary
theory, and be content with the briefest excursions into literature, rhetoric
and education, however fascinating these kindred subjects may at times
appear.

This being my purpose, I have also refrained from specifically discussing
whether the theories of the ancients were right or wrong, whether, for
example, poetry should benefit as well as give delight, and what that
benefit should be, or how far great literature demands technical training
in the art as well as native genius. My opinion on such subjects would

carry no authority and be, I imagine, of very little interest to any reader. Nor have I deliberately drawn any comparisons with modern methods of literary criticism, a field in which my knowledge is very limited. This does not mean that I have studiously avoided expressing opinions of my own or followed the example of the student who, when examined in English poetry, began by stating that he was not going to be trapped into making a value-judgement! Some may think that on matters classical I have expressed myself only too vigorously, and I have made no great effort to avoid expressing here and there other opinions where these seemed relevant. Overall, however, I have tried to simply tell the tale I believe myself qualified to tell and to avoid irritating the reader with irrelevant opinions of mine on other matters.

The bibliography contains only those titles referred to in the notes, and a few of general interest which may or may not have been referred to. On such a vast subject, a complete bibliography would become a book in itself. This, I think, would only confuse the reader. Where author and page only occur in the notes, the reference is to the first work mentioned in the bibliography under that author's name. For the rest, abbreviated but easily recognizable titles, or periodical number and page will make the reference obvious.

I take this opportunity to express my gratitude to the Guggenheim Foundation for granting me a Fellowship for the session 1959-60, which greatly facilitated the completion of this book; to the Princeton Institute for Advanced Study for making me a member of the Institute for that session; and to my college for giving me leave of absence at that and other times. I am also much indebted to a number of colleagues who read parts of this book in manuscript and made helpful suggestions at various times, in particular to the late Robert J. Getty whose unfailing generosity and many kindnesses were a great help to me on this as on so many other occasions.

G.M.A.G.

CHAPTER I

The Beginnings of Criticism

HOMER

Greek literature begins, for us, with the Homeric epic, and, because we know nothing of their antecedents, the *Iliad* and the *Odyssey* seem to us nothing short of a literary miracle. Clearly, however, they must be the culmination of a long poetic tradition which goes back several centuries and presupposes some critical thinking and literary techniques, however empirical. These we cannot recover, nor do we need to go into the complicated questions of date[1] and authorship. For our purpose it is enough to know that, as far as Greece in the Classical Age was concerned, the Homeric epic was there from the beginning, that the Greeks of the fifth century and earlier were brought up on Homer, whose influence was all pervasive in the development of Greek literature and indeed in their whole attitude to life as well as to poetry. The Homeric heroes were the heroes of every schoolboy centuries before Alexander the Great imagined himself a second Achilles and slept with the *Iliad* under his pillow. The Greeks were fortunate indeed that their first introduction to ethics, religion and literature was by way of poetry universally recognized as supreme.

Not the least important part of the many-sided Homeric inheritance is the honoured place the poets occupy in Homeric society. There are no bards in the Achaean camp before Troy, but when the envoys come to beg Achilles to return to the battle, they find him 'delighting his heart with a clear-toned lyre' and 'singing the famous deeds of men', the κλέα ἀνδρῶν. He is reciting, or perhaps even composing, an epic lay.[2] Clearly, poetry and song are not beneath the dignity of the greatest hero of them all.

---

[1] Herodotus (2, 53) considers Homer and Hesiod as roughly contemporary and dates them four hundred years before his time, 'and no more'. This means mid-ninth century. The question has been debated ever since. Modern scholars tend to date the Homeric epics towards the end of the eighth century, the *Odyssey* somewhat later, but there is no unanimity on the subject. Hesiod is then somewhat later still. On the whole question see *A Companion to Homer*, ed. A. J. B. Wace and F. H. Stubbings, especially Ch. 7 (J. A. Davison) and Ch. 3 (Sir Maurice Bowra).

[2] *Iliad* 9, 186–9. φόρμιγγι λιγείη a recurrent epithet applied to the lyre, the voice of an orator or of the Muses. It is always a complimentary epithet, even when applied to Thersites (*Iliad* 2, 246) by Odysseus, who says in effect: 'Thersites, you babbler, though you are a clear-voiced speaker, hold back; do not, all by yourself, quarrel with kings.'

In the *Odyssey* there are two bards, Phemius in the palace of Odysseus and Demodocus at the court of Alcinous. Demodocus is blind – this may be the source of the legend of a blind Homer – and he is treated with every mark of respect. As Odysseus puts it, 'bards are honoured and respected by all who live upon the earth. The Muse taught them their lays; she loves the tribe of singers',[1] and king Alcinous is proud of his court poet (*Od.* 8, 250):

> Come, Phaeacian dancers, the best of you strike up, that the stranger, on his return home, may tell his friends how we excel in navigation, fleetness of foot, dance and song.

As for Phemius, he sings to the suitors in Odysseus' absence, and even that tough company 'listened in silence as he sang the baneful return of the Achaeans from Troy'.[2] When the suitors have been killed Phemius begs for his life, but with no great humility:

> Pity me, Odysseus and respect me. I am a suppliant before you. If you kill me who sing of gods and men, you will yourself suffer for it. I am self-taught, and a god has furnished my mind with many a tale. I will methinks, sing for you as for a god. Do not wish my death.[3]

What makes the bard an object of respect and indeed of reverence is that he is directly inspired by the Muses and Apollo and, by his songs, confers immortality on men. The notion of poetic inspiration has had a long life; to us it is only a rather trite metaphor to express the unexplainable, but Homer meant it literally, and it is this inspiration which accounts for the magic spell of poetry over the hearer, as well as for the ecstasy of the poet.

When Homer invokes the Muses on his own account, everything is inspiration and he speaks as if the poet were but a passive instrument. Even the facts of the story come from the Muses:

> I could not tell of, nor name, the multitude of them, not if I had ten tongues, ten mouths, a voice unbreakable and a heart of bronze within me, if the Olympian Muses, the daughters of aegis-bearing Zeus, did not put me in mind of all those who went to Ilium.[4]

---

[1] *Od.* 8, 479-81. For the respect shown to Demodocus see also 43-106, 248-66, 470-535.

[2] *Od.* 1, 325.

[3] *Od.* 22, 344: σὺ δέ μ' αἴδεο καί μ' ἐλέησον: αἰδώς is the feeling of respect or veneration one feels before the gods or the sense of inner shame one feels when behaving unworthily. The bard, inspired by the gods, is a proper object of αἰδώς. Phemius is asking Odysseus' pity for his plight and respect for his profession. For the poet as dispenser of immortality see *Iliad* 6, 357-8, *Odyssey* 8, 579-80 quoted by Bowra (*Companion* 72) who says: 'This is the nearest approach in the Homeric poems to a theory of poetry.'

[4] *Iliad* 2, 484-94, at the beginning of the Catalogue of ships. Apart from the brief formal

He is not quite so modest on behalf of Demodocus and Phemius. We have just heard the latter claim to be self-taught as well as inspired, and elsewhere we find that the poet sings only when he has a mind to, and chooses a theme at will from his repertory[1] to please his audience. The only aim or purpose of poetry, in Homer, is to give pleasure, and the word ἡδύς pleasant or sweet, occurs at almost every mention of it. Moreover, it is not only the story which is the gift of the Muse, but the words, and the voice as well, i.e. the *sound* of it, that total music of words to which the Greeks always remained highly sensitive. As Eumaeus says to Penelope of the unknown stranger who is Odysseus (*Od.* 17, 518):

> Like a poet who has learned from the gods lovely words (ἔπε᾽ ἱμερόεντα) to sing to mortals who are insatiably eager to hear him whenever he may sing, so he charmed me with his tales as he sat in my house.

And as early as Homer, significantly, the roator in Council is spoken of in the same terms as the poet. So old Nestor is introduced at the climax of the quarrel between Agamemnon and Achilles:

> And Nestor arose among them, the man of pleasing words, the clear-voiced councillor of the Pylians. Sweeter than honey flowed his voice from his lips. . . .[2]

This too is very Greek.

The gift of the Muses then is threefold: the story, the lovely words, the clear and pleasing voice; it is the combination of all three which stirs the emotions, sometimes unbearably as when Penelope asks Phemius not to sing of the return of the Achaeans, or when Odysseus covers his head to hide his tears when Demodocus sings of Troy's fall[3] – a first glimpse of the paradoxical pleasure of tragedy when, as Plato was to put it, 'we feel pleasure and yet we weep'.

The poet can express himself in different kinds of poetry, for Homer already knows of several genres. Epic lays are naturally the most frequently referred to, but there is also the paean in praise of Apollo, the marriage song, the harvest song, the *thrênos* or lamentation. We note that the epic is recited or 'sung' to the accompaniment of the lyre, and the other genres are choral in nature or sung against a choral background.

---

invocations at the very beginning of the *Iliad* and the *Odyssey*, and an equally brief one towards the end of the Catalogue (*Il.* 2, 761), there are only three more, namely 11, 218; 14, 508, and 16, 112. None of these adds anything. Then there is the story of Thamyris who boasted he could outdo the Muses in song and was duly punished for his impiety (2, 594-600).

[1] E.g. *Od.* 1, 347: ὅππῃ οἱ νόος ὄρνυται; 8, 45: ὅππῃ θυμὸς ἐποτρύνῃσιν ἀείδειν.

[2] *Iliad* 1, 247-9: τοῖσι δὲ Νέστωρ | ἡδυεπὴς ἀνόρουσε λιγὺς Πυλίων ἀγορητής | τοῦ καὶ ἀπὸ γλώσσης μέλιτος γλυκίων ῥέεν αὐδή.

[3] *Od.* 1, 337 and 8, 523.

There is also the lay of Demodocus in the eighth book of the *Odyssey* on the illicit love affair between Ares and Aphrodite which is in fact a comic parody of a hymn, thus presupposing the hymn. This reminds us that Aristotle attributed to Homer the *Margites*, a mock epic. At any rate we know that Homer not only laughed at his gods, mighty powers as they were, but also on occasion at his heroes. Homer is of course not concerned to give us a list of poetic genres; they are mentioned incidentally, but obviously they are clearly distinguished. The Greek instinct for analysis and classification was already at work.

Homer also knows, in practice if not in theory, a number of different styles of oratory. We have the very different speeches of Odysseus, Phoenix and Ajax in the ninth book of the *Iliad* as well as countless other examples. We also have the clear contrast between the plain and the abundant styles, as they were to be called later, in the description given by Antenor of the earlier visit to Troy of Odysseus and Menelaus (*Iliad* 3, 213):

> Menelaus spoke briefly.[1] He said little, but that very clearly; he was a man of few words, but these hit the mark . . . when the wily Odysseus . . . raised his mighty voice his words flowed like snowflakes in winter, and no man would rival him. . . .

This passage became a commonplace with the teachers of rhetoric in later centuries. So did many others; for later critics found in Homer many passages to illustrate their theories, techniques and figures of speech, and for the most part they were right to find them there, as it is Homer's word-magic[2] which made him *the* poet for two thousand years, and still one of the very greatest to this day.

HESIOD

When we turn from Homer to Hesiod,[3] the only other early epic poet whose works are extant, we find ourselves in a very different world. Life in Boeotia was much poorer and more primitive than in the heroic world which Homer depicted or the Ionian feudal society in which he probably lived. Moreover, Hesiod's purpose is clearly didactic. The *Works and Days*

---

[1] ἐπιτροχάδην ἀγόρευε does *not* mean 'trippingly, fluently, glibly' as L.S.J. translate, for none of these adverbs suits Menelaus at all, but *succinctly* or briefly. Cf. *Od.* 18, 26, the only other Homeric example, where it probably means: 'how he dismisses the matter in a few words'. The same meaning suits the passages of Dionysius where he uses ἐπιτρόχαλος and ἐπιτροχασμένα, namely *Composition* 18; *Demosthenes* 40 and *Thucydides* 16, though the meaning 'quickly' also occurs, a natural extension.

[2] E. E. Sikes (*The Greek View of Poetry*, p. 3) has drawn attention to the frequent use of θέλγειν in this connexion, 'to charm, to enchant'.

[3] The name Hesiod is here used for the Boeotian school of epic poets where the works attributed to Hesiod certainly originated, whether all of them were written by him or not.

gives moral advice and sets forth the tasks of the farmer at the different
seasons of the year; the *Theogony* deals with the birth, parentage and
powers of the gods, and tries to bring some order into their chaotic
relationships. Yet Hesiod is well aware of the charm of poetry, and, as the
Muses give pleasure to the gods by their songs, so the poet must presumably entertain his hearers as well as instruct them.[1] The poet is here also
the favourite of the Muses, and indeed Hesiod claims a very special
personal inspiration. The Muses, the daughters of Zeus and Memory
(*Theogony* 22):

> ... one day taught Hesiod a beautiful song as he pastured his flock on
> the slopes of holy Helicon. And to me, even me, the Olympian Muses,
> the daughters of aegis-bearing Zeus first spoke these words: 'Rustic
> shepherds, creatures of shame, mere bellies, we know how to utter
> many false things which are like the truth, but also know, when we
> wish, how to utter the truth.'[2] Thus spoke the daughters of great Zeus,
> they of ready speech. They plucked a branch from a flourishing bay
> tree and gave it to me as a staff, a wonder to behold. They breathed
> into me song divinely sweet that I might glorify the future and the
> past; they bade me sing of the race of the blessed immortals, and of
> themselves first and last.

We note, for the first time, the distinction between truth and fiction, both
inspired. There are nine Muses in Hesiod as in Homer, and Hesiod gives
their names (*Theog.* 75):

> Thus sang the Muses who dwelt on Olympus, Clio, Euterpe, Thalia,
> Melpomene, Terpsichore, Erato, Polymnia, Ourania, and Calliope
> who is the eldest of them all.

Except for singling out Calliope, later the epic Muse, Hesiod does not
differentiate them as they were differentiated later when each Muse presided over a different kind of literature.[3] A beautiful voice is still a part of

[1] *Theogony* 37-42, 51, 94-103.

[2] This is sometimes interpreted in terms of rivalry between the Hesiodic and the Homeric
poets (e.g. by Sikes, 6-7), i.e. Hesiod speaks truth while Homer speaks 'lies'. But we have no
reason to think that Hesiod regarded the legends of the Trojan war as unhistorical, or that he
would claim that the *Theogony* was to be taken as literal truth. The contrast seems much more
general.

[3] The usual classification, for us at least, dates from Roman times: Clio as the Muse of
history, Euterpe of lyric poetry, Thalia of comedy, Melpomene of tragedy, Polymnia of the
hymn, Terpsichore of the choral song and the dance, Erato of love poetry, Urania of astronomy.
This one scientific Muse was no doubt a later explanation of her name. The idea of such
departmentalization, however, is much older, as is proved by a tantalizing passage in Plato's
Phaedrus (259 b-d). Referring to the legend that at the birth of the Muses certain mortals,
overpowered with delight, sang night and day, forgetting to eat or drink, Socrates tells how
such persons, at their death, were transformed by the Muses into grasshoppers and how they

the Muses' gift and the wise councillor, more explicitly than in Homer, shares the inspiration of the poet (*Theog.* 80):

> Calliope attends upon kings revered. Whenever the daughters of great Zeus honour with their presence the birth of one descended from god-nurtured kings, they pour a sweet dew upon his tongue, and honeyed words flow from his lips.

The gift of the poet is parallel to this (ibid. 94):

> To the Muses and Apollo we owe the presence on earth of men of song and of those who play the lyre, while the kings are from Zeus. Blessed is he whom the Muses love; sweet speech flows from his lips. When sorrow comes upon a heart unused to grief, and anguish distresses, then the poet, the squire of the Muses, sings the famed deeds of men of old (κλέα προτέρων ἀνθρώπων) and the other forgets his anxiety and does not remember his cares, for the gift of the Muses diverts him.

This claim of Hesiod for equality with kings, or at least with the feudal kinglets of Boeotia, is more vehement than in Homer, more arrogant, perhaps because less securely recognized than was the high social position of poets in Homeric society. In Homer, it is more taken for granted.

Homer and Hesiod are poets, not critics, but they do express an attitude to poetry which is very Greek, and we find in them the seeds of later controversies such as the part of art as against inspiration, whether poetry should entertain or instruct (or both), the theory of literary genres, and the like. Both express the Greek love of beautiful words; in both we find the same emphasis on the voice as well as on the words and the matter; the question of the poet's, or rather the Muses', relation to truth is also raised for the first time.

THE HOMERIC HYMNS

The Homeric Hymns may be considered as a kind of appendix to the old epic poetry. The collection consists of thirty-three hexameter invocations to various gods. Most of them are very short but a few are longish narrative stories about the life of the god they address. They were written at various times, some perhaps as late as the fourth century B.C.

report to the goddesses 'who honours each of them. To Terpsichore they report on those who honour her in the choral dance and thus make them dearer to her, to Erato those who honour her in erotic songs, and so to the other Muses according to the kind of honour due to each, and to the eldest, Calliope, and the next in age, Urania, those who spend their time in philosophy....' What a pity that Plato did not complete his list in detail! For all we know, he may have invented the notion of departmentalized Muses.

Only one passage need be noted here. It occurs in the hymn to Apollo which Thucydides (3, 104) quotes as the work of Homer, and which must therefore be quite old, early seventh century at the latest. It is of interest to us because we find in it the word μιμεῖσθαι used for the first time of artistic 'imitation'. In a description of a festival at Delos, the poet tells us of a choral competition where the Delian maidens, in the service of the god (158):

> first celebrate Apollo in song, then Leto, and Artemis the shooter of arrows. Calling to mind the men and women of old they sing a hymn and charm (θέλγουσι) the tribes of men. They know how to *imitate* the speech of all and they dance to the rattle of castanets. Any spectator would think himself to be singing, so fitting is the beautiful song.

μιμεῖσθαι is here usually taken to refer to mimicry, the imitation of dialects or tricks of speech. Even so, the maidens are imitating the actual, and the performance is praised for its realism. The passage thus foreshadows the later theories of art as imitation.

THE AGE OF LYRIC

The seventh and sixth centuries B.C., the 'Lyric Age' of Greece when personal poetry reached its highest development, is a frustrating subject of study for the student of literature who has to be satisfied with scanty fragments from the great poets of the period; for the student of literary theory and criticism the frustration is even greater. The kinds of poetry multiplied, both monodic and choral, all kinds of lyric metres were dis-covered to express the feelings of the individual which had now become a fit subject for poetry. It is certain that the Greeks' lively, critical and analytic mind was applied to poetry, for these writers were certainly highly conscious as technicians. But only the faintest echoes of this activity are heard in very much later writers. By the end of the seventh century, for example, the Nome (a kind of melody and monody) was carefully divided by Terpander into seven separate parts, each with its own function; other kinds of poetry, the hymn, the paean, the prosodion or poem of thanks, the dithyramb, the epinician ode and the rest[1] were no doubt subjected to similar study. But we find no trace of any theory of poetry or serious criticism.

Poetic contests, already flourishing in the time of Hesiod, multiplied and became a regular feature of the panhellenic and local festivals; they were an early method of publication. Greek artists, like Greek athletes,

---

[1] For the different types of poetry in this period see H. W. Smyth, *Greek Melic Poets*, introduction, and for the nome of Terpander ibid. xiv. For the seventh and sixth centuries generally see A. R. Burn, *The Lyric Age of Greece* (London, 1960).

were highly competitive, and the competition was usually between individuals and for a prize. The poet continued to invoke the Muses and Apollo, but increasing emphasis was placed upon his art and skill, so that poetry became recognized as a craft among other crafts, and Solon could speak of it as among the natural occupations of men: some are merchants, some work the land while 'another who has been taught the gifts of the Muses, knows the measures of the lovely skill',[1] and others again are physicians. It must be during this period too that the word ποιητής, maker, and its cognate ποίησις came to be used without qualification to mean poet and poetry, replacing ἀοιδός, for poetry was coming to be *the* creative skill, though the first example of that usage is not found in our extant texts till much later.[2]

MORAL CRITICISM

In a society where poetry holds a vital place and where education largely consists of poetry and music, the poet becomes a teacher and is naturally held responsible for the social and moral effect of his work. The Olympian gods of ancient Greece had no great concern for the morals of their worshippers. Apart from a few traditional requirements like hospitality, respect for parents, expiation of blood guilt and the sanctity of an oath, their main concern was that proper rites be paid to them. There was no preaching in the temples, and men naturally turned to their poets (the only literature they knew) for guidance in the art of living. Hence the Greeks felt that the poets were the teachers of men, and it was very natural that criticism of poetry should begin as moral criticism, that when men's ideas of the gods became more sophisticated, the Homeric divinities should be the first to draw the critic's fire. Thus began what Plato was to call 'the ancient quarrel between poetry and philosophy'.[3] It was the philosopher-poet Xenophanes who, at the end of the sixth century, first ridiculed anthropomorphism and poured scorn on the gods of the epic. 'Men of sense must hymn the gods with tales of good omen and words that are pure, ... not speak of battles of Titans, Giants and Centaurs, fictions of the ancients.' And again: 'Homer and Hesiod attributed to the gods all things that bring shame and censure to men: theft, adultery and deception.' The same kind of criticism is found in Heraclitus.[4]

[1] Solon fr. 13, 51-52: ἄλλος Ὀλυμπιαδῶν Μουσῶν πάρα δῶρα διδαχθείς | ἱμερτῆς σοφίης μέτρον ἐπιστάμενος. Note that even the gift of the Muse has to be *learned*; the word σοφία means skill in Homer and early poetry, the later τέχνη. The classical poet inherited this claim to σοφία which then meant *wisdom*, and this is the claim which Plato was to dispute.

[2] Sikes, p. 4, points out that the word ποιητής in this sense is first found in Herodotus and then in Aristophanes.   [3] *Rep.* 607 b.

[4] Xenophanes fr. 1 and 11. Cf. also 14, 15, 32 and 34; Heraclitus fr. 40 and 42 (Diels). See also Heraclitus fr. 57 for the first explicit reference to the poet as teacher: διδάσκαλος δὲ πλείστων Ἡσίοδος though he is being ironical, cf. fr. 107.

This concern with the moral and social effects of poetry is quite legitimate; indeed where poetry is a potent social force it is inevitable; it becomes a 'moral fallacy' in criticism only when social and artistic criteria are confused, and we shall see that Greek critics often did confuse them. On the other hand, literary theory which neglects the responsibility of the artist to the community is very incomplete. Art for art's sake is a concept which can only arise when poetry has ceased to have any influence upon society. Certainly all Greek critics were concerned with the influence of literature on the morals and education of the community.

PINDAR

The first fifth-century lyric poet whose works are extant both echoed the criticism of Homer and certainly accepted the moral responsibility of the poet. The odes of Pindar (518-438 B.C.), written for the most part to celebrate victories in athletic contests, are interspersed with moral and philosophical reflections. He also reflects upon the nature and methods of his craft; indeed he has been called 'the earliest European literary critic'.[1] As an aristocrat, he realizes in his own person Hesiod's claim of parity with kings. There is indeed a hieratic tone about his poetry when he writes as a 'prophet of the Muses'.[2]

Pindar claims inspiration from the Muses (sometimes from the Graces, Apollo, or the gods), but he was not the man to think of himself as a passive instrument; with him inspiration is a permanent state rather than a temporary 'possession' by a god; it is nearly identified with inborn talent, which is then directed by the poet himself.[3] He is proud of poetry as the dispenser of immortality, and the magic words of the poet far outlive the deeds which caused them to be written.[4]

The subject must excite the poet to both thought and passion – 'We shall not praise a more glorious contest than Olympia whence the famous song besets the minds ($\mu\eta\tau\acute{\iota}\epsilon\sigma\sigma\iota$) of wise poets.'[5] Pindar expresses the worship of physical prowess and the glory of the great national games. He despises technique and training; everything in poetry is natural talent,

---

[1] By Gilbert Norwood, *Pindar*, p. 165. The whole section: 'Pindar on the Art of Poetry' should be read in this connexion, and I am much indebted to it.

[2] fr. 150 (Sandys).

[3] At *Nemean* 3, 26-29. He calls upon his $\theta\upsilon\mu\acute{o}s$ to 'summon the Muse' – $Mo\hat{\iota}\sigma a\nu$ $\phi\acute{\epsilon}\rho\epsilon\iota\nu$ – to honour the race of Aeacus, and the first person singular is much in evidence, e.g. *Olympian* 9, 22-28. See also *Ol.* 1, 4 where he calls on his $\mathring{\eta}\tau o\rho$ (heart or spirit); *Nem.* 5, 20, etc.

[4] *Nem.* 4 ad init.: 'Wise ($\sigma o\phi a\acute{\iota}$) songs, the daughters of the Muses *charm* as they touch him . . . the word lives longer than deeds; whatever the tongue, by favour of the Graces, draws from the depth of the mind.'

[5] The word $\sigma\acute{o}\phi os$, which he applies to songs, Muses or poets, seems to oscillate between the earlier meaning of skilful and the later meaning of wise. *Ol.* 1, 7-9. Cf., for the effect of the theme on the poet, *Nem.* 4, 35.

and this is in agreement with his aristocratic outlook and his general philosophy of inborn worth.[1]

Because of his high conception of the dignity of his calling, Pindar is much exercised over the relation of poetry to truth, both moral truth and factual truth.[2] He was evidently disturbed by Homer's stories of the gods. He corrects the legend that Tantalus served his son Pelops as food for the gods and exclaims: 'It is not for me to call one of the blessed gods a cannibal. This I avoid.' He seems to wonder that men inspired should tell such false tales:

> The Grace of Song who fashions for mortals all things that are sweet, adds honour to these stories and often causes the incredible to be credited. The days to come are the wisest witness, but I say it is seemly that man should tell noble things of the gods – the guilt is less.[3]

Elsewhere he blames Homer for extolling Odysseus at the expense of Ajax, and declares (N. 7, 22):

> His falsehoods, through winged skill, have dignity. His skill (σοφία) beguiles and leads astray with stories, and the greatest mass of men are blind at heart.

Here he is concerned with the moral effect of untruth, but he himself carefully strives for factual accuracy also, as when he gives (O. 9, 65) the list of victors at the first Olympian games. He seems to feel that 'even inspiration cannot dispense with accuracy'.[4] and is clearly puzzled by the relation between truth and fiction, as others were after him.

Pindar speaks of the 'rule' or 'law' of his odes, and seems to consider it peculiarly his own. This τέθμος seems connected with brevity, with the limits of length or time at his disposal, with the need to leave certain things unsaid, and above all with the part of a story selected for description.

---

[1] E.g. *Ol.* 9, 100: 'All that comes by nature is best (τὸ δὲ φυᾷ κράτιστον ἅπαν); many seek to attain fame by virtues that are taught, but whatever is without (the gift of) gods is no worse for remaining unspoken.' Cf. *Ol.* 2, 86 and *Nem.* 3, 40.

[2] Plutarch tells us some anecdotes which illustrate this problem. There is the story of how Solon went to see a play of Thespis (apocryphal because Solon died about 560 B.C., and the first tragedy of Thespis can hardly have been performed before 535 B.C., *Solon* 29): After the performance, he spoke to Thespis and asked him if he was not ashamed to tell such lies before so many people. When Thespis replied that there was no harm in saying and acting such things in play, Solon struck the ground with his stick and said: 'If we praise that kind of play and esteem it like this, we shall soon find it in our business contracts.' The dramatic illusion is illustrated by the answer of Simonides who was asked 'Why are the Thessalians the only people you cannot deceive?' and replied: 'They are too stupid for me to deceive' (*De Audiendis Poetis* 15 D), and Plutarch continues:
Gorgias said that tragedy is deceit, and that he who deceives is a better man (δικαιότερος) than he who does not, and he who is deceived is wiser than he who is not.

[3] *Ol.* 1, 30-35 and 52-53. Cf. *Ol.* 9, 35-39.

[4] Norwood's phrase (p. 166) to render αὔξεται καὶ Μοῖσα δι' ἀγγελίας ὀρθᾶς (*Pyth.* 4, 279).

He adds that this is understood only by a few, and it seems to be a novelty. The most attractive suggestion as to the nature of this 'law' is given by Norwood:

> He worked in strong reaction against his great predecessor Stesichorus, whom Quintilian compares with Homer, saying, indeed, that he sustained on his lyre the weight of epic poetry. Pindar invented the brief ode – not merely an ode shortened by omissions, a feat too simple for boasting; but an ode shortened by a new manner of handling narrative. Instead of telling the whole story in detail according to the now familiar manner which Stesichorus had inherited from Homer, he selected a highly significant portion and elaborated that by picturesque detail and direct moral comment, giving it structure and climax. . . . In short: Pindar invented the dramatic lyric.[1]

Whether this attractive suggestion be correct or not, we clearly have here a poet-critic, brooding over the technique of his art. In this he was not alone for there are clear traces of lively comment and criticism between contemporary poets in the early fifth century. We have a fragment of Simonides (556-468 B.C.), alleged to refer to Pindar, in which the older poet said: 'The new wine is not yet proved better than last year's vintage', and we find Pindar's answer in the ninth Olympian (47): 'Arouse the clear breath of song, praise old wine but the flowers of song that are new.' We also find two references to crows and jackdaws who chatter below as the eagle of poetry soars aloft.[2] The eagle is obviously Pindar himself; who the crows are we cannot be sure, nor how far either he or they soared above vituperation into criticism. The poetess Corinna, however, came close to it, if we may trust Plutarch's story[3] that she rebuked Pindar in his youth because he didn't tell a story, which was the function of poetry, but concentrated on verbal ornament. Taking her criticism to heart, the young poet composed a song which told a number of stories at once, and Corinna laughed and said, 'One should sow with the hand, not with the whole sack.' If Corinna's epigram is genuine one is tempted to believe it to have been a more general criticism – for Pindar's glittering language at times certainly gives the impression of sowing 'with the whole sack'!

These are but faint echoes of a critical activity which must have been considerable; we may add to them another famous saying of Simonides, that painting was silent poetry, while poetry was vocal painting,[4] and the somewhat later *obiter dictum* of Herodotus that the *Cypria* was not the

[1] Norwood 169-70, where see further details on Pindar's claims to originality. For τέθμος see *Pyth.* 1, 81; 4, 247; 9, 77; *Isthm.* 1, 60; 6, 19; also *Ol.* 7, 88 and *Nem.* 4, 33.
[2] *Ol.* 2, 87; *Nem.* 3, 80-82; see also *Nem.* 8, 20-22 on the dangers of originality.
[3] Plutarch, *De Glor. Ath.* 347 F.
[4] Plutarch, ibid. 346 F (cf. 18 A). The whole passage is worth quoting, though only the

work of Homer, because Paris' journey from Sparta to Troy is there much
shorter, and that, while Homer knew the story of Helen's stay in Egypt,
he preferred not to use it because it was not suitable to the epic,[1] perhaps
the first mention of the notion of appropriateness in literary criticism.
But this is very little.

THE TRAGEDIANS

Nor do we get very much direct help from the tragedians, and yet it is
obvious that the development of tragedy from the *Suppliants* of Aeschylus
to the *Oedipus Coloneus* of Sophocles (the last play we possess, produced
in 401, after the death of its author, who had survived Euripides) cannot
have been an unconscious process or due entirely to differences of temperament. Clearly, Aeschylus, Sophocles and Euripides must have reflected
on the changes they made, and made them deliberately, even though they
may not have realized fully the *ultimate* consequences of these changes.
This was obviously the case in the more obvious reforms, as when Aristotle
tells us that:

> Aeschylus was the first to introduce a second actor; he also made the
> chorus less important and gave first place to the spoken parts. Sopho-
> cles added both a third actor and painted scenery.[2]

or when he tells us later[3] that Sophocles said that 'he made his characters
what they ought to be while Euripides made them what they were'. This
argues a theoretical difference between the two poets as to the proper
function of tragedy.

What Aeschylus meant when he said that his tragedies were 'slices from
the great banquet of Homer' is not certain. If he meant that he took his
subjects from Homeric legends, this is both obvious and only partially
true; if he meant that he took a story from Homer and then gave it a
dramatic structure and significance of its own,[4] the same can be said.

bare statement can be attributed to Simonides with any confidence, and certainly the references
to Thucydides obviously cannot be his:

> Simonides calls painting silent poetry, and poetry painting which speaks, for the actions
> which painters depict as happening, writers narrate and record as having happened. The
> former by means of colour and shape, the latter by means of words and phrases, represent
> (δηλοῦσι) the same things and differ only in the materials used and the manner of their
> imitation (μιμήσεως); both have the same end in view and the best historian is he who
> makes his narration like a picture by an imaginative description of his characters and their
> emotions.
>
> Indeed Thucydides always strives for such vividness and makes his hearer into a spectator;
> he is eager to stir up in his readers the astonishment and anxieties of an eye-witness.

[1] Herodotus 2, 116: οὐ γὰρ ὁμοίως ἐς τὴν ἐποποιίην εὐπρεπὴς ἦν.
[2] *Poetics* 4 (1449 a 15).
[3] Ibid. 25 (1460 b 35).
[4] See Norwood p. 266, note 24. Norwood considers the translation 'slices' misleading

Perhaps he only meant to express his indebtedness in a less specific way, and that debt was indeed considerable, for Homer had shown how to dramatize a story. About three-fifths of the *Iliad* and the *Odyssey* are in direct speech; large sections of the epic could be put on the stage practically without change, and Homer has deservedly been called the 'master of tragedy'.[1] Indeed tragedy united within itself the two chief genres of poetry which Greece had so far developed, the dramatic epic and the lyric. It is foolish to suppose that the great tragedians were not aware of the fact.

Our extant tragedies cover a period of about seventy years. Every classical student can point to the main changes in the form and the spirit of tragedy during that period: the diminishing importance of the chorus, the greater depth of characterization, the increasing realism, and so on. The changes are clear over the period as a whole in spite of differences between individual plays which of course do not conform to so easy a pattern. Some of the changes reflected the outlook of the Athenian society which was itself changing rapidly, and each of the three dramatists does, by and large, reflect a different climate of thought and feeling: Aeschylus reflects the earlier years of the century when the growth of culture was making new and insistent demands upon the old religion; he expresses the new responsibilities which came with freedom from fear of the Persians; Sophocles was thirty years younger and lived his middle years in the great period of expansion and optimism of the Periclean age – 'many are the marvels of the world but none more marvellous than man'[2]; Euripides represents the generation of the Peloponnesian War, the age of the Sophists, the new thought, the new scepticism, the new psychology and humanism. He was only fifteen years younger than Sophocles, and died first, but he obviously represents a later climate of thought. Aristophanes is our witness that the Athenians were very conscious of these differences; we may be sure that they were perceived by the great tragedians as well as by their audience, that they were frequent topics of conversation among a people so intellectually buoyant as the fifth-century Athenians, that plenty of theories were put forward, and that the three poets themselves reflected at length upon their art, Aeschylus and Euripides perhaps even more deeply than Sophocles. One could no doubt try to deduce theory from practice, especially as they not infrequently

because it ignores that a dramatist gives a new structure to the story he may borrow. 'If Aeschylus had meant "slices" he would have said τόμοι, not τεμάχη. τέμαχος, which only in late Greek appears as a synonym of τόμος, meant a slice (of fish) cut off and fried as a separate meal; the frying corresponds to the dramatic treatment of the original story. Aeschylus uttered an epigram, not a stupidity.' The saying is in Athenaeus 8, 347 E: τὰς ἑαυτοῦ τραγῳδίας τεμάχη εἶναι τῶν Ὁμήρου μεγαλῶν δείπνων.

[1] Plato, *Republic* 10 (598 d): ἐπισκεπτέον τήν τε τραγῳδίαν καὶ τὸν ἡγεμόνα αὐτῆς Ὅμηρον.
[2] *Antigone* 332.

dramatized the same legends,[1] but this would be highly subjective if it
were to take us beyond the usual differences discussed in every textbook.

The text of the tragedies gives us very little of critical importance. This
is natural enough, though the reflective nature of the choral odes might
have led to reflections on poetry. This is not the case. There are only two
general references to poetry of any interest in Euripides. In *Andromache* the
chorus is disapproving of two women in the house of Neoptolemus; they
develop the theme by saying that one commander is better than two in
the city, one author better than two to write a song (476); at sea one
middling pilot is better than a pair of wise men. Perhaps Euripides had
unfortunate experiences in collaboration!

The other reference is not in an ode but in the appeal for help which
Adrastus addresses to Theseus in the *Suppliants*; it occurs after a lacuna
(180-3) so that the application of the thought is obscure, though the
meaning is clear.

> So must a minstrel if he composes a poem, be himself joyful; if he is
> not, but is filled with private woe, he cannot bring joy to others.

This is an interesting point: the poet must feel the emotions he wishes to
communicate, a problem we shall see again in Aristotle, and in later critics
who apply it to both poets and orators.[2]

Where the tragedians treat the same story as a predecessor, it is possible
to find implied criticism of the earlier play. Euripides, however, goes
further and on two occasions makes such criticisms all but explicit. When,
in the *Phoenician Women*, Eteocles is planning the defence of Thebes
against his brother Polyneices and his allies, he says that he will place a
chieftain at each of the seven gates, but 'it would take a long time ($\delta\iota\alpha\tau\rho\iota\beta\dot{\eta}$
$\pi o\lambda\lambda\dot{\eta}$) to name each one, with the enemy at the gates. I will go, that we
may not be idle' (751-3). This is obviously a sarcastic reference to the
Seven Against Thebes, where a catalogue of the captains takes a very long
time indeed! (375-676). The criticism is of the slow tempo of Aeschylean
drama,[3] and we shall meet it again.

Similarly, when the old man, in Euripides' *Electra*, says that someone
has made offerings at Agamemnon's tomb, it surely must be Orestes, and
might Electra not recognize him by the lock of hair he left there, since he

---

[1] We have only one example among the extant plays where the same basic plot is treated
by all three tragedians, *The Libation Bearers* of Aeschylus, the *Electra* of Sophocles and the
Electra of Euripides.

[2] In both cases Euripides is accused of bringing in his own irrelevant thoughts. But to a
Greek writer a comparison with poetry is as natural as one with navigation or politics, and in
the *Suppliants*, Adrastus may be saying: 'I cannot make you feel hopeful, being myself in
despair, any more than a poet can communicate a joy he does not feel.'

[3] One may compare Euripides, *Suppliants* 849-50, where criticism of the same scene in
Aeschylus is probably intended.

is her brother, or by his kindred footstep, or by something she weaved for him before he left, Electra dismisses these suggested tokens of recognition as utterly ridiculous (518-43). But they are precisely the tokens which lead to the recognition of Orestes in Aeschylus' *Libation Bearers*. Clearly Euripides is criticizing the older playwright for his lack of realism.[1] The techniques of recognition were probably discussed in Athens long before Aristotle wrote the *Poetics*.

THE SOPHISTS

With the growth of democracy in the fifth century the road to power lay open for the man who could sway the assembly and the law courts where juries often consisted of several hundred men. So a great demand for education arose, especially in the art of speech, and professors of rhetoric naturally sprang up to fill the demand. The study of oratory originated in Sicily where the names of Empedocles, Tisias and Corax are associated with its beginnings. The contribution of Empedocles, whom we know better as a philosopher, is obscure. Corax and Tisias were the authors of the first textbooks on rhetoric, but Aristotle tells us that Corax at least concerned himself only with a study of probable arguments for the guidance of pleaders.[2] This close association of rhetoric with the courts at its very birth should be remembered, for it gave the study of the art of prose a slant which influenced it for centuries.

The professors of rhetoric were soon attracted to Athens, and there gave a completely new direction to the discussion and study of literature. The sophists, as they were called,[3] were all concerned with the study of language since all of them were teachers of the art of speech. Protagoras specialized in grammatical inquiries, the study of moods and tenses, the difference between wish, question, statement, command, etc., and it is probably in this context that we should read his well-known remark that Homer was wrong to address the Muse in the imperative at the beginning of his epics. Protagoras also studied different types of argument, and, if we can trust Plato, he was not above quoting the poets for his own purposes, a common Greek habit.[4] Prodicus' specialty was the exact use

[1] Some modern critics have found this in such intolerably bad taste that they have tried to delete part or all of this passage. See J. D. Denniston's edition of *Electra* pp. 112-15.

[2] *Rhetoric* 2, 24, 11 (1402 a 18).

[3] The origin of the name is obscure, familiar as it is to us in Plato who is responsible for its pejorative sense. Originally the term means 'one who makes wise' or a teacher of wisdom, and we should again remember that σοφία had not entirely lost its earlier meaning of skilful.

[4] For Protagoras' grammatical studies see Diogenes Laertius 9, 52, for the criticism of Homer's μῆνιν ἄειδε θεά and ἄνδρα μοι ἔννεπε Μοῦσα (the first words of the *Iliad* and *Odyssey* respectively) see Aristotle, *Poetics* 19, 5 (1456 b 15), and on quotations from the poets Plato, *Protagoras* 339 ff. On Protagoras generally see, besides Plato's dialogue, D. Loenen, *Protagoras and the Greek Community*. Loenen, however, perhaps exaggerates the importance of his subject.

and definition of words, which endeared him to Socrates. His precise manner of speaking is vividly parodied by Plato in the *Protagoras* (337 a-c) where it is in strong contrast to the flowery grandiloquence of Hippias. The latter was the sophist who appeared at Olympia with everything he wore made by himself. He claimed encyclopedic knowledge and his works included books on grammar and criticism, though his criticism of Homer seems to have paid most attention to the morality of Homeric characters.[1] This indeed was the fashion of the time.

Here we may in passing note two statements of the same period. One is from a short anonymous work of obviously sophistic origin usually dated late in the fifth century. It repeats the statement elsewhere attributed to Gorgias that the best writer of tragedy, like the best painter, is the one whose imitation of reality most successfully deceives, and adds that poets are not concerned with truth but only aim at giving pleasure. The other statement is the famous saying of Democritus the atomist philosopher, that the successful poet is out of his mind, possessed by a god, and that sane poets should be banished from Helicon. This is a restatement of the doctrine of inspiration in its extreme form; it would have pleased neither Pindar nor, one imagines, the tragedians.[2]

The most important sophist, however, was Gorgias of Leontini who came to Athens in 427 B.C. with all the tricks of his rhetorical trade and took the city by storm. He made explicit the claim implied in the teachings of all the sophists, namely that prose-speech was a sister art to poetry. In this they were really reviving a claim already granted, as we have seen, by both Homer and Hesiod, whose orator in council shared with the poets the inspiration of the Muses.

Gorgias was the first theorist of the art of writing prose. Like most originators, he went too far and his name became synonymous with poetical diction and exaggerated mannerisms. The figures of speech mostly associated with his name are the trope, over-bold metaphors, *allegoria* or to say one thing and mean another, *hypallage* or the use of one word for another, *catachresis* or to use words by analogy, repetition of words, resumption of an argument, *parisosis* or the use of balanced clauses, *apostrophe* or addressing some person or divinity, and antithesis.[3] Most of these, as well as homoioteleuta, rhythms and jingles, can be seen in a fragment of a funeral speech – an exercise in the rhetoric of display – and

---

[1] See Plato, *Hippias Minor*, ad init.

[2] The anonymous treatise is known as *Dissoi Logoi*, giving two opposing arguments on every question. It will be found in Diels[6] 2, 90 (pp. 405 ff., in particular 411-12). The statement of Democritus is referred to by Horace, *Ars Poetica* 296, and Cicero, *De Divinatione* 1, 37, 80, also quoted by Diels 2, p. 146.

[3] See Suidas, quoted by Diels under Gorgias, A2; and the *Encomium of Helen* in Diels fr. 11, Gorgias' funeral speech being fr. 6.

a translation will give some idea of the artificial nature of his style, even
without the rhythms and repetitions of sounds which cannot be rendered:

> What did these men lack that men should have? What was present in
> them that should have been absent? Would that I could express what I
> wish, that I could wish what I should, escaping the nemesis of the
> gods, avoiding human envy. Divine was their courage, human but
> their mortality. Many times they preferred gentle fairness to aggressive
> justice, many times right judgement to strict legality. This they thought
> the most divine and universal law: rightly and at the right time to
> speak or be silent, to act or be inactive. Two necessary things they
> practised above all: judgement and strength, in deliberation the former,
> in action the latter. They protected those whose misfortunes were
> undeserved, as they punished those who were undeservedly fortunate.
> Bold when required, angry when seemly, by their mind's intelligence
> they checked the rashness of their strength. Insolent to the insolent,
> moderate to the moderate, fearless before the fearless, dangerous in
> danger. As witness of this they set up trophies over their enemies,
> statues to Zeus, offerings of themselves – not without experience of
> natural combat and lawful love, of armed struggle and the beauties of
> peace, proud in their righteousness before the gods, pious in their care
> for their parents, just in equality to their fellows, devoted in loyalty to
> their friends. They are dead, but our longing continues for them
> immortally, mortal though our bodies be.

The most interesting fragment of Gorgias, however, is his *Encomium of
Helen*, a true ἐπίδειξις or show-piece, for the term *epideictic* seems to have
been used as a critical term precisely to apply to those displays of rhetorical
virtuosity on paradoxical subjects which became a regular practice of the
professors of rhetoric. Later, when Aristotle recognized three kinds of
rhetoric: deliberative, forensic and epideictic, the last division came to
include all that did not fit into the other two, and confusion followed. In
the *Encomium of Helen*, however, a paradoxical subject for a Greek audience if there ever was one, we have epideictic in the true sense, its only
purpose being to display the author's cleverness. Helen is represented as
quite blameless when she followed Paris to Troy, for her flight was due to
one of four causes: it may have been the will of the gods, or she was taken
by force, or Paris persuaded her, or she loved him so much that she could
not help herself. It is in discussing the third possibility that Gorgias speaks
of the power of the Word (*Logos*); he makes a number of remarks of a
critical nature which raise some basic ideas more fully treated by Plato
and Aristotle. Let us look at some of the sections of this remarkable
fragment:

(8) The Word is mighty in its power; its body is small and invisible but the deeds it performs are divine. It can *end fear*, remove pain, bring joy, *increase pity*. . . .

We note the power of speech to rouse the emotions, and the special reference to pity and fear as well as what Aristotle was to call 'other such emotions'. The power of *Logos* over men became a commonplace of the schools.

(9) But one must also give proof to satisfy the mind. All poetry I believe to be metrical speech (λόγον ἔχοντα μέτρον). Upon those who hear it comes a shudder of *fear*, tearful *pity* and a longing for lamentation; through words the soul comes to feel a sorrow of its own at the good or ill fortune of others. . . .

As *Logos* means speech in general, we have here the claim that prose and verse differ only in the latter being metrical; the emotions associated with tragedy can also be aroused by oratory. We note that the contriver of *logoi* must satisfy the mind as well as appeal to emotion. Here we should remember that *Logos* refers to content as well as words. It means reason as well as speech. The emphasis on tragedy is natural since it was *the* poetic art form of the day.

(10) It is through words that inspired songs bring pleasure and chase away pain. The power of song, together with the soul's judgement, persuades and moves as if by magic. Magic is based on two things, errors of soul and deception of the mind.

(11) How many men have persuaded others, and of how many things, by fashioning a false argument. If all men remembered the past, understood the present and foresaw the future the Word would not be what it is now, but, as it is, it easily influences those who do not remember the past, examine the present or divine the future. . . .

The aim of *Logos* is pleasure; it is not concerned with truth; indeed its power lies in exploiting the failings, mental and emotional, of men. This is the amorality of the rhetoricians which disgusted Plato. It is true that Gorgias goes on to blame the persuader of evil, but that, one feels, is due to his paradoxical subject: he has set out to exonerate Helen, so he must lay the blame on Paris.

(12) The Word which persuades the soul compels it to believe what is said and to praise what is done. The one who persuades is the wrongdoer, for he uses compulsion – it is vain to blame him who is persuaded. He is compelled by the Word.

One remembers that in the *Gorgias* of Plato (436 d – 457 d), Gorgias says that rhetoric is an instrument which requires skill and training for its use, but that the teacher of rhetoric is no more to blame for its misuse than the teacher of fencing is responsible if his pupil uses his acquired skill to commit murder. When pressed, however, he contradicts himself there also, for he admits casually that if any pupil should come to him who does not know good from evil, he will, of course, teach him that too.

(13) ... we must learn the compelling contests of arguments in which one argument delighted and persuaded a great multitude, *because it was composed with skill, not because it was spoken with truth*. ...

(14) The power of *the Word is to the soul as medicines are to the body*. As different medicines draw out different humors from the body and bring an end now to disease and now to life, so it is with words; some bring pain, some joy, others fear, others again make men bold, while some by evil persuasion drug and bewitch the soul.

The parallel with medicine is noteworthy, for Plato and Aristotle both claim that philosophy heals the soul. Hence Plato's concern in the *Gorgias* to show that the analogy is false: rhetoric is not analogous to medicine but to cookery, its aim is not health but pleasure.

Enough has been quoted to show the tantalizing nature of this fragment; if Gorgias reflected deeply on the ideas here barely mentioned he must have had theories on the nature of language. After reading it we also can understand Plato's attitude better. It makes us wish Gorgias' book on the art of speaking were extant. To it probably belongs the advice, approved by Aristotle, that when your opponent is in earnest, you should undermine his effect by making the audience laugh, but be serious when your opponent is playful.[1] Yet Gorgias' book might well disappoint us, for Aristotle also tells[2] us that the methods of education of Gorgias and other rhetoricians was thoroughly unscientific and consisted almost exclusively of making their pupils learn certain set pieces by heart. The brilliance of even the great sophists was superficial; they taught how to be successful on an intellectual level parallel to that, in our own day, of courses on 'how to win friends and influence people', only in their case it should be phrased 'how to persuade people and be somebody in your city'. All later references to Gorgias are to his stylistic excesses; there are none to his methods of teaching.

The most important name among the next generation of sophists is Thrasymachus of Chalcedon. He seems to have paid even more attention

[1] *Rhet.* 3, 18 (1419 b 3). [2] *Soph. El.* 34 (183 b 36).

to rhythm, and to have favoured paeonic feet at the beginning and end of clauses, so that, Cicero tells us, his prose was apt to break up into rhythmic *clausulae* to the point of monotony. He wrote on methods of arousing pity and was masterly at playing upon the passions of an audience. Presumably in opposition to Gorgias, he attempted to develop a prose diction which was neither too poetical nor too colloquial, and he had a talent for organizing his thought and expressing each point succinctly and clearly before passing on to the next. This is the same Thrasymachus whom we meet in the first book of Plato's *Republic* as the apostle of might as right.[1]

Because they helped to undermine the traditional values of Athens, the sophists provoked the anger of Aristophanes. Plato despised them because of their shallow thinking and also because, although they claimed equality with the poets as artists and as teachers, they refused to accept any moral responsibility for what they taught. The strictures of the comedian and the philosopher are justified from their point of view, yet they should not blind us to the very real contribution of the sophists.

In teaching rhetoric they filled a real need. To the traditional education which consisted mostly of physical training, music, and poetry, they added the study of language both grammatical and stylistic, as these two aspects were not yet differentiated. The Athenians were well prepared for such study; they knew their Homer and their tragedians[2]; they had listened to great orators in the assembly. The conscious theoretical study of what they had practised for so long must have fascinated them, and this helps to explain the success of Gorgias. From now on Greek writers knew what they were doing and did it deliberately (did this contribute to the decline of poetry?). One can exaggerate the influence of theory upon practice but the great prose writers of the fourth century, from Thucydides on, were unusually deliberate artists. Few would deny that the influence of Gorgias, and of rhetorical theory in general, upon the tortured

[1] For Thrasymachus on rhythm see Aristotle's *Rhetoric* 3, 8, 4 (1409 a 2) and Cicero, *Orator* 39, and 174-5. For his stirring the passions, *Phaedrus* 267 c-d. He is usually credited with originating the periodic style on the authority of Theophrastus as quoted by Dionysius of Halicarnassus, *Lysias* 6. As he shares the quality there described with Lysias, and in *Lysias* 8 that orator is specifically said *not* to write in the periodic style, the usual interpretation of the earlier passage is clearly wrong; I believe that the quality attributed to both him and Lysias is a certain compactness in the expression of ideas. In another passage of Dion. of Hal., namely *Demosthenes* 3, Thrasymachus is supposed, again on the authority of Theophrastus, to be the originator of the middle style, but I believe what is in question in that part of the Demosthenes is not style as a whole (i.e. diction *and* word-arrangement) but only diction or the choice of words. For a full discussion of these passages, and of Thrasymachus generally, I refer the reader to my article in *AJP* 73 (1952), 251-67. Theodorus of Byzantium is a third name often coupled with Gorgias and Thrasymachus, but of him we know practically nothing. See also below, p. 213 and note 3.

[2] How familiar the Athenians were with their tragic poetry is shown by the story told by Plutarch (*Nicias* 29) that some of the Athenians enslaved at Syracuse in 412 B.C. earned their freedom by reciting choral odes from the plays of Euripides.

style of Thucydides and the smooth, balanced period of Isocrates, or that the sophists, and Gorgias in particular, were in large part the originators of that conscious search for the best form of expression which culminated in the supreme artistry of Plato[1] and the nervous power of Demosthenes. Moreover, by linguistic analysis and exegesis, they also contributed to a fuller understanding of poetry itself,[2] though not, it seems, to the making of it.

[1] The deliberate care of Plato is illustrated by the story told by Dionysius of Halicarnassus (*Composition*, 25) that, when Plato died, tablets found among his belongings showed how he had tried many word-orders for the simple sentence which begins the *Republic*. (Cf. Diog. Laert. 3, 37.)

[2] *Protagoras* 338 e, where the sophist is made to say: 'I think, Socrates, that skill in dealing with poetry is a very important part of a man's education. By this I mean that he should be able to understand what is correctly composed and what is not, and that he should know how to distinguish between the two and, when asked, be able to account for the distinction.' The criticism of poetry was a regular part of the sophists' stock in trade. Cf. *Prot.* 347 a and *Hippias Minor* 363 c.

CHAPTER II

Comedy: Aristophanes

The only extant examples of fifth-century comic drama are the comedies of Aristophanes so that we have no standard of comparison, but his claim to have introduced a new type of comedy[1] may well be justified, for his plays are not only supremely clever comedies of situation, but also social satire of a very high order. He does not hesitate to lampoon the foibles of individuals, but the central idea of his great comedies concerns the community as a whole. The exploitation of the Athenian allies, war and peace, the Athenian fondness for litigation, the position of women in society; each of these provides the subject of at least one comedy. In fact Aristophanes was as able a dramatizer of ideas in his own medium as Euripides was in his, and his old rival Cratinus coined the word εὐριπιδαριστοφανίζειν[2] 'to write like Euripides and Aristophanes at once', thus implying, one presumes, that the comic poet wrote like his old enemy even while criticizing him.

In view of the important place of poetry, and of tragic drama in particular, in the social life of Athens, it was entirely natural that comedies of this nature should pay considerable attention to poetry and drama. Literary allusions, criticisms and parodies abound throughout, and Aristophanes clearly expected his audience to recognize them, to an extent quite impossible on our own comic stage. Moreover, two whole comedies have literary subjects: the *Thesmaphoriazusae* which satirizes Euripides, and the *Frogs* with its contest between Aeschylus and Euripides for the Chair of Tragedy in Hades; there are also several literary scenes in the other plays. We do not, of course, expect impartial judgements from Aristophanes, but his criticisms are often acute and he incidentally formulates a number of critical principles which we meet here for the first time.

He was also the first, as far as we know, to give clear expression to the old Greek feeling that poets are teachers. As Aeschylus puts it in the *Frogs* (1054-5): 'Children are taught at school, but poets are the teachers of men', and Aristophanes willingly accepted this responsibility for himself. He does not hesitate to criticize the policies or leaders of the nation. In the *Acharnians*, Dicaiopolis, who has made a separate peace with Sparta, begins his defence (498) with an appeal to the spectators not to resent the

---

[1] *Clouds* 518-62; cf. *Knights* 507-50.   [2] Cratinus fr. 307 (Edmonds).

discussion of public affairs on the comic stage and in the parabasis of the same play (the Chorus traditionally addresses the audience on behalf of the poet in part of the parabasis) Aristophanes claims that his frank and disinterested criticism and advice benefit the city (630-64). Twenty years later, with the self-confidence of an established reputation, he boldly suggests that the Athenians who had been disfranchised after the oligarchic revolutions should be reinstated so that all Athenians together could fight side by side to save their city.[1] Although such completely serious passages are rare, even in the parabasis, yet a serious undercurrent is common enough below the surface of uproarious fun.

There is an interesting literary scene in the *Acharnians*, the first real attack on Euripides. Dicaiopolis wants to look as pitiful as possible when pleading his case, and he has the brilliant idea of borrowing from Euripides some of the rags in which Euripidean characters so often appear; he goes to call on him with this purpose in mind (393-489).

The slave who answers the door has obviously been infected by his master's subtlety of speech when he says that Euripides is 'within and not within', by which he means that the tragedian is upstairs but his mind is away gathering ideas. Dicaiopolis is lost in admiration, finally secures an audience and persuades the poet to lend him rags 'from the old play'. Does he mean Oineus? No, somebody much more beggarly. Phoenix? No. Philoctetes? Bellerophon? Neither. It must then be Telephus. The rags are brought out. Dicaiopolis, pleading the tough assignment before him, then asks for the cap, the staff, the tin cup, until Euripides exclaims in dismay: 'You're taking my whole tragedy, man!'

The main criticism here is of the realism of Euripides which, as some thought and think, degraded tragedy from the heroic to an everyday level.[2] There are also incidental parodies of the poet's sophistic subtleties.

The famous attack on Socrates in the *Clouds* is mainly an attack on the rhetorical education of the sophists, with which the real Socrates had nothing to do, but Aristophanes brings in philosophy, the new poetry, Euripides, the new music and cheerfully lumps them all together.[3] So Strepsiades has to submit to grammatical studies and worship the new philosophical gods. Then the great debate between the right and the wrong *Logoi* is full of Euripidean echoes. The quarrel between Strepsiades

[1] *Frogs* 686-705.

[2] A typical comment by R. C. Jebb in *The Growth and Influence of Classical Poetry*, p. 223: '... the light of common day was let in upon the tragic stage, with disastrous results for dramatic effects.'

[3] At 316-18. The 'idle men' ἀργοί who worship the Clouds are the philosophers; among the gifts of the new goddesses, γνώμη and νοῦς are clearly philosophic terms, and διάλεξις probably Socratic, whereas τεράτεια, περίλεξις, κροῦσις are rhetorical. This is shortly to be followed by quotations from the new poets. And so on, with a good deal of Socratic vocabulary, e.g. ψυχή (319), διαιρῶν καὶ σκοπῶν (742).

and his son started when the boy, being more modernly educated, wants to quote from Euripides instead of from old Simonides or Aeschylus.[1] He then argues from animal life in the manner of the younger sophists, to justify the most outrageous conduct.

We need not endorse Aristophanes' condemnation of it all, but he was to a large degree justified in linking together these different aspects of the new thought, for they all challenged tradition, whether social, political, religious, educational, musical or literary. And he was certainly right to see in Euripides the representative of the new scepticism on the tragic stage.

In the *Thesmaphoriazusae* (The Women at the Thesmaphoria) Euripides has discovered that the women are plotting vengeance on him for all the dreadful things he has said about them. He wants a spy on the premises. He comes to ask Agathon, the younger tragedian, whom we also meet in Plato's *Symposium*, unbearded as he still is, to attend disguised as a woman. He finds Agathon's slave about to sacrifice before his master begins to write, and the slave calls upon all men and all nature to be silent; for Agathon of the beautiful words (καλλιεπής) is laying the keel of a new play; he is turning new words on the lathe, rounding them off, etc. etc. Euripides waits while the younger man comes out and sings a choral ode for women, a pretty invocation to the gods.

The whole effect is of preciosity and effeminacy. Agathon is even dressed as a woman (148):

> I wear clothes to go with my thoughts; a poet must adjust his ways to his compositions. If he writes a play for women his body must share their ways . . . what we have not, *imitation* (mimêsis) will hunt up for us.

These words inevitably lead to some very dubious jokes, but there is a serious point in this buffoonery, namely the need for a dramatist to identify himself with his characters, to think their thoughts and adopt their ways, and also that the nature of the poetry depends upon the nature of the poet.[2]

Later in the play, when Mnesilochus has accepted to spy on the women (and has had to be shaved for the occasion), been discovered and put under guard, Euripides tries to rescue him and each attempt parodies a situation in a Euripidean tragedy, namely in *Palamedes*, the *Helen* and the *Andromeda*. Now parody does not necessarily imply condemnation or even criticism, but it can be a powerful critical weapon, and Aristophanes was a past master in its use, especially the parody of situation. The most

---

[1] Note how scornful the young man is of Aeschylus' 'bombast': ψόφου πλέων, ἀξύστατον, στόμφακα, κρημνοποιόν (1367).

[2] 167: ὅμοια γὰρ ποιεῖν ἀνάγκη τῇ φύσει, a principle here burlesqued by suggesting that this is why the plays of Phrynichus are beautiful, those of Theognis frigid, and so on.

superb example is at the beginning of the *Peace*. Euripides, in his *Bellero-phon*, had made his hero ride up to heaven on the winged Pegasus. How he managed this on the stage we do not know for we do not have the play. In Aristophanes, Trygaeus, fed up with the war, decides to ride up to heaven too to remonstrate with Zeus on the state of Greece. As *his* Pegasus he is fattening up an enormous beetle, and we see him starting up upon it with many a quotation from the *Bellerophon* (so the scholiasts tell us). To the astonishment of Hermes, and ours, he actually gets there. The whole scene is uproariously funny. We cannot tell how deadly the parody was, but here and elsewhere Aristophanes seems to be ridiculing Euripides' original attempts to enact impossible situations, his love of novelty and his bold stage-experiments. The chief purpose of these parodies is obviously to amuse, but their success requires an audience thoroughly familiar with the originals.

Shortly after the death of Euripides, Aristophanes produced the *Frogs*. It is the most important critical document we possess from the fifth century, and probably the most amusing in the whole history of criticism. Dionysus, the god of tragedy, visits Heracles, who, as an old traveller to the underworld, may be able to give him useful hints; he explains that he has been reading the *Andromeda*[1] and has decided to go down to Hades to fetch Euripides back, for he was a skilful poet ($\pi o\iota\eta\tau o\hat{v}$ $\delta\epsilon\xi\iota o\hat{v}$, 71). Heracles asks what's wrong with those now living, and they review them briefly. What of Iophon, the son of Sophocles? Well, he's the only good thing left but we cannot be sure yet. Why not fetch back Sophocles instead of Euripides? We'll just wait and see what Iophon is like on his own; besides, Euripides is such a clever rogue, he'll find ways to help in his escape, whereas Sophocles was always such an easy-going fellow.[2] Where's Agathon? He's left us to join the banquets of the blessed; a pity, he was a good poet and his friends miss him. Xenocles? Pythangelus?

Heracles: Aren't there other little lads writing innumerable tragedies, more loquacious than Euripides by a mile?
Dionysus: Yes, tiny grapes not worth the picking, mere chatterboxes; they produce one play, befoul tragedy once, and are never heard of again. You won't find a creative poet, look where you will.

[1] The *Andromeda* is not extant, but it was very popular in antiquity. It seems, to have been a tale of romantic love, an unusual subject. See Lucian, *How To Write History* ad init.
[2] Sophocles died after Euripides, not long before the performance of the *Frogs*, and this is usually thought to account for the little notice which is taken of him in this play. Actually, however, three antagonists would have been awkward. In any case the contrast between Aeschylus as the representative of old Athens (he had died half a century before) and Euripides as the representative of the new is much clearer and more dramatic. Sophocles was not an easy butt of comedy, and references to him in the comedies are very few.

Heracles: How do you mean, creative?

Dionysus: By creative I mean one who will venture some such bold
phrase as 'Ether, halls of Zeus', or 'the foot of time', speak
of a mind unwilling to take a sacred oath, the tongue
having forsworn itself without the mind.

Heracles: You like these things?

Dionysus: I'm quite crazy about them.

Heracles thinks they're all nonsense, but as Dionysus rudely reminds him,
he is hardly an expert: 'You teach me to eat.'

The whole scene makes clear that Aristophanes, who had ridiculed and
satirized Euripides on the stage for over twenty years, fully recognized his
genius and unhesitatingly classes him with Aeschylus and Sophocles as one
of the three great tragedians of Athens. That verdict has never been disputed. We should note that in this scene there is no question of any moral
judgement.

After a number of ludicrous adventures Dionysus has arrived in the
underworld, and it is now suddenly discovered that a great contest is
being prepared. In Hades every craft has its recognized master who dines
at Pluto's table. Aeschylus was the master of tragedy, but Euripides, who
has lately arrived, is terribly popular with all the knaves and rogues who
make up the demos of the underworld, and is challenging him for the
Chair of Tragedy (τραγωδικὸς θρόνος, 709). As for Sophocles, he reveres
Aeschylus and will only enter the lists if Euripides should win. They were
lacking a competent chairman, but who more appropriate than the god of
tragedy, Dionysus himself?

So the great contest begins. It puts before us two different views of
poetry and tragedy which are perennial and irreconcilable. True, the
differences between the two tragedians are due, in part, to the difference
of date. The tempo of Aeschylean tragedy was already archaic by 405 B.C.
and so was a good deal of his language, while the rhetorical techniques
of Euripides belong to the age of the sophists. Yet the plays of Aeschylus
were still greatly admired and could be produced in competition with
living dramatists, a privilege which, in 405, had been granted to no other
dead poet. Essentially, however, the conflict goes much deeper, for it
illustrates the opposition of the romantic idealist to the realist, the former
believing that many true things are better ignored, the latter that the
truth, the whole truth, is ultimately beneficial. This opposition extends to
both matter, language, and style. The grand manner of Aeschylus requires
dignified, stately language; the realism of Euripides inevitably uses everyday speech. It is part of Aristophanes' greatness that, in spite of all his
prejudices in favour of Aeschylus, he could see the greatness and the
attraction of both.

There is a preliminary skirmish (814-74), prayers and preparations (875-904), a general engagement (905-1098), and then three separate assaults on specific points, namely the use of the *prologos* (1119-250), prosody and music (1251-363), and diction (1364-413).

The preliminary skirmish touches on points more fully debated later; it also contains Aeschylus' one witticism. He is, he says, at a disadvantage because his own plays survived him, while those of Euripides died with him and are therefore readily available in the Underworld!

The two contestants then each say a prayer. Aeschylus prays to Demeter, while Euripides invokes his new gods: Aether, the Twisting Tongue, and the Upturned Nose.

The first point of attack is the slow tempo and choral nature of Aeschylean tragedy. Some character, be it Achilles or Niobe, stands there veiled while the chorus sing a string of odes, and the audience wonder who it may be. Then, when the play is half over, he speaks a dozen tremendous words which no one understands. As for Euripides (939):

> When I took over from you our art, swollen with bombastic words and heavy phrases, I had to take some weight off her first and put her on a reducing diet of light verse, exercise and white beets, and give her chatterjuice strained from my books.

His characters, he goes on, name themselves right away; they do things from the first, and all of them talk, woman, slave, master, maiden or old crone. 'That is the democratic way. I taught all of them to talk', and they all know the techniques of talking. Their actions too are of an everyday sort which the audience understand, and so can check for themselves. But this is precisely what disgusts Aeschylus.

Euripides agrees that a poet should be admired 'for his skill, his advice, *and because we make men better*' (1009). This, says Aeschylus, is precisely what his own martial plays do, whereas Euripides, with his immoral plots, his Phaedras and Sthenoboeas, makes them a good deal worse. And here comes a famous passage (1052):

Euripides: Do you mean that my story of Phaedra is untrue?
Aeschylus: No by Zeus. It certainly is true, but the poet should veil depravity, not teach it by bringing it on the stage. *Children have schoolmasters to tell them, the poets are the teachers of men.* Therefore we should speak what is good.

Fine themes and fine words to suit them, that is the poet's function. And he mentions again Euripides' beggars in rags, the everlasting chattering and questioning which everybody apes nowadays instead of exercising in the gymnasium.

Up to this point Aeschylus' criticisms are based on moral grounds, while Euripides' are artistic, for even he could hardly attack the moral effect of Aeschylus' plays (perhaps the real Euripides might have done so, but Aristophanes certainly would not). Having agreed that poets are to be commended for poetic skill *and* moral teaching Euripides has dealt with the former, Aeschylus with the latter.

From now on, however, we are mainly concerned with artistic criteria, and specific points.

First the *prologos*, i.e. that part of a tragedy which precedes the entrance of the chorus. Using the new methods of exegesis developed by the sophists, Euripides makes two charges against Aeschylus: obscurity and tautology, and proves them both. He shows that the first lines of the *Libation Bearers* can be interpreted in two different ways, and that there are two unnecessary words in three lines (1126). Aeschylus' counter-attack is also twofold. The first point is trifling, namely that Euripides should not speak of 'once happy Oedipus', for he was wretched from birth. The second is much more important, and its comic effect is shattering. He gets Euripides to quote the first lines of several plays and fits in the phrase 'and lost his oil-flask' within the first sentence, e.g. (1205)

> Euripides: Aegyptus, as our common legends tell,
> Sailed with his fifty children o'er the seas,
> Arrived in Argos ...
> Aeschylus: ... Lost his flask of oil.

The process is repeated half a dozen times, with any play Euripides cares to choose. The effect is very funny, but what does it mean? A Euripidean drama usually begins with a straight narrative to acquaint the audience with the story, or the particular version of it which the poet is adopting. Now in a straight narrative, neutral in emotional tone, a half line consisting of verb and object can before long be fitted in. The choice of the oil-flask, so common a piece of personal property in Greece, breaks the tragic dignity; it might just as well (as Aristophanes himself tells us at 1203) have been a blanket or a lunch kit. Aeschylus seems to mean that the Euripidean *prologos* stands outside the play and is in fact too much like a prologue in the modern sense, and also perhaps that the rhythm is monotonous, with frequent pauses in the middle of the third foot. This criticism, though it is often undeserved, has been repeated in almost every textbook.[1]

The second specific criticism concerns the lyric metres of the two poets. Euripides criticizes the monotony of Aeschylean lyrics; they can almost be reduced to one and he reduces the major part of a number of lines to

---

[1] 'Euripides' might have made a better defence. Where the first speech of the play is more emotional, the oil-flask trick doesn't work, e.g. *Alcestis* or *Medea*.

the last four-and-a-half feet of a Homeric hexameter.[1] Aeschylus replies by condemning modern variations in music and rhythm, of which he gives a number of examples from Euripides. The details are obscure but the main intention is clear. He then goes on to compose a parody of a Euripidean lyric monody. The meaning of this seems to be that the younger dramatist wastes great poetry on paltry subjects. 'A poor spinning girl lost her domestic cock and wishes to search the cottage of her neighbour Glyce whom she suspects of stealing it. That is all. But it is sung in strains that might befit a falling dynasty or some tremendous catastrophe of nations.'[2] Euripides here again is accused of debasing tragedy.

The third and last attack concerns the diction of the two poets, and it is judged by the comic device of bringing out scales and weighing the lines which the two adversaries throw into them. This is broad farce and the result is a foregone conclusion: the words of Aeschylus are the weightier. There was no need here for a serious judgement, only to point to the difference.

What is remarkable is that at the end of this prolonged contest Dionysus refuses to choose (1411):

> My friends, I am not going to judge between these men, for I don't want to be the enemy of either. I think the one so clever, and I like the other so.

With another abrupt change in the plot, Dionysus *now* tells us he came down to Hades to fetch the poet who would give the best advice to the city. After hearing them both, Dionysus still is unable to choose and finally decides on the basis of his own feelings only, and chooses Aeschylus.[3] Aristophanes could hardly have made it clearer that both are great poets, and that no choice is possible on aesthetic or artistic grounds. This is indeed a compliment to Euripides, after persecuting him on the stage for nearly a quarter of a century.

In this remarkable contest, which is the last critical scene in Aristophanes, it should be noted that both sides hit the mark and that, for all his pre-

---

[1] This is the interpretation of Benjamin Rogers in his edition of the *Frogs*, xxv-xxix.
[2] Ibid. xxxiv.
[3] That the decision is not made on artistic grounds is clear from the passage just quoted. But, in spite of what many commentators say, it is not made on the grounds of the advice they give either, and this is more surprising, for here (i.e. as a teacher of men) one would have expected Aeschylus to win. Yet at 1434, *after* Aeschylus' advice that one should not rear a lion's whelp, but, if one has, it's better to yield to him Dionysus says he is still in doubt (δυσκρίτως ἔχω) because Euripides' advice is so clever (σοφῶς), Aeschylus' so clear (σαφῶς). After more obscure suggestions, Pluto presses for a decision, and Dionysus says he will choose the one whom he *likes* best – ὃν ἡ ψυχὴ θέλει. This means exactly the same as τῷ δ' ἥδομαι in 1413, and the decision is therefore explicitly subjective, it is based neither on poetic merit nor on moral-didactic grounds.

judices in favour of Aeschylus, the comic poet is a remarkably impartial judge. Here and elsewhere he uses a number of critical terms not previously used in our texts.[1] Moral judgements are intermingled with the artistic, but the two are not really confused. As the critical ideas here dramatized are expected to be appreciated by the audience, it is clear that they must have been topics of conversation in Athens at the time.

The notion of *mimêsis* or imitation so amusingly ridiculed in the scene with Agathon, for example, was probably no invention of Aristophanes,[2] though the particular application of it obviously was; and with this goes the idea that the poet must identify himself with his characters, that the nature of the poetry depends on the nature of the poet, as also that the poet must feel the emotions he wishes to arouse. Incidentally, the impression we get of Agathon 'of the beautiful words' is one of preciosity, and is entirely compatible with the Agathon of Plato's *Symposium*.[3] The criticisms of Euripides in particular, of his realism, his sophistic diction, his non-dramatic prologue, and the like, have been repeated in every textbook ancient and modern.

How far was Aristophanes original in all this? We cannot be sure, for no other comedies of this period have survived. The available fragments show quite clearly that poets and poetry were frequently mentioned on the comic stage, and that quite a few comedies had literary subjects, but we know nothing of the plots. Epic legends were obviously burlesqued, the by now archaic language of the epic and the solemn language of older tragedies were frequently ridiculed. Opinions were often expressed about poets, but the standard of criticism in the fragments is no higher than the well-known encomium of Sophocles in Phrynichus' *Muses* (produced in competition with the *Frogs* in 405) which states that Sophocles was happy indeed, lived a long time, and wrote many lovely tragedies,[4] or the fragment of Philemon a century later which says that if the dead have perception 'I'd gladly suffer hanging to see Euripides'. Aristophanes' dislike of modernistic music with its trills and variations, is echoed by others, and the most interesting of these fragments is from Pherecrates,[5] who

---

[1] Among the words used by later critics which are first applied to literature by Aristophanes we find, for example, ψυχρός, frigid, in *Thesmaph.* 170 and 848; ἀστεῖον, probably in the older sense of elegant rather than that of witticism, in *Frogs* 901 and elsewhere; εἰκών, image or simile (?), ibid. 906; στωμυλία and στωμύλλω, ibid. 1069-71 and 1310; στοιβή, padding, ibid. 1178; στόμφαξ, bombastic, in *Clouds* 1367. See on this subject J. D. Denniston in CQ 21 (1927), 113-21.

[2] In *Thesmaph.* 155, quoted above, ἃ δ' οὐ κεκτήμεθα μίμησις ἤδη ταῦτα συνθηρεύεται the word μίμησις seems dragged in, as if it were a semi-technical term slightly misused. We shall see the word reappearing in contemporary Socratic conversations recorded by Xenophon (see p. 37).

[3] For all we know about Agathon see P. Lévêque's *Agathon*.

[4] Fragm. 31 (Edmonds).

[5] Fragm. 145 (Edmonds).

represents Mousikê complaining at length of the indignities she suffers at the hands of recent lovers. Yet there is no indication in the extant fragments that other comic writers showed any critical acumen to compare with Aristophanes. On the other hand, it is well to remember that such fragments as we have from lost plays of Aristophanes himself give us no indication of critical genius either.[1]

Nor do the fragments of fourth-century comedies add very much. Antiphanes (c. 388-311 B.C.) approaches criticism when he deplores the fact that contemporary poets no longer write their own music, and by contrast praises Philoxenus:

> Philoxenus stands out among all poets, in the first place his words are everywhere his own and new; then, his tunes are full of suitable variations. He was like a god among men; he knew what music really is. . . .[2]

And the well-known (fr. 191) complaint of a comic poet:

> Tragedy is altogether a blessed thing to write; to begin with, the plots are known to the audience before a word is said, and all the poet has to do is to remind them. 'Oedipus' says he, and they know all the rest: his father Laius, his mother Iocasta, his daughter, his sons, what will happen to him, what he has done. Or again, let someone say 'Alcmaeon', and right away he's aware of his children, that he killed his mother in a fit of madness, and that Adrastus will come on in a fury, go away again and come back.
>
> And when tragedians have nothing more they can say, and their plots have collapsed, they raise the machine[3] – as easy as lifting a finger – and the audience is quite satisfied. Our situation is entirely different; we have to invent everything: new names, new plots, new speeches, the past and the present, how things will turn out and how they began. If a Chremes or a Pheidon omits any of this, he is hissed off the stage, but a Peleus or a Teucer may do so.

---

[1] For a thorough examination of the fragments of comedy from the point of view of literary criticism see G. W. Baker's 'De Comicis Graecis Litterarum Iudiciis'. For the collected fragments: J. M. Edmonds, *The Fragments of Attic Comedy*.

[2] fr. 209 (Edmonds).

[3] The accusation that tragedians bring on the *deus e machina* for no other purpose than to get them out of difficulties with their plots is also found in Plato's *Cratylus* 425 d: 'Unless, like the tragedians take refuge in bringing on the gods when they have got into difficulties. . . .' It is a casual reference and neither passage should be interpreted as a serious accusation, since both are humorous. Yet it has been taken seriously and repeated *ad nauseam*, especially against Euripides, who makes greater use of the *deus e machina*. Actually, he brings in the gods at the end of plays for quite different, and much more worthy, reasons. See my *The Drama of Euripides* (London, 1941; repr. 1961), 73-78.

It seems very unlikely, however, that any later writer of comedies reached Aristophanes' stature as a critic. It is true that such fragments as we possess come from the works of later antiquarians who selected passages to explain rare words, or, as in Athenaeus, some rare dish, which explains in part why references to cooks and fishmongers are so very numerous in our comic fragments. If remarks of real critical importance had been frequent in later comedies, it seems very unlikely that no record of them would have survived, since many of the comedies themselves did survive into Roman times. We may therefore conclude that the combination of comic genius with acute critical insight which we find in Aristophanes was not repeated.

CHAPTER III

Thucydides, Socrates, Isocrates

Within a year of the performance of the *Frogs* the Athenians had lost the war against Sparta, and that defeat marks a turning point in Greek literary history. As Aristophanes had realized, the great days of tragedy had ended with the death of Euripides and Sophocles. And Aristophanes himself may be said to have outlived himself: he went on writing comedies until his death in the middle eighties but his heart was no longer in it. The parabasis has disappeared in the two comedies still extant from this period and the choral part is restricted to vanishing-point. The *Ecclesiazusae* is a last and not very successful attempt at social satire, while the *Plutus* already belongs to the Middle Comedy which has no political colouring or personal invective. It is often said that the fifth century is the century of poetry and the fourth the century of prose, and to this comedy is not really an exception for its verse came as close to prose as poetry can do.

There is an opposite exception, however. History is the one prose genre which reached its highest development in the fifth century. Herodotus probably completed his History of the Persian Wars shortly after 431 and Thucydides was writing his account of the Peloponnesian War during the last years of the century. He probably died about 400. Herodotus does not indulge in any theoretical discussion. He begins by stating only that he is publishing the results of his investigation ($\iota\sigma\tauo\rho\iota\eta$) in order that the great deeds of both Greeks and barbarians, and the causes of the war, shall not be deprived of their due fame. The historian, like the epic poet, whose descendant he feels himself to be, is the dispenser of immortality. Herodotus was a great traveller, and it is being increasingly recognized that in practice he took great pains to establish the facts in that vast picture of events which he draws, and that, in spite of certain weaknesses as in the field of military strategy, he deserves his title of the father of history.

Thucydides, however, is as conscious and deliberate an artist in his own genre as Pindar and Aristophanes were in theirs, and explicitly concerned with its aims and methods. He is anxious to differentiate his conception of history from that of his predecessors, including Herodotus. The famous chapters in the first book (20-22) where he does so are in effect a statement of the historian's duty, the only such statement from classical Greece.

He begins by showing the inadequacy of oral tradition, his example being that of the Athenian tyrannicides Harmodius and Aristogeiton (here Herodotus' account agrees with his, V, 55); then, after correcting errors in Herodotus on a couple of other matters, Thucydides describes his own practice:

> Most men take no great pains to discover the truth and accept the common version of events, but my reader will make no mistake if he believes, from the evidence I have given, that the events were such as I have described them. He should not put more trust either in the poets who celebrate events by magnifying them or in story-tellers who compose their work to please their audience rather than to give a truthful account. He will realize that absolute proof is impossible where the lapse of time has successfully turned most events into legends, but that the account I have given, based on the clearest available evidence, is satisfactory in view of the fact that these things happened long ago.

Thucydides is here speaking of the past, even the distant past. He claims that he, unlike his predecessors, has examined all the available evidence, and given as probable an account as possible. Story-tellers, λογόγραφοι was a term often applied to earlier historians, including Herodotus. The latter's fondness for a good story is well known, but it is not always realized that in preserving these stories, even when he does not believe them, Herodotus has at times preserved information of value, whereas Thucydides, trusting his own valuation of the evidence, gives what he considers the true account, but rarely the evidence on which it is based, or the evidence he has rejected, which might be of value to us.[1]

He then turns to his main theme, the Peloponnesian War which he himself lived through:

> I know that men always believe that any present war in which they may be engaged is the greatest ever, and then, when it is over, they think the wars of old more deserving of wonder, yet I think that those who analyse the actions of this war will clearly realize that it came to be the greatest of them all.

Thus he comments on the importance of his subject. Then comes the famous passage:

> As for the speeches made on each occasion either before or after hostilities had begun, it was difficult both for me, where I had heard them myself, and for my other informants to recall precisely what was

---

[1] This point is well brought out by W. P. Wallace in *Phoenix* 1964, pp. 251-61.

said. I therefore recorded what, in my opinion, each speaker needed to say ($\tau\grave{a}$ $\delta\acute{e}o\nu\tau a$)[1] in the particular circumstances, while at the same time I kept as close as possible to the general trend of what was actually said.

As for the actions of the war, I did not deem it right to rely on any chance source of information or on my own impressions, but I have sought to attain the greatest possible accuracy in recording each of the events which I had myself witnessed and those reported to me by others. I found this a difficult task because eye-witnesses gave different accounts of the same actions according to the nature of their sympathies or of their memory.

The absence of an element of romance in my account of what happened may well make it less attractive to listen to, but all who wish to attain a clear view of the past, and also of the same or similar events which, human nature being what is it, will recur in the future – if these people consider my work useful, I shall be content. It is written to be a possession of lasting value, not a work competing for an immediate hearing.

The last two paragraphs deal with events and the meaning is plain. Thucydides lays upon the historian the duty to sift his evidence most painstakingly, to allow for bias, and to mistrust the memory of eye-witnesses, including his own. Nor must he repeat unreliable stories, however attractive. One may feel that the historian did not always live up to this himself, that, for example, he did not make sufficient allowance for his own bias against Cleon in the Sphacteria affair, but the theory at least is clear and beyond dispute.

This is not quite the case with what he says about speeches, which has been the subject of prolonged controversy.[2] We should note first that he

---

[1] $\acute{\omega}s$ δ' $\ddot{a}\nu$ $\acute{e}\delta\acute{o}\kappa o\nu\nu$ $\acute{e}\mu o\grave{\iota}$ $\ddot{e}\kappa a\sigma\tau o\iota$ $\pi\epsilon\rho\grave{\iota}$ $\tau\hat{\omega}\nu$ $\grave{a}\epsilon\grave{\iota}$ $\pi a\rho\acute{o}\nu\tau\omega\nu$ $\tau\grave{a}$ $\delta\acute{e}o\nu\tau a$ $\mu\acute{a}\lambda\iota\sigma\tau$' $\epsilon\acute{\iota}\pi\epsilon\hat{\iota}\nu$. Both Gomme in his *Commentary* and Andrewes in his *Phoenix* article translate $\tau\grave{a}$ $\delta\acute{e}o\nu\tau a$ as referring to form and not matter, i.e. 'They are written as I thought each speaker would most fittingly speak about the particular occasion . . .' (Andrewes). This seems to me somewhat perverse, and I agree with Grosskinsky (*Das Progamm* p. 33, quoted by Andrewes) that this is not the natural meaning of the Greek. Moreover, it is surely admitted that the manner and style of the speeches is Thucydides' own. What Thucydides is saying is that he puts into the speaker's mouth the arguments which the particular circumstances call for, and that when he has received a reliable report he sticks to the general trend of the actual speech. In any case, most speeches would naturally be relevant to the circumstances, and therefore include most of $\tau\grave{a}$ $\delta\acute{e}o\nu\tau a$. For the use of this word we may compare Plato, *Phaedrus* 234 e, where the expression $\tau\grave{a}$ $\delta\acute{e}o\nu\tau a$ clearly refers to content in contrast with manner and style.

[2] A very full discussion of the text of ch. 22 will be found in A. Grosskinsky's *Das Programm des Thukydides*. See also Gomme's *Commentary* pp. 140-50 (vol. 1), and A. Andrewes' 'The Mytelene Debate' in *Phoenix* 1962, 64-85. Many other useful references will be found in all three authors. For the style of Thucydides' speeches and their relation to the contemporary love of debate, see Jacqueline De Romilly's chapter 'Discours antithétiques' in her *Histoire et Raison* pp. 180-239. Gomme holds the view that Thucydides did try to report the general

does not even conceive of writing history without speeches; they are essential to the genre and he accepts from Herodotus the Homeric inheritance of dramatization through direct speech. A modern historian would not think of introducing a speech unless he had a verbatim report at hand, but this limitation is quite foreign to the ancients. Thucydides, however, here also departs from precedent by imposing two limitations upon himself. What is said must be entirely suitable to the particular circumstances: he will restrict himself to what each speaker *should* have said (τὰ δέοντα), taking all the circumstances into account. And further he will *as far as possible* restrict himself to the general argument of the actual speech. This must mean that where he has had a fairly full report he will give us the main trend of the argument, though he feels free to add something here and there which *should* have been said. Clearly, in those cases, it was possible to give an account generally faithful to the original. Obviously, this second limitation cannot apply where the historian did not receive a reliable report of the speech actually made, or only the barest outline. He would no doubt be faithful to this outline, but fill it in as he thought fit, and, where no reliable report was available at all, he would presumably feel free to invent the kind of speech which *he* would have made, under all the circumstances. None of this, of course, refers to the *style* of the speeches, which is Thucydidean throughout.

The theory seems fairly clear. How far Thucydides lived up to it is for students of the historian to decide. He obviously did not believe that his predecessors observed these limitations, either in their speeches or in their account of the facts. Most readers of Herodotus (the only text we have for comparison) would agree with him and assume that Herodotus would not have claimed for his speeches even the kind of historical truth which Thucydides claims for his, though of this we cannot be sure.[1]

Thucydides' account of his method is the more important in that it was neglected by the historians of the next two centuries who, after Xenophon, seem to have had no great respect for historical truth, and received too rhetorical a training to accept limitations on speeches, which would have

tenor of what was actually said, while Andrewes thinks that he did so more faithfully in the earlier part of the History, less in the later part, the Melian dialogue being an example of free composition. (One might argue, however, that Thucydides might not have considered the Melian dialogue as speeches within the meaning of 1, 22, or that his limitations do not apply where he wants to dramatize by direct speech a situation where no speeches were actually made.) De Romilly tends to the theory of free compositions, and see her *Thucydide et l'impérialisme* pp. 203-59 for a full discussion of the Corinthian and Athenian speeches in the first book, and also of the Melian dialogue. Grosskinsky would interpret περὶ τῶν ἀεὶ παρόντων to apply to the general state of affairs as well as to the particular occasion.

[1] We should not forget, however, that Herodotus explicitly states that his most improbable debate on the relative merits of democracy, oligarchy and monarchy (3, 80-82) did in fact take place, where he talks of 'those Greeks who do not believe that Otanes advised the seven Persians that the Persians should adopt democracy' (6, 43, 3).

hampered them in rhetorical display. We shall have to wait more than two hundred years for any further discussion of historiography in our extant texts.

The Socratic Circle

We have traced several kinds of approaches to literature, mainly poetry, through the fifth century. At its beginning Xenophanes and Heraclitus were concerned with content, with the moral effect of poetry upon the individual and the community; towards its end, the sophists are concerned exclusively with form or style. It was left for the poets themselves, Pindar and Aristophanes in particular, to be concerned with both aspects of poetry, with form as well as with content. The two approaches, the philosophical and the rhetorical, continue side by side through the fourth century; both also gain in depth: Plato and Aristotle, while still concerned with the moral effect of literature, also establish important critical principles, while Isocrates, though a teacher of rhetoric, is not satisfied with the study of style alone but wants his pupils to develop a moral philosophy of life. Nevertheless, the two points of view remain distinct, and it is the rhetorical, not the philosophic approach which triumphs in the end and dominates both education and criticism in Hellenistic and Roman times.

The first critical writings of the fourth century came from the Socratic circle, but we know little more than their titles. Crito wrote on poetry, Glaucon (Plato's brother) on Euripides and Aristophanes, Simmias on the epic; Antisthenes, who was a pupil of Gorgias as well as (probably later) a disciple of Socrates, wrote on style and language as well as on Homer and on contemporary orators such as Lysias and Isocrates.[1] He seems to have combined rhetorical display with moral criticism and his work on style seems to have been mainly concerned with grammar. We have no evidence beyond the titles as to the nature of the others' writings.

Socrates himself, of course, had written nothing. There is, however, a passage in Xenophon's *Memorabilia* (3, 10) which probably goes back to the historic Socrates and which throws an interesting light on the theory of art as imitation of life. Socrates is talking to the sculptor Parrhasius; it is common ground between them that the sculptor imitates actual things he sees, but Socrates points out, first, that he need not confine himself to one model but can combine, in a beautiful statue for example, characteristics which in life belong to different individuals. Further, when Parrhasius says it is obviously impossible for him to represent the soul,

---

[1] For Antisthenes see Diogenes Laertius VI, 1-19, especially the list of his writings; also H. J. Lulofs, *De Antisthenis Studiis Rhetoricis* (Amsterdam dissertation 1900). For the critical writings of the other Socratics see E. Egger, *Essai sur l'histoire de la critique grecque* p. 31.

Socrates goes on to show that he does in fact 'imitate' facial expressions and bodily stances which express the feelings, so that the sculptor does imitate the character of the soul (τὸ τῆς ψυχῆς ἦθος) as well as of the body. The notion of art as imitation is thus already broadened in two ways: the artist can combine what is separate in actual life, and even the visual arts can, to some extent at least, represent the non-physical through its physical expression.

This is the only passage on art which, we may be fairly sure, is Socratic. Beyond this we must rely on the dialogues of Plato, and the problem of where Socrates ends and Plato begins is notoriously insoluble. This is regrettable, for Socrates belongs to the fifth century while Plato, who was twenty-eight at the time of Socrates' death in 399 and probably did not begin writing till later, belongs mainly to the fourth. That his dialogues profess to re-create the fifth-century climate of ideas is a further complication. We may feel that the *Apology* has a special claim to be historical, but even there we cannot be sure of any particular passage. It will be best therefore to deal with Plato's works as a whole.

Isocrates

Before we do this, however, we should consider here a great fourth-century figure whose very longevity makes him difficult to place in any chronological sequence. Isocrates[1] was born in Athens in 436, eight years before Plato. He opened his school in the late nineties of the fourth century, some years before the Academy. There he taught for over fifty years and was still writing when he died in 338, the year in which the battle of Chaeronea made Philip of Macedon master of Greece. He was then ninety-eight. Plato had died about eight years before at the ripe age of eighty-two. Aristotle was now forty-seven and well established in the Lyceum. The *Poetics* may already have been written, the *Rhetoric* may have followed shortly after.

Except for his own peculiar style, Isocrates did not contribute much directly to literary theory or criticism, but his indirect influence can hardly be exaggerated because it was his kind of education which triumphed over all others and dominated the Graeco-Roman world.[2] He defined it as 'learning to speak (and write) well on noble subjects'. The idea was not new; it derived from Gorgias whose pupil Isocrates was. His contemporary influence was great, and among his pupils were famous orators and statesmen like Isaeus, Lycurgus and Hypereides, the historians Ephorus

---

[1] For Isocrates see H. I. Marrou, *Histoire de l'éducation* 121-36, and W. Jaeger, *Paideia* vol. 3, 46-155. We are the more entitled to call him a fourth-century figure in that he apparently was with Gorgias in Thessaly during the last ten years of the Peloponnesian War.

[2] Marrou, 122.

and Theopompus, the best general of the century Timotheus, Theodectes the friend of Aristotle, as well as Speusippus, Plato's nephew and successor.

Isocrates has suffered from being the contemporary of the two greatest philosophers and of the greatest orator of Greece. He called his course of training *philosophia* and himself *philosophos*, but he had no claim to the title in the Platonic or Aristotelian sense[1]; he was included by the Alexandrians in the canonic list of the ten Attic orators although a physical handicap prevented his speaking in public; his style, though perfect of its kind, bears no comparison with that of either Demosthenes or Plato. He preached the unity of Greece against the Persians under some such leader as Philip of Macedon. Such a point of view was very sensible, but it makes him cut a sorry figure in the history books beside Demosthenes the passionate defender of Athens as an independent city state. This is natural enough; Isocrates' patriotism was constant and sincere, but it never caused him to write an inelegant sentence.

He is the Greek apostle of a general education.[2] By noble subjects he meant subjects of importance to the state and he had nothing but contempt for the teachers of forensic rhetoric who restricted themselves to private cases in court, also for the philosophers who discussed useless subjects about which the knowledge they profess is unattainable. Moreover, to speak (λέγειν) includes to write, even more obviously in Isocrates than in other authors, since his own works, though cast in the form of speeches, were meant to be read. But then reading, for the ancients, meant reading aloud, so that they always *heard* all forms of literature.

The formula went something like this: in order to speak well you must know what can be known about your subject, so that education teaches you to think as well as to speak.[3] Where complete knowledge is not possible, one must develop the capacity to foresee the consequences of a particular course of action. Further, it was a commonplace that to speak well the speaker must make a good impression on his audience; the pupil must therefore want to be a good man in order to do so. Hence Isocratean education also aims at developing character. Beyond this he does not go, and when he raises the question of what kinds of knowledge one should acquire, what arts or crafts should be studied, he never answers it. We find instead glowing rhetorical passages on the power of *Logos* as

[1] It is important to remember that Isocrates was about fifty when Plato opened the Academy. He uses the word φιλοσοφία in its general fifth-century sense (cp. Thucydides 2, 40, 1 and Herodotus 1, 30, 2), and meant by it the training of the mind. See, e.g., *Antidosis* 304 where he uses both φιλοσοφία and that other Socratic phrase τῆς ψυχῆς ἐπιμέλεια of his own form of education. *Antidosis* 271-82 gives a clear idea of what Isocrates calls philosophy.

[2] For the nature of his education – ἡ τῶν λόγων παιδεία, ἡ περὶ λόγων φιλοσοφία etc. – and also his criticisms of other teachers see especially *Antidosis* 45-50, 258-69; *Helen* 1-14 and *Against the Sophists*, passim.

[3] τὸ φρονεῖν εὖ καὶ λέγειν: e.g. *Antidosis* 244 cf. 207 and 277.

the source of all good and all progress in human life, and of all thought as well, since thought is the soul speaking to itself. Indeed Isocrates' theory of education often seems a mere playing on the various meanings of the Greek word *logos*: speech, words, thought, and also reason.[1]

But if he is very vague on the content of this education, and is always pulling us back to the surafce of things, Isocrates gives a fairly adequate description of what he considers to be an educated man: it is the man who is able to express himself elegantly, who manages the everyday business of life well, shows good judgement in his decisions and can foresee their consequences, who is just and tolerant in his relations to others, who can control the urge to pleasure, is not defeated by misfortune nor corrupted by good luck, and who esteems the favours of chance no higher than the rewards of merit. Above all, it is the man who can give sound advice to the state.[2]

Isocrates' references to other kinds of education are nearly always contemptuous, for he was nothing if not complacent, and he querulously resented all criticism. He feels very superior to the professional rhetoricians who make rules about everything (there is very little on rhetorical techniques in his extant works) and also to those who seek impossible knowledge, who believe all virtues to be one (Plato?) and to those who write on laws (Plato and Aristotle?). The pursuit of geometry, astronomy and 'eristic dialogues' may keep young men out of mischief but he considered it quite useless for grown men. This must refer to the Academy. For the 'eristics', a somewhat ill-defined class which may include different people at different times but must primarily refer to the logic-chopping sophists satirized by Plato in the *Euthydemus*, he has no regard whatever.[3] The difference between Isocrates' and Plato's conceptions of education is obvious, and indeed perennial: it is that between the believer in a general education and the believer in education in depth. Yet it is, I believe, a mistake to speak of any deep hostility between them, and the only certain reference to Isocrates in Plato is gently ironical, though certainly no eulogy.[4]

---

[1] *Antidosis* 278, on the need for a good character, and *Antidosis* 253-57, *Panegyricus* 47-50 for praise of *Logos* where one would expect more detail on his methods.

[2] *Panathenaicus* 30-32.

[3] See *Against the Sophists, passim*; *Helen*, ad init. The contrast with philosophers is rather. well put at *Antidosis* 84: 'They exhort people to a virtue and a wisdom which others do not know and they themselves dispute about, I exhort people to a virtue which all men recognize', and cf. 266.

[4] At *Phaedrus* 278 e Isocrates is mentioned as a friend of Socrates who has more talent than Lysias, and is of nobler character. Socrates adds that he would not be surprised if, as the years go by and he persists in his present type of writing, Isocrates will be as superior to his predecessors as an adult to children, but if he were not satisfied with this, a higher impulse could lead him to higher things, 'for the man's mind has a certain philosophical capacity' – φύσει γὰρ ὦ φίλε, ἔνεστί τις φιλοσοφία τῇ τοῦ ἀνδρὸς διανοίᾳ. If we remember that the *Phaedrus*

We know very little of Isocrates' teaching methods. The full course apparently took three to four years, and it seems probable that he never had more than about eight or nine pupils at a time. The course was evidently intensive and each pupil must have received a great deal of personal attention.[1] The formal teaching must have been purely rhetorical and linguistic. Other kinds of knowledge which Isocrates expected his pupils to possess were no doubt picked up incidentally in discussions of the content of rhetorical exercises. They criticized each other from the point of view of style also, perhaps of various styles, though there can be little doubt that the style of Isocrates himself was the pattern they were to follow, since it became recognized as the style of his school as well as his own.[2] A good deal of reading and criticism of various authors, both poets and prose-writers, also took place. Isocrates' own speeches were, he tells us, discussed and corrected with his pupils, though one wonders how far they would dare to go and how far the master welcomed their criticisms. He does not, however, exaggerate the role of the teacher, for of the three requirements of success, natural talent, training in the art, and practice, it is natural talent which he regards as the most important.[3]

We have no systematic statement of Isocrates' stylistic theory, but from his own practice and from scattered references in his works we have a very good idea. He is the perfect practitioner of the periodic style, with balanced clauses of equal length, deliberate contrasts and studied antitheses, frequent homoioteleuta, a smooth word-order which avoids awkward, rough collocations of sound and above all any hiatus, i.e. to follow a word which ends with a vowel by one which begins with one. This avoidance of hiatus is the best-known affectation of Isocrates, emphasized by all later critics. The very smoothness of his word order and the balanced nature of his periods became a weakness and led to a monotonous style without power or passion.

cannot have been written much before 370 when Isocrates was 66, and Plato 58, we must see this as a barbed compliment. Plato recognizes the prominence of Isocrates in his own field, but he has wasted his talent for philosophy (in the Platonic sense). On the other hand it is not an attack either. It is not hostile, in fact almost friendly, but definitely ironical. On the whole subject of Isocrates' relations with Plato see Jaeger op. cit. 147-52 with my review in *AJP* 68 (1947), 212-13, and R. Hackforth, *Plato's Phaedrus* (Cambridge, 1952), 167-8.

[1] For the number of pupils see Marrou, op. cit. 129 and note; also R. Johnson's 'A Note on the Number of Isocrates' Pupils' in *AJP* 78 (1957), pp. 297-300. For Isocrates' methods of teaching see the same author's 'Isocrates' Methods of Teaching' in *AJP* 80 (1959), 25-36, with its discussion of *Antidosis* 180-8.

[2] *Against the Sophists* 18. The good teacher must be a model ($\pi\alpha\rho\acute{\alpha}\delta\epsilon\iota\gamma\mu\alpha$) which his students must be able to imitate ($\mu\iota\mu\epsilon\hat{\iota}\sigma\theta\alpha\iota$). This is, in embryo, the later theory of rhetorical imitation or emulation which is so prominent in Dionysius, Cicero and Quintilian. See also *Antidosis* 206.

[3] *Antidosis* 185-8, for the importance of natural talent, and *Panathenaicus* 200, *To Philip* 17, for criticism in the school.

Isocrates did not adopt the poetic diction of Gorgias, but he recognizes that epideictic, i.e. display rhetoric like his own, is somehwat akin to poetry and music, that it admits a more poetic and varied diction, more novel ideas and more ornamentation than the forensic type does.[1] He himself, however, is sparing in his use of metaphors and tropes, his chief ornamentation being the elaborate structure of his periods and the smoothness of his word arrangement.

Like most teachers of rhetoric, Isocrates is said to have written a text-book on the art. Cicero and Quintilian knew of such a book, but Cicero had not seen it and Quintilian doubts whether it is genuine.[2] All we have of that kind is a doubtful extract in a Byzantine rhetorician[3]:

> From the Art of Isocrates we learn what kinds of style and diction are said to be pure. He thought so highly of purity of expression that in his own Art he gives the following advice about it: 'Our diction must avoid clashing vowels, for these have a limping effect; nor should we end one word and begin the next with the same syllable, e.g. εἰποῦσα σαφῆ, ἤλικα καλά, ἔνθα Θαλῆς. We should not use the same connecting particles in close proximity, while the answering particle must follow its leader without delay. We should use a word either metaphorically or else the most beautiful or the least newly coined, or the best-known. Altogether, prose should not be mere prose, for that is too dry, nor metrical, for that is too obvious, but it should be mixed with every kind of rhythm. In narrative we should make our first, second and other points in order, and not leave the first unfinished to pass on to another and then come back from the last to the first.'

Some of this advice is certainly Isocratean, the avoidance of the hiatus (as any forger would know), and the repeated syllables are akin to this. The full use of connecting particles also sounds genuine. The confused sentence about metaphors and that about prose and rhythm sound more Aristotelian than Isocratic, though the last sentence about orderly narrative again sounds like Isocrates.

He advised his students to read the poets – what Greek could avoid doing so? – but his references to poetry are few and far between, and one doubts whether he had much feeling for it. He expatiates on the difficulties of the prose-writer:

> Many embellishments are available to the poets: they can bring in the gods to associate with men, to talk with them, to help whomever they

---

[1] *Antidosis* 46-47. *Panegyricus* 11-12.

[2] Cicero, *De Inventione* 2, 2 (7); Quintilian 2, 15, 4.

[3] Maximus Planudes, probably thirteenth century, in his notes on Hermogenes, in Walz, *Rhetores Graeci* 5, 469, also in the Benseler-Blass edition of Isocrates, 2, 275.

please. They can describe these things not only in current language but they may use strange words, new words, metaphors; they embroider their poetry with every kind of ornament, omitting none. None of these are allowed to the prose-writers, who must restrict themselves to words that are customary in public life and to ideas directly related to their subject. The poets, moreover, compose everything with metre and rhythm while prose-writers do without them. Yet metre and rhythm have so strong an appeal that even where diction and ideas are poor, the audience is attracted by the rhythm and the measure. The power of these is shown by the fact that if you destroy the metre of the most popular poetry, leaving words and ideas as they are, the poems will appear much inferior to their present renown. (*Evagoras* 9-11.)

This is a typical passage, for Isocrates is writing with a purpose. He is emphasizing the difficulties of what he claims to be a new genre,[1] the prose encomium of a contemporary. In such a context it is perhaps unfair to point out that he displays only a rudimentary understanding of the differences between poetry and prose. He also attacks Homer for his scandalous stories about the gods, and he has an almost Platonic passage on how poets and prose-writers whose aim is only to please must write fiction, not truth, and not attempt to give advice.[2] Elsewhere he blames the poets for their immoral stories about the gods. These scattered references show little interest in poetry, but then Isocrates was not a very imaginative man, except when rewriting history to suit his purpose.

When contrasting himself with other writers, he enumerates the kinds of things they write and he gives at times almost a list of prose genres.[3] These lists of his, however, are rather casual, never clearly thought out or exhaustive. He lists (1) myths and fiction generally, (2) paradoxical writings which include Socratic dialogues, the encomia of the sophists on such paradoxical subjects as salt or the bumblebee, (3) history, (4) forensic and perhaps deliberative political oratory, and, contrasted with all this (5) speeches like his own which gave advice to the state on important subjects. Actually, a much more specific list of different genres could easily have been drawn up by this time. He does however accept the theory of

[1] But see D. R. Stuart's chapter on 'The Pretensions of Isocrates' in his *Epochs of Greek and Roman Biography* (Berkeley, 1928), 91-118.

[2] *To Nicocles* 48-49. The passage, by the way, is not in defence of Homer and the tragedians but ironically commends them for realizing they must please the crowd.

Once he is on the point of discussing the function of Homer and Hesiod in education but does not pursue the subject, and it is clear what he was about to say was not complimentary! For Homer's stories about the gods see *Busiris* 38-40.

[3] See *Panathenaicus* ad init., *Antidosis* 45-46 and a discussion of these passages in Stanley Wilcox, 'Isocrates' Genera of Prose', *AJP* 64 (1943), 427-31.

genres, each with its own special laws, as when he rebukes Polycrates for
not restricting himself, in writing an encomium, to what was flattering his
subject, or to what was derogatory in his attack on Socrates for 'you must,
as everybody knows, exaggerate the virtues of your subject in an encomium
and do the opposite in an accusation . . .'.[1] His own eulogies certainly
follow this rule.

He also claims the right to digress in his introductions,[2] and his own
digressions at the beginning of some of his words are quite deliberate;
this is the natural place for them as when he discusses, at the beginning of
the *Panegyricus*, how a skilful speaker can make what is great appear common, extol the commonplace, deal in a new way with an old subject or
with a new subject in the old way – rather an odd introduction to a serious
work, as Longinus was to point out, and not one to inspire confidence.[3]
Isocrates did not want his pupils to be ever looking for some new subject.
The aim should not be to speak on a topic never dealt with before, for this
search for originality leads to the ridiculous encomia of the sophists on
salt and bumblebees; the thing to do is to speak better than anyone has
done before.[4]

It is easy to underestimate Isocrates and to see in his great fame and
influence the triumph of the superficial and the commonplace; compared
to Plato and Aristotle he was both. It is equally easy to exaggerate his
merits and to regard him as the apostle of common sense, of a justified
scepticism as to the possibility of philosophic knowledge, and to extol him
as the man who established a new kind of education and 'a new moral
code' for Greece. There is half a truth in each of these contrary views. He
was not a great thinker, a great orator, a great critic or a great writer, but
he must have been a very great teacher. He was the first of a series of great
professors who equated higher education with rhetoric, the art of self-
expression in words. There is obvious truth in his view that if you seek to
speak well on noble subjects you will be driven to seek what knowledge
you can on these subjects and even want to improve your character so as
to be listened to. We, too, insist that our methods of education 'develop

[1] *Busiris* 4.
[2] *Panegyricus* 13.
[3] See Longinus, *On The Sublime* 38, 2.
[4] *Helen* 12, *Panegyricus* 7-8.

Three other theoretical statements are attributed to Isocrates: (1) Quintilian (2, 15, 4),
quotes as his the definition of rhetoric as πειθοῦς δημιουργός, the artificer of persuasion,
which is also used by Plato; (2) Dionysius of Halicarnassus says (*Lysias* 16 end) he is following
Isocrates and his school when he enumerates five sections of a speech: the exordium, the
statement, the narrative, the proof and the peroration; (3) Quintilian also quotes as Isocratean
the advice that the narrative should be clear, brief and plausible (4, 2, 31). But Quintilian may
be confusing the narrative with the statement of fact (πρόθεσις) and the advice to be brief
probably related only to this (which is often considered as a part of the narrative).

moral character' without being very clear how this is to come about. Isocrates' weakness here is that he is so very vague in his description of this education and left it to others, Aristotle and Cicero in particular, to fill this void. But, for all that, the man who speaks well on noble subjects – the *vir bonus dicendi peritus* as the Romans called him – remained the ideal of the ancient world. By creating this ideal Isocrates gave new life to the basic ideas of the fifth-century sophists, refined them, and passed them on to the Graeco-Roman world.

CHAPTER IV

Plato

Because Plato banished the poets (or most of them) from his ideal state, poets and critics have often been as impatient with him as he was with poetry. George Saintsbury, for example, gave him a bare three pages in his *History of Criticism*,[1] and almost completely ignored his positive contribution. Scholars of this century have, fortunately, made a greater effort to understand Plato's attitude and have rightly put more emphasis on the second part of the *Phaedrus* and on the *Laws*.[2]

To understand Plato's attitude, it is essential to keep in mind that it springs from a profound belief in the power of poetry and the fine arts to mould character and to influence the moral attitudes of the community; in modern terms we should think of movies and television to which the theatre in Athens was the nearest equivalent as a means of mass communication. We should remember the place which the poets, and Homer in particular, held in Greek education. When Plato says in the *Republic* (401 b) that not only poets, but painters, architects and musicians must not represent in their works what is base, licentious or mean, it is

in order that our guardians shall not be nurtured among images of vice as in an evil pasture, little by little and day by day feeding on evil herbs from many sources and imperceptibly gathering a mass of evil in their very soul. We must seek out artists with an inborn gift to represent what is naturally beautiful and gracious, so that our youth, living as in a healthy place, shall be improved from every side whenever they see or hear works of beauty, as a breeze coming from salubrious climes brings health, and thus from childhood on they shall be led to sympathy and harmony with, and love of, the beauty of reason.

It is because he so ardently believes in the influence of the fine arts for good that Plato is so afraid of their evil influence when misdirected.

---

[1] London, 1908, 17-20. Vernon Hall's *Short History of Literary Criticism*, 1963, also has the negative view.

[2] E.g., J. W. H. Atkins, *Literary Criticism in Antiquity*, vol. 1, 33-70; W. Chase Greene, 'Plato's View of Poetry' in *HSCP* 1918; to a lesser extent E. E. Sikes, *The Greek View of Poetry*. See also the chapter on Art in my *Plato's Thought*. For the effect of contemporary realism in art upon Plato's general attitude see P. M. Schuhl, *Platon et l'Art de son Temps*.

Moreover, he was the first to develop a theory of literature and of its place in society. As in so many fields he was the first to raise problems of capital importance; that he did not always find the completely right answer was inevitable, but this should not blind us to his greatness in boldly raising them, or to the fact (too often forgotten) that in many cases we have not yet found the answers ourselves, more than two thousand years later. This is particularly true in the case of censorship of the arts.

As the spiritual heir of Socrates and himself the founder of a new kind of higher education, it was natural for Plato to investigate the old claims of the poets, or rather the claims made on behalf of the poets as 'the teachers of men'. Plato was bound to examine also the claims of those new teachers, the sophists and rhetoricians to whom the young had turned for the art of self-expression. His investigation goes through three main stages. Briefly in the *Apology*, more fully in the *Ion*, he raises the question whether poets rely on art (i.e. knowledge) or on inspiration; in the *Gorgias* and the *Republic* he approaches rhetoric and poetry (and he insists they are but two sides of the same problem[1]) as an educator and a social reformer, and it is from this point of view that he examines their art, its nature and its influence. While he incidentally says a number of things which are both revealing and important in other ways, the social aspect is dominant throughout. It is only later, especially in the *Phaedrus* and the *Laws* that he examines literature for its own sake. The social responsibility of the artist is still of vital importance, but Plato now goes beyond this, examines the nature of 'rhetoric' and poetry, puts forward some critical theories and prepares the way for Aristotle. In the great myth of the *Phaedrus* he again deals with inspiration, this time in depth.

The *Apology* does little more than raise the question whether poets know what they write about. It will be remembered that Socrates is seeking to understand the oracle which said that no man in Greece was wiser than he. So he went to people who obviously knew things he did not know, among them the politicians and the poets. To his surprise he found that anyone present could explain the poets' meaning better than they could themselves. So he came to the conclusion that 'they did not compose their poems through wisdom but by some natural gift or divine possession,[2]

[1] The sophists and the rhetoricians are identified in *Gorgias* 520 a; oratory is closely linked with music and poetry 501 d – 502 d as different kinds of δημηγορία or public speaking. See also *Phaedrus* 234 d and 236 d where the word ποιητής is applied to the orator Lysias, and 258 d where the subject of the critical part of the dialogue is said to be the art of writing well, whether in prose or poetry.

[2] 22 b: οὐ σοφίᾳ ποιοῖεν ἃ ποιοῖεν ἀλλὰ φύσει τινι καὶ ἐνθουσιάζοντες. . . . It is worth noting that the word σοφία had shifted its meaning. In Homer it meant skill, and he can speak of the σοφία of any craftsman. So when the term is used of poets by Hesiod or Solon it means no more than what Aristophanes called the skill, δεξιότης, of the poet (*Frogs* 1009). In Pindar the

like seers and diviners, for these too say many fine things, but do not understand what they are saying'.

The notion of inspiration was not now quite as simple as in Homer, and in any case it was ambivalent for a Greek. It has been well said in this connexion that 'possession by a god was not the highest of destinies to the Hellenic mind. It recalled too vividly the frenzy of wine and the delirium of love. To Plato, above all, intent upon the equable life controlled by reason, possession was dangerous, if not despicable.'[1] Despicable is too strong a word, and in his more poetic and mythical moods Plato did speak of inspiration with respect, but Socrates is here obviously ironical, and the general Greek attitude to the gods makes that irony more natural.

The poet's claim to σοφία is further examined in the *Ion*. Ion is a rhapsode and Socrates defines the craft (τέχνη) of the rhapsode as 'to understand the thought of the poet as well as the words', for 'the rhapsode must interpret the thought of the poet to his audience'.[2] This requires knowing other poets as well as Homer, since they write on the same subjects.[3] What Socrates is saying in effect is that good criticism (as we may well translate τέχνη ῥαψωδική in this context) requires a thorough understanding of *all* poets.

Ion, however, claims knowledge of Homer only, but then he cannot lecture on Homer, or recite him, with knowledge at all, for as in the other arts you cannot understand the work of one artist without knowing that of others. He must, like the poet himself, rely on inspiration (θεία δύναμις) and of this purely emotional appeal Socrates proceeds to give a remarkable description (533 d-e):

> It is no art or craft (τέχνη, which requires special knowledge) which enables you to talk well on Homer, but a divine power which moves you, like that of the magnet. This not only attracts iron rings, but imbues those rings with its own power to attract other rings, with the result that sometimes a long chain of such rings are suspended from one another, and the power to attract in all of them derives from the magnet.
>
> So the Muse herself inspires men, and the inspiration passes from them to others, till we have a whole chain of men possessed.

σοφία of the poet had something of the wider meaning; by the end of the fifth century and certainly in the fourth the claim to σοφία for the poet is not a claim to a special skill, but to wisdom.

[1] W. P. Johnston, *Greek Literary Criticism*, p. 14.

[2] 530 b-c. At least that is what a rhapsode should be, but if we can believe Xenophon (*Symposium* 3, 6 and *Memorabilia* 4, 2, 10), Socrates had no high opinion of rhapsodes.

[3] The reason is not a very good one, but the statement is interesting and we may well accept it, especially as Ion claims not only to recite Homer but to 'talk about' Homer better than anyone else. In any case, as for the Greeks the contests among poets were the natural means of publication, to judge a poet you had also to know his competitors.

It is in a state of possession that poets compose their beautiful poems; they are no more rational than Corybants in their ecstatic dances in worship of Cybele, or than Bacchanals in a state of frenzy. 'The poet is a light, winged and holy thing' and it is only when in an irrational state of possession that he can compose at all.[1] He communicates his ecstasy to the rhapsode who is the poet's interpreter as the poet is the interpreter of the gods, and the rhapsode in turn communicates it to his hearers. Because the state of possession is irrational, poets can often compose only one kind of poetry, or even only one good poem. Ion agrees that he is beside himself when enacting scenes of Homer, in a state of high emotion, possessed by the pity and fear which he awakens in his audience.[2]

However, he still lays claim to knowledge, and the rest of the dialogue deals with the knowledge of different craftsmen which Ion admits he does not possess, so that the doctor is a better critic of medical passages in Homer, the charioteer of the chariot races, the general of strategy, and so on. In the end, he is satisfied that his special ability is a divine gift, not knowledge.[3] By implication the claim sometimes made for the poets, that they were masters of every craft represented in their poems, is also disallowed. Whatever Homer teaches, we feel, it is not medicine or charioteering or any other craft, not even the art of war.

The whole process, illustrated by the simile of the magnet, is purely emotional; it has nothing to do with reason or knowledge; the critical faculty is completely dormant and it is precisely this emotional surrender uncontrolled by reason which Plato distrusts and believes to be dangerous. He will deal more fully with it in the *Republic*. We should note, however, that the *Ion* is full of references to the *beauty* of poetry and to the many fine things which the poets say. Plato's attitude to poetry is always ambivalent.

In the *Gorgias* he turns his attention to the new teachers of the art of prose, the rhetoricians. He examines the nature of their craft (τέχνη). If it is a craft it must involve special knowledge. What is this knowledge? Challenged to define rhetoric, Gorgias says it is the art of persuasion (453 a). Socrates then distinguishes two kinds of persuasion: the one is based on knowledge and teaches something, the other merely makes people believe something and requires no knowledge in the persuader. This last is the persuasion of the orator, and the distinction is all the more important as

[1] 534 b: κοῦφον γὰρ χρῆμα ποιητής ἐστι καὶ οὐ πρότερον οἷός τε ποιεῖν πρὶν ἂν ἔνθεός τε γένηται καὶ ἔκφρων καὶ ὁ νοῦς μηκέτι ἐν αὐτῷ ἐνῇ.
[2] 535 c. This is the first mention of the later commonplace that the poet and the actor (and the orator) must feel the emotions they seek to communicate. Note also the emphasis on *pity and fear* which we have already met in Gorgias (*supra*, p. 18).
[3] εἰ δὲ μὴ τεχνικὸς εἶ, ἀλλὰ θείᾳ μοίρᾳ κατεχόμενος ... (542 a).

the orator deals with matter involving right and wrong. Gorgias points out, however, that the orator can persuade far more successfully than the expert, and quite logically suggests that the teacher of rhetoric should not be blamed if his pupil misuses his skill any more than a fencing master if his pupil uses his skill to commit murder (456 d). However, when he is faced with the consequences of this position – that orators know nothing of good or evil – he blandly remarks that if any of his pupils should be so ignorant, he will teach them this as well (460 a). When the contradiction is pointed out (for now he accepts the responsibility which he denied just before) he retires from the discussion.

His pupil Polus takes his place and now Socrates puts his case much more bluntly. Rhetoric is not a τέχνη (art or craft) at all, because it is not based on knowledge and does not aim at what is good, as real crafts do. Four genuine crafts minister to mankind: gymnastic and medicine which look after the body; law-making and corrective justice which look after the soul. To each of these corresponds a counterfeit which merely aims at flattery and pleasure, not at the good. Gymnastic makes the body healthy, its counterfeit, cosmetics, makes it only appear so. Medicine restores health, cookery gives the feeling of health, not the reality. Law-making seeks to prescribe the good life, and justice to restore it. But the counterfeits, sophistry and rhetoric, aim only at pleasure in an empirical way, for the real good of the soul they care not at all, indeed they have no knowledge of it.[1] Gorgias had boasted that the rhetorician could be more persuasive than the expert; no wonder, says Socrates, a pastry cook will always get more votes than the doctor on a matter of diet from an assembly of ignorant children! What people think they desire (ἃ δοκεῖ) is not always what they really want (ἃ βούλεται, 466 d). Sophists and orators never provide more than the former. This leads to the great discussion on the good life which takes up the rest of the *Gorgias*.

Thus does Socrates put the sophists and rhetoricians in their place. Gorgias had said that the words of the rhetorician worked upon the soul as medicines worked upon the body, but Socrates refuses to accept this: the sophists are not doctors of the soul, only cooks who seek to give immediate pleasure. They have no real knowledge. Neither did the poets, but they at least could claim to be inspired. As before, Plato is concerned with content only, not with the means of persuasion provided by form and style. Much of what is said here can also be applied to the poets.[2]

In the second book of the *Republic* Plato is discussing the education of his

---

[1] 465 c–e. In making rhetoric the counterfeit of corrective justice Socrates is obviously thinking of the rhetoricians' boast that they could make the worse case appear the better in a court of law.   [2] See p. 47, note 1, above.

guardians and he states at once that the immoral stories of Homer and other poets about gods and heroes must be censored. This criticism of the poets was by now traditional, but the problem had become more urgent. Ideas about the gods had changed since Homer, but he had kept his place in the education of the young. The sophists had taught people to argue from the behaviour of the gods to their own and this helped to bring the Homeric legends into disrepute. More responsible thinkers, by attacking these tales, also attacked the sanctity of Homer. The ordinary Athenians seem to have resented both attitudes.[1] The educational problem was real. To Plato the gods can never be the cause of evils; heroes should behave with dignity and self-control; therefore neither gods nor heroes must be said to behave badly (387 b):

> We shall ask Homer and the other poets not to be annoyed if we expunge things of that kind. It is not that these things are not poetical and pleasing for the majority of men to hear; indeed the more poetical they are the less they must be heard by children or by men who must be free men and fear servitude more than death.

This is the first hint of another, and an artistic, standard of criticism, but it is the social effects which now occupy the philosopher exclusively. Heroes must not be depicted as giving way to excessive emotions, whether laughter or tears.

After the principle of censorship has been firmly established, Plato also applies it to literary forms. Poets and story-tellers[2] proceed either by narration, or by impersonation ($\mu\iota\mu\dot\eta\sigma\epsilon\iota$) or a mixture of both, any direct speech being counted as impersonation.[3] Drama proceeds entirely by impersonation, while epic would come under the mixed kind. We have seen that Plato was suspicious of the emotional appeal of poetry and this obviously seemed to him much more intense where the parts were *acted* (393 c). The author identifies himself with his characters, the actor or rhapsode, as the next link in the chain, goes through a similar process, and inspires the audience to do the same. And because Plato firmly believes that we become like what we 'imitate' (395 c-d) – in modern terms, that by identifying with a gangster in a film we do not work our gangsterish tendencies out of our system but, on the contrary, increase them – Plato will not allow the impersonation of evil characters at all. Moreover we lose our singleness of character by impersonating different types.[4] He then

---

[1] For the unpopularity of the Sophists see *Meno* 91 c.

[2] He speaks of $\mu\upsilon\theta\dot\delta\lambda\omicron\gamma\omicron\iota$ $\ddot\eta$ $\pi\omicron\iota\eta\tau\alpha\acute\iota$ 'poets and storytellers'. The former wrote also in prose, so that all literature is included, though Plato has poetry mainly in mind (392 d).

[3] This makes us realize that the rhapsodes must have dramatized the speeches in recitation. This is also the impression given by Ion.

[4] 397 e: οὐκ ἔστιν διπλοῦς ἀνὴρ παρ' ἡμῖν, οὐδὲ πολλαπλοῦς, ἐπειδὴ ἕκαστος ἐν πράττει.

applies the same principles to music: we shall only retain those musical modes which represent or 'imitate' the brave man's actions in war and peace. And so we come to banish the 'imitative' poets from our republic (398 a):

> As for the man who, in his cleverness (ὑπὸ σοφίας) can become every sort of person and imitate all things – if such a man should arrive in our city and want to exhibit his works, we would do him reverence as to someone holy, wondrous, and delightful, but we would tell him that we have no one like him in our city, that it is not lawful for such a one to be there. We would anoint his head with myrrh, crown him with wreaths – and send him away to another city. We ourselves would employ a more austere and less delightful poet or story-teller for our own good, one who would imitate for us the speech of a worthy man, and tell his tales in accordance with the principles we have laid down when we first undertook to educate our guardians.

Thus does Plato ban all poetry which relies on impersonation only – that is, all drama – and forbid all dramatization of evil, all direct speech on the part of bad characters. Nor should we forget that he has already banned all excessive displays of emotion, which would exclude a good deal of lyric poetry and a good deal of Homer, beside his Olympus. What remains? By exercising our ingenuity we can get a certain amount under the wire: edifying stories, some lyric poetry, hymns and paeans, and a kind of bowdlerized drama and epic, but I doubt if Plato himself took the trouble to work it out.

What he is doing is to put before us a perennial social and educational problem: the need for censorship of the arts and especially of literature; he does so with a vividness which tempts us to concentrate our attention upon details and to forget the fundamentals. The principle of censorship which he was the first to formulate has been accepted by every civilized state except his own, for laws against libel, blasphemy or obscenity are also a form of censorship. It is comic to find commentators blaming Plato without giving any thought to the practices of their own countries. His application of the principle goes too far, and Aristotle will correct some of his exaggerations, but this does not lessen the importance of this first theoretical discussion of the artist's responsibility to society by one who was both a great artist and a great social philosopher. It is a discussion which the world has never been able to forget, and it is perhaps because we ourselves have not found a satisfactory answer to the problem that commentators are so very ready to ridicule Plato's solution, which is admittedly defective.

He discusses poetry again in the tenth book of the *Republic*. He has now, in the central books, explained his theory of eternal Forms and the nature of the philosopher who has knowledge of these, the only true statesman and the only true teacher. He has also clarified his theory of the three parts of the soul: the reason, the spirited part, and the passions. It is in the light of these metaphysical and psychological theories that he looks at poetry again.

He warns us at once that he is going to use the word *mimêsis* in a broader sense.[1] What he now means he explains quite carefully by the famous illustration of the three beds: there is the Form of bed made by the god, there is the actual bed made by the carpenter, and then there is the picture of a bed made by the painter. This is third in degree of reality and so the painter is at two removes[2] from true reality and *his* bed is an imitation of an imitation – and, at that, seen only from a particular angle.

This is the famous theory of art as 'imitation', which condemns the products of art to the same low degree of reality as images in a mirror (596 d-e). Plato means much the same thing as the ordinary man to whom a picture isn't 'real', and he means that art imitates life, which in a general sense it undoubtedly does. He is concerned to prove the inferiority of the poet to the philosopher who has knowledge of the Forms whereas the poet does not even have knowledge of the particulars which are themselves but imitations of the Forms. And he proceeds to confirm this by another illustration: the horseman knows how to use a bridle, the bridle-maker does not but he trusts the instructions of the horseman, has a right opinion about it, and makes it. The painter does not even know that, but can only 'imitate' or (make a picture of) the bridle. So that in knowledge too he is third, he has neither knowledge nor true opinion of what the bridle should be. Plato says, it is true, that the good poet should have knowledge of his model (598 e) but on the one hand, his condemnations include all actual poets and other artists (602 b) and, on the other, anyone who has true knowledge is a philosopher and has other things to do, since the artist's work is but 'play'.[3]

Plato pursues his attack upon the claims of the poet with great gusto, now on psychological grounds, and this brings us back to the other meaning of *mimêsis* as emotional identification.[4] The accusation now is

---

[1] This is obvious where Socrates asks for a definition of *mimêsis* as a whole (ὅλως), 595 c.

[2] In Greek the *third* from the truth, for they always counted the first member of a series. So the day after tomorrow is to them the *third* day from today.

[3] 602 b: ἀλλ᾽ εἶναι παιδίαν τινα οὐ σπουδὴν τὴν μίμησιν.

[4] The two meanings are not unconnected. When the poet represents an angry man on the stage he impersonates him, identifies himself with him and at the same time 'imitates' anger as he knows it in life.

that poetry appeals to the passions and emotions without control by reason. We identify ourselves emotionally (συμπάσχοντες, 605 d) and the more violently we are affected the more we praise the poet. The passions and emotions which decent people control in their own lives are given free rein in the theatre, with disastrous results for the moral character of our citizens. The poet obviously appeals to the lowest part of the soul. This we cannot allow, he must be controlled by censorship.

Plato enlarges upon this emotional appeal, the greatest danger he sees in poetry, and he is obviously thinking mainly of epic and tragedy. Throughout, however, he recognizes the charm of poetry, and when he condemns 'the Muse of pleasure' (607 a) it is with regret, and if anyone can defend poetry, we shall gladly listen and repeal our sentence of banishment if the defence is successful.[1]

The discussion of art in the tenth book reaffirms, expands, and supports what was said in the third. The one new theory is that of art as imitation of things in the actual world of phenomena. We must not be misled by Plato's use of painting to illustrate the point into believing him to mean that tragedy can only dramatize scenes which have actually happened in every detail. This is obviously nonsense, and we saw that Socrates in Xenophon did allow for different combinations at least. What Plato insists on, however, is that neither the poet nor other artists can imitate the Forms directly, and, in the actual discussions of art he never does allow this possibility. To imitate the Forms the poet would need to acquire philosophic knowledge, and no actual poets possessed it, but there is nothing in Plato's philosophy which would prevent the existence of a poet-philosopher, indeed Plato himself was both.

Even in the *Republic*, when he is not specifically discussing the arts, Plato does express himself as if the 'imitation' of the Forms by the artist were possible. Not only does Socrates speak (488 a) of artists who combine different parts of existing things to make something which did not exist, but when challenged to show that his ideal state is practicable he asks (472 d)

> Do you think that a man is any the less a good painter if he paints a picture such as the most beautiful man would be and if, having made every detail fit, he cannot prove that such a man exists?

Socrates goes even further when defending the thesis that philosophers should rule; he says (484 e) that those who are without knowledge of any true reality (the Forms) are like the blind, and that they cannot, '*as a painter can*, fix their eyes on what is most true' and thus establish our laws and customs. And again elsewhere (500 e) he compares the philosophers

[1] 607 c-d, and cf. 595 b-c at the beginning of the book.

to 'painters who use the divine model'.[1] Moreover the Republic itself is
said to be (592 b):

> perhaps a pattern laid up in heaven for him who will to look upon,
> and as he looks on it, to govern his own soul. It matters not whether
> it exists anywhere, or ever will exist . . .

Plato did, it seems, conceive of another kind of art, and another kind of
politics, but neither, alas, existed, or so he thought.

The beginning of the *Phaedrus* (229 b) raises the question of the allegorical
interpretation of poetical myths. Socrates and Phaedrus are walking along
the river Ilissus, and the younger man exclaims that this is surely the place
from which the maiden Oreithyia was snatched by Boreas; he then turns
to Socrates: 'Do you believe this story to be true?' Socrates does not give a
direct reply but says that if he did not believe it he could no doubt
rationalize the myth by saying that she was blown down from the rocks
by the North Wind and died, and that this was the origin of the story.
The only trouble, he adds, with this kind of thing is that you then have
to find similar explanations for all the tales, stories and monsters of mythology, which would take quite a lot of time. He prefers to spend his on
worthier pursuits such as attaining self-knowledge.

Plato never did have the time for this type of rationalizing, and he
obviously considered it an inadequate defence of the poets. He had already
said in the *Republic* that he would not tolerate stories of quarrels among
the gods 'whether composed as allegories or without allegory',[2] for a
child cannot appreciate the difference, and first impressions are hard to
efface.

When Plato thus rejected it as useless, allegorical explanation of the
myths was already an old established practice.[3] Its origins are obscure but
we can trace it back as far as the beginning of the sixth century. Indeed, in
a sense, the Homeric gods are allegorical by nature, as many of them were
personifications of natural forces.

Allegorical explanations seem to have arisen in two ways. A people who
are fond of quoting poetry are inevitably led to quote it for their own
purposes, as the sophists notoriously did, and even Plato does at times.
They then seek the authority of the old poets for their own ideas, and

[1] οἱ τῷ θείῳ παραδείγματι χρώμενοι ζώγραφοι. Here we have a metaphor which does not
strictly imply that painters do this.
[2] 378 d: οὔτ' ἐν ὑπονοίαις πεποιημένας οὔτε ἄνευ ὑπονοίας. ὑπονοία (lit. under-meaning) is
the classical term for allegory, which in Roman times was called ἀλληγορία (to say one thing
and mean another).
[3] See J. Tate, 'The Beginnings of Greek Allegory' in *CR* 41 (1927), 214-15. The two kinds
of allegory are discussed by the same author in a series of interesting articles in *CQ* 23 (1929),
142-54; 24 (1930), 1-10; 27 (1933), 74-80 and 158-61; 28 (1934), 105-14.

allegorical interpretation is often a very effective way of doing this.
Already in the fifth century, philosophers made free use of allegory in
interpreting Homer.[1] Democritus said that Athena was Wisdom and that
she was called Tritogeneia because wisdom consists of three parts: to plan
well, to speak well, and to act well.[2] The Stoics were later to develop
allegorizing to a fine art and attempt to make Homer into a good Stoic.

The second kind of allegory aims to defend the poet and came to be
used when Homer was condemned for his immoral stories from the sixth
century on. This is the type of allegory Plato had in mind in the *Republic*.

Both kinds were helped by plays on words, particularly on the names
of the gods, and sought help from the pseudo-science of etymology to
which, in the fifth century, the new interest in language gave a new
impetus. Already Heraclitus had played on the name of Zeus as Life (the
accusative $Z\hat{\eta}\nu a$ and the infinitive $\zeta\hat{\eta}\nu$).[3] We see in the *Cratylus* that Plato
refused to take etymology any more seriously than allegory itself.[4]
Serious men, as he says elsewhere, should be able to discover the truth
together without complicating their search by irrelevant discussions of
what poets mean.[5]

The *Phaedrus* is formally a critical discussion of three speeches: one which
purports to be by the orator Lysias[6] on the paradoxical subject that a youth
should grant his favours to one who does not love him rather than to one
who does – a typical sophistic display piece; then a speech by Socrates on
the same subject, and finally Socrates' palinode on Eros, the great myth
which forms the central part of the dialogue.

The myth is relevant here only as a vindication of that high emotional
state of which Plato has hitherto been so suspicious. It is true that the
careful reader of the *Republic* realizes that the philosophic life is motivated
by passion for truth but the emphasis was certainly on control by reason.[7]
In the *Phaedrus* there are four kinds of 'madness' ($\mu a\nu i a$, a strong word)
or possession which are gifts of the gods, and among these (245 a):

> The third kind of possession or madness comes from the Muses. It lays
> hold of a gentle and virgin soul, rouses and inspires it to song and
> poetry, and adorns innumerable great deeds of the ancients to educate

[1] Diels on Metrodorus (48, 3) and Theogenes (72, 2).   [2] Diels Fragm. 2.
[3] Diels fr. 32. For other interpretations, Diels' Index s.v. *Zeús*.
[4] There are a few more points of interest in the *Cratylus*. At 425 d we have the first reference
to tragedians using the *deus e machina* to get them out of difficulties; there is also a discussion
of *mimêsis* and it is pointed out that an imitation or image can never reproduce the model
perfectly, for then it would be a replica, not an image or imitation (432 b).
[5] *Protagoras* 347 b – 348 a.
[6] Whether this is a genuine speech by Lysias or a parody we cannot tell, though one feels
that Plato would enjoy writing a parody and is less likely to transcribe a real speech.
[7] See my *Plato's Thought*, 129-37.

their posterity. Whoever comes to the gates of poetry without the Muses' madness, believing that technical skill will make him an adequate poet, is himself ineffectual and the poetry of this sane man vanishes before that of those who are mad.

And, as Socrates has just stated (244 d), 'the madness that is from the gods is a finer thing than human sanity'.

'Madness which comes from the gods' expresses in mythical language much the same as passion directed by reason, and there is no contradiction with the *Republic* in this rehabilitation of inspiration but there is a considerable difference of emphasis. This is the first time that Plato has recognized, at least in his discussions of poetry and the arts, the necessity of passionate intensity on the part of the artist and spoken of inspiration with respect. He is now talking like his older contemporary Democritus (c. 460-370 B.C.),[1] but it is the only time he does so.

We may note in passing that when, later in the myth (248 d-e), Plato gives a list of human lives in a descending scale according to the degree to which they have shared the vision of Reality (which all human beings share to some extent) the poet has been promoted above the maker of beds! He comes in the sixth place, after the philosopher who is the true μουσικός, after the law-abiding ruler, the man of affairs or politician, the doctor or gymnastic trainer and the seer, but before the farmer or artisan, and well ahead of those perverters of the truth, the sophist or demagogue, and the tyrant or despot.

It is idle to attach much importance to the details of either a Platonic myth or a Platonic illustration, and few poets would derive any great satisfaction from being promoted above the bridle-makers. But at least this passage of the Phaedrus-myth should warn us not to attach too much importance to the fact that in the *Republic* poets were ranked below artisans. The myth should not be forgotten, however, when we consider the critical and more pedestrian part of the dialogue.

In his first brief comments on the Lysian speech, Socrates was quite ready to admire the manner of the speech, its clarity and compactness, its precise and well turned phrases, but he had paid but little attention to content, which seemed to him somewhat repetitious. Here we have the first formulation of the difference between form and content, which was to become so commonplace.[2]

---

[1] Cicero, *De Divinatione* I, 37, 80: *negat enim sine furore Democritus quemquam poetam magnum esse posse, quod idem dicit Plato*, and Horace, *Ars Poetica* 296: *excludit sanos Helicone poetas Democritus*. No one has explained how Democritus reconciled this statement that poets must be mad with his atomic theory. Diogenes Laertius 9, 46-49 names a number of works by Democritus on poetry, song and language, but we know nothing whatever of their contents.

[2] The form is here called διάθεσις, the content εὕρεσις, which is also the later term (236 a). That this is the contrast is quite clear where Socrates says that when the ideas are commonplace,

Socrates now sets out to investigate 'how to write well', whether in verse or prose.[1] First of all the writer (or speaker) must know his subject. This the rhetoricians denied, as Phaedrus reminds us; they maintained that to persuade the crowd one need not know the truth but only what the crowd believes. Socrates says they are wrong for two reasons: (a) the man who does not know the truth is not likely to give good advice, and (b) even if the intention is to deceive, one is more likely to be successful if one knows the truth. This is the old quarrel of the *Gorgias*, and we are still concerned with content only (259 e – 263 d).

The second point is that you must define your subject (263 d – 264 b). This Lysias did not do, whereas Socrates did define the kind of love he was talking about. Thirdly, every *logos* or discourse must have a definite structure with every part in its proper place (264 c):

> Every *logos* should be like a living organism (ζῷον) and have a body of its own; it should not be without head or feet, it should have a middle and extremities which should be appropriate to each other and to the whole work.[2]

Socrates quotes as an example of bad work the following epitaph the lines of which can be shifted into any order:

> I am a bronzen maiden, on Midas' grave I lie,
> Till stop the flowing waters, as long as trees grow tall,
> Forever here remaining, on this lamented tomb
> To those who pass by saying: Midas is buried here.

Fourthly, all the scattered parts of the work must look to the Form or Idea of the whole. This means that the writer must have the capacity to analyse logically or, as Plato puts it, divide his subject 'according to the Forms', divide it 'along the joints' and not hack it into unmeaning pieces (265 e). Without this capacity to analyse there is no understanding of any subject. Socrates shows that his own speeches were properly subdivided in this way.

---

one admires only the διάθεσις, but when the matter is also difficult to discover (εὑρεῖν) one should also admire the εὕρεσις. διάθεσις here quite obviously includes the points which Socrates is willing to admire at 234 e, namely clarity (σαφῆ), compactness (στρογγύλα), and precisely turned phrases (ἀκριβῶς ἕκαστα τῶν ὀνομάτων ἀποτετόρνευται). These same terms reappear in later appraisals of Lysias, notably in Dionysius' essay on the orator.

[1] 258 d: τίς οὖν ὁ τρόπος τοῦ καλῶς τε καὶ μὴ γράφειν ... ἐν μέτρῳ ὡς ποιητὴς ἢ ἄνευ μέτρου ὡς ἰδιώτης and at 259 e he uses the phrase καλῶς λέγειν τε καὶ γράφειν. We cannot here translate καλῶς as 'beautifully' because it has a wider connotation and for Plato it refers to content and moral effect as well as to beauty.

[2] Plato has already used this principle at *Rep.* 4, 420 c-d, where he says his aim is not the happiness of any particular group in the state but of the state as a whole, as in making a statue one does not beautify any one part at the expense of the whole.

Then, fifthly, Plato turns to a subject he has so far ignored, namely the techniques of the art. He begins by being severely critical of the writers on rhetoric who, not having the kind of understanding he has been describing, confuse a technical vocabulary with art itself, and ignore the fundamentals of their own craft.[1] He also ridicules the claims of Tisias and Gorgias that they could make things seem important or unimportant, speak briefly or at length on any subject, which made Prodicus say that he knew only the craft of necessary words (267 b), and Socrates pours scorn on the writings of Thrasymachus on how to stir up emotions such as pity or anger (267 c-d).

All these tricks, says Plato, do not constitute an art or craft (τέχνη). What would a doctor say to one who claimed to know medicine because he knew the effect of every drug, if he had no idea *when* to prescribe them? Or again

> What if a man came to Sophocles and Euripides and said that he knows how to speak at length on trifling subjects and briefly on important subjects, that he can at will make pitiful or, on the contrary, frightening and threatening speeches,[2] and so on, that in teaching these things he considers he teaches how to compose tragedies? I think, Socrates, that they would laugh at anyone who thinks that tragedy is anything less than the organization of those elements together so that they fit in with each other and with the whole work.

A musician would be equally contemptuous of someone who knew only his notes and thought he knew music. These are the prerequisites of the art of music, not the art itself.

This is a very interesting passage because while thus vehemently denying that the rhetoric as taught is an art or craft (τέχνη), Plato is by implication recognizing that the tragedy of Sophocles and Euripides *is* a *technê*, (as are the music of Adrastus and the oratory of Pericles) like the medicine of Hippocrates[3]; that these men did possess that dialectical

---

[1] At 266 d – 267 d Plato mentions a number of technical terms, selected at random from rhetorical textbooks, which is interesting because it shows how elaborate the jargon of rhetoricians had already become early in the fourth century. The list is as follows: προοίμιον (exordium), διήγησις (narrative), μαρτυρία (testimony), τεκμήριον (argumentative proof), τὰ εἰκότα (probabilities), πίστωσις (proof), ἐπιπίστωσις (supplementary proof), ἔλεγχος (refutation), ἐπεξέλεγχος (supplementary refutation), ὑποδήλωσις (insinuation), παρέπαινος (indirect praise), παράψογος (indirect censure), διπλασιολογία (repetition), γνωμολογία (maxim), εἰκονολογία (simile), ὀρθοέπεια (correct speech), ἐπάνοδος (recapitulation). This is obviously but a casual selection from a much larger number of technical terms.

[2] Note once again the emphasis on pity and fear as the main emotions aroused.

[3] 269 a, and cf. 270 a where Pericles is said to have been the greatest of orators because of his friendship with Anaxagoras, which gave him an understanding of nature. For Hippocrates see 270 b.

knowledge which he is denying to the professional rhetoricians. This is a definite advance on the harsh condemnations of the *Republic*.[1]

All our evidence tends to show that Plato's strictures on the rhetorical technicians were justified, that they concentrated on tricks of speech and arguments, that their advice to pleaders concentrated on technical tricks and was completely amoral. We have only to think of Gorgias' *Encomium of Helen* and the *Rhetorica ad Alexandrum*.

Plato now sets out to examine the requirements of the real *art* of rhetoric.[2] He begins by a statement we have also met in Isocrates,[3] namely that it requires natural ability, knowledge (ἐπιστήμη) and practice, but of course he interprets the formula differently, especially knowledge.

Any *technê* must study the object of its concern, analyse it into its parts, know how it acts on other things and is affected by them. Otherwise it is not a *technê* but an empirical routine (270 b-d). Now rhetoric is concerned with the human mind. The true rhetor must therefore study human psychology and know the various kinds of soul. He must also analyse the different kinds of arguments and ways of speech, and know how each kind of mind is affected by each of them. Without this knowledge there can be no art or craft or speech (speaking or writing) but only a kind of empirical routine.

Once the rhetor does possess this knowledge and has sufficient practice, knows the right occasion for speaking or keeping silent, and can thus apply the techniques now taught by the rhetoricians at the proper time and the appropriate occasion, *then* he has acquired the art. This none of our teachers of rhetoric possess, indeed they deny the need for these things.

[1] There is a passage in the *Sophist* (235 a – 236 c and 265 a – 268 d) where Plato also speaks of *mimêsis* based on knowledge. In the course of a diaeresis in which he is trying to track down the sophist by a process of dichotomies, he divides image-making into εἰκαστική, the making of exact copies, and φαναστική, the making of images which only look like the original. He then divides the latter into those who use tools to make their images, and those who use their body and voice for the purpose. Here one assumes that for once the painter and sculptor part company with the actor and speaker, and the term *mimêsis* is in this passage used to describe the second class only. These 'imitators' are then further subdivided into those who have knowledge of their model and those who have not, and the ignorant further differentiated into one class who have no intention to deceive and those who have, these deliberate deceivers being demagogues and sophists.

One should not press the details too far. Both τέχνη and *mimêsis* are clearly used in other than their usual senses. Nevertheless the class of imitators by voice and body obviously includes drama, and it is interesting to find that some of them have knowledge. This is not unlike the difference between Sophocles and Euripides as against the mere technicians in the *Phaedrus* or the artist in the *Laws* who is also granted knowledge of both models and techniques. We should also note that among the ignorant imitators some are allowed at least good intentions.

For further implications of the meaning of *mimêsis* in this passage see J. A. Philip's 'Mimêsis in the Sophistês of Plato'.

[2] 269 c: τὴν τοῦ τῷ ὄντι ῥητορικοῦ τε καὶ πιθανοῦ τέχνην . . .

[3] See above, p. 72.

Plato seems to be trying hard to be practical, to isolate the true art of rhetoric and its requirements. And that he is being practical is proved by the fact that the method he sets out here is largely the method followed by Aristotle in his *Rhetoric*. But, as Aristotle once remarked in a different context, however much Plato wants to be practical, he soon swings back to the ideal.[1] When he reasserts in the end that argument from probability is not enough and that his orator must know the truth, we are reminded by his very language that there is only one kind of knowledge of Truth, and that is the knowledge of the Forms, which requires much labour, 'a labour which the sane man must undertake not in order to speak to, and act with, other men, but in order to be able to speak things pleasing to the gods, and to do everything, as far as he is able, to please them' (273 e). Our speakers and writers have become philosophers on the way, and Plato hints that they will have better things to do. That is why he ends the *Phaedrus* with the story of Teuth which doubts the efficacy of the written word, inferior as it is to the joint search for truth in living discourse.

In his old age Plato discussed *mousikê*, poetry and music, once more. He approaches it in the second book of the *Laws* from the point of view of the educator, as in the *Republic*, but the later discussion is much more fruitful and suggestive.

The educational function of *mousikê* in training the emotions of the young before they reach the age of reason is here also strongly emphasized (653 a-c), but this is now distinguished from its recreational function. Emotional control is apt to slacken at various times in life and (653 d):

> The gods, taking pity upon the human race and its labours, established the round of divine festivals for them as periods of rest from their labours and granted that the Muses, their leader Apollo, and Dionysus be our companions at these festivals, in order that this control might be restored . . .

This correction of emotional imbalance, the recreational function of *mousikê*, is a very important addition to the Platonic theory of art and it foreshadows the Aristotelian *catharsis* which, at least in the *Politics*, is also a function of recreation. As so often in Plato, it is not elaborated.

The origin of music and poetry is then equated with the gradual control, by rhythm and harmony, of the random cries and movements of infancy, for the sense of rhythm and harmony is a special gift of the gods to humanity (653 d):

---

[1] *Politics* 2, 6, 4 (1265 a 3-4). Aristotle is talking of the *Laws* and its tendency to revert to the ideal Republic.

No young creature is able to keep silent or keep its body still; it is
always ready to move and utter cries, skipping or leaping about,
playing and dancing with pleasure, uttering every kind of sound.
Other animals have no perception in these activities of any order or
disorder which is called rhythm and harmony. But to us the gods
whom we mentioned as our partners in the dance have granted the
pleasurable sense of rhythm and harmony by means of which they stir
us and lead our choirs, linking us together in song and dance ... shall
we agree then that our first education is through the Muses and Apollo?

Thus the arts are rooted in human nature and human life: when we speak,
every one of us practises the art of expression in words; when we move,
every one of us is to some extent a dancer. Music and poetry are but the
culmination of the process which imposes rhythm and harmony on the
random cries and uncoordinated movements of the human infant.[1] It is
in this sense that 'the well educated man is he who can sing and dance well'
(654 b).

   With his conception of art as an integral and important part of life, it is
natural enough that, when Plato now considers the three criteria by which
it must be judged, the moral content and moral effect of the production
should retain its importance and so he insists that a 'beautiful' song must
be of 'beautiful' things,[2] that the song of the brave man is beautiful, that of
the coward is ugly (654 e).

   The second criterion of good art is the pleasure it gives, and this is much
more sympathetically dealt with than in the earlier works.[3] Plato now
freely admits that good art must give pleasure, but of course it must be the
pleasure of the right people. Small children like puppet shows, older
children prefer comedy; youths, educated women and perhaps the
majority like tragedy, old men prefer the epic (658 e). We will surely
agree that good art cannot be judged, to put it in modern terms, by box
office receipts.

   Plato does not want the judges in artistic contests to be swayed by the
mob. They must be its teachers, not its pupil, and so should the poets.[4]
While discussing pleasure Plato has an interesting passage (655 c-e) where

   [1] Cf. the gradual control of human soul's movements in *Timaeus* (47) as rhythm and
harmony are parallel to the imprinting of *Logos* or Reason upon Chaos, which is then related
to the orderly motions of the stars.
   [2] The Greek term καλός (654 c and *passim*) unites the two ideas, the beautiful and the good,
they always merge in Plato as the Good and the Beautiful are but two aspects of the same
Reality.
   [3] This is true of pleasure in general. As Plato says at 663 b-c, no one will choose actions in
which pleasure does not predominate and it is the task of the lawgiver to show that the best
life is also the most pleasurable. See also *Laws* 732 e – 733 d and my *Plato's Thought*, 83-86.
   [4] 659 b. οὐ γὰρ μαθητὴς ἀλλὰ διδάσκαλος τῶν θεατῶν μᾶλλον ὁ κριτής...

he insists that our appreciation must be sincere if it is to be beneficial. Only too often when their character and training are at odds, men praise one type of performance and secretly enjoy another, or say that the one is good, the other pleasurable. We should enjoy what we praise if we are integrated personalities. You become like what you enjoy (656 b) for bad art is like bad company. One cannot, in other words, really enjoy great art from a sense of duty, and it is no use pretending that one does.

There is, however, a third criterion which the critic or judge must take into account, and here for the first time Plato introduces an aesthetic criterion, even though it appears to be formulated somewhat crudely as ὀρθότης, i.e. the rightness or correctness of the imitation, its truth to life. Since the products of art are all imitations and images[1]

> it seems that in each case the critic, if he is not to fall into error, must know what the work is. For if he does not know its nature, i.e. what its intention is, of what it truly is an image, he can hardly know how far it succeeds correctly in what it intends to do. (668 c)

The critic must also know the nature of the model in order to be able to judge the image or imitation of it. He must, for example, know the nature of man in order to be able to judge a dramatic or other image of a man. And although Plato again uses painting and sculpture as his main illustrations (668 e), and talks in terms of measurements and the like, it is a mistake to understand his ὀρθότης or 'correctness' in too narrow a sense. It certainly includes a great deal, explicitly good and consistent characterization, the appropriateness of character to words and tune, and the like.

In fact Plato is near to requiring once more from his artist and his judge the complete philosophic knowledge of life (the Forms are not mentioned in the Laws). At least his critic must have that knowledge since he is ultimately responsible for the morals of the community. The poet must know the techniques of his art, the appropriateness of his words and tunes to each other and to the whole work. He need not, however, have knowledge of the social effect of his art[2] but then he must obey the lawgiver as censor.

---

[1] 668 b. It is interesting that Plato introduces the theory of imitation as a truism which everyone will accept, poets, audiences and actors.

[2] 670 e: τὸ γὰρ τρίτον οὐδεμία ἀνάγκη ποιητῇ γιγνώσκειν, εἴτε καλὸν εἴτε μὴ καλὸν τὸ μίμημα. Cf. 801 c-d. Throughout the discussion καλόν and καλῶς refer to content, i.e. whether it is a work that will have a good influence. Plato confuses us by changing his terminology, however. At 667 a the three criteria are χάρις, ὀρθότης and ὠφελία, i.e. pleasure, correctness and usefulness (whether it benefits people). At 668 c, the critic must know the nature of the composition, οὐσία = ὅτι ποτ᾽ ἐστι (τὸ ποίημα), for if he does not know this, namely τί βούλεται its intention or of what it is an image (ὅτου ποτ᾽ ἔστιν εἰκὼν ὄντως and all this is included under οὐσία) he cannot know whether it is 'correct'. In this passage Plato is explaining what he

This, Plato's last discussion of the arts, brings in a number of new ideas and some of them take us half-way to Aristotle. The vital importance of the arts in the formation of character remains, but another function is added, cultural recreation which helps to restore emotional balance where it has been lost. The origins of poetry and music are traced back to the effect of the specifically human sense of rhythm and harmony upon the random cries and movements of infants. Pleasure now becomes a necessary and respectable criterion of good art. We also find a new and specifically artistic criterion, 'correctness' which, fairly interpreted, has great possibilities. Finally, though censorship remains, and it looks as if the critic will need philosophic knowledge of reality, the poet need not possess it and it is at least possible to be a great artist without being a philosopher.

There are a few more incidental but significant references to poetry in the *Laws*. Plato objects to music without words or dance (669 e); music alone was a contemporary development fully recognized by the time Aristotle wrote the *Politics*. We may note in passing that he objects to colour-metaphors in musical criticism (655 a). The perpetual desire to please the mob spoils artistic production and leads to a 'theatrocracy' instead of an aristocracy of taste (700 a – 701 d). Plato wants to keep the different genres fixed and quotes the example of Egypt (799 a) and he objects to excessive appeals to the emotions (800 d). The board of censors shall consist of the officer in charge of education (the chief functionary of state) and a board of men over fifty (801 d); they will select for performance representations of the good life, hymns to the gods, encomia of the great dead and so on (801 e). Indiscriminate learning of poetry by rote is condemned (810 e – 811 c); when searching for an example of what might be so learned he suggests the *Laws* itself, as a model for educators for it too is somehow inspired.[1]

There is also a brief reference to comedy in a final discussion of censorship (816 d-e). Here Plato is unusually uncertain, almost embarrassed, and he seems to look on comedy as a necessary evil. To know what is serious one must know what is laughable, if only so that one should not inadvertently say or do something ridiculous. However, acting in comedies, and probably writing them also, will be a task for foreigners and slaves,[2]

means by the nature of the work and includes the *aim* or *intention* of the artist. Then at 669 a-b he states again that the critic must know three things (pleasure is now left out) namely (*a*) ὅ τί ἐστι, again the nature of the *work* in the sense just explained, which here seems to *include* the knowledge of the model, (*b*) whether it is correct, ὡς ὀρθῶς, and (*c*) ὡς εὖ which is here equivalent to καλῶς, or to ὠφελία, i.e. its good effect. ὡς εὖ cannot refer to technical perfection, since this ὡς ὀρθῶς; it must refer to the beneficient effect. It is this same τρίτον which need not concern the poet at 670 e.

[1] 811 c: οὐκ ἄνευ τινος ἐπιπνοίας θεῶν.

[2] 816 e: μιμεῖσθαι which in comedy is forbidden to citizens probably means both writing comedies and acting in them.

no citizen should be seen to learn comedy, and it should remain, for our citizens, something unfamiliar. This is little enough.

There is, however, one other passage in Plato which is at least more enlightening, in the *Philebus* (48 a – 49 c). The pleasure of tragedy is quoted there as an example of mixed pleasures, 'when we enjoy it and weep at the same time'. The case of comedy is not so clear, but it is found that here too pain is involved, for comedy always involves spite or envy (φθόνος) which is a painful feeling and makes us laugh at the misfortunes of others. Ridicule is bound up with self-ignorance, be it of one's possessions, one's physical appearance or one's mentality, and those who thus do not know themselves are the proper butts of comedy, provided only that they are not so powerful that fear displaces laughter. Thus is pain mixed with pleasure, not only in dirges, tragedies and comedies on the stage, but 'in the whole tragedy and comedy of life'.

It is curious that Plato, so adept at humour, irony, sarcasm and even farce, should have reflected so little on the nature of the comic. It is even more curious, though this may be accidental, that we have very little more on this subject from Aristotle or any other Greek writer.

CHAPTER V

Aristotle

Plato's method is synoptic, Aristotle's analytic. Plato always sees every subject in its relation to every other, as part of the whole domain of knowledge. Aristotle deals with every branch of knowledge by itself, usually in a separate treatise, and keeps strictly within the limits he has set himself. The *Poetics*, for example, deals with the criteria of good poetry, especially tragedy. The function of poetry in society does not arise and is not explicitly dealt with. This does not mean that Aristotle considers it unimportant, only that the subject is treated elsewhere, in the *Politics*, and the conclusions of that discussion are taken for granted in the *Poetics*.

Aristotle was a member of Plato's Academy for twenty years. As has often been said, he starts where Plato left off, and, where he disagrees, his discussions are frequently slanted to answer Plato. Plato found it hard, as we have seen, to recognize any knowledge which was not philosophic knowledge. Aristotle's *Ethics* are largely concerned to prove that one can live a good and useful life without being a philosopher; hence the emphasis on ethical virtue and practical wisdom. The *Rhetoric* shows the kind of limited knowledge which it is necessary for the orator and public man to possess. It also analyses the art of expression in words, rhetoric, as the *Poetics* analyses the art of tragedy. But in neither case is that, for Aristotle, the whole story. Both works to a large extent explain, refine and improve Platonic theories.

THE *POLITICS*

It is in the last part of the *Politics* that Aristotle takes up the problem which so exercised Plato, namely the social function of *mousikê*, poetry and music, and incidentally of the other fine arts. He is discussing education; he therefore approaches the problem from the same point of view as Plato usually does, and establishes much the same kind of censorship.[1] His rulers too must see to it that only stories with the right moral are told to children, and not tolerate ugly language ($\alpha i \sigma \chi \rho o \lambda o \gamma i \alpha$) in the state, for ugly words

---

[1] *Politics* 7, 17 (1336 a-b). For $\alpha i \sigma \chi \rho o \lambda o \gamma \epsilon \hat{\iota} \nu$, 1336 b 4-5, and for comedy 1336 b 10-20. Indeed Aristotle goes further than Plato, for he decrees serious penalties for bad language (1336 b 9-13)!

and ugly deeds are closely akin. If an awkward exception is made for comedy, because it is sanctioned by custom at certain festivals of the gods, only adult males may attend the performances. It is completely taken for granted that art is 'imitation', *mimêsis*, of life in the Platonic sense.[1]

The main discussion of education is in the last chapters of the eighth book. The customary subjects are said to be reading, writing, physical training and *mousikê*,[2] which obviously includes both poetry and music, and the word continues to be used in this sense. Aristotle is here concerned with the social function of both music and poetry.

Mousikê has three functions, the first two being the same as in Plato's *Laws*, the educational and the recreational. Aristotle, however, adds a third: *mousikê* also has a part to play in the proper use of leisure. He makes a sharp distinction between recreation or play on the one hand, and leisure on the other. Recreation is rest and refreshment which we all need after toil; it has a healing function and restores the body and the mind. Leisure is the time which remains after we have done our work and *after* necessary recreation. Education for leisure is important and here too *mousikê* has a vital role. It is not only, as is too often thought, a provider of pleasure; it also helps to provide happiness, for the right use of leisure is on a much higher plane than recreation, a plane to which most of us only rise occasionally, the kind of life which Aristotle calls διαγωγή. We might call this the cultural function of *mousikê*, but unfortunately Aristotle does not pursue the subject beyond saying that *mousikê* also contributes to wisdom.[3]

---

[1] 1336 b 10: μήτε ἄγαλμα μήτε γραφὴν εἶναι τοιούτων μίμησιν, and then immediately goes on to speak of comedy which is clearly included under *mimêsis*. So with μίμησις and ὁμοιώματα in book eight chs. 5 and 6. If Aristotle here and in the *Poetics* had disagreed with Plato's use of *mimêsis*, he would undoubtedly have emphasized the difference.

[2] That *mousikê* is here used for poetry *and* music is obvious, for poetry could not be left out of a list of subjects of Greek education (1337 b 24-25). And the word continues to be used in this, the usual sense, throughout the discussion, for Aristotle deals with physical training in ch. 4 and with *mousikê* in ch. 5. In 1342 a 18 '*mousikê* in the theatre' and ὁ θεατής, the 'spectator' obviously include drama. Moreover, even in ch. 6, where he is primarily discussing musical modes, and one is tempted to translate by music, the flute is excluded 'because flute-playing does not permit words' which makes it very clear that when discussing the other musical modes he is thinking of songs, i.e. music *and* poetry. It is very unfortunate therefore that throughout the discussion, the standard translations of Jowett and Barker translate *mousikê* by 'music'. In 1340 a 13: ἀκροώμενοι τῶν μιμησέων γίγνονται συμπαθεῖς καὶ χωρὶς τῶν ῥυθμῶν καὶ τῶν μελῶν αὐτῶν means 'All men are roused to emotional sympathy when they hear imitations, even without rhythm or melody', i.e. speeches in prose, *not* 'mere imitative sounds' (Barker) whatever they might be. At 1339 b 20 *mousikê* with or without *melôdia* does *not* mean music, whether instrumental or accompanied by the voice (Barker) or music, whether with or without song, but 'poetry whether with or without music'. Again, the imitations of anger, gentleness, courage and moderation which are nearest to the actual are ἐν τοῖς ῥυθμοῖς καὶ τοῖς μέλεσιν, 'in poetry and song' and clearly include drama and lyric; it does *not* refer to 'musical times and tunes' (Barker).

The meaning of *mousikê* is important for this is the only discussion of its kind in Aristotle.

[3] 1339 a 25-26: ἢ πρὸς διαγωγήν τι συμβάλλεται καὶ πρὸς φρόνησιν...

The educational function is to Aristotle the most important. As in Plato, it trains the emotions and teaches us to take delight in moral actions and good character. Our children, says Aristotle, should be trained to play musical instruments, not indeed to exhibit themselves in professional contests which is unbecoming, but sufficiently to be good judges and critics of 'musical' performances when they get older. This instrumental training is also useful to keep children out of mischief and of course it has a direct influence upon character.[1]

It is when dealing with the recreational function of *mousikê* that Aristotle discusses *catharsis*, and in the *Politics* it is limited to that second function. Recreation, Plato had said, aimed at restoring emotional balance, and this is also the result of *catharsis*.[2] Unlike Plato, however, Aristotle allows highly emotional performances for recreational purposes (attended only by adults) which would be quite unsuitable for the education of children. But there must be no citizens among the performers.[3]

He is here concerned with the same problem of emotional identification as Plato was. Any kind of presentation or imitation arouses us to *sympatheia* (feeling with), a much stronger word than our 'sympathy', and some excite us to the point of possession.[4] But whereas Plato continued to believe that 'we become like what we imitate', Aristotle thought that at these performances the very intensity of emotional excitement would, by a process of catharsis, purge away the excess of emotion, work it out of our system as it were.[5]

He refers us to the *Poetics* for a fuller explanation of catharsis. One may therefore assume that the word was there used in the same general sense, though several kinds may well have been distinguished. As that fuller explanation, if it was ever written, is lost, we have only the passage in the *Politics* which is, fortunately, fairly explicit (1342 a 5):

[1] On the educational value of *mousikê* generally, see ch. 5 and 6, 1339 a 11 – 1341 b 35. For the effect on character 1339 a 15-28 and *passim*. On instrumental training, 1341 a 1 – b 19; on keeping children out of mischief (like the rattle of Archytas), 1340 b 26-30; and Aristotle adds song (ᾄδοντας) to instruments at 1340 b 20-26 in order to become good critics.

[2] That catharsis is restricted to recreation, for which it is almost a synonym, is quite clear. Compare, for example, πότερον παιδείαν ἢ παιδιὰν ἢ διαγωγήν at 1339 b 14 with 1341 b 38: παιδείας ἕνεκεν καὶ καθάρσεως . . . τρίτον δὲ πρὸς διαγωγήν. And see πρὸς ἀνάπαυσιν at 1342 a 23.

[3] 1342 a 3: πρὸς μὲν τὴν παιδείαν ταῖς ἠθικωτάταις πρὸς δὲ ἀκρόασιν ἑτέρων χειρουργούντων καὶ ταῖς πρακτικαῖς καὶ ταῖς ἐνθουσιαστικαῖς. We remember that the citizens in the *Laws* were not to act in comedies (or write them?). See above, pp. 64-5.

[4] ἐνθουσιασμός. See 1340 a 7-14.

[5] Plato recognizes a similar purging or releasing of emotion, not in the effects of *mousikê* but in the curing of religious frenzy at *Laws* 790 e – 791 b. He has been describing how babies can be quietened by being rocked and compares this effect of external motions with 'the healing of Corybants' and 'the curing of Bachants who are beside themselves' by a combination of dancing and music 'to overcome inner fear and frenzy' (φόβεραν . . καὶ μανικὴν κίνησιν). They too recover their emotional poise. Aristotle may well have had this passage in mind.

An emotion which strongly affects a few souls is present in all in varying degrees, for example pity and fear, and also the feeling of ecstasy or possession, to which some people are particularly liable. We see that such people, when they come under the influence of religious music and are affected by songs which drive the soul to frenzy, are restored as if under medical treatment and purge. Now people much given to pity and fear, and emotional people generally, must be affected in the same way; they all undergo a kind of purge and pleasurable relief. And others share the same experience to the extent that they share such emotions.

In the same way cathartic songs give men a pleasure which is harmless. For this reason we must provide for such songs and tunes actors to enact the *mousikê* of the theatre.

Spectators are of two kinds; some are free and educated men, some are vulgar, mechanics, general labourers and the like. These last we must provide with contests and spectacles for their recreation. Just as their souls are perverted from their natural state, so there are perversions of music, songs which are intense and exaggerated. Each derives pleasure from what is akin to his nature.[1] We must therefore allow the performers to perform this kind of *mousikê*, for this kind of spectator.

The meaning of catharsis is here quite clear. Highly emotional and intense performances will be allowed so that those whose emotions are out of control will have them stirred up further and reach a crisis which will purge away the excess and restore them to a more normal and balanced state. The emotions chiefly mentioned are pity, fear and an ecstatic sense of being 'possessed'. We should also note that this process is intended for 'vulgar mechanics, labourers and the like', and that the cultured man whose passions are under control (like Aristotle) has little need of this homoeopathic treatment; if affected at all, he will be so only to a much lesser degree.

As already mentioned, this is the only *general* discussion of *mousikê* in Aristotle. He follows Plato in the need for censorship, as well as in the educational and recreational functions of *mousikê*, but he adds a third, the cultural function, and, while the general aim of recreation is the same, the method employed is entirely different: his idea of catharsis is quite new when applied to musical and poetic contests, and he allows many kinds of cathartic performances which Plato would never have tolerated.

[1] Cf. *Laws* 655 d 5 – 656 a 4, discussed above, p. 65.

THE *POETICS*[1]

The *Poetics* as we have it is fragmentary. We have already seen that the *Politics* refers us to it for a fuller explanation of catharsis. The *Rhetoric* also says that the different forms of the comic have been dealt with in the *Poetics*.[2] Neither of these discussions occurs in the extant text. Then also, the first sentence of the *Poetics* itself says that its 'subject is the art of poetry in general and its different genres, the specific power of each genre'. This promise is not kept: the *Poetics* deals with tragedy fully, and only incidentally with some other genres such as epic, comedy and history, but always in comparison with tragedy. It has therefore been frequently assumed that there was at least another book in which some of these problems were dealt with.[3]

In style the *Poetics* is very uneven, often abrupt, repetitive, even ungrammatical, sometimes contradictory, so that it has been supposed that a number of later additions were made by Aristotle himself, as one might do in the margin of lecture notes.[4]

Art as Imitation

That all art was imitation was a truism to Plato,[5] though the metaphysical and psychological consequences which he drew from this in the tenth book of the *Republic* were obviously his own. Aristotle repeats the main principle that all kinds of poetry, music and dancing, and the plastic arts as well, are forms of imitation. He too states this not as a theory to be established but as something to be taken for granted and a basis for further theories. There is no suggestion that he is using the word *mimêsis* in any novel sense[6]; clearly he means that the situations, actions, characters and

---

[1] The actual title is *On the Art of Poetry*, but *Poetics* is now hallowed by usage. The standard editions are Ingram Bywater's and Alfred Gudeman's. On controversial passages I shall simply indicate the different interpretations, and the reader is referred to these editions for a full discussion of the differing views without any further mention of these editions. The same is true of G. F. Else's *Aristotle's Poetics, The Argument* wherein the discussions also follow the text. S. H. Butcher's *Aristotle's Theory of Poetry and Fine Art* is also useful but less specific. The reader is also referred to my translation, *Aristotle on Poetry and Style* for a fuller discussion of particular passages. None of these will be further referred to in the notes except for a special reason. I should also draw attention to a very useful little book by Humphrey House, *Aristotle's Poetics* which discusses various aspects of Aristotle's theories, and to *Tragedy* by F. L. Lucas.

[2] *Rhet*. 3, 18,7 (1419 b 6): εἴρηται πόσα εἴδη γελοίων ἐν τοῖς περὶ ποιητκιῆς and c.f.I, 11,29 (1372 a 1-2).

[3] Ingenious attempts have been made to reconstruct the missing book, especially by Lane Cooper, *An Aristotelian Theory of Comedy*. A. Ph. McMahon, on the other hand, does not believe that the second book was ever written, see *HSCP* 28 (1917), 1-46.

[4] See, for example, D. De Montmollin, *La Poétique d' Aristote* and G. F. Else, *passim*, also F. Solmsen in *CQ 29* (1935).   [5] *Laws* 668 b-c and see above, p. 63.

[6] Aristotle in fact uses *mimêsis* in both Platonic senses. Usually it is in the general sense of

emotions portrayed or evoked must strike one as true to life. As so often, however, Aristotle broadens and clarifies the Platonic theory where he later says that, when accused of untruth, the poet may reply that he is imitating things as they are, as they were, as they ought to be, or as men thought they were, i.e. representing the present, the past, the ideal, or men's beliefs about them. Even so, however, we must still feel the picture to be true to something actual, which is the essence of the theory and the justification of the continued use of the word *mimêsis* as imitation; this feeling is lost in the alternative translation as 'representation'. By thus broadening the concept, however, Aristotle avoids the narrow interpretation of *mimêsis* as copying which Plato's use of painting in illustration seems at times to imply and which is nonsensical. This theory of imitation, be it noted, was not challenged in antiquity.[1]

If all art is imitation, then different arts are species of that genus and should be distinguished by meaningful differences in 'the nature of the imitation'. So Aristotle proceeds to suggest that the basis for such classification should be three essential principles of difference between various kinds[2]: differences in the model they imitate, in the means or medium they use, and in the manner in which they do it. Now all musical and literary arts imitate by means of speech, rhythm and music, whether used together or separately (as dancing uses rhythm alone). The manner of imitation is whether the poet uses impersonation only, narrative only, or a mixture of the two.[3] The differences based on the nature of the model correspond to what we would call differences in subject matter, but Aristotle gives a curious twist to this when he goes on to say that the difference here depends on whether the artist represents men as they are, as better or as worse. This becomes a moral difference: epic and tragedy represent men as better, comedy and parody as worse. Pauson the painter represented men as they are.[4]

Aristotle's point is that any classification of kinds of literature based on these three principles of difference will be far more significant than the usual distinctions into prose or verse or according to particular metres

imitation of life, and when he first speaks of dramatic impersonation (ch. 3 ad init.) he avoids the term *mimêsis* for it. In a later passage, however, he is not so careful where (1460 a 8) he says that Homer rarely speaks in his own person, οὐ γάρ ἐστι κατὰ ταῦτα μιμητής, for then he is not an imitator, i.e. impersonator, while others take a personal part throughout, μιμοῦνται δὲ ὀλίγα καὶ ὀλιγάκις, i.e. they but rarely *impersonate*.

[1] Except by Philodemus. See below, pp. 195-6.

[2] Aristotle is here seeking to divide the arts κατ᾽ ἄρθρα or κατ᾽ εἴδη as Plato put it in *Phaedrus* 265 e. See above, p. 58.

[3] This is the same distinction made by Plato in *Rep.* 3, 392 c, except that Aristotle phrases it differently; to him the mixture is a form of narration.

[4] The first three chapters of the *Poetics* deal with these three principles of classification of imitations.

(Homer and Empedocles both wrote hexameters but they have nothing significant in common). Having made this clear, however, he does not himself offer us such a classification except that he uses the differences in the model as a main distinction between tragedy and comedy, for 'tragedy imitates men who are better, comedy imitates men who are worse than we know them today' (1448 a 17).

Like Plato, he seeks the origins of poetry in human nature itself, and differences in human nature also account for the two main divisions of poetry as it developed. He attributes the birth of poetry to two main causes, first, that man is by nature the most imitative of animals, and that humanity is gifted with a sense of rhythm and melody.[1] Because he is so imitative, man will enjoy both the making of imitations and the contemplation of them. This latter pleasure is often due to the pleasure of recognizing the model in the image, though there are other pleasures involved in the contemplation of the image's workmanship, and here presumably the sense of rhythm and melody is involved.

Differences of human character account for the fact of two main streams of poetry when

> The more serious-minded imitated the noble deeds of noble men; the
> more common imitated the actions of the less noble.

One stream accounts for invective, lampoons, and ultimately comedy, the other for hymns, encomia, the epic, and ultimately tragedy. Yet both streams are said to derive from Homer, whose *Margites* is in the same relation to comedy as the *Iliad* and the *Odyssey* are to tragedy![2] Tragedy and comedy are then the culminating forms of each stream. Comedy was developed from the phallic songs, and tragedy from the dithyramb.[3]

Comedy, Epic and Tragedy
Aristotle defines comedy first, and the definition should be kept in mind

---

[1] This sense of melody and rhythm is the same as the sense of harmony and rhythm which Plato said was a special gift of the gods to mankind in *Laws* 654 (see above, pp. 61-2). The other cause that man is naturally imitative, is an addition of Aristotle, ch. 4 (1448 b 4-24). When he goes on to say that this feeling for rhythm, led to the development of poetry from 'random utterances' – ἐκ τῶν αὐτοσχεδιασμάτων he is again very close to Plato (above, p. 62).

[2] This seems to contradict the statement that different kinds of poetry arose from the character of the poet. Aristotle presumably thinks that this was generally so, although not in Homer's case who stood above them all. The *Margites* seems to have been a mock epic about the man who knew many things and knew them all badly (Plato, *Alcibiades* 2, 147 b); only half a dozen lines remain. It seems to have been written in hexameters interspersed with iambics. It was (probably wrongly) attributed to Homer but must at least have been very old. See T. W. Allen, *Homeri Opera* (Oxford text) 5, 152-9.

[3] This origin of tragedy from 'the leaders of the dithyramb' via the satyr play has often been doubted. See Pickard-Cambridge, *Dithyramb, Tragedy and Comedy*[2] (89-97) for a full discussion of the evidence. S. M. Adams found support for Aristotle in Pindar, *Phoenix* 9 (1955)

when reading that of tragedy, because, though simpler and less complete, it raises some of the same problems (1449 a 31):

> Comedy, as already mentioned, is an imitation of men who are inferior though not altogether vicious, but the ridiculous is a species of ugliness. It is a sort of flaw and ugliness, which is painless and not destructive. An obvious example is the comic mask, ugly and twisted but not painful to look at.

Aristotle does not explain. The statement that the flaw (*hamartêma*) must not be so ugly as to be painful is reminiscent of Plato's statement that laughter is replaced by fear if the butt of comedy (lacking in self-knowledge) is too powerful. So here, overpowering ugliness is repellent and therefore painful, not funny.[1] We should also note that inferior men are morally inferior since they have a degree of vice, though they are not excessively vicious. So the objects imitated by comedy, when contrasted with those of tragedy, were described earlier in terms which at least include moral inferiority.[2]

It is clear that the intention of this incomplete definition is to contrast it with tragedy about to be defined. It is not a complete definition of comedy but concentrates on describing the object of imitation of comedy which to Aristotle is the basic difference with tragedy. He goes on to mention the epic which has the same objects of imitation as tragedy and there specifies *another* point of difference, which is the reason why epic is mentioned here (1449 b 9):

> As far as being an imitation in verse of good men is concerned, epic agrees with tragedy. They differ in that epic only uses one meter and is in narrative form. They also differ in length, for tragedy tries to confine itself as much as possible within one revolution of the sun, or a little more, whereas the time of an epic is unlimited. This, however, was at first also true of tragedy.

That is, since, unlike comedy, epic does imitate the same models as tragedy (the noble deeds of noble men) it differs in other ways. The last of these, an almost casual reference that tragedy nowadays tries to limit its action to one day or thereabouts,[3] is the only reference to the illfated 'unity of time' of later criticism. It is obviously *not* a statement of what tragedy

---

[1] See Philebus 48 a – 49 c and above, p. 65.

[2] Ch. 2, where the better and worse models are clearly morally so, being explained by κακίᾳ καὶ ἀρετῇ, vice and virtue.

[3] Else (pp. 210-19) suggests that Aristotle is not talking about the supposed time of the action, but the length of time occupied by the performance. This is certainly a possible translation, but he then has to take the next clause, ἢ μικρὸν ἐξαλλάττειν as a substantival clause, as if Aristotle had said 'and to vary but little'. This seems unlikely.

should do, only of what it usually does. Unity of place is never mentioned at all, and we shall see that unity of plot is the only unity on which Aristotle does insist.

The Definition of Tragedy

Having thus made clear where comedy and epic differ from tragedy, Aristotle proceeds to define it (1449 b 21):

> Epic poetry and comedy we shall deal with later; let us now take up the definition of tragedy which emerges from what has been said. A tragedy, then, is an imitation of a good action, complete and of a certain length, by means of language sweetened for each of its parts separately; it relies in its various elements[1] upon acting, not narrative; through pity and fear it achieves the catharsis of such emotions.

Aristotle himself explains, in the following sentence, that the phrase 'sweetened language' refers to rhythm, song and music, and 'for each part separately' means that some parts of a tragedy have only the rhythm of poetry while other parts (the choral odes) have song and music as well. Unfortunately, he does not help us directly with the expressions that are really controversial. Yet I believe that if we concentrate on what Aristotle actually says, and not on what we should like him to say, there is little ground for controversy.

Some commentators like to think that Aristotle's criteria in the *Poetics* are purely aesthetic and that he is quite free of what they call 'the moral fallacy' in the appreciation of poetry. This would be very strange, for Aristotle is a Greek, and he is certainly not free of the 'Platonic fallacy' in the *Politics*. But even if we restrict ourselves to the *Poetics*, there are plenty of moral judgements. I have translated 'a tragedy is the imitation of a good action', i.e. morally good. The Greek adjective is *spoudaios*, and it is, of course, the action of the whole drama that is in question. When the word is applied to characters, or men, or their actions elsewhere in the *Poetics*, it always has moral connotations. So has the 'inferior' model of comedy, and this meaning carries over when, a few lines later, tragedy is said to be the imitation of men who are more *spoudaioi*.[2] This means better men. To

---

[1] I give the Greek of this celebrated definition: ἔστιν οὖν τραγῳδία μίμησις πράξεως σπουδαίας καὶ τελείας μέγεθος ἐχούσης ἡδυσμένῳ λόγῳ χωρὶς ἑκάστῳ τῶν εἰδῶν ἐν τοῖς μορίοις δρώντων καὶ οὐ δι' ἀγγελίας δι' ἐλέου καὶ φόβου περαίνουσα τὴν τῶν τοιούτων παθημάτων κάθαρσιν. My translation takes the words ἐν τοῖς μορίοις closely with what follows, and in the same sense as six lines later where Aristotle is explaining his definition. For a justification of this see *Phoenix* 12 (1958). The difference from the usual translation 'in language embellished with each kind of artistic ornament, the several kinds being found in different parts of the play; in the form of action not of narrative' (Butcher) is not one of substance, but of the exact meaning of the Greek.

[2] See above, p. 73, and note 2. We may add that where Aristotle is discussing the

translate this as 'men of a higher type', or 'superior' men, is very puzzling. It would certainly have puzzled Aristotle to understand how one can be a higher type of man without being a better man morally, intellectually and in every other way. And so with actions. Commentators are about equally divided nowadays between 'a morally good action' and a 'serious action', but if we lay aside our prejudices, the first is, in my view, the only correct translation.

The other main difficulty is the meaning of catharsis. Here the choice lies between 'the purging of such emotions' (which I have adopted) and 'the purification of such emotions'. The first is a medical metaphor, the second an Orphic one; both are possible meanings. Here again we have no right to ignore the passage at the end of the *Politics* where the sense of purgation is perfectly clear, and which specifically refers to the *Poetics* for a 'clearer' explanation, not for a completely different meaning.[1] Perhaps we need not pursue the matter further, for most modern commentators now interpret it as 'purging'. Even if we did not have the *Politics*, the purification of pity and fear is a strange idea for Aristotle, the son of a doctor and the most un-Orphic and unmystic of men. Some have probably been misled by the modern notion of disinterested pity, which is quite un-Aristotelian. To Aristotle pity is a kind of fear, is not disinterested, and is not a desirable thing at all.[2] Purging is clearly right.

The rest of the definition is clear. We are by now quite familiar with the meaning of 'imitation', and we can fully agree that a tragedy should be an entity, its action complete and of a certain length. Nor is there any reasonable doubt that the 'pity and fear and such emotions'[3] are those of the spectators. The rousing of pity and fear in their audience was, as we have seen, the recognized goal of the art of words, of orator, rhapsode and poet. Besides, Aristotle, in the *Politics* at least, was answering Plato and evolved the theory of catharsis in that context. There is no doubt as to whose emotions are there purged.

---

representation of evil on the stage, he says that to decide whether a passage is 'good or bad', we should see it in relation to the whole, etc. Nearly all translators there translate *spoudaion* as morally good. Butcher's 'poetically right' is not possible and in any case does not help him with 'serious' here.

[1] See above, p. 68. There is a very full discussion of the possible meanings of catharsis in Bywater pp. 152-61.

[2] See *Rhetoric* 2, 8 (1385 b 13): 'Let pity be a kind of pain we feel at the sight of a fatal or painful evil in one who does not deserve it, an evil one might expect to befall oneself or those close to one. *Clearly, to feel pity, a person must think that he himself, or someone belonging to him, is liable to suffer some evil....*'

[3] We should note, however, that Else (pp. 225-32 and 423-52) translates 'the purification of those painful or fatal acts which have that quality'. This is a new version of the 'purification' theory only now it is that of the actions. A similar suggestion has been made by S. Albertis in *Archives de Philosophie* 21 (1958). This interpretation has not had a good reception and is, to me, quite unconvincing.

Catharsis for Whom?

One minor puzzle remains. In the *Politics* it is mainly the emotions of 'vulgar artisans, labourers and the like' which, being in a state of unbalance, were purged by cathartic *mousikê*. There is no hint of this in the *Poetics* and it may seem frivolous to raise it in this connexion but the problem should be faced. We may find comfort in the reflection that even in the *Politics* what violently affected the unbalanced affected other men, whose feelings of pity and fear and 'possession' were less strong, to a lesser degree. This is not very satisfactory, for then 'the educated man' would be much less affected by even the most superb tragedy. Here, I think, the promised clearer explanation of catharsis, did we have it, would most probably have helped, and it might well have told us of different ways in which different kinds of people might be affected by poetry, all of which, as different kinds of catharsis, would have been classed under the generic term. This might have made the theory much more acceptable than the bald statement at the end of the definition can do. In this connexion it is also helpful to remember that we find in the *Problems* that even good men suffer from unbalance of various kinds, in particular that the 'melancholic' temperament, which includes 'men distinguished in philosophy, politics, poetry and the arts', suffers from excess of black bile.[1] So by the time he wrote the *Poetics* Aristotle may have realized that we could all do with catharsis of one kind or another and universalized the concept. If he did, we may be very sure that he fully analysed its different kinds. In the absence of his explanation, however, any attempt to clarify the problem further is mere guesswork.

The Elements of Tragedy

Aristotle recognizes six, and only six, significant 'parts' or elements in a tragedy: plot, characterization, language, thought, spectacle and music. Three of these are summarily dealt with. Indeed he does not deal with music at all, but merely says that its effect is plain to everyone. Of the spectacle, what we should call the staging or production, i.e. the visual effects, he is unduly contemptuous (1450 b 17):

> The spectacle does indeed stir the emotions of the audience, but it is the least artistic element; it has least to do with the poet's craft, for the power of the tragedy can be felt even without the performance or the actors.[2] The working out of visual effects belongs more to the property man's craft than to that of the poet.

[1] See the interesting study of catharsis, its origns in Plato and its relation to Aristotle's psychology and physiology in Jeanne Croissant's *Aristote et les Mystères*, 75-111.

[2] This is a minor contradiction, for if acting is required by definition, the spectacle is an

He also deprecates the rousing of pity and fear by spectacular means rather than by the plot structure, and a play which relies entirely on the spectacle to stir the audience has nothing in common with a tragedy (1353 b 1-10), for the effect is not so much fear as amazed horror. He does, however, allow elsewhere that the poet must pay attention to the staging as a necessary concomitant of tragedy, and try to visualize the performance, particularly the positions and gestures of the actors (1455 a 22-30).

Thought is obviously present when characters prove a point or utter a general truth. For the expression of thought which is in effect the art of rhetoric, Aristotle simply refers us to his *Rhetoric* (1456 a 33 – b 18).

The Plot

The most important elements are plot and character, the discussion of which occupies the thirteen central chapters. To Aristotle the plot, the structure of the action, is by far the most important; since tragedy is the imitation of an action, the action *is* the imitation, the 'soul' of a tragedy.[1] It is *possible* to have a tragedy without characterization, but without plot there can be no drama (1450 a 15-25).

The story or plot must be *one*; there must, that is, be unity of plot. This is the only kind of unity Aristotle requires, but on this he insists emphatically. And it must be a real unity which is not achieved, as some people think, by merely being the story of one person. The unity must be such that if any one incident is deleted or displaced, the whole tragedy is dislocated. In other words, the unity must be organic, with a definite place and function for every part and every part in its place, and the connexion between them must be inevitable, or at least probable. This connexion should not be too obvious beforehand, for there should be an element of surprise, but the design must be seen clearly after the event. An *appearance* of inevitability may be sufficient to achieve unity as in the story of Mitys' statue falling upon and killing his murderer. Plots that are episodic, i.e. without probable or necessary connexion between events, must at all costs be avoided.[2]

integral part of the tragedy and important to the dramatist, and if the effect of the tragedy can be felt by reading it, spectacle should *not* be an essential part of tragedy. Aristotle is of course thinking of reading aloud, since silent reading was unknown. This would allow a certain amount of acting, and the hearer could presumably imagine the performance, as the poet is told he should at 1454 b 15-18 and 1455 a 22-30.

[1] 1450 a 37: ἀρχὴ μὲν οὖν καὶ οἷον ψυχὴ ὁ μῦθος τῆς τραγῳδίας, δεύτερον δὲ τὰ ἤθη.

[2] The emphasis on unity of plot pervades the whole discussion, particularly ch. 8 (1451 a 15-36) and the comparison with epic plots (1456 a 7-15). The episodic plot is rejected at 1451 b 33-34. For the element of surprise and the story of Mitys see 1452 a 1-11, and for the probable or inevitable connexion between events κατὰ τὸ εἰκὸς καὶ ἀναγκαῖον 1151 a 13 and *passim*.

Aristotle again discusses defective plots which do achieve certain dramatic and tragic effects but not the best in ch. 18, 1456 a 21 – 'as when a clever but wicked man like Sisyphus is

As for the length of the story, it must be short enough to be grasped and easily remembered as a whole, and it must be long enough to allow for the necessary change of fortune in accordance with what is probable or inevitable. Within those limits, the longer the better (1451 a 5-11).

Peripety and Recognition

The events must be such as to arouse pity and fear, the change of fortune preferably from good fortune to bad. While it must be a single story, yet the structure of the plot may be simple or complex. The latter is preferable, and it means that the change of fortune is accompanied by Reversal (*peripeteia*) and Recognition (*anagnôrisis*). Aristotle gives as an example of peripeteia the scene with the messenger from Corinth, in the *Oedipus Tyrannus*. Oedipus had fled Corinth because of an oracle that he would slay his father and marry his mother; even when he hears of the death of the king of Corinth he refuses to return for fear that the second part of the oracle might still come true. The messenger tries to put his fears at rest by telling him that he was not the child of Polybus and Meropa but a foundling; it is this information which leads to the discovery that the oracle has already been fulfilled. Peripeteia then means that as the plot seemed to be moving in one direction there is a sudden *turn* of events and it moves in another.

Recognition in its most common form is the recognition of persons, the discovery of a bond, usually of kinship, with someone thought to be an enemy, whom one is about to injure or has injured. Aristotle himself points out that the term is capable of a broader application:

> There are, to be sure, other kinds of recognition, the knowledge acquired may be of inanimate objects, indeed of anything; one may recognize that someone has, or has not, done something. . . .

In this wider sense one might translate *anagnôrisis* by discovery or disclosure, and this is much more suited to modern drama, but it is the 'recognition between persons' which, except for that one hint, Aristotle discusses and has mainly in mind.

The best type of plot then is complex in the sense that it is complicated by recognition and peripeteia, and both should arise directly out of the action, without seeming to be contrived by the dramatist.[1]

deceived or a brave villain is defeated'. The defect may be because both are villains and thus not good tragic heroes, or because their fall into misfortune is *not* due to any 'flaw' in their character since Sisyphus' deception is not due to lack of brains nor the other's defeat to lack of bravery, i.e. the misfortune is in no way related to their *hamartia*.

1 The whole discussion of complex plots, peripety and recognition will be found in chs. 10 and 11.

The Tragic Character

Aristotle then proceeds to deal with the change of fortune and this leads him to the character of the tragic hero whose fortunes are changed (ch. 13). He begins by rejecting both the saint and the complete villain as tragic heroes. For a thoroughly good man to fall into misfortune is merely shocking; for the villain to become prosperous is, 'of all things the least tragic'; for the villain to come to misfortune may be satisfying but not tragic. None of these changes arouses pity and fear:

> We feel pity for a man who does not deserve his misfortune, we fear for somebody *like ourselves*; neither feeling is here involved.

To enjoy a tragedy, in other words, we must be able to identify emotionally with the hero, but both saint and villain are too remote from us.

> This leaves a character in between those two; a man who is neither outstanding in virtue and righteousness, one who does not fall into misfortune through vice and wickedness, but through some *hamartia*, and one who is famous and prosperous like Oedipus and Thyestes and the famous men of such families.

A few lines further on we are told that the best kind of plot requires change from good fortune to bad fortune 'not through wickedness but through a great *hamartia*'. The problem is the meaning of *hamartia* which has been variously interpreted as 'a moral flaw', 'an error of judgement' or a mere 'mistake'.

Now it is clear that Aristotle is describing the tragic character, and that *hamartia* should be a part of that character. A mere mistake which corresponds to no inner fault, on the other hand, is purely external, and cannot make the change of fortune 'probable or inevitable'. It is possible for a man to be the victim of circumstances, but his response to them must spring from something within himself. Aristotle does *not* say that the misfortune is the hero's fault, only that some *hamartia* in himself make his tragedy come about, and thereby makes it probable if not inevitable dramatically. This rules out 'mistake'.

When commentators wonder whether *hamartia* means *either* a moral weakness *or* an error of judgement, they are reading into Aristotle a modern dichotomy between brains and moral character which would seem unnatural to him. The flaw is one of personality, and the human personality includes both moral character and the human mind. In other words the flaw or weakness may be one of either mind or morals. It must be sufficient to bring about the tragedy, i.e. to make it dramatically satisfying, but it need not involve any moral responsibility. It is quite vain to seek for a *hamartia* in Oedipus, moral or otherwise, which makes him responsible for his misfortune, but we can certainly find in him a certain impatience, obstinacy, even arrogance, which make the development of the plot seem natural and dramatically satisfying. The whole controversy as to whether the *hamartia* is a moral flaw or an intellectual one is beside the point. It can be either, or even both.[1]

Nor should we forget the comic flaw which must in some way be parallel. Comic characters are by definition morally inferior, and the painless ugliness which is not vicious brings them *up*, one imagines, towards the common human level of 'men as they are', more like ourselves. Tragic heroes are great and noble, but the weakness which is their flaw brings them more *down* towards the common level, prevents them being so noble and saintly that we could not identify with them either. What use Aristotle made of the personality flaw in comedy we cannot tell, any more than what use he made of the comic catharsis, if indeed there was such a thing.[2]

The other characteristic of the tragic hero, that he should be among the great ones of the earth, is natural enough and enhances the dignity of the tragic stage. Most tragic heroes through the ages have, until very recently, been of that kind. Nor is there any contradiction with the requirement that they be 'like ourselves', for in the dreamland of the theatre we find no obstacle to identifying ourselves with kings and princes, provided only that they have some human weakness which brings them closer to us.[3]

There is another discussion of tragic characters, where Aristotle is not thinking exclusively of the tragic hero, but of tragic characters in general. Here he states four requirements.[4] The first of these brings another shock to those who want to acquit Aristotle of any moral purpose, for he says the characters must be *good*. Some have suggested that this only means useful to the purpose of the play or good of its kind, but these are clearly mistranslations, for Aristotle himself goes on to say that 'words and action express character, as we said, if they involve a moral choice, and the character is good when the choice is good'. Here he seems to have gone back to Plato's prohibition of evil on the stage but he qualifies this at once

[1] Else (378-85) equates *hamartia* with ignorance of the relationship before recognition, and makes ὁ μέταξυ the character 'who falls between the *undeserving sufferer* and the *sufferer who is like us*', but since these two are not in any way opposed, and might be the same, this interpretation does not make sense to me, and *hamartia* on his interpretation adds nothing to ἄγνοια.

[2] Those interested in speculations on the subject should read Lane Cooper's *An Aristotelian Theory of Comedy* where they will find a valuable collection of ancient passages on comedy and then the author practically rewrites most of the *Poetics* to apply to comedy, a most imaginative reconstruction.

[3] It should be noted that Oedipus and Thyestes are mentioned as examples only of members of great families, *not* as examples of the flaw.

[4] Ch. 15, 1454 a 15-36. There is here far more agreement between commentators that moral character *is* involved, for Aristotle's own words make this perfectly clear. Potts has good of its kind', however.

when he cites Menelaus in the *Orestes* of Euripides as a character *unnecessarily* evil. He qualifies it further where[1] he says that one should not consider only whether any particular action or speech is morally right or wrong, but judge it in relation to the character concerned, 'the person affected or addressed, the time, the means, the purpose, for it may help to achieve a greater good or avoid a greater evil', i.e. in relation to the play as a whole.

The second requirement for tragic characters is that they should be appropriate or true to type. A man should be manly but manliness is not suitable for a woman, nor should she be an accomplished speaker. Here he gives as examples a lamentation of Odysseus (unsuitable for a hero) and a speech of Melanippe (too philosophical for a woman).

The third requirement is that characters should be like (life). This is an essential requirement of any imitation. Unfortunately he gives no example here and it might mean like their prototypes in legend, i.e. Achilles must be wrathful, Medea jealous and so on. But these legendary figures were considered to be historical characters in any case, so the difference is not significant.

Finally, the character should be consistent throughout the play. And here Aristotle makes his meaning plain by a good phrase: where inconsistency is a character trait, the person should be consistently inconsistent. Iphigenia in the *Iphigenia at Aulis* of Euripides is an example of an inconsistent character (1454 a 33-36):

> In characterization as in plot structure, one should always aim at what is either probable or inevitable so that a character will act in a probable or unavoidable manner.

Then Aristotle seems to remember that he had said that the characters of tragedy were better than life, and he tries to reconcile these seemingly discordant views by saying that we should imitate good portrait painters who 'can reproduce the characteristics of their subject in a good likeness which is nonetheless more beautiful than the original' (1454 b 8-14).

Characterization is discussed under plot, to which it is really subsidiary since it arises out of the actions and Aristotle goes into considerable detail about the best tragic plots and situations. He advises the dramatization of the old legends, but he recognizes that this is not essential because these legends are in any case familiar only to few people, and Agathon has shown that the plot can be completely invented (1451 b 15-26).

We have seen that the story must be one. A double plot, as in the *Odyssey* where the good are rewarded and the bad punished is therefore

---

[1] 1461 a 4-9, εἰ σπουδαῖον ἢ φαῦλον must here mean good or bad, though Butcher translates, 'poetically right' but this hardly makes sense in the context, and see 1461 b 19-23.

not the best kind, and this kind of denouement, which is put in to please the groundlings, is closer to comedy where the greatest enemies are reconciled and 'nobody kills anybody'.[1]

Only that kind of plot will arouse pity and fear (except in so far as suffering is in itself pitiful) where the suffering is inflicted by people whose relationship should imply affection. The relationship may be known all the time and the suffering inflicted in spite of it (Medea); it may be recognized after the event (Oedipus); it may be discovered before the event and the deed done in spite of it; or it may be discovered and the deed prevented. The worst of all is where the facts are known from the beginning and then the deed is not done. Every reader now expects Aristotle, who has insisted on an unhappy ending and compared the opposite to comedy, to say that the best is where the full discovery comes after the deed is done (Oedipus) but, by one of these strange reversals of which he is sometimes capable, he suddenly says that the best type is where the relationship is discovered in time and the deed prevented![2]

Aristotle has a strong dislike of the supernatural, since every event must follow the other as probable or inevitable. He wants to restrict the supernatural to events outside the play, that is, in the past or the future. Gods may be allowed to tell of the distant past or to foretell the future, but supernatural interventions within the play like the chariot sent by Helios for Medea's escape (and he might have added Poseidon's bull who kills Hippolytus) must be avoided. Within the play itself, there must be nothing irrational or inexplicable (ἄλογον, 1454 a 37 – b 8).

He is critical of contemporary tragedians, and when, at the end of his discussion of the plot, he suddenly speaks of four types of tragedy, these are types by which actual and probably contemporary tragedies may be classified because of their exaggerations of a particular aspect, for he clearly disapproves of every type but one. The first is the complex tragedy, i.e. the tragedy with a complex plot (with peripety and recognition and of

---

[1] 1453 a 30-39. Aristotle is obviously right that the mere triumph of the hero over the villains does not make good tragedy, and the ancient critics tended to look upon the *Odyssey* as akin to comedy, but why does he refer to it as having a double plot? Does he mean that the events in Ithaca and the adventures of Odysseus divide our attention, or simply that the hero triumphs and the villains are punished. Aristotle is, of course, not suggesting that nobody kills anybody at the end of the *Odyssey*! What he says is that the double plot is more *like* comedy and that in *comedies* no one kills anyone.

[2] The contradiction is startling indeed and no satisfactory explanation has been offered. Bywater suggests that Aristotle is now using a moral criterion and that he is now thinking not of the emotions of the audience but of their moral sensibility, but no such thing is suggested anywhere and we have seen that Aristotle had the moral criterion in mind before and in any case such a distinction is quite foreign to him. Gudeman denies any contradiction because Aristotle is not here concerned with plot-structure, nor with the emotions. But Aristotle *is* discussing plot here, and he has been concerned with emotions all the time! We must recognize this as one of those puzzling contradictions which do occur in Aristotle occasionally.

this he approves), it is in fact the type he has been building up and recommending all along; the second is the tragedy of mere suffering ($\pi\alpha\theta\eta\tau\iota\kappa\acute{\eta}$), and he has told us that *pathos* or suffering is not enough; the third is the tragedy of character, but to him character should remain subordinated to plot; the fourth is the spectacular tragedy which he has earlier dismissed with contempt as not tragedy at all. He admits that each kind has had good poets but he reaffirms that the basic requirement of tragedy is the plot, and one may surely conclude that his own classification by different types of plot, simple, complex, etc. is much to be preferred.[1]

Language

He has now dealt with five of the six elements of tragedy, or rather he has dealt with plot and characters, dismissed two elements, spectacle and music, and (ch. 19) referred us to the *Rhetoric* for thought. He then deals with language or diction in three chapters (20-22) which are mostly about grammar and linguistics and are of little broader interest except for two things, the treatment of metaphor and a few but illuminating remarks on diction proper.

> The language, to be effective, should be lucid without being common. Now the most lucid language consists of current words, but it is common. . . . Unusual words, on the other hand, give dignity to the language and avoid the commonplace. By unusual I mean strange words, metaphors, lengthened forms, anything contrary to common usage, but if all one's words are of that kind the result is riddles or gibberish. . . . What we need is a mixed diction.

This is exactly the same advice as he gives to prose writers in the *Rhetoric*. The difference is of degree only as poets are allowed a good deal more ornamentation.

The discussion of metaphors shows that Aristotle uses the word in a wider sense than we do, and he seems to include any kind of transference of epithet and the like. His classification of metaphors is somewhat mechanical (proportional, from genus to species, species to genus, etc.) and he nowhere says what a metaphor is. We shall find a more lively discussion of this in the *Rhetoric*.

Tragedy and History

While we do not posses the discussion of comedy which Aristotle pro-

---

[1] 1455 b 33 – 1456 a 7. The text is uncertain where the fourth type is mentioned. I have followed Bywater and read ὄψις. Some editors read ἁπλῆ, the simple plot tragedy, but this, too has been called inferior to the complex in ch. 13, so that in any case the last three types are inferior. The example given favours the spectacular rather than the simple.

mised, we do have a fairly lengthy comparison of epic with tragedy and some *obiter dicta* on history; both are illuminating but we feel that the philosopher's powerful analytical brain is concentrating on tragedy, and that these other genres remain on the periphery of his field of vision. The result is that epic becomes a kind of inferior tragedy and history is not distinguished from chronicle. Neither genre is treated for its own sake (1451 a 37):

> It is not the business of the poet to relate actual events, but what might happen or could happen in accordance with probability or necessity. The historian and the poet differ, not because the one writes verse and the other prose – the work of Herodotus, put into verse, would still be history – but because the one relates what happened, the other what might happen. That is why poetry is more akin to philosophy and a better thing than history, for poetry deals *more* with universals, history with the particular events. The particular event is, for example, what Alcibiades did or had done to him; whereas the universal is what kind of thing will inevitably, or probably, happen to a certain kind of person. . . .

And in a later passage, where he compares the structure of the epic with that of history, he adds (1459 a 22):

> History has to expound not one action but one period of time and all that happens within that period to one or more persons, however tenuous the connection between those events. The battle of Salamis and that of the Carthaginians in Sicily took place at the same time, but there was no common purpose. Similarly, events may follow one another in time without any common end in view.

Aristotle then goes on to criticize epic poets for adopting a historical structure. If we regard these statements as concerned with poetry, we may readily admit that poets are *more* concerned with general truths and not bound by actual events, which the historian obviously must be. The emphasis on facts may even be a rebuke to contemporary historians who seem to have had no excessive respect for historical truth. And we should be prepared to accept from a philosopher that what deals with universal truths is better and more important than what deals with fact, though we need not agree with him. But as a theoretical statement about the writing of history (and we have no other from Aristotle) it is woefully inadequate. No historian could give *all* the events of a given period, he must obviously select them. And Thucydides would have disagreed that history could do no more than chronicle events. It is a mistake to try to extract from these statements any Aristotelian theory of history, though one suspects he would have disagreed with Thucydides. It is a great pity that we do not have from Aristotle a serious discussion of history. It might well have been very different; even as it is he does allow the historian *some* concern with universals.

Tragedy and Epic

To epic Aristotle devotes three chapters, two of which (23 and 24) make some acute comments and come close to considering epic for its own sake, but the third (26) is spoiled by a rather naive desire to prove (as against Plato) that tragedy is a higher form of poetic art than the epic. Aristotle is never at his best when arguing against Plato. He begins by comparing epic with tragedy (1459 a 17):

> Clearly, narrative imitation in one poetic metre must have a dramatic plot-structure centred upon one complete action; it must have a beginning, a middle part, and an end, in order, as one organic whole, to provide its own kind of pleasure. . . .

He then proceeds to contrast a proper epic plot structure with that of a history, as we saw, and praises Homer who did not treat of the whole Trojan War, which would have been too long to be grasped as one subject, but took as his theme one part of it which is then adorned with many incidents; yet Homer, he adds, preserves, unlike other epic poets, the essential unity of his plot. Aristotle does make clear that this unity is different from that of tragedy for the epic form allows several parts of the action to come to a head simultaneously and allows for more variation.

Epic also has greater length, and Aristotle suggests that the proper length might be equal to 'the tragedies which a poet presents for one performance' (i.e. three tragedies and one satyr-play) which is about one-third of the *Iliad* and, curiously, about the length of Apollonius' *Argonautica*. Epic also has greater scope for the marvellous and the irrational, because we do not *see* the story enacted, and it can thus give a greater sense of the marvellous, which is pleasant. Even here the philosopher advises caution, and the supernatural or unexplainable should only be used when the desired effect cannot be attained in any other way, not for its own sake; it should be avoided where possible or else lie outside the part of the story which is dramatized (as in tragedy). However, 'what is impossible but credible must be preferred to what is possible but unconvincing' (1460 a 27).

When, however, Aristotle says that: 'the different types of epic should be the same as the types of tragedy: either simple or complex, either an epic of character or of suffering', we feel he is applying to the epic categories which derive from tragedy. The feeling grows when he adds (1459 b 14):

As for the plot structure of each poem, the *Iliad* is simple and an epic of suffering, the *Odyssey* is complex – recognition occurs throughout – and an epic of character.

It is quite true that there is no recognition in the *Iliad* and that in this respect it is simple in the Aristotelian sense, but even on the basis of Aristotle's own formula, it is highly questionable to say that it has no peripeteia, and equally questionable whether we can find any in the *Odyssey*. Aristotle seems to be ignoring this, and thinking only of recognition. To call the *Odyssey* an epic of character (ἠθική) is equally dubious, for characterization is at least as good in the *Iliad*. Aristotle probably means that it is on a lower plane of intensity, but that is not the meaning of the word elsewhere in the *Poetics*. One is equally puzzled to find the *Iliad* called παθητική, for a 'pathetic' tragedy was not, hitherto, much esteemed.[1] One is tempted to conclude that Aristotle preferred the *Odyssey*, which would be very strange; one would have thought that the *Iliad* dealt more in universals and was 'more akin to philosophy'. The truth seems to be that Aristotle is misled by forms of classification not intended for the epic in the first place, and not very suited to it.

We are also told that the hexameter is the only possible meter for the epic, and that Homer alone among epic poets knows to speak in his own person very rarely, so that Aristotle evidently approves of Homer's fondness for dramatized direct speech, and all would agree with the philosopher that Homer's characterization is superb.

In the last chapter, as already mentioned, Aristotle tries to prove that tragedy is the better or higher form of art. He first replies to the criticism that tragedy is more vulgar because it 'imitates everything', and because both the actors and flute players have to throw themselves about. This, says Aristotle, quite rightly, is a foolish argument for they need not do so, and it is in any case a criticism of the performers, not of the poets; it is just degenerate contemporary histrionics, and the rhapsodes can be just as bad.

No, tragedy is superior because (*a*) it has all the elements of the epic (plot, character, thought, language) and music and spectacle besides; (*b*) it fulfills the purpose of its imitation more economically, and what is compact is more pleasing[2]; (*c*) epic has less unity, and its theme is 'watered down' because of its greater length, it is less truly the imitation of one

---

[1] As used by later critics the word ἠθικός as against παθητικός, came to refer to a lower emotional level as well as writing in character (the two being often combined, as in Lysias). This meaning, which we know from Quintilian (6, 2, 8-24) and find in 'Longinus' is, it would seem, not entirely foreign to Aristotle. See below, pp. 291-2.

[2] 1462 a 19. If 'an imitation which attains its end in a shorter space' is more pleasing, was Aristotle right to say that as long as the theme could be grasped as a whole, the longer the better (1451 a 10)?

action; and (*d*) every kind of art must arouse its own particular pleasure, and tragedy does this better.

The arguments about greater economy and unity are interesting. As for each art and its own pleasure, Aristotle began this discussion by saying that epic too had its own proper pleasure, but he did not tell us what it was or how it was obtained. One is left with the uncomfortable feeling that he considered this to be the same as that of tragedy and the epic to be merely an inferior form of tragic art. I do not believe that Aristotle would ever have done so, or even left the impression that he did, if he had ever made the epic the subject of a separate study.

Criticism

A quite separate chapter (25) deals with certain problems raised by the literary critics of the day. Many of the objections he tries to answer are matters of extreme detail and rather picayune, of the kind we connect with Zoilus, a contemporary of Aristotle, who came to be known as *Homeromastix*, the Scourge of Homer, and it is worth noting that all the specific criticisms answered by Aristotle, much on the same level, in this chapter, concern Homer. Sometimes they are mere matters of punctuation, or a word may be used in an unusual sense, or metaphorically, or it may be a matter of usage. Here are two examples: some critic had raised the question why Apollo sent his poisoned shafts upon the mules first, for what had they done? Aristotle suggests in all seriousness that the word οὐρῆες may not mean mules at all, but sentinels; or again when Achilles receives the envoys and tells Patroclus to 'mix a stronger wine' some critics were obviously shocked, as only drunkards drank their wine neat; Aristotle suggests that perhaps the word ζωρότερον in this case meant 'more quickly'. There is no evidence for the suggested meaning in either case. This part of the chapter makes clear that the loss of a good many works in the fourth century with literary titles, and not only those of Zoilus, is perhaps not much to be regretted; they probably contained little more than this kind of criticism and moral diatribes on behalf of or against Homeric and other literary characters or their authors. It is most unlikely that any of these critical works made any important contribution or were on the level of what we find in Plato and in Aristotle.

This chapter, however, is the work of Aristotle, and so it also contains some important remarks of a more general nature. One of the most interesting is his insistence that every art or craft should have its own standard of what is right (1460 b 13):

> . . . we allow the poet many modifications of language. What is right for a poet is not right for a politician; indeed what is right in poetry is not right in any other craft.

Then there is the distinction between intrinsic and incidental faults (ἁμαρτίαι) in art. If an artist picks a subject and cannot deal with it ably, then his art is at fault. But if he makes a mistake in medicine (Homer might make one of his doctors give an inflammatory instead of a soothing poultice), that is an incidental fault. Aristotle expresses this somewhat curiously where he says that in the second case the flaw is 'in the model' or that the artist picks 'the wrong model', but his essential meaning is perfectly clear: 'it is a lesser fault not to know that a hind has no horns than to make a bad picture of it'. He is surely right to say that critics should keep this distinction in mind.

He returns to the problem of the relation of poetry to truth, and it is here that he quotes as an answer the words of Sophocles 'that he made his characters as they ought to be, while Euripides made them as they are'. The poet may also answer that he is depicting things as they used to be, or even as men say or think they are, so that Xenophanes' criticism of Homer's gods is not valid.

Part of the answer to Plato about the representation of evil on the stage, which we have already discussed, also occurs in this chapter, as well as the proper use of the impossible or unexplainable to attain certain effects, and here he condemns the appearance of Aegeus in the *Medea* as an unexplained coincidence and the wickedness of Menelaus in the *Orestes* (again) as unnecessary.

Finally, there is a delightful warning which not only ancient critics were apt to forget (1461 b 1):

> The proper method of criticism is the opposite of that mentioned by Glaucon who says that critics unreasonably make certain assumptions beforehand, condemn the poet out of hand and argue on the assumption that he said what they think he said, which they do not like.

Miscellaneous Advice

There are, in the *Poetics*, a number of short sections which cannot be related to any of the main ideas, yet deal with important points. A number of these occur in one chapter (17) where Aristotle seems to turn away for a moment from his discussion of the elements of tragedy to give somewhat scattered advice to tragic writers. After saying that the poet should try to visualize the performance to avoid awkwardness, he wrote the only sentence in the *Poetics* which considers the personality and feelings of the writer (1455 a 32):

> Given equal natural talent (ἐκ τῆς αὐτῆς φύσεως), those dramatists are most convincing who themselves feel the emotions they are trying to

communicate; one who is himself distressed communicates distress, one who is angry communicates anger most realistically. Hence the art of poetry requires either high natural gifts or an unbalanced nature; the latter poet becomes one character after another, the former preserves his critical sense.[1]

We have here a clear contrast between two ways in which the poet shares the emotions of his characters. One type of dramatist loses himself in one character after another, identifies completely. The other does so to a lesser extent, enough to share the character's feelings, yet he retains his own personality and critical sense. There can be little doubt that Aristotle would prefer the latter, and think him the better artist, but he does not say so.

Then comes the curious advice that 'the dramatist must first set out the outline of his story; he will then name his characters and construct the necessary incidents', and we are given such an outline in the case of the *Iphigenia in Tauris* and of the *Odyssey*; these outlines are very bare indeed. One may well doubt whether any worthwhile dramatist has ever proceeded in this systematic manner, but what Aristotle seems to mean is that the dramatist must keep the outline of the plot clearly in mind to be sure that every incident 'belongs to the story', i.e. develops the main theme and is not an extraneous episode. This is sound enough advice.[2]

Every tragedy, we are told, should first build up the dramatic situation and then unravel it (1455 b 24):

In every tragedy there is involvement and unravelling. What has happened before the play begins, and some events within it, constitutes the involvement, the rest is unravelling. I mean that the involvement extends from the beginning to the part which immediately precedes the change to good or bad fortune, while the unravelling extends from where the change of fortune begins to the end.

It is here also implied that every incident should contribute to one or the other. The unravelling or 'untying' is clearly more than what we call *dénouement*. Greek plays being so much shorter than ours, much less time could be given to 'involvement', nor was this necessary, as most of the legends were known at least in outline.

There is also his famous advice on the part to be played by the chorus (1456 a 25):

---

[1] The text is doubtful but the main contrast between the poet who loses himself in his characters and the one who retains his critical sense is quite clear. See my translation p. 34 and note 1.
[2] So Else well explains the passage (505-6).

The chorus must be considered to be one of the actors, a part of the play, and share in the action not as in Euripides but as in Sophocles. In later dramatists the choral odes are no more part of this plot than of any other tragedy; they are mere interludes, a practice started by Agathon. Yet what difference is there between singing an interlude and inserting a speech or a whole scene from another play?

This sentence of Aristotle is probably responsible for a good deal of the criticism of Euripides for the irrelevance of his choral odes, which has been very much exaggerated.[1] It may be worth pointing out therefore that Aristotle is making a double contrast: Agathon's choral odes are often mere interludes and in this he is contrasted with Sophocles *and* Euripides whose odes are relevant. However, the manner of relevance is better in Sophocles than in Euripides, presumably because it is closer and more direct.

It is obvious to the most casual reader that the *Poetics* represents a tremendous advance in critical thinking on anything which preceded it. Aristotle brings the full power of his analytic mind to bear upon the art of tragedy, and to some extent upon poetry in general, and the result is the first formulation – if by no means always a perfect formulation – of many deeply seminal ideas which are at the very root of poetic appreciation. These ideas, as well as their implications, have been discussed, developed and refined for two millennia, and the temptation to read some of these refinements back into the texts, and to interpret these texts in the light of them, is almost irresistible. Yet it must be resisted, for it contributes nothing but confusion to our understanding of Aristotle or of the history of literary appreciation.

His theory of catharsis is an obvious example.[2] There is no doubt that the witnessing of great tragedy does result in a kind of 'cleansing' of our minds and feelings, but to call this 'the purging away of pity and fear and such emotions' is clearly inadequate. Yet that is what Aristotle does call it and the various 'purification' interpretations are due to later thought.

---

[1] Aristotle's attitude to Euripides is, like that of most critics, ambivalent. He calls him 'the most tragic of the poets' because he has many unhappy endings and perhaps also because of the nature of his tragic heroes (1453 a 23-30, see my translation p. 25, note 4) but he adds 'though he manages his plays badly in other respects', and elsewhere he disapproves of Menelaus in the *Orestes* as unnecessarily evil, of the intervention of the supernatural in the *Medea* and of inconsistency in the character of Iphigenia at Aulis (1454 a 25-32); the arrival of Aegeus in *Medea* is fortuitous (1461 b 21) and Aristotle *seems* to agree with Sophocles' implied criticism of Euripidean realism (1460 b 35). On the other hand he praises the recognition of Orestes by Iphigenia (1455 a 18) but not that of Iphigenia by Orestes (1454 b 32).

[2] For a delightfully irreverent discussion of catharsis see F. L. Lucas' *Tragedy*, ch. 3 (pp. 35 ff.).

The tragic hero is often at odds with himself, and the theory of *hamartia* opens the door to all kinds of psychological studies of the tragic character, but *hamartia* alone is no solution. There is a very strong element of 'imitation of life' in all the fine arts, yet not quite in the sense in which Plato and Aristotle meant it. Recognition is important in the development of most tragedies, and Aristotle himself hints at the wider sense of discovery or disclosure, but so to translate *anagnôrisis* is a misinterpretation, if not as disastrous as to translate *peripeteia* by 'the irony of events'.

Yet there is also much which we can accept unaltered: the insistence on unity of plot so wisely emphasized, the fact that heroes of tragedy must be sufficiently 'like ourselves' to allow emotional *sympatheia*, the recognition that the four aspects of tragedy which are the basis of a classification of actual dramas – complexity of plot, suffering, character, and spectacle – must be present in every play, and many other things, not to mention such *obiter dicta* as Agathon's 'it is probable for the improbable to happen', 'what is impossible but convincing should be preferred to what is possible but unconvincing', and the like.[1]

Every thinker, even an Aristotle, is limited by the thought and the circumstances of his times. Aristotle did not know, and did not conceive of, tragedy written in prose. One suspects he would have approved, for he welcomes, in the *Rhetoric*, the fact that the poets themselves are giving up highly poetic language. In any case, he comes very close to the heart of the matter when he says that 'it is the plot, not the verse, which makes a (tragic) poet'.[2] It is misleading too to study the *Poetics* as if nothing had come before it. Aristotle's thought, here as elsewhere, is rooted in the philosophy of Plato. He goes far beyond him, but many a misinterpretation has been due to ignoring the roots of his thinking.

Aristotle has another limitation more his own: it seems obvious that he had very little feeling for poetry as such. (Tragic) poetry was to him 'more philosophic' than history, but only because of its content, and it always remained much inferior to philosophy itself. He analyses it unemotionally and always with a touch of the supercilious. It is this very lack of emotion which led him to some of his most striking analyses, but from the author of the greatest work on poetry in the classical centuries such statements as that prose writers at first adopted a poetical vocabulary 'because poets, though they said silly things, seemed to have acquired their reputations through their language', or that the rich should be discouraged from wasting their substance on useless public services 'such as dramatic performances, torch-races, and the like', or again his statement that deliberate ambiguity is practised by 'people who have nothing to say but pretend they have; such people usually write poetry, as Empedocles

---

[1] 1461 b 10-15 and 1456 a 24   [2] 1451 b 27-28.

did' are indeed surprising. Nor should we forget his frequent references to the 'depravity of the audiences', which makes style and ornamentation necessary, but 'nobody teaches geometry that way!'[1] It is this curious attitude which now and then makes us feel that in the philosopher's discussions of tragedy, and of poetry in general, there is something missing, something rather important. Aristotle never gets excited about poetry, whereas Plato cannot mention poetry without excitement. This attitude does not in any way detract from his greatness, or from the greatness of the *Poetics*, but to keep it in mind will help our understanding of this supremely illuminating but at times curiously unsatisfying book.

THE *RHETORIC*

'Rhetoric' was for the ancients the art of speech and writing generally, and Aristotle makes very clear that this is the subject of his treatise when he introduces it by saying that rhetoric is an art which all men practise since all men engage in argument, criticism, accusation and defence, some at random, some with conscious method. In the *Poetics* he referred us to the Rhetoric for a study of how to express thought in words, even in poetry. It is true that the study of language, because of its origins, was slanted to oratory, and that the orator remained *the* practitioner of the art of prose as the tragedian was, for Aristotle, *the* poet, so that prose is discussed in oratorical terms, but this should not mislead us; a great deal of 'rhetorical' theory, in Aristotle as in other critics, is equally applicable not only to the art of writing prose but to poetry as well.

Aristotle is very critical of the professional teachers of rhetoric because they concentrate on technicalities and on oratory in courts of law; they miss the essence of their subject which is a study of the means of persuasion, and they ignore that deliberative or political oratory is a higher form of their art. The *Rhetoric* is the kind of book the rhetoricians should have written; it might be said to put the kind of education Isocrates practised in his school on a more philosophical basis; it provides a solid foundation which Isocrates neglected, even though there was evidently some hostility between the two schools. In part it is also an answer to Plato's accusations, for it insists that rhetoric is an art, and a useful one. These are clear Platonic echoes[2] in an early passage which may be summarized as follows:

Truth and justice are more potent than their opposites and if those who

---

[1] For the quotations in this paragraph see *Rhet.* 3, 1, 9 (1404 a 24), *Politics* 5, 8, 20 (1309 a 20), *Rhet.* 3, 4, 4 (1407 a 33-35) and *Rhet.* 3, 1 (1404 a 8-12).

[2] *Rhet.* 1, 1 (1355 a 21). See W. Rhys Roberts, in *CP* 19 (1924). The defence of rhetoric summarized in the text is that put up by Gorgias in Plato's dialogue—but Aristotle of course does not fall into Gorgias' illogicality (above, p. 50).

defend them are defeated by wrong decisions the blame is theirs, because they have neglected rhetoric. Even the most exact knowledge will not enable one to persuade a crowd, for in speaking to them one must argue from common assumptions. There is no shame attached to defending oneself with one's fists, why be ashamed to defend oneself with words? Certainly, ability to speak can be used for evil purposes, but so can any skill or possession except virtue itself.

Aristotle is here using exactly the same arguments as Gorgias did in Plato's dialogue, arguments which were never answered because Gorgias was tricked into contradicting himself. The *Rhetoric* is an answer to Plato also in a much deeper sense; in the first two books Aristotle sets forth the kinds of limited knowledge the orator-statesman must possess: i.e. how to be a good orator without being a philosopher. More than this, the *Rhetoric* in the main follows in those books the method indicated in the *Phaedrus*, where Plato required the orator to study the human soul, to classify human emotions and all forms of argument. This is precisely the path which Aristotle follows,[1] and his classifications are indeed 'by the joints' and meaningful.

Having defined rhetoric as 'the faculty of discovering the available means of persuasion in each case' Aristotle then divides these means of persuasion or proofs into external proofs based on evidence and those to be discovered which depend upon the art (ἔντεχνοι, 1355 b 35-39). The latter are of three kinds: those depending on the impression made by the character of the speaker, those depending on the emotions aroused in the hearers, and those discovered in the circumstances of the case – i.e. proofs related to speaker, audience and content.

Such clear logical classifications must have been in strong contrast to the empirical lists of the rhetoricians and where they occur in later critics we may be sure of Aristotelian or at least Peripatetic influence. So with his clear distinction between arguing by analogy, i.e. from one example (παραδεῖγμα) to another and the *enthymeme* which is the rhetorical syllogism, based on probability (ch. 2). He establishes once and for all the standard formula of the three kinds of rhetoric: the deliberative, the forensic and the epideictic. The first is concerned with the future, aims to persuade to a certain course of action, and deals with the advantageous or harmful; the forensic deals with the past, aims to accuse or defend, and deals with what is just or unjust; epideictic is concerned with the present, aims to praise or blame, and deals with the beautiful and the ugly (ch. 3). This formula had its dangers: the first two divisions are clear-cut, but

---

[1] The manner in which Aristotle followed Plato's advice, with reservations, is excellently described by F. Solmsen in *CP* 33 (1938), 402-4.

epideictic very much less so; as defined by Aristotle it is intended to include encomia, funeral speeches, and sophistic display speeches. When the formula became thoroughly established, everything in prose which was not forensic or deliberative came to be included under epideictic, i.e. display rhetoric, including the writing of history and even of philosophy. Aristotle does not seem to intend history, and certainly did not intend philosophy to be included in this classification. The later inclusion of history was unfortunate, for later critics came to look upon it as a form of display on the part of the writer (which it often was) and even as akin to poetry.

Aristotle then goes on to deal with the kind of human affairs and the objects of human desire which the orator (or writer) must know since his arguments must be drawn from such knowledge. The second book describes human emotions and states of mind, and as he is describing the ordinary man's feelings there is much here which helps us to understand the Greek view of life; the description of youth, the elderly and the middle-aged (this last, being a mean between the other two, is of course the most desirable), once read, sticks in the memory. The full description of fear (2, 5) and of pity (2, 8) is especially relevant to the *Poetics*. The last part of the second book gives full analyses of the use of maxims, enthymemes, and refutations. But all this belongs more to the study of rhetoric in the stricter sense.[1]

Having dealt with content and argumentation in the first two books, Aristotle turns, as he tells us at the beginning of the third, to style (λέξις) and structure (τάξις). He first, however, deals very briefly with delivery (the Greek word ὑπόκρισις also means acting), a subject obviously distasteful to him but the power of which he knew must be recognized. Actors nowadays, he tells us, are getting more important than poets, and the same will very soon be true in the assembly and the courts, 'because

[1] There are a very few passages in the first two books of the *Rhetoric*, which have a certain relevance to matters dealt with in the *Poetics*. I, II, 22 (1371 b 4-11) repeats what is said about the pleasure given by imitations because we recognize the model in the imitation (painting, sculpture, and poetry), because it is pleasant to learn; then also περιπετείαι (sudden changes?) and narrow escapes from danger are pleasant because they make us marvel (θαυμάζειν).

At I, II, 6 (1370 a 27) pleasure is said to reside in perception, and imagination (φαντασία) is a weak kind of perception, pleasure accompanies both hopeful expectation and recollection and so 'lovers enjoy talking and writing about their beloved'.

There are two particular points in the description of fear (2, 5) which deserve special emphasis. At 1382 b 25 we find 'all things are fearful which are pitiful when they happen, or are about to happen, to others', and a little further on (1383 a 8), 'whenever you want to make your hearers afraid, you must make them feel they are likely to suffer, as even greater men than they have suffered, and that people like themselves (ὁμοίους) have suffered or are suffering...'.

We may also note in passing that he quotes in full (1402 a 10) Agathon's saying that it is probable for the improbable to happen: τάχ' ἄν τις εἰκὸς αὐτὸ τοῦτ' εἶναι λέγοι βροτοῖσι πολλὰ τυγχάνειν οὐκ εἰκότα.

of the depravity of audiences'. We cannot afford to neglect delivery any more than style. He mentions that Thrasymachus has written about delivery and adds that nowadays the success of written work depends more on style than on content. He then dismisses the whole subject with the words: 'Nobody teaches geometry that way!' (1403 b 20 – 1404 a 19).

'Words imitate, and the voice is the most imitative part of man.' The poets were first in the field, and as their reputation was due not to what they said but to the language used, it was natural for Gorgias to reproduce poetic diction in prose. Indeed, uncultured people still admire poetic prose, for they do not realize that *the language of poetry is different from that of prose.* Yet the poets themselves now use the iambic metre because it is the nearest to conversation, and, except for epic writers, they have largely abandoned a poetic vocabulary (1404 a 20-39).

Aristotle will only recognize one virtue or excellence (ἀρετή) of style, which is lucidity, since the purpose of speech is to make one's meaning clear. He does indeed recognize other qualities and discusses them at length, but lucidity is the only specific *aretê* or excellence which fulfills the proper function of speech. Now current words make for clarity but the result is somewhat common, so we must use unusual expressions, though not as freely as poets do, to ornament our speech and make it more pleasing, but the audience must not be aware of artifice, we must appear to speak naturally, not in a studied manner. Artifice is successful when the artist composes in the terms of common speech. Euripides does this and was the first to point the way (1404 b 25).

This is probably the first reference in our texts to art hiding itself. It is also the first time we meet this criticism (favourable in this case) of Euripides: that he used simple language and attained his effects mostly by the arrangement of words. From now on the basic distinction in stylistic formulae is between the choice of words and their arrangement, and we note that Aristotle is using the technical terms which became stereotyped later, ἐκλέγειν for the choice of words and συντίθεναι for the arrangement of them. Prose cannot use the devices of poetry freely, it must rely mainly on current words, and on metaphor as its chief ornament. Aristotle discusses the metaphor at some length[1]:

> The metaphor above all is lucid, pleasing, and strange too to a high degree; moreover, *one cannot learn its use from anyone else* . . . it must not be far-fetched but we must give names to things which have none by transference from things closely akin and similar to them, and the kinship must be realized as soon as uttered. . . . Good metaphors can

---

[1] Ch. 2, 7-13 (1405 a 3 – b 20) and ch. 10, 7 to end (1411 a 1 – b 21), the later passage being mainly a number of examples.

usually be made from successful riddles, for metaphors are a kind of riddle.

Aristotle's favourite is, here as in the *Poetics*, the proportionate metaphor, where *a* is to *b* as *b* is to *c*, so that *a* and *c* can be transferred. The wine cup is to Dionysus as the shield is to Ares, so the cup may be called the shield of Dionysus, old age the evening of life, and so on. The most famous example he gives is Pericles' saying, when many youths had perished in battle, that the year had lost its spring. But when Aristotle has given the classic difference between simile and metaphor (1406 b 20: 'Achilles leapt like a lion' is a simile whereas 'a lion, he leapt' is a metaphor), he goes on to say that *the simile* is more poetic and rarely to be used in prose. He obviously has the elaborate *Homeric* simile in mind, for it is simply not true that 'he leapt like a lion' is less appropriate in prose than 'a lion, he leapt'.

Aristotle is very conscious of the importance of semantics, whether you call Orestes his father's avenger or a matricide, and he illustrates it by the anecdote about Simonides who refused to write an ode for a victor in a mule race, saying he would not write an ode to 'half-donkeys', but when the fee was made high enough he composed the ode which begins: 'All hail, daughters of storm-footed steeds.' The philosopher drily comments that they were still the daughters of donkeys (1405 b 20-26).

Frigidity is caused by bad taste, and there are four causes of it: extravagant use of compounds, excessive use of rare words, epithets too long, too frequent or inappropriate, and poor metaphors. Examples are given from Gorgias and Lycophron, and from Alcidamas for whom 'epithets were not mere seasoning, they were the whole dish'. Most of the examples of frigidity would offend modern taste as well, but we would not blame Alcidamas for calling the *Odyssey* 'a beautiful mirror of human life'. This far-fetched metaphor has, on the contrary, become trite.[1]

So far (chs. 1-4) Aristotle has been discussing the first essential requirement of style, or, more strictly, of diction, namely lucidity without meanness. He now states the second requirement, the very basis of a good style, namely, as he puts it with conscious meiosis, to write Greek (ἑλληνίζειν), and it is interesting that the same essentials of good Greek are still found in our composition books, namely the right use of connecting particles, the use of specific, not general, terms, the avoidance of all ambiguity, and correct genders and numbers.

---

[1] Here (ch. 3) as in the *Poetics* Aristotle says that compound words are most suited to the dithyramb, rare words to the epic and metaphors to iambic poetry (no doubt because it is most akin to prose). These frequent references to, and quotations from, poetry should constantly remind us that the general discussion of style in the third book applies to all prose, and to poetry as well.

The third requirement is the principle of appropriateness (πρέπον), a term already well developed which we shall meet at every turn in later critics. Our language must be suited to the subject, and to the emotions we arouse – an angry man uses more violent words and harsher sounds than one who expresses pity. Generally speaking, when expressing strong emotions we can depart further from simple everyday language, for then we are closer to poetry, and poetry is highly emotional.[1] 'An audience always shares the feelings of a passionate speaker, even if there is nothing in what he is saying.'[2] One's language must be appropriate to the subject, to the speaker (i.e. be in character), as well as to the emotions one wishes to arouse.

All the foregoing have been concerned with λέξις in the sense of diction or the choice of words. Aristotle now goes on to deal with problems of λέξις[3] in the sense of word-arrangement, and the first of these is prose-rhythm. His general principle, that prose should have rhythm but not meter is accepted by all later critics. He pays special attention to the beginning and end of clauses, and recommends the paeonic, i.e. ‿◡◡◡ at the beginning and ◡◡◡‿ at the end. By thus equating prose-rhythm with actual feet Aristotle gave a bad example. Later critics followed and extended this method, often analysing whole clauses into feet, though they continued to pay particular attention to the first and the last few syllables. What really matters in prose-rhythm is not the occurrence of particular feet (except that an excess of them is bad) but the general effect, the relative number of long and short syllables and the like. Yet Aristotle's general principle is obviously right, and he is also right that the weight of the last few syllables of a clause or sentence is important (ch. 8).

Then comes (ch. 9) the structure of the sentence. Here he establishes the main difference between the loose or strung-along style (λέξις εἰρομένη, i.e. like beads on a string) and the periodic. The first is the older way of

---

[1] 3, 7, 11 (1408 b 19) ἔνθεον γὰρ ἡ ποίησις – poetry is a kind of frenzy. The phrase does not in this context mean 'inspired' or 'divine' or the like, but it is equivalent to ἐνθουσιασμός, sense of possession, a high pitch of excitement.

[2] 1408 a 23. Another example of quiet irony is in chapter 6, where Aristotle interrupts his general advice in order to analyse the ways of achieving ὄγκος weight in diction. It is hard to avoid the impression of irony here, as when he says that this is achieved by referring to a thing by circumlocution, by using the definition rather than the name, e.g. by not saying 'circle' but 'a plane figure equidistant from the centre'. Certainly, he is not advising ὄγκος as a generally desirable quality but analysing the ways of attaining it, e.g. by using more epithets and metaphors (while not being too poetical), by using the plural for the singular, as poets do, by avoiding asyndeta, by the use of conjunctive clauses, and by using privative adjectives (ἐκ στερήσεως) such as lyre-less music, which process, he says, can go on ad infinitum.

[3] We have seen that Aristotle distinguished word-arrangement from choice of words (the standard later formula) but only casually and he still uses λέξις to cover both. It is in fact the general term for style in Aristotle and in most critics, and can be used to include any aspect of it.

writing in which the sentences have no real structure at all; it is not very pleasing because of its lack of form. The periodic on the other hand constructs its sentences to correspond to the thought. Indeed Aristotle's definition of a period is that sense and sentence end together, so that he allows periods of one clause only, but as a rule he uses the word to indicate sentences of at least two clauses, logically construed, and therefore easier to remember. Here too we must observe due measure; a succession of very short sentences makes the reader stumble, too many long ones leave him panting behind.

The period of several clauses may be simply divided into clauses (διῃρημένη λέξις), or the clauses may be equal and antithetical. *Parisosis* refers to clauses of equal length, *paromoiosis* to clauses which begin or end with similar sounds. Aristotle then gives a number of examples, many of which, naturally, come from Isocrates who, as we have seen, paid the most careful attention to the balanced nature of his periods.

The discussion of style ends with an attempt (chs. 10-11) to account for the appeal of particularly happy or pleasing sayings (ἀστεῖα). Their success is largely due, as it was in the *Poetics*, to man's general delight in learning, by which is meant that any expression which makes us realize something we did not see before gives us delight. Similes have that effect, and so do metaphors, for they make us see a new similarity or, as we would say, a new association of ideas. So with arguments or enthymemes: the obvious have little appeal, but rather those which are fresh, yet understood as soon as uttered. Antithesis has something of the same effect. 'The more briefly and antithetically a thing is said, the more appreciated. We learn rather through antithesis, while brevity makes the process quicker.'[1] Aristotle then gives numerous examples, particularly of metaphors, and draws particular attention to Homer's 'active' metaphors which personify the inanimate, like 'the eager spear' or 'the shameless rock', etc. Another desirable quality is vividness, when our words bring things before the very eyes of our audience. Riddles or semi-riddles too appeal to the delight in learning as when Stesichorus threatened the Locrians by saying: 'Your grasshoppers will sing to themselves on the ground.'[2] This is akin to the comic use of the unexpected, to play on words, and to hyperbole.

Aristotle fully realizes, however, that there is not one perfect style for all occasions, and that the different kinds of 'rhetoric' require different methods. His main distinction (a rather unusual one in ancient times) is between spoken and written work. We need proficiency in both if we are to be able to speak Greek and to communicate with our fellows in

---

[1] 3, 11, 9 (1412 b 21-25).
[2] 3, 11, 6 (1412 a 24). Meaning: 'I will ravage your country.' This became a stock example in the schools.

writing. The written style must be more exact, for the spoken word can rely on acting or delivery. The most exact poets like Chaeremon and Licymnius are easily read, but generally speaking written works seem thin on the platform, while speeches that go over well often fall flat in the study, where the advantages of delivery are lost. Hence repetition and *asyndeta* are to be avoided in written prose where there can be no variation of tone, whereas in delivery asyndeton makes for amplification; it seems to say much in a short time.[1] Speaking before a crowd is like making a sketch to be seen at a distance, and preciseness is there out of place. Forensic oratory is more precise, especially before one judge, where a histrionic delivery is inadvisable. In fact preciseness varies inversely to reliance on delivery. That is why epideictic or show oratory is most like writing, while political rhetoric is most different. As for length, it is obvious that one should not be too brief nor too verbose, but attain the mean and the appropriate.[2]

The remaining chapters of the *Rhetoric* deal with τάξις or the arrangement of a speech into its different parts. This is much more in the nature of direct advice to rhetoricians and need not detain us long. We can appreciate the greatness of Aristotle, however, if we compare even this part of his work with other technical treatises, and in particular with the *Rhetorica ad Alexandrum* which has been preserved among his works. That short treatise, now known to date from the fourth century, though certainly not Aristotle's own,[3] is conceived on much the same plan, but it is, in comparison, incredibly dull. It is repetitive, practically without illustrations, whereas Aristotle abounds in apt and enlightening examples; moreover, there is not a glimmer of any moral outlook anywhere in it, but it gives, throughout, the most unscrupulous advice. Such advice, let it be noted, is not lacking in Aristotle himself; certain of the more analytical chapters are full of it when they state how to influence a jury to one's own advantage, and particularly in these concluding chapters; but these chapters are only part of the whole, they are set in a framework which does set out the aim and purpose of rhetoric as a whole and which certainly expresses a highly moral view of life. If the *Rhetorica ad Alexandrum* may be taken as an example of the contemporary 'arts' of rhetoric, and it is the only

[1] Asyndeton consists in leaving out the connectives. In Greek, where they were usually put in, this was a conscious figure of speech. One of Aristotle's examples here (1414 a 3) is the repetition of the name Nireus at the beginning of three lines of the *Iliad* (2, 671-3) without connectives. This too became a stock example.

[2] Aristotle refuses to recognize brevity, magnificence and some other qualities of style (1414 a 20-28); it all depends on the particular circumstances.

[3] For the *Rhetorica ad Alexandrum* see the text and translation by H. Rackham in the Loeb library. It is now proved to be a fourth-century text because fragments of it occur in Hibeh papyrus 26, published by Grenfell and Hunt, Part I, 114-38. The author is generally thought to be Anaximenes, but this ascription is doubtful. See my *A Greek Critic*, pp. 156-8.

technical treatise we possess which is at all contemporary, then the rhetorical writers fully deserve the contempt with which both Plato and Aristotle refer to them.

We feel this contempt again in the chapter where Aristotle establishes the number of parts or sections which a speech contains. Essentially, he says, there are only two, the statement of the case and the proofs or demonstration.[1] The numerous subdivisions found in contemporary rhetoricians are quite ridiculous; they are certainly not found in every kind of rhetoric, nor even in every kind of forensic speech. However, one may recognize as reasonable a fourfold division into exordium, statement or narrative, proof, and epilogue; and he proceeds to examine the function of each of these four parts in turn.[2]

The exordium of a speech (ch. 14) is like a prologue in poetry or a prelude in music. There is a tendency to digress here – see the *Helen* of Isocrates – 'but even if a speaker digresses, it is appropriate that the whole speech should not be in one key (ὁμοειδῆ)'. The proper function of the exordium is to state the purpose of the speech; the rest is only to remedy the weaknesses of the audience. Having stated his ideal, Aristotle proceeds to analyse all the possible ways to incite prejudice in the jury[3] though he repeats that all this is really extraneous, and that a sensible audience should not need much of an exordium!

Narrative is most useful in forensic speeches where it must show character and emotion, least useful in political oratory. In epideictic displays it should not all come at once. He opposes the current advice that narrative should be brief: 'As the man said to the baker who asked him whether he should make his loaf hard or soft: "Why, can't you make it just right?"' (1416 b 30-32).

Proofs (ch. 17-18) are least useful in display speeches, when the facts are taken for granted and we rely mostly on amplification. Examples are more suited to political rhetoric, argument to forensic. Maxims are also

---

[1] Ch. 13. The two essential parts he prefers are πρόθεσις and πίστις. The four he finally adopts are προοίμιον, πρόθεσις or διήγησις, πίστις and ἐπίλογος. The ridiculous subdivisions he notes and discards are ἀντιπαραβολή (contrast), ἐπάνοδος (recapitulation); from Theodorus of Byzantium he quotes ἐπιδιήγησις (supplementary narrative), προδιήγησις (preliminary narrative), ἔλεγχος (refutation), ἐπεξέλεγχος (supplementary refutation); from Licymnius ἐπούρησις (a blowing forward), ἀποπλάνησις (digression), ὄζοι (ramifications). The spirit of this chapter is very similar to that of *Phaedrus* 266 D – 267 D, see above, p. 59.

[2] Dionysius of Halicarnassus, *Lysias* 16 (489), attributes such a fourfold division of speeches, with, however, the addition of the statement, to Isocrates and his school. It would then be pre-Aristotelian in origin. See F. Solmsen in *AJP* 62 (1941), p. 37, n. 8. Even so, however, we should not consider it to indicate Isocratean influence whenever we meet it in later critics, since it is also in Aristotle, and therefore might derive from him, directly or indirectly.

[3] Part of ch. 14 and the whole of ch. 15 consider ways to remove or increase slander. A curiously formal chapter where every new point is introduced by ἄλλος (τόπος) much in the manner of the textbooks.

to be used. And here Aristotle notes that political or deliberative rhetoric is more difficult than forensic, for it looks to the future, not to the past 'which is known even to soothsayers, as Epimenedes said'. Within the category of proof also comes the use of questions – to which it is safer to give your own answers – and the use of ridicule and jests, about which Aristotle once more refers us to the *Poetics* in vain, and repeats the advice of Gorgias 'to confound your opponents' seriousness with jests, and his jests by being serious' (1419 b 4).

As for the epilogue (ch. 19) its purpose is fourfold, to dispose the hearer in your favour, to amplify or depreciate certain points, to excite the emotions of the audience, to recall the salient points. Recapitulation is therefore in place here, not in the exordium, contrary to the usual opinion. Asyndeton is also in place.

And here, abruptly, the *Rhetoric* ends.

There can be no doubt that Aristotle's logical, analytic approach to rhetoric was something quite new and a tremendous advance upon anything that preceded it. All the evidence we have – the *Rhetorica ad Alexandrum*, the remarks of both Plato and Aristotle about contemporary rhetoricians, the practices of Gorgias and Isocrates – clearly shows that the 'arts' or textbooks of the rhetoricians were little more than lists of empirical oratorical tricks or arguments. The scientific approach is clear in Aristotle's careful definition of the art not as the art of persuasion (for the most careful and perfect speech may fail to persuade) but as the ability to discover the possible means of persuasion, and the verb he employs ($\theta\epsilon\omega\rho\epsilon\hat{\imath}\nu$) is used of philosophic contemplation; we see the scientific approach again in his classification of 'artistic' proofs as depending upon the character of the speaker, the audience's emotional reactions and those to be found in the circumstances of the case itself; in his careful comparison of rhetoric with dialectic, of the enthymene with the syllogism. The three kinds of rhetoric, the forensic, the deliberative, and the epideictic were recognized in practice but even this division may not have been theoretically formulated, and the careful analysis of different $\tau\acute{o}\pi o\iota$ according to the kinds of argument was undoubtedly his own. The same is no doubt true of his analysis of sentence structure into the strung-along style and the periodic, whether loose or antithetical. All this soon became accepted in the schools, as well as his requirement of prose-rhythm, and it is quite obvious that, while the *Poetics* seems to have been lost for some generations, the *Rhetoric* had a continuing influence, both direct and indirect.

But if Aristotle's philosophical approach enabled him to make a great contribution to literary and stylistic theory, it also has a certain weakness. His interest being theoretical, he naturally expounds his theories and literature is merely used to provide illustrations. In his own case the method was less deductive than it appears, for his theories were undoubtedly based upon the study and analysis of many literary works, as his custom was also in other fields. In less able and less philosophical hands, however, the method was apt to degenerate into the statement of *a priori* theories, lists of figures of speech and thought and the like, treating literature merely as a treasure house of illustrations of rhetorical tenets, and never looking at it for its own sake. Aristotle must bear some responsibility for initiating or continuing this method.

There were then, as we saw, two approaches to literary theory in the late fifth and fourth centuries; the philosophical and the rhetorical. Aristotle may be said to have brought them together in the *Rhetoric*. This is the last work we possess from the hand of a philosopher, and he makes this fusion with considerable success. The contribution of the two great philosophers to literary theory was considerable, yet it is difficult not to be disappointed. Neither Plato nor Aristotle even attempt to define the nature of poetry. Aristotle may have done so in his lost dialogue on the poets or in lost parts of the *Poetics*, but if so, no trace of it remains, and there are other essentials which seem to be missing. With Plato the fault lies in his persistent concern with the social responsibility of the poet and the writer; also, he is temperamentally incapable of compromise, so that he can recognize no knowledge but the highest. Yet of his deep feeling for poetry there is no doubt. With Aristotle the opposite is the case: he is fully prepared to accept as sufficient for the poet and the writer a practical kind of knowledge; his clear and acute mind sees many things which no one had seen before, and some of these are still of very great significance, but there is a lack of feeling for poetry and for style which leaves one somewhat frustrated and dissatisfied.

Nevertheless both philosophers together made an original contribution which in depth and breadth of view was not to be equalled for many centuries.

CHAPTER VI

Theophrastus

With the probable exception of Demetrius *On Style*,[1] we have no extant critical texts after Aristotle and the *Rhetorica ad Alexandrum* in the fourth century B.C. until we come to the writers of the first century B.C. This lack of original works is especially tantalizing in the case of Theophrastus, the nephew and successor of Aristotle, with whom his name is constantly coupled as an important Peripatetic critic. We know that he wrote on poetry and style and many attempts have naturally been made to reconstruct his theories on the basis of later references to him, but such reconstructions are often based on flimsy evidence and seem to exaggerate the differences between the two philosophers.

The first-century writers on literary theory and criticism in Rome – the author of *Ad Herennium*, Cicero, Dionysius of Halicarnassus – freely use critical formulae, by their time well established, which obviously derive from earlier Greek sources. Some of these formulae can be traced back to Aristotle himself, and the temptation is strong to trace back others to Theophrastus' book περὶ λέξεως. Two formulae in particular have been conjecturally attributed to him, namely an exclusive list of four 'virtues', ἀρεταί, of style, and also the formula of 'three styles'. Before we deal with these conjectures, however, let us first examine what we actually *know* about Theophrastus' critical theories.

He took over the presidency of the Lyceum when Aristotle left Athens in 323 B.C. He belongs not to the Hellenistic but the classical period. Like Aristotle, he wrote on a great variety of subjects, and some of his works, notably on plants, are extant. We also have *The Characters*, a short book of thirty-six very brief sketches of different types of men, graphic, humorous, and altogether delightful, which *may* have been written, as has often been thought, as psychological helps for orators and writers. Of his works on rhetoric, poetry and style, however, nothing remains, apart from what is found quoted in later writers, and direct quotations are rare.

The views of Theophrastus, where we can be sure of them, are always in essential agreement with those of Aristotle. Both discussed the general

---

[1] For Demetrius see the next chapter.

themes[1] with which an orator has to deal and the commonplaces in which
he should be trained in order to do so[2]; both disliked the continuous or
strung-along sentence structure and preferred the periodic[3]; the advice to
mitigate the boldness of metaphors by introducing them by 'as if', 'if one
may put it that way' and the like was given by both of them.[4] Like his
master, Theophrastus was aware of the great influence of *mousikê* in the
forming of character.[5]

We have statements from both philosophers on beautiful words which,
while not couched in exactly the same terms, state that words are beautiful
because of their sound, their meaning, or their associations, i.e. the mental
picture they evoke.[6] They both discuss maxims which Aristotle defines as
general statements as to what is to be done and avoided in human life,
and which express either a generally accepted view or a paradoxical one.
Here Aristotle goes on to further distinctions and is more detailed, but
the general view is the same.[7]

This does not mean that Theophrastus was a mere echo of Aristotle: he
often elaborates and clarifies the views of his teacher. He dealt more fully
with delivery, a subject Aristotle deplores and curtly dismisses.[8] He may
well have been more keenly aware of historical development in matters of
style, for he noted the changes in historical style brought about by Herodotus and Thucydides.[9]

Theophrastus seems to have shared Aristotle's prejudice against epideictic, for he stated, in this following his master, that epideictic had
nothing to do with practical affairs and was concerned only to give
pleasure.[10] This assumes his acceptance of the Aristotelian theory of three
kinds of rhetoric. Quintilian quotes Theophrastus as saying that one may
seek the matter of one's exordium from one's opponent's speech[11]; this
probably comes from a discussion of the exordium, and we may assume
that Theophrastus discussed the four parts of a speech – the exordium,

[1] Theon, *Prolegomena* in Walz 1, 165 and the discussion of subject matter in Aristotle, *Rhet.*
1, 4 ff.

[2] *Rhet.* 2, 18, 2 (1391 b 22 ff.) and 2, 19; also the references to Theophrastus in Alexander's
Commentary on the Topics (Berlin edition 1891) where see Index Nominum under Theophrastus.

[3] *Rhet.* 3, 9, 2 (1409 a 24) and Cicero, *Orator* 228.

[4] *On the Sublime* 32, 3. This advice is apparently not found in our texts of Aristotle.

[5] Plutarch, *De Recta Ratione Audendi* 38 A, and J. Croissant, *Aristote et les mystères* 113-116.

[6] *Rhet.* 3, 2, 13 (1405 b 6-20) and Demetrius 173-174; also Dionysius of Halicarnassus,
Composition 16. See *TAPA* 83 (1952) 172-183 for a fuller discussion of problems concerning
Theophrastus and for fuller references. Beauty of words p. 173.

[7] *Rhet.* 2, 21 and *TAPA* 1952, p. 174.

[8] Our authority for this is late but specific. See H. Rabe, *Prolegomenon Sylloge* p. 177
(Walz 6, 35-36), and cp. *Rhet.* 3, 1, 3-7 (1403 b 20 – 1404 a 19).

[9] Cicero, *Orator* 39.

[10] Quintilian 3, 7, 1.

[11] Quintilian 4, 1, 32.

narrative, proof and peroration – a formula which, whatever its ultimate origin, is, as we saw, discussed at length at the end of Aristotle's *Rhetoric*.

Cicero tells us that Theophrastus discussed prose-rhythm more fully than Aristotle, and there is an interesting reference in Demetrius which seems to prove that Theophrastus went beyond the recognition of feet at the beginning or end of a clause, for he recognized a paeonic rhythm in clauses which did not begin or end with paeonic feet.[1] If Theophrastus thus paid more attention to general prose-rhythm rather than particular feet, he considerably refined the Aristotelian theory of rhythm in prose, an improvement which later critics ignored at their peril.

When Quintilian[2] quotes Theophrastus as saying that the reading of poetry is very profitable for speakers, and that many have followed him in giving this advice, this must mean that he put greater emphasis on poetry in the education of the orator than is implied in Aristotle.

Perhaps the most pleasing of all the actual fragments quoted from Theophrastus is where he said that some things should be left to the hearer's (or reader's) imagination[3]:

> You must not state everything with precise and lengthy elaboration; leave some things for your hearer to infer and work out for himself. When he grasps what you have omitted he will be more than a hearer, he will be a witness on your behalf, and a friendly witness because he thinks himself rather clever and you have given him a chance to exercise his intelligence. To say everything is to convict your hearer of stupidity, as if you were talking to a fool.

Demetrius[4] also quotes Theophrastus' definition of frigidity as that which 'exceeds the form of expression appropriate to the subject', i.e. over-elaborate language. This is quite in the spirit of Aristotle's discussion of frigidity of diction, which Demetrius proceeds to quote. We should note that it is frigidity of *diction* which both philosophers have in mind and that the fault lies in *inappropriately* dignified language, a fault against the quality of πρέπον or appropriateness, closely connected as this is with the Aristotelian concept of the mean between two extremes. We remember Aristotle's advice that diction, both in poetry and prose, should be

---

[1] *De Oratore* 3, 184; *Orator* 172: *Theophrastus vero eisdem de rebus accuratius*; Demetrius 41.
[2] Quintilian 10, 1, 27.   [3] Demetrius 222.
[4] Demetrius 114. The example given, ἀπυνδάκωτος οὐ τραπεζοῦται κύλιξ for ἀπύθμενος ἐπὶ τραπέζης οὐ τίθεται κύλιξ may well come from Theophrastus. So too the comment that 'so small a matter cannot carry such a weight of language'. Demetrius goes on to discuss Aristotle's analysis of different kinds of frigidity, with no implication of any difference between the two writers. To Demetrius the vice of frigidity is one to which the grand manner is particularly liable. This does not, of course, commit Theophrastus to the same theory or to the same use of μεγαλοπρεπής. Cf. *Rhet.* 3, 3.

clear but not lowly, i.e. with some ornamentation.[1] And dignity (τὸ μεγαλοπρεπές), Theophrastus is also quoted as saying, is attained in three ways: in diction, word-arrangement and the use of figures.[2]

This last quotation is of special interest in that it clearly makes the distinction between the choice of words or diction on the one hand, and their arrangement on the other, which was to become the chief division of style in later critics. This distinction was already implied in Aristotle where he said that Euripides achieved his effects not by his choice of words, since he used an ordinary vocabulary, but by their arrangement.[3] The use of σχήματα for figures of speech is also interesting as Aristotle did not use the word in that sense.

Ammonius, a late commentator on Aristotle,[4] quotes Theophrastus as saying that every speech has two aspects, the content and the effect upon the audience; the philosopher is mainly concerned with the first, the poet or rhetorician mainly with the second: they *choose* their words for effect and *arrange* them harmoniously, and they charm their audience by these means as well as by means of 'lucidity, pleasantness and other qualities such as length or brevity, using them all appropriately'. The basic distinction here too is in Aristotle[5] who distinguishes the language of instruction ('nobody teaches geometry that way') from stylized rhetoric πρὸς ἀκροατήν which must take the depravity of audiences into account. We should not seek here the origin of the concept of the simple style, for the simple style is as much a product of art as any other, and its prototype is not a philosopher but an orator, namely Lysias. Aristotle, it is true, left us with the feeling that the orator *ought* to speak like a philosopher, whereas Theophrastus makes a clear distinction between them, and this does distinguish literature more clearly from what might be called the language of instruction. The distinction is not clearcut but a question of emphasis; basically it is Aristotelian.

So far we have found Theophrastus repeating and interpreting Aristotelian concepts with interesting additions of his own, but nowhere departing from or contradicting Aristotelian theory. If, however, later formulae such as that of four virtues of style or that of the three styles are to be attributed to him, this will no longer be true, since Aristotle recognized only one *aretê* or virtue of style, lucidity, and only one style appropriate to deal with a particular subject before a particular audience, always a

[1] *Rhet.* 3, 2, 1 (1404 b 1-4); cf. *Poetics* 22, 1 (1458 a 19).
[2] Dionysius, *Isocrates* 3 (ad init.). I have shown in *AJP* 73 (1952) that the use of the word μεγαλοπρεπής does not imply any theory of three styles.
[3] *Rhet.* 3, 2, 5 (1404 b 24-36) and see above, p. 95.
[4] In his commentary on *De Interpretatione* Berlin ed. (A. Busse) 1897, 65, 22. For text and discussion see *AJP* (1952) 177-8 and references there.
[5] *Rhet.* 3, 1, 5-6 (1404 a 1-12).

mean between two extremes. Let us be clear that it is the formulae, not the ideas they contain, which are in question.

No one disputes that Theophrastus must have discussed purity of language (to write Greek, as Aristotle called it, which the Romans translated *latinitas*), lucidity (*the* virtue of Aristotle), appropriateness (πρέπον) and ornamentation, since they were all discussed by Aristotle. The only question at issue is whether he had an exclusive list of *four* virtues, and called them by that name (ἀρεταί), thus using the word in an un-Aristotelian sense. The importance of the question is easily exaggerated. The teaching of rhetoric was highly formalized in Hellenistic and later times and it was natural enough for the teachers of rhetoric to attach great importance to precise formulae; even slight differences in these, or a slightly different technical vocabulary, was all that distinguished them from one another. It was their only claim to originality, but there is no need for students of the period to be infected with this disease of formu-laitis. One feels in any case that Theophrastus like Aristotle, would have too much sense to pick out four essential qualities and no more, and that he is unlikely to have used the word *aretê* in this un-Aristotelian and loose way. The evidence in favour of attributing this formula to him is a passage of Cicero who, when discussing the simple style, says it can have latinity, clarity, appropriateness, but not that 'which Theophrastus placed fourth among the good qualities (*in laudibus*), namely ornamentation'.[1] Does this imply an exclusive list of four? And does *laudes* here mean *virtutes*? The latter point is certainly very doubtful. The former is possible but not necessary. There is very little in the way of evidence elsewhere. Cicero is in any case notoriously careless in his use of technical terms.[2] While it would be interesting to know where the theory of four (and only four) excellences of style originated we cannot with any certainty attribute it to Theophrastus, and in any case it would add little or nothing to his critical ideas but merely convict him of a certain rigidity of thought. He obviously discussed other qualities of style as well.

The formula of three styles is even less likely to have originated with him. It occurs in the first century only in Roman writers where each style has its own diction *and* word arrangement; even then every writer or speaker is expected to use all three styles at different times, so that the

---

[1] *Orat.* 79: *sermo purus erit et Latinus, dilucide planeque dicetur, quid deceat circumspicietur; unum aberit quod quartum numerat Theophrastus in orationis laudibus; ornatum illud, suave et affluens.*

[2] Cicero uses *virtutes dicendi*, e.g. in *Orat.* 139 where, however, the list is quite different. Still another list, then called *lumina*, occurs in *De Partit. Orat.* 19, namely *dilucidum, breve, probabile, illustre, suave.* On the other hand in *De Orat.* 1, 144 he uses the four qualities listed here but calls them *ornamenta.* For other examples of a loose use of technical terms see below, pp. 177-9.

notion of three equally acceptable styles, plain, grand, and intermediate, is largely a myth, though no doubt individual writers tend to one rather than the others. The main evidence here is alleged to be a passage of Dionysius of Halicarnassus which quotes Theophrastus as saying that Thrasymachus of Chalcedon originated a τρίτη λέξις, between the poetic and the simple. I have argued at length elsewhere that, in this context, λέξις here refers to diction and that what Theophrastus attributed to Thrasymachus is only a middle kind of diction between the poetic language of a Gorgias and the simple language of a Lysias.[1] This does mean that Theophrastus recognized three kinds of diction, the grand (Gorgias), the plain (Lysias), and the intermediate (Thrasymachus). This is quite Aristotelian, nor does it imply approval of all three. Indeed to understand τρίτη λέξις as implying a full-fledged formula of three styles proves too much; it traces the formula back not only to Theophrastus but to Thrasymachus as well, right back into the fifth century!

It would seem then that the formula of four 'virtues' of style should probably not be attributed to Theophrastus, while that of the three styles should certainly not be traced back to him except in the very limited sense that he recognized that prose writers did use plain language, poetic language, and a language in between the two, and it is more than likely that he approved of the mean between the other two, as a faithful follower of Aristotle naturally would.

We know very little more about Theophrastus as a critic. He seems to have praised Thrasymachus also for the ability to express his ideas clearly and compactly.[2] Plutarch tells us he did not think very highly of Demosthenes' delivery, a verdict which was apparently shared by Demetrius of Phalerum and the fashionable circle in Athens to which Demetrius belonged.[3] Theophrastus also praised the capacity to speak extempore though he recognized the danger of relying upon one's ability to do so. Finally, to Dionysius' surprise and indignation, he condemned Lysias for vulgar elaboration and poetic diction on the basis of his *On Behalf of Nicias*, which Dionysius regarded as obviously spurious.[4]

One more reference should be mentioned which clearly attributes to Theophrastus a statement at variance with Aristotle as we know him. The Latin grammarian Diomedes (fourth century A.D.) says that Theophrastus defined tragedy as 'a reversal of fortune at the heroic level'.[5] Such popular

---

[1] *Demosthenes* 3 (ad init.) and *AJP* 73 (1952), 263-6, where see references.
[2] This I believe to be the meaning of the 'virtue' described in *Lysi s* 6 by Dionysius as συστρέφουσα τὰ νοήματα καὶ στρογγύλως ἐκφέρουσα. It is often wrongly interpreted to mean the periodic style. See above, p. 20, note 1.
[3] Plutarch, *Demosthenes* ch. 10 and 11; *Praecepta gerendae reipublicae* 8. Also F. Wehrli, *Demetrius von Phaleron* p. 35.   [4] Dionysius, *Lysias* ch. 14.
[5] *Grammatici Latini* (Keck) 1, 487: τραγωδία ἐστιν ἡρωϊκῆς τύχης περίστασις.

definitions of both tragedy and comedy occur elsewhere in our grammarians and scholiasts, but the attribution to Theophrastus is found only in Diomedes, even though other definitions can be found with a much more Aristotelian ring.[1] None of them, compared with that of the *Poetics*, seems very complete. If Diomedes is to be trusted, we must suppose that Theophrastus did thus define tragedy in a popular work, probably to distinguish it from comedy. Indeed, it has even been suggested that the definition may ultimately derive from a popular work of Aristotle's own, though this is pure conjecture.[2] Un-Aristotelian in its incompleteness, it does not actually contradict the *Poetics* but rather extracts from it two obvious features and no more.

Such is the incomplete picture available to us of the work of Theophrastus in the field of criticism. It is disappointing as well as fragmentary. We should remember that, in spite of the books on linguistic and literary subjects credited to him,[3] his main interests lay in other fields. If he had originated some of the later theories now often credited to him and strayed far from the Aristotelian fold, some definite traces of this would surely have survived among the numerous references to him in our texts, nor would his name have been so uniformly linked with that of Aristotle. His critical works were widely read, no doubt deservedly, but in all essentials they seem to have been a restatement, with clarifications and elaborations, of the theories of his master. We should not be led to attribute to him later theories and formulae in the teeth of the evidence; the old tradition was probably right and is well summarized in the words of Quintilian (3, 1, 15): *Theophrastus quoque, Aristotelis discipulus, de rhetorice diligenter scripsit.*

[1] See A. Ph. McMahon in *HSCP* 28 (1917), 1-46.
[2] McMahon, ibid. 45.
[3] For a list of the works of Theophrastus see Diogenes Laertius 5, 42-50.

CHAPTER VII

Demetrius On Style

The treatise known as Demetrius *On Style*, περὶ ἑρμηνείας is the only
extant critical text which in all probability belongs to Hellenistic times.
The manuscript tradition attributes it to Demetrius of Phalerum, the
friend of Theophrastus who ruled Athens on behalf of the Macedonian
king Cassander from 317 to 307 B.C. and then retired to the court of
Ptolemy Soter in Alexandria where he may have helped to establish the
great Museum library. His authorship of *On Style* is recognized as extremely unlikely, and the treatise, being thus left fatherless, has been
assigned to various dates and authors. At the beginning of this century
most scholars were inclined to bring it down to Roman times, somewhere
in the first century B.C. or A.D. or even later. Recent scholarship, however,
tends to revert to an earlier date, late third or second century B.C. I have
argued elsewhere for a date about 270 B.C. or not much later, and for an
author personally acquainted with the relevant works of Aristotle and
Theophrastus, and indeed with those of Demetrius of Phalerum as well.[1]
That the treatise is Hellenistic seems certain; it does not link up with any
movement we can trace in the Hellenistic centuries but rather with what
had gone before so that it seems appropriate to deal with it here. We may
as well, for the sake of convenience, call the author Demetrius, though
not the Phalerean. The name is common enough.

On Style is conveniently divided into 303 short numbered paragraphs,
and its general plan is clear: first, an introductory section on the structure
of sentences (1-35); this is followed by a discussion of four specific
χαρακτῆρες i.e. styles or manners of writing, namely the grand, impressive
or elevated (μεγαλοπρεπής, 38-113), the elegant or polished (γλαφυρός,
128-85), the plain or simple (ἰσχνός, 190-235), and the forceful or intense
(δεινός). Each of these is considered from the point of view of subject-
matter – though of this very little is said – of diction and of word-arrange-

---

[1] See my annotated translation, *A Greek Critic: Demetrius On Style*, especially the introduction pp. 39-56, and the two appendices. The two chief editors, L. Radermacher and W. Rhys
Roberts, would date the work in the first or second century A.D. For more recent opinions
see F. Boll in *Rhein. M.* 72 (1917) 25-33 and W. Kroll, *R.E.* Suppl. 7 (Stuttgart, 1940) 1077 ff.
For further references see *A Greek Critic* p. 22 note 26. Catharina Augustyniak in her *De
tribus et quattuor dicendi generibus* returns to the earlier opinion. The main arguments will be
briefly stated at the end of this chapter.

ment. Each style also has a neighbouring vice into which the unwary may fall: frigidity neighbours upon grandeur, affectation is close to elegance, aridity to plainness, and coarseness to forcefulness. These vices too are briefly discussed.

The introductory section owes much to Aristotle's discussion of sentence structure in the third book of the *Rhetoric*, but Demetrius does not hesitate to change the terminology or to add ideas of his own. He puts much more emphasis on the clauses which, he says, must, like Aristotle's periods, correspond to the thought. Generally, clauses should be moderate in length, unless special effects are sought. For example, brevity can be forceful and 'every master is monosyllabic to his slaves whereas supplications and lamentations are lengthy', also 'a maxim (γνώμη) expanded in length becomes an instructive piece of information or a piece of rhetoric instead of a maxim' (8-9). Demetrius adopts Aristotle's distinction between the periodic and the loose style, but he uses a simpler term to indicate the latter,[1] and says no period should consist of more than four clauses (16). He then introduces a threefold classification of periods as conversational, historical and rhetorical, each more involved than the preceding; the conversational is very close to the loose style (21), a good example of this being the first period of Plato's *Republic*.

The way in which Aristotle is used in this section, as elsewhere, seems to argue personal knowledge of the *Rhetoric*, and a readiness to use him for the author's own purposes, which is not characteristic of a member of the school.[2]

When we come to the discussion of the four χαρακτῆρες, we should realize that the translation 'styles' is somewhat misleading, partly because we currently use the word more subjectively as something peculiar to an individual writer while the ancients thought of it more objectively, and partly because the word 'style' has, in the history of ancient criticism, been closely associated with the more rigid later formula of the three styles (the plain, the grand and the intermediate).[3] The good 'orator' must then be able to use each of the three at the proper time. They are not, however, used together. The Greek word χαρακτήρ is very general in meaning and Demetrius is much less specific in his use of it, for he applies it not only to the four main 'characters' discussed, but also to the corresponding vices, so that he speaks of the frigid χαρακτήρ, the arid, and so on. He also applies the word to the epistolary 'style' or manner. Moreover, his main 'styles', except for the plain and the grand, can be mixed, i.e. used *at the same time* so that the elegant can combine with both the plain and the

[1] 12: διηρημένη (ἑρμηνεία) for Aristotle's λέξις εἰρομένη.
[2] For Demetrius' unusual attitude to Aristotle see *A Greek Critic* pp. 32-38.
[3] See pp. 107-8 and 138 above

grand, and the grand alone cannot mix with the plain.[1] His 'styles' in fact are more like qualities[2] or elements of style, than like the more rigid styles of the three-style formula. Demetrius is not extending the formula but dealing with a different subject.[3]

It should also be noted that the categories of ancient criticism are not quite the same as our own. The distinction between style and content is simple enough; we have seen that it can be traced back to Plato,[4] but the further subdivision of style itself into word-choice (λέξις, later ἐκλογή ὀνομάτων) and word-arrangement (σύνθεσις), which is here used explicitly for the first time, may well puzzle a modern reader. Word-choice in ancient critics not only refers to the use of current or unusual words, neologisms, compound words and the like, but also to the use of words expressing passion and character, so that writing in character is partly a matter of word-choice. It also includes the use of different forms, cases or tenses, the use of loaded words, metaphors and similes, and even the use of few words or many. *Synthesis* or word-arrangement, on the other hand, is mainly concerned with three things: the sound or music of words in juxtaposition, the structure of clauses and sentences, and above all the resulting rhythm. This division of style into word-choice and word-arrangement is, as we saw, implicit in Aristotle[5]; it may very well have been made explicit by Theophrastus. Demetrius further includes the use of figures of speech under word-arrangement (59).

When he deals with these figures, and recommends a number of them as contributing to this style or that, we find that the same figures are not infrequently appropriate to different styles – asyndeton, for example, or *anaphora* (repetition of the same word at the beginning or end of con-secutive clauses) may be elegant in one place, impressive in another, and then again forceful later.[6] This is, of course, quite true, but there must then be a difference in tone, context or other factors and Demetrius ought

---

[1] Demetrius has been held to contradict himself for at 36 he states that the plain and the grand do not mix but are opposite extremes (ἐναντιωτάτω) while at 258 he says that the force-ful and the elegant seem or are thought to be opposite extremes (ἐναντιώτατοι). The contradic-tion is purely verbal for at 36 he says that all the other styles except the grand mix with the plain; he does not say anywhere that the elegant can be mixed with the forceful. One must conclude therefore that there are two impossible combinations, the plain and the grand and also the elegant and the forceful. The contradiction is that two sets of styles are said to be ἐναντιώτατοι.

[2] That Demetrius' styles are more like qualities has often been noted. F. Solmsen, for example in *Hermes* 66 (1931) attempts to link the four styles of Demetrius with the four virtues often attributed to Theophrastus, and δεινότης is often spoken of as a quality by Dionysius. See also R. Altschul, p. 31, note 21, and Stroux, p. 104.

[3] There is little force, therefore, in making it an argument for a late date that a four-style formula must be a later variation of the three-style formula, e.g. Augustyanak, pp. 23-33 and Rhys Roberts, p. 51.

[4] Above, p. 57.   [5] Above, p. 95.

[6] For *anaphora* cf. 61, 141 and 268. On this see *A Greek Critic* pp. 27-28.

to have analysed these differences to account for the different effects. He does not do so; this is an obvious weakness but he is at least a better critic for realizing that the same devices do not have the same effect in different contexts, and for not trying to restrict each figure to one style only. He seems aware of the difficulty when for example, he says that 'Sappho can use even the most forceful figures charmingly' (140) or again, when commenting on her use of hyperbole, e.g., 'more golden than gold': 'it is a most admirable feature of the divine Sappho's art that she extracts great charm from the use of devices in themselves questionable and difficult' (127). Our author has great sensitivity, and his feelings are nearly always right, though his explanations are often incomplete, even at times illogical.

His practical advice is good; his numerous illustrations are apt and at times illuminating. In his discussion of the grand style for example, where he begins with word-arrangement and specifically with rhythm, he follows Aristotle's predilection for the paeon at the beginning and the end of clauses (Aristotle, however, did not link this advice with any particular style). He then adds (41), following Theophrastus, that a clause may be paeonic in a general sense without specifically beginning or ending with a paeon. This realization of a general rhythmic effect in prose which does not involve analysing a clause exactly into feet is an important improvement on Aristotle, in this case derived from Theophrastus.

Periods, as we would expect, contribute to the grand manner, but they must have a definite structure with well marked clauses, for 'long journeys seem shorter if one stops frequently at an inn, while a deserted road makes even a short journey seem long' (47). So too, harsh-sounding words, singly or in juxtaposition, make for grandeur (48-49), and we should not, in the smooth manner of Isocrates, avoid all hiatus; its use should, however, be deliberate, for frequent and haphazard vowel-collisions 'interrupt our flow with stops and jerks' (68). In the same section on the grand manner he points out that the less vivid words should come first, the more vivid later, in ascending order as it were (50-52), that connectives should correspond exactly (53), and that expletives which are mere 'fillers' should be avoided at all costs (55).

The discussion of metaphor is of special interest (78-90). Demetrius has been blamed because he goes beyond the requirements of the grand style which he is here discussing. This accusation is deserved. He does have a way of discussing a subject more fully than is immediately necessary, the first time it comes up, but this is not a serious fault. In this instance, he follows Aristotle in attaching great importance to the use of metaphor and in saying that they must not be far-fetched or too numerous. Like Aristotle, he favours active metaphors which to some extent personify inanimate objects. Then he improves on Aristotle in two respects: he points out that metaphors are not always interchangeable (he obviously has Aristotle's proportionate metaphor in mind): you can, for example, speak of the foot of a mountain but not of the slope of a man.

Then he makes a neat correction. We remember Aristotle's puzzling statement that a metaphor is safer in prose, and a simile more poetical. Demetrius very sensibly reverses this (80): 'when a metaphor is too bold, we can change it into a simile, which is safer', and he then adds: 'when we turn a metaphor into a simile . . . we must aim at brevity and add only the word "like" before it; otherwise it will not be a simile but a poetic comparison', by which he obviously means the extended Homeric simile. This clears up the difficulty, for it was the failure to distinguish the ordinary simile from the Homeric which led Aristotle into confusion.[1]

Diction in the grand style will naturally include unusual words, compounds and new onomatopoeic coinages. Among the figures recommended for this style are *allêgoria* or veiled meanings (99): e.g. 'their grasshoppers will sing from the ground' an example also used by Aristotle for 'I shall ravage their country'; *epiphônêma* (106), i.e. an ornamental addition when the sense is already complete, and hyperbole. All these can enhance impressiveness, but they must be used with caution. On poetic vocabulary Demetrius makes an interesting point when he says that Herodotus borrows words from the poets wholesale, whereas when Thucydides uses a poetic word he integrates it into the context of his ideas and thus makes it his own (113).

Frigidity, ψυχρότης, the vice neighbour to the grand manner, is discussed at some length (114-27). Theophrastus defined it, we are told, as that which 'overshoots its appropriate expression', i.e. the use of language too elevated for the thought expressed. Aristotle's four causes of frigid diction are quoted,[2] namely the excessive use of epithets, dithyrambic compounds, an exaggeratedly unusual vocabulary, and poor metaphors. Demetrius then adds an excess of metrical phrases as a further cause of frigidity, and (119):

> In general, frigidity is like boastfulness. The boaster lays claim to qualities he does not possess, undeterred by his lack of them; and the writer who speaks weightily of trivial matters is like one who boasts about trifles. To discuss matters of no importance in an exalted style is like beautifying a pestle, as the saying is.

[1] See above, p. 96.
[2] Demetrius says he is quoting Aristotle's four causes of frigidity but then a short lacuna follows and *two* causes only are quoted; the reference to *Rhet*. 3, 3, 1-4 (1405 b) is, however, very clear and the other two reasons must be added. In Aristotle frigidity is not linked with any particular style

Thus far the grand style and its neighbouring vice; their meaning is plain to all. It is more difficult, however, to extract the one basic idea of the elegant or polished style, and the author seems to be guilty of some confusion. He describes elegance (128) as 'a certain bright playfulness of expression' and immediately divides it into two kinds: the charm of the first is 'serious and dignified as in poetry', the second is 'more commonplace and comic, like jests'. About the first there is little difficulty: the illustrations, i.e. the Homeric scene of Nausicaa playing among her handmaidens and a number of passages from Sappho and other lyric poets, clearly have charm, grace and an elegant dexterity of expression; they are playful because they are on a lower emotional plane than the heroic passages of Homer or the more passionate poems of Sappho. This 'bright playfulness' merges into wit; a good many witticisms have elegance and charm. Indeed, as one looks over the examples of milder witticisms, one might doubt whether they are witticisms, or merely elegant and charming, e.g. the quotation from Sophron (147): 'the boys are pelting the men with leaves and twigs as innumerable as, they say, my dear, were the darts which the Trojans showered upon Ajax.'

But, because elegant charm and witticisms both have playfulness and dexterity of expression, Demetrius has been led to include all witticisms under elegance, even those that are grim and brutal, though he himself describes the result as forcefulness (130-1). The passage from Lysias (128, cf. 262) about the old woman 'whose teeth were easier to count than her fingers' is witty but neither elegant, charming nor gracious, and this is even more true of the Cyclops' promise to eat 'Nobody' last, which makes the scene 'more awe-inspiring' (φοβερώτερος, 130). These more brutal witticisms properly belong to the forceful style where indeed we shall meet some of them again. Demetrius seems aware of his difficulty, for he actually discusses the *difference* between elegant charm and comic laughter, but he does not clear it up (163-9): he tells us that the charming writer wants to delight us, the comedian to make us laugh. He should have gone on to say that a writer may well have both aims in view and that only when he succeeds in both at once can his witticism be counted as elegant. He does not say so, however: his analysis is once again deficient, and here the result is definitely confusing.

We have so little on comedy and wit in ancient writers that even the few points made here should be noted: the difference between the elegant and the bitter witticism just mentioned; that a witticism can increase the grimness of a passage, a usage at which Xenophon, we are told, was particularly apt; or a witticism may brighten a distasteful subject as when Xenophon said of Aglaitadas 'It is easier to strike fire from you than laughter' (134), and this is called the most effective kind of wit (135).

Other kinds of witticisms are also mentioned, namely double meanings, like the description of the sleeping Amazon (138) with her bow and arrows ready, her shield as her pillow, 'and they do not loosen their girdles'. Or again the witty use of *allēgoria* where old men are said to be 'ready to weigh anchor'; the use of saws and proverbs, and the comic use of hyperbole. In the use of all these devices good taste is important, for 'a man's jokes are an indication of his character; they may well indicate a lack of seriousness or self-control' (171). We may also note that stylistic ornament is inadvisable in jests, for it distracts attention (165).

As for the more serious and poetic elegance, Demetrius gives a number of illustrations under the usual headings of content, word-choice and word-arrangement. Some subjects, a garden of the Nymphs, a bridal-song and the like, have a charm of their own which even a bad writer can hardly spoil, though a good writer will increase it (132). The diction is obviously important: a happy metaphor or simile, an elaborate compound or an unusual derivative may contribute to both elegance and humour (142-5), and so can an appropriate fable or hyperbole. Above all, beautiful words, beautiful in sound, meaning or associations, greatly contribute to the charm of a passage.[1] Rhythm too is important, but it must not be obvious. We may note in passing that 'no previous writer has had anything to say about elegant word-arrangement' (179).

Affectation (κακόζηλος), the vice neighbouring on elegance, is briefly dealt with. It may be due to the thought expressed ('a Centaur riding himself'), to a wrong choice of words, or to a poor word-arrangement, especially to feeble rhythms like those of Sotades (186-9).

In his treatment of the simple style Demetrius varies his approach. The usual formula is almost discarded: except for the bald statement (190) that the subject-matter should be simple also, the words current and usual, and a very short section on word arrangement (204-8) wherein he advises the avoidance of long clauses, clashing vowels and unusual figures, he concentrates on three qualities characteristic of the simple style, namely clarity (191-203), vividness (209-20) and persuasiveness (221-2). The treatment of these is somewhat undistinguished and without surprises: the unusual is to be avoided throughout, in diction, in structure, and in the use of figures. There is again some confusion of thought where vividness is said to require putting in *all* the details whereas the examples show that it is the *selection of significant detail* which is required. We have already noted the quotation from Theophrastus (222, under persuasiveness) that one should not spell out everything in precise detail but leave some things for the hearer to work out and understand for himself.[2]

---

[1] Demetrius here (173) quotes a description of the kinds of beauty in words from Theophrastus. See above, p. 104.   [2] Above, p. 105.

One section of this chapter, however (223-35), is of considerable interest. It deals with the proper style to be used in writing letters. Demetrius does not agree with Artemon who, he tells us, published Aristotle's correspondence,[1] that letters, being as it were one side of a dialogue, should be written in a conversational style (224):

> A letter should be written rather more carefully than dialogue, though not obviously so. Dialogue imitates impromptu conversation, whereas *a letter is a piece of writing which is sent to someone as a kind of gift*. . . . Disjointed sentences frequently occur in conversation but they are out of place in letters.

Letters, however, have one point of contact with dialogue, that they should be in character (227):

> You might say that everyone draws, in his letters, a picture of his own personality. A writer's character can be seen in all his works, but nowhere so clearly as in his correspondence.

He makes another good point (228):

> Letters which are too long and too dignified in language are in fact not letters at all, but treatises which are addressed to somebody as an afterthought.

It follows that the sentence-structure should not be heavily periodic, for then it becomes a speech. This is not only ridiculous but unfriendly, 'for, as the saying goes, one should call a spade a spade[2] among friends'. Only certain kinds of subject-matter are appropriate in letters; discussions of logic or natural science are not (232):

> The beauty of a letter lies in the affection and courtesy it expresses. Old saws or proverbs may be quoted, but these are the only kind of wisdom it should contain because proverbs are a kind of common popular wisdom. A writer who expounds general reflections and urges a way of life on you is not chatting with a friend in a letter but preaching *ex cathedra*.[3]

Letters are written at times to cities and potentates (234), and in these the style will be more elevated, but even so they should not become treatises 'like the letters of Aristotle to Alexander, or Plato's to the friends of Dion'. The final conclusion is that 'the style of letters should be a mixture of the plain and the elegant'.

[1] The identity of this Artemon has been much disputed. See p. 120, note 1.

[2] The Greek saying is to call figs figs (229).

[3] ἐκ μηχανῆς: speaking as a god from the machine' refers to the epiphanies of the gods in the theatre, often foretelling the future.

This charming discussion of the proper epistolary style is the only one
of its kind in classical texts, even though letter-writing quite early became
a recognized literary genre, not only the writing of genuine letters but
of imaginary letters by important personages. Demetrius seems to be
thinking only of genuine letters but his principles would also apply to
the others. As a literary genre, letter-writing of both kinds may well go
back to the fourth if not the fifth century.[1] We have no other discussion
of it till centuries later, and then nothing as good as this.

The chapter on the simple style closes, as it must, with a few paragraphs
(236-9) on the neighbouring vice, in this case aridity (ξηρός). This may be
due to baldness of thought, e.g. 'Xerxes came down with all his men'
instead of 'with the man-power of all Asia', or to poor and dry diction, or
to a word-arrangement with too many short phrases, or to abrupt,
premature endings. There is also a combination which Demetrius calls
ξηροκακοζηλία which combines affectation of ideas with aridity of expression.

When we come to the fourth and last style, forcefulness or intensity, we
find that it has a good deal in common with the grand manner. Demetrius
tells us himself that the diction will be much the same, though used with
different intent (272); a number of the same figures are used, indeed one
or two of the same examples occur in both chapters. Yet there are obvious
and clear differences, and the grand manner is not necessarily forceful.
Forcefulness is more vehement and abrupt; it involves a heightening
emotional tension and we are not surprised to find a number of examples
from Demosthenes whereas no Demosthenic passages illustrate the other
styles.

The chief difference seems to be that forcefulness demands brevity and
terseness: short phrases instead of clauses, for 'length destroys vehemence'
(241). Even when we use periods, and a succession of periods can be forceful (251), they must be short, not more than two clauses, and with clear,
well marked endings. Rhetorical devices such as antithesis, paromoiosis,
balanced clauses and so on must be avoided as incompatible with strong
emotion, but discordant combinations of sound, hiatus, a jerky and forced,
unnatural order of words, lack of connectives, all these can contribute to
forcefulness which requires a histrionic delivery. We also find some new
figures not mentioned before such as ironic euphemism, *epinome* (dwelling
on, or rather hammering away at, a subject), and the *klimax* or ladder of
which the famous Demosthenic example is quoted:

[1] On this subject see H. Koskennieni's 'Studien zur Idee und Phraseologie des griechischen
Briefes bis 400 n. Chr.' and J. Sykutris' 'Epistolographie' in *RE*. In his essay on Lysias ch. 1
Dionysius of Halicarnassus mentions the orator's performances in the epistolary genre.
Lysias was born *c.* 459 and died 380 B.C. so that letter-writing as a genre may well date as
early as the late fifth century.

I did not say these things and then not move a motion; I did not move a motion and then not go as an envoy; I did not go as an envoy and then not persuade the Thebans. . . .[1]

The violent and bitter witticisms mistakenly discussed under elegance here come into their own, and in this connexion Demetrius quotes several examples from the orator Demades who, he says, practised a peculiar kind of forcefulness which was a combination of strong, expressive words, veiled meaning and hyperbole (282-6). For example

Alexander is not dead, men of Athens, for the smell of his corpse would cover the world.
The power of Macedon, with Alexander gone, is but a blinded Cyclops.
Our city is no longer the fighting sailor of our ancestors, but a slippered old crone gulping her gruel.

The vice neighbouring on forcefulness is coarseness (ἄχαρις, 302-4). It may be coarseness of subject, i.e. the mention of unmentionable things, a word-arrangement too jerky and disconnected, or a diction inappropriate and in bad taste. And, like the grand and the forceful, so frigidity and coarseness too are close neighbours.

Such are the highlights[2] of this curious treatise. Its author is no genius, but an educated scholar with a good knowledge of Greek literature, both classical and early Alexandrine, who shows what the objective, somewhat formula-ridden techniques of Greek criticism can accomplish. He is no philosopher, but no mere rhetorician either; his interest is in literature, not in courtroom procedures, cases, or arguments, and his book is literary theory and criticism properly so called. He is certainly no mere copyist or excerptor from other (unknown) sources; and he knew his Aristotle and his Theophrastus at first hand – or so it seems to me. He shows considerable independence of mind, and even his weaknesses are personal, not of the kind which one repeats at second hand. That he often uses illustrations also found elsewhere (whether in Aristotle or in later authors) is no argument to the contrary, for every ancient critic does this down the centuries, even Longinus. If a perfect illustration has been found, why look for

[1] The Greek is much more terse (270), with carefully balanced connectives: οὐκ εἶπον μὲν ταῦτα, οὐκ ἔγραψα δέ, οὐδ' ἔγραψα μέν, οὐκ ἐπρέσβευσα δέ, οὐδ' ἐπρέσβευσα μέν, οὐκ ἔπεισα δὲ τοὺς Θηβαίους (On the Crown 179). The figure consists of a series of steps, each repeated before proceeding to the next, ab, bc, cd and so on. We may also note the jerky rhythm of the second to the fifth clause and the more solid ending of the last.
[2] I have omitted in particular mention of one figure, innuendo (τὸ κατεσχηματισμένον), which implies much more than it says. This is discussed at some length (287-95) as appropriate when addressing potentates, or a dangerous assembly. It often results in forcefulness. This leads to a discussion of different modes of speech – question, suggestion, accusation, etc. – the one true digression in the book (296-301).

another probably less perfect? If, as I believe, the treatise can be dated in early Hellenistic times, or indeed any time before 100 B.C., its interest is considerably enhanced, for it is then the only extant critical work between the fourth century B.C. on the one hand and the Greek and Roman critics of the first century on the other.

This is not the place to argue the case for an early date, but the position may perhaps be briefly summarized.[1]

There are two good reasons to consider the traditional authorship of Demetrius of Phalerum very improbable, if not impossible. The first is the evidence of Hermippus, quoted by Diogenes Laertius (5, 58). He states that Ptolemy Philadelphus, on his accession, banished the Phalerean (who had opposed his succession) to the country under guard, where he 'lived in discouragement'. Hermippus continues: 'He was somehow bitten in the hand by an asp, while he was asleep, and died.' Cicero refers to Demetrius as one of those who owed their death to the enmity of a despot.[2] These passages imply that he was murdered, it would seem shortly after 283 B.C. Now internal references make it quite clear that our treatise cannot have been written before 275 B.C. at the very earliest. The other potent argument is that the treatise is not written in Attic (in spite of occasional conscious Atticisms) but in the kind of Greek which approximates the *koinê* and it is very unlikely that Demetrius of Phalerum, an Athenian and the friend of Theophrastus, would write that kind of Greek even after thirty years in Alexandria.

Those who would date our treatise in the first century B.C. or later rely very heavily on the language used and have listed a number of words and expressions which do not occur elsewhere till Roman times. Their arguments are not, in my opinion, convincing, for we have no contemporary texts as a basis of comparison, so that we have very little idea what kind of Greek might be written in Alexandria in the third century. The subject is highly technical and uncertain as it requires the examination of a large number of words and expressions. I can only say that such an examination has convinced me that the linguistic arguments for a late date are weak.

My chief reasons for believing the date of our treatise to be early Hellenistic are: (i) our author's attitude to Aristotle is quite unlike that of the critics of the first century or later; (ii) so is his attitude to Demosthenes who later was considered the paragon of all the styles; (iii) he shows a familiarity with persons and events of the later fourth and early third

---

[1] For a full discussion of the various views as to the date which are here briefly mentioned I must refer the reader to *A Greek Critic*, introduction and appendices. Since its publication, a later date has been suggested by G. P. Goold in *TAPA* 1961 and by J. M. Rist in *Phoenix* 1964. I do not find their arguments convincing, and my answer to them will be found in *Phoenix* 18, 1964.

[2] *Pro Rabio Postumo* 9, 23.

centuries which is more compatible with oral than written tradition, and references to contemporaries are quite natural in a highly literate, scholarly and controversial circle such as we know to have existed in and around the Museum; (iv) there are a number of points of contact with the known stylistic theories of Demetrius of Phalerum which argue some acquaintance with him or his work. As for external evidence (v) there is I believe a strong probability that Philodemus in the first century B.C. was acquainted with the treatise and in fact believed Demetrius of Phalerum to be the author.

The negative evidence is also strong: (vi) 'Demetrius' shows no concern for, indeed a complete unawareness of, the questions which agitated critics like Dionysius of Halicarnassus, Cicero and Horace in the first century B.C. and their successors. There is not a word about Asianism or Atticism, about Analogy or Anomaly, about rhetorical *mimêsis* or the education of the orator, and the whole critical formulaic system is very much simpler.

Complete certainty is of course impossible of attainment but on the basis of these and for other less striking reasons I believe 270 B.C. or not much later to be the likely date. Its links with the Classical period are much stronger than any link with a much later date.

CHAPTER VIII

Alexandria

Our lack of texts for the third and second centuries B.C. makes the study of stylistic and literary theory during that time very uncertain. We can, however, from references in later authors and from the mass of *scholia* or editorial notes in our much later manuscripts, trace, if only in outline, certain major developments such as the rise of the Asiatic style, the growth of literary scholarship in the Museum at Alexandria and with it the discovery of certain critical principles, the general attitude of the philosophical schools towards literature and rhetoric, and the resurgence of rhetorical teaching in the second and first centuries. Moreover, here and there throughout this period there flits, on the edges of our field of vision, some uncertain and unsubstantial ghost conjured up to perplex us from the charred remains of Philodemus.

ASIANISM: HEGESIAS

As a result of Alexander's conquests the Greek language, together with Greek ideas and practices, spread all over the Middle East until Greek became the common language, the *koinê*, of the whole region. In the process it lost some of its precision and subtlety until it became the simpler form of Greek which we know as the language of the New Testament. At the same time there arose, somewhat paradoxically, a more flowery and redundant style which came to be known as Asiatic. The name was probably not in use until much later, and certainly the controversy between Asianism and Atticism belongs to the first century B.C.[1] but the thing itself was very much earlier. As Cicero was to put it in the *Brutus* (13, 51):

> Once eloquence set out from the Piraeus to travel all over the islands and all of Asia, it came into contact with other ways of life and lost the healthy sanity of Attic diction as well as the capacity of speaking well. Then came those Asiatic orators whose style lacks succinctness and is excessively redundant though its rapidity and abundance are not to be despised. The Rhodians, however, remained saner and more like Attic orators.

See Wilamowitz, 'Asianismus und Atticismus' in *Hermes* 35 (1900), 1-52.

He had said in the *De Oratore* (3, 11, 43):

> Any uneducated Athenian will easily surpass the most learned Asiatic not so much in his choice of words as in the way he speaks them; it is not so much a matter of good as of pleasing speech.

Quintilian (12, 10, 16) more than a century after Cicero, said that some people traced the origin of the Asiatic style to the fact that, as Greek spread, some Asians were eager to acquire a reputation as orators before they had sufficient command over the language so that they were apt to speak in paraphrases because they were at a loss for words, and then later persisted in the practice. He himself rather believes that the differences in style were due to differences in taste:

> The Athenians were too polished and refined to tolerate empty or redundant phrases, whereas the Asiatics, a more boastful and bombastic people, swelled with desire for a more vainglorious eloquence.

Whatever the cause, the Asiatic style was obviously flowery and pleonastic. One thinks of such a process of degeneration as slow and gradual, but it must have started before the end of the fourth century, for Cicero quotes Demetrius of Phalerum himself as no longer pure Attic in style. Moreover all the critics associate Asianism especially with the name of Hegesias of Magnesia who flourished, be it noted, as early as the middle of the third century. No critic has a good word to say for him; they all accuse him of lack of taste, and the vices particularly associated with his name are the breaking up of his sentences into short, all but metrical, clauses and the use of unnecessary words to round out the rhythm, the result being not unlike a succession of short verses.[1] Clearly Asianism, whatever it was called, if indeed it had a name at that time, was, in origin, early Hellenistic. We know from Cicero that it continued to flourish and, in the first century, it was the bugbear of Greek and Roman critics alike.

LITERARY SCHOLARSHIP IN ALEXANDRIA

Meanwhile the great library of the Museum had been established at Alexandria about 285 B.C. It flourished under royal patronage and soon became the recognized centre of Greek literary scholarship which may be said to have been born there. The kings of Egypt deliberately set out to collect the best manuscripts of all the great Greek authors and entrusted to the best scholars of the Greek world, attracted by their patronage, the

---

[1] See Cicero, *Orator* 69, 230: *sunt etiam qui illo vitio quod ab Hegesia maxime fluxit, infrigendis concidendisque numeris in quoddam genus abiectum incidant versiculorum simillimum*, and ibid. 67, 226. Dionysius of Halicarnassus quotes (*Composition* 18, U-R II, 80-82) a fairly long extract from Hegesias as the ultimate in poor rhythm, and a shorter fragment is found in Strabo (9, 1, 6).

For the Asianism-Atticism controversy see below, pp. 181-4.

task of establishing authoritative texts of them, and cataloguing them. Upon the basis of these catalogues the first real histories of literature came to be written.

The early years of the Museum (Μουσεῖον, i.e. temple of the Muses) was the golden period of Alexandrine Greek literature, the age of Callimachus, Theocritus and Apollonius of Rhodes. It was a scholarly and learned literature which had a great deal of influence on Roman poets but never caught the imagination of succeeding ages to the same extent as the Greek classics of earlier generations. Apollonius' epic is extant, we have some idylls of Theocritus, and considerable fragments of the poetry of Callimachus, but little else. The prose works of all kinds are lost, and so are the great works of literary scholarship. The critical principles which the Alexandrians evolved must be painstakingly rescued bit by bit from fragmentary references in the *scholia*, the notes of Greek editors in the margins of our manuscripts centuries later. There the comments of the great critics of Alexandria are preserved but in mutilated, abbreviated, distorted and frequently anonymous form. The most fruitful field of this kind is the Homeric scholia, and the patient and careful study of these by modern scholars helped by later commentaries such as those of Eustathius in the twelfth century, which are extant, has rescued some important and illuminating material on Alexandrian scholarship. One can trace the process of transmission through a long chain of later commentators such as Didymus and Aristonicus in the time of Augustus, to Herodian and Nicanor a century and a half later, then to a compiler of all four in the third century, and so to our Byzantine manuscripts.[1]

While we cannot always be sure of the contribution of each of the great Alexandrians, we can certainly trace a gradual and consistent improvement of critical methods which culminates in Aristarchus of Byzantium who became chief librarian of the Museum in 180 B.C.

The first librarian was Zenodotus. He was also the first Alexandrian editor of Homer. We cannot be sure what state the text of Homer was in before Zenodotus began to work on him, yet to judge from the general (though by no means complete) agreement of quotations in earlier writers with the received text from our manuscripts it seems that there was a generally accepted vulgate.[2] Zenodotus indulged in 'athetizing', in fact he

[1] Great work in this field was done by K. Lehrs, *De Aristarchi Studiis Homericis*; by A Roemer, in his *Aristarchs Athetezen in der Homerkritik* and also *Die Homerexegese Aristarchs in ihren Grundzügen*. See also N. Wecklein *Ueber Zenodot und Aristarch* and A. Severyns, *Le Cycle épique dans l'école d'Aristarque*, in this last the reader will find a clear and brief account of the process of transmission pp. 1-28.

[2] This does not mean that there were not many other versions. For the freedom with which changes could be made see Plutarch *Alcibiades* 7, but, on the other hand, J. Labarbe, *L'Homère de Platon*, pp. 409 ff.

invented the process, and marked with the sign – or *obelos* the lines which he rejected. This he did often on subjective grounds, and it is easy to ridicule him. For example, he athetized the words of Nausicaa to her handmaidens at the appearance of Odysseus bathed and beautified by Athena, wishing that she might have such a man for her husband; this being, Zenodotus thought, most unmaidenly.[1] Of the same kind is his condemnation of the violent insults ('You drunkard with the face of a dog and the heart of a deer . . .') hurled by Achilles at Agamemnon just before he swears by the sceptre that he will retire from the fight. Zenodotus thought them unseemly for a hero.[2]

We should remember in his favour, however, that, though he marked the lines as spurious, Zenodotus still, unlike some modern editors, included them in his text. He questioned but did not delete. And his successors were, if to a lesser extent, capable of equal folly, for we are expressly told that Aristophanes of Byzantium and even the great Aristarchus agreed with his deletion of Achilles' brutal wish, when he sends Patroclus into battle, that no Trojan or Greek might survive and they two alone might raze Troy. The Alexandrians said that these lines were inserted by men who maintained that there was homosexuality in Homer and that Patroclus was the beloved of Achilles.[3] This is foolish for the lines do not leave that impression, and we have here an early example of prudish critics wishing to excise from the text something that exists only in their own mind!

Zenodotus' criticism, however, was not all of this kind; a good deal of it was linguistic. This too may have shown a certain lack of historical perspective when judged by later standards, so that one may sympathize with Timon of Phlius who, when asked where one could find a good Homeric text, replied that it was essential to get one which had not been corrected by the critics![4] Nevertheless, the work of Zenodotus was a great step forward; it was a tremendous task to establish a critical text of Homer. His criticism was at least an improvement on that of Zoilus and his like.[5]

The second great Alexandrian was Callimachus. He may never have been chief librarian but he was closely connected with the Museum. He was both a literary scholar and a poet; in his poetry he from time to time expressed ideas about literature which were characteristic of his day. His chief scholarly work was a vast collection of πίνακες or memoranda on all classical Greek authors. This collection was undoubtedly based on the great library's catalogues; it was probably in different sections correspond-

[1] Plutarch, *De Audiendis Poetis* 27 c.
[2] See Lehrs, p. 29.
[3] Homer, *Iliad* 16, 97-100, discussed by Roemer, *Athetezen*, p. 61.
[4] Diogenes Laertius 9, 113 quoted by P. Cauer, *Grundfragen der Homerkritik*, p. 70
[5] See above, p. 87.

ing to the chief literary genres; the different authors were then treated
under such genre-headings as tragedy, comedy, philosophy, medicine,
and so on, with biographical details, lists of works considered genuine or
spurious, and brief discussions of all their works. This vast collection was
a mine of information on which many later compilers drew for their
own work. It was in fact the first attempt at a history of Greek classical
literature.[1]

It is in his poetry, however, that we must look for incidental and often
fragmentary remarks which reflect the literary tastes of the day, for
Callimachus seems to have achieved in Museum circles a position not
unlike that of an unofficial dean of letters. The Greek literature of Alexandria could never be a popular literature since it was written by foreigners
in the land of Egypt, writing in the foreign language of the court, and
completely cut off from the life of the people. It was a learned literature,
written largely by men of letters for men of letters, all of them very conscious of the supreme achievements of their great predecessors, and somewhat inhibited by them, conscious of their inability to compete with the
greatest. Hence the Alexandrian tendency to make up for lack of genius
by careful workmanship; hence too their tendency to write in the smaller
genres: the hymn, the epigram, the pastoral, the lyric, the epyllion;
hence too their desire for praise from fellow cognoscenti and their contempt for the vulgar crowd whom they could neither know nor understand. Such a literature does not seek to teach but to entertain; in Alexandria the classical concept of the poets as the teachers of their people was
inevitably challenged. It is against this background that Callimachus'
remarks on poetry must be judged and understood.

Such was, for example, his advice to budding poets not to travel upon
the highways already overcrowded with the chariots of others but rather
to find literary byways of their own.[2] This, taken in conjunction with his
other well known saying that a big book was a big nuisance,[3] reflects the
Alexandrian preference for shorter genres and opposes any attempt to
write in the great genres of epic, and probably tragedy also. This advice is
meant to apply only to creative writing, not to works of scholarship or
science of which many were written. Even in the creative literary field,
however, Callimachus' advice was not universally accepted. Tragedies
were still written in great numbers, and Apollonius Rhodius disregarded
Callimachus when writing his epic of the Golden Fleece, *The Argonautica*,
in four very long books, thereby provoking Callimachus and starting a

[1] For the nature of Callimachus' πίνακες and their influence see P. Moraux, *Les Listes
anciennes* p. 221; and their use by later authors in R. Pfeiffer's *Callimachus*, fragm. 429-56.

[2] Fragm. 1, 25-30 (Pfeiffer). The advice is conceived as given to the poet by Apollo. Cf.
Epigram 28 (Pfeiffer).

[3] Athenaeus 72 a. Cf. Hymn to Apollo 105-13 on large but muddy rivers.

bitter feud.[1] Callimachus is supposed to have driven Apollonius to retire to Rhodes for some years. However, time gave the younger man his revenge; not only did he return to Alexandria to be chief librarian which Callimachus may never have been, but his work has survived whole.

There is no reason to think, however, that Apollonius was alone in his opposition. In fact a fragment of commentary on Callimachus' *Aitiai* was found on a papyrus some thirty years ago which lists a number of his opponents among them Praxiphanes the Peripatetic against whom we know that he wrote a book and the shadowy figure of Neoptolemus whom we find criticized in Philodemus. Neoptolemus certainly believed that poetry should not only delight the reader and play upon his emotions but also benefit him. He is also said to be the originator of a threefold formula which reappears in later writers and grammarians and which is also supposedly found in Horace's *Art of Poetry*.

It is a critical scheme which distinguishes three aspects for poetic criticism, namely the poem, the poetry and the poet: techniques were discussed under the first, content under the second, and the faults and virtues of the poet under the third. We need not follow Philodemus in condemning such a scheme as completely absurd, but it is worth noting that it is only a more or less convenient triad of headings which by itself tells us nothing about the ideas of either poet or critic, since it is the ideas expressed under the headings, not the headings themselves, which are significant, both in Horace and Neoptolemus. Far more interesting is the suggestion, for which there is some evidence, that Neoptolemus was a defender of long poems and probably on the side of Apollonius as against Callimachus.[2]

Another great scholar and chief librarian was Eratosthenes (275-194 B.C.), one of the world's most successful polymaths. His most famous book was his *Geographica*, but he was also a distinguished mathematician, an astronomer, and a literary scholar of some importance. His friends called him *Pentathlos* after the test of athletic versatility at Olympia, but the less well disposed nicknamed him *Bêta* implying that, though he was distinguished in many fields, he was a master of none.[3] He wrote nine books on comedy which, if extant, would be invaluable. He seems to have been

---

[1] On this famous quarrel see: Pfeiffer, *Callimachus* vol. 2, xli-xlii. See also index s.v. Apollonius Rhodius.

[2] For Neoptolemus see C. Jensen's *Philodemus über die Gedichte*, pp. 93-127, and C. O. Brink *Horace On Poetry* pp. 43-74, where the fragmentary evidence of Philodemus is discussed anew. See also Brink's article on 'Callimachus and Aristotle' in *CQ* 1946, 11-26 where he proves that A. Rostagni's conception of Callimachus as an Aristotelian simply does not fit the facts, and that, while the careful scholarship of the Alexandrians may well have been developed under Peripatetic influence, Aristotelian ideas had no influence whatever upon the critical ideas of Callimachus and his circle.

[3] On this and Eratosthenes generally see E. P. Wolfer, *Eratosthenes von Kyrene als Mathematiker und Philosoph*, Groningen, 1954.

unimpressed by tradition and to have expressed himself vigorously. As a geographer, he said that the itinerary of Odysseus' wanderings would be known when the cobbler was found who sewed the bag in which Aeacus imprisoned the winds! In this he incurred the displeasure, nearly two centuries later, of that other geographer Strabo who also strongly opposed Eratosthenes' view that the aim of poetry is to give pleasure, not to instruct,[1] so that poetry should be judged by the delight it gives, its only excellence being its capacity to imitate life in words. Being an expert in strategy, agriculture or rhetoric is, said Eratosthenes, of no use to a poet, and critics should not waste their time establishing the truth of a poet's facts. Eratosthenes evidently supported this thesis by proving Homer wrong in fact on a number of points, including the mouths of the Nile. This typically Alexandrian view, though refreshingly different from the classical, is, in Eratosthenes' uncompromising form, hard to maintain as long as poetry is truly significant in the life of any society. Poor dull Strabo is very naive in many of his objections, but he is ultimately right. At least a good deal can be said (and has been much better said) for his more utilitarian point of view.

With Aristophanes of Byzantium we come into the second century B.C. One of his more dubious titles to fame is that he invented the Greek accents. They were intended to preserve the already fading pitch-accentuation of classical Greek and his system has survived to this day to plague every student of Greek. He also inaugurated a much clearer and more thorough use of punctuation signs. His edition of Homer is believed to have begun a reaction against the too free athetizings of Zenodotus. In this connexion he invented a much fuller system of editorial symbols which, further improved by Aristarchus, survives in our manuscripts.[2] He also edited Hesiod, Pindar and the other lyric poets. He wrote on tragedy and on his namesake the great comic poet; the short critical notices which precede the texts of the dramas in our editions are believed to derive from him. It is interesting to note that the doctrine of what is suitable to different genres is fairly rigid in these 'hypotheses' as the

---

[1] Strabo 1, 2, 3: ποιητὴν γὰρ ἔφη πάντα στοχάζεσθαι ψυχαγωγίας, οὐ διδασκαλίας and 1, 2 17: μὴ κρίνειν πρὸς διάνοιαν τὰ ποιήματα μηδ' ἱστορίαν ἀπ' αὐτῶν ζητεῖν. The other statements of Eratosthenes referred to are to be found in the same discussion of Strabo, 1, 2, 3-22, who says everyone regards Homer's poetry as a φιλοσόφημα.

[2] We saw that Zenodotus used the *obelos* (-) to mark a line as un-Homeric. Aristophanes added the asterisk *, to indicate that the sense is incomplete, a T as an obelos applying to several lines and the antisigma, ƆƆ, to indicate unnecessary repetitions. Aristarchus added the diplê, >, to draw attention to a problem of exegesis, the dotted diplê, >̣ to show where he differed from Zenodotus. Unlike Zenodotus, he used the asterisk for a passage wrongly repeated elsewhere, and the antisigma to indicate that the order had been disturbed, and a simple dot for a suspected passage. (J. E. Sandys, *A History of Classical Scholarship*[3], Cambridge 1903, vol. I, pp. 126 and 132.)

Alcestis and the *Orestes* of Euripides, for example, are there adversely criticized for their happy endings as more suitable to comedy. Clearly, the Alexandrians had a definite theory of literary genres and it is probably their definitions of tragedy and comedy which go on being repeated in simplified form by the scholiasts and grammarians of the Roman empire. Ultimately they derive from the Lyceum, as for example that tragedy depicted events at a heroic level, while comedy remained on a more everyday level and used everyday language.[1] In such definitions we can trace a thread of ideas from the Lyceum, through the Alexandrians and the later grammarians right to our own day. It is also Aristophanes who is said to have exclaimed: 'O life, O Menander, which of you imitated the other?'[2] Beside all this, Aristophanes was also a famous grammarian and wrote a book on Analogy, in which no doubt he sought to formulate those rules of grammar which the Stoics, as Anomalists, so persistently denied.

The greatest of all Alexandrian scholars was undoubtedly Aristarchus of Byzantium. His name became a household word and men marvelled at his ability to get into a writer's mind.[3] When he became chief librarian in 180 B.C. work on the classical texts had been going on for a full century; methods of criticism and exegesis had gradually developed and improved; we shall not go far wrong in attributing the best of them to him, though we should remember that our evidence is scanty, that some of them at least probably originated with his predecessors, and that his great fame may well, at times, have obscured their deserts. Most of our evidence comes, as already noted, from Homeric scholia and commentaries.[4] Aristarchus' edition and commentary became the most famous, and if his own textual readings are thought to have had little permanent effect, this may well have been due to his more conservative hesitation to amend the text. Indeed it has sometimes been thought that he incorporated few if any of his own emendations.[5]

He saw – and this was perhaps his greatest contribution – that the Homeric epic had to be interpreted by itself,[6] that the comparison of various passages in Homer was more helpful in grasping the exact mean-

---

[1] On the whole subject of these popular definitions of tragedy and comedy, their origin and influence see A. Ph. McMahon, in *HSCP* 40 (1929) 97-202, and for Aristophanes of Byzantium in particular pp. 105-8.

[2] ὦ Μένανδρε καὶ βίε, πότερος ἂν ὑμῶν πότερον ἀπεμιμήσατο, attributed to him by Syrianus in Walz 4, 101 (Rabe 2, 23).

[3] See Horace, *Ars Poetica* 450 and Athenaeus 634 c.

[4] See the works mentioned on p. 124, note 1, above, and P. Cauer's *Grundfragen* ch. 3. It is Cauer's contention that Roemer unjustifiably favours Aristarchus at the expense of his predecessors. So N. Wecklein who seeks to rehabilitate Zenodotus in his *Zenodotus und Aristarch*.

[5] See Cauer pp. 58-70.

[6] Roemer, *Homerexegese* p. 16: Ὅμηρον ἐξ Ὁμήρου σαφηνίζειν and 179-81.

ing of Homeric phrases than quotation from later authors, and that
neither in language, mythology nor social customs were differences with
later times a sufficient reason for correction or deletion. In this way he
established, for example, that φόβος in Homer does not mean fear but
rout, and that the verb φοβεῖσθαι means to flee and not to fear; that certain
Homeric constructions were sound, though different from later usage.
He realized the difficulty of the words that occur only once, the ἅπαξ
λεγόμενα, and that they had to be explained rather than excised. Like
Aristotle, he recognized several kinds of metaphors and noted Homer's
fondness for personifying inanimate objects.[1] He pointed out that metaphors must be based on what is seen and known, not on what is obscure.

Like Aristotle too,[2] Aristarchus realized that Homer must be interpreted
in the light of the social customs of his day or, more exactly, by those of
the heroic age he describes. This principle cannot be ignored in our
estimates of Homer's characters, many of whom say and do things which
the critics of Alexandria considered improper. He noted that Homeric
society represents a simple life where heroes and kings perform a great
many menial tasks themselves; they drive their own chariots, carve their
own meat, and Nausicaa washes the family clothes. To insist upon these
differences represents a welcome progress in historical perspective, without which criticism can go sadly astray.

The same is true of actions or words which shock the moral sensibilities
of a later age. We saw that Zenodotus thought Nausicaa most unladylike
in expressing a wish for a husband like Odysseus. King Antinous came
under similar censure for offering her in marriage to a man about whom
he knew practically nothing[3]; the Homeric custom which led the
daughters of the house to give visiting heroes their bath incurred similar
objections; and the same feeling of impropriety had led to the emendation
of Telemachus' words: 'I wouldn't expect this to happen even if the gods
wished it' into 'unless the gods should wish it', an emendation later rejected, probably by Aristarchus, because 'the exaggeration is in character'.
Even the gods were not allowed to speak with impropriety and Hephaistus'
reference to Hera as 'bitch-faced' was corrected into the more customary
'cow-eyed'.

It was no small progress in critical thinking to reject such emendations
and to justify the original readings as in accordance with the social customs
of the heroic age or as in character.

Indeed, Aristarchus and his school established as a critical principle the
need to judge any statement in relation to the person who makes it, and

[1] Roemer, *Homerexegese* 24-26 and cf. Aristotle, *Rhetoric* 3, 11, 2 (1411 b 32 ff.).
[2] *Poetics* 25, 7 (1461 a 2) and fragm. 142-79 (Rose), and Roemer, *Homerexegese* pp. 185-9.
[3] *Odyssey* 7, 311-15 and Roemer's *Athetezen* 331, and, for other examples of ἀπρεπῆ, 316-37.

not to attribute to the poet things which may be untrue or inconsistent with what is said elsewhere but are, perhaps for that very reason, appropriate and in character.[1] An interesting example of this is the passage in which Menelaus is called a poor fighter, a passage which Plato uses for his own purposes in the *Symposium*.[2] Aristarchus pointed out very properly that the speaker, Apollo, is no friend of Menelaus, that he is trying to encourage Hector and to shame him into fighting because Menelaus killed a friend of his. As Athenaeus put it, 'when something is said in Homer, it is not necessarily said by Homer'.[3]

All this is good criticism. So was the insistence on a certain poetic licence, ποιητικὴ ἀρέσκεια, which should excuse minor contradictions, as when Agamemnon's sword is called silver-studded in one place and gold-studded in another.[4] If the poet wants to give Agamemnon three daughters instead of two, or devise lovely names for them, that is entirely his affair. It was something gained to free the epic, and traditional poetry of all kinds, from the claims of an exaggerated historicity. Here Eratosthenes had given a lead, and the relation of poetry to history had been discussed by Aristotle.[5]

Further, the poet must be allowed to deal with different events at different lengths, to omit irrelevant details, or details which the hearer can perfectly well supply for himself. When Zeus on Ida suddenly addresses Apollo, whom we last saw on the battlefield, the poet is not obliged to tell us how Apollo got there.[6] This seems in part an application of Theophrastus' advice to leave some things to your reader's imagination.

Aristarchus also took a stand on wider issues. He was a strong champion of the unity of Homer as against the separatists who, even then, considered the *Odyssey* to be by a later author; he may have discussed the artistic unity of each poem as a work of art, and the contribution made by the characters of Achilles and Hector to the unity of the *Iliad*.

[1] We must judge, that is, by τὸ πρόσωπον τὸ λέγον. This is an extension of Aristotle's advice that any evil on the stage must be judged in relation to the character speaking or acting, and to the play as a whole (*Poetics* 25, 8, 1461 a 5, above, p. 81). See Roemer, *Homerexegese* p. 223 and Hans Dachs, *Die Λύσις ἐκ τοῦ προσώπου*.

[2] *Iliad* 17, 588 and *Symposium* 174 b.

[3] Athenaeus 178 d: οὐ γὰρ εἴ τι λέγεται παρ' Ὁμήρου, τοῦθ' Ὅμηρος λέγει.

[4] *Iliad* 2, 45 and 11, 29-30. Roemer, *Homerexegese* pp. 225-31.

[5] *Poetics* ch. 9 (1451 a 37).

[6] A distinction was made between passages in which the poet himself refers to something as having happened which he did not mention at the time, which is *paraleipsis*, and those passages when he tells us the beginning or end of a sequence of events but never mentions the other steps. This is the true σιώπησις. Not telling us how Apollo came to be on Ida is an example of the latter; but when Paris tells Hector that Helen has been urging him with gentle words to go back to the battlefield, and nothing has been said about this before, this is *paraleipsis*, and no true σιώπησις. See Roemer, *Homerexegese* 239-48 and R. Meinel, κατὰ τὸ σιωπώμενον. This last also contains an appraisal of Roemer's methods.

Further than this it would be rash to go, but enough has been said to show that the great scholars of Alexandria, and Aristarchus in particular, made a lasting contribution to the development of both exact scholarship and literary criticism. Their contribution to the latter frequently followed suggestions which were first made by Aristotle and the earlier Peripatetics. The pupils of Aristarchus continued his work, though the emphasis in the generations that followed was often placed on grammar and linguistics. It was a famous pupil of Aristarchus, Dionysius Thrax, who published, towards the end of the second century, the short but famous Greek grammar which remained the basis of all works on Greek accidence for many centuries.

Alexandria continued to be a centre of learning and literary scholarship under the early Roman emperors. It was not without rivals, the chief of which was the group of scholars attracted to Pergamum and its library by the patronage of the Attalid kings from the late third century B.C. onwards. Its chief representative is Crates of Mallos, a contemporary of Aristarchus, probably the first head of the Pergamum library, and he too edited and published books on the classical writers of Greece. He visited Rome about 168 B.C. and, kept there for a while by a broken leg, he lectured with great success while recovering. Crates and his colleagues in Pergamum seem to have largely adopted the language theories of the Stoics, and as a result to have adopted the empirical 'anomalist' point of view, in opposition to the more dogmatic (as they claimed) 'analogist' views of Aristarchus and the Alexandrians. It was probably through Crates that 'anomalism' came to Rome, and the whole controversy followed and was transferred to Latin, as we can see later in Varro. Crates wrote on the Attic dialect, and seems to have developed a theory which subordinated *grammatikē* or the interpretation of texts to a much broader concept of linguistic study which he termed *kritikē*; it included a study of style and linguistic science generally, but our information is too scanty to make any real valuation of the contribution of Crates, and of the Pergamum school generally, to literary theory and criticism.[1]

[1] The evidence, such as it is, will be found in the study of H. J. Mette: *Parateresis*.

CHAPTER IX

The Schools of Philosophy

While Alexandria became the literary and scientific centre of the Greek world, the philosophers remained in Athens. During the Hellenistic and the Roman centuries, schools of philosophy were established and flourished in many cities, but, however high the reputation of those teachers abroad, the Academy remained the spiritual home of the Platonists as the Lyceum remained that of the Peripatetics, and also, though not so completely, the Stoa that of the Stoics and the Garden that of the Epicureans. By the end of the fourth century, 'philosophy' was clearly distinguished from rhetoric and the word was used in the modern sense, as Plato and Aristotle had used it. No longer would a teacher of rhetoric call his system of education *philosophia*, as Isocrates had done. Indeed, Isocrates had no successors. Schools of rhetoric no doubt continued, but none of them attained a comparable influence or reputation, at least until the time of Hermagoras (fl. 150 B.C.). The philosophers retained the theoretical initiative up to that time; theories of poetry and rhetoric were initiated by them, and it has been said that philosophy played a more dominant role in the education of the young during this period than it was ever to do again.[1]

The attitude of the various schools towards the art of speech, however, whether in poetry or prose, were anything but uniform. Contemporary with Aristotle, and before the founding of the Epicurean school, we find the somewhat lonely figure of Nausiphanes of Teos, follower of Democritus and teacher of Epicurus, who apparently attempted to include rhetoric in his philosophy and held the unusual view that the study of nature was the best training for the orator. This, of course, was only his version of the view that the good speaker needs knowledge, and that the philosopher is therefore the best orator – a view which can be traced back to Plato and was to be adopted, in a different form, by the Stoics. Nausiphanes may be considered the last of the city-state philosophers, for he wanted his pupils to take part in public life. What he meant by the study of nature is not very clear in our sources; obviously it included natural philosophy, but it may also have included the nature of man in the sense

---

[1] By H. von Arnim in his *Leben und Werke des Dio von Prusa* p. 80. The first chapter of this work (pp. 4-114) gives an extremely illuminating survey of the relations between philosophers sophists and rhetoricians from the fifth to the first century B.C.

that Plato had advised psychology as necessary to the orator and Aristotle had worked out in the *Rhetoric* how much knowledge a political orator required. Our evidence for Nausiphanes is fragmentary and unsatisfying[1]; he seems to have thought that the logical methods of philosophic inquiry could and should be applied to rhetoric.

Epicurus, as his manner was, reacted violently against the teaching of Nausiphanes, as he reacted against all the arts. Believing as he did that the wise man should not endanger his imperturbability by engaging in public affairs, he regarded rhetoric as useless at best, and was entirely out of sympathy with any study of style. Not until the first century, in Philodemus and his teacher Zeno, do we find any trace of sympathy with the art of language, whether in poetry or prose, among the Epicureans. Even then, however, public speaking, political or forensic, was condemned as useless or worse. With this exception, the Epicureans made little or no contribution to any theory of literature or criticism.[2]

THE ACADEMY

The Academy did not do much better. It is true that we are told that Xenocrates, Plato's pupil, defined rhetoric as 'the art of speaking well'[3] but what conclusions he drew from this definition we do not know. Certainly, the philosophers of the early Academy, by and large, seem to have retained all Plato's prejudices and to have looked down upon rhetoric, and probably poetry, with Platonic contempt. They were notorious for their opposition to rhetoric and many of the usual arguments against it were quoted from them.[4] Unlike Plato himself, however, they made little or no contribution to literary theory or criticism and we have no evidence of any serious attempt to develop the seeds that Plato had sown. By and large, this was left to the Peripatetics. There may have been some relaxation of hostility towards rhetoric when in the late third century the Academy adopted a modified form of scepticism and taught its pupils to argue on both sides of every question, though they would probably have regarded this as training in logic and dialectic, rather than in rhetoric. Further, a more friendly attitude to rhetoric probably developed under Philo of Larissa, the teacher of Cicero – but that belongs to a later period.

[1] Mainly Philodemus in his *Rhetorica*, Sudhaus II, pp. 1-44; for a discussion of Nausiphanes see von Arnim's *Dio*, pp. 43-63.

[2] That the evidence for Epicurean views of poetry belongs to a later period can be seen, for example, in Ph. De Lacy's 'The Epicurean Analysis of Language', *AJP* 60 (1939), pp. 85-92.

[3] Sextus Empiricus, *Adv. Math.* 2, 6. According to him the definition was common to Xenocrates and the Sophists. Xenocrates' definition: ἐπιστήμη τοῦ εὖ λέγειν certainly implies knowledge, and it is quite probable that, like Plato, he denied that rhetoricians possessed this knowledge.

[4] Sextus Empiricus, *Adv. Math.* 2, 12. 20. 43.

The Stoics, on the other hand, did take an interest in rhetoric, but the difference was more apparent than real, for their interest was mainly logical and linguistic, and they had, as Cicero tells us, no feeling for style.[1]

Their interest in etymology was great. They believed that there was a natural relation between things and their original or true (ἔτυμα) names, a relationship which was usually believed to be onomatopoeic. Here they were opposed by the grammarians of Alexandria for whom etymology was only the historical study of words. Nor were the Stoics in sympathy with Alexandrian attempt to discover the laws (νόμοι) which governed derivation and inflexion. Beyond the original correspondence between names and things they saw only the corruptions brought by time and habit. They were 'anomalists' where the Alexandrians were 'analogists', and this famous controversy occupied the minds of many generations of philologists. The dispute seems somewhat academic to us, brought up as we are from childhood to think of language as governed by grammatical rules with exceptions (a conception which has its own artificiality when applied to living language) but the Anomalists and Analogists carried on their controversy in the Hellenistic and then the Roman world with fanatic exaggerations on both sides, with an emotional intensity no doubt increased by school rivalries, and with appeals to cosmic principles which set the cultured world at odds. We shall consider this question further when dealing with Varro.

From Aristotle the Stoics adopted the idea that rhetoric was parallel to dialectic though they defined them differently; they were students of logic, of different forms of expression, and they interpreted 'the art of speaking well' as the art of saying what is true. This required knowledge, so that only the Stoic philosopher who had that knowledge was, or could be, a good speaker.[2] To them rhetoric was to say what one had to say and, with this emphasis on content simply expressed, it is natural enough that it was the Stoics who added brevity to the list of rhetorical virtues.[3] Their interest in words seems to have led them to write on tropes and figures. The theories of figures of speech did not originate with them – we have seen that the word σχῆμα was used in this sense by Theophrastus, though not by Aristotle – but it may well be that Stoic studies of figures formed the basis of those lists of them which play so prominent a part in the writings of later critics.[4]

[1] Cicero, De Orat. 2, 159-61 and Brutus 117-19.
[2] This view is ridiculed by Philodemus in the Hypomnêmatikon. Sudhaus II, pp. 197-230.
[3] Diog. Laert. 7, 59.
[4] See K. Barwick, Probleme des Stoischen Sprachlehre pp. 88-111; C. N. Smiley, 'Seneca and the Stoic Theory of Style' pp. 54-55.

In poetry, as in prose, the Stoics[1] attached more importance to content than to form, though they acknowledged that poetic elaboration, which appealed to the emotions of the unphilosophical, might prepare them for the truths of philosophy. The poet could present a general truth in mythical, individualized form: the anthropomorphic gods of Homer, for example, might dispose people to believe in the gods. But the poets did not as a rule speak the literal truth and often had to be interpreted allegorically. We have seen that the practice of allegorical interpretation was at least as old as the fifth century, but the Stoics made the most consistent use of it. It enabled them to find in Homer, for example, the most surprising confirmation of Stoic doctrines.[2]

While the meaning of the poem appealed to the mind, the sound of it appealed to the ear and aroused the emotions. Now the Stoics' belief in an original onomatopoeic relation between the name-sound and the thing – a relation corrupted but not entirely lost – naturally led them to feel that the sound pattern itself might correspond to the meaning and affect the emotions in a particular way. It is therefore not surprising to find Stoic theorists attaching great importance to euphony as a vital factor in poetry, and Philodemus attributes such a theory of euphony both to Ariston of Chios (250 B.C.) and to Crates of Mallos who lived nearly a hundred years later.[3] Philodemus objects that poetic form is thus judged by the practised ear and no longer a matter of rational judgement. It may be, however, that the Stoic wise man's less emotional reaction to the beauty of sound patterns, whether in poetry or music, was not devoid of a rational element,[4] for it seems to have involved an appreciation of the appropriateness of this pattern to the thought-content. The details are uncertain, but it is clear from our evidence that some Stoics at least made a real effort to develop a theory of poetry,[5] as well as of rhetoric. The details, however, are very obscure, nor was there one generally accepted Stoic theory.

[1] For an enlightening attempt to bring the scattered reference to poetry from Stoic writers into focus see Ph. De Lacy's 'Stoic Views of Poetry' pp. 241-71. All necessary references will be found in this article.

[2] Ariston of Chios, expressly identified as a Stoic by Philodemus (Jensen, p. 33), stated that Homer could be called a good poet only καταχρηστικῶς. As De Lacy points out (*Stoic Views*, pp. 260-2) the practice of allegory, itself considered a figure, is closely connected with other figures which indicate the use of words in a different than their primary sense, such as *katachrêsis, metalêpsis, ainigma, emphasis, symbolon*, etc.; it may also have led the Stoics to the study of the various kinds of ambiguity or *amphibolia*.

[3] For Ariston see Philodemus περὶ ποιημάτων 5, col. xiv-xxi (Jensen, pp. 33-49) and for Crates xxi-xxvi (Jensen, pp. 49-59 and 146-70).

[4] See De Lacy, *Stoic Views*, pp. 250-4.

[5] Ariston also, it seems, made a somewhat unique effort (as far as we can tell) to transfer to poetry the Stoic doctrine of things indifferent (ἀδιάφορα) so that many poems were neither good nor bad. He also said that, although good composition was not enough to make a good poem (that no doubt needed good content too), bad composition was enough to make it bad.

THE PERIPATETICS

It was the Peripatetics who undoubtedly had the greatest influence on literary and rhetorical theory. Aristotle and Theophrastus are frequently quoted together as the source of Peripatetic critical ideas, and, though their successors went on writing on rhetoric, there is little or no evidence that they made any very original contribution.[1] As we examine the critical formulae which are obviously well established by the first century, most of them are derived from Aristotle or are at least permeated by ideas which can be traced back to him and Theophrastus, though the precise formulation is often later and its exact origin is uncertain.[2] Aristotle, as we have seen, had established rhetorical education on a firmer philosophic base; his analysis of the sources of arguments (τόποι) from the psychological point of view, of the difference between the dialectal syllogism and the enthymeme, of proofs as based on demonstration of fact, on the character of the speaker or on playing upon the feelings of the hearers – all this and much more is quite unique and wherever we find this more philosophic approach we are entitled to see its ultimate source in the *Rhetoric* of Aristotle.

Of the formulae themselves some are taken over from him unchanged, as the three kinds of rhetoric (the deliberative, the forensic and the epideictic) were taken over by the Stoics and are met with, in the same form, in almost every textbook down the centuries. The Aristotelian division of proofs into the external proofs which do not depend upon the art of the orator (ἄτεχνοι) and those which he has to find and elaborate for himself (ἔντεχνοι) became equally commonplace.

Other formulae are of more obscure origin. Regularly, in first-century writers, the art of Rhetoric is divided into five parts: invention (*inventio*, εὕρεσις), arrangement of subject matter (*dispositio*, τάξις), style (*elocutio*, λέξις), delivery (*actio*, ὑπόκρισις), and memory (*memoria*, μνήμη). Who first used this exact formula we do not know, but invention, the discovery of what to say, of what arguments to use, is clearly the subject of the first two books of the *Rhetoric*; arrangement of material is explicitly dealt with in the last seven chapters of the third where style is also dealt with in the first twelve chapters. And all three parts are mentioned together (except that he does not use the term εὕρεσις) as *the* three factors to be dealt with in a discussion of speech in the introductory paragraph of the same book.[3]

---

[1] The Peripatetic school seems to have degenerated and fallen far below Aristotelian and Theophrastean standards of scholarship in the third century. It is doubtful whether even the writings of Aristotle were freely available to the Peripatetics themselves. See I. Düring, *Aristotle in the ancient literary tradition* pp. 462 ff. and P. Moraux, *Les listes anciennes* pp. 240 on. [2] See F. Solmsen's 'The Aristotelian Tradition' pp. 35-50 and 169-90.

[3] *Rhet.* 3, 1, 1: τριά ἐστιν ἃ δεῖ πραγματευθῆναι περὶ τὸν λόγον, ἓν μὲν ἐκ τίνων αἱ πίστεις ἔσονται, δεύτερον δὲ περὶ τὴν λέξιν, τρίτον δὲ πῶς χρὴ τάξαι τὰ μέρη τοῦ λόγου.

Moreover, Aristotle mentions delivery as the third factor in an alternative classification just below (one which omits word-arrangement) and, though he himself deals with it very briefly, we know that Theophrastus wrote on the subject at greater length. So four of the five parts of the famous formula were discussed at length by the two great Peripatetics. Somebody added memory – a less important addition since it is necessary in every art. Who did so? We do not know, but it is reasonable to suppose that the whole formula arose in the Peripatetic school.[1] Certainly the main ideas were Peripatetic.

The same is true of the formula of the four virtues of style: we have seen reason to doubt that Theophrastus had an exclusive formula of four ἀρεταί, but, whether he did or not, the four ideas: correct language, lucidity, appropriateness, and ornamentation were certainly discussed by him, as they were by Aristotle along with a number of others. In the first century and later, the number of 'virtues' were usually five, and our authorities imply that the Stoics added brevity to the other four,[2] which is indeed likely since they disliked ornamentation. Aristotle had refused to consider brevity a desirable quality, for there are times when it is unsuitable. Here again *all* these qualities were discussed by Aristotle, some more fully than others. The formula itself may be regarded as deriving from several sources; by whom it was originally formulated is unknown – nor is the matter one of great importance, but the Peripatetic influence is undeniable.

The origin of the notorious formula of the 'three styles' is even more obscure, and likely to remain so. Both Aristotle and Theophrastus recognized the difference between plain and adorned diction but the right style for Aristotle, and probably for Theophrastus, remained a mean between those two extremes – even though Aristotle recognized that different kinds of rhetoric required differences of style. We also know that Theophrastus drew a clear distinction between, on the one hand, the simple language of philosophy which was concerned with the exposition of its subject matter, and, on the other hand, the language of poetry and rhetoric, which was mainly intended to affect the audience. The doctrine of the three styles may conceivably have developed from one or other of those theories,[3] or from a combination of both, when the strictly Aristotelian doctrine of the best style as a mean lost its hold. But in the present state of our knowledge it is wiser not to claim Peripatetic influence on this particular formula, or indeed on the ideas it formalizes.

---

[1] The addition is less likely to have been made by a Stoic, for Diogenes Laertius quotes the formula as Stoic omitting memory (7, 43).

[2] Diog. Laert. 7, 59.

[3] G. L. Hendrickson, 'The Origin and Meaning of the Ancient Characters of Style', in *AJP* 26 (1905), 248-90.

There is another formula which we find in Aristotle and which recurs through the centuries, namely that of the four parts or sections of a speech: exordium, narrative, proofs and peroration. It has recently been suggested that this formula, unlike that of the five parts, is not truly Aristotelian, but characteristic of Isocrates; that its recurrence in later authors argues Isocratean influence. Aristotle, we are told had broken with the tradition of organizing the rhetorical material under the heading of *partes orationis*; he relegated this traditional method to his last six chapters and he is there reproducing a system of the alternative, 'Isocratean' type, probably following Theodectes.[1]

This contention raises an interesting point regarding the approach of traditional rhetorical textbooks. There is no doubt that the formula of different sections of a speech is pre-Aristotelian, indeed pre-Platonic. But our evidence does *not* prove that the early rhetoricians made this formula the structural basis of their work; nor do we hear of any one of them who restricted himself to four parts,[2] or any similar number. As for the theory of the sections of a speech in Isocrates, Dionysius of Halicarnassus does credit 'Isocrates and his followers' with such a theory, but of five parts, the Aristotelian four and *prothesis* (cf. *Rhet.* 3, 13, 2). The variation is of no great importance, but again Dionysius does *not* either say or imply that Isocrates used this as the basic structure of his system. We also know from Quintilian (4, 2, 31) that 'the majority of writers, especially those of Isocrates' school, want the narrative to be clear, brief and plausible (*verisimilis*)'. This again only proves that Isocrates and his followers discussed what the characteristic qualities of the narrative, and probably of other sections of a speech, should be.

---

[1] F. Solmsen's 'The Aristotelian Tradition' 35-50; also his 'Drei Rekonstruktionen' pp 144-51, and K. Barwick: 'Die Gliederung der rhetorischen τέχνη und die Horazische Epistula ad Pisones' 1-43.

[2] Plato, *Phaedrus* 266-7, speaking of what is contained in the rhetorical textbooks, does mention first the sections of a speech, and the first three are exordium, narrative and proofs. But he then goes on to add a great many other subdivisions (sixteen in all) from various rhetoricians. This does not sound as if any one of them had a clear-cut, logical scheme, and their inexperience in the methods of *diairesis*, mentioned just before (266 c), seems to imply that they had not. Socrates then goes on to mention certain figures (repetition, figures of speech, etc.) and emotional appeals without any suggestion that these were discussed under the heading of the parts of a speech. Similarly Aristotle, where he blames the writers of rhetorical textbooks for neglecting proofs and concentrating on 'frills' (προσθῆκαι) such as emotional appeals, does not imply the subordination of these to the parts of a speech (*Rhet.* 1, 1, 3). A little later (1, 1, 8) he says that they are being technical about irrelevancies when they define other things, '*as for example* what should be contained in the exordium, the narrative *and every one* of the other parts'. In the third book (ch. 13), as is well known, he ridicules the numerous divisions current among the rhetoricians (νῦν δὲ διαιροῦσι γελοίως, which does *not* mean 'the division now generally made is absurd' but 'their present divisions are ridiculous') and he goes on to speak not only of a narrative and epilogue but (in the same and following sentences) of a great many more.

Finally there is Theodectes, a pupil of Isocrates and a friend of Aristotle, who is credited by two anonymous documents of certainly late, but uncertain, date with the theory that 'it is the task of the orator to write his exordium to conciliate, his narrative to convince, his argument to prove, and his recapitulation to remind (his audience)'.[1]

It is clear from all this that the old rhetorical technicians did have various formulae of the sections of a speech, it seems rather numerous sections, and that they discussed the purpose of the various sections; that Isocrates spoke of five such sections (in his case at least one may doubt whether he made them the basis of his system, for he was not a systematic man); and that Theodectes may well have had a theory of four sections.[2]

Admittedly, the whole manner and style of the last six chapters of the *Rhetoric* are different from most of the rest.[3] These chapters seem to be conceived and developed in the amoral manner more typical of the rhetoricians, and Aristotle reminds us in the course of this very discussion that he does not think much of this approach.[4] It may well be that he based these chapters on the work of his friend. On the other hand, no one has suggested that these chapters were not written by Aristotle, and there are plenty of Aristotelian touches in them.[5] Since, then, the formula of the four sections was at least adopted by him – and made part of his *Rhetoric*, it is hard to see how the occurrence of the formula in later authors can be interpreted as an indication of *non*-Aristotelian influence. At most we can say that when this formula is made the structural basis of the whole work, as frequently occurs in later rhetoricians,[6] and the more philosophic parts of the *Rhetoric* are ignored, this approach is typical of the more rhetorical, technical works, but we are not justified in calling it Isocratean. Where, however, the four-sections formula is mixed with others, as for example in Cicero, it is as likely to be derived from Peripatetic as from other sources. For, as the formula is discussed at length in the *Rhetoric*, it

[1] H. Rabe, *Prolegomenon Sylloge* (Teubner, 1931). The two passages do not quite correspond (p. 32 and p. 216) but both mention Theodectes, both imply the four-parts formula and both link it with ἔργον τοῦ ῥήτορος which suggests that the formula was of some importance.

[2] There was a widespread belief in antiquity that the *technê* of Theodectes was written by Aristotle, as Quintilian tells us (2, 15, 10). Barwick evolves a theory that this τέχνη consisted of two books by Aristotle and one by Theodectes, on the sections of a speech, which last was then the basis of the last six chapters of the *Rhetoric*. Solmsen suggests, more sensibly, that Aristotle collected the writings on rhetoric of Theodectes, probably after his death and then used part of them in the same last chapters (*Hermes* 67, p. 145).

[3] But not from all. This drier, more technical manner does occur in other parts even of the *Rhetoric*, not to mention other works. See, for example, the discussion of different τόποι in 2, 25. In any case, it is a bold man who would base any argument on Aristotle's style.

[4] *Rhet.* III, 14, 8 (1415 b 4) and cf. ch. 13 and I. 1, 3-9 (1354 a 11 – b 21).

[5] For example his insistence on enthymemes in 17, 5-8 (1418 a 1-17) and 12-13 (1418a 38-63) and the proofs based on ἦθος and πάθος in the same chapter.

[6] A good example of this approach is the little work known as the *Anonymus Seguerianus*, Spengel-Hammer I, Part 2, 352-98.

must have remained part of the Peripatetic inheritance. We are therefore justified in saying that Peripatetic ideas are contained in this formula also.

There is one considerable gap in our knowledge of Peripatetic literary theory, namely their theory of Comedy. As we have seen, the second book of the *Poetics*, where the Aristotelian theories of laughter were to be dealt with, if it was ever written, is lost, and we have only scattered comments in the *Poetics* and elsewhere.[1] However, among the mass of undated and anonymous works that have been preserved, there is a very short and mystifying document, the so-called *Tractatus Coislinianus* which seems to contain at least some Aristotelian echoes.[2] The terminology is Aristotelian; it contains some things that Aristotle said, some things he may have said, but other things which he could not have said under any circumstances. It reads like a very confused and late epitome of a work which may have reflected the views of Aristotle more clearly. Most of it makes little sense and adds nothing to our knowledge, but it does contain a skeleton analysis of various ways to provoke laughter which argues a well-thought-out theory of comedy, though it is probably incomplete and uncertain in some details.

Laughter is said to be provoked either by the language (ἀπὸ τῆς λέξεως) or by the situation (ἀπὸ τῶν πραγμάτων). Witty language is then analysed into seven different kinds: it is due to (i) the use of homonyms, or (ii) synonyms, (iii) verbosity, (iv) paronyms, i.e. either lengthened or clipped forms, (v) diminutives, (vi) changed words, either in sound or by using words of the same root, and (vii) wrong gender or other wrong category.[3]

Laughter due to the situation is analysed into nine species: (i) making one thing appear like another, whether better or worse, (ii) deception, (iii) impossibility, (iv) reaching a possible end through illogical means, (v) the unexpected, (vi) presenting characters as worse than they are, (vii) vulgar dances, (viii) a worse choice is made when a better was possible, (ix) lack of logical sequence.

A moment's thought will show that, though the author himself is not very logical – vulgar dances are obviously not on the same level as the other kinds of comedy of situation – and a few details are doubtful, there lurks somewhere behind this skeleton a thought-out and interesting theory of comedy. Indeed Starkie and Rutherford have clothed the skeleton with life by illustrating the various species of each.[4] The main division is clearly Aristotelian, and many of the species are obviously sound.

---

[1] See above, p. 70.
[2] See note at end of this chapter.
[3] The text and meaning of VI is uncertain. On VII Bernays rightly points out that, if the term σχῆμα is Aristotelian, it cannot refer to figure of speech. *Zwei Abhandlungen* 176-7.
[4] See note at end of this chapter.

The *Tractatus* makes a few more Aristotelian points as when it distinguishes comedy from insult, or requires the diction of comedy to be popular and ordinary. The three types of comic characters, the buffoon, the boaster and the ironic man are also of interest. It should be emphasized, however, that a good deal of the *Tractatus* hardly makes sense, that it can only be used with the greatest caution, and that none of the details can, without further evidence, be credited to Aristotle or to the Peripatetics, as some scholars have been tempted to do. It is only because of the lack of better evidence that this mystifying document has been given a somewhat spurious importance.

THE REVIVAL OF RHETORIC: HERMAGORAS

Thus from the time of Theophrastus through the third century, the development of rhetorical theories was in the hands of the philosophers rather than of the rhetoricians, who receive little mention in later writers.[1] Towards the middle of the second century there came a change and the school of Hermagoras in Athens attained a high reputation and influence such as no rhetorical school had had since Isocrates. It was the time when the Romans (the fall of Corinth in 145 B.C. marks the complete subjugation of Greece) came to Greece in search of culture as well as conquest. But the Romans were a practical people, and abstract philosophy made little appeal to them. It is suggestive[2] that at this very time the 'ancient quarrel' between the schools of philosophy and those of rhetoric seems to have flared up again, and that we find *all* the philosophers arguing that rhetoric is not a *technê*, and therefore no proper subject to teach.[3] Not only Carneades the Academic, but Diogenes of Babylon, the Stoic, and even Critolaus the Peripatetic, now argue to this effect.[4] It is not very much later that there was a renewed interest in rhetoric among the Epicureans, as we shall see when dealing with Philodemus.

---

[1] This is very much the impression Quintilian conveys in his brief historical survey; he mentions Isocrates after the fifth-century rhetoricians and then remarks on the diverse paths followed by the school of Isocrates and the Lyceum, where Aristotle, in Isocrates' old age, took to teaching rhetoric in the afternoon. He also mentions Theodectes without linking him with Isocrates, and then Theophrastus. So far he is obviously thinking of the fourth century. And it is from the time of Theophrastus on (*hinc*) that 'the philosophers devoted themselves more to the study of rhetoric than the rhetoricians themselves, especially the leaders of the Peripatetics and Stoics'. The next stage comes with Hermagoras (3, 1, 13-16).

[2] For this point of view see von Arnim's *Dio*, pp. 88-89. He points out that the rhetoricians were expelled from Rome by decrees of the Senate in 161 B.C.

[3] How standardized these arguments became is well shown by the parallels given by Radermacher between the arguments quoted by Philodemus from earlier philosophers, and those found in Lucian's *Parasitism as an Art* more than two centuries later. Sudhaus' *Supplementum* XXIII ff.

[4] For Critolaus see Sudhaus' *Supplementum* pp. IX-XXVI (Radermacher) and for Diogenes ibid. pp. XXXIV ff., and *Rhetorica* I, 202 ff.

This concerted attack at the very time when the school of Hermagoras was flourishing can hardly have been coincidental.[1] It seems that Hermagoras was not only reviving the study of rhetoric but definitely encroaching upon the philosophers' preserves. He divided the subject-matter of the orator into general (θέσεις) and particular (ὑποθέσεις) questions. The former included all the scientific and ethical problems which were generally agreed to be the subject-matter of philosophical, not rhetorical discussions. As examples Cicero[2] gives: Is there any good except righteousness? Are the senses reliable? What is the shape of the world? What is the size of the sun?

On the other hand, while Hermagoras said that the end of rhetoric was to persuade,[3] he seems to have restricted himself to the means of persuasion to be found in the subject matter. He was concerned with the classification of the different kinds of themes, issues, arguments and the like, and Cicero tells us that he was of little help in matters of style.[4] Quintilian quotes him frequently,[5] always as an expert on the analysis, classification and nomenclature of arguments, and in this field he is an influential and important source both for Cicero's more technical books and for later rhetoricians.

Hermagoras' main theory seems to have been an analysis of the different kinds of στάσις (constitutio or status, i.e. the general basis of argument in a particular case) of which he had four: the issue of fact, i.e. whether the deed was done or not (coniecturalis); the issue of definition, i.e. the deed was done but its nature must be determined (definitiva – e.g. was it murder?) the qualitative issue (generalis, e.g. was it justified? was it legal?); and finally the issue of demurrer (translativa, e.g. is it the proper court or the proper charge?). This last kind of στάσις was original with Hermagoras.[6] He then had further subdivisions, but into these we need not go; they belong to the history of rhetoric in the strict sense, indeed largely to the history of jurisprudence.

[1] For a study of Hermagoras' teaching and collected references to him, see G. Thiele, *Hermagoras;* also D. Matthes in *Lustrum* 3 (1958) 58–214, and his *Hermagoras, Fragmenta,* Leipzig (Teubner), 1962.

[2] The youthful Cicero, who seems to criticize Hermagoras with all the exuberance of a youth attacking a master he is largely following, makes this point in *De Inventione* I, 6, 8: 'Quas quaestiones procul ab oratoris officio remotas facile omnes intellegere existimamus. Nam quibus in rebus summa ingenia philosophorum plurimo cum labore consumpta intellegimus, eas sicut aliquas parvas res oratori attribuere magna amentia videtur.' In his more mature works he himself assigns an important part in rhetoric to such general questions.

[3] Quintilian 2, 15, 14.

[4] *Brutus* 263: . . . Ex hac inopi ad ornandum, sed ad inveniendum expedita Hermagorae, disciplina. And cf. 271.

[5] Quintilian 2, 21, 21; 3, 3, 9; 3, 5, 4 and 14; 3, 6; 3, 21, 56–61; 3, 11, 1–2 and 18–22; 5, 9, 12; 9, 2, 106.

[6] *De Inv.* I, 11, 16. This classification is the same as that which Cicero uses frequently, i.e. an sit, quid sit, qualis sit? except that Cicero usually omits the fourth, e.g. *Partitiones* 33–51 and 104; *Topica* 87–90; *De Oratore* 1, 139 and 2, 103.

It is interesting to find that he also used the formula of the sections of a speech, for he advised a digression before the peroration, something extraneous to the case which nevertheless would impress the audience, and here again Cicero disagrees with him.[1]

The importance of Hermagoras lies in the fact that he seems to have initiated the resurgence of rhetoric and of the rhetorical schools which was to continue into the Roman world and vitally affect Roman education and Latin literature as a whole. He also typifies, in one department of rhetoric at any rate, those over-subtle technicalities against which the Romans so consistently rebelled but which they never were able to shake off. It has been suggested that he wrote under Stoic influence, but by this time the various schools had influenced each other continually for well over a century and their individual traditions can no longer be disentangled. The age of Eclecticism now begins; even in Ethics and Metaphysics all schools, except the Epicureans, were affected by it, and the educated Roman was always inclined to take what appealed to him from every school. This was even more true in literary and rhetorical theory; even Neoptolemus in the previous century is believed by Jensen to be an Academic while Rostagni and Brink think he was a Peripatetic. The rhetorical theories and formulae, along with lists of figures, have become standardized, and the often slight variations in names of figures, for example, are the only tokens of a not impressive originality in later rhetorical works.

NOTE ON
THE *TRACTATUS COISLINIANUS*

This very short treatise – Bernays' reproduction of it takes less than three pages – was first published in 1839 and has been edited, translated and commented on by a number of scholars since.[2] As it is one of the very few Greek texts on Comedy that have been preserved, it has naturally attracted much attention and one is tempted to use it to reconstruct the Aristotelian

[1] *De Inv.* I, 51, 97. In the same youthful work I, 9, 12, Cicero also criticizes him for using the formula of the three kinds of rhetoric as subdivisions of the third type of στάσις, and says he had an unphilosophic mind: 'Nunc vero ea vis est in homine ut ei multo rhetoricam citius quis ademerit quam philosophiam concesserit; . . .' The first of these criticisms shows that the στάσεις formed the basic structural formula of Hermagoras' work.

[2] By J. A. Cramer in his *Anecdota Graeca Bibl. Paris.* (Oxford 1839). It is fully discussed by J. Bernays in his *Zwei Abhandlungen*, 135-86; and his text is used in this section. See also in G. Kaibel's *Die Prolegomena περὶ κωμῳδίας*. It is enthusiastically hailed as contributing to our knowledge of Aristotle's theory of comedy by W. M. Starkie, *The Acharnians* xxxviii-xxiv, and W. Rutherford, *A Chapter in the History of Annotation* pp. 435-55, but it should be noted that they concern themselves mainly with the analysis of comic laughter in sections 2-3 of the *Tractatus*. The contrary view is held by A. P. McMahon in *HSCP* 28 (1917), pp. 29-34.

theory of comedy,[1] especially as its terminology is obviously Aristotelian.
This, however, is a risky procedure; though a number of points can be
traced back to the *Poetics* and other works of Aristotle, the author is at
times singularly confused in mind, at times quite un-Aristotelian. Moreover, if he had had the missing book of the *Poetics*, the discussion of
Comedy, it is incredible that he should have devised such a confused
definition of comedy; as it stands, the definition is clearly a rather stupid
attempt to apply to comedy the various points made in Aristotle's famous
definition of tragedy, obviously without understanding them.

   The date of this treatise is quite uncertain. Attempts have been made to
date it or its source in the first century B.C., partly at least on the basis of
similarities with Cicero's discussion of the comic in *De Oratore* II, 216-90,[2]
but this is quite unconvincing and the *Tractatus* reads much more like a
much later epitome of some better work, or indeed of several works, with
very patchy results.

   The little treatise begins with a completely un-Aristotelian division of
poetry into two main classes, the imitative and the non-imitative, with
subdivisions as follows:

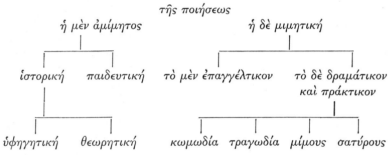

If we can interpret ποίησις here as including both prose and poetry, the
concept of non-imitative ποίησις including history and instruction (the
prose of the philosophers and the schools which however would also
include such poetry as that of Empedocles, Parmenides and Lucretius) is
of some interest, as indeed is the subdividing of history into that which
preaches by examples and that which aims merely at establishing the facts.
The right-hand division of mimetic poetry into narrative (epic) and drama
(comedy, tragedy, mimes and satyr-plays) is more orthodox. Though
suggestive, the whole classification is, of course, incomplete. In any case,
it is quite un-Peripatetic and should warn us at once against assuming

   [1] As is done by Lane Cooper in his *An Aristotelian Theory of Comedy*. He practically rewrites *The Poetics* to apply to comedy, a striking piece of imaginative writing which is often
suggestive but largely fanciful.
   [2] W. L. Grant shows convincingly that the parallels in Cicero are insignificant, in *AJP* 69
(1948), 80-86.

without other evidence any Aristotelian background for anything our author says.

There follows a curious description of tragedy: 'Tragedy destroys the fearful emotions of the soul through pity and fear, and (that) it wishes to moderate fear. It has sorrow for its mother.'[1]

This at least makes some sense. It is followed by a definition of comedy which, as it stands, makes very little sense indeed:

κωμῳδία ἐστὶ μίμησις πράξεως γελοίου καὶ ἀμοίρου μεγέθους χωρὶς ἑκάστου μορίων ἐν τοῖς εἴδεσι δρῶντος καὶ δι' ἀπαγγελίας δι' ἡδονῆς καὶ γέλωτος περαίνουσα τὴν τοιούτων παθημάτων κάθαρσιν· ἔχει δὲ μητέρα τὸν γέλωτα.

Without the Aristotelian definition of tragedy before us we could have no idea of what our author is even trying to say. With it, we see that he is mechanically trying to transfer to comedy what is there said of tragedy, whether it fits or no; even so, the singular δρῶντος has nothing to agree with and is presumably a genitive absolute (for Aristotle's δρώντων) and surely δι' ἀπαγγελίας requires a negative before it, as in Aristotle, unless indeed our author means that there is acting *and* narrative (messengers' speeches?) in different parts of the comedy. This extraordinary farrago could surely *not* have happened if our author had had Aristotle's definition of comedy or a second book of the *Poetics* before him. It seems to prove, on the contrary, that he had no more than we, and was trying to make do with it.[2] If we must try a translation of this scribbling, it will run something as follows:

Comedy is an imitation of a laughable action, (and) of undivided and completed length, each of its parts separately sweetened in language in the parts, through acting and ⟨not?⟩ through narrative. By means of pleasure and laughter it achieves the catharsis of such emotions. It has laughter for its mother.

The first and second clauses insist on the importance of plot in comedy as in tragedy and might well represent a Peripatetic tradition; the second clause which corresponds to the clause about the use of 'rhythm, melody and song' to sweeten language in tragedy might conceivably make sense

[1] ἡ τραγῳδία ὑφαιρεῖ τὰ φόβερα παθήματα ψυχῆς δι' οἴκτου καὶ δέους καὶ (ὅτι) συμμετρίαν θέλει ἔχειν τοῦ φόβου ἔχει δὲ μητέρα τὴν λύπην. This reads like a comment on the Aristotelian definition of tragedy, an attempt to explain catharsis as purgation, and then as moderation, and the mysterious ὅτι seems to indicate our author is quoting. The last clause does not mean much and completely ignores Aristotle's saying that tragedy had its own peculiar pleasure.
[2] So Bernays (p. 146): 'kurz das ganze Machwerk beweist nur, dass der Verfertiger desselben in seinem Exemplar der Poetik eben so wenig wie wir in dem unsrigen eine Aristotelische Definition der Komödie vorfand.'

if properly expressed. Presumably comedy as well as tragedy, to Aristotle, would be through acting and *not* narrative. But neither pleasure or laughter are properly παθήματα (passions or emotions) and what 'such emotions' here may mean is left completely obscure.[1]

Then follows the analysis of the sources of laughter discussed in the text. Here we suddenly find ourselves upon a much higher level. The Greek terms for the subdivisions of γέλως ἀπὸ λέξεως are, in the order they are translated on p. 141: κατὰ ὁμωνυμίαν, συνωνυμίαν, ἀδολεσχίαν, παρωνυμίαν, παρὰ πρόσθεσιν καὶ ἀφαίρεσιν, ὑποκόρισμα, ἐξαλλάγην (Cramer has ἐξαναλλάγην), subdivided into φώνη or τοῖς ὁμογένεσιν and finally σχῆμα λέξεως.[2] In the same order, the subdivisions of γέλως ἐκ τῶν πραγμάτων are (i) ἐκ τῆς ὁμοιώσεως πρὸς τὸ χεῖρον and πρὸς τὸ βέλτιον; (ii) ἐκ τῆς ἀπατῆς; (iii) ἐκ τοῦ ἀδυνάτου; (iv) ἐκ τοῦ δυνατοῦ καὶ ἀνακολούθου; (v) ἐκ τοῦ παρὰ προσδοκίαν; (vi) ἐκ τοῦ κατασκευάζειν τὰ πρόσωπα πρὸς τὸ μοχθηρόν; (vii) ἐκ τοῦ χρῆσθαι φορτικῇ ὀρχήσει; (viii) ὅταν τις τῶν ἐξουσίαν ἐχόντων παρεὶς τὰ μέγιστα φαυλότητα λαμβάνει, and finally (ix) ὅταν ἀσυνάρτητος ὁ λόγος ᾖ καὶ μηδεμίαν ἀκολουθίαν ἔχει.

The fourth section states the difference between mere abuse (λοιδορία) and comedy. 'Abuse explicitly condemns present evils while comedy needs what is called innuendo' (ἔμφασις). Though Aristotle could not have used the term,[3] the distinction reflects his preference for the newer type of comedy.[4] This is also true of the next sentence or section which states that the jester (ὁ σκώπτων, the term is more appropriate to the old comedy) tries to convict one of sins of soul and body, though this sentiment reflects rather a defense of the old comedy.

We are next told (6) that as tragedy wants to achieve a moderation of fear, so comedy wants a moderate amount of laughter.[5] This presumably is the effect of catharsis. Our author then divides 'the matter of comedy' (ὕλη a somewhat inappropriate word) into the six elements of tragedy which we know in the *Poetics*, namely plot, character, thought, diction, song, and spectacle, and makes a comment on each:

---

[1] Lane Cooper (p. 67) suggests that the emotions purged by comedy would, in Aristotle, have been envy and anger. This may well be, especially if we remember the connexion of φθόνος with comedy in Plato (*Philebus* 48 a ff. and above, p. 65), but there is no trace of this in the *Tractatus*.

[2] This sevenfold division of γέλως ἀπὸ λέξεως is also preserved in the Scholia on Dionysius Thrax; together with the formal division of comedy into prologue, etc., but it only has the first two subdivisions of the comic of situation.

[3] The word is here used in the later sense of hidden meaning or innuendo explained by Quintilian 8, 2, 11, and 8, 3, 83-86 altiorem praebens intellectum quam quem verba per se ipsa declarant; see also 9, 2, 64.

[4] See his distinction between comedy and the *iambeion* at *Poetics* 5, 1449 b 8 and 9, 1451 b 14 and, more specifically, *Nic. Ethics* 4, 1128 a 20 ff. See also Bernays 148-53.

[5] σύμμετρα τοῦ φόβου θέλει εἶναι ἐν τραγῳδίαις καὶ τοῦ γελοίου ἐν ταῖς κωμῳδίαις. The subject of θέλει is obscure, but I have ignored minor grammatical difficulties; they abound.

A comic plot is one which is built around a laughable action.

The characters of comedy are the buffoon, the ironical man and the boaster.

Thought is of two kinds: maxim and proof (and he divides proof, πίστεις, into oaths, agreements, testimonies, tortures and laws).

Here we must pause a moment: the comic plot is simple enough; the characters here given are frequently met with, but maxims and proof by no means exhaust thought; and in the five kinds of proof we recognize with a shock the five kinds of external proof of the *Rhetoric* and they really do not fit, though no doubt they could be used on the comic stage, especially if we remember how numberless were the 'recognitions' of later comedy. Our author (or his source), having been told in the *Poetics* (1456 a 34) to look to the *Rhetoric* for the means of expressing thought, mechanically transcribes something he found there even if this does not make very much sense, as Bernays suggests.[1] The text then continues:

Comic diction is ordinary and popular. The comic poet must speak his own native language, through his characters, and speak his own dialect himself.

The former statement is, one imagines, quite Aristotelian since he welcomed the change to less poetic language in tragedy itself, though he would probably have added that it must not sink too low but remain an appropriate mean. The second statement goes with it and probably means that in comedy the language is uniform, and does not change, as in tragedy, to Doric in choral lyrics. After a couple of unenlightening comments on music and spectacle we find the surprising statement:

Plot, diction and music are seen in all comedies, thoughts, character, and spectacle in a few.

The author is presumably using thought, character and spectacle to mean a great deal of each. Still 'a few' is surprising. There follows a purely formal division into 'the parts of comedy', prologue, choral part, *epeisodia* and *exodos* and an explanation of each term. This exactly corresponds to the formal parts of tragedy in the twelfth chapter of the *Poetics*, though these definitions are not as appropriate to comedy, and the treatise ends with the post-Aristotelian division of comedy into the old, the new and the middle:

[1] Bernays, pp. 155-6 and cf. *Rhet.* 2, 21 (1394 a 22), and the discussion of πίστεις generally, and for the five kinds of πίστις 1, 15, 3 (1375 a 24). At other points too Bernays explains how some sayings of Aristotle in the *Rhetoric* are mechanically and inappropriately transferred

The old is that which abounds in the ridiculous.

The new is that which has given that up, and inclines to the more serious (πρὸς τὸ σέμνον).

The middle is a mixture of the two.

Such is the content of this confused little treatise, with its curious mixture of sense and nonsense, of obviously Peripatetic and obviously un-Peripatetic observations. The compiler, or his source (or sources), was clearly familiar with the *Poetics* as we have it and with parts of the *Rhetoric* as well, but, equally clearly, he did not understand them very well. There is no reason to think that he drew on Aristotelian sources which we do not possess, and we are certainly not justified in reconstructing such sources from what he tells us, except for his classification of the sources of laughter which does seem to reproduce the theories of people much more intelligent than himself. They may quite likely have been Peripatetics.

CHAPTER X

Roman Beginnings

The study of language and letters (*grammatica*) was at one time neither practised nor indeed esteemed in Rome, a rude and warlike community with as yet little leisure for liberal studies. The beginnings of such study were mediocre, as the first teachers, both poets and half-Greeks themselves (I mean Livius and Ennius who are known to have taught both languages at home and abroad), did no more than interpret the Greeks or give readings of whatever they had themselves composed in Latin. . . .[1]

Suetonius (*c.* A.D. 69-140) goes on to trace the awakening of literary studies in Rome to the visit of Crates of Mallos 'about the time of Ennius' death' (169 B.C.). The influence of Pergamum on Rome, symbolized by the visit of Crates, was important, and Suetonius no doubt means *grammatica* as a formal study, but even so he is less than fair to the literary pioneers of the third century. The first of these, Livius Andronicus, was indeed an Italian Greek from Tarentum (*c.* 284-204). He wrote comedy, tragedy and lyric, and translated the *Odyssey* into the primitive accentuated Saturnian metre. There were a number of dramatic performances of plays more or less freely translated from the Greek at the end of the third century and the beginning of the second, i.e. after the second Punic War.

The second name which has survived is that of Naevius (270-201 B.C.), a Latin who wrote plays modelled upon the Greek but not it seems, mere word for word translations; he also composed, still in Saturnian metre, an account of the first Punic War. According to Aulius Gellius (I, 24) he boasted in his epitaph that at his death Rome forgot how to speak Latin.

It is to Ennius (239-169 B.C.), however, that Suetonius' words do much less than justice. He too wrote Greek tragedies and comedies in Latin, but his great fame rested upon an epic history of Rome and of the second Punic War for which he adopted the Homeric hexameter and naturalized it, so to speak, into a Roman metre. His language and rhythms are often heavy and laboured, and quite un-Homeric, but the power of a great poet comes

---

[1] These are the opening words of Suetonius' *De Grammaticis*. *Grammatica* includes far more than our word grammar, not only linguistics but the study and exegesis of poetry and prose works. For Varro's definition of the subject and the importance of the *grammatici* in Roman education see below, pp. 163-4.

through; some of his majestic lines are even today stamped upon the memory of every Latinist. His influence was very great, and it is largely under that influence that the Roman writers gave up their native metres and very soon adopted those of Greece. This was a momentous step, the more so that Greek scansion is based on the time factor (i.e. the length or shortness of syllables), whereas the native metres depended on stress-accentuation. Thus the dependence of Latin literature, in matters of form, was permanently established.

The effects of this dependence were, of course, manifold. Plautus was a slightly older contemporary of Ennius and the metre of second-century Latin comedy remained unaffected – both his comedies and those of Terence are written in accentuated senarii – but in content it was completely dependent upon Greek models, so much so indeed that scholars have frequently used Latin comedies to reconstruct the plots of lost comedies of Menander. Throughout the history of Latin literature Roman poets drew their inspiration from Greek models, and reproduced their themes with varying degrees of fidelity to the originals. We should remember, however, that in ancient times, both Greek and Roman, the notion of originality was very different from ours. Greek poets frequently drew their inspiration from Homer, Greek tragedy re-enacted old legends drawn from the Homeric or Cyclic saga, and the three great tragedians frequently wrote plays which re-enacted legends already dramatized by their predecessors or contemporaries. This applied not only to plots or situations, but also to language and expression; poets and other writers freely borrowed phrases from one another, and deliberately changed and improved them. Known poetry was a common possession upon which all could draw and to which all contributed according to their talent. What more natural then, when Greek poetry came to Rome, than that they should draw as freely upon it as did the Greeks themselves?

The nature of this dependence changed from direct translation to adaptation as Latin literature developed, and from adaptation to making the Greek borrowings into something quite different. On the one hand, the formal dependence, in matters of genres and metres for example, remained absolute, but on the other hand, from the very first, the spirit and the resulting product were quite different. Plautus might borrow the whole of his plot from a Greek comic poet, but the result was Roman and not Greek; even on the purely formal side, the hexameters of Ennius were very different from those of Homer. The same is true within Latin literature itself, for the hexameters of Virgil are very different again, and Virgil borrowed expressions and phrases from both Homer and Ennius. We must therefore keep in mind both the quite different general attitude to originality and plagiarism and also the peculiar Roman dependence upon

Greek literature in order to understand both Latin literature and Roman literary theory. Later, the practice of recitation and the declamations of the rhetorical schools, as well as the rhetorical theory of *mimêsis*, which at its best was emulation and at its worst the imitation of particular stylistic turns and devices, much reinforced this dependence upon predecessors, both Greek and Latin.[1]

We have seen that the Alexandrians themselves were already inhibited by their classical inheritance, and that Callimachus advised them not to compete in the greater genres – tragedy and epic in particular – where they had inherited perfection. When Roman literature began to develop in the second century, they inherited not only the classical Greek literature but Alexandrian poetry as well, and besides this, a fully developed system of literary theory and criticism, and a language much more developed and sophisticated than their own. In Greece the great creative period came first, theory and criticism followed, but this was impossible in Rome. The inevitable result is that Latin literature was from the first much more self-conscious and self-critical. Their first poets were also their first critics, and we find in the fragments of Lucilius the satirist, for example, a good deal of thought obviously given to language and literature. The literary genres were set by the Greeks and it was a long time before the Romans ventured beyond them. Similarly, in literary and rhetorical criticism and theory, they inherit and restate rather than originate.

Fortunately, they inherited controversy as well as theory; the Alexandrians, as we have seen, did not always agree among themselves, and the Romans did not allow themselves to be intimidated by Callimachus from trying the great genres of antiquity, especially the epic which seems to have been particularly suited to their temperament. Here were the seeds of that quarrel between those who, in the first century, wanted to model Roman poetry upon the great works of the classical period – Homer and the tragedians mainly – and those who wished to model themselves upon the smaller products of Alexandrian poetry and theory. All of them, however, seem to have agreed with the Alexandrians in putting the emphasis on *ars* or τέχνη, poetry as hard work, as technical proficiency requiring special knowledge and training, rather than on native creative genius. This is inevitable in a period of theory and criticism and the Romans, in view of their inheritance, could not have avoided it.

The result of this emphasis is a tendency for literature to become esoteric, written by those who know for those who know. In this the Romans did not go so far as the Alexandrians, but even in the golden age

---

[1] On this whole subject see W. Kroll, *Studien zur Verständnis der römischen Literatur* especially ch. 7, 'Originalität und Nachahmung'; also A. M. Guillemin, 'L'imitation dans les littératures antiques'.

of Rome no literature except oratory, which was directly concerned with matters political and directly appealed to the people, was ever an integral part of the people's life as poetry had been in Athens. This is partly due to a difference in national character. The Romans were not a poetic or artistic race, and they knew it, but the tendency was reinforced by considering poetry as largely a matter of training and techniques.

The Romans were very much aware that Greek was a more supple and sophisticated language than their own. Lucretius insisted again and again on the difficulty of expressing philosophical ideas in Latin. So did Cicero; he deliberately set out to create a Latin philosophical vocabulary which largely became the European vocabulary; and he did the same with Rhetoric. Horace's repeated emphasis on the responsibility of the poet to enrich the language should be read in this context, for he was keenly aware that to restrict Roman poets to the language used by their ancestors was suicidal. More than a century later we shall find Quintilian still aware of the lack of suppleness in Latin, which had to make up in forcefulness what it lacked in subtlety.

Latin literature was therefore the self-conscious creation of men who were thoroughly familiar with a kindred literature which they knew to be far more developed than their own. The educated Romans of the late Republic and the early Empire were bilingual. They deliberately set out to forge their own language into an instrument by means of which they could hope to rival the Greeks with masterpieces of their own which, imitative in all external matters of form, would yet breathe the Roman spirit and celebrate Rome's achievement. Their inevitable sense of inferiority in literary matters would probably have been fatal to the success of their endeavour had it not been accompanied by a sense of their own greatness in other fields of endeavour where the Greeks had failed, and perhaps also by their sense of superiority, as conquerors, to the contemporary heirs of the greatness of Greece.

PLAUTUS

Roman comedy does not provide us with very much in the way of theory, and it is a mistake to attempt to read any theory into the few casual literary jokes in the comedies of Plautus. For example, a character who is hard up for money and advice says he is going to do what poets do, for poets, once they have their tablets in hand, discover things that are not there at all and make the untrue appear true. To solemnly extract from this any theory of the suspension of disbelief in the theatre[1] seems somewhat heavy-handed and pedantic. In the prologue of the *Amphitryo* Hermes says that since the gods are going to take part this must be a

[1] *Pseudolus* 401-5; and see D'Alton, p. 2, n. 5.

tragedy, but if the audience doesn't want a tragedy we'll make it a comedy or, better still, let's call it a tragicomedy.[1] The use of this neologism is interesting, but it hardly involves a theory of a new genre.

Plautus makes one point, however, which seems to imply a deliberate theory, and he repeats it. In the prologue of two different plays,[2] he announces that he is *not* going to tell the audience how things are going to turn out (one of the usual functions of the prologue). Moreover, some of his other plays have no prologue at all. This means that Plautus is deliberately developing the sound dramatic technique of withholding the outcome to the end, and also that of making the necessary background information emerge in the course of the play itself.

TERENCE

With Terence, younger by a generation, we find ourselves in the very different atmosphere of the Scipionic circle, a group of men of letters who gathered around the younger Scipio, the conqueror of Carthage, in the middle of the second century B.C. in Rome. Here, certainly, there was plenty of literary discussion. There were Terence, Polybius the historian, Lucilius the satirist, Panaetius the philosopher, Scipio's friend Laelius, and others. Lovers of Greek literature to a man, they yet opposed a too slavish conformity to Greek models; above all they insisted on *latinitas*, the speaking and writing of good Latin. They also seem to have favoured a simple manner of writing, which may have been due to the Stoic influence of Panaetius.

Naturally, as a member of the circle, Terence takes pride in the purity of his language. He adopted as his own the technique of Plautus in his prologues. Indeed Terence goes further; he says nothing at all about the plot in his prologues,[3] but uses them as a vehicle of literary controversy with a rival group of comic writers older than himself who had a much more boisterous, Plautine conception of comedy.[4] They resented Terence as a rather precious young upstart who enjoyed distinguished patronage. So it is in Terence's prologues that we find his account of the controversy and of his own critical ideas; his enemies said that if it were not for their attacks on him, he would have had no material for his prologues.[5]

The main charge brought against Terence is, to us, disconcerting. They

---

Amphitryo 50-63, D'Alton, p. 9.

[2] The *Trinummus* and the *Asinaria*.

[3] *Adelphi* 22.

[4] His chief opponent, whom he does not name, was one Luscius Lanuvinus, an older playwright of whose work nothing remains.

[5] *Phormio* 13-15. In using his prologues for this purpose, Terence was probably influenced by the rhetorical rule that a speech began by an introduction which should be used to conciliate the audience.

do not criticize him because he followed Greek models, for they all did that, but because he does not stick to them closely enough; indeed that he goes so far as to put scenes from *several* Greek comedies into *one* of his own. This is the famous charge of *contaminatio*. It is hard to see the point of this accusation, unless they felt that the supply of Greek comedies would run out if the practice continued! Terence's defence is to plead guilty, but he quotes precedents from Naevius, Plautus and Ennius, and he says he would rather imitate their carelessness than the 'murky labours' of his critics.[1] However, when a comedy derives from a single Greek original, he is careful to say so.[2] He also retorted that his chief rival was a good translator but only managed to turn good Greek into inferior Latin plays.[3]

He was also accused of plagiarism. This again does not mean plagiarizing from the Greeks, which was praiseworthy enough, but using a plot already used by a Roman predecessor. Terence defends himself in all earnest, and says that, while it is true that Plautus had used the plot of Diphilus' *Dying Together*, he had *not* used the particular scene which Terence now had put in his *Adelphi*; moreover, to forestall criticism, he had translated it 'word for word'.[4] Elsewhere he says that the flatterer and the braggart in his own *Eunuch* do *not* derive from Naevius' or Plautus' comedies of the same name, but from the *Colax* of Menander – 'if this be a sin, it is due to the poet's negligence, not a deliberate intention to plagiarize'.[5] Terence and his critics obviously agree that to translate from the Greek is right and proper, but to imitate a plot or even a scene previously used by a Roman playwright is a literary crime. One could have no better illustration of the peculiar relationship between Latin and Greek literature.

Another accusation brought against Terence points to a real difference between his comedies and those of his predecessors. His plays were said to be too simple in style and too smooth in composition.[6] If this refers to his language, he is proud of it[7] but he takes the charge to apply to his plots, and his reply is to pour scorn upon the noisy and fantastic scenes of the others, e.g. a youth talking to a hind pursued by dogs, and upon the conventional nature of their characters, all acting at the top of their voices,[8] the angry old man, the greedy parasite, and so on. To his own plays he

---

[1] *Andria* 9-21; *Heauton.* 16-21.

[2] *Heauton.* 4: Ex integra Graeca integram comoediam hodie sum acturus; cf. *Phormio* 24-28.

[3] *Eunuch* 8.

[4] Verbum de verbo expressum est, *Adelphi* 11, and the whole passage, 1-14.

[5] *Eunuch* 23-28: si id est peccatum, peccatum imprudentia est poetae, non quo furtum facere studuerit.

[6] *Phormio* 4-5, fabulas tenui esse oratione et scriptura levi; the word tenuis we meet later to describe the' plain' style.

[7] *Heauton.* 46: in hoc est pura oratio.

[8] *Heauton.* 30-40; cf. *Eunuch* 35-40.

applies the epithet *stataria*,[1] meaning that they are quiet, standing still, as it were, in strong contrast to wild comedies in perpetual motion. He does not seek to entertain by continuous excitement but provides a calmer sort of pleasure. We need not take seriously the accusation that 'men of rank' write his comedies for him.[2] His reply, that everybody in the state makes use of these men so why should not he, is obviously humorous.

All this controversy is confined to the prologues. No more than in Plautus should we look for literary significance where none is intended.[3] What he does say, however, implies a thought-out theory of comedy: his claim to have established a new, less boisterous type of comedy, his theory that a dramatist should unfold the background of his plot as the action proceeds, his vindication of good *latinitas* on the stage, the greater freedom he claims to at least combine Greek originals – all these are forward steps in both the practice and the theory of the genre.

POLYBIUS

Another member of the Scipionic circle who made an important contribution to literary theory is the historian Polybius. His universal history of the times set out to show why the Romans were becoming the masters of the Mediterranean world, and he is still our main authority for the Punic Wars. He was an Achaean Greek who had played an important role in the Achaean league when he was brought to Rome with other hostages in 168 B.C. During the sixteen years that he was kept in Rome he became an intimate of the elder Scipio and the tutor of his sons.

Polybius formulated a theory of historiography in sharp contrast to Hellenistic practice, and his twelfth book is devoted to this and to unsparing criticism of Hellenistic historians, Timaeus in particular.[4] History, as we saw, was often classed under the heading of epideictic rhetoric, along with encomium and its opposite; it was generally written from a very partial point of view with perpetual straining for stylistic effects. Both tendencies can be traced back to Isocrates who did not scruple to manipulate historical facts to prove his point, and the first Hellenistic

---

[1] *Heauton.* 35: adeste aequo animo, date potestatem mihi statariam agere ut liceat per silentium.

[2] *Heauton.* 24.

[3] When, for example, Gnatho claims to be a new type of parasite (*Eunuch* 232-54); when Pamphilius says we must keep our secret, unlike what happens in comedy where everybody knows everything (*Hecyra* 866, 872); when there is talk of a wonderful scheme to pretend that a foundling is legitimate (*Andria* 218-25) there may be an implied criticism of comedy conventions. But Greek comedies were full of that kind of joke and we should not attach too much importance to them.

[4] On this subject see E. Norden: *Die Antike Kunstproza* 1, 81 ff. and C. Wunderer, *Polybius, Lebens und Weltanschauung am dem Zweiten Jahrhundert*, especially 29-39; and F. W. Walbank, *A Historical Commentary on Polybius*, vol. 1, 6-16.

historians such as Theopompus and Euphorus were his pupils. However, the tendency to partiality was more widespread, and Peripatetic prejudice against Alexander obviously coloured Callisthenes' account of his campaigns. All our evidence shows that the writing of history, from the fourth century on, was more rhetorical than historical.

To Polybius, however, the historian's fidelity to truth was the first essential and should know no compromise: 'as a living animal becomes ineffective when deprived of his eyesight, so history, if truth be taken away, is but a useless tale'.[1] Philinus, he says, was partial to Carthage as Fabius was partial to Rome; both their histories of the first Punic War are thereby made ridiculous.[2] Polybius himself, friend as he became of the Romans, does not hesitate to discuss their faults[3]: even his account of the younger Scipio is not all praise.

He held three things to be necessary for the historian: the study of the documentary evidence, actual familiarity with the terrain, and understanding of political events. He understood documentary evidence in the modern sense, not merely the reading of books; indeed he had nothing but contempt for those who write history from books alone. The historian must interview witnesses and make every effort to discover the truth.[4] As for surveying the ground, Polybius was a tireless traveller and went to see for himself whenever he could. To appreciate events, he held that the historian must have had personal experience of politics and of strategy.[5] This he himself possessed and he jeers at the mistakes in other historians which were entirely due to their ignorance of practical politics.

> Plato says that human affairs will be successfully managed when philosophers are kings, or kings study philosophy. I would say that history will be competently written when men of practical experience undertake to write it, and when they consider it not as an incidental occupation but as an essential and honourable pursuit worthy of the devotion of a lifetime, or when prospective historians consider practical experience indispensable to their craft.[6]

Polybius had the Stoic's dislike of both rhetorical devices and emotional appeal. Hence the sharp line he draws between history and tragedy, and his criticism of Phylarchus' emotionalism.[7] Hence also his dislike of those

[1] 1, 14, 6; cf. 12, 12, 3. [2] 1, 14-15.
[3] E.g. 1, 37; 1, 39, 12; 1, 64, 6. [4] 12, 25e and 27.
[5] 12, 4 c; 12, 25 g – 25 h and 27, 7 where he states that personal inquiry (πολυπραγμοσύνη) is the most important part of history.
[6] 12, 28, 1-5.
[7] 2, 56, 6-12, where he blames Phylarchus for exploiting dramatic situations with the sole aim of stirring the emotions of his readers, thus writing like the tragedians, καθάπερ οἱ τραγῳδιόγραφοι. He then goes on to contrast the purpose (τὸ τέλος) of history and tragedy. Tragedy aims to thrill and excite for the moment while history aims to persuade and instruct

rhetorical display speeches which Hellenistic historians, bad imitators of
Thucydides, inserted into their histories without much regard to the
particular circumstances or the character of the speaker.[1]

> What was actually said should be told, but the historian who omits
> what was said and the reason for it, and inserts in its place untrue
> displays of rhetoric and irrelevant matter destroys what is the particular
> characteristic of history.

Even worse are those fantastic scenes where historians imitate tragic poets
and bring the gods into sober history to get them out of the confusion
which their own ignorance has generated.[2] Polybius obviously feels deeply
on the subject of history to which he devoted many years of unsparing
labour. His conception of it, however, goes far beyond a mere recital of
events; the historian must account for these and make the reader understand causes and motives. Only in this way can history be useful to public
men, and all men will then benefit from a knowledge of the past, find
pleasure in it, as well as being able to endure better the vicissitudes of
fortune by the example of others.[3] The best kind of history to Polybius is
universal history, the kind he writes, for it more fully displays the working
of cause and effect. Moreover, the universal historian is less likely to
magnify the importance of particular events or personalities than one
whose vision is limited to one place or one campaign. He is also less likely
to slip into encomium or personal attack.[4]

It is generally admitted that Polybius made every attempt to live up to
his ideal of impartial truthfulness, though opinions differ as to how far he
succeeded. He seems to have been swayed by his Achaean patriotism in
dealing with the enemies of the Achaean league, and even in theory he
seems to admit that patriotism may colour a historian's account, though

its students. The term 'tragic history' has been used by scholars to refer to Hellenistic emotional
history which Polybius is here criticizing and this type of history has been alleged to have had
a theoretical base in Peripatetic literary theory, or maybe Isocratean, and that such theories
of history deliberately applied to history-writing some of the principles which Aristotle
applied to tragedy. That the Hellenistic historians wrote dramatically as well as rhetorically is
not in doubt, but the evidence for a thought-out theory of 'tragic history' is very doubtful
indeed. It rests upon a fragment of Duris (historian, pupil of Theophrastus) which can be
variously interpreted, Jacoby *F.G.H.* 76 F 1. F. W. Walbank in *Historia* 9 (1960) 216-34
examines the factors which led to a certain confusion between tragedy and history and
concludes that the use of the phrase 'tragic history' as referring to a special school of history
is a distortion and should be dropped. However, see C. O. Brink in *Proc. Cambridge Philol. Soc.*
186 (N.S. 6), 1960, 14-19.

[1] 12, 25, b. Polybius himself used speeches; his theory of them agrees with Thucydides and
it is the later Hellenistic rhetorical historians whom he is criticizing.

[2] 3, 48, 8-9.

[3] See 3, 6 for a discussion of causes, also 12, 25, i, 9; for the usefulness of history e.g. 2, 56,
11-13 and 3, 31.

[4] On universal history 3, 32; 7, 7, 6; 29, 12; etc.

he must not falsify his facts. More important, however, is his admission that in a special work on Philopoemen, the Achaean general, he had magnified his deeds. But then he was writing an encomium, as he tells us himself, so that, presumably, the laws of history no longer held.[1]

Except for the brief remarks of Thucydides, this is the first extant discussion of history. It would seem that later historians had at least to pay lip-service to historical truth, though 'tragic history' was by no means dead and both Greek and Roman historians continued to be under powerful rhetorical influence. Lucian, three hundred years after Polybius, will be equally strong in his condemnation.

LUCILIUS

The last member of the Scipionic circle who need concern us is Lucilius (180-103 B.C.) the father of Roman satire. From him we have a number of very short fragments, mostly preserved by the grammarians with little or nothing to indicate their context. This is tantalizing, but we must resist the temptation to invent a context for them, which is likely to be misleading. For example, we find him laughing at Scipio's affectation,[2] and also drawing a satiric picture of Scipio attended by a host of followers in the street.[3] On this we might build a theory of enmity between them, if we did not happen to know that their relations were friendly.

The elder Pliny tells us that Lucilius was the first Roman with a critical sense of style,[4] and it is indeed regrettable that his meaning is so often obscured by the scrappy nature of his fragments. He clearly had a keen interest in language and literary style, and he reflects the discussions of his circle on these matters. We can, for example, trace his preoccupation with pure latinity, for we have a number of lines on proper spelling; he objects to Accius' way of writing aa for a long a, and he insists on ei for i in the nominative plural.[5] Reflecting the same interest in language are his

---

[1] On patriotism see 16, 14, 6; on his work on Philopoemen 10, 21, 8: 'as the nature of the former work, being an encomium, required a narrative of his deeds under various headings with some amplification of them ($\mu\epsilon\tau'$ $\alpha\dot{\nu}\xi\dot{\eta}\sigma\epsilon\omega\varsigma$) so the nature of this history, impartial in blame and praise, demands a true account based on evidence and the reasons for either blame or praise.'

Walbank p. 16 discusses the whole question of Polybius' reliability and comes to the following conclusion about the *Histories*: 'A slight concession (in principle) to politic piety and (in practice) to local patriotism, a limited success in retailing the real contents of some of his reported speeches, a readiness to embrace the terminology (but not the emotional attitudes) of tragic history in the interests of $\tau\dot{o}$ $\tau\epsilon\rho\pi\nu\acute{o}\nu$ or moral edification – these probably represent the sum of what a critic of Polybius' truthfulness can assemble. They amount in total to very little, and leave the overwhelming impression of a reliable and conscientious writer. . . .'

[2] 983-4 (963-4). The numbers of the lines are those in E. H. Warmington, *Remains of Old Latin* (Loeb) vol. 3, which is the most easily available in English, and gives the context in which the fragments are found. The numbers added in brackets are those in the standard edition of F. Marx.

[3] 254-8 (1138-42).   [4] *N.H.* Praef. 7.   [5] 368-96 (358-81).

accusations of provincialism and rusticity against certain authors,[1] as also
the list of solecisms which we are told he made.[2]

Concerning style we have a well-known description of the overelaborate
style of one Albucius, quoted three times by Cicero:

> How beautifully his expressions are put together like bits of mosaic
> artfully set down in a floor of wriggly pattern.[3]

and he mocked the same Albucius for wanting to be Greek in everything.[4]
His humorous use of monstrous compounds in the manner of Pacuvius
and Ennius, and his dislike of overelaborate rhetoric,[5] also seem to reflect
the Scipionic preference for simplicity in writing. So does the ridiculing
of the Isocratean fondness for *homoioteleuton*, or ending successive clauses
with the same sound.[6]

There is also a fairly elaborate distinction made between *poema* to refer
to a short poem, or a few lines of poetry, and *poesis* which is reserved for
a long poem, and this same usage is found in other critical writings.[7] This
is as far as we can safely go. It would take a bold man to deduce from such
scattered remains without context any consistent theory of language or
style, especially in a satirist who may be stating something only to ridicule
it. To adapt the phrase of Aristarchus, all that is said in Lucilius need not be
said by Lucilius, however much we may regret the loss of his satires, some
of which, if extant, would certainly reflect the critical ideas of his time.

There were other literary scholars in Rome in the second century, but
our information about them is even more scanty. The poet Accius, for
example (170-85 B.C.), wrote a critical history of Roman drama with
special reference to the dates of their performance. Our sources indicate
that he made some elementary mistakes, as when he places the first performance of a Roman drama in 197 B.C., which is obviously too late, or
when he placed Hesiod before Homer. His reputation, however, stood
high in the first century, and traces of him can be found in Livy and
Horace, who repeated some of his errors.[8] Another famous but shadowy
figure is that of Lucius Aelius Stilco, the teacher of Varro who was the
greatest scholar of them all.

VARRO

Marcus Terentius Varro (116-27 B.C.) was a decade older than Cicero and

[1] 232 (1130) and Quintilian 1, 5, 56.   [2] 397 (1100).
[3] 84-85 (84-85).   [4] 87-93 (88-94).
[5] 86 (86).   [6] 186-93 (181-8).
[7] 401-10 (338-47). Similar distinctions between ποίημα and ποίησις occur in Philodemus
(about Neoptolemus) and Varro. For a discussion on the possible significance of these see C. O
Brink, *Horace on Poetry*, pp. 61-74.
[8] See G. L. Hendrickson in *AJP* 19 (1898).

survived him by about fifteen years. His reputation for erudition was un-
equalled in Rome and he wrote a large number of books on a great many
subjects. His treatise on agriculture, *De Re Rustica*, is extant. He was the
author of *Menippean Satires*, named after the Cynic writer Menippus
(third century B.C.); these were a medley of prose and verse on topical
subjects, probably mostly literary, of which only the scantiest fragments
remain. He also wrote a large number of works on grammar, language
and literature, on which his fame mainly rests. These included his *De
Lingua Latina*, originally in twenty-five books, of which six books remain.[1] There can be no doubt that Varro's interests were mainly linguistic,
for it is as an authority on the use and meaning of words that he is most
often quoted. The extant books deal with etymology and Anomaly, two
subjects of particular interest to the Stoics. Rome was in closer touch with
Pergamum than with Alexandria and, as we saw, the Stoics were dominant
in Pergamum. We remember that Suetonius dated the beginnings of
literary studies in Rome from the visit of Crates from Pergamum. It has
even been suggested that the main divisions of the *De Lingua Latina* followed
a Stoic pattern.[2]

The last three of the extant books present us with the fullest available
discussion of the controversy between the Anomalists and the Analogists.[3]
The arguments of the Anomalist are expounded in the eighth book, those
of the Analogist in the ninth, and the tenth gives Varro's own position.
The Anomalist's position is essentially negative: he piles up the obvious
irregularities in the formation of derivatives, in the declension of nouns
and the conjugation of verbs to prove that there are no laws of language
and that custom and usage are the only criteria of correct speech. He also
insists that in language, as in all other things, pleasure comes from variety,
a theory which he expounds at considerable length. Basically, the Anomalist simply denies both the existence and the desirability of any laws or
rules in language.

The Analogist's position is much more sensible and much more en-
lightened. Most of his arguments are attributed to Aristarchus who did
not deny the existence or importance of custom and usage; on the contrary,
he made the rules of analogy depend on them in their application, but,
where custom allows, the rules of analogy should be followed. The
Analogist has no difficulty in proving that there is in fact much more
regularity in derivations and declensions than Anomalists allow. He too
can appeal to general principles and he points out that there is regularity
as well as variety in all things and that nothing is ever discovered by

[1] See R. G. Kent, *Varro on the Latin Language*.
[2] See H. Dahlmann's *Varro und die hellenistische Sprachtheorie* 1-87.
[3] See the interesting article of F. H. Colson, in *CQ* 13 (1919), 24-36.

blindly following custom. These appeals to cosmic principles are then followed by specific advice such as that the root of a noun is to be found in oblique cases rather than in the nominative, thus enabling us to perceive regularity behind the apparent changes and variety. The Analogists were seeking to establish grammatical rules; sometimes they went too far and used regularly derived forms which were in fact outlandish, but their basic principles were sound.

Varro himself, in the tenth book, adopts a modified Analogism and seeks to explain how far it is justified. His position, made clear only by implication, is probably best expressed by the statement elsewhere attributed to him,[1] that good latinity depended on four factors: natural correspondence between name and object, conformity with the rules of grammar, customary usage, and the authority of great writers. His illustrations are all Latin. He is applying to Latin ideas and theories inherited from Greece.

Of Varro's other works we know very little. If we possessed his *De Poematis*, it would no doubt throw a good deal of light on Hellenistic theories of poetry, but the fragments are too scanty to allow any reliable conjectures on what kind of light it might have thrown. There is a fragment (398 B) which makes the familiar distinction between *poema* as a brief piece of verse and *poesis* as a large complete work like the *Iliad*. The fragment then goes on to define *poeticê* as the art of poetry itself.[2] This triple division, however, cannot safely be related either to the *ars-artifex* formula or the triad *poema, poesis, poeta* associated with Neoptolemus by Philodemus, both of which some scholars, as we shall see, have tried to find in Horace. We should always keep in mind that a slight shift in meaning, or a minimal difference in terminology, was a matter of great importance to different critics in so formulized a study as ancient rhetoric and criticism, especially in Hellenistic times.

When Varro is reported to have said (fr. 399 B) that in comedy Caecilius deserved the palm for plot, Terence for characterization and Plautus for his language, no conclusions as to Varro's literary theory can be drawn from this, especially when, as is the case for this and the previous fragment, the quotation comes from a Menippean satire and we are quite ignorant of the context.

We do know, however, that Varro made a list of the Plautine comedies which he considered genuine and that he based his verdict on internal evidence, using Plautus' wit and language as criteria,[3] and this implies a

---

[1] *Grammatici Latini* (Keil) vol. 1, p. 439: Latinitas constat ... natura, analogia, consuetudine auctoritate.
[2] For a discussion of the possible implications, and of such other evidence as may be thought to be available, see H. Dahlmann's *Varro's Schrift De Poematis*, especially 26 ff. See also p. 160, note 7, above.   [3] Aulus Gellius, *Noctes Atticae* 3, 3, 2-4.

thorough study of the comedies. His definition of *grammatica* is also of importance to make us understand the function and place of the *grammatici* in Roman education. Varro defined it as the study of poets, historians and orators, and its aim as the capacity to read well (aloud of course), to interpret and explain, to establish a correct text, and to evaluate the works studied.[1]

Finally, there is an interesting reference in Aulius Gellius where he is discussing the three styles, which he links with three neighbouring vices; Gellius quotes Varro as saying that Pacuvius was an example of copiousness, Lucilius of simplicity, and Terence of the intermediate style.[2] Now quite apart from the value of these judgements (one might have expected Terence to be the example of simplicity), if Gellius is quoting correctly, then Varro's was the first extant example of the use of the three-style formula, and the first, moreover, to classify authors in accordance with it. The formula is found in the *Ad Herennium* and in Cicero who were Varro's contemporaries. It is also of interest to note that Varro's examples are *poets*, thus making it clear that the formula, from the first, was applied to literature as a whole, not merely to rhetoric or prose.

The Roman writers who contributed to literary criticism and theory in the last two generations of the republic and the early empire were all – with the exception of Horace – more closely tied to the art of rhetoric than the Greek critics had been or continued to be. This is no accident. Oratory was, of all forms of literature, the most congenial to the Roman temperament, and it is only in Roman times that Isocrates' theory of education as 'learning to speak well on great subjects' came into its own, when rhetorical and higher education became synonymous terms. Rhetoric now claimed all literature as its province and poetry came to be looked upon as rhetoric in verse. Roman poetry was always more influenced by rhetoric than Greek poetry had been; this influence can be felt even in the Augustans and it increased rapidly in the age of silver Latin; even philosophy became ancillary to rhetoric. To Cicero, oratory was the highest form of literature; Seneca the elder was a camp follower of the rhetorical school, even if a critical one; Tacitus was as much an orator as a historian; and Quintilian was the imperial professor of the art. Rhetoric as an art was a Greek discovery, textbooks on rhetoric had been written in increasing

[1] *Lectio, narratio, emendatio, iudicium*, each of which he defines (fr. 236, Funaioli), and fr. 234 where the four officia of *grammatica* are described as *scribere, legere, intellegere, probare*, where *scribere* takes the place of *emendare*.

[2] *Noct. Att.* 6, 14: et in carmine et in soluta oratione genera dicendi probabilia sunt tria, quae Graeci χαρακτῆρας vocant, nominaque eis fecerunt ἁδρόν, ἰσχνόν, μέσον, nos quoque quem primum posuimus uberem vocamus, secundum gracilem, tertium mediocrem ... vera autem et propria huiusce modi formarum exempla in Latina lingua M. Varro esse dicit ubertatis Pacuvium, gracilitatis Lucilium, mediocritatis Terentium.

numbers from the time of Gorgias, and there were rhetorical schools, no doubt, through the Hellenistic centuries, but they were not the whole of higher education in practice. Poetics and rhetorical theory were separate subjects for Hellenistic critics, and indeed they still are so in Philodemus. Dionysius of Halicarnassus' interests are literary as much as rhetorical, even though he shares the rhetorical slant of the times, and this is obviously true of Longinus. With the Romans rhetoric predominates to a greater degree, and it might be argued that even Horace's discussion of poetry shows the influence of his rhetorical education.

It is a pity that we do not know more about the work, and the works, of the *grammatici* who might be called the secondary school teachers of Rome. The young Roman boys came to them after they had learned to read and write with the *ludi magister* who looked after their elementary education. There were both Greek and Latin *grammatici* in Rome and the Romans attended both types of school. It is here that they were trained in literature and language. They read the poets, the historians and the orators; as Varro told us, the texts were explained to them, their literary judgement was trained. The teachers were mainly slaves or freedmen, but a number of them were scholars of considerable reputation. Young men of literary tastes gathered around them and formed in effect a literary circle where their own compositions were often presented for criticism. It was in these circles, and there only, that a love for, and familiarity with, literature for its own sake had much chance of developing, though even here it is probable that in view of the influence of Pergamum, there was a good deal of emphasis on grammatical exegesis. As we have seen, the criticism of literature, from the days of Zoilus on, was often somewhat picayune and defensive. The Alexandrians had moved beyond this, but Rome's connexion with Alexandria was comparatively late. Furthermore, the Stoic practice of allegorical interpretations must often have had a deadening effect. Nevertheless, the *grammatici* played a vital role in spreading appreciation of poetry and literature over a large section of the community, and continued to do so under the empire.[1]

The study of literature for its own sake never made a very wide popular appeal to the Romans, and when the rhetorical schools established themselves as a further educational stage, probably during the lifetime of Cicero, the *grammatici* were soon overshadowed by the rhetoricians. Before this time they had to some extent taught rhetoric themselves, and at what age the boy should move from the *grammaticus* to the *rhetor* was still a matter of controversy in the age of Quintilian. It was not, however, so much a matter of encroachment by rhetoric upon the time spent with the grammaticus as that the study of literature became more and more slanted

[1] On this whole subject see H. I. Marrou, *Histoire de l'éducation dans l'antiquité*[2], pp. 369-79.

towards the ultimate aim of rhetoric, so that those aspects of criticism and language, and those authors, who were directly useful to the orator received most attention. In our critical texts the slant is only too obvious. On the other hand, we should not forget that, to men like Cicero and Quintilian, the art of rhetoric covered the whole art of self-expression.

THE *AD HERENNIUM*

The first Latin text we should examine is an anonymous document, preserved among the works of Cicero but certainly not by him, a treatise addressed to one Herennius and probably written in the eighties of the first century B.C.[1] Our examination of it will be brief because it is written completely from the point of view of the rhetorician. It is interesting, however, as the first attempt we possess to translate all the technical terms into Latin and to give Latin illustrations at all points; usually, though not always, these illustrations are made up by the author himself, a practice he justifies at some length in the introduction to the fourth and last book.

The treatment of *inventio*, i.e. the different types of issues and arguments treated by Hermagoras two generations earlier, is lengthy: it takes us through the first two books and well into the third (to 3, 15); a brief section on the arrangement of arguments follows (3, 16-18); the next subject is delivery (3, 19-27), then memory with a discussion of a contemporary mnemonic system (3, 28-40). Only with the fourth book do we come to the discussion of style though it is true that this book is the longest.

Our unknown author begins by declaring that he will omit the unnecessary technicalities introduced by the Greek professionals, but as half the work consists of a highly technical discussion of issues and arguments, and another quarter (4, 19-69) of an equally technical discussion of forty-five figures of thought and nineteen figures of speech, we are inclined to wonder how much he can have omitted! We shall meet this impatience with Greek technicalities again. In this connexion we may note that he says at the end that rhetoric is not everything, and that he has also pursued 'other and better studies' (4, 69), presumably philosophy.

We find in this treatise most of the usual formulae. As already mentioned, the general plan is based on the five-part formula which we shall meet again in Cicero and Dionysius, namely invention, order, style, memory and delivery, and the inverted order here is no doubt intended to emphasize the importance of style. The three kinds of rhetoric, forensic, deliberative and epideictic, also appear (1, 2) and so do the means of attaining proficiency (1, 3), namely theory, practice, and imitation (i.e.

[1] See H. Caplan's edition. Caplan dates it (xxvi) about 86-82 B.C.

emulation). The sections-of-a-speech formula is here subordinated to the different kinds of causes, and the number of sections is here six, namely exordium, narrative, division, proofs, refutations and peroration.

The three-style formula is discussed at length (4, 11-16) with examples and neighbouring vices (as in Demetrius). Our author refers, as we saw that Varro may have done, to three acceptable styles (*figurae*). The grand style is here called *gravis* (solemn) while its neighbouring vice is *figura sufflata* (overblown); the middle style is *mediocris*, its fault *genus dissolutum*, slack. The simple style, *figura attenuata*, is apt to fail and become *genus aridum et exsanque*, dry and bloodless. It is important to note, however, that every orator must be able to use all the styles, each at the appropriate moment:

> it is necessary, when speaking, to vary one's style, so that the grand will be followed by the intermediate, this by the plain, and then change them again, so as to avoid satiety without difficulty.

Then there is a somewhat confused reference to the formula of qualities (4, 17-19). Neither the word *virtus* nor any other likely translation of ἀρετή is used, but we are told that good style requires three 'things' (*res*), namely *elegantia*, *compositio*, and *dignitas*. The first of these, *elegantia*, is then subdivided into *latinitas* and *explanatio* which clearly means clarity in the context, and we thus have the first two usual qualities; the way of introducing them may just be an idiosyncrasy of the author or of a source which he is following. But then we have *compositio* and as it is said to consist of avoiding hiatus or excessive repetition of letters[1] and words, hyperbaton, and excessively long periods, the word is obviously used to translate σύνθεσις or word-arrangement. How does this come to be sandwiched between qualities? Then *dignitas* would seem an obvious quality, and a very Roman one, but as the whole discussion of figures which follows is subsumed under it, it seems to have a much wider meaning and to be nearly equivalent to κατασκευή, elaboration or ornamentation, which Cicero will call *ornamentum*. This does appear in lists of virtues of style elsewhere. We may also note the absence of appropriateness (πρέπον, *decorum*) and of the Stoic virtue of brevity, although this last is often omitted from a list of virtues.

The confusion, especially in the use of *compositio*, usually so firmly established as a subsection of style, the other being the choice of words, is hard to account for. It may serve to remind us, however, that the formulae as we know them were not as rigidly applied or universally accepted at the beginning of the first century, and therefore in Hellenistic times, as

---

[1] The example of such repetition of letters is the line of Ennius: 'O Tite, tute, Tati, tibi tanta, tyranne tulisti' (4, 12, 18).

the paucity of our sources leads us to believe. There are a number of other puzzling details in the *Ad Herennium*, but these belong rather to the history of courtroom oratory, and to consider them here would lead us too far astray.

This treatise is particularly remarkable in its almost desperate desire to be Roman at least in terminology and illustrations, and as independent of the Greeks as was humanly possible. With this in mind, we must now turn to our anonymous author's much greater contemporary.

CHAPTER XI

Cicero: The Education of the Orator

When Cicero, then in his early fifties, dedicated the *De Oratore* to his brother in 55 B.C., he said that Quintus had often urged him to write a serious book on the art of speaking 'because the unfinished and unpolished work which escaped from my notebooks when I was little more than a boy[1] is hardly worthy of my present years or of the reputation I have acquired in so many important cases'. The early unfinished work must be the *De Inventione*, which must then have been published when Cicero was, at most, in his early twenties. It is a study of *inventio* only, that is, of various types of issues and arguments to be used on different occasions; but the introductory chapters to each of its two books clearly express some important general principles to which Cicero remained faithful to the end of his life.

The introduction to the second book might well be called the creed of an eclectic; it is typical of the times as well as of Cicero, and he followed this method in philosophy as well as in rhetoric. He tells the story of the painter Zeuxis who, before proceeding to paint a picture of Helen of Troy, chose, from the most beautiful women of Croton, not one model but five. Cicero continues[2]:

> So when I wanted to write a book on the art of speech, I did not have one model before me to follow in every particular. I assembled all the writers on the subject, excerpted from them the best advice which each seemed to give and so extracted what was best from many minds. Each one of these, deservedly famous and of high repute, was in some respects the best, but not one was best in everything. In view of this it seemed silly to neglect one man's good advice because some error of his irritated me, or to adopt the faults of another merely because I followed his good advice.

> If in other fields of study also men would take whatever is most appropriate from many sources rather than attach themselves to one teacher, their arrogance would be less offensive, their faults less enduring, and their ignorance less distressing.

[1] *De Orat.* I, 5. *pueris aut adolescentulis nobis.*
[2] *De Invent.* 2, 4–5.

There is no reason to doubt that this is a true account of Cicero's method. He undoubtedly read a great deal. We should not, however, picture him working like a modern scholar, carefully verifying his references at every step. That was not Cicero's way, nor indeed the way of ancient writers generally. They trusted their well-trained memory, and Cicero's memory was excellent, but not infallible. When he goes on immediately to mention a book of Aristotle which contained a careful statement of all previous rhetors' theories, so that people consulted it rather than them, it is natural to suppose that this work – a τεχνῶν συναγωγή or Collection of Arts of Rhetoric – was among those he possessed, especially as he almost immediately goes on to state that he had *not* seen a textbook by Isocrates which was extant. Nor would Cicero have credited his Antonius[1] with having read both Aristotle's *Collection of Arts* and his *Rhetoric* if he had not read them himself. Indeed this is probably what the passage is intended to convey. The matter is of some importance, for Cicero's treatment of rhetoric has many affinities with that of Aristotle and we have no right to assume that he had not read him.[2] The same is true of the works of Hermagoras and others.

The first book of *De Inventione* starts with what is in effect a reworking of the old commonplace, as old as Gorgias at least, on the blessings of eloquence, of the Logos, but it is a reworking with a difference. Cicero states without equivocation that mere rhetoric does more harm than good, a statement which his modern readers would do well to remember if they are to understand his point of view:

> Prolonged reflection on this subject leads me to this conclusion above all others: I believe that wisdom without eloquence is of little use to the community, but that eloquence without wisdom mostly does great harm, and never does any good.

Cicero goes on to plead for the study of moral philosophy as well as of the art of speech. Both are needed, and this is the basic principle of all his thinking and writing on education. It is interesting to find it so clearly formulated so early in his life. He then proceeds to argue that the power to persuade played a great role in leading men from savagery to civilization 'and served the highest interests of mankind'. He traces 'the origin of the evil', mere rhetoric, to the time when the power to persuade fell into the hands of unscrupulous men, 'shrewd men' trained in the law courts, without regard for truth, who then managed to control public affairs, so that wise men retired to their study (1, 3, 4):

---

[1] *De Orat.* 2, 160. We know from his *Topica*, ad init., that the *Topics* of Aristotle were in Cicero's library at Tusculum.

[2] F. Solmsen makes this clear in *CP* 33 (1938), 401-2.

And so, when rash and reckless men grasped the helm of the ship of state, violent and disastrous shipwrecks naturally followed. Eloquence then incurred such odium and disrepute that the most gifted men turned from the strife and tumult of public life as from turbulent tempests to seek harbour in some quiet and studious pursuit.

The Platonic echoes are clear and obvious,[1] but Cicero was a Roman and a statesman; the academic ivory tower was not for him. He dedicated his whole political life to finding some *concordia ordinum*, some basis of agreement between the saner elements in the state to save the dying republic. He failed. After that failure, he repeated his plea for a system of education which would ally the pursuit of wisdom with that of eloquence. If we remember that the word *orator*, for Cicero at least, had inherited the political overtones of the Greek ῥήτωρ, the Platonic echoes continue, even though the plea this time comes from the forum outside rather than from inside the philosopher's study, and is in part directed to the philosophers themselves. This is the basic appeal of the *De Oratore* in 55 B.C.; it is found again in the *Orator* in 46, towards the end of Cicero's life.[2]

Cicero's plea was of course very different from Plato's. He did not want his orator to be a philosopher in the Platonic sense; nor did he endorse the Stoic view that only the philosopher was the perfect speaker. But he did want his orator to have enough knowledge of philosophy, history, jurisprudence, and even science, to be able, as Isocrates had put it, to speak well on great subjects. When he says that he owes to the Academy whatever he may be as an orator,[3] he does not mean that the study of philosophy by itself makes a great orator, for he is always careful to add that it must be supplemented by specifically rhetorical studies.[4] These must be pursued in the rhetorical schools, but the rhetorical school alone cannot make an orator either. From this point of view his plea for a general education is a protest against the over-subtle technical training of the schools of rhetoric where nothing else was taught. Hence he often speaks with contempt of these *officinae rhetorum* or rhetorical workshops, not because this technical training is superfluous, but because by itself it is woefully inadequate.[5] Thus it is, in a sense, true that Cicero was trying to rescue rhetoric from being 'a mere scholastic study of the processes of argument and of the technique of style' and was restoring an earlier and more classical tradition.[6] This statement, however, needs qualification, for rhetorical scholasti-

[1] For the ship of state cf. *Rep.* 6, 488 a-d; taking refuge from the storm reminds one of *Rep.* 6, 496 d, and the clever lawyer of *Theaet.* 172 e ff.

[2] *De Orat.* 3, 56-95 and 122-31; *Orator* 11-19, 61-64.

[3] *Orator* 12: *et fateor me oratorem . . . non ex rhetorum officinis sed ex Academiae spatiis exstitisse.*

[4] *De Orat.* 3, 80 and 142-3; *Orator* 14-17, 64.

[5] *De Orat.* 1, 24 and 102-5; 2, 75-77; 3, 75 and 92-95.

[6] J. W. H. Atkins, *Literary Criticism* 2, 23.

cism was not a Hellenistic development; it was as old as rhetoric itself. The tradition which Cicero is supposed to have restored is that of Isocrates,[1] but again there is a difference, for, though Isocrates was certainly no mere technician and did try to communicate to his pupils a philosophy of life, we have seen that he never explained what training or knowledge was required. Cicero, however, had also read Aristotle, and while adopting the ideal of Isocrates, based it, not in detail but in principle, upon the kind of requirements outlined by Aristotle.

It is easy to ridicule the general education of the orator, even as preached by Cicero. It is always easy, for specialists in particular, to ridicule any attempt to impart general culture. In modern terms one might describe the Ciceronian curriculum as a thorough general training in philosophy (including logic, ethics, and psychology), in political science, history, and law, with a stiff Honour course in the art of speech in both Latin and Greek. Cicero is fully aware that this theory of education, and particularly his requirements in philosophy and law, would startle his contemporaries,[2] but he insists again and again that rhetoric without educational background – eloquence without wisdom as he put it in the *De Inventione* – is useless or worse. Living in a utilitarian society, Cicero, like all of us, tries to justify the time to be spent on these 'academic' subjects on the grounds of their practical utility to 'the orator'. He does better, however, when he justifies the study of history on the simple ground that 'not to know what happened before you were born is to remain for ever a child'.[3]

---

[1] See H. M. Hubbell, *The Influence of Isocrates on Cicero, Dionysius and Aristides* and, by the same author, 'Isocrates and the Epicureans'.

[2] *Orator* 12-17. See also the objections of Scaevola and Antonius in *De Oratore* 1, 35-44 and 80-96.

[3] *Orator* 120. For the practical utility of the knowledge he requires in the orator see ibid. 16-17 and 115-19.

Cicero attached great importance to history; its *exempla* or examples of noble conduct were not only useful to the orator but could also exercise a moral influence upon the reader. He puts in the mouth of his Antonius an uncompromising statement of the laws of history-writing in the *De Oratore* (2, 62 cf. ibid. 36). The historian must tell the truth without fear or favour; his chronology must be clear, he must describe the terrain, the causes of events, men's motives and plans, their actions and their consequences. Cicero is also fully aware of the difference between history and encomium (*Ad Att.* 1, 19, 10). All this is excellent and worthy of Polybius.

Unfortunately for the orator, however, there is extant a letter of his to his friend Lucceius, *Ad Fam.* 5, 12, who wrote a history of the Italian and Civil Wars asking him to write a special monograph on the Catiline conspiracy and Cicero's consulship rather than merely include them in a larger work. In this letter, we are told 'He requests Lucceius to ignore the laws of history, and to set forth his achievements in a more favourable light than is warranted by a rigid regard for the truth. What he in fact demands is that the laws of encomium rather than those of history proper should be applied to the monograph . . .' (D'Alton, p. 519). Once more we have poor Cicero betrayed by his private correspondence!

This harsh verdict, which is only too commonly accepted, s based on two sentences. In the first Cicero says that a special monograph, with the author's attention on one theme and one

To regard Cicero's rhetorical works merely as a protest against the
elaborate technicalities of the professional technicians is, however, an oversimplification. The *De Inventione*, apart from the introductions, consists of
two whole books on the different kinds of cases, issues, and arguments,
and is highly technical. This, as we have seen, is an early work. When he
wrote the *De Oratore*, we are told that 'he was dissatisfied with his first
essay on rhetorical theory as too narrow and immature, and was no longer
content with the mere technical precepts of the rhetoricians'.[1] This was in
55 B.C., and it is true enough that the *De Oratore*, as well as the *Brutus* and
the *Orator*, written a decade later, are much broader in conception and are
largely concerned with matters of principle. But the argument about
maturity is not very convincing when we find that his last two rhetorical
works, the *Partitiones Oratoriae* and the *Topica*, written in 45 and 44
respectively, are just as technical again! The *Partitiones* roughly covers the
whole field, but style is dealt with very briefly and by far the greater part
of the treatise deals again with kinds of cases, issues, and arguments, while
the *Topica* once more, as the title implies, deals with sources of arguments
or *loci*, that is, with *inventio*.[2] At this point we may remember that the

person, will deal with events in a fuller and more elaborate manner, *omnia uberiora atque
ornatoria futura sint*. He then gracefully apologizes for asking Lucceius thus to elaborate his
actions (*ornare mea*), which may not be thought to deserve it. *Ornare* in such a context does
not mean 'to eulogize'. Cicero had complained to Atticus that Atticus' own account of the
consulship was too bald and its only ornament was that it had none, *ornata hoc ipso quod
ornamenta neglexerunt*, as women's best perfume is to have none (*Ad Att.* 2, 1, 1). We know
that Atticus practised the simple style, and Cicero thought his consulship deserved to be
'written up', elaborated in matter and manner. This is the obvious meaning of *ornare*.
   Cicero then goes on to say that, having transgressed the bounds of modesty (*verecundiae*)
this far, he might as well go on to be even more shameless. He repeats his request that Lucceius
should elaborate (*ornare*) his account more than he perhaps feels like doing, and in this (*in eo*)
overlook the laws of writing history, also that, though he has shown he is not the man to be
swayed by friendship (any more than Xenophon's Hercules by pleasure), yet if this friendship
makes him see Cicero's actions in a favourable light, he will not spurn this but give in to this
friendship 'a wee bit more' (*plusculum*, a colloquial word, and a humorous one) than strict
truth would allow. If interpreted too seriously, this is damning, but it is not meant too seriously,
as the word *plusculum* should warn us. Cicero is *not* asking for an encomium, he is certainly
not asking Lucceius to falsify the facts, he is rather thinking of the interpretation of them. It is
no more than saying: 'I know you will not be swayed from the path of truth by our friendship,
but be just a bit easy on me.' There is nothing very shameful in that. The best account of the
passage is that of A. M. Guillemin in *REL* 16 (1938), 96 ff. She also points out that to ask to
secure immortality in someone's writings was a compliment to the writer, that the whole
tone is urbane, and that Cicero's letter was carefully written, meant to be read by others, and
therefore not likely to contain a request which would make Cicero look ridiculous. See also
B. L. Ullman in *TAPA* 73 (1942), 44-45.
   [1] J. F. D'Alton, p. 149.
   [2] The aim of the *Topica* is somewhat puzzling because at first sight it 'professes to be a
translation or adaptation of the *Topics* of Aristotle ... but it bears little resemblance to this
treatise' (Hubbell in Loeb edition, p. 377). If we look carefully at what Cicero actually says in
the introduction, the puzzle, I believe, explains itself. It is written at the request of Trebatius,
who, in browsing through Cicero's library had found a copy of Aristotle's *Topics*, and

unknown author of the *Ad Herennium* also begins by expressing contempt for the technicalities of Greek writers and then becomes highly technical himself. We find Quintilian doing much the same thing, and we may be tempted to conclude that, however impatient the Romans were with the Greek technicians, they were quite unable to shake off their influence.

This is true, but in Cicero's case the explanation is inadequate, for he does shake off the technicians in his three great central works. We may then notice that all his more technical works deal in great detail with the discovery of arguments or with their arrangement, with *inventio* and *dispositio*, but that, with one exception, he nowhere deals with matters of style in any technical detail. The exception is the discussion of prose-rhythm at the end of the *Orator* and for this there are special reasons since, as we shall see, he is defending himself. The truth seems to be that Cicero the lawyer had patience in plenty to deal with the technicalities of his trade as any good lawyer must have, but that Cicero the orator and stylist had very little patience indeed for technicalities of style. In the third book of the *De Oratore*, for example, Crassus is supposed to deal with style exclusively but he deals at great length with the relation of oratory to philosophy; even when he is dealing with style itself, he prefers to discuss general principles; when he must deal with specific technical points such as figures of thought and speech, he reels off a long list of them without illustration or explanation[1] as if to say: 'All this you know as well as I do.' It is particularly when dealing with matters of style that Cicero, here and elsewhere, expresses his contempt for the technicians.

That Cicero's technical works to a very large extent merely reproduce the theories of Hellenistic writers is obvious; in the *De Inventione* he takes, with youthful zest, any opportunity to criticize Hermagoras,[2] but he is

immediately asked Cicero to explain it. 'And when I had explained the meaning of the book to you, that the method of finding arguments (*disciplinam inveniendorum argumentorum*), so that we should attain them without error and by a rational system, was discovered by Aristotle and contained in these books, you, modestly as always but as I could see with great eagerness, requested that I should discuss these things (*illa*) with you.' They had, that is, already discussed the *Topics* of Aristotle to some extent, and the further request was not so much for a discussion of that book, as of the whole subject. The *illa* refers to the whole subject – *disciplina inveniendorum argumentorum* – or, specifically, *argumenta*. Cicero is on a voyage to Greece and has no books with him. As always, his debt to Aristotle does not consist of specific details but of general principles, and he proceeds to classify topics in his own way without further reference to Aristotle. Trebatius' request then was for a general discussion rather than for an explanation or commentary on Aristotle's book. As Hubbell translates: 'you begged me to teach you the subject'.

[1] *De Oratore* 3, 202-8; cf. *Orator* 136-9.
[2] *De Inv.* 1, 8 where he criticizes Hermagoras for assigning general questions (θέσεις) to the orator whereas they are matters for philosophers (though Cicero himself adopts Hermagoras' view in later works, e.g., *De Orat.* 3, 106-7 and 120, and *Orator* 125). He also criticizes Hermagoras for making the main division of kinds of oratory a mere subdivision of *constitutio generalis* (*De Inv.* 1, 12).

obviously heavily dependent upon the works of that rhetorician. In the last chapter of the *Partitiones* he tells his son that he has explained to him all the divisions of oratory which originated in the Academy, and the *Topica* begins by acknowledging his debt to Aristotle. Throughout his other works he often mentions Greek sources and makes little claim to originality. Scholars have assumed that his plea for a wider education which should combine rhetoric and philosophy is also directly derived from some one Hellenistic source. It obviously does not reflect the attitude of a rhetorical school; it is not Stoic or Epicurean, nor have we any reason to call it Peripatetic. On the other hand Cicero frequently acknowledges his debt to the Academy, and the suggestion has been made repeatedly that he must be reflecting the views of the contemporary Academy, and in particular those of Philo of Larissa or Antiochus of Ascalon.[1] That Cicero's philosophical eclecticism largely derives from the Academy is generally recognized (indeed he tells us so himself); and Philo, then head of the Academy, taught both rhetoric and philosophy,[2] but we have no evidence at all that he held any such view of the education of the orator as Cicero does, or indeed that he discussed the subject. The same is true of Antiochus.

It was natural enough for a philosophical school which wanted to attract Roman students to add some courses on rhetoric to its curriculum, but it seems extremely unlikely that *any* school of philosophy should thus subordinate philosophy to rhetoric, extol practical education at the expense of the contemplative, or admit that its teaching must be supplemented by purely rhetorical studies. What Cicero is advising is very much the kind of education he had himself received, very much the education of Roman gentlemen in the late second and early first century, though more exacting. It is Roman rather than Greek, and it seems both natural and probable that it was Cicero who first gave it theoretical expression. If so, he was not restoring a Classical tradition but creating one; he has some claim to be called the father of Classical humanism, and he created it very largely by combining the Isocratean ideal of education with the Aristotelian requirements for competence in oratory. Here too he failed, and the divorce between rhetoric and philosophy continued; with the development of the practice of declamation it went in fact from bad to worse. In actual practice, however, the educated Romans of the Augustan age did combine their rhetorical training with literary and philosophical interests, though the philosophy was more Stoic than Academic. Cicero, very quick-witted himself, no doubt underestimated the difficulties; it is

---

[1] H. von Arnim, *Dio von Prusa* 97-114; Wilamowitz in *Hermes* 35 (1900), 43, n. 2; Kroll in *Rh.M.* 58 (1903), 552-97; H.K. Schulte, *Orator* 111-12; but see Solmsen in *CP* 33 (1938), 399.
[2] Cicero, *Tusc. Disp.* 2, 3 (9).

not true that 'what you cannot learn quickly you will never learn at all'.[1]

Training in oratory, as Cicero conceived it, covered the art of self-expression in all its genres, for the orator had to use the techniques of them all. He had to learn both style and delivery, and master the ways of arousing the emotions of his audience as well. Indeed, oratory was to Cicero the most difficult of all genres, so that great orators were fewer than artists of any other kind, and he enlarges on 'the incredible magnitude' of the task (De Oratore 1, 17):

> He must acquire knowledge of most things, for without it his flow of words is empty of content and ridiculous; he must shape his discourse both by selecting the right words and arranging them; he must have a thorough knowledge of the emotions with which nature has endowed man because the power and purpose of eloquence depend entirely upon his capacity to calm or to excite the minds of his listeners; and to this he must add a certain charm and wit, an erudition worthy of a free man, swiftness and brevity both in challenge and reply combined with subtle charm and purity of language; he must, moreover, understand the past and the force of example which it provides; he cannot neglect the knowledge of law and jurisprudence. Why say more of delivery? . . . Why speak of memory which treasures all these things?

In passages like this Cicero gives a better defence than anyone else has ever done of the rhetorical education of his day. And, though he and his successors attacked certain aspects of this education, in his case its narrow technical nature, in later writers the artificial nature of school exercises, we have no record of any protest against the basic principle that the art of self-expression was the right and proper main subject of higher education. As described by Cicero, there is a good deal to be said for this education. The art of speech is over-emphasized, yet can anyone deny that the capacity to use one's own language well is, or at least should be, a characteristic of the educated man, or that the man of general culture, the synoptic man, is badly needed in an age of over-specialization, however difficult it may be to produce him? Cicero wanted his orator to be such a man, and he certainly was such a man himself, magnificently.

The list of subjects to be pursued – philosophy, political science, history, law, and rhetoric both Latin and Greek – does not seem, at first sight, to include literary studies. We may be sure that Cicero would have been horrified at any such omission. For him literature is obviously included under rhetoric. When he himself turns to writing on philosophy, he is not

---

[1] De Orat. 3, 90: res quiden se mea sententia sic habet ut nisi quod quisque cito potuerit, numquam omnino possit perdiscere; cf. ibid. 123.

aware that he is inexperienced in this artistic form, though we may note that his best philosophic writings are those where he writes as an advocate, the *De Finibus* for example, where he first puts the case for Stoicism or Epicureanism and follows this up by putting the case against it.

To him the experience of the successful orator included all forms of expression. He probably did not agree with his Antonius who wished to restrict oratory to public speaking in the courts or the assemblies, but he did, one imagines, agree when Antonius said that those other kinds of 'rhetoric' are but child's play for any intelligent man of general culture who has been trained in the battles of the courts.[1] We find the same attitude in an interesting passage of the *Orator* (61-68) where Cicero attempts to explain how the orator differs from the philosopher, the sophist, the historian, and the poet. Many philosophers write very well in their calm, dispassionate way, but they do not have to sway an audience; the sophist in his display speeches can make far greater use of ornamentations and use all devices more openly, and much the same is true of the historian. As for the poet, the difference no longer lies in the rhythm since orators now also use rhythm, but the poet is to be commended in that '*he seeks to attain the virtues of the orator while limited by the verse-form*' (67); and the poet can also use ornaments such as metaphors and archaisms more freely (cf. 201-2). Essentially, however, the orator has been trained to do all that these other kinds of writers do, and to sway the crowd besides.

Certainly the study of literature is included in the Ciceronian curriculum, but the rhetorical purpose of its inclusion and the rhetorical slant given to its study were potentially dangerous to literature itself and to literary criticism as well; Roman literature did in fact become more and more rhetorical. Thus literature was subordinated to the purposes of one particular literary kind.

We should recognize, however, that oratory is an important form of literature, though we need not agree with Cicero that it is the highest form. We shall then more fully recognize that many of the rhetorical formulae which he employs can be applied beyond the field of rhetoric. Take for example the most general formula of the five parts of rhetoric: invention, disposition, style, delivery, and memory.[2] The last is sometimes omitted because it is a factor in all arts, crafts, and sciences; it is perhaps more needed in oral speech though no literary genre can really do without it. As for delivery, we no longer expect an author to be able to speak his own work (and that is a pity), but even we are disconcerted if a poet

---

[1] *De Orat.* 2, 72: *omnium ceterarum rerum oratio . . . ludus est homini non hebeti neque inexercitato neque communium litterarum et politioris humanitatis experti.*

[2] This general formula, with minor variations, is used in *De Oratore* 1, 64, 113, 142, 187; 2, 79; *Brutus* 215-16; *Orator* 43-60; *De Optimo* 4-6; *Partitiones* 1-4. Memory is omitted in *Brutus* 110 and *De Oratore* 1, 213.

cannot give a reading of his own poetry. This is because we know that rhythm is an important element in poetry, but the ancients knew what we are apt to forget, that rhythm is also an important element in literary prose. Cicero would have considered a writer who was unaware of his own rhythms as thoroughly uneducated in the art of language, and he would have been right. This is not to say that rhythm should be studied by all writers in minute detail as the ancients advocated, but quite obviously it should be an important element in the study and criticism of any literary genre. The reader does not need to know how effects are obtained but, as Cicero said, it is the business of the critic to know it.[1]

Inventio, or considering what to say, obviously applies to all kinds of literature, and *iudicium*, to select from what can be said what should be said on the particular occasion, is sometimes added as a separate heading.[2] The discussions of this part of the formula, however, were more strictly rhetorical because they concerned themselves specifically with the analysis of issues and arguments in judicial cases and, to a much lesser extent, in deliberative and epideictic rhetoric. On this subject Cicero could be very technical indeed.

Cicero prefers to discuss the style of individuals rather than style in the abstract. In the *Brutus* he gives us brief estimates of his predecessors in oratory; sometimes contemporary pairs such as Crassus and Antonius are contrasted with each other. These estimates embody various rhetorical formulae: not only the general formula we are discussing but also others such as the qualities or virtues of style, the three styles, and the three duties of the orator, namely to instruct, to please, and to arouse the emotions.

When using the formulae, Cicero is extremely careless in his terminology. This is usually attributed to the speed with which he wrote or to the fact that he was following different authorities at different times. We know that he wrote his philosophical and rhetorical works very fast; they were largely a drug to make him forget the emptiness of his life when public affairs were denied to him. Yet his rhetorical works were carefully planned and executed,[3] and the extent to which he was merely translating has probably been exaggerated. He changes his terms and varies his formulae not so much because he is careless, but rather because he is interested in ideas rather than in precise terminology and uses whatever words or formula best express his meaning at the particular moment.

The customary *officia*, duties, of the orator are three: *docere* to instruct, *delectare* to entertain, and *movere* to stir the emotions (e.g., *Brutus* 185-200).

---

[1] *Brutus* 187.

[2] *Orator* 44: *invenire et iudicare*, and cf. *Topica* 6.

[3] He himself was still highly pleased with the *De Oratore* ten years later. See *Ad Atticum*, 13, 19, 4: *sunt etiam de oratore nostri tres, mihi vehementer probati*. Rackham points out that this is very different from the way he spoke of his philosophical works (Loeb transl. vol. 1, pp. ix-x).

The terms may change, and in *De Oratore* 2, 114 and 121 we have *probare, conciliare, flectere*, which is not quite equivalent, for to conciliate is not the same as to entertain.[1] The order may be changed (ibid. 129) and sometimes Cicero uses two terms instead of three, namely *docere* and *movere*, but these are called *laudes*, good qualities, not *officia*. A truly startling change, however, occurs in *De Oratore* 1, 130 where the three duties are said to be *decere, movere, delectare*, i.e., to speak appropriately, to stir, and to delight. This variation seems to be unique, as *decere* usually belongs to the formula of the qualities or virtues of style, where it frequently recurs. These virtues are usually four: correctness of language (*Latine*), clarity (*dilucide*), appropriateness (*apte*), and adornment (*ornate*).[2]

But this very list of virtues, called *laudes* or *virtutes*, or indeed *ornamenta*, may change (*Partit.* 19-21); other qualities such as brevity, vividness, *hilaritas*, or even *significatio* (= ἔμφασις, to mean more than you say) may be substituted, as in *Orator* 139; or the list may have five virtues instead of four.[3] At the beginning of the *De Optimo Genere Oratorum* Cicero maintains that it is a mistake to speak of genres of oratory, *genera oratorum*, as there are genres of poetry (tragedy, comedy, epic, etc.), for the only *genera* in oratory are the plain, the grand, and the intermediate, a formula which may tell us something about individuals, but very little about the art of oratory (*de re*). This seems to completely confuse the theory of genres (forensic, deliberative, etc.) with the quite different formula of styles which Cicero usually calls *genera dicendi*, and of which he himself makes considerable use elsewhere (*Orator* 20-21; 69; 75-99) in theoretical discussion. The reason is that in the *De Optimo* he is concerned to show that there is only one best way to speak at a particular time on a particular subject in a particular kind of speech or in a particular part of a speech. So he discards both formulae, taking them as one, or rather he rejects *genera* in both senses at once: *oratorem genere non divido, perfectum enim*

---

[1] Alain Michel, in *Rhétorique et Philosophie chez Cicéron*, seeks to account for the difference by linking *conciliare* with content and *delectare* with style (p. 155): 'Dans le *De Oratore* Antoine, qui traite des procédés de l'invention, distingue trois devoirs pour l'orateur: *probare, conciliare, movere*. Le mot *delectare* en revanche n'est employé qu'à propos de la *dictio*.' We may note in passing that *dictio* in Cicero usually refers to diction, i.e., choice of words, rather than to style as a whole, which is *elocutio*. It is quite true that Antonius is supposed to deal with subject-matter, but a good many of his remarks are of a general kind, and the generality of this one is not qualified in any way: *ita omnis ratio dicendi tribus ad persuadendum rebus est nixa: ut probemus vera esse quae defendimus, ut conciliemus eos nobis, qui audiunt; ut animos eorum ad quemcumque causa postulabit motum vocemus.* I do not believe that Michel's linking of *conciliare* exclusively with *inventio* and *delectare* with style can be maintained.

[2] As, for example, in *Orator* 79, the passage often used as evidence for a formula of four virtues of style in Theophrastus. See *TAPA* 83 (1952), 180-1.

[3] For differing forms of this formula see also *De Orat.* 1, 144 and 229; 3, 37; *Partitiones* 19-21. Particular virtues are discussed in *Brutus* 133, 210-14 and 258-62 (*latinitas*), *Orator* 70-74 (*decorum*).

quaero. As for the three-styles formula itself, the styles are called *colores*, *habitus*, and *figurae*, as well as *genera dicendi* in *De Oratore* 3, 199 (the term *colores* at least is surprising). Cicero's probably deliberate carelessness in the use of technical terms does make the use of his text to reconstruct the precise formulae of his Greek predecessors somewhat hazardous. Impatience with precise technical terminology is not unusual in a man who is mainly interested in ideas.

Cicero not only wants his potential orator to study philosophy; he wants him, as a result of that training, to approach rhetoric itself in a more philosophical manner, and this broader approach is certainly his own in his three major works: the *De Oratore*, the *Brutus*, and the *Orator*. The *De Oratore* is in three books of which the first is largely a debate, set in 91 B.C., between the two outstanding orators of the day, Licinius Crassus and Marcus Antonius, on the nature of oratory and the kind of training it requires. Crassus takes the view which we have seen to be Cicero's, while Antonius takes a narrower view. In the second book Antonius discusses *inventio*, and Crassus deals with style in the third, but a great many general ideas are incidentally discussed. The *Brutus*, which is a history of Roman eloquence given by Cicero himself in conversation with Brutus and Atticus, shows a considerable sense of historical development.[1] As has often been pointed out, this development culminates, at least by implication, in Cicero himself – a view for which the great orator had a good deal of justification. Echoes of contemporary criticism of Ciceronian oratory can be found in both treatises, and his last great work, the *Orator*, is a more open defence of his style and theories. This is in the form of a letter to Brutus. The *Brutus* is largely expository, but the *De Oratore* makes excellent use of the dialogue form to enliven even dry academic discussions.

Such questions as whether rhetoric is or is not an *ars*, one of the perennial problems of ancient rhetoric, often lead to very dull discussions (as, for example, in the second book of Quintilian), but Cicero enlivens the argument by the clash of opinions and personalities. Crassus maintains that it is an art, Antonius, who poses as a self-made orator, denies it. The question is settled by a compromise: rhetoric is not an 'art' in the scientific sense that its rules cover all cases and are infallible, but it is an *ars* – the Greek τέχνη – in the sense that general principles can be established which apply for the most part. One can be an orator without this knowledge, but one cannot be consistently good, as Antonius was, without both knowledge and technical training, and we soon find that Antonius' ignorance of both Greek literature and the craft of oratory was largely

---

[1] See in particular *Brutus* 70–76 and cf. *De Oratore* 2, 92–96, where we also find the idea that every age has its distinctive style; *quid causae ... cur aetates extulerint singulae singula prope genera dicendi* (92).

protective camouflage.[1] The solution was not original; we find it, though differently applied, in Philodemus, and it goes back in Aristotle.[2]

There are, indeed, many Aristotelian echoes, but the Aristotelian influence is felt even more in the general, more philosophical approach to rhetoric. Peripatetic influence upon stylistic studies was considerable, but after Aristotle we know of no one before Cicero who so clearly insisted on the need to base the study of commonplaces and arguments upon a study of human psychology.[3] It is therefore significant that, when he uses the old rhetorical formula of the parts or sections of a speech (the number varies betwen four and seven but the formula is essentially the same) he protests that those qualities which can reasonably be said to be characteristic of particular parts – as πάθος, emotional appeal, is of the exordium and the peroration, and persuasiveness of the narrative – should not be restricted to those parts but also belong to the speech as a whole. One should conciliate the audience in one's exordium certainly but one must never lose sight of this aim throughout the discourse. And so with the other qualities.[4]

When Cicero discusses the three styles,[5] he always makes it plain that the perfect orator must be able to use all three wherever suitable and he goes so far as to identify each style with a particular function of the orator. One should instruct (docere) in the plain style, entertain (delectare) in the mean style, and stir the emotions (movere) in the grand style. The greatness of Demosthenes was that he could use every style as the occasion demanded, and Cicero makes the same claim for himself, and with good reason. Nevertheless the grand, copious, passionate rhetoric was his special forte, and to him it is the essential, the true, the supreme rhetoric. He adopts the Aristotelian classification of the means of persuasion as of three kinds: those based on evidence, i.e., factual proof, those due to the impression made by the character of the speaker, and successful appeals to

[1] The question of oratory as an art is raised by Antonius De Orat. 1, 92-93 and further discussed at 109-10, 145-6, taken up again in 2, 28-33 and 232. For Antonius and the untutored orator, see De Orat. 2, 1-6.

[2] For Philodemus see below, and Aristotle Rhet. ad init.

[3] On the whole subject of Cicero's more Aristotelian approach see Solmsen in CP 33 (1938), 390-404 and AJP 62 (1941), 169-90.

[4] Antonius deals with the parts or sections in De Orat. 2, 311-32, and at once emphasizes that various aims apply to all parts, as he already said in 79-82. The parts are also briefly discussed in Orator 122-5; Partitiones 28-60; a very brief mention in Topica 97-98. In the De Invent. 1, 19 we have six and these are the framework of discussion to the end of the book (20-109).

[5] No use is made of the three style formula in the De Oratore, where it is only briefly mentioned by Crassus in 2, 200. In the Brutus 201-2 we have two genera described, the plain and the grand, with the corresponding vices: aridity (inopia et ieiunitas) and flatulence (inflatum et corruptum). In the Orator, and there only, we have the three styles fully described (20-22; 75-99) and they are linked with the three officia oratoris at 69; the use of them emphatically linked with appropriateness in 70-74.

the emotions of the audience. This analysis is based on essential differences in the nature of the means of persuasion and is much more philosophical than endless lists of arguments for any particular occasion in the manner of Hermagoras. Again, there is no evidence that any teacher of rhetoric since Aristotle had adopted it before Cicero.[1] Other Aristotelian echoes occur throughout the rhetorical works: Cicero freely acknowledges his indebtedness and was right to claim that his own views combined the ideas of Isocrates with those of Aristotle.[2] He himself was greatly pleased with his achievement, as he had every right to be.

Ciceronian eloquence, however, did not go unchallenged, and the main opposition came from a group of writers who disliked the copious grandiloquence of his style, which they called 'Asiatic'.[3] They prided themselves on an 'Attic' style, by which they meant the simple style of Lysias. This was the famous Asiatic-Atticist controversy. The composition of the 'Atticist' group is somewhat uncertain: the poet and orator Calvus certainly belonged to it and Brutus' name is clearly linked with his. Tacitus speaks of an exchange of letters between both of them and Cicero[4]:

Clearly, even Cicero had his detractors who thought him swollen and turgid, not succinct enough, far too exuberant and copious, in fact,

---

[1] See Philodemus, *Rhetorica* (Sudhaus, 1, 370): τοῦτο δὲ μόνον (i.e., how to arouse and calm the passions) ὡς οὐ πρόσηκον ἑαυτοῖς οὐκ ἐγχείρησαι τοὺς ῥήτορας ἐκ τῶν Ἀριστοτέλους μετενεγκεῖν and see once more Solmsen in *CP* 33 (1938), 393-402.

[2] Cicero seems to claim originality when (*Ad Fam.* 1, 9, 23) he says that the three books of the *De Oratore*: *abhorrent . . . a communibus praeceptis atque omnium antiquorum et Aristoteliam et Isocratiam rationem oratoriam complectuntur*, i.e., they do not follow the usual precepts but embrace the systems of the ancients, both Aristotelian and Isocratean. The claim to originality seems at first sight much weakened by *De Inventione* 2, 6-8, where Cicero says of the Aristotelian and the Isocratean schools:

> *ex his duabis diversis sicut familiis, quarum altera cum versaretur in philosophia nonnullam rhetoricae quoque artis sibi curam assumebat, altera vero omnis in dicendi erat studio et praeceptione occupata,* unum quoddam est conflatum genus a posterioribus *qui ab utrisque ea quae commode dici videbantur in suas artes contulerunt; quos ipsos simul atque illos superiores nos nobis omnes, quoad facultas tulit, proposuimus et ex nostro quoque nonnihil in commune contulimus.*

But Cicero is not saying more than that later rhetoricians drew upon both the Peripatetic and the Isocratean schools and that their theories derived from both, which is obviously true. He does not here imply, surely, that his own *later* system, which is certainly a conflation of both, must be attributed wholesale to some earlier authority.

[3] Quintilian 12, 10, 12-14, where it is clearly stated that some of his contemporaries called Cicero 'Asiatic' (*tumidum et Asianum et redundantem*). Quintilian then goes on to discuss the Asiatic-Atticist controversy and the three styles, his point of view being the same as Cicero's (cf. 12, 10, 58-72). So Cicero, as we saw, uses the three style formula only in the *Orator* where he is defending his own (see above, pp. 178-9). For the most enlightening discussion of the Atticist-Asiatic controversy see Wilamowitz in *Hermes* 35 (1900), 1-52. For some account of various views see A. Desmouliez in *REL* 30 (1952), 168-85.

[4] Tacitus, *Dialogus* 18. On this correspondence see G. L. Hendrickson in *AJP* 47 (1926), 234-58.

not Attic enough. You have surely read the letters Calvus and Brutus sent to Cicero; from these one can gather easily enough that Cicero considered Calvus bloodless and thin (*exsanguem et attritum*) and Brutus tedious and disjointed (*otiosum atque disiunctum*) while Calvus criticized Cicero as loose and flabby (*solutum et enervem*) and Brutus called him – to quote his own words – 'feeble and emasculated' (*fractum atque elumbem*).

Tacitus' (or rather Aper's) comment is that all three of them were right! Caesar, the champion of pure latinity seems also to have been connected with the Atticist group, so was Asinius Pollio, and Catullus may have been. But the grounds of opposition were diverse. If Calvus was an 'Atticist', Brutus probably was not[1]; the Stoic contempt for style is not the same as the desire for a simple style; the truly plain style is, as Cicero well knew, difficult to achieve (*Orator* 76). Nor is there any necessary connexion between a belief in Analogy (Caesar wrote a book on the subject) and a simple style. Yet in practice all these might find themselves united in opposition to the grand and less precise manner of Cicero.

We can, by implication, follow the progress of the quarrel in Cicero's own works. There is no reference to Atticists in the *De Oratore* and only one purely historical reference to the loss of good taste when Greek oratory spread into Asia (3, 43). But when Crassus comes to deal with the qualities of style, he dismisses the first two, good Latinity and clarity, somewhat superciliously (3, 38): 'We are not trying to teach rhetoric to anyone who cannot speak, nor can we hope that anyone who cannot speak Latin will adorn his speech, or that anyone whose speech we cannot understand can say anything we can admire.' It has been suggested[2] that this cavalier dismissal of both good latinity and of clarity was itself provocative, and indeed that it provoked Caesar to write his *De Analogia*. This work was written shortly afterwards and dedicated to Cicero, as we know from the *Brutus*, where it is described by Atticus (253) as a most careful treatise on good latinity which state that 'the choice of words is the source of eloquence'. It may be in deference to Caesar's views that in the *Brutus* as a whole more attention seems to be paid to good latinity as an important quality in Cicero's judgement of various orators, and it is strongly emphasized in the judgement on Caesar's own style which is put in the mouth of Atticus (252-3 and 258). Thus the courtesies are preserved,

[1] This would seem to follow from the words put into Brutus' mouth by Cicero (*Brutus* 284): 'Our friend Calvus wanted it said that he is an Attic orator; hence that leanness of style which he deliberately cultivated.' Calvus had died shortly before this was written in 46 B.C. For the uncertain composition of the Atticist group see W. Kroll's edition of the *Orator* p. 11 and notes.
[2] See G. L. Hendrickson in *CP* I (1906), 97-120.

as they always were between Caesar and Cicero; the term Asiatic is still used in the *Brutus* in its proper sense, and if the Asiatic style is said to be unwholesome, the celerity and abundance of some Asiatics is 'not to be despised' (51). Indeed Hortensius, the famous orator, an older contemporary of whom Cicero speaks with affection and respect, is said to practise the *genus Asiaticum* (325). This is divided into two kinds: one style which is given to short, sharp, epigrammatic clauses (*sententiae*), balanced and charming rather than dignified, while the other kind, 'now current all over Asia', is rather excited and volatile, abundant, ornate, and flowery in its flow of words. *Hortensius is said to have excelled in both kinds.* True, Cicero says that his vibrant excitement is more suited to youth, so that Hortensius was not as good in his later years, but this is still dispassionate criticism, and Cicero still speaks of 'an admirable flow' in Asiatics.

It was his condescending estimate of Calvus, the leader of the Atticists, who had recently died, which probably embittered the dispute. Calvus, he said, was well-trained in theory and careful in practice but so given to self-criticism and introspection that the very fear of error made him lose all vitality.[1] Cicero then launches his first attack on the self-styled Atticists (284-91): the absence of vices of style is certainly Attic; bombast is certainly to be condemned, but if the polished simplicity of Lysias is Attic, so is Demosthenes, and a great many others. To pick out the simple style as the only Attic style is absurd. Cicero is of course perfectly right; the self-styled Atticists have no exclusive right to the name. But he cannot help adding that their simple style will be precious little use before a popular court; in any case their claim is not new: even Hegesias claimed an Attic style! Much the same attack is repeated in *De Optimo Genere Oratorum* 7-10.[2]

Whatever the cause, the battle must have become heated in this year 46 B.C. – perhaps it was at this point that they called Cicero himself an Asiatic – for in the *Orator* (23-32) the references to the Atticists are more contemptuous and the denunciations of Asianism much more violent.

> We must warn those people whose unskilled speech is so frequently heard, who either want to be called Attic or themselves speak in the Attic manner, that their greatest admiration should be for Demosthenes . . . and that they should measure eloquence by his power rather than by their own weakness.

Demosthenes of course could practise every style, and it is in this context

---

[1] *Brutus* 283: *inquirens in se atque ipse sese observans metuensque ne vitiosum colligeret etiam verum sanguinem deperdebat.* Cf. *exsanguis* in the quotation from Tacitus above.

[2] The *De Optimo Genere Oratorum* is an introduction to a translation of Demosthenes' *On the Crown* and also the speech of Aeschines. It is doubtful whether the translations were ever written. See G. L. Hendrickson in *AJP* 47 (1926), 109-23.

that we have the only full description of the three styles by Cicero. Nor
has he now a good word to say for the Asiatics: 'So Caria and Phrygia
and Mysia, countries without polish or elegance, developed a fatty kind
of diction (*tamquam adipatae dictionis genus*) best suited to their ears. . . .'
How would the Athenians have listened to an orator 'who began to sing-
song (*canere*) in a voice that both sank and shrieked in the Asiatic manner'?
Cicero seems eager to dissociate the Asiatic from the grand manner, so
often his own, and he goes on pouring ridicule upon Atticist pretensions.
Thus far we can follow the Atticist-Asiatic controversy. We shall find
echoes of it in Dionysius a generation later, and even in Quintilian a
century later. The whole *Orator* can be considered from this point of view
as a defence of Ciceronian eloquence against contemporary attacks. Even
the long technical discussion of prose-rhythm is part of that defence – for
the plain style makes no use of rhythm,[1] while the Asiatics used it excessively.

The discussion of rhythm naturally forms part of the treatment of
collocatio, the arrangement of words, which, as always, has three aims: the
harmony of sound which should result from the juxtaposition of words,
the shape and structure of the sentence attained through the interrelation
of clauses, and the rhythm. The first two are dealt with first (149-67). The
sentence-structure must not be over-elaborate or the result of obvious
effort; as for sound, though Latin will allow *hiatus* it tends to contraction
and elision; we must be guided by custom rather than rules in the use of
unusual forms (an implied criticism of the Analogists); in all matters of
sound the ear is the best judge (159). Returning to structure, Cicero considers that the words themselves often dictate it 'either spontaneously,
because of the antithesis between component parts, or from the use of
words that are naturally symmetrical in form, and so spontaneous
rhythms often arise'. He then passes to rhythm proper (168-234) and
claims to deal with the subject more fully than anyone had done before
(226).

Cicero felt strongly on the subject of prose-rhythm; conscious rhythm,
especially at the beginning and end of clauses, was a recent import into
Latin prose (171), 'though it has won approval among the Greeks for
nearly four hundred years' (that is, ever since Gorgias). In Latin, it was
largely developed by Cicero himself. Here he was opposed not only by
the Atticists who no doubt considered it a feature of Asianism (which, if
exaggerated, it was) but also by those literary patriots and reactionaries
who wanted the old Roman writers, rather than the Greeks, to be the

[1] *Orator* 77. He makes a final attack, in the same contemptuous tone at 234-6, and it is also
significant that at the very end (237) he implies pretty clearly that he does not expect Brutus
to agree with him. But then Brutus' style was not distinguished.

models of their contemporaries. Cicero maintains that the 'ancients' would have used it if they had known it – 'if Ennius could despise what was old in his day . . . why should not I?' Deliberate archaizing is surely absurd.

> As for those who are not aware of rhythm in a well balanced period, I do not know what kind of ears they have, or indeed what is human about them! My ears certainly rejoice in a full, well finished period, resent what is truncated, and dislike what is redundant. Why do I say *my* ears? I have often seen the crowd exclaim when the words fell into a balanced rhythm. For the ear expects the words and the sense to march together (168).

That the Roman crowds had cheered Cicero to the echoes there is no doubt, but it is hard to believe that his rhythms were the main reason for their cheering, though it may well have been a contributory if unconscious factor. Certainly, later critics ridiculed some of his favourite rhythmical endings, like the famous *esse videatur*.[1]

He briefly reviews the critical history of prose-rhythm to convince his opponents by the weight of authority. Like Aristotle and every critic since, he emphasizes that metre must be avoided in prose, but rhythm there must be (188). Like all ancient critics he analyses prose-rhythm by reducing it to metrical feet, a quite unsatisfactory process except at the beginning or end of a clause. He recognizes, however, that prose-rhythm can only approximate metre and must not have frequently recurrent metrical patterns. His theory is not without flaws and even inconsistencies. He adopts the Aristotelian classification of metrical feet by time (188, cf. *Rhet.* 3, 8; 1409 a 3) which differentiates them by the time-ratio between two parts of one foot, either 1 to 1 (spondee, dactyl), 2 to 1 (iambus, trochee), or 3 to 2 (paeon). This leads him to blame Ephorus for not seeing that dactyls and spondees are equivalent, which they obviously are not, even on his own premisses. He first says (194) that it is better to end a clause with long rather than short syllables, and therefore rejects the tribach, but then later says that it makes no difference whether the last syllable is long or short (214 and 217), the short being lengthened anyway. Quintilian is more subtle here, for he sees that there is still a difference.[2] Yet Cicero does display some independence, for he does not endorse Aristotle's predilection for the paeon, but prefers the dichoreus (i.e., $-\cup-\cup$, choreus being Cicero's name for the trochee) or the cretic, feet for

---

[1] See Tacitus, *Dialogus* 23; Quint. 10, 2, 18.

[2] Quintilian (9, 4, 93-94) says that, although a concluding short syllable is considered to be equivalent to a long one, there is in fact a real difference between the two: *aures tamen consulens meas intelligo multum referre verene longa sit quae cludit, an pro longa*, and he quotes *dicere incipientem terrere* as in fact less full (*plenum*) than *ausus est confiteri*.

which the classical Greek critics showed no great liking,[1] but at the same time condemns their excessive use by the Asiatics (212–13).

The rhythm must follow the balance and structure of the sentence without obvious effort; it must not, therefore, be obtained at the cost of an unnatural order of words or of padding with *inania verba*, as in Hegesias (226). There must be no monotonous repetitions of the same concluding rhythms, as in Hierocles and Menecles (231). This emphasis on the difference between his own practice and that of the Asiatics is significant. Moreover, epideictic rhetoric can naturally make a much freer use of rhythm than forensic or political rhetoric, where it should be used very sparingly until you are master of your audience (210).

There are weaknesses in this theoretical exposition; one may feel that it does not give enough weight to the differences between the Latin language and the Greek, and that Cicero is more independent in practice than in theory, but it was probably the first theoretical exposition of prose-rhythm in Latin and Cicero obviously attaches great importance to this aspect of his style. His general principles are sound enough and he was trying to educate his compatriots who were much less sensitive than the Greeks in this respect. The excessive use of rhythmic *clausulae* in later authors can hardly be blamed on Cicero.

Rhythmical prose was characteristic of the grand, passionate style, and it is the grand style he is defending in his last and most bitter attack upon the Atticists at the end of the *Orator*:

No one who could speak in this manner has ever been unwilling to do so; those who speak differently are unable to speak like this. And so they became Atticists, as if Demosthenes was an Asiatic.[2]

Cicero is no believer in esoteric art. For him the crowd is the only judge of an orator's capacity,[3] and we feel him yearning for the days of his own oratorical glory when he describes the reactions of the crowd when the great orator speaks.[4]

Aristotle had said that the poet should feel the emotions he is trying to communicate; so Cicero insists that the orator must do likewise, indeed it

[1] Bornecque, *Les Clausules métriques* p. 26 points out that these feet were affected by the Asiatics. He suggests that Aristotle was probably Cicero's main authority up to section 206, that for the later part of the discussion Cicero chiefly relied on Asiatic sources and his own experience, and that this may account for some contradictions. See also P. Wuilleumier in *REL* 7 (1929), 170–80.

[2] *Orator* 234. What Cicero actually says is: *quasi vero Trallianus fuerit Demosthenes*, i.e. 'as if Demosthenes was a Trallian'. Tralles was a city in Caria, and the home of certain Asiatic orators.

[3] *Brutus* 184–9.

[4] *Brutus* 290.

is inevitable that he should do so: 'the listener will never be set on fire unless there is fire in the words that reach him',[1] and we can readily see that the delivery of one of his great, passionate orations was for him as exhausting an emotional experience as the performance of a great actor. Small wonder that the peroration was always entrusted to him.[2]

In one respect, however, he attacks the Atticists on their own ground. Wit and humour were particularly suited to the simple style. Indeed Attic wit was famous, but not one of them shows any talent in this direction – unworthy 'Attics' as they are.[3] Cicero himself had a great reputation as a wit and made free use of witticisms in his speeches, but he only once discusses the subject at any length, as a kind of digression in the middle of Antonius' discussion of *inventio*, in the second book of the *De Oratore* (2, 216-90). There we do have a substantial treatment of wit and its proper use by orators, put in the mouth of Julius Caesar Strabo, who had made a study of the subject. It is worth noting that Strabo states categorically that he had found no worthwhile discussion of the subject of laughter by any Greek writer, only collections of jokes. Those who had tried to discuss the subject methodically failed utterly.[4] This should prevent us from looking for any *one* source which Cicero is allegedly reproducing here; it also should be sufficient proof that he did *not* have before him any treatise on laughter by Aristotle (such as the lost second book of the *Poetics*) or Theophrastus, for he would never have dismissed a work of either so contemptuously, any more than a work of Panaetius the Stoic, whom he highly respected, or of Philo of Larissa for that matter.

As usual, significant ideas or general distinctions are discussed first – and then we get a rather casual list of types of jests which is probably derived from those Hellenistic works, but the illustrations of each kind are taken from Roman orators.

Strabo begins by making an interesting distinction between a humorous or sarcastic tone which pervades all one says on a particular occasion, and witticisms proper, which are sudden, sharp, and brief. The former is here called *cavillatio* and the examples given from Crassus (223-6) seem to be of prolonged sarcasm, though a milder kind of irony is also included (227) under this heading. Short, sharp wit, on the other hand, is *dicacitas*. The same distinction is also made in the *Orator*.[5] It has something of the dis-

---

[1] *Orator* 132, cf. *De Oratore* 2, 189-96.

[2] *Orator* 130.

[3] *Orator* 89-90. On the whole subject see Mary A. Grant, *The Ancient Rhetorical Theories of the Laughable*, A. Haury, *L'ironie et l'humour chez Cicéron*.

[4] *De Oratore* 2, 217: *itaque cum quosdam Graecos inscriptos libros esse vidissem de ridiculis, non nullam in spem veneram posse me ex eis aliquid discere; inveni autem ridicula et salsa multa Graecorum . . . sed qui eius rei rationem quandam conati sunt artemque tradere, sic insulsi exstiterunt, ut nihil aliud eorum nisi ipsa insulsitas rideatur. . . .*

[5] *Orator* 87, but the terminology is different. In the *De Oratore*, *facetiae* and *iocus* are the

tinction between humour and wit in English, except that the pervasive *cavillatio* includes much more than humour.[1] The difficulty of the subject is emphasized, and Strabo says there can be no *ars* of it, while Antonius (who, we remember, had maintained earlier that there was no *ars* of rhetoric either) suggests that general rules may be discovered which are sufficient to give some guidance.

One such rule is when *not* to make a joke, for nothing is harder for a wit than to refrain from making a sally he has thought of (221). This avoidance of the unseemly is also emphasized in the *Orator* (88), where we are told that the orator must not make too many jokes lest he appear a buffoon; he must avoid jokes that are improper or angry, he must not laugh at misfortunes, at crime, at himself, or the judges, or on the wrong occasion, for all this is inappropriate (*indecorum*). The avoidance of the cruel or improper joke, the difference between wit and buffoonery can be traced back to Aristotle.[2] Carefully prepared witticisms brought from home are much less effective than those which spontaneously come to mind under provocation.[3]

Strabo now (235) proceeds methodically and announces five headings: the nature of the joke; what causes it; whether the orator should provoke it; how far he should do so; and what its different kinds are. The first he dismisses as not germane to his subject and proceeds to the second: what makes people laugh? People laugh, we are told, at ugliness or deformity,[4] but only if these are not very serious: one does not laugh at criminals, for one hates them; nor does one laugh at real misery, for one pities it (238). This is obviously reminiscent of Aristotle's comic flaw, and looks back beyond him to Plato.

generic terms for all kinds of wit (2, 216), which is then divided into *cavillatio* and *dicacitas*. This last term retains the same meaning in the *Orator*, but *cavillatio* is replaced by *facetiae*, and the generic term is *sales*.

[1] It is so translated by H. M. Hubbell in the *Orator* (Loeb edition) with 'pleasantry' as the generic term. Rackham in the *De Oratore* speaks of two kinds of wit, 'irony' being the pervasive and 'raillery' the sharper kind. It is impossible to find exact equivalents.

[2] See *Ethics* 4, 8 (1128 a) and *Rhet.* 3, 18, 7 (1419 b 3, where a brief reference to γελοῖον occurs in the discussion of the third part of the speech, the proof). There is a striking phrase in *Rhet.* 2, 12, 16 (1389 b 10) where εὐτραπελία is said to be πεπαιδευμένη ὕβρις. The same distinction between right and wrong jesting is made in Cicero's *De Officiis* 1, 103-4, where the right type of jest is said to be *elegans, urbanum, ingeniosum, facetum*, while the joke to be avoided *illiberale, petulans, flagitiosum, obscaenum*. The right joke is also made at the right time and *remisso animo*, i.e., without heat. So the author of the *Ad Herennium* discusses the jest under delivery 3, 13, 23; it belongs to the *sermo*, i.e., is to be spoken in a conversational, not a passionate tone. We now see more clearly why Cicero considers wit to belong mainly to the simple style.

[3] *De Oratore* 2, 230 and *Orator* 89.

[4] 236: *turpitudine et deformitate*; *turpitudo* seems a translation of αἰσχρός, which means both ugly and shameful, and thus refers to both moral and physical ugliness, and *deformitas* is put in to express the latter. On this whole section cf. Aristotle's definition of comedy in *Poetics* ch. 5 and what Plato said in *Philebus* 48 a ff.

We can agree with Cicero that the orator will use laughter, that he will do so either to secure the goodwill of his audience, or their admiration of his wit or clever repartee, the impression made by an orator being, as we know, an important factor in his success. Witticisms may also be used to embarrass the opponent, to lighten the severe or gloomy atmosphere, or indeed to gloss over a point made by the other side. In some of this at least Cicero is expressing ideas which were generally accepted, for in the *Ad Herennium* we find the comic discussed under the exordium, as a form of *insinuatio* or 'subtle approach',[1] and it is said to be used in three ways: (*a*) when one has a bad case (much what Cicero means by glossing over an argument that cannot be disproved), (*b*) when the audience has already been convinced by one's opponent, and (*c*) when the judges are tired out by previous speeches. We note again that Cicero is not tied down by the parts-of-a-speech formula, that his discussion is more general, more thorough, and more interesting.

As to how far the orator should go in his jesting, we have already seen that some subjects such as extreme ugliness are not proper topics for laughter; the good orator will avoid all that is unseemly or inappropriate to the occasion, to the feelings of the audience, or his own (cf. *Orator* 88). He must not be funny to excess. It is all a matter of taste. The most important thing, several times repeated, is to know what jokes not to make.[2]

In proceeding at this point to give a number of examples of different kinds of jokes, Strabo begins by distinguishing between jokes of substance (*in re*) and verbal wit (*in verbo*),[3] though the best are of both kinds at once (248). We first have examples of the two most obvious kinds of substantive jests: the funny story or anecdote, and mimicry or caricature (*depravata imitatio*, 242), but the orator must be particularly careful, he must suggest rather than act out his imitation. All this requires a most delicate touch; in fact the very same words can be serious or witty in intention according to circumstances (248), which is often the point.

Seven kinds of verbal wit are noted (253-63): ambiguity, the unexpected, the play on words, the clever quotation, taking literally what is not so meant, the figurative or inverted meaning (by allegory, metaphor,

---

[1] Caplan's translation of *insinuatio* in his Loeb edition. The reference is to *Ad Herennium* I, 9-10.

[2] See *De Oratore* 2, 237-9, 242, 244, 251-2, *Orator* 88, *De Officiis* I, 103-4.

[3] The same distinction is made in the *Tractatus Coislinianus*, but there are few parallels between the subheads in the *Tractatus* and in Cicero (see above, p. 143). It is interesting to note that this distinction, however, is not made in the *Ad Herennium*, though there is, as one might expect, some correspondence between its types of jest and Cicero's. It is, however, not very close. Cicero gives about seven kinds of jokes *in verbo* and thirteen *in re*, a total of twenty. The *Ad Herennium* has seventeen kinds, undifferentiated, ten of which roughly correspond to types cited by Cicero, though several of the terms differ. Inevitably, one or two, like the *praeter expectationem* (παρὰ προσδοκίαν) occur in all three lists.

or irony), and the verbal contradiction. Jests of substance are, we are told, generally funnier, and of these we find about twenty species,[1] of which some are common enough, like the witty anecdote, understatement or overstatement, while others seem more like an attempt to describe a particular witticism that has come to mind. However, many more kinds could apparently be dug up from the Greek textbooks (288).

> A good many other kinds are collected by the Greeks, but I think I've described too many kinds already – for those which are expressed by the force and sense of a word are definite and limited in number, and these, as I said before, are admired rather than laughed at. As for those witticisms that concern the matter and sense, one can classify them *ad infinitum* but they fall into a few main kinds: deceiving of expectation, ridiculing other people's character, and pointing to the ridiculous in one's own; pointing to a likeness to the more unseemly; being ironical; saying something slightly absurd, and criticizing folly – all this provokes laughter. So the man who wants to speak wittily must be, as it were, suited by nature and manners to these kinds of jests so that his very features can be adapted to every kind of jesting. Indeed, the more austere and morose his expression, the more witty his jokes usually seem.

This fairly lengthy discussion of the comic is the more important in that it is the only full treatment of the subject we possess before Quintilian. This is no doubt accidental and yet the definite statement at the beginning that there are no Greek sources which do more than list jokes under different headings would seem to indicate that notable discussions of the comic were at least very rare. Cicero gives us an adequate but not very

---

[1] The complete list seems to be as follows: (i) *narratio*, the funny story or anecdote; (ii) *ex similitudine*, a comparison or caricature; (iii) *minuendi aut augendi causa*, understatement or overstatement; (iv) an obscure meaning clarified by some hint or word: Cornelius, an excelsent military commander but a financially corrupt man, thanked Fabricius for securing his election as consul in war-time. 'There's nothing to thank me for,' answered Fabricius, 'if I'd rather be plundered than sold into slavery'; (v) *dissimulatio* or irony; (vi) calling a bad thing by a good name, which is akin to irony; (vii) *subabsurdum*, saying something ridiculous, or apparently absurd; (viii) pretending not to understand: when asked his opinion of a certain man who had been caught in adultery, Pontidius said, 'He is slow'; (ix) to turn the jest against the jester; (x) suggestion of a joke, but obscure: a friend was lamenting that his wife had hanged herself from his fig tree, the other said, 'I'd be grateful for some cuttings from that tree'; (xi) bad-tempered jests spoken suavely; (xii) the patient jest: a man carrying a box bumped into Cato, then shouted 'Look out!' 'Why', said Cato, 'are you carrying something else?' (xiii) a neat witty reproof: a man who was assigned a well-known but stupid counsel said to the praetor, 'Please assign him to my opponent, then I shan't need any'; (xiv) to give a full explanation which does not fit the occasion; (xv) *discrepantia*, inconsequence: 'This man lacks nothing – except money and honesty'; (xvi) the unexpected turn – *praeter expectationem*; (xvii) seeming to yield a point without actually doing so; (xviii) wishing for the impossible; (xix) giving an answer that is not wanted.

profound discussion, and he does try to rise above mere technicalities. The passage of the *De Oratore* does not link wit with any particular style, but the *Orator*, as we saw, links it with the simple style. This does not mean that it was to be entirely avoided in the intermediate or even the grand style but more care would there have to be exercised to avoid the cruel and the scurrilous. In fact Cicero himself used witticisms freely and he has often been accused of not living up to his own advice.

In evaluating the rhetorical works of Cicero, a sharp distinction must be drawn between his general treatises and his more technical studies: the *De Inventione*, the *Topica* and the *Partitiones Oratoriae*. The *De Inventione* was written in early youth when he apparently intended to cover the whole field of rhetoric in this manner, a task he never completed. We have seen that, even at that early age, he clearly formulated certain general principles which he was to follow consistently. The other two technical works were written at the end of his life. He was then being eagerly consulted in his retirement by young Romans who hoped to become famous orators, and one must suppose that these books were written to provide them with what Cicero considered the minimum technical equipment for the understanding and practice of argumentation in the courts. All three works are mainly of interest to the historian of professional rhetoric and courtroom practice, and certainly a lawyer could still find much in them to interest him, but they contribute little to the history of literature or criticism, or to the more general questions and controversies of his own time.

Between the *De Inventione* and his next work on oratory, the three books of the *De Oratore*, lie the whole thirty years of Cicero's brilliant legal and political career, two aspects of his life that can hardly be separated. And indeed he would not have wished to separate them, for his own point of view was certainly synoptic; any attempt to divorce literature from life, rhetoric from literature, politics from rhetoric, any of these from philosophy and education, would have seemed to him quite artificial and regrettable. To him the highest form of literature was oratory, the orator was the statesman, and the true philosopher should be a combination of all these. That he himself achieved high distinction in each of these fields is undeniable.

Cicero was a Roman. Therefore to him, as to his contemporaries, philosophy meant little except in so far as it brought immediate help in solving practical problems. His philosophical works, superb pieces of popularization as they are, are limited in their scope and understanding. His oratorical works suffer from no such handicap. At the time he wrote the *De Oratore*, the *Brutus*, the *Orator*, he was universally recognized as the greatest Roman orator, and even his enemies attacked him as such. He was also deeply concerned with the education of Roman youth and impatient with the educational methods of his day. To us these works seem at times to go into considerable technical details; they are, in fact, infinitely less technical than any other strictly rhetorical works we possess in either Latin or Greek. It is important to realize this if we are to understand where Cicero is putting his emphasis. The essential question for him is: by what methods can Rome produce men who can express themselves effectively and who will at the same time see the terribly important problems of Roman society in perspective and be able to find the right solutions? It is the combination of this deep and genuine anxiety with his unique experience in the art of language and in affairs of state – it is this combination which breathes life into the dry and analytical formulae which he transmits from the Greeks, and which also enables him to contribute a good deal of his own.[1]

[1] Except for minor alterations, this chapter was first published as an article in *Phoenix* 16 (1962), 234-57, and I thank the editors for permission to reproduce it here.

CHAPTER XII

Philodemus

Excavations at Herculaneum have brought to light, from the middle of the eighteenth century on, a large number of papyrus rolls thought to be manuscripts from the library of Philodemus. A number of these contain works by the philosopher himself, but the rolls were badly damaged by fire and quite illegible in part. Even the best preserved parts are charred at the edges and otherwise damaged so that the text is full of lacunae and can only be restored by filling in gaps by conjecture based on the number of missing letters. These conjectures can at best be only probable restorations. The most relevant works for our purposes are the fifth book of Philodemus' *Poetics*, published by C. Jensen in 1923 and the remains of four books of the *Rhetorica* restored by Sudhaus.[1] These restorations are brilliant, and for the most part generally accepted, though before one builds on them it is always necessary to examine the text carefully to see how much can be regarded as certain. The matter is further complicated by Philodemus' method: he nearly always quotes from earlier critics and then criticizes their views so that his own must be gleaned from incidental comments in the course of the discussion.

He thus throws light on the critical theories held by various writers on poetry and rhetoric during the third and second centuries B.C., but it is a flickering and uncertain light; even when we can be sure whose views he is discussing it is difficult if not impossible, because of the many lacunae, to be sure where the particular discussion begins or ends. Scholars have largely used Philodemus as a source for earlier theories and somewhat neglected his own.[2] Yet his own views are of considerable interest and in

---

[1] *Philodemus über die Gedichte, fünftes buch*, by Christian Jensen, and *Philodemi volumina rhetorica* by Siegfried Sudhaus. For a useful translation of the rhetorical fragments and a discussion of Philodemus' rhetorical theories see H. M. Hubbell, *The Rhetoric of Philodemus*.

[2] For example, Jensen's edition of the fifth book has three substantial appendices: the first discusses the theories of Neoptolemus as reconstructed from Philodemus, the second deals in the same way with the views of Ariston of Chios, and the third with those of Crates of Pergamum, but there is no discussion of Philodemus' own views. (The uncertain nature of the evidence is well illustrated by the fact that an early section in Philodemus which Jensen here takes as dealing with the theories of Neoptolemus he later believed these to originate with Heraclides of Pontus, in *Sitzungsbeichte Pruss. Akad. d. Wiss.* 1936, 292-320.) Atkins, in his *Literary Criticism in Antiquity* says (vol. 2, p. 55) 'herein perhaps lies the real and permanent value of the work (i.e. the *Poetics* of Philodemus); it helps in reconstructing some of the earlier doctrines.'

many ways unique in their opposition to traditional theories. They are hard to establish, for it is usually easier to be sure of what he rejects. Yet a careful study of the fragments, particularly of the fifth book on poetry and the rhetorical works, does reveal theories of poetry and of prose literature which we find nowhere else, even though our knowledge of them must, because of the nature of the evidence, remain frustrating in its incompleteness.[1]

Philodemus was both a philosopher and a poet, the author of many treatises on philosophy from the Epicurean point of view and of light erotic and somewhat improper verse. Some of his epigrams are preserved in the Greek anthology,[2] and he was well known in Rome as a poet, indeed he seems to have had some influence on the Augustans.[3] Born in Gadara in 110 B.C., he studied in Athens under Zeno of Sidon, whose lectures Cicero attended when in Athens, in 79-78 B.C. Cicero says that Zeno was, for an Epicurean, an unusually good writer, and Philodemus obviously shared with his teacher a lively interest in literature which was quite unusual among Epicureans. It is from Zeno, as he tells us himself, that he derived the theory that epideictic rhetoric was an art, and this view was attacked by other members of the school. Indeed Philodemus' first work on the subject, the *Hypomnêmatikon*, which was published anonymously, was thought to be Zeno's and attacked as such, notably at Rhodes.[4]

Philodemus established himself in Rome in the household of L. Calpurnius Piso, who was consul in 58 B.C. Cicero knew him as a man of culture and learning,[5] though in his speech against Piso he affects to believe that the Epicurean's philosophy and advice were a bad influence upon his patron. Even there, however, Cicero's personal references to Philodemus are restrained, not to say complimentary, certainly to his poetry if not to himself.[6] It was Piso who presented Philodemus with the villa at Hercu-

[1] The originality of Philodemus' views on poetry has, however, been recognized by L. P. Wilkinson in his article, 'Philodemus and Poetry' and by N. A. Greenberg in an unfortunately unpublished thesis, *The Poetic Theory of Philodemus*, summarized in *HSCP* 1957; also and above all by A. Rostagni in his 'Filodemo contro l'estetica classica', see *Scritti Minori* I 394-446, but Rostagni as usual goes far beyond his evidence.

[2] *Greek Anthology*, ed. W. R. Paton, 5 vols. Most of the epigrams are in books V, X, and XI, vols. 1 and 4.

[3] See J. R. M. Tait's *Philodemus' Influence on the Latin Poets*, Bryn Mawr diss. 1941; G. L. Hendrickson, in *AJP* 39 (1918), 27-41; Alfred Körte, in *Rhein. Mus.* 45 (1890) 172-7.

[4] For this controversy see the fragments in Sudhaus I, 77-120 and Hubbell 277-84. The nature of the argument seems to indicate (as Hubbell points out) that Philodemus was *not* able to find a clear statement in Epicurus or other leaders of the school that sophistic or epideictic rhetoric was a τέχνη. The fragments of the *Hypomnêmatikon* will be found in Sudhaus II, 196-303.

[5] *De Finibus* 2, 35, 119: familiares nostros, credo, Sironem et Philodemum, cum optimos viros, tum homines doctissimos (Torquatus speaking).

In Pisonem 28, 68-70: est quidam Graecus qui cum isto vivit, homo, ut vere dicam – sic

laneum. Virgil was for a while a member of Philodemus' school at
Naples, attracted perhaps by the unusual combination of poetry and
philosophy. Certainly the dual personality of Philodemus as a serious-
minded philosopher and a writer of light verse is relevant to his poetic
theory.

ON POETRY

He repeatedly protests, for example, against requiring a moral and educational purpose from a poet, and his own poetry obviously had none.
Where poetry does teach something, he insists, it is incidentally, and the
quality of the poetry is not affected thereby. Philodemus makes great
play of those who seek a didactic purpose in Homer, and of those who,
while not quite venturing to say that the Homeric poems are not good
poetry declare Homeric poetry great only when interpreted allegorically.[1]
He is here opposing both the widely held Greek view that the poets were
the teachers of men, and also the Stoic habit of allegorical interpretation.

When poetry is not required to teach or benefit the reader, there is
naturally less need for the poet to have a reliable knowledge of life and
nature, or for his poetry to be regarded as an imitation of them. We shall
therefore not be surprised to find Philodemus ridiculing theories which
require all kinds of knowledge from the poet,[2] or any direct relation

enim cognovi – humanus, sed tamdiu quamdiu cum aliis est aut ipse secum . . . est autem is
de quo loquor non philosophia solum, sed etiam ceteris studiis quae fere ceteros Epicureoa
neglegere dicunt, perpolitus. Poema porro facit ita festivum, ita concinnum, ita elegans,
nihil ut fieri possit argutius. Philodemus is not actually named in the passage, but the identification made by Asconius has never been doubted, indeed it is obvious.

[1] In the following notes the references will be given, for the fifth book of the περὶ
ποιημάτων as J. followed by a number meaning the page or pages in Jensen's edition. Where
the exact reference is required the column numbers will be added, and the line number, both in
brackets. For the opposition to views which require poetry to teach or benefit see J. 5-11; 33
(XIII, 10-27); for Homer and Antimachus as good only in a sense see J. 35 (from XIV, 29)
and 37 (XV, 1-7) where Philodemus opposes the view of some critic that:

We call the poems of Homer and Archilochus good with some indulgence (μετὰ
συγγνώμης), those which express wise and instructive ideas we call good unambiguously
and to a higher degree, one might say in the full sense, while the others are called good
only in a sense (or where interpreted allegorically).

The word translated 'in a sense is καταχρηστικῶς, for the meaning of which see Ph. De Lacy
in AJP 69 (1948) 260 and note 108. As an example of the kind of text we have to deal with
I append the Greek of the above. Note that the letters in square brackets are conjectural
restorations convincing as they are in this case. This is a fair specimen:

καὶ μετὰ συγγνώμης τὰ Ὁμήρου καὶ [Αρχι] λ[όχ]ο[υ χ]ρηστὰ ποιήματα [λεγ]οντων ἡμῶν,
τὰ δὲ σ[οφὰς ἔχοντα και π]αιδευτικὰς ἀναμφιλέκ[τω]ς, καὶ π[ο]υ μᾶλλον, ἴσω[s δε]
καὶ κυ[ρ]ίως, ἐκείνων καταχρ[ησ]τικῶς προσ[αγ]ορευομένων.

See also J. 65 (XXIX, 8-22).

[2] J. 11-13 (from II, 11 to III, 5). This reads like a *reductio ad absurdum* of the *mimêsis* theory,
i.e poetry as imitation of life.

between poetry and reality,[1] whether in the sense of direct representation of life and events, or in a vaguer sense. Nor would he thus restrict the subjects which a poet may treat, and he allows not only fiction which is like life but subjects of pure imagination.[2] He does admit, however, that the choice of subject is part of the poet's art.[3]

Perhaps most interesting is Philodemus' contention that a poem must be judged as a whole, in all its aspects at once; it has of course both form and content but these cannot be separated, for they are closely interrelated, and, inevitably, affect one another.[4] Poets can and do, in a general way, borrow their subject-matter, but the matter itself becomes different if it is differently expressed, so that when Sophocles and Euripides each write a tragedy on the same subject, even that subject is *not* identical.[5] Hence, while he agrees that poor technique (σύνθεσις τῆς λέξεως) is enough to make a poem bad,[6] good technique is not enough to make it good; indeed composition cannot be judged by itself, and one cannot legitimately say that a poem is good in technique and poor in subject or vice versa. If a poem is good, it is so as a certain content or idea expressed in a certain way; poetry is not like a dress which can be put on a particular idea, it is the very shape of it. Philodemus admits that the subject must be well thought out, the words be suitable and the style good, but it is the fusion of these three which is the poem.[7] Hence he is always protesting against the fragmentation of criticism, the judging of a poem by a set of rules (θέματα) or requirements, some of which apply to one aspect and some to another, be it diction, choice of subject, or whatever else.[8] He denies the validity of the *metathesis* encouraged by the grammarians, i.e. rearranging the words to show that the original order was best; to him a change even in the word-order implies other changes, even of subject.[9] This insistence on unity is the protest of the poet, rather than of the philosopher, against the critical methods of contemporary grammarians and critics, against the Peripatetic as well as the Stoic tradition. Philodemus can do this and remain a faithful Epicurean, because the Epicureans had done very little theorizing on the subject, nor did they recognize poetry as important or beneficial.

It follows from this insistence upon the unity of a poem, and the need to judge it as a whole, that Philodemus opposes those critics who would

---

[1] J. 9-11 (from I, 31); 17 ad init.; 19 (VI, 25-28).

[2] J. 21 (VII, 23-29).   [3] J. 21 (VII, 15-19 and 29-31).

[4] J. 27-29 (X, 33 – XI, 4): Neoptolemus was wrong to separate style from content; and cf. 23, 25 (VIII, 33 – IX, 10); also pp. 42-47 and p. 59 (XXVI, 4-7).

[5] This point is well brought out by Greenberg in a discussion (*The Poetic Theory* pp. 155 ff.) of certain fragments of other books published by J. Heidman in *Der Papyrus* 1676.

[6] J. 43 (XVIII, 1-17).   [7] J. 27 (especially X, 27-32).

[8] J. 51 (XXII, esp. 24-30).   [9] See Greenberg in *TAPA* 89 (1958), 262-70.

isolate a few qualities as essential, be it brevity and vividness or, in great poetry (tragedy and epic), magnificence and the like.[1] For this too is a kind of fragmentation. So is the emphasis which 'the critics' (οἱ κριτικοί) placed upon the *sound* of words, singly or in combination, and their viewing euphony as the one essential.[2] Here again Philodemus is in opposition to both Stoic and Peripatetic traditions, and, when he says that it is impossible to imitate things by particular words,[3] he probably has in mind the Stoic belief in a direct relation, at least originally, between the name and the thing.

But Philodemus' main objection against the 'euphonists' was that they made the practised ear the judge of euphony, and, in the case of those he calls the κριτικοί, of the composition as a whole, indeed of the poem itself,[4] so that poetry is no longer a conscious art or *technê*, and the judgement of it becomes entirely the concern of the senses and the emotions. Philodemus is no irrationalist or intuitionist.[5] He insists that poetry must be judged by the mind and reason (λόγῳ); it follows from its being a conscious art that the mind is also active in the writing of it. There are definite standards (σκόποι) which poetry must attain and by which it must be judged.[6]

Unfortunately, we have only a very partial and obscure statement of what these standards are. He does tell us that the thought should not be too wise or too vulgar but somewhere between the two, and the language should 'imitate that of useful instruction'.[7] Philodemus evidently did not regard poetry as the right vehicle for philosophic instruction. It has been suggested that, when he said this, he cannot have read Lucretius, but it may very well be that the urbane writer of light verse who explicitly denies any didactic or moral purpose to poetry disapproved of Lucretius, as indeed, from his point of view, he must have done.[8] As for the requirement that poetic language should imitate that of useful instruction, we should remember that, in Aristotle and Theophrastus,[9] the language of useful instruction is that of the philosopher who avoids ornamentation, and Philodemus seems to mean that poetry should be simple and straight-

---

[1] J. 15; cf. J. 61 (XXVII, 6-25).   [2] J. 47 (esp. XX, 22-34).
[3] J. 71 (esp. XXIII, 16-20).   [4] J. 47-49 (XX, 22 – XXI, 22).
[5] In this respect Rostagni seems to go too far in likening Philodemus to modern aesthetic intuition in *Scritti Minori* I, 356-71. It is clearly stated as Philodemus' view in J. 47 (XX, 21-26) that criticism is a function of reason as intellect (λόγῳ). See also J. 47 (XX, 23) and 53 (XXIII, 30-35).
[6] J. 53 (XXIII, 1).   [7] J. 53 (XXIII, 1-11).
[8] See Ph. De Lacy in *AJP* 60 (1939), 91, note 29: 'There is no evidence to connect Lucretius with any contemporary Epicurean school. Apparently he used only literary sources....' He also shows (p. 87) why the Epicureans disapproved of poetry as a vehicle for philosophic instruction.
[9] Above, p. 106.

forward in expression, which would appear to agree with his own practice. He has also admitted that the subject must be well thought out, the words appropriate, the style good, though all these, as we have seen, must be judged not separately but in relation to each other. Critical principles must be of a general nature and apply to the poem as a whole.

Philodemus recognized a body of old poetry, obviously including the Homeric epic, to be clearly good poetry and this enabled him to reject any critical theories which did not recognize them as such[1]; but he very rightly ridiculed those who defined good poetry merely as poetry which was like those models.[2] Such a definition is absurd, for the greatness of Homer himself is thus not accounted for. One does not, he tells us, define justice as the imitation of Aristides, wisdom as that of Epicurus, or politics as that of Pericles. And he seems to cast further aspersions upon the rhetorical theory of 'imitation' or emulation as applied to poetry when he points out that no poet, however great, is uniformly great in every genre, or even in his own.[3] One should therefore imitate with discretion.

Thus far we can go with fair certainty, but beyond this we are in the realm of doubtful restorations and highly conjectural interpretations. When he agrees that there is no 'natural good' in a poem ($\phi\upsilon\sigma\iota\kappa\grave{o}\nu$ $\check{a}\gamma\alpha\theta o\nu$) we may reasonably surmise that he is opposing the Stoic view that a poem embodies the expression of the divineGood orLogos wor king in the world, though the passage as it stands is puzzling.[4] Jensen[5] links Philodemus' insistence on generally valid principles of criticism with the Epicurean theory of concepts ($\check{\epsilon}\nu\nuo\iota\alpha\iota$) so that poetry is true poetry if it conforms to those concepts which are, as it were, a composite impression resulting from previous perceptions. But here the text does not help us, and where Philodemus does use the word $\check{\epsilon}\nu\nuo\iota\alpha\iota$ it would seem to be in a non-technical sense.[6] There is the striking passage[7] where Philodemus seems to tell us that besides good technique he agrees that good poetry requires passion in the poet ($\tau\grave{o}$ $\pi\acute{a}\theta os$ $\tauo\hat{\upsilon}$ $\pi o\iota\eta\tauo\hat{\upsilon}$), and we might draw interesting inferences from this were it not that it is a conjecture of which not a single letter is clear in the text, and that Jensen himself later conjectures $\sigma\tau\acute{\iota}\beta os$[8] 'the path of the poet' which has of course no more authority than $\pi\acute{a}\theta os$. The context would seem to require rather a reference to 'content' as against form or technique. There is also a rather confused passage which appears to mean that poetry must be judged as poetry (by its own art) and that mistakes against other arts should be forgiven, thus repeating the distinction made by Aristotle between intrinsic and inci-

[1] J. 41 (XVII, 6-10); also J. 65 (XXIX, 9-16).
[2] J. 67-69 (from XXX, 24).
[3] J. 75 (XXXIV, 13-24).
[4] J. 51 (XXII, 18-21).
[5] p. 157.
[6] J. 51 (XXII, 15) and J. 67 (XXX, 34).
[7] J. 21 (VII, 20).
[8] In S. B. Pruss. Akad. 1936, 292-320.

dental faults, but the text is uncertain and has been interpreted differently.[1]

All this, and much else, is doubtful, but we have enough definite evidence of the critical theories discussed above to show that Philodemus was a critic of considerable originality and of highly unorthodox views. The man who maintained that poetry did *not* have an educational or moralizing function, that it need *not* be an imitation of life or have any clear relation to actual truth, that a poem must be judged as a whole and that the usual criticism, which considered every aspect of a poem under special rules and postulates was blind to the real nature of poetry, that excessive emphasis on sound and euphony was mistaken, that both criticism and poetry itself were matters for the intellect rather than the senses, that there were definite standards to be met, and finally that poetry was not philosophy and yet should be simple in language and thought – such a man was not afraid to attack common assumptions. We may say, of course, that the originality was not his but due to the sources he copied. That he used other sources he tells us himself, though not for any of the above ideas. Some may well have been due to his teacher Zeno whom he much admired – in the *Rhetorica* he explicitly declares himself indebted to him – and he may have done so in the lost parts of his work on poetry. But as far as our evidence goes, on poetry at any rate he expresses very sensible criticisms of prevailing ideas. This criticism is found nowhere else in extant sources; practically no notice was taken of it; his contemporaries, Cicero, Dionysius and Horace, contradict him at every turn and expound the orthodox views without mentioning him.[2] This in no way diminishes his importance.

---

[1] J. 43-45 (from XVIII, 27):

[ἀτ]οπώ[τε]ρον δ[έ] τὸ λέγειν ὅσα παρὰ τὰ[ς τ]έχ[ν]ας ἔχε[ι] κἂν ἀστείως ἦι συνκειμένα φαῦλ[α] εἶναι καὶ μὴ δεῖ[ν π]ο[ημάτ]ων [κρίνεσθ]αι π[α]ρὰ τὴν μόνην [και] κυρίως λεγομένην ἐ[πὶ τού]τοις τέχνην ἐπ[ὶ δ' ἄλλ]ων σὺ[ν ἀ]λλαι[ς] κ[αλῶς] πεποιη[μέν]α παρὰ τὰ[ς] ἄλλας . . .

which appears to mean:

> It is even more absurd to say that what contravenes certain arts is bad even if it is well composed; and that what is good and successful and sound in the best poems should not be judged in accordance with the one art properly so-called concerning them while other matters should be judged well performed in relation with other arts . . .

[2] There may be some echoes of Philodemus in Cicero, but they have little or no influence upon the course of the discussion or the opinions of the orator. Rostagni (*Scritti Minori* I 372-93) points to a few possible ones. In the *De Oratore* Antonius has discussed content (*res*) and Crassus, who is to discuss style, remarks that content and words should not be thus separated, since every discourse consists of both (*ex re et verbis*): words have no place without matter and matter cannot be revealed without words (3, 19 ff.) and, a little later, repeats that such separation is like separating body and soul. The other echo is Cicero's use of the word sophist to mean the practitioners of epideictic rhetoric (*Orator* 37-42) – a Philodemean use it is true, but epideictic, especially as encomia or their opposite, had long been recognized as the special province of the sophists. There is also Cicero's reference to certain Greeks who separated

His views on rhetoric were as unorthodox as his views on poetry; they show the same independence of mind, though not perhaps the same depth of perception or understanding.

The earlier work, the *Hypomnêmatikon*, consists of an interesting attempt to distinguish clearly between the sophist or teacher of rhetoric and the politician (the orator in the usual sense), and between the politician and the philosopher. It is to a large extent a polemic against rhetoric in favour of philosophy, a subject which also occupies the greater part of books two and seven of the *Rhetorica*. The *Hypomnêmatikon* seems to begin,[1] appropriately enough, with a statement that the possessor of one *technê*, or art or craft, cannot perform the work of another, and soon proceeds to discuss the view of Diogenes of Babylon (240-152 B.C.) that the (Stoic) philosopher is the only perfect orator, politician, etc. Philodemus naturally rejects this Stoic view; Epicureans did not claim that philosophy trained politicians. Nor does he have any difficulty in showing that politicians are not philosophers. He then makes a point to which he will return (and which applies to poetry as well as rhetoric) that bad morals do not prevent good artistry,[2] although many orators have deserved well of their country. The fact is, he says, that the word good in such a phrase as a good orator is ambiguous, for it can be used in a technical or a moral sense.[3]

Philodemus is here opposing the Ciceronian view, inherited from Isocrates, that rhetorical education ensures good morals, the traditional concept of the orator first defined by Cato as *vir bonus dicendi peritus* which will still be defended by Quintilian a century and a half later.[4] This, to Philodemus is confused thinking, and he attacks it with much the same arguments as we do, namely that proficiency in rhetoric has nothing to do with moral character. It is foolish, he insists, to claim that the student of rhetoric is morally better than his contemporaries: this is not only a patent falsehood; it makes no more sense than to say that a musician becomes a better musician by studying rhetoric.[5]

Most important to us is the distinction Philodemus makes between the forensic and deliberative rhetoric from epideictic and left them, and them only, as the province of the orator. Philodemus of course did so, and denied they were arts, as against epideictic which he maintained was. Of this more important point there is no mention in Cicero's passage, and the reference may be more general, but even if we admit that in all these cases Philodemus is in the orator's mind, and he may have been, it is a poor harvest.

[1] Sudhaus II, 197 ff. All the volume and page references in what follows are to Sudhaus' Teubner edition.

[2] II, 226 (xxi): ὄντες πονηροί, τεχνῖται δὲ ὅμως οὐ κωλύονται διαφορώτατοι πάντων ὑπάρχειν, and the following pages. See also I, 223-4 (XLIII a).

[3] This is clearly the meaning of II, 235 where τεχνίτης ἀγαθός is contrasted with κατὰ τὸ ἦθος (ἀγαθός), though the text is in a bad state.

[4] Above, pp. 169-71, and for Quintilian below, pp. 304-5.

[5] II, 269 and on to 272.

orator and the sophist, and this is also the subject of the first two books of the *Rhetorica*.[1] By 'sophist' Philodemus means the professional teacher of rhetoric. He denies that political rhetoric is an art or, as he puts it, that persuasion can be taught; no general principles apply even for the most part; politics deals only with particular occasions and is purely empirical. The rhetorical teachers claim to teach political and forensic rhetoric, but they do not do so in fact.

What they do teach, and what therefore *is* an art, is the art of epideictic rhetoric, the art of writing and making display speeches, in other words the art of style. This is not concerned to persuade; in fact its practitioners are quite unable to shine in court or before the assembly, where men are concerned with content and anxious to make the right decision, whereas in display oratory the audience is free from such preoccupations and pays more attention to the words, to figures of style, etc., and he has an interesting quotation from Epicurus to this effect.[2] It is true that rhetorical experts may make a man a more pleasing speaker even before the people, but this is only an accessory help, just as a politician may gain something from the study of poetry or philosophy.[3] Yet philosophy and poetry are not political rhetoric; neither is Sophistic.

By thus clearly separating what he calls sophistic from political or forensic rhetoric – at times he denies that it should be included under rhetoric at all – Philodemus comes very close to the concept of *belles lettres*[4] and if his theory had been generally accepted, literary criticism might have been less influenced by rhetoric and become a separate study. However, the development of higher education as rhetoric in the first century B.C. was against him.

Unfortunately, Philodemus does not (in the extant remains) describe this sophistic at all adequately. We do find the following:

> Then came the art of beautiful speech – they called it persuasive speech, but the art was that of beautiful speech. Speech is a gift of nature, but beautiful speech is the gift of art.[5]

He then goes on to say that while it is possible to speak spontaneously in

---

[1] II, 233-46, also I, 1-146; II, 65-130.

[2] II, 256 (iii*a*). Cf. I, 50 (XXIII, 33 – XXIV, 9). That the rhetors do not shine ἐν δήμοις κα δικαστηρίοις see I, 42-43. It is quite clear from the whole discussion at I, 77-104 that Philodemus could not quote either from Epicurus or Metrodorus a clear statement that they regarded 'sophistic' as an art.

[3] II, 253 (XLVIII, 24 ff.).

[4] At I, 122 (XXII, 29) we find the following definition: ἡ σοφιστικὴ ῥητορικὴ τέχνη τίς ἐστι περί τε τὰς ἀποδείξεις οἵας αὐτοὶ ποιοῦνται καὶ τὰς τῶν λόγων διαθέσεις οἵων αὐτοὶ γράφουσί τε καὶ σχεδιάζουσιν.

[5] II, 190-1 (fr. I).

a clear, convincing and beautiful manner, yet to speak like that often requires art.[1]

This art of speech is not a *technê* in the same sense as an exact science; its principles and general rules do not apply without exception, but it does have rules and principles which generally apply, though a certain amount of contingency or guess work will remain. An exact science is a $\pi\alpha\gamma\acute{\iota}\alpha$ $\tau\acute{\epsilon}\chi\nu\eta$ a fixed art, but sophistic is a $\sigma\tau o\chi\alpha\sigma\tau\iota\kappa\grave{\eta}$ $\tau\acute{\epsilon}\chi\nu\eta$, a guessing or approximate *technê*.[2] This is essentially the distinction made by Aristotle in the *Rhetoric* and repeated by Cicero. But to Philodemus rhetoric, i.e. the art of persuasion, is no *technê* at all, for persuasion is sheer guess work.[3]

But if he recognized that 'sophistic' or epideictic rhetoric was, or could be, an art, he does not admit that the teaching of it has any more to do with ethics than poetry, music or any other craft. Ethics, presumably, remains the province of the philosopher. So he makes short shrift of the claims of epideictic orators that their encomia are in praise of virtue and that they thus persuade men to practise it.[4] The sophists do not in any case have the philosophical knowledge to know which are the praiseworthy things; besides, they praise things indiscriminately, and often the wrong things quite deliberately, Clytemnestra rather than Penelope, monsters like Polyphemus, and so on. Their claim to praise virtue is not justified by the facts; their motive is only to show off their virtuosity. The result is that not only the ordinary rhetorical education, but also sophistic rhetoric which Philodemus recognizes as the art of beautiful speech, are both divorced from morality and philosophy, a point of view not found in any other writer of the period.

Only the first part of the fourth book deals with style, but it is for the most part highly fragmentary and tantalizing.[5] The first few intelligible fragments, however, do put forward the theory that there is one naturally beautiful way to express things – $\phi\acute{\upsilon}\sigma\epsilon\iota$ $\kappa\alpha\lambda\grave{o}s$ $\lambda\acute{o}\gamma os$ which apparently consists in using current or proper names; it is the way of the philosopher rather than that of the orator or sophist.[6] This must mean that Philodemus considers the simple manner to be the best also in prose and he goes on to say that this makes it unnecessary to seek styles that have been arbitrarily established. This is as well, he continues, for there are many of these styles, nor is any one of them universally effective; some prefer that of Isocrates, others that of Thucydides, and so on. It would be hard to know whom to follow. He praises the manner of grammarians and philosophers who do not get involved in rhetorical technicalities.

After these general remarks, Philodemus does deal with style more

---

[1] II, 192 (fr. V).   [2] I, 68-77; cf. I, 26, and cp. Cicero p. 179 above.
[3] II, 116 (fr. VIII).   [4] I, 213-21.
[5] I, 147-81.   [6] I, 149 (IV) and 151-3 (VII and X).

PHILODEMUS 203

specifically, but the text is unsatisfactory. However, he seems to be following the general formula of the four qualities or virtues, for correct language ('Ελληνικὴ ἑρμησεία)[1] is mentioned first and includes the avoidance of linguistic errors. This, however, is no monopoly of the 'sophists' who are themselves guilty of many mistakes. He then goes on to discuss clarity, or rather, in the text as we have it, obscurity (ἀσάφεια): obscurity may be deliberate if one has nothing to say or, if involuntary, may be due to the desire for variety, digressions, poetic or tropical language, or to solecisms, archaisms and the like, faults of which the philosopher (with his simple manner) is free.[2] It may also be due to lack of mastery of one's subject, of the proper value of words, of sentence structure, to incorrect language or not using words in their proper sense.

There is a brief reference to appropriateness (τὸ πρέπον, the third virtue) but the context is missing and it may only be incidental.[3] Here the text breaks off, but the next lot of fragments begin with a criticism of the sophists for excessive use of certain figures such as homoioteleuta, homoioptota and the like, which would certainly come under the fourth virtue, ornamentation, as would what follows.[4]

An interesting short sentence refers to a division of ornamentation into three kinds: (a) tropes, that is metaphor, allēgoria and the like, (b) schēma, which here clearly means sentence structure: periods, clauses, phrases (kommata) and their interrelations, and (c) plasma or style, of which he seems to mention four kinds: the copious (ἁδρογραφία), the plain (ἰσχνότης), the grand (μέγεθος)[5] and the elegant (γλαφυρότης). This is the first mention by a Greek author of the formula of several styles.[6] Here, unfortunately, the text again breaks off, and the passage which no doubt dealt more fully with these styles is lost. So is that which dealt with sentence structure. Something is left of the treatment of metaphor but the text is uncertain and it deals entirely with the views of others except for a general statement that metaphors may be used.[7] A probable classification of allegoriai into enigmatic, ironical and proverbial is legible enough to be

[1] I, 154 (XI).   [2] I, 158 (XV, 20).   [3] I, 161 (XIX, 9).

[4] I, 164 (III, 10). Sudhaus' restoration of the text here makes Philodemus speak of ἐγκατάσκευος λόγος, ornamentation, and wonder whether a diction cannot be fashioned from common speech to express both πάθη and ἦθη of the elaborate style, thus again emphasizing the possibilities of simple speech. However, the text seems too uncertain to base anything on this.

[5] The word μέγεθος at I, 165 (IV, 4) is a conjecture, only the first letter being apparently established. Radermacher, in Rhein. Mus. 54 (1899), p. 361, n. 1, followed by Hubbell (p. 298) reads μεσότητα and equates this with γλαφυρότης. This reduces the styles to three, but involves using ἤ in two senses, and the text would seem to require four styles.

[6] If ἁδ]ρο[γρα]φία is taken to mean forcefulness, we might see here a reference to the four styles of Demetrius, but the text is too uncertain. See Phoenix 18 (1964), p. 296.

[7] At least the passage I, 181 (XXII, 15-24) implies one should not shun them entirely. At I, 172 (XIII), we find a reference to metaphors which personify: i.e. ἀπ' ἐμψύχων [ἐπ' ἄψυ]χα ... ὁ [καὶ] ἔμπαλιν, and there is a reference to farfetched metaphors at I, 179 (XX, 15).

tantalizing.[1] There follows a section on delivery which does not contain anything unusual.

This is all we possess of a discussion of style. It is very little; its most important feature is Philodemus' thinly disguised contempt for all elaboration in prose[2] and his clear insistence that there is a naturally (simple and) beautiful way of saying things. This attitude is of course characteristic of the Epicurean point of view.

Though he insisted that sophistic rhetoric is an art and that Epicurus and Metrodorus said so, Philodemus does not concede the 'sophists' very much and has no sympathy with their claims.[3] We have already seen that he denied all moral value to orations of praise or blame, and that he would not allow that 'sophists' could teach either political or forensic rhetoric, which were in any case unteachable. We have seen him criticize them for their incorrect speech, and their lavish use of ornamentation. In another passage[4] he states that sensible sophists restrict themselves to teaching the function of the different parts of speech in the realm of politics (he is presumably being ironical, since he states again and again that they cannot teach political rhetoric) but the more stupid crowd of them profess to teach this for every kind of speaking. Either they think these subdivisions of a speech are to be used only in politics, which is wrong, for everybody uses them; or they think that they are the only ones to teach methods to deal with every kind of subject, which is absurd, for they give no help in other subjects where the same rules do not apply; or again they believe that they are the only ones to have published studies on these subjects, which is not true. And Philodemus is equally contemptuous of the rhetorical teachers' claim that they teach how to find all possible arguments on every subject – how could they find the best arguments in medicine or music?

What the sophists claim to teach – political oratory – they cannot teach. What they can (or at least could) teach, the art of beautiful speech which one may call epideictic rhetoric, they teach very badly. Really beautiful speech, the natural way to say things, the φύσει καλὸς λόγος, is in the end the way of the philosopher rather than that of the sophist. And so the polemic against rhetoric in favour of philosophy permeates, one might almost say vitiates, the whole work, even in its more technical parts. It also obscures Philodemus' more important contributions to

[1] I, 181 (XXIII).

[2] Besides the passage about the φύσει καλὸς λόγος there are a number of incidental remarks which show contempt for the rhetorical devices of the sophists and indeed for the sophists themselves as against philosophers; such are I, 153 (X, 1-12); 155 (XII, 1-4); 156 (XIII, 15); 158 (XV, 18-24); 162 (I, 8-17); 185 (IV^a, 2-6).

[3] As pointed out in Sudhaus' Supplement p. xxvii.

[4] I, 201-9 (XX^a, 12 – XXVII^a).

criticism, namely the attempt to disentangle the art of beautiful speech
from the influence of rhetoric, and his very sensible refutation of the
identification of the good man with the good orator. His Epicurean outlook, however, in the end seems to betray him into a theory not so very
different from the Stoic view he so contemptuously refutes: that the
philosopher, only now it is the Epicurean, is the best practitioner of the
art of beautiful speech.

Perhaps it is because of the polemical nature of the *Rhetorica* that Philodemus does not seem to have felt the need for any synthesis between his
theories on the art of prose and his theory of poetry. No doubt our
evidence is fragmentary but it shows no trace of any such synthesis.
Moreover, there could be no such synthesis between poetry as he conceived it and rhetoric in the general sense since the aim of rhetoric is to
persuade whereas poetry had, to him, no practical aim. The value of
poetry – though what this value is was left very vague – lies in its fusion of
the cognitive and the emotional appeals of language, between form and
content. Persuasion on the other hand is, or should be, a purely rational
process; emotional appeals only obscure and confuse the issues, and the
orator has no more right than the philosophers to use imaginative and
emotional language.[1] This difference, however, does not apply to his
sophistic or epideictic speech which he clearly regards as the art of
beautiful prose. Here too the performance is an end in itself, no more
concerned with persuasion than poetry was.

There are, obviously, many points of contact between the two arts: the
morals of the writer, whether of poetry or prose, are irrelevant to his art,
and in both cases Philodemus opposes those theories which require from
the writer a good deal of knowledge.[2] In both poetry and prose he inclines
to the simple manner; this is the probable meaning of the naturally
beautiful speech – φύσει καλὸς λόγος – in the *Rhetorica*; and 'the language
of useful instruction', which the poet is advised to imitate in the *Poetics*,
probably also refers to simple language. His strong and repeated objection
to euphony as the only test of good poetry seems to be briefly echoed in
the *Rhetorica* where he states that it is impossible to imitate things by

[1] See De Lacy in *AJP* 60 (1939), p. 89; 'The Epicurean analysis of rhetoric differs from the
analysis of poetry in that rhetoric makes illegitimate use of the devices suitable to poetry.
True poetry is an expression complete in itself and not concerned with any end external to
itself. Rhetoric, on the other hand, has a practical purpose, the persuasion of the auditor.
It uses emotional appeal to support what should be a purely cognitive problem. From the
philosophic point of view it is objectionable because the emotional appeal interferes with the
truth of the statements involved. Rhetoric is unnecessarily obscure.'

[2] See the whole argument against Nausiphanes who held a knowledge of Nature made the
best orator, II, 1–44, but the text is very fragmentary and it is hard to make out how much of
this actually discusses the theories of Nausiphanes. His name does occur, however, on p. 24
(XXIX, 15) and probably on p. 5 (XIII, 4, 10).

words. In both cases he dislikes a lot of rules and regulations; whether the postulates of the critics or the precepts of the 'sophists'. Finally, as good poetry is not didactic or useful, except incidentally, so the art of sophistic rhetoric is not intended to persuade or to deal with what is useful; the aim of both is beauty and pleasure only. If we possessed the two works in full, we might find this last point developed into a theory of literature as such, but there is no trace of such a development in the extant fragments. We might also find other points of contact expanded and related to both poetry and prose. Nothing is said, for example, of the importance of content, of the subject treated, in our fragments on rhetoric. Presumably, a piece of beautiful prose must also be judged as such, not fragmented into content, style, etc. considered separately. It is not likely, however, that a real synthesis was made, for surely some trace of it would have been found in our texts. And although one hesitates to judge from even a large number of mutilated fragments, while we know that Philodemus was a poet of some talent, his *Rhetorica*, as far as we have it, does nothing to substantiate his claim that the philosopher was the best practitioner of the art of beautiful prose!

CHAPTER XIII

Dionysius of Halicarnassus

Dionysius of Halicarnassus settled in Rome about 30 B.C. Cicero had died thirteen years before; and Philodemus more recently; Virgil and Horace were well started on their literary careers; Mark Antony had been defeated the previous year and the now unchallenged power of Octavian, soon to become Augustus, was bringing peace to the Roman world after three generations of civil strife. Dionysius greatly admired Rome and the Romans, and he settled down to writing the history of early Rome in twenty books, the *Roman Antiquities*, to show why the Romans had become masters of the world, and to make their early history available to Greek readers.[1] This he certainly considered his major work, but his reputation as a historian is not high; in practice he was too much under the influence of the Hellenistic view of history as a form of epideictic rhetoric akin to poetry – a view against which we have seen Polybius vigorously protesting a century before. But Dionysius also published critical essays, presumably during his stay of more than twenty years in Rome, and these are of very great importance in the history of literary criticism and theory. He belonged to a literary circle of which we know little, except that it included Caecilius of Calacte, another famous critic of the day whose works are unfortunately lost.[2] In this circle the method of comparative criticism, which we can see developing in Dionysius' essays, seems to have originated. These critics broke away from encomium and condemnation (recognized forms of epideictic); they discussed the faults as well as the merits of their subjects, and attempted to reach a true valuation of an author's style, illustrated by close analysis and by comparison with the style of others. This kind of criticism was unusual, and Dionysius finds it necessary to defend the method even in his later works.[3]

He inevitably shared the rhetorical slant of his contemporaries, both

---

[1] *Roman Antiquities* I, 5.

[2] Caecilius of Calacte was a Sicilian and possibly a Jew. Like Dionysius, he was a historian as well as a literary critic; his critical work too was of the same kind: he wrote against Asianism, on the ten Attic orators, comparative studies of Demosthenes and Cicero, of Demosthenes and Aeschines; he also wrote on figures and on rhetoric generally. It was his work περὶ ὕψους which caused 'Longinus' to write the famous treatise with the same title. See W. Rhys Roberts in *AJP* 18 (1897) 302-12; and E. Ofenloch, *Caecilii Calactini Fragmenta*.

[3] *Letter to Pompey* ch. 1 and *Thucydides* 1-5.

Greek and Roman, and his works are meant to contribute to the education of the 'orator', but he is a man of letters rather than a professional rhetorician. It is generally thought that he had a school of rhetoric, but this is doubtful. It is true that, in the *Composition*, he tells the young Melitius Rufus, to whom the work is addressed, that they will pursue the subject further 'in our daily exercises'[1] but this only proves that he acted as tutor in a Roman family, a not unusual position for an educated Greek; it does not prove him a professional rhetor. On the other hand, he frequently hurries on to another subject to avoid becoming too technical and is explicitly eager to differentiate his literary essays from the professional textbooks in a way which implies that he was not himself a schoolmaster.[2] Rhetoric to him means the art of writing as well as the art of speaking,[3] and the true rhetoric, as in Cicero, is 'philosophical rhetoric', indeed the 'true philosophy'.[4] He has an unbounded admiration for Isocrates, indeed he is an Isocratean rather than a Ciceronian, for he gives us no clear conception of the education which he desires, at least in his extant works.

The subject may, however, have been discussed in what was probably his first work, now lost, *On Polticial Philosophy*[5] in which, as we can easily deduce from his views elsewhere, he must have argued that a training in rhetoric was the right training for public life, thus taking position with Cicero against the Epicureans in general and Philodemus in particular.[6]

Dionysius also wrote works of historical literary scholarship, investigations of the genuineness of the speeches of the orators, and of this type of work we have two extant examples: the *First Letter to Ammaeus* and the essay on *Dinarchus*. The letter is probably an early work; it briefly and neatly disproves the contention of an un-named Peripatetic philosopher that Demosthenes owed his greatness as an orator to the teachings of Aristotle. By references to the dates of the works and life of the two men, Dionysius disproves the Peripatetic claim.[7] The *Dinarchus* on the other

---

[1] *Composition* ch. 20 (U-R I, 94, 5): ταῦτ' ἐν ταῖς καθ' ἡμέραν γυμνασίαις προσυποθήσομαι. See M. Egger *Denys D'Halicarnasse* 7-8. Even Asinius Pollio acted as tutor to his own grandson, Sen. *Controv*. IV. Pref. 3. Where precise reference to the text of Dionysius is needed in this chapter, the page and line references will be Usener-Radermacher's Teubner text.

[2] See, for example, *Letter to Ammaeus* II, ch. 1 (U-R I, 422, 2-6) where he reluctantly complies with Ammaeus' request to be more precise, τὸ διδασκαλικὸν σχῆμα λαβὼν ἀντὶ τοῦ ἀποδεικτικοῦ, and *Demosthenes* 6 (U-R I, 231, 20): μή ποτε εἰς τοὺς σχολικοὺς ἐκβῇ χαρακτῆρας ἐκ τῶν ὑπομνηματικῶν.

[3] E.g. *Lysias* 2 (U-R I, 10, 2): τοῖς βουλομένοις καθαρῶς γράφειν καὶ λέγειν ἐκεῖνον τὸν ἄνδρα ποιεῖσθαι παράδειγμα ταύτης τῆς ἀρετῆς, *Thucyd*. ch. 1 U-R I, 325, and *passim*.

[4] *Isocrates* 1-2 and 4 (ἀληθινὴ φιλοσοφία at U-R I, 61, 5) and the following chapters.

[5] In *Thucydides* 2 (U-R I, 327, 20) he says he never wrote a book to attack anybody except that his περὶ πολιτικῆς φιλοσοφίας was written in opposition to those who unfairly attacked 'political philosophy'.

[6] See above, pp. 200-1. Dionysius' hostility to Epicurus is also referred to in Diogenes Laertius X, 3. See also *Composition* 24 (U-R II, 122, 8-12).

[7] In the last chapter he tries to prove too much by finding a reference to the trial 'On the

hand is late, for Dionysius explains why he had not dealt with this orator before; Dinarchus, he says, was not an originator but an imitator of various styles; Dionysius here combines a brief critical essay with an investigation of the speeches and gives a list of the genuine and the spurious, based largely on their dates and the presence or absence of the orator in Athens at those times. This gives us a fairly good idea of the nature of his other works on similar subjects, which are now lost. Caecilius too is frequently quoted as an authority on the genuine speeches of the orators.

Dionysius himself mentions a number of essays which he had written or intended to write. Some of these may never have been completed, some were written and are lost. What we do possess, however, makes up a considerable body of critical work, more than we have from any other Greek critic. There is an epitome of a work *On Imitation*, mostly of the second book from which he himself also quotes longish extracts. The third book, on methods of imitation, is lost. From his work *On the Ancient Orators* we have the preface, the three essays on *Lysias*, *Isocrates* and *Isaeus* which constituted the first book, and that on the style of Demosthenes from the second. The *Letter to Pompey* follows. The essay on *Composition* (word-arrangement) must have been written before or at the same time as the *Demosthenes*. We also have a substantial essay on *Thucydides*, to which the *Second Letter to Ammaeus* is an addendum. Both the cross-references in the works themselves and the obvious development in critical techniques, which has been clearly shown to exist,[1] make it almost certain that the extant essays were written in something like the above order, with the *First Letter to Ammaeus* near the beginning and the *Dinarchus* probably last.

The first book *On Imitation*[2] apparently discussed the nature of rhetoric in general, and the respective claims of talent, training and practice, but practically nothing remains. The second book, in an attempt to guide would-be writers and orators, stated what authors were to be imitated, and in what respects, and gave brief critical valuations of them, somewhat as Quintilian does in the much admired tenth book of his *Institutio Oratoria*, but Dionysius more freely compared writers with one another. An epitome is an unreliable basis for judgement, but Dionysius quotes at some length in the *Letter to Pompey* (3) what he had said about the historians, and in particular a lengthy discussion of the comparative merits of Herodotus and Thucydides. This well-known passage undoubtedly shows

Crown' in Aristotle's *Rhet.* 2, 23, (1397 b 7) thus proving that the *Rhetoric* was written later. If Aristotle there refers to the orator at all, it is not to that trial. See Egger pp. 140-1. For a study of the chronology of the letter see R. Sealy in *REG* 68 (1955), 77-120.

[1] By S. F. Bonner in *The Literary Treatises of Dionysius of Halicarnassus*, especially ch. 2. Bonner's chronological order seems by far the most likely.

[2] What remains of the περὶ μιμήσεως will be found in Usener-Radermacher II, pp. 197-217.

Dionysius at his worst and weakest. He applies to the two historians a highly elaborate critical formula point by point, compares them, and scores a plus or minus mark, as it were, in each case. He also gives free rein here to his moralistic and rhetorical prejudices. As an example of this mechanical and not very intelligent criticism, it provides a starting-point for the study of Dionysius' method:

A. TREATMENT OF SUBJECT-MATTER

1. *Choice of subject:* Herodotus is better; he chose the glorious Persian wars, while Thucydides chose a war fatal to Greece, which should not have taken place, and had better been forgotten.
2. *Where to begin and end:* Herodotus better. Thucydides starts with the misfortunes of Greece; as an Athenian he should have started with the great deeds of Athens. The end is abrupt.
3. *Selection of material:* Herodotus better; he rests his audience with digressions; Thucydides goes on and on breathlessly; only very occasionally does he have a digression.
4. *Arrangement of material:* Herodotus better; he finishes one topic before he goes on to the next; Thucydides' chronological exposition by summers and winters breaks all continuity.
5. *Attitude of the author:* Herodotus rejoices in Greek successes, sympathizes with their defeats; Thucydides' grudging attitude to Athens, due to his exile, is obvious.

Herodotus is therefore altogether better in the treatment of subject-matter.

B. STYLISTIC QUALITIES

1. *Purity of language:* Both are excellent.
2. *Lucidity:* (this section is lost in the *Letter*, but from the fragments of *Imitation* we know Herodotus was said to be better, as indeed one would expect).
3. *Brevity:* Thucydides better here, though Dionysius slyly adds that brevity is a virtue only if accompanied by lucidity.

These are the essential qualities, the others add ornament to the style.

4. *Vividness:* Both good.
5. *Rendering character and passion:* Thucydides better at arousing passions, Herodotus at rendering character.
6. *Loftiness:* Both are equal.
7. *Force and tension:* Thucydides better here.
8. *Persuasive charm:* Herodotus better: the language of Herodotus aims at naturalness, while Thucydides wants to be forceful.

9. *Appropriateness:* Herodotus better; Thucydides always uses the same style, especially in the speeches.

Even this numbered summary is not unfair to Dionysius. The limitations of this kind of formalized criticism are obvious, even if Dionysius were right on every count. There are inherent contradictions in the formula itself: appropriateness is said to be the most important of all qualities, yet it is not an essential quality, while brevity is. The prejudices of the critic in the treatment of subject-matter need not be emphasized; the only legitimate criticism is the section concerning Thucydides' chronological arrangement.

In the following chapters of the letter the formula is applied only in part to Xenophon as an imitator of Herodotus, and to Philistus as an imitator of Thucydides, and though Philistus is inferior in almost every respect, Dionysius adds that he is 'a more useful model for forensic oratory', which was no doubt true, but reminds us vividly of the purpose of these formulae. If we may trust the epitome, such comparisons were less used for the other authors who were briefly characterized. Perhaps it was inevitable that comparative criticism should begin by such soulless point by point comparisons, but this, as will be obvious, was only the starting-point. Nor did the *Imitation* slavishly apply identical formulae to every author; even in this work's brief descriptions, and even in epitome, qualities emerge which are characteristic of the author and do not belong to the formula, as in the brief reference to Alcaeus, in whom we should observe, we are told, 'a natural grandeur, brevity, charm and intensity, as well as the use of figures allied with clarity in so far as it is not obscured by his dialect; above all, his is the *éthos* of political composition; if you abstract the metre, what remains is political rhetoric'.[1]

We should be clear about this concept of 'imitation', $\mu\iota\mu\eta\sigma\iota\varsigma$. It does not mean slavish copying in Dionysius any more than in Cicero or Quintilian. We should probably translate it by 'emulation'. There is nothing wrong with encouraging prospective speakers or writers to read the great authors of the past, nor indeed in pointing out what particular qualities in each author are to be admired, or even emulated. An interesting passage in the *Dinarchus* makes it abundantly clear that Dionysius knew the difference between right and wrong 'imitation'. After explaining why the speeches of that author can be identified, precisely because they are *mere* imitations and therefore always inferior to their models, he continues (ch. 7; U-R I, 307, 7):

An imitation is related to the ancient models in two different ways: the first relationship is the natural result of being for a long time in

[1] U-R II, 205, 16-21.

close contact with the model and living with it, the second resembles it but results from the application of rhetorical rules. About the first kind there is little one can say, about the second one can say only that all the models have a natural grace and charm of their own, while their contrived imitations, even if they are as perfect as imitations can be, always have something laboured and unnatural about them.

This is a very good description of the difference between true emulation and the imitation of particular qualities or stylistic devices. Whether Dionysius saw this as clearly when he began to write we do not know, though we are not justified in assuming that he did not. It is very certain, however, that he was not thinking only of 'rhetoric' in the sense of public speaking but that he explicitly wanted to guide in 'imitation' all prospective writers as well.[1] The 'rhetorical' slant is undeniable, but we must not think of Dionysius as narrower than he is.

The short preface to the work on the *Ancient Orators* is a violent tirade against that Asianism which, he says, has corrupted Greek eloquence since the death of Alexander the Great, and Dionysius hails the revival of 'the ancient philosophic rhetoric' after two centuries of decay, a revival for which he gives credit to Rome and the rulers of Rome 'educated men of noble discernment', who have already brought about the writing of many worth-while histories, great speeches, works of philosophy and other literature in Latin and Greek; before long they will secure the complete rout of Asianism and the triumph of good taste. Clearly, Dionysius sees his own essays as a contribution to this struggle.

The intended compliment to the circle of Augustus then ruling in Rome is obvious, but Dionysius seems to be speaking in a broader perspective and the writers of the previous generation, men like Caesar, Cicero and their contemporaries, are, one imagines, meant to be included. Cicero above all was surely one of those who published great speeches and philosophical works, and was largely responsible for the revival of 'philosophic rhetoric'. We can the more easily admit this if we realize that, though a violent opponent of Asianism, Dionysius is not taking the position of the Roman Atticists whom we have met in Cicero. His great admiration for Demosthenes is enough to separate him from them. He is an Atticist only in the same sense as Cicero: he believed the great Attic writers to be the best models.

That Dionysius does not mention Cicero means nothing. Greek critics and rhetoricians hardly ever mentioned Roman writers. They did not need to, for their concern was with Greek literature. Moreover, few Greeks knew Latin, though Dionysius did learn it in Rome. There may

See p. 208, note 3, above.

also have been an element of discretion towards the masters of the world in this silence; the Greeks were not likely to put any Latin writers on a par with their own great Classics (even the Romans very rarely did) and silence saved embarrassment. Whatever the reason, the fact is well established. The Romans, of course, had no such inhibition, but then educated Romans were bilingual, and they fully recognized their debt to Greece.

Dionysius' purpose is to select the best orators *and historians*,[1] to study their choice of style and the characteristics which should be imitated or avoided in each writer. And he adds that he has not found any such previous works, though he has searched for them; he means, presumably, impartial studies of individual writers. The claim to originality is, so far as we know, justified, and it is particularly interesting in relation to his con-temporaries, for Caecilius, as we saw, is credited with a work on the ten Attic orators and with a comparative study of Cicero and Demosthenes. If these had been already published, Dionysius' claim to originality would merely have made him ridiculous.

The first essay, the *Lysias*, is interesting: it applies to that orator, with some variations, very much the formula we met in the *Letter to Pompey*,[2] but the result is infinitely more alive and there is some very good criticism. Each quality is fully explained and a good deal of what we find here is repeated in all the histories of literature and rhetoric. After a short bio-graphical sketch (his regular practice), Dionysius emphasizes the good qualities of Lysias, and vividly expresses his own enthusiasm. In purity of language Lysias is superior to all but Isocrates and 'I would advise all who want to become *writers and speakers* to take Lysias as the pattern of this virtue'. Lysias always uses current, simple language without tropes or elaboration, yet he has dignity and nobility when dealing with important subjects. He is both lucid and brief, an unusual combination in which both Thucydides *and Demosthenes* are his inferiors (3-4). He eschews all irrele-vance in subject-matter, has an exquisite judgement of what material to use (5) and a neat, compact terseness in the expression of particular ideas (6).[3] He is praised for his vividness (7), his sense of character, appropriate-

---

[1] U-R I, 6, 21 ff.

[2] Except that he begins with the stylistic qualities or virtues (1-15) and then proceeds to the treatment of subject-matter (15). The choice of subject, the beginning and end, and the attitude of the author are omitted (they hardly apply to a forensic orator), and we have the more common εὕρεσις, κρίσις and τάξις, i.e. Cicero's *inventio, iudicium* and *dispositio*. It should be noted that, though the main division is quite clear, Dionysius deals under qualities with certain aspects of πραγματικόν. Lucidity and brevity, for example, are discussed both as regards style and the handling of material in 3-5. The division into style and subject-matter is artificial, and they inevitably overlap.

[3] In ch. 6 Dionysius discusses 'an admirable virtue which Theophrastus said originated with Thrasymachus, but I think it began with Lysias', and defines it as: ἡ συστρέφουσα τὰ νοήματα καὶ στρογγύλως ἐκφέρουσα λέξις. This is usually interpreted to be the periodic style. I have argued at length in *AJP* 73 (1952) 255-61 that this interpretation does violence to the Greek

ness and the rest, but Dionysius freely admits that the orator is lacking in tenseness, forcefulness and all the qualities that go with a grand and impressive style (13).

All this is good criticism, but it is only a more able, lively and sensitive application of the same critical formulae. At one point, however, Dionysius rises above formulae, namely in his discussion of Lysias' characteristic charm (χάρις, 10-12). Here he realizes that he is faced with a quality which pervades every aspect of Lysias' writing: 'it is easily perceived, obvious to expert and layman alike, but very difficult even for the most skilled in speech to explain.'[1] And he goes on to say that there are many such qualities which can be appreciated only by prolonged familiarity and by trained feelings – as is also the case in music. What is more, Lysias' charm is the surest guide in the recognition of his genuine speeches. This passage is of the first importance; one could ask for no clearer recognition of the limitations of Dionysius' own formal methods of criticism. He is of course perfectly right about Lysias' charm.

But even if theory cannot have the last word, a good many words before the last rightly belong to it, and Dionysius, after a brief recapitulation of Lysias' virtues and weaknesses, goes on to deal with the handling of subject-matter (partly already incidentally dealt with).[2] This is more formal and brief: Lysias is good at invention and judgement, but too simple in arrangement, without elaboration, figures or tropes.

Then (17) Dionysius suddenly switches to another formula, that of the four sections of a speech[3] and examines his author from this point of view. This is largely repetitive, for we get, to a large extent, the same qualities from a different point of view; yet it is fairly lively. As we would expect, Lysias' talents make him excellent in the exordium (the textbooks, says

and is thoroughly unsatisfactory; Dionysius is referring to the capacity to express thoughts succinctly and compactly. Egger was quite right (48-9) when he translated: 'l'élocution qui resserre les pensées et les arrondit' and see his note 1 on page 49. I will only emphasize here that this quality is said to be essential to forensic oratory, which the periodic style emphatically is not; that we are told that few imitated it except Demosthenes, yet Isocrates is the chief exponent of the periodic style and if that style is here referred to it is incredible that he should be ignored. Further, and this I failed to point out before, in ch. 8 we are explicitly told that Lysias did *not* use the periodic style: Dionysius is there showing Lysias to be supreme in the rendering of character (ἠθοποιία) and he goes on to say that for this reason he uses current diction and a simple word-arrangement, realizing that periods are unsuitable (U-R I, 15, 21): καὶ συντίθησί γε αὐτὴν (i.e. λέξιν) ἀφελῶς πάνυ καὶ ἁπλῶς ὁρῶν ὅτι οὐκ ἐν τῇ περιόδῳ καὶ τοῖς ῥύθμοις ἀλλ᾽ ἐν τῇ διαλελυμένῃ λέξει γίγνεται τὸ ἦθος. This puts the matter beyond all doubt: Dionysius can hardly claim Lysias to be the originator of periods in ch. 6 and then state in ch. 8 that Lysias does not use a periodic style!

[1] U-R I, 18, 11-14. Note particularly on p. 19, 8: χρόνῳ πόλλῳ καὶ μάκρᾳ τρίβῃ καὶ ἀλόγῳ πάθει τὴν ἄλογον συνάσκειν αἴσθησιν. Dionysius is certainly not one of those who maintained that criticism is purely a matter of rules.

[2] See p. 213, note 2, above.

[3] For this formula see above, pp. 139-40.

Dionysius, must have had him in mind when they drew up their requirements); he is also a master of narrative, good at the kind of proofs which rely on the circumstances of the case or on the expression of character, but weak on passion, whether in proofs or peroration (18-19). This section is formal, but by no means dry, and very readable.

The last part of the essay (20-31) consists of illustrations from three different kinds of speeches. Dionysius gives enough of the circumstances to make his extracts intelligible. His comments are of a general nature only but the passages are well-chosen and excellently illustrate the points he has made. We shall see that he deepens and develops this illustrative method in later works.

Altogether, the *Lysias* is the most conventional of the extant works, yet in its own way it is very successful. Perhaps because he came to realize in this study the obvious limitations of the method, Dionysius never again uses the formula of qualities as the structural basis of so considerable a part of an essay. Part of the attractiveness of the *Lysias* is also that Dionysius is consistently right in his judgements, which is by no means always the case.

The *Isocrates*, which followed, certainly shows some advances in technique, in particular the more detailed analysis of illustrative quotations, but as a piece of literary criticism it is much inferior to the *Lysias*. The difficulty seems to be that while Dionysius has an unbounded admiration for Isocrates as the real founder of philosophic rhetoric, and all but worships him for the moral effect of his speeches and educational method, he cannot admire his style, especially his word-arrangement, and he is too honest a critic to pretend to do so. The biographical sketch soon becomes a hymn of praise of the educator, but the formula of qualities has gone dead: one chapter (2) suffices for it and we need our scoring-board again: Isocrates is as good as Lysias in purity of language, preciseness, using current vocabulary (though he uses more tropes), clarity, vividness, the expression of character, persuasiveness and appropriateness; but less brief, less compact, slower; for his carefully balanced periodic structure, his avoidance of hiatus, etc., not a good word is said.

We then make a new start (3) with Theophrastus' formula of word-choice, word-arrangement and the use of figures. Isocrates is good at the first, but poor at the other two and there is some pretty harsh criticism of his style – followed by praise for his elevation, dignity and impressiveness, and a comparison of him to Pheidias and Polycleitus, while Lysias has the slighter charm of Calamis, but it is not very clear whether Dionysius is still thinking of style, for, if so, what does this dignity consist of except perhaps the actual language, i.e. choice of words?

One almost hears a sigh of relief as Dionysius passes on to subject-matter, for Isocrates is as good as Lysias in invention and judgement of what to use, and actually better at arrangement of content, working on his proofs, etc. As for the choice of subject . . . here Dionysius suddenly sails off into a paean of praise of the moral effect of Isocrates' speeches; who can avoid being a better man for reading the *Panegyricus*? And so on and so on, for seven chapters! No doubt Dionysius is perfectly sincere even if he is 'consciously producing propaganda for the Augustan program of social reform',[1] but for the one item, i.e., choice of subject, all this is somewhat out of proportion!

We come to earth for a recapitulation of results. Isocrates is superior to Lysias only in choice of subject and arrangement of subject-matter, but nothing is said in favour of his word-arrangement. Dionysius shows his discomfort by pointing out that others too have adversely criticized Isocrates. Nor is there one word of praise for Isocrates' style in the last third of the essay (14-20) where passages are quoted in illustration; the same awkwardness prevails: in one instance (17) the comments are purely ethical, while in another we are told to overlook Isocrates' weaknesses and concentrate on his strong points (15) but no stylistic strong points are mentioned! We should note, however, that in several cases a passage is analysed sentence by sentence (e.g. 14 and 20) to show why such balanced clause-structure becomes very monotonous. This is something new in depth of method and it will be developed further.

Apart from this, however, the essay is no advance on the *Lysias*, quite the contrary. The qualities in which we are told Isocrates is the equal of Lysias are nowhere described or illustrated. Two points are fully made: Isocrates' word-arrangement is very poor; Isocrates' moral effect is magnificent. It would seem that Dionysius the 'philosopher' and Dionysius the literary critic are at odds, but they do not compose their differences; indeed they do not even admit them.

Criticism by illustration is then further developed in the *Isaeus* where nearly three-quarters of the essay are given over to it (5-18). Moreover, as we are told that the style of Isaeus is very like that of Lysias and that it is often hard to distinguish them, parallel passages of the two authors are set side by side and the differences studied in some detail. Dionysius is not here in conflict with himself; the moralist has nothing to do here and the field is left free for the critic. As in the *Isocrates*, the use of the quality-formula is, if not perfunctory, at any rate very brief and restricted to one chapter (3). In most qualities, we are there told, Lysias and Isaeus are very much alike, but Lysias is more simple, more natural and better at expressing character; Isaeus is more contrived, more exact, more elaborate in word-arrangement, less charming but more forceful. It is this forcefulness in particular which makes him the forerunner of Demosthenes; he also uses more figures and more rhetorical tricks which are apt to arouse suspicion.

This is the usual list of plus and minus scores, but we now proceed to concrete illustration of these points. Detailed comparisons of passages and sentences very neatly illustrate Dionysius' exact meaning. For Isaeus' use of figures no corresponding examples can be given from Lysias, so passages from Demosthenes are given instead and the comparisons, as it were, look forward as well as backward. We see how close Isaeus is to Lysias in some respects, how close to Demosthenes in others, which was the very reason why he was chosen as the subject of a special essay. Behind these illustrations is the formula of the parts of a speech; we are given first exordia, then narratives, then proofs, and told that Isaeus introduced more variety in his use of these parts: his narratives are not always in one piece, but sometimes broken up and intermingled with proof of particular points. This whole section is lively, well presented and altogether excellent criticism.

We now come to the περὶ συνθέσεως, On Word-Arrangement, usually known as On Composition, which was written either before, or concurrently with, the essay on Demosthenes. It is a work of literary theory rather than criticism, dealing as it does with only one aspect of style, namely word-arrangement which, as we know, consists of the sound of words in their various combinations, the structure of sentences, and rhythm. Dionysius here concerns himself particularly with the first and last of these, that is, with the music of language, to which the Greeks were so very sensitive, and which he felt had not been adequately dealt with by any of his predecessors.[1] It has certainly not received much attention in modern times.[2] This makes the treatise of very special interest and it is undoubtedly our critic's masterpiece. He begins by stressing the importance of his subject, and quotes passages from Homer and Herodotus to prove his point; he may well be accused of ignoring other factors in his enthusiasm, but when he rewrites a short quotation from the first chapter of Herodotus by rearranging the order of words in the manner first of Thucydides and then of Hegesias (4), he certainly proves his main thesis,

[1] Ch. 1 (U-R II, 21-23). The claim to originality is emphatic and, as far as we know, justified. It is true that Demetrius had a good deal to say on the subject of σύνθεσις and the kinds appropriate to each of his 'styles', but even if Dionysius knew the treatise On Style, it does not deal with word-arrangement as such. Cicero, as we saw, dealt with rhythm at length at the end of the Orator. but this is only a part of word-arrangement. Dionysius also condemns post-classical Greek writers for paying too little attention to word-arrangement, and mentions Polybius among those who are almost unreadable because of their neglect of it.

[2] Rhys Roberts, in his edition p. 32 refers to Robert Louis Stevenson's essay, Some Technical Elements of Style in Literature. That short work is of very special interest to readers of Dionysius, and shows some very close parallels, although it is believed that Stevenson was not familiar with Dionysius.

and the parallels from other arts such as architecture, carpentry and embroidery legitimately emphasize the importance of the arrangement of one's material which, in writing or speaking, consists of words. Surprisingly, Dionysius states that there is no natural order of words in Greek (5), and, if here also he appears to exaggerate, it is at least true that the natural order is much less important in an inflected language, in which far more variations are possible.

One should, we are told, aim at charm and beauty (10), but these are not the same. Thucydides' word-arrangement mainly produces beauty, that of Xenophon charm, and when Dionysius adds that Herodotus achieves both, he is foreshadowing the three styles of word-arrangement of the later chapters. Particular attention must be paid to melody or pitch, to rhythm, to variety, and to appropriateness as the means to a successful arrangement (11).

Dionysius analyses the music of language into its elements; not only words and syllables but individual letter-sounds contribute to the total aesthetic effect, and each has its individual value: long vowels are more pleasing than short; labials than gutturals, and so on, and he has a particular aversion to sibilants. This careful analysis (14), which incidentally gives us a good deal of information on Greek pronunciation, is very striking, and he again emphasizes the limitations of analysis when he points out that scansion is based on the difference between long syllables and short, but that the first syllables of ὅδος, ῥόδος, τρόπος and στρόφος, though all short, have in fact different time values (15).

> What is the substance of my argument?[1] That the interwoven letters determine the varying quality of the syllables as the combined syllables determine the diverse nature of the words, and the arrangement of the words determines the many shapes of discourse. It follows that beautiful language inevitably contains beautiful words, and that the beauty of words is due to that of the syllables and letters while pleasing language is the result, for the most part, of words and syllables and letters which please the ear. The particular differences which express the different characters, passions, dispositions and actions of persons derive their quality from the original interweaving of letters.

Dionysius analyses (17) rhythm into its elements with the same thoroughness, i.e. metrical feet, and explains the aesthetic value of each foot. He shows the same preference for long syllables here as he showed for long sounds, but here too tries to prove too much when he reduces sentences of Plato or Demosthenes to a succession of feet, for, while it is true that the rhythms of prose are no less real for being irregular, it is their

[1] U-R II, 63, 4 (Rhys Roberts, p. 160).

general effect which is significant as Theophrastus had realized.[1] Moreover, very different feet can be found in the same sentence with equal ease, depending on the method of division, where one starts, and the like. Nevertheless, Dionysius is right in principle: different prose rhythms, resulting from the different arrangement of words, produce very different aesthetic and emotional effects. Nor would one deny the need for variety (19) in sound as in rhythm, or that the total language-music should be appropriate to the content and the emotional effect one wishes to produce (20). This whole general discussion culminates in a splendid appraisal of the well-known lines of Homer which describe the torture of Sisyphus in Hades, condemned to push a large rock up a hill, but ever prevented from succeeding in his task (20, U-R II, 90-92):

– – –∪∪ – – – ∪∪ – ∪∪ – ◡

και μην Σισυφον εισειδον κρατερ᾽ αλγε᾽ εχοντα

–– – – – ∪ ∪ –∪∪ – ∪∪ – ◡

λααν βασταζοντα πελωριον αμφοτεροισιν

– ∪∪ – – – ∪∪ – – – ∪ ∪ – ◡

η τοι ο μεν σκηριπτομενος χερσιν τε ποσιν τε

–∪ ∪ – – – ∪ ∪ – ∪∪ – ∪∪ – ◡

λααν ανω ωθεσκε ποτι λοφον· αλλ᾽ οτε μελλοι

– ∪∪ – ∪∪ – ∪ ∪ – – – ∪ ∪ –◡

ακρον υπερβαλεειν τοτ᾽ επεστρεψασκε κραταιις

– ∪∪ – ∪ ∪– ∪ – – – ∪ –◡

αυτις επειτα πεδονδε κυλινδετο λαας αναιδης.[2]

Dionysius comments in detail on the number of long syllables and feet, on the necessary pauses between sounds which cannot be run together, in the first five lines. These express the straining of Sisyphus to push the stone uphill, in contrast to the dactylic last line where rapid short syllables and longer words that run easily together render the motion of the stone rolling down into the plain.

It is at this point that Dionysius introduces his theory of three styles of word-arrangement. He is quite clear that these are only generic types and he fully realizes that there are infinite varieties of each type. He states emphatically that, as in our looks, so in our style, each of us is different from all others. This needs to be emphasized, for it is often ignored, and Dionysius blamed where he does not deserve it. Nevertheless, there are,

---

[1] Above, p. 105, and rhythm in Cicero, pp. 184-6.

[2] The translation of the passage (*Odyssey* 11, 593-8) is 'And I saw Sysiphus heavily labouring, pushing a massive rock with both hands; straining with hands and feet, he was heaving the rock up the slope, but just as he was about to hurl it over the top and heaving in his might, the shameless stone would roll down again into the plain.'

he says, three generic styles of Arrangement: the austere, the elegant and the intermediate. His description of them is very striking. First comes the austere (22):

> The words should be securely planted and occupy strong positions so that each can be seen from all sides and the parts of speech separated by appreciable intervals and perceptible time. Harsh and clashing juxtapositions are frequently not avoided – the result being like rough-hewn blocks of building-stone put together without squaring or smoothing, in their natural state. The time is often lengthened by using large, wide-stepping words with broad effects, for a sequence of short syllables is uncongenial to this style except where it is sometimes unavoidable. Such then are the effects to be pursued and desired in the use of particular words.
>
> Similarly, the structure of clauses aims at dignified and impressive rhythms; the clauses are not equally balanced or similar in sound; they do not slavishly follow a rigid sequence but shine forth in noble independence, reflecting nature rather than art, expressing passion rather than character.[1]
>
> The composition of the period does not even attempt, for the most part, to complete the sense; if this should accidentally happen, their naturalness and unstudied character is emphasized; no unnecessary words are added to round off the sentence or clarify the meaning; no care is taken to end the period with ostentatious smoothness, nor measure its length to conform to that of the speaker's breath, or to obtain any other effect of this kind.
>
> The following also belong to this kind of word-arrangement: rapid changes of case, diversified figures, lack of connectives and articles, frequent disregard of grammatical sequence. It is not in the least flowery, but proud, independent, unadorned, with the patina of archaic beauty.

To illustrate his meaning Dionysius comments in fascinating detail upon a longish fragment of Pindar and the first twenty-five lines of Thucydides' History – he also mentions Antimachus, Aeschylus, and Antiphon as using this type of word-arrangement in their various literary genres.

In strong contrast is the other extreme, the smooth, flowery, elegant Arrangement of Isocrates (23):

> It does not want each word to be seen from all around, or all words to be broadly and securely planted with long time-intervals between

---

[1] On the implications of the words for passion and character, πάθος and ἦθος, see pp. 291-2.

them; it altogether dislikes a steady slowness. It rather seeks movement in its language, with the words flowing into one another without independent positions, like a river that never stands still. The parts of speech should run together and combine, giving as far as possible the impression of one unit of speech. This is achieved by well-adjusted rhythms which prevent perceptible intervals of time between the words, the result being, in this respect, like finely woven linen or like paintings in which light and shade merge into one another. All the words should be euphonious and smooth, soft as a maiden's cheek, without harsh or clashing syllables. All that which is bold or hazardous is avoided.

Not only are the words carefully joined and fitted together but the clauses too are well interwoven and it all ends with the period. No clauses will be too long or too short, and the measure of the period is that of a man's breath. No passage without periods, no period without clauses, no clauses without symmetry are tolerated. The rhythms are not the longest but the intermediate, or even shorter. The periods must end rhythmically, and move forward regularly, so that their arrangement has the opposite effect from that of the words, for these run together whereas the periods are clearly separated so that they can be distinctly seen. The most archaic figures are avoided as are all those which are stately, weighty or have an old-time flavour, while full use is made of figures that are rich and seductive, deceptive to a large extent, and affected. In general, this style of word-arrangement is, in all important respects, the opposite of the one first described, and there is no point in repeating myself.

The examples of this style of word-arrangement chosen for comment are Sappho's famous ode to Aphrodite (preserved for us here only) and a passage of the *Areopagiticus* of Isocrates. Other authors mentioned as exponents of it are Hesiod in epic, Anacreon and Simonides in lyric, and Euripides in tragedy.

The third or mixed word-arrangement Dionysius finds harder to describe; as elsewhere, he is not very clear whether it is an Aristotelian mean or a mixture, though he tends to favour the latter meaning and insists again that it is but a generic term for many varieties which avoid the excesses and combine the advantages of both the extremes. This type of word-arrangement is therefore to be considered the best. It is that of Homer, Stesichorus, Alcaeus, Sophocles, Herodotus, Demosthenes, Plato, and Aristotle.

The last two chapters of the *Composition* raise the question why some prose is poetic and some poetry like prose. Unfortunately Dionysius sticks to his subject, i.e. word-arrangement, in considering this question and indeed to one aspect of it, namely rhythm. He therefore merely says that prose approaches poetry when it is definitely rhythmical, and poetry is like prose when it resolves its metres, when its clauses do not correspond to the rhythmical pattern but over-step it by enjambement. This likeness need not be a fault in either case, and examples are given from Homer, Euripides and Simonides. All this is no doubt true enough, but, while it raises an important critical problem, it gives only a very partial answer to a single aspect of it.

Dionysius is well aware that some of his readers will find it hard to believe that great writers consciously concern themselves with such minutiae of sound and rhythm as he has been expounding. Modern readers are likely to be even more incredulous, for few of us believe that literary genius consists of an infinite capacity for taking pains. Dionysius reminds us that Isocrates took ten years to compose his *Panegyricus* and he tells how, at Plato's death, tablets were found which showed him to have tried out many different word-orders for the simple sentence which begins the *Republic*. We are not surprised, he tells us, that painters and sculptors should take much pains with details. Is it then so surprising that Demosthenes was careful of euphony, and used no word at random? Moreover (U-R II, 193, 4):

> When we learn to read, we first learn the names of letters, then their shapes and values; then the syllables and their properties; after this the words and their inflections – their longer and shorter forms and their declensions. . . . Then we begin to read and write, slowly at first, and syllable by syllable. When, in due process of time, the forms of words are fixed in our minds, we read easily and get through any book handed to us without stumbling, with incredible speed and ease. We must suppose that the same is true as regards the euphony of clauses and the arrangement of words for those who are trained to this. It is not unreasonable for those without experience or training in this or any other task to be surprised and incredulous when anyone else does something supremely well because he has mastered the art.

This view deserves consideration, and the Greeks were certainly highly conscious literary artists ever since Homer. Furthermore, even where the artist acts instinctively, the critic must still explain the nature of his success.

With the *Demosthenes* we return to the essays on one author, and we begin, as usual, with a biographical note, but the orator's handling of subject-matter is delayed to another work and we are concerned only with style. Moreover, the formula of qualities is nowhere used as a basis of criticism though the qualities themselves appear, as is natural, in comments on comparative passages. The sections of-a-speech formula is not used but the superiority of Demosthenes is established on the basis of a three style formula, three styles of composition in the second part, and three styles of diction in the first.

Here we face a problem of structure and meaning. If the first part discusses 'the three styles' ($\lambda\acute{\epsilon}\xi\epsilon\iota\varsigma$) including both word-choice and word-arrangement, and the second part word-arrangement, there is a lack of unity in the essay of which Dionysius seems himself quite unaware. Moreover, Demosthenes is said to practise *all three* kinds of *lexis*, but the intermediate kind of word-arrangement.[1] The two formulae cannot be telescoped: Isocrates, for example, practises the smooth or flowery word-arrangement, which is an extreme, but has the intermediate type of diction. Plato's diction is strongly criticized in the first part, but, in the second part, as always in Dionysius, his word-arrangement is said to be admirable.[2] These contradictions are not really resolved by supposing, as is generally done, that Dionysius wrote the first thirty-four chapters, then interrupted himself to write the *Composition*, and after that wrote a special essay on the word-arrangement of Demosthenes. He then tacked it on to the first part where it did not fit.

I have argued elsewhere[3] that the main subject of the first part is not style in the inclusive sense, but *language* or *diction*, that this is clearly the case in the first eight chapters, though when he comes to use passages in illustration Dionysius certainly adds comments which also deal with word-arrangement. Nevertheless he had diction mainly in mind in the

---

[1] The difference here, however, is more verbal than real, since the intermediate type of *lexis* uses both extremes at different times (as Isocrates and Plato are said to do), while the intermediate type of word-arrangement is a mixture of the extremes. Nevertheless, this is a further difference of conception which undermines the unity of the work if we understand the *lexis* of the first part to include not only diction but also the word-arrangement of the second.

[2] U-R I, 223, 9: ὁ Πλάτων ὁ θαυμάσιος (ch. 42). Cf. *Composition* 18 where Plato's word-arrangement is highly praised and he is called δαιμονιώτατος in this respect (U-R II, 77, 3). See also the comments in the *Letter to Pompey*, on the criticism of Plato in the *Demosthenes* (ch. 2, especially U-R II, 227; and 230, 13 ff.) where Dionysius explicitly states that he did not criticize Plato's way of handling his material 'and within the department of style only his excessively figurative and dithyrambic *language*'.

[3] *AJP* 73 (1952), 261-6. I there argued at length that the word λέξις in the first part of the treatise and certainly in the first eight chapters *means* diction and should be so translated. It is perhaps better to say that under this very general term λέξις, Dionysius discusses three kinds of language and that it is language which he *has in mind* in the first part. We have already seen (p. 213, note 2, above) that even when his categories are quite clear, he occasionally discusses under one head, briefly, what belongs to another. Certainly the critcial terms used throughout the first eight chapters, and the qualities attributed to Demosthenes in 8, are all of a kind usually applied to the *language* of an author. Where σύνθεσις is mentioned, it is that of Isocrates and it is said to spoil his effects when he uses the noble type of diction (ch. 4. U-R I, 135, 18 – 136, 9). It should also be noted that a middle diction is not a new idea to Dionysius and that where he contrasts Sophocles and Euripides in his *Imitation*, the κεκραμένη μεσότης which he attributes to Euripides definitely refers to language (U-R II, 206, 23).

first part, and so could naturally proceed to discuss mainly word-arrangement in the second. It is certainly not unusual for him to wander beyond the boundaries of his immediate subject. The word 'diction' however is perhaps too restrictive; 'language' is a better word, for ἐκλογὴ ὀνομάτων included, as we have already seen, not only the choice of words, but writing in character, expressing passion, using tropes and metaphors, and in fact came to include almost everything which is not specifically word-arrangement or figures; it is usually under *eklogē* that the quality-formula was used in earlier essays. We need not then imagine Dionysius writing the *Composition* between chapters thirty-four and thirty-five of the *Demosthenes*.

The technique of comparative criticism is further developed in this essay on Demosthenes; short passages, sometimes single sentences, are analysed and often rewritten (a technique we have met in *Isaeus* and *Composition* but which is here more frequent) to show clearly what certain criticisms mean. The one great weakness of the essay, however, is that it is too nearly an encomium on Demosthenes; he was occasionally adversely criticized in earlier essays[1]; here he can do no wrong. *All* styles of language *and* of word-arrangement are used by him more perfectly than by any other author. Dionysius is mostly shrewd and mostly right in his judgements, but such consistent adulation becomes tiresome.

Dionysius then begins his essay by establishing three kinds of diction and gives illustrations of each but he does not, unfortunately, comment on them: first that of Thucydides, unusual, uncommon, elaborate with various kinds of ornamentation; the second is that of Lysias, plain, simple, using the current language of conversation. The third kind is intermediate between those two extremes or a mixture of the two (here too Dionysius rather confuses the two concepts). This intermediate diction is illustrated by an extract from Thrasymachus whom Theophrastus regarded as its originator[2] and is attributed also to Plato and Isocrates who are said to use the simple and the elaborate kind in different passages. However the smooth, elegant arrangement of Isocrates with its elaborately balanced

---

[1] E.g. in *Lysias* 4 (U-R I, 12, 15) where both Demosthenes and Thucydides are said to be inferior to Lysias in lucidity. In ch. 6 (I, 14, 14) Demosthenes is said to be less simple and clear in compactness of expression (see p. 213, note 3); and in *Isaeus* 4 (I, 97, 2-9) both Isaeus and Demosthenes are said to arouse suspicion because of their rhetorical devices. We find no such censure in the present essay, for Bonner (pp. 68-69) is mistaken when he says that in the ninth chapter Dionysius is adversely criticizing passages of Demosthenes and rewriting in order to make his objections clear. What Dionysius is doing is to prove that Demosthenes in certain passages uses the elaborate or Thucydidean style of diction (I, 145, 4-6). He points out where certain expressions do indeed belong to this style, and rewrites *to show how Demosthenes would have put it if he had been using the simple style of diction*. There is no adverse criticism or objection. This is quite clear from such sentences as (145, 24): 'if it had been necessary to speak simply and without elaboration, he would have spoken as follows . . .', which occur throughout.

[2] See p. 20 note 1 and p. 108 above.

clauses is said to spoil the effect of his noble language, while Plato's language is apt to be at times too poetical, too verbose and obscure, his Greek poorer altogether. From all these imperfect forms of diction Demosthenes developed his own which possesses all the good qualities of all the others (8). Dionysius quotes passages from Demosthenes to illustrate each of the three styles of diction. It is here that he begins also to rewrite, but the rewriting is meant only to clarify; it need imply no unfavourable criticism.[1] The point is that the orator could vary his language to suit particular circumstances, or a particular audience (15) and yet at the same time avoid excess in either direction. To prove this we have detailed comparisons with extracts from Lysias, Isocrates and Plato.

Unfortunately the Platonic passages (24-30) are from the *Menexenus* which, if genuine, is nowadays mostly regarded as a rhetorical parody. Apart from this, in the case of Plato, the criticisms seem much less sensible and less fair in detail, and our critic does not live up to his promise to compare only the best passages from different authors. He is too determined to prove the superiority of Demosthenes.

The second part of the essay need not detain us long. It repeats (36-41) almost word for word the description of the three styles of word-arrangement from the *Composition*; we have examples of the smooth type from Isocrates, of the austere from Thucydides, and from Herodotus of the intermediate. Demosthenes, too, practised the mean or mixed type, and detailed analyses show how he varied his word-arrangement sometimes from sentence to sentence, and that he was fully aware of the importance of pitch, length, variety and appropriateness, factors discussed more fully in the *Composition* to which Dionysius refers the reader. Once again he repeats that the ear is the best judge of the music of language and insists again that Demosthenes was consciously artistic in these details (48). After a few words on the importance of delivery, Dionysius disposes of Aeschines' criticisms of Demosthenes with ease (55-6), but he probably admits lack of wit in Demosthenes, though the text is unfortunately uncertain at this point (I, 247, 15 ff.).

The *Letter to Pompey* was elicited by a protest against the criticism of Plato contained in the *Demosthenes*. In reply, Dionysius makes a spirited defence of his method of comparative criticism. Critical essays are not bound by the conventions of the encomium or the denunciation but should express the impartial truth. He disclaims any intention of 'running down' Plato in the manner of Zoilus, and insists on the purity of his own motives (1-2). The other main interest of the letter is the long quotations on the historians from his work on *Imitation*, which we have already discussed.

[1] See p. 224, note 1 above.

The *Thucydides* is almost certainly the last major essay we possess, and it is interesting to note that Dionysius still finds it necessary to defend his right to criticize impartially, to mention faults as well as virtues. He also stresses that one need not be a great artist before being entitled to criticize; indeed even the layman is entitled to do so, since, in so far as literature appeals to the ear and the emotions, he is the best judge (1-4). We also find in this essay a much more developed attempt to judge Thucydides in direct relation to the earlier historians and see him in his historical setting. The early historians all wrote simply, without artistic elaboration; their subjects too were simpler: the history of one city or one people; they made no attempt to eliminate the mythical or legendary. Then came Herodotus, who represents a second stage of development in both matter and style (5-6), and then Thucydides.

The general formula provides the basic structure of the discussion of the *Thucydides* which is in three parts: first τὸ πραγματικόν, the handling of material, then τὸ λεκτικόν or style, then 'proofs', i.e. illustrative quotations. We begin with choice of subject: Thucydides considered the subjects of most of his predecessors too narrow, that of Herodotus too broad, and so he chose the history of one war (6). This picture of Thucydides in search of a subject may seem naive, but at least the moral censures of the *Imitation* have disappeared.[1] We then have nearly three chapters (6-8) commending the historian's respect for the truth and the pains he took to establish it, his desire to be impartial, and his hope that his History may be 'a possession for ever' and of use to mankind.

The arrangement of material (οἰκονομία) is subdivided in a new way: (i) διαίρεσις, the general method of arrangement, (ii) τάξις which (surprisingly) here refers only to the adequacy of beginning and end, and (iii) ἐξεργασία, the elaboration of particular events. These are legitimate critical categories and each judgement is strengthened by quotation and analysis.

Dionysius still considers (9) that Thucydides' chronological arrangement is confusing, and he backs his opinion by a careful analysis of the third book to show how the story of Mytelene is several times interrupted, as are other events. He then (10) turns to the first book and here too he documents his belief that the beginning of the History is confused and disordered: What Thucydides considered the true reason of the war does not appear until his ninety-seventh chapter: Dionysius would have preferred a more natural chronological order. As for ending with the battle of Cynossema, it seems strange that it never occurred to Dionysius that the History might have been left unfinished.

To ἐξεργασία (why some events or situations are treated at great length

---

[1] διάθεσις, the attitude of the writer to his subject, has also been dropped.

while others, equally important, are but briefly mentioned) Dionysius
devotes six longish chapters (13-18). This topic was not mentioned in
earlier works, and, obviously, the criticism is justified from the strictly
historical point of view. The capture of Melos was no more important
than that of Scione (v, 32), yet the latter is barely mentioned whereas for
Melos we have the whole Melian dialogue at the end of the fifth book.
The occasion of the famous funeral speech of Pericles (ὁ δὲ δὴ περιβόητος
ἐπιτάφιος, 18) is a trivial engagement at the beginning of the war, and
Dionysius gives a number of other examples of over-elaboration. The
answer is, of course, that Dionysius is blind to dramatic values in Thucydides, as many critics have been since. The Melian dialogue is where it is
because Thucydides wants to emphasize the pride and arrogance of Athens
just before the Sicilian expedition; while the funeral speech gives, at the
beginning of the war, a statement of the ideals of Athens by its great
leader. Indeed Dionysius nearly gives this answer himself when he says
that no doubt the historian wanted a funeral speech by Pericles, who died
shortly after,[1] but he does not consider that this answers his objection. He
finds (19) the same arbitrary amplification of events in the introduction of
the first book, and he boldly rewrites to make his point clear, omitting
chapters two to twenty, thus conforming much better to the 'rhetorical'
idea of the nature of an exordium, as he tells us himself (20).

He then turns to the consideration of style; he first reminds his readers
of the main formulae (22),[2] and again gives an account of the development
of history-writing from this point of view (23). Here we proceed on the
subdivision into word-choice, word-arrangement and the use of figures;
the word-choice and word-arrangement of Thucydides are very briefly
characterized (we had a fuller study of them in the *Composition* and the
Demosthenes). This is followed by a mere list of figures without explanation
or illustrations. This is rather surprising in view of the habit of illustrating
his statement which Dionysius had developed, and his friend Ammaeus
evidently found it as unsatisfying as we do. He asked for explanations,
and Dionysius complied with no very good grace, in the *Second Letter to*

---

[1] Ch. 18, U-R I, 352, 24.
[2] Style (λέξις) is as usual divided into ἐκλογή ὀνομάτων, word-choice, and σύνθεσις, word-
arrangement, but the subdivisions are different. *Ekloge* is here of two kinds, current language
and figurative language, while *synthesis* covers (*a*) phrases and clauses and periods, i.e. sentence-
structure, and (*b*) the use of figures, but as figures are explicitly said (U-R I, 358, 17) to apply
to single words as well as combinations of words, this should belong to both sections. He then
barely mentions that there are two kinds of virtues, the essential and the non-essential, and
then somewhat impatiently says these have all received plenty of study. The purpose of this
incomplete summary of formulae is obscure, for while he makes a brief use of the first in the
following chapter it is in a different form (23), and *he does not use the formula of qualities at all.*
One feels he briefly mentions the formulae for form's sake, and then goes on to other (and
better) things.

Ammaeus, which is, in effect, an addendum to this chapter, illustrating it point by point. It makes extremely interesting reading for anyone familiar with Thucydides.[1]

The list of figures is followed by a brief summary which gives four main characteristics of the historian's style: poetic vocabulary, variety in the use of figures, harsh word-arrangement, and swift condensation of expression (τὸ τάχυ τῶν σημασιῶν). As 'colouring' of the Thucydidean style are mentioned: astringency (στριφνόν), succinctness, sharpness, severity, weight, force, awesomeness and, above all, passion. 'When his ability matches his intention, the result is completely right and inspired, otherwise . . . the condensed expression leads to obscurity and other faults' (I, 363, 18).

The next twenty chapters are the 'proofs', i.e. passages from Thucydides to illustrate his virtues and his weaknesses, and, for the most part, Dionysius' judgements agree with those of modern commentators. He selects, for example, as a perfect example of Thucydides at his best (27) the famous description of the naval battle in the harbour of Syracuse (VII, 69-72), while, on the other hand, the equally famous chapter on the state of Greece (III, 82), analysed in fascinating detail, is not undeservedly quoted as exemplifying Thucydidean obscurity, rhetorical ornamentation and tortured syntax (28-33). Dionysius considers that Thucydides is at his best in straight narrative, and that his speeches are much more uneven. Several are analysed both for matter and for style. That of the Plataeans to Archidamus (II, 71-75) is said to be excellent (36), as is (42) their other (III, 53-59) but the speech of Hermocrates (VI, 76-80) is in part severely criticized (48). So is the second speech of Pericles in the second book (II, 60-64), and here we part company with our critic for his main objection is that while the words put in Pericles' mouth may express Thucydides' idea of him, no statesman would have been so unconciliatory in the circumstances (44-46). Dionysius has his eye too much on the rules of the rhetoricians. Then, the Melian dialogue is altogether too much for him! The moralist has hitherto been commendably kept in check by the critic, but here he overcomes him (37-41). No Athenian general could have expressed such arrogant, brutal, impious sentiments! That is probably quite true, as is the criticism that Thucydides is not keeping to his promise of sticking closely to what was actually said, but Dionysius quite fails to appreciate the historian's dramatic purpose, and he cannot refrain from repeating his earlier accusation of malice on the part of Thucydides towards his native city. Dionysius' last comment on the more elaborate speeches is worth quoting: no one talks that way in court, in the assembly or in conversation and if anyone did, 'not even their mothers and fathers could endure their displeasing language, but on hearing them would need interpreters, as if they were speaking a foreign tongue' (I, 409, 1-5).

There were some people in Dionysius' day who considered Thucydides the best model for historical if not for all writing; some of Dionysius' criticisms of the historian had no doubt been made before, at least in a general way, and they had something to say in his defence. Dionysius deals with these defenders briefly but adequately (50-51). They said that history is written for the educated only. This, says Dionysius, would make history the exclusive possession of the few; moreover, those who understand everything Thucydides wrote without syntatical notes are very few indeed! Nor is it true that he wrote the language of his day, for none of his contemporaries wrote like that. History may be to some extent poetic in diction, but it is not poetry. No other historian imitated Thucydides' style; Demosthenes did so, but we are given a passage from each of them to show that the orator avoids the excesses of the historian. Dionysius has some ironical words (52) about contemporary imitators of Thucydides who make a good thing out of it. By all means let us imitate his brevity and forcefulness, his intensity and impressive power, but not his obscurity in language and his excessive use of elaborate figures (I, 417, 20).

The great weakness of the rhetorical kind of criticism through the centuries was that it focused attention upon this or that quality of style, upon this or that aspect in the handling of subject-matter and used great literature merely as a storehouse of examples for the successful application of the formulae. Dionysius was no genius who could free himself entirely from this weakness and even he fails to appreciate or to evaluate a work as a whole. This is why he is blind to the dramatic purpose and the dramatic power of Thucydides, yet if this had been pointed out to him he would doubtless have replied that history is not drama and the two genres should not be confused. For the same reason he fails to appreciate the many-sided irony and humour of Plato. He fails to get into the mind of his author, with the result that, in the case of Thucydides and Plato, his criticisms often seem naive and unimaginative, and there is more to the greatness of Demosthenes than, for all his enthusiasm, he manages to convey.

Within these basic limitations, however, he is a far better critic than most of his predecessors. His essays differ from the textbooks of the rhetoricians in that he does keep his eye on his author throughout; he does not use his author merely to illustrate a particular formula or figure but his formulae to explain his author, and he himself clearly realized that the only kind of criticism he knows has serious limitations, when he described the charm of Lysias. He is quite right to insist, and to go on insisting, that criticism must see the faults as well as the virtues of an author's style, and that the critic has the right, indeed the duty, to be truthful and impartial. He developed a method of comparative criticism which, as far as the objective criticism of style was concerned, was eminently successful, and which, in its painstaking and detailed analyses, is wholly admirable. Several of his essays were probably far more controversial than we realize. His balanced judgement of Lysias, which freely admitted the orator's defects as well as admired his virtues, must have shocked Lysias' 'Atticist' admirers, and what seems to us excessive adulation of Demosthenes was probably addressed to the same group. The *Thucydides* too is admittedly controversial; we have pointed out its limitations but we should not allow our admiration for the great historian to blind us to the fact that a great many of Dionysius' stylistic criticisms are completely justified. Thucydides *is* obscure, often unnecessarily so. And if Dionysius does not fully understand the historical developments which led Thucydides to write as he did just at that moment in the history of the Greek language, he yet makes a gallant attempt to understand the historical developments in 'rhetoric' which led up both to Thucydides and to Demosthenes.

Above all, however, Dionysius has written one great book which is essential to our understanding of Greek prose style. The *Composition* proves him a literary theorist of considerable merit and gives us an insight into that language-music which is essential to all great poetry and prose. Not the least attractive merit of this work, indeed in all his works, is his own lively enthusiasm, that personal note in his undoubted love of great literature, a note very rare in ancient criticism. This makes him, with all his weaknesses, second only to Longinus in the direct if sometimes provocative and irritating appeal which he makes even to us, and which fully explains his great reputation in antiquity.

CHAPTER XIV

Horace

We know that Horace's *Satires* were published about 30 B.C., shortly after he obtained the patronage of Maecenas. Two of them, the fourth and tenth of the first book, are of literary interest as a defence and discussion of satire as a genre. From 30 to 23 B.C. Horace devoted himself to lyric poetry and the first three books of *Odes* appeared in 23 B.C. About three years later, in the first book of *Epistles*, we find him refusing to write more (lyric) poetry and giving his reasons in a letter to Maecenas (II, 1); and also violently resenting the cool reception given to *Odes* (II, 19). So far the dates are fairly clear. This is no longer true of the second book which contains the literary letters: one to Augustus, one to Florus and the famous Letter to the Pisos on the art of poetry. This last is 476 verses long and entirely devoted to the subject. The Letter to Florus and the *Ars Poetica* seem to belong to the time when he was not writing lyrics to which he turned again with the *Carmen Saeculare* in 17 B.C. and the fourth book of odes, published in 14. The letter to Augustus would seem to be after he started writing lyric poetry again or later. This, however, might also be true of the *Ars Poetica* and if we deal with the letter to Augustus last, it is as a matter of convenience rather than of conviction.

The fourth satire, then, begins a defence of the genre (without using the name *satura*) by an appeal to its famous Roman originator Lucilius. The poets of the Old Greek Comedy, we are told, did not hesitate to denounce anyone[1] who deserved it and in this, as in everything else except their metre Lucilius followed their example. He was witty, discriminating and . . . unpolished (*durus componere versus*). This was his failing; he wrote

---

[1] These personal invectives – τὸ ὀνομαστὶ κωμῳδεῖν – which Aristotle disliked (*Eth. Nic.* 4, 8, 6. 1128 a 22) disappeared in New Comedy and were replaced by innuendo (ὑπόνοια). If the word *poetae* is used deliberately in 1 (Heinze's note) while Horace disclaims the title for himself, for satire in general and for New Comedy (for this is the kind of comedy referred to at 45), it would seem that he links Lucilius more to the Old Comedy (6: hinc *omnis* pendet), and himself with the New. This implied contrast is somewhat confused, however, by including Lucilius with himself as writing satire which is *not* poetry at 57. For an analysis of this satire as 'a protest against the prevalent conception of satire' and a programme for a new and more urbane kind, rather than a reply to critics see G. L. Hendrickson in *AJP* 21 (1900), 121-42. For the opposite view Niall Rudd in *AJP* 76 (1955), 165-75. For a general discussion of all the literary satires and letters treated in this chapter see E. Fraenkel's *Horace*, C. O. Brink's *Horace on Poetry* and C. Bekker, *Das Spätwerk des Horaz*.

too much too fast. His flow was muddy and verbose; he was too lazy to endure the pains of writing well.

This sudden, unexpected criticism of Lucilius comes as a shock to any reader, as it is meant to do. Horace does not pursue his criticism further. Instead he continues his attack on careless verbosity by mentioning a contemporary who challenged him to a contest of speed, and disclaims any capacity in that direction or any desire to obtain the plaudits of the crowd; his works are not recited in public for the very reason that so many people dislike this kind of writing. Take any crowd, he says, and you will find many vices to expose; so they hate the poet as a madman bent on harming friend and foe alike.

Horace replies that, in the first place, he does not claim to be a poet. His verse is more like conversation (*sermoni propiora*); he leaves poetry to those more divinely endowed. He notes that it is an open question whether comedy itself can rightly be called poetry, for it is only every day language versified; this is true of both Lucilius' work and his own, whereas great poetry remains great when its metre is broken up, and he quotes Ennius to make his point.

Horace is quite sincere in this disclaimer, as far as his satires and later his letters are concerned. They are not poetry in the same sense as tragedy and epic, for example. And the reference to (later) comedy comes in naturally, for we have seen that critics generally put it on a lower level as a more natural and simple representation of every day life.

The innocent have nothing to fear, and in any case Horace's satires, he continues, are not published, only read to a few friends when pressed, so the accusation that he enjoys hurting people does not hold. This is somewhat disingenuous for even a private reading can be a source of fruity gossip, but he is more serious when he denies that he indulges in malice, backbiting, insinuations, and the like. That is the kind of person one should guard against. To ridicule Rufillus and Gargonius because the former smells of scent while the other smells like a goat (a quotation from an earlier satire, perhaps somewhat ruefully introduced) is quite a different thing surely.

This habit of noting men's failings, the poet tells us, was encouraged by his father as a part of his education – and Horace inevitably names some examples which he was warned not to follow. He was saved from many faults that way and he now amuses himself by writing down these things. This surely is a harmless foible. If you can't forgive this (so the satire ends) all the poets will be after you in a body.

Horace does not, in this poem, criticize Lucilius again after his first outburst. Yet criticism is obviously implied. He insists upon the close connexion between Lucilius and the invective of old comedy, while a

milder form of satire seems to be what he is defending. Throughout, he
claims the right to make personal attacks, but there is at least an implied
promise to use this right with moderation, and we know that attacks upon
named individuals tend to be fewer in later satires and disappear completely in the letters.[1] Lucilius showed no such moderation, he *did* widely
publish his writings and his personal attacks could *not* always be defended
on grounds of public morality. The only open criticism of Lucilius then
is of this style, but by implication he is criticized for his violence. We
should not forget that Horace, writing well before 30 B.C., is comparatively
young, not yet an established poet.

In any case, the criticism of Lucilius obviously annoyed some literary
circles in Rome, and Horace returns to the subject and to the nature of
satire, in the tenth. He is now much more explicit and more sure of himself, both in criticism and in his constructive theory,[2] but he is also more
generous in recognizing the greatness of his predecessor, though he claims
that he had always recognized it. No one, he says, is surely so inept an
admirer of Lucilius as to deny that he wrote with too little care and too
much speed.[3] Then come more constructive suggestions (7):

> It is not enough to ridicule and raise a laugh, though there is some
> virtue in that. We must be brief so that our sentences will run smoothly,
> unhampered by words which are but a burden on weary ears. Our
> conversational tone, though often playful, must at times be serious
> and we must play the part of a poet or an orator. Now and again we
> must be urbane, check our force and deliberately restrain it. Ridicule,
> in matters of importance, is a stronger and a sharper weapon than
> bitterness.

We can learn this, he continues, from the writers of Old Comedy, whom
critics like that fop Hermogenes never read, 'nor that ape whose only skill
is to mouth the words of Calvus and Catullus'.

The admirer of Lucilius now (23) replies that, at any rate, Lucilius'
habit of mixing Greek words with Latin was attractive, but Horace will

[1] For the significance of names in the satires see Niall Rudd in *CQ* NS. 10 (1960), 161-78.
[2] As Eduard Fraenkel well puts it, p. 128, 'To come from Satire IV to Satire X is not unlike
meeting again, after an interval of a few years, one whom we had known as a very young
man. The shape and colour of his face are still the same, but its lines are now more firmly
drawn and there is in it a determined expression which we had not noticed before.'
[3] This is the beginning of the tenth satire as now accepted. It is preceded by eight lines which
are almost unanimously rejected but occur in all the manuscripts. For an interesting defence
of them as written by Horace but probably discarded, see G. L. Hendrickson, in *CP* 11 (1916),
249-69. In two further articles of the same title, *CP* 12 (1917), 77-92 and 329-50, Hendrickson
argued that Valerius Cato was one of the circle of admirers of Lucilius, Calvus and Catullus
whom Horace is opposing throughout this satire. For Satire X see also Hendrickson in *Studies
in honour of Basil L. Gildersleeve* 161-8.

have none of it.[1] Such a mixture, he says, is no more acceptable in a poem than in a lawcourt. He keeps the emotional tone in check, however, by telling us that in his young days he used to write poetry in Greek himself, until Quirinus, the ancestral god of Rome, appeared in a dream and pointed out that he was making no great contribution there; so now, while others write on mighty subjects he is content with this more playful genre, with satires which do not have to satisfy demanding judges or struggle for success in the theatre. He leaves the higher kinds of poetry to others: 'comedy to Fundanius, tragedy to Pollio, epic to Varius', and 'the rustic Camenae rejoice to grant gentle and playful elegance to Virgil'.[2] Satire, 'which Varro had tried in vain', was the only genre where Horace felt he could do better – though recognizing the superiority of its founder (*inventore minor*). He would not venture to dispute Lucilius' crown, but he repeats that the older poet was muddy and verbose. Why not?[3] Was Homer faultless? Lucilius himself, and Ennius as well, never hesitated to criticize their predecessors. Granted that Lucilius was more urbane and careful than earlier Roman poets who wrote before Greek influence made itself felt, yet if he was writing today he would have pruned his work with more care and shown a more cultivated taste (71).

Horace again insists that he does not seek popular acclaim but the good opinion of the select, and among those whose opinions he values he mentions Varius, Maecenas, Virgil, Pollio, Messala and others. Among those he despises are Hermogenes Tigellius, Fannius, 'that bug Pantilius', and the Demetrius who may be the 'ape' mentioned above.

The group whom Horace wishes to please belong to the literary circles of Maecenas, Pollio and Messala, literary patrons and authors who were creating Augustan literature, and we may note in this connexion that Horace's hostility to those who uncritically worshipped the older Roman authors like Lucilius and Ennius (here once coupled together) comes to the fore. We shall see that he will always oppose those who excessively admire the old Roman poets. By and large, the Augustans took the great classical

---

[1] One might quote Cicero to the same effect: *Orator* 164: *qua re bonitate potius nostrorum verborum utamur quam splendore Graecorum. . . .*

[2] Here occurs the famous sentence: *Molle atque facetum Vergilio adnuerunt gaudentes rure, Camenae*, i.e. the Muses of the countryside had granted to Virgil the qualities expressed by the words *molle* and *facetum*. Commenting on the last word and its use in this very passage, Quintilian says (6, 3, 20): 'The word *facetus* is not only applied, in my opinion, to the comic for then Horace would not have said that nature had endowed Virgil with the gift of the kind of song that is *facetum*. The epithet, I believe, rather implies a certain grace and cultured elegance (*decoris magis et excultae elegantiae*).' We should probably translate 'gentle and playful elegance', remembering that, at the time Horace wrote, only the *Eclogues* were published. See, in particular, H. J. Rose, The *Eclogues of Virgil* p. 24; also C. N. Jackson, *HSCP* 25 (1914), 117-37 and Ch. Knapp in *AJP* 38 (1917), 194-9.

[3] One remembers how Dionysius too, Horace's contemporary, had to insist on his right of frank criticism of Greek authors. See above, pp. 225-6.

Greek poets as their models, and thought of themselves as developing
Latin literature beyond the point reached by their predecessors.

The membership of the other group, whom Horace opposes, is less
clear. Presumably it included the worshippers of Lucilius, but the reference
to Calvus and Catullus implies that it also included those 'moderns' who
followed Alexandrian rather than classical models and accepted the preference of Callimachus and his circle for shorter poems, epigrams,
lampoons, the epyllion, etc., perhaps also the Alexandrian view of poetry
as something remote from social and political life.

The differences between the two groups, however, are not clear-cut.
Virgil's *Bucolics* were obviously influenced by Theocritus. Calvus was, we
know, an Atticist, and Horace clearly wants the satirist to practise the
simple style. He was himself to write short poems and his contempt for
the vulgar crowd is Alexandrian and Callimachean, not classical. On the
other hand, Catullus had imitated Sappho as well as Callimachus. Rival
factions there certainly were, but their literary views, theories and tastes
were not always in clear opposition at all points.

The first satire of the second book is a humorous apology both for satire
and for not writing high poetry to celebrate the deeds of Augustus.
Horace professes to consult the old and respected jurisconsult, Trebatius
Testa, about his dilemma. Some people say his satire is bitter and goes
beyond the law (*extra leges*, a pleasant pun which, meaning the law of the
genre, also hints at possible legal penalties); others say he is just feeble and
his verses worthless. The old man advises him to stop writing, or swim
the Tiber three times a day, which are both impossible, and then suggests
writing poetry about Augustus' victories but Horace says he just hasn't
that kind of talent. So Trebatius warns him that 'bad poems' may bring
unpleasant consequences. Bad poems yes, says Horace, but what about
good poems which the Emperor likes? Well then, of course, people will
laugh and you'll be acquitted.

The bantering tone should be noted, for Horace seems here quite un-
worried by criticism, or by any pressing invitation from the Emperor to
write real poetry about him. Neither subject is, as a rule, so lightly dismissed.

The first book of the *Epistles* was published in 20 B.C. The introductory
letter is again addressed to Maecenas. Horace explains that he is now too
old for real poetry and that his interest has turned to philosophical
questions (broadly speaking, it is philosophy which he mostly discusses in
this book). The nineteenth letter, however, is very different; it is in effect
a satire, except that no names are mentioned, for in it Horace protests,

angrily, against the critics by whom the three books of his Odes had been
coolly received. There is a passage of considerable interest where he sets
out his claim to originality (21-34). He begins by making a valid distinction
between the kind of purely external 'imitation' which his own work has
had to suffer from 'a slavish crew', and the kind of imitation he himself
practised[1] when he was the first to bring the iambics of Archilochus into
Latin literature, thus initiating a new genre (the *Epodes*), and so with the
Alcaic metre. Here too he was a pioneer, i.e. in his *Odes*.

Then he tries to answer the question why so many people praise and
enjoy his poetry in private but criticize it in public. It is, he says, because
I don't seek public acclaim, I won't buy it by dinners or gifts of old clothes;
I don't go round to placate the tribe of grammatici, I don't give public
recitations; if I suggest that my poetry is too slight to be recited in a big
lecture hall, these people won't believe me, they say that I keep my work
for the Emperor's ear alone. I hesitate to show my contempt for these
critics, fearing physical assault. So I temporize, for I cannot stand the angry
hostilities of these public contests.

Who the critics were we do not know, they probably overlapped with
the group named in the tenth satire, but for a poet who despised popular
acclaim, Horace seems singularly bitter when he gets a bad press!

In the later letter to Florus (II.2) we find Horace again making excuses for
not writing 'poetry': he simply cannot write any more odes; when he was
young and poor he had to write poetry but not now; he feels his age;
different people want different genres from him; and anyway how can
he write in the noise and bustle of Rome? Mutual admiration societies
have no further attraction for him. Besides, writing poetry is hard work.

Then (109) his tone suddenly becomes more serious as he enlarges on
the heavy labour of the poet and the part he must play in creating and
enriching the language – a subject to which he will return in the letter to
the Pisos. The poet must be his own honest critic and judge the fitness of
words as a censor judges members of the Senate. He must be bold enough
to discard words of little beauty or dignity even if they are still embedded
in the language and hard to remove; he must bring back into the light
again the more beautiful words used by the grand old writers which are
now abandoned and deserted; and he must admit such new words as usage
will sanction. The poet's language should flow like a strong and pure
stream,[2] and improve the language of Latium: he must prune what is too

[1] One is reminded of the passage in the *Dinarchus*, where Dionysius distinguishes two kinds
of 'imitation'. See above, pp. 211-2.
[2] The poet's language must flow 'strong and clear like a pure stream' – *vehemens et liquidus
puroque simillimus amni* – which reminds one by contrast of Horace's criticism of Lucilius as

florid and luxuriant; smoothen what is too harsh, delete whatever is lacking in power. All this may seem like play, but it is torturing labour for the poet.

Then Horace returns to his excuses; all this he will leave to younger men, and busy himself with philosophizing.

So far then we have had from Horace a strong defence of satire as a literary genre, and at the same time a development of this genre into something more urbane, less bitter and less given to personal denunciations. From this the creation of another kindred genre, the epistle, similar in form but different in content has developed, a vehicle intended for the expression of general reflections about life. When Horace spoke of Lucilius as the heir to ancient comedy he knew very well that the inheritance was indirect, by way of writers like Bion of Borysthenes in the fourth century (he himself calls his satires Bionean)[1] and other Cynic writers who also preached by means of wit and ridicule and whose style was called serio-comic ($\gamma\epsilon\lambda o\iota o\sigma\pi o\upsilon\delta a\hat{\iota}o\nu$). Horace's intention when he deliberately ignored these intermediate writings, was probably twofold: he likes to find classical rather than later models for his writings, and he wanted to link Lucilius with the old comedy's personal invective which he himself would gradually (though not uniformly) abandon.

We have had a clear distinction made between true poetry and the *sermones* (both satires and letters) and a frank statement that he has not the talent necessary for these higher flights, which are mainly represented by tragedy and epic.

We also have had an interesting insistence upon the peculiar responsibility of the poet for the health and life of the language, and through the language, of the community. In other ways too Horace's poets, high and low, have a responsibility to society.

The notion of originality as we find it here granted to Lucilius (*inventor*) was not that he invented satire but that he was the first to introduce it into Latin, and Horace himself claims an originality of the same kind for his epodes and his Alcaic and other odes.

But what of the odes as a genre. Are they high poetry? Horace does not tell us, though his statement, after 23, that he has now retired from the labours of 'poetry' to confine himself to epistles, imply that they are, and this accords with the claims to immortality as a poet which he makes for himself in the odes. It is interesting too that though their length and precise technical elaboration would satisfy Alexandrian canons, it is the early classical lyrists whom he takes as his models and claims as their ancestors.

---

muddy, *lutulentus*, as Brink notes (p. 159, n. 3). He also notes that the stream-metaphor recurs in Horace and recalls Callimachus' commendation of a pure, small spring, *Hymn to Apollo* 108.

[1] *Bionei sermones* in the Letter to Florus 60.

ARS POETICA

We now turn to that delightful but mystifying document, the letter to the Pisos, father and sons (who have never been definitely identified). The title *Ars Poetica*, though not Horatian, is already used by Quintilian.[1] It is a misleading title, for, as we have seen, *ars* or τέχνη was the name given to the rhetorical textbooks, and it makes us expect the kind of logical structure of the parts which is quite foreign to a Horatian epistle, also a completeness of treatment which is absent. The letter is no more a complete discussion of poetry than is Aristotle's *Poetics* and, like Aristotle, Horace makes a number of general statements of wide application, but he concentrates his attention upon the two major genres, drama and the epic. Elegiacs and lyrics, for example, are only mentioned in passing; they are not discussed at all. In fact Horace says nothing about the types of poetry of which he was himself a master. We do not expect any discussion of *sermones*, but what of the odes? Why does the great lyric poet not discuss lyric poetry? This question has never been answered. Is it Aristotelian influence? Does his dislike of Callimachus' aversion to the writing of tragedies and epic cause him to take the opposite position? Is he following some earlier authority? Or is the answer simply that this *is* a letter to the Pisos and that the father or the sons' interests were directed to tragedy and epic? In that case their special interest in satyr-plays might explain the surprisingly long section on that type of drama.

We do not know, but the lack of any discussion of Horace's own type of poetry means that he himself is not directly involved and this accounts for a certain remoteness. The *Ars* does not have the fire or the intensity of the earlier defences of satire as a legitimate genre.

That a great many points made in the epistle derive directly or indirectly from Aristotle is universally admitted. Now, whatever the precise historical facts behind Strabo's well-known story[2] that Theophrastus bequeathed his library, including Aristotle's works, to Neleus, and that the books were hidden and neglected at Skepsis until, via the library of one Apellikon, they came to Rome in the time of Sulla and were then edited by Tyrannio and Andronicus, there is no doubt that many Aristotelian texts suddenly appeared in Rome about that time, and that Andronicus' edition of them became the received text of later commentators. The editing was going on about the middle of the first century. Horace must have been aware of it and he might well have read some Aristotle. There are, in the *Ars Poetica*, a great many points of contact with the *Poetics*, but they are peri-

---

[1] Quintilian 8, 3, 60: *Horatius in prima parte libri de arte poetica*, and the dedication of the *Institutio* par. 2.

[2] Strabo 13, 1, 54 (608-9) and Plutarch, *Sulla* 26. The story is discussed with some scepticism by P. Moraux, pp. 1-6 and 311-21; but see I. Düring, pp. 382, 393.

pheral, nothing recalls its principal theories, such as catharsis for example, or *hamartia* or recognition. It seems therefore most unlikely that Horace had read the *Poetics*. The same is true of the *Rhetoric*, and in any case this was much less relevant to his subject. Whatever is Aristotelian can easily be accounted for by an intermediate source or sources (perhaps Neoptolemus). In other cases, like the contrasted description of youth and old age, the similarity may be coincidental.

Broadly speaking, Horace is doing for poetry, especially dramatic and epic poetry, what Cicero did for prose. He is making available to his compatriots, in Latin, general Greek classical theories and advice.[1] This is a natural thing for him to do, since he so ardently believed that Roman poets should take the classical Greek poets as their models.

We must not look for original ideas in the *Ars Poetica*, even less so than in Cicero, who discusses in his rhetorical works an art of which he is the greatest Latin exponent, whereas Horace tends to restrict himself to genres which he never practised. It should be frankly admitted that all that Horace says has been said before, in Greek. This does not mean that the ideas are not his; we all make our own, and often passionately believe in, ideas we have not ourselves originated. Intellectual originality is a very rare quality which, in things literary and artistic, the Romans did not even profess to possess. They knew their own greatness; they had no need to stake false claims. On the other hand, there is no need to believe that Horace, any more than Cicero, was slavishly following one source. He no doubt took what he believed to be relevant and right, possibly from several sources, and omitted what he considered irrelevant or disagreed with. He nowhere, for example, discusses metaphor, which, since Aristotle, was a regular part of any discussion of word-choice. Many of the critical theories and formulae were, in any case, common property by this time.

What makes the *Ars Poetica* so very delightful is Horace's unsurpassed gift for the happy phrase or image, and many of them have passed into the common language of mankind. Horace passionately believed that Latin poetry, in the hands of his friends, Varius, Virgil and others, was blossoming into its golden age (as indeed it was) and that it had a better chance of developing further by emulating the great writers of the golden age of Greece rather than those of a less creative period, and by not letting itself be inhibited by the theorists and critics of the Callimachean school. Much as it owed to the Greeks in externals Latin literature was to be Roman in matter and spirit. Horace's philhellenism was never Graecomania, any more than Scipio's or Cicero's.

[1] A great many parallels have been worked out in detail by G. C. Fiske and Mary L. Grant in *Cicero's De Oratore and Horace's Ars Poetica*.

The mystifying aspect of the letter is the absence – or apparent absence – of any systematic plan or structure to the work. Horace passes from one subject to another quite freely; sometimes abruptly, sometimes by means of elaborate transitions which glide from one topic to another imperceptibly so that we are hardly aware of a change of subject. This casual informality is obviously deliberate. Yet we know that in the satires and letters, and often in the odes as well, Horace is not as casual as he seems, and that often, behind it all, a systematic structure of ideas can be discovered. Hence many attempts have been made to find such a structure here also, but there is no unanimity as to what that structure is. The problem is complicated by the statement of Porphyrio, a third-century commentator, that Horace, in the *Ars Poetica*, 'gathered together the precepts of Neoptolemus of Paros, not all of them, but the most important'.[1] Moreover, Horace was inevitably familiar with the formulae of rhetorical teaching, and as some of these, wholly or in part, can also be applied to poetry, he almost inevitably must have had them in mind. After all, even Aristotle in the *Poetics* refers us to the *Rhetoric* for the expression of ideas in verse as well as in prose. Besides, a good many of the precepts here enunciated by Horace for poetry are equally applicable to a work in prose. The nature of poetry, the poetic imagination, and other essential factors which distinguish poetry from prose are not discussed by Horace any more than by Aristotle. Poetry to the ancients was largely a matter of genres; it never occurred to Aristotle or Horace, for example, that a tragedy might be written in prose.

Horace seems to make a new start at verse 304 and to introduce the last part of the poem by saying that, while not writing poetry himself, he will yet advise the poet 'whence poetry is derived, what nurtures and forms a poet, what is appropriate and what is not, where excellence or error will lead him'. Eduard Norden suggested in 1905[2] that this indicated a main division of the *Ars* corresponding to the *ars-artifex* (art-poet) formula which was thought to have been used by other critics and technical writers as a structural basis for their works on poetry and rhetoric, so that all that follows 304 is concerned with the poet, while the preceding part is concerned with the art (1–303). This somewhat artificial division was then given new life, and the statement of Porphyrio new meaning, when Christian Jensen restored, in the badly damaged papyri of Philodemus' *Poetics*[3] the name of Neoptolemus (a very convincing restoration) who was there credited with a threefold formula, namely πόημα, πόησις,

---

[1] *in quem librum congessit praecepta Neoptolemi* τοῦ Παριανοῦ *de arte poetica, non quidem omnia sed eminentissima.*

[2] *Hermes* 40 (1905), 481–528. See also K. Barwick in *Hermes* 57 (1922), 1–62, esv. 43–62.

[3] Jensen, *Philodemus über die Gedichte*, pp. 93–127.

ποητής (poem, poetry, poet) as divisions of the art of poetry. Neoptolemus apparently discussed style under *poema*, content under *poesis*, and ποητής was then identical with the second part of Norden's division in the *Ars*, from 304 to the end. The other division Jensen placed at line 45, content or *poesis* being discussed at the beginning, and 46-294 dealing with style or poema. Having thus forced Neoptolemus' structural triad upon Horace, Jensen then proceeded to use Horace to reconstruct the theories of Neoptolemus.

The elusive structure of so famous a poem set a fascinating problem to scholars, and much has been written on the subject in various countries in the last two generations. The reader is referred to C. O. Brink's recent book, *Horace on the Art of Poetry* for a full and interesting review of the whole controversy. Brink too applies Neoptolemus' threefold formula to the *Ars*, accepts Norden's division at 304, or thereabout, but he considers 1-40 as introductory and outside the scheme; 41-118 is then concerned mainly with style (*poema*) and 119 to 294 with content (*poesis*) which at least preserves Neoptolemus' order. The last section is, as before, *ad poetam*. This modernized Neoptolemic view comes nearer to a solution of the problem because, although its author does not always escape the temptation of seeing Neoptolemus lurking under every pronouncement, he does try to distinguish between the probable and the merely possible, he does recognize that Horace's 'gliding transitions' deliberately obscure changes of subject and hide the structural skeleton, he acknowledges that Horace's special preoccupations alone may account for certain passages, and that certain recurrent concepts cut across boundary lines and provide additional patterns. If due weight is given to these concessions, the Neoptolemic theory becomes much less objectionable.[1]

It should be mentioned here, however, that the very existence of the *poema-poesis-poetes* structure has been denied, even in Neoptolemus himself.[2] I should myself, be inclined to accept it even in Horace's work, pro-

[1] We have already said something of Brink's reconstruction of Neoptolemus' theories when discussing criticism in Alexandria (above, p. 126 and p. 127, note 2). As regards the structure of the *Ars Poetica*, due weight should be given to his last chapter which recognizes other structural patterns, for when he is using Horace to reconstruct Neoptolemus he is himself inclined to go too far as when he suggests that Neoptolemus too may have 'placed certain overriding demands such as the principle of unity at the beginning of his treatise, and later reiterated them whenever it was expedient to do so' (p. 139). Such a supposition is surely unnecessary, for it suggests that Horace followed Neoptolemus somewhat slavishly, which is hard to believe. Similarly, the notion of *decorum* was such a commonplace in the first century as in Cicero and Dionysius, that it is unnecessary to trace it back to Aristotle through Neoptolemus (e.g. p. 96).

[2] See H. D. Dahlman in *Varros Schrift de Poematis* who maintains that there is no evidence that the work of Neoptolemus or any other Hellenistic critic was built on the bipartite or tripartite formula and that what has been taken for a structural formula was merely a series of definitions in the introduction to critical works. The evidence is in any case very much later.

vided that due allowance is also made for simple associations of ideas and it is recognized that the rhetorical formulae of the day were also present to Horace's mind. At any rate, whatever scheme or structure the *Ars Poetica* may have should emerge from the work itself, and perhaps only the student who approaches it in blissful ignorance of scholarly theories can be an unbiased judge in this matter. The summary of the poem which will follow shortly may enable the reader to make such a judgement. There we will leave the problem of structure, remembering that formulae are less important than the ideas they contain, and that it is in any case the latter which are, or should be, our main concern.

We will approach the work from a different angle. It is obvious that Horace, in the course of the letter, chooses to emphasize a number of topics by dwelling on them and that he deliberately uses the figure which the rhetoricians call *amplificatio* or *epimoné* to put them in relief. Let us look at these topics first, since he evidently thought them important. Some of them we have already met.

The first such topic (49-71) is the right of the poet to use new words where necessary, a licence freely accorded to the poets in the time of Caecilius and Plautus which should not be denied to Varius and Virgil; surely they have as much right to enrich the language as Cato and Ennius had,

> The forests change as the years go by and this year's foliage falls; so words grow old and die, and words newly born have the vigour of youth . . .

and Horace goes on to illustrate this idea by reflecting on the mortality of all human achievements, a beautiful passage. This links up with his attacks on the uncritical worship of early Roman poets who wrote in more primitive days and before the full effects of Greek culture were felt. It also reminds us of that almost solemn passage in the letter to Florus about the poet's influence on, and responsibility for, the life of a language. It is especially topical in Rome, because Roman writers were very conscious of the beauty of Greek, of its greater development and adaptability. We

N. A. Greenberg in 'The Use of Poiema and Poiesis', accepts Dahlmann's view, draws attention to the fact that Porphyrio speaks of *praecepta*, *not the organizational principle* of Neoptolemus, and investigates what these precepts may be.

Recently, Carl Bekker, *Das Spätwerk des Horaz* (Göttingen, 1963) has proposed a different threefold division of the *Ars Poetica*, namely 1-40, 41-250 and 251-476. He points out (which is certainly true) that his first and last division are much more in Horace's style, enlivened by dialogue and the like, and give expression to many general philosophical ideas which we find elsewhere in Horace, here applied to poetry. This leaves 41-250 and in this central part, which is much more technical, Horace is following a previous source, probably Neoptolemus. A. Ardizzoni in Ποίημα points out on pp. 31-40 that the words *poema* and *poesis* are used by Horace in quite different senses than by Neoptolemus according to Philodemus.

meet this feeling in Lucretius, Cicero and others, and it still worried Quintilian. Horace knows that those who uncritically worshipped the old Roman writers stood in the way of progress.

The second topic, amplified but not quite at such length, comes (99-113) where it has just been stated that the genres must be respected, that comedy and comic diction are different from tragedy. Horace then enunciates a principle also found in Aristotle and Cicero that the actor (and the poet) must *feel* the emotions he is trying to communicate; just as in life we feel anger or sorrow before we express them by words and play of features, so the process must be repeated in dramatic performances. This passage stands almost by itself (as a similar statement does in Aristotle).[1] Ancient literary theory is generally so objective, deals so much with the product rather than with its creator that anything which goes beyond this should be noted. Here the statement is, as it were, sandwiched between more usual references to appropriate diction.

Another topic, this time amplified at considerable length in two different places (155-78 and 310-18) is that dramatic characters must be true to life. The first passage emphasizes differences due to age and gives us a striking description of youth contrasted with old age (161-76), while the second emphasizes the differences due to one's station in life or relationships. Both passages express the Platonic-Aristotelian theory of art as imitation of life (*doctus imitator*, 318) and both are closely related to the emphasis on content as against style; indeed the conclusion of the second leads directly to the statement that 'a moral tale adorned with attractive commonplaces' (general statements of moral import) is the way to success (319-22) as opposed to 'melodious trifles'. Nor is this an isolated sentiment for Horace had already emphasized that the choice of subject was the most important thing, and that everything else would follow (40-41). This almost Stoic insistence on content as against style is very Roman and natural enough in Horace (had he not before this turned to philosophy in the letters?). He seems to be speaking in conscious opposition to those who put the emphasis on artistic elaboration, the Alexandrian critics perhaps and also to Philodemus who denied the theory of imitation and the need for knowledge of life in the poet.[2] Of course, Horace, of all men, knows well enough that artistry is needed and when he raises the question later whether a poet should edify or give pleasure, he will say he should do both (332-5 and 343-6).

Then there is what we might call the need-for-training-correction-and-criticism theme which runs through the last part of the poem and leads to

[1] See above, pp. 88-9.
[2] See p. 195, above.

various elaborations or amplifications of its different aspects. It links up with the inadequacies of early Roman poetry which Horace is never tired of pointing out. He dwells again upon the careless and primitive nature of Accius' and Ennius' poetry and the lack of criticism of Roman poets (258-64), and also on the need to study Greek models to overcome this (267-9), then cites Plautus as an example of carelessness. A more sophisticated age needs to be frank in its criticism (270-4).

The first amplification of this general theme occurs where the incapacity of Roman poets to bear the labour of correction is said to have deprived Latium of potential greatness (289-91), followed by a direct appeal to the young Pisos (an appeal to the young generation really) to correct their work again and again in every detail. The contrary view was that of Democritus when he said that there are no sane poets on Helicon – thus preaching that poetry is a matter of native genius only. The baneful effects of this are shown in the amusing picture of the phony poets, those who believe that long hair, a beard, dirty nails and lack of personal hygiene make a genius.

A little later, we find a contrast between the Greeks, endowed both with native genius (*ingenium*) and artistic skill, and the little school scene where the Roman boy learns only to love money and is complimented upon his financial arithmetic, thus creating in Rome a climate inimical to good poetry (323-32).

Then, from 347 on, Horace concentrates upon this general theme almost entirely. Some mistakes can be allowed and forgiven, but not repeated ones (347-60), for second-rate poetry is never necessary; we can do without it (366-78). This leads to the need for training and correction again (379-90).

After an excursus on the benefits of poetry, we return to our theme at 412 and stay with it. First the need for training which is as necessary to poetry as to any other skill (412-18), then criticism, and on this aspect Horace now dwells at length. First we have the picture of the rich poet who gathers his yes-men together and gets praised to the skies; this is bad criticism or rather no criticism at all (419-35). Then a vivid presentation of the honest and true critic, enlivened by dialogue (435-52). The whole passage 419-52 is a double panelled *amplificatio* on the nature of criticism. The three needs, for training, for criticism, for prolonged correction, are but three aspects of the same need, and they emphasize the need for *ars*, i.e. technical knowledge and training, in strong contrast to the Democritean theory which Horace considers so very dangerous for his compatriots because it is precisely in patience and technique, not in native genius that they are lacking. The humorous picture of the mad poet with which the *Ars* now ends takes on a new significance from this context.

The excursus on the benefits which poetry has brought to mankind (391-407) is the working over and applying to poetry in particular of the old commonplace of the power of *Logos*, the Word, which we know to be as old as Gorgias and have also met in Cicero.[1] It is brought into a Roman context at the end, namely that poetry is so vital and important a human activity that you should not be ashamed of 'the Muse who plays upon the lyre and the singer Apollo' (406). Horace is clearly combating a very real prejudice against mere poetry on the part of the Romans.

There is, finally, a further passage which may not qualify as an *amplificatio* in the technical sense but enough emphasis is put upon it to bring it into sharp relief (202-18). It describes the dangerous degeneration of theatre audiences from an earlier time when life in Rome was more simple and sober, before she became the conquering metropolis of the Mediterranean world. The picture is partly fanciful, for what we know of Roman audiences, in the time of Plautus and Terence and earlier, does not encourage us to think that they were ever very discriminating. The passage also reminds one of the theme of musical degeneration so frequent in Greek texts from Aristophanes through the fourth century. As so often, Horace is echoing a Greek theme but at the same time making it highly relevant to a Roman context. There is no doubt that the power of Rome which made the golden age of literature possible brought with it prosperity, luxury and the love of possessions. When Horace says it made theatre audiences more demanding and less discriminating he may be speaking strict truth.[2] Drama and literature were probably affected and Horace was indeed closer to the end of Latin poetry's highest level of achievement than he knew. For once, Horace himself appears as a *laudator temporis acti*, and the passage exemplifies that yearning of the Romans generally for the ethics of a much simpler age long past which could never return.

The emphasis which Horace puts upon these general themes, a quite deliberate emphasis, makes one see his general critical position more clearly, and the way most of them are obviously related to the contemporary background makes one realize that the *Ars Poetica* is a more controversial document than it at first appears. The emphasis on revision, hard work, and criticism is natural to Horace, for though his poetic genius has been doubted – and it is one of his most attractive qualities that he doubted it himself – his workmanship has always been recognized as supremely successful. He regards poetry as a serious pursuit, not something gentlemen can successfully practise in their spare time (as many Roman gentlemen did, both then and later). It requires great knowledge of life, infinite pains, and considerable training. In this he is fighting

[1] Above, p, 169.
[2] Cicero, *De Legibus* 2, 15, 39 and Quintilian 1, 10, 31.

Roman prejudice, and Roman impatience with technicalities. Yet he is himself a Roman, and he too feels that poetry should be socially responsible and socially beneficial, with an important part to play in society. His insistence on technical excellence is almost Alexandrian, but his insistence on socially useful and moral content is more classical, more on the side of the philosophers.

Let us now look at the letter as a whole. As the document is brief, the following summary will give the reader a more complete picture, and will also enable him to follow the sequence of ideas and search for his own pattern or plan. Following his own advice, Horace plunges *in medias res*:

> If to a human head a painter should want to join a horse's neck, or spread many-coloured feathers over limbs gathered all from different sources, so that what is a shapely woman becomes a black fish below, and you were invited to see his work, my friends, could you restrain your laughter? Believe me, a book whose meaningless images, like the nightmare of sickness, are conceived so that neither head nor foot belongs to one form, is very like that painting. 'Painters and poets' you may say 'have always had the same freedom to be as daring as they like.' I know, and myself both claim and grant that freedom, but not to the extent of joining the monstrous to the peaceful, to pair serpents with birds, or lambs with tigers (1-13).

These first lines are clear: a work of art must have unity, the parts must be appropriate to the whole. It must be one, as Aristotle said of tragedy, or, as Plato put it, it must be a ζῷον, an organism. Horace elaborates the same idea by protesting that a purple patch (*purpureus pannus*) must not be introduced, however beautiful in itself or whatever scope it gives to the author's particular talent, after a promising beginning, if it is not relevant to the particular subject. And the passage ends with the generalized statement: 'Choose whatever subject you wish, provided it be simple and one.'

But then, without transition,[1] there follows the unconnected idea that the attempt to achieve a desired quality of style often lands one in a neighbouring fault[2]:

> I try to be brief, and become obscure; a man who tries to be smooth

---

[1] It is interesting to find so abrupt a switch so early in the poem. The next point has nothing whatever to do with the notion of unity or plot and is on a purely stylistic point. I cannot see any association of ideas which accounts for the new subject. One almost feels Horace is warning us not to look for any logical sequence. He then returns to unity, and it is the illustration of the search for variety which brings us back to unity, a purely external transition.

[2] For the 'neighbouring vices' see Demetrius 114, *Ad Herennium*, 4, 10-11 (15-16), Seneca, *Controv.* 7, Praef. 9, and *On the Sublime* ch. 3.

lacks vigour and spirit; one who aims at grandeur becomes turgid; if
he wants to avoid storms, his timidity makes him crawl along the
ground; and one who seeks too much variation on one theme paints a
dolphin in the forest or a boar upon the ocean. The desire to avoid one
fault leads to another, if art be absent.[1]

The background here seems to be the notion of vices neighbouring upon
virtues which was something of a commonplace, and its last illustration
brings us back to the notion of unity and to the thought that every
part must be developed so as to fit into the whole and not be overelaborated at the expense of the whole.[2] Many a sculptor is good at
particular details – be it hair or nails – but he cannot make a whole statue.
This is like having beautiful hair or eyes with a crooked nose (37).

Somewhat abruptly again, Horace now turns (38) to the choice of
subject. The writer should carefully consider this and be sure that it is
within his powers, for if the subject is well chosen, then neither the power
of expression (*facundia*) nor lucid order (*ordo*, the arrangement of content)
will desert him. For the beauty and excellence of order requires 'that he
should say now what now needs to be said' (43) and this should be the aim
of the poet.

It seems natural for the choice of words to follow the choice of subject,
though the combination of words is mentioned in the same breath, for a
new combination makes even an old word seem new (47-48). And now
comes the insistence on the right to coin new words when needed and the
splendid passage, already mentioned, on language as a living thing and
the mortality of all human achievements (48-72), ending with:

. . . all the works of man will perish, as must once honoured, charming,
popular ways of speech. Many words now dead will live again, if
usage wishes, for usage is the arbiter, the law and norm of speech.

Diction is now followed by word-arrangement, which in poetry is
metre. (Here Horace seems for a brief moment to be following the
inventio, dispositio, dictio, compositio formula.) Homer showed the hexameter to be the right metre for epic, elegy was first used for mourning,
then for thanks at a prayer fulfilled, though the question of who originated
it is still undecided (*sub iudice*). Archilochus first used iambics for lampoons
and it was then taken over by comedy and tragedy as a metre suited to
conversation, action and overcoming the noise of the theatre. To lyric

[1] The emphatic position, at the end of the line and paragraph of the word *ars* (i.e. technical
knowledge and training) – *si caret arte* – should be noted. It introduces early an idea much
emphasized later.
[2] Cf. Plato. *Rep.* 4. 420 c-d.

metres was entrusted paeans to gods and heroes and the celebration of
athletic victories, then love and wine which occupy the young.

Having thus tied in different metres with different kinds of song, it is
natural that the theory of genres should be mentioned, with the requirement that the laws of the genres should be respected (85), in tone and subject-matter. It is at this point that our general view seems to narrow to
the theatre, as the two dramatic genres, comedy and tragedy, are the
only two used in illustration (89-98). The matter, the emotions, must be
treated differently, on the comic and on the tragic stage, though at excep-
tional moments they come close to each other. Moreover the actor (and
the poet) must feel and display the emotions they wish to communicate to
the audience,[1] for if the language is unsuited to the emotions portrayed,
you'll be laughed off the stage. Characterization concerns what is said and
how it is said and it seems incorrect to suggest that the whole passage on
genres, and what is appropriate to them is concerned only with style,
though it is true that the last part of it emphasizes diction.

We are now definitely settled in the theatre, and the mention of characters and how they must be represented very naturally leads to mention
of the plot itself, still in terms of characters of the old legends. Here (125)
Horace is more restrictive than Aristotle,[2] for, though he admits the
possibility of fictitious characters (i.e. not belonging to the usual legends)
and advises that these, if dramatized, must be consistent with themselves,
he believes this to be difficult indeed, and strongly advises (129) that one
should pick one's characters (and plots) from Homer. This mention of the
epic should not disturb us for in the following section illustrations are
taken from the epic as well as from drama,[3] the two genres being closely
allied, a relationship that goes back at least as far as Plato who called
Homer the first tragedian, and in any case epic and tragedy were regarded
as the two kinds of high poetry, as we have already seen.

The dramatist will be able to make the old stories his own if he does not
imitate the lesser poets or translate word for word, which would involve
him in unnecessary difficulties. He should be particularly careful how he
begins his tale.[4] He must not promise too much or his mountainous

[1] 101-11. Cf. *Poetics* 17 (1455 a 30); Cicero *De Oratore* 2, 189. Above, p. 243 note 1.

[2] The whole section reminds one of Aristotle's four requirements for tragic characters
(*Poetics* 15 ad init.), that they should be good, true to type, true to life, and consistent (above,
p. 80). Horace has three of these, namely (i) true to type, e.g. Achilles or Medea, (ii) consistent, though this is mentioned only in connexion with fictitious characters (119-27), and
(iii) true to life (152 ff.). For Aristotle on fictitious characters see *Poetics* 9 (1451 b 24).

[3] As Brink has pointed out pp. 7-8.

[4] One is reminded of Dionysius' emphasis on the right beginning, see above (p. 210) and
of Antonius' statement in Cicero on the importance of a good beginning in *De Oratore* 2, 313 ff.
That the exordium in poetry and prose had a similar function had been noted by Aristotle,
Rhet. 3, 14, 5-6 (1415 a 8-25).

travail will lead only to the birth of a mouse! Begin simply like Homer, do not begin too far back or begin a tale of Troy with the miraculous birth of Helen from an egg. Homer plunges straight into the middle of his story. What he cannot tell successfully he leaves out, he mixes truth and fiction so well that beginning, middle and end fit together without discrepancy (136-52). After this advice on how to begin a tale, where Horace seems to have the epic mainly in mind, we return to the characters of drama and the need for them to be true to life; this is now amplified by the passage which dwells on the difference between youth and age[1] a difference which, along with all others, must be reproduced on the stage (153-78).

We now suddenly come to a passage of miscellaneous advice to tragic writers (179-201): (1) as things seen impress one more vividly than things heard, certain things – Medea's murder of her children, for example, or the banquet of Atreus, or such incredible things as Procne changing into a bird – had better not be enacted; (2) the play should have five 'acts', neither more or less; (3) no god should appear unless he is needed to untie the knotted action; (4) no more than three actors should have speaking parts; (5) the chorus should play its part in the action, its odes should not be irrelevant to the story, and, further, it should always be on the side of justice and virtue.

Murder was not allowed on the Greek stage but reported by messengers, and we remember Aristotle's advice that nothing unexplainable or irrational (ἄλογον) should take place on the stage.[2] That the epiphanies of the gods often helped the tragedians out of their difficulties was an accusation made by the comic poets, but it was not deserved, by the great tragedians at least.[3] Horace, however, seems to accept this as their proper function. The three actor convention was, of course, Greek. The need for the choral part to be relevant reproduces what Aristotle said in the *Poetics*,[4] but their moral function is not Aristotelian. Neither is the five-act requirement.[5] Both of these last two points probably derive from an Alexandrian source, though the moral duty of the chorus might well have been added by Horace himself.

Consideration of the chorus' part naturally leads to the music which accompanied their odes, and, in a passage already noted for its emphasis, Horace states that this music has degenerated from the simpler days of old

---

[1] See above, p. 239, where the similarity to Aristotle, *Rhet.* 2, 12-14, 1389 a 3 ff. is noted.

[2] *Poetics* 15 (1454 a 36 – b 8).

[3] On this use being made of the gods see above, p. 31 note 3.

[4] *Poetics* 18, 1456 a 26 and above, p. 90.

[5] By *actus* Horace presumably means the parts of the play separated by choral odes or interludes. As there was no chorus in Roman comedy, Donatus has a hard time applying the rule to Terence. See W. Beare in *Hermathena* 67 (1946), 52-59.

as power and luxury grew, and the audiences included boors and knaves cheek by jowl with the worthy and the cultured (202-19). He undoubtedly was thinking of the Roman stage, but the passage also echoes similar complaints in Greek writers from Aristophanes on. One is reminded, too, of the Aristotelian tendency to blame 'the depravity of audiences' as well as of Horace's own frequently expressed contempt for the vulgar crowd.[1]

Horace now abruptly turns to discuss the satyr-play, and the attention he gives it, as a genre intermediate between tragedy and comedy (220-51) is puzzling. As usual, however, some of the things he says can be applied far beyond the genre immediately under discussion. The transition is meant to be humorous rather than historical (which it obviously is not) when he says that tragedians introduced the satyr-play to keep an unruly audience in their seats. He insists that the proprieties must be preserved, the gods of tragedy must not be made to speak the earthy language of the taverns, nor on the other hand wander in the clouds. Tragedy among the satyrs is rather like a Roman matron bidden to dance on a holiday; she must not sink to the everyday language of comedy. In a satyr-play (240):

> My song would be composed in words everybody knows, so that anyone could hope to do as well, but, should he try, he will perspire profusely and toil in vain, so great is the power of sequence and phrasing, such the honour which words from the common stock can attain.[2]

Vulgarity will not be given the prize by the solid citizenry of Rome. Horace seems to have only the satyr-play in mind, but he gives here an excellent description of his own poetry, at least in the satires and epistles. They too were a genre between everyday conversation and high poetry.

The mention of the choice of language not unnaturally brings us back to word-arrangement and metre, and we are given a fanciful picture of the iambus and the iambic trimeter only gradually and reluctantly admitting the spondee, especially to the fourth and second feet, and this gives Horace an opportunity to criticize the heavy spondaic metres of Accius and Ennius and to express again his opposition to those whose excessive admiration for the early and more primitive Roman poetry turns them away from the Greek models they should study day and night (251-71). He claims a more refined taste for himself and his contemporaries.

The mention of Greek models leads to a brief glance at the history of the development of Greek comedy and tragedy – a somewhat confused

---

[1] E.g. *Odes* 3, 1. 'odi profanum vulgus et arceo,' and we are reminded of his frequent denials, in the *Satires* and *Letters* that he seeks public acclaim. See above, p. 234.

[2] Cf. Cicero's description of the simple style, and also Dionysius, *Lysias*.

HORACE 251

glance which mixes the history of the two, and speaks of the old comedy being suppressed by law, which is inaccurate. The purpose of this passage (275-84), however, is presumably to point out that Greek drama too had to develop and that it is not the more primitive which is the more admirable. Roman literature would do as well, if only the Romans had the patience (285):

> Our poets left nothing untried, nor were their merits least when they dared to follow no longer in the footsteps of the Greeks but to celebrate Roman deeds on the tragic and the comic stage. Latium would have been as famous for its literature as for its brave deeds of war, if only the labour and delay involved in polishing their work had not irked every one of our poets.

And he warns the young Pisos of the necessity to polish and correct literary work to the last detail (*ad unguem*, 294). Democritus' saying that sane poets have no place on Helicon and that native genius outweighs art and training has led to a mass of long-haired, unwashed, dyspeptic people who think themselves poets if they look like a genius. If that's the price of being a poet, Horace will have none of it! (303)

However, if not a poet he can still, like a whetstone which cannot itself cut anything but can sharpen other instruments, advise poets as to the sources of poetry, what nurtures and makes a poet, what is appropriate, what is not, and whither excellence and error will lead (304-8).[1]

The source and first principle of good writing is wisdom. The Socratic dialogues will provide the subjects (*rem*, 310) and words will willingly follow a subject well chosen. Horace then enlarges again upon the need for the poet to observe and understand life, this time from the angle of different duties and professions (319-22):

> Sometimes a tale shining with commonplaces and the right moral, though it have no charm, dignity or art, pleases the people more and lives longer than verses poor in content or melodious trifles.

Thus the practical Roman, but he goes on at once to express his admiration for the native genius and the artistic finish of the Greeks' high poetry, and contrasts with this the Roman love of money and possessions which is inculcated into them from their early years. In such an atmosphere, how can we hope for poetry worth preserving (323-31)?

Poets want either to benefit or delight their hearers, or to do both at once (333-4). Horace interrupts the consideration of this question to insist on brevity, and adds that fiction must remain close to life. Our young bloods will reject the impossible, while our elders will pass by any poetry

This is the point where Horace is supposed to turn from the art to the poet. Above, p. 240.

that is not useful, and (thus reverting to the previous subject) it is the work which is both useful and charming which will be successful with publishers and public alike (343-6).[1]

Some faults are inevitable and may be forgiven, but repeated faults will not. To be occasionally good, like Choerilus, is not enough. Even Homer nods, but poetry, like painting, is of two kinds: that which can only be looked at from a distance and that which will bear close and repeated scrutiny (365). We may have to make do with the second-rate in some things when the best is not available, but the mediocre poet finds no forgiveness 'from men or gods or bookshops' – he is someone we can do without (366-78). Those not trained to other pursuits refrain from them, but everybody thinks he can write poetry (384).

> You will not say or compose anything against the will of Minerva. Such is your decision and your intent. But if you should write something one day nonetheless, submit it to Maecius' judgement, or your father's, or mine, and keep it among your tablets for nine years. You can destroy what you have not published; once you let your words go out, they cannot be recalled (390).

Then comes the passage on the benefits that poetry has conferred upon mankind[2] since Orpheus (391-406) with the conclusion that one should not be ashamed to practise it. The old problem is briefly mentioned: is good poetry due to native ability or to *ars* (technical knowledge and training)?[3] The answer is that both are needed (408-11). Poetry needs training as much as does chariot-racing for which the young will give up much (415).

Horace then draws a picture of the wealthy poet who is praised by his friends in exchange for favours received, but who will never know honest criticism (419-37) and, in contrast, the duty of a friend to be an honest critic, a very Aristarchus (438-50).

As so often, Horace ends the poem on a lighter note, and we have an amusing picture of the poet eagerly hunting out victims to recite to, as mad as Empedocles who threw himself into the crater of Etna. If a poet falls into a hole he may be doing the same thing, so don't pull him out. Why he should go on writing is a mystery. Better avoid him or he'll stick to you like a leech and never let you go.

---

[1] This is Cicero's *docere* and *delectare*, and those who believe Horace to have this rhetorical formula at the back of his mind could point out that he has already dealt with *movere* 88-115. The question as to whether poets should teach as well as delight is a very old problem. It was debated with new vigour in Alexandria and also in Philodemus (above, pp. 128 and 195).

[2] The passage is discussed above, p. 245, and cf. e.g. Cicero *De Inventione* ad init. and p. 169, above.

[3] Cf. the long discussion whether rhetoric is an *ars* in Cicero, *De Oratore* 2. Above, p. 179.

Horace discusses poetry once more in the *Letter to Augustus*, and it is fitting that we should end our consideration of him as a critic with this document in which he shares with his Emperor his concern, his hopes and his fears for the future of Roman poetry in which both men were so profoundly interested. Horace preserves the conversational style which he had made so very much his own, but a public letter to the emperor is inevitably a more formal document and he develops his subject in a fuller and more consecutive manner.

The first eighteen lines are in a sense a dedication, and even this is not irrelevant for, though Horace does not specifically say so, it was Augustus who provided the peace and prosperity which made the golden age of Latin literature possible. Unlike many heroes of old, says Horace, Augustus is honoured by his people while still alive. In this the people are wise but they are foolish to honour poetry only if it is remote from them in space or time (a typically easy transition). They will admire any extant bit of primitive latinity, Twelve Tables and all, but dislike anything contemporary. Here we are on familiar ground, but that Horace gives this subject pride of place and develops it at considerable length (20-90) shows that he still believed it to be of vital importance. We should also note that this uncritical worship of the Roman ancients is not restricted to a literary coterie but a very widespread prejudice, at least among the older generation (*cuncti paene patres*).[1] Horace is sarcastic – how many years must one be dead to become an ancient? – and he is angry (76):

> What makes me indignant is that a work is condemned, not because it is thought to be poor in style or lacking in beauty, but because it is recent.

The next passage, with its parallel pictures of classical Greece and earlier Rome, expresses, by implication rather than explicitly, the Augustan ideal of a literature which would combine the artistic perfection of the Greeks with the sturdy devotion to duty of an earlier Rome, a literature which would give both delight and responsible moral guidance, be both pleasurable and useful as he put it in the *Ars Poetica*. Horace forces the contrast somewhat when he describes Greece at peace enjoying its games and poetry, lyric and dramatic 'like a small girl playing under the eye of her nurse' (99), capricious in her taste and irresponsible; but he also emphasizes, on the Roman side, that the sturdy devotion was that of an earlier day. It is probably to emphasize the dangers involved on either side that he describes Greece with what seems patronizing condescen-

---

[1] Note *populus* at 18, *vulgus* at 63, *patres* at 81 (the older generation, not the senate) and *senes* at 85.

sion.[1] He has shown elsewhere that he has no illusions about contemporary Roman taste, and he clearly notes here (109-10) that the Romans are changing for the worse – and everybody is in a fever to write poetry.

This provides a transition to another favourite subject: that poetry requires training in the art as much as medicine or navigation. This is not here enlarged upon and Horace turns to the function of the poet in society, – so that even the craze to write has its good points.

As the poet's chief passion is to write, he will be an example of how external misfortunes should be endured. He may not make a good soldier but he is useful in other ways; he is largely responsible for the education of the young, he teaches them their language and to appreciate the proper use of it. Through his works the poet is a teacher of morals, of the right feelings towards the gods, how to pray to them, as men did in early times when the harvest was in (140).

This naturally brings before us a picture of primitive Roman poetry devoted to these celebrations and to rustic banter. This kind of poetry itself, we are told, degenerated into malicious slander which had to be restrained by law, and was thus reformed.

Then came Greek influence, and 'captured Greece captured her rude conqueror, and brought the arts to rural Latium' (156-7). The Romans gave up their rude Saturnian metres, but the process was a long one and 'traces of the country remain to this day'. The Roman came to the study of Greek late; after the Punic Wars he investigated what useful contributions Greek tragedy could make and whether he could worthily (*digne*) translate it. He was pleased with the result, being by nature bold and of noble spirit (*sublimis*), but he was afraid to correct his work, he thought this below his dignity (*turpem lituram*). Comedy seemed easier, but this too is difficult and once more Plautus is blamed, in spite of all his dramatic skill, for his slipshod versification. There follows another violent and prolonged attack on the Roman theatre audiences (182-207) and their lack of poetic appreciation. Horace makes it very clear that he greatly admires the dramatists but he cannot face the theatre. However, even those who write only to be read deserve the emperor's attention (214-18).

The last part of the letter returns to Augustus both as parton of the arts and the subject of song (219-70). Poets are often bothersome, but they are the providers of immortality. Augustus is declared fortunate indeed to have such poets as Varius and Virgil to celebrate his great deeds.

We know that Augustus wanted Horace to write that kind of poetry,

---

[1] Which makes Fraenkel (p. 390) point out that, in spite of the Roman's genuine admiration for Greek superiority in the arts, there is 'always the possibility of a change of front. . . . It can always happen that those who shortly before have been treated as revered masters will, without warning, be put in their place and become mere *Graeculi*.'

and that the poet to some extent complied, in his own way, when he wrote the great patriotic odes of the fourth book, but further than that he refused to go. Here he neatly excuses himself once more: such subjects are beyond his powers; it is better not to write than to write badly, and surely no one wants to be pictured, whether in bronze or words, by a poor artist.

This letter is much more than a request for imperial patronage for poetry, or than a letter written to Augustus because he had requested one.[1] It is a basic restatement of Horace's sincere belief that Roman literature needed the Greek classical influence, and above all that it must be freed from the fetters of archaistic worship of early poetry. He knew Latin contemporary poetry had risen to great heights, he hoped it could rise still higher, but he fully realized the danger that it might degenerate instead, as it very soon did.

[1] Suetonius (?) in his *Life of Horace* tells us that Augustus, 'after he had read some epistles (of Horace) and noted that none of them mentioned him, complained to the poet: "Know that I am angry with you because in all your writings of this kind you don't talk to me at all. Are you afraid to be discredited by posterity if you appear friendly with me..."' and that this letter was the result.

CHAPTER XV

From Augustus to Nero

The Augustan age in Roman literature did not survive the Emperor, he survived it. When Augustus died in A.D. 14, Livy, it is true, was still completing his great history of Rome in one hundred and forty-two books, but most of this monumental work had been written and published years ago. Livy died in A.D. 17; Ovid was to linger a year longer in hopeless exile by the Black Sea, but Ovid in any case was never a true Augustan, either in spirit or style, and it is not without significance that he appears as a declaimer in the rhetorical schools, a very accomplished one, in the pages of the elder Seneca.[1] The other great poets of the reign had gone long ago, the last being Horace who had died in 8 B.C., twenty-two years before Augustus.[2] No writer of great fame was to follow until the early and happier years of Nero's reign in the middle of the first century, when suddenly we find another famous group, Persius, Seneca the philosopher, Lucan and Petronius.[3]

But Latin literature had changed by then, and one thing that all first-century writers have in common is a deep concern for the decay of 'eloquence'. They are very conscious of a breakdown in the Roman way of life; they unanimously deplore the luxury and greed rampant in imperial Rome and make it responsible for the decadence of literature and oratory. The denunciation of luxury was not new – we find it in Livy[4] – but, as the empire imposed peace upon the Roman world, prosperity increased

[1] *Controv.* II, 2 (10), 8-12. The subject of the *controversia* may be added to those given below as one which obviously would appeal to Ovid: 'A husband and his wife swore that if anything happened to either of them, the other would commit suicide. Travelling abroad, the husband sent a messenger to his wife, announcing his death. The wife hurled herself from a height. She recovers, and her father orders her to leave her husband. She refuses. Her father disinherits her.' Seneca quotes a number of sayings of Ovid, and gives some examples of how he adapted some sayings of the famous rhetorician Latro in his poetry. He also tells us that Ovid rarely took part in *controversiae* unless they had psychological interest, but preferred the *suasoriae*, because he didn't like arguing. The particular controversia took place at the school of Arellius Fiscus when Ovid was still a boy. 'He had a polished, becoming and amiable talent. Even then his speech was like verses put into prose. . . .' The whole passage is of considerable interest.   [2] Virgil and Tibullus had died in 19 B.C., Propertius in 16 B.C.

[3] The idea of the first few years of Nero's reign as the promise of a new 'Augustan' era, and the philosopher Seneca's hope that Nero would be a second Augustus is developed by Paul Faidier in *Les Etudes Classiques*, 1934, pp. 1-16.

[4] Livy deplored the luxuriousness of his day in his preface: '. . . donec ad haec tempora quibus nec vitia nostra nec remedia pati possumus . . . nuper divitiae avaritiam et abundantes

and the concentration of wealth in Rome must have strikingly increased also. Contemporaries certainly believed it to be responsible for the degeneration of morals and the barrenness of literature. The old Roman virtues still remained the Roman ethical ideal, but this ideal had less and less relation to actual life – a divorce not unknown in other societies and never conducive either to settled conditions or to great art, at least when it becomes so obvious that men are aware of it, as the first-century writers certainly were.[1]

There were other factors, the most obvious being the loss of freedom which contemporary writers naturally are less inclined to mention. Even under Augustus, who still could be friends with those who differed from him and at times showed remarkable patience and good humour, books were burned by order of the Senate, and his patience had limits, as Ovid and others discovered.[2] Under Tiberius and his successors the situation rapidly deteriorated.[3] Oratory was probably the first genre to feel the change. Banished from the forum and the senate where the fate of Rome was no longer decided, and very largely also from the courts as more and more cases were tried before a single judge instead of a jury, rhetoric took refuge in the schools. This process began as early as the last years of Cicero; it was contemporary with the development of new methods of rhetorical education which were to affect all Latin literature. Against these methods too the writers of the first century protested with almost equal unanimity, but in vain.

SENECA THE ELDER

To understand the peculiar forms of education which developed in the

voluptates desiderium per luxum atque libidinem pereundi perdendique omnia invexere.' It is interesting that even in Livy's style there can already be traced 'much that heralds the Latin of Tacitus; Livy, as an index of the changes coming over prose, stands appropriately, both in time and manner, between the republican and the "silver" Latinity', Wight Duff[3], Vol. I, p. 481.

[1] It has often been suggested that the decadence of morals and eloquence became a commonplace which every writer was almost bound to develop, and hence that these general sentiments need not be taken too seriously. This, I think, misunderstands the nature of *loci communes* or τόποι. Except in school exercises, or when pleading a case, no reputable writer would develop such a 'commonplace' unless he meant it. The treatment might be quite conventional, but the sentiments were genuine. The only exception among the writers we shall deal with might be Petronius, because one can never be sure, especially with the fragmentary state of his text, what his genuine sentiments are. Yet commentators are fairly unanimous in the belief that on matt ers of literature his characters express his serious feelings disreputable as those characters are.

[2] Seneca, *Controv.* 10, *Praef.* 4-8 mentions that T. Labienus, whose outspoken Pompeian opinions earned him the nickname of 'Rabienus' (the Madman) was the first to have his books burnt and committed suicide. Seneca has just told us (ibid. 3) that some speeches of Scaurus were also burnt by order of the Senate. Strangely enough, the old man indulges in an indignant tirade against such an intellectual crime in the case of Labienus but says that the fire wa probably a good thing for Scaurus' reputation! [3] Tacitus, *Annals* I, 72

schools during the reign of Augustus, and their effect on the style of later writers, we must turn to a much neglected but important work, the *Controversiae* and *Suasoriae*[1] by the elder Seneca, the father of the better-known Seneca the philosopher. The elder Seneca was born about 57 B.C. in Spain. He came to Rome to complete his education at the age of fifteen and lived there the rest of his long life except for fifteen years (13 B.C.-A.D. 2) which he spent in his native land. He died about A.D. 37 at the ripe age of around ninety-four. He wrote a history of Rome to the death of Tiberius, which is unfortunately lost. In his nineties he wrote, for the benefit of his sons, his reminiscences of the declamations in the schools of famous rhetors, discussed the way various topics were handled by the professionals, and recorded the bright sayings of many of them. It is almost unbelievable to us that he is writing from memory, though he evidently had a remarkable one, but that is unimportant. The original work consisted of ten books of *controversiae* and two of *suasoriae*, with a preface to each book. About half the work is lost, but a good deal remains; his introductions, with their pen-pictures of famous rhetors of the late first century B.C. and early first century A.D., as well as his own comments and reflections, there and throughout, give us a real insight into the education of the day – an insight much needed to understand the period.

There had always been rhetorical exercises in the schools, and it is no doubt in this sense that Quintilian[2] tells us that some people date the origin of *declamationes* from the time of Demetrius of Phalerum. But Seneca[3] says quite specifically that the *declamatio* as he knew it developed after Cicero's day, within his own lifetime. Its special characteristics seem to have been twofold: the public nature of the performance and the increasingly artificial nature of the subjects proposed. A rhetor's pupils would declaim before friends and fond parents, but the really social events and important occasions would be when the professionals, even rival professionals, performed. Society gathered to hear them, famous orators on occasion took part, and the emperor had been known to be present. Nor did the audience hesitate to express its approval or disapproval by comment and applause.

Declamations were of two kinds. The *suasoria* was a speech of advice to

---

[1] The full title of the work is: *Oratorum et rhetorum sententiae, divisiones, colores suasoriarum et controversiarum*. The most easily available text is Bornecque's edition.

[2] II, 4, 41: has fictas ad imitationem fori consiliorumque materias apud Graecos dicere circa Demetrium Phalerea institutum fere constat.

[3] *Controv.* 1, *Praef.* 12. Seneca distinguishes three stages in the history of declamations: the pre-Ciceronian *thesis* or general question, the Ciceronian *causa*, and the *controversia*, which he says is more recent. Suetonius too speaks of the old type of *controversia* more closely linked with an actual event, and a newer type. *De Rhet.* ch. 1. For a discussion of the passage of Seneca and the history of declamations see S. F. Bonner's *Roman Declamations in the late Republic and early Empire* pp. 1-50.

a historical character in a historical or imaginary situation. It was often spoken in character. Among the titles preserved by Seneca are, for example: 'After all others have fled, the three hundred Spartans at Thermopylae deliberate whether to flee or take a stand' – 'Should Cicero beg Antony for his life', and this last was refined by Cicero's old enemy Pollio, to the indignation of Seneca (VI, 14), into: 'Antony has promised to spare Cicero's life if Cicero will burn all his speeches'; advise Cicero! – 'Agamemnon deliberates whether to sacrifice Iphigenia.'

The *controversia* on the other hand was a speech for the plaintiff or the defendant in an imaginary lawsuit. This might, and originally did, prepare the pupil for the law-courts. Only the cases became more and more artificially imaginary.[1] The law is stated first, and that too is often imagined, then the circumstances. The given circumstances could not be altered but the orator could deal with them in his own way. Indeed Seneca usually reports the debates under three heads: the *sententiae*, i.e. the bright sayings and epigrams of the various professionals; the *colores*, i.e. the particular slant or colouring given to the attack or defence; and the *divisiones*, i.e. the different arguments or approaches to be used by the speaker. Here we have a great many subjects to choose from, one more fantastic than the other. Here are a few representative examples. 'A Vestal Virgin has been hurled from the Tarpeian rock for unchastity. She survives. Is she to be thrown down again?'[2] This is fairly reasonable. 'The punishment for rape is that the woman may demand the man's death or make him marry her. A man raped two women in one night. The first wants him executed. The second wants to marry him.'[3] This is rather more fanciful. And one example of the more complicated kind. Law: 'Children who do not provide for their parents are liable to imprisonment.' Case: 'A man killed one of his brothers who was a tyrant. He killed another brother whom he caught in adultery with his wife (both tyrants and adulterers could be killed without being guilty of murder). He is then taken prisoner by pirates. He writes to his father to ransom him. The father refuses, indeed he writes to the pirates to say he will pay twice the sum they ask on condition that they cut off both his son's hands. The pirates free him instead. Later, the father loses his money. The son then refuses to provide for him. The father brings the son to court.'[4]

It is difficult for us to understand that not only rival professors of rhetoric took part in these performances, but that they became fashionable events attended by prominent public men and leaders at the bar, who not infrequently performed at them. Undoubtedly, for people with a thorough

---

[1] Bonner, however (pp. 84-132), maintains that the majority of the subjects are much more closely related to actual Roman law and customs than is generally believed.

[2] *Controv.* I, 3.   [3] *Controv.* I, 5.   [4] *Controv.* I, 7.

training in rhetoric, there was a certain entertainment value. In any case, those were difficult times, and Roman intellectuals probably welcomed a harmless occupation which did not get them into trouble with the powers that be, and which, they were convinced, had at least some educational value.

This it no doubt had. It must have developed a certain quickness of wit and the art of speaking in public. Some historians have worried about the effect on the pupils' morals but this was probably minimal. However, if we remember that the very same topics were discussed again and again in different schools and at different times, that many sessions were public, and that the declamation became the most important school exercise, it is at once obvious that the speakers would strain to find some new point to make, the more ingenious the better. Certainly, clever epigrams and striking phrases were the fashion of the day; this may have affected Roman morals; it certainly affected Latin literary style, for every writer was trained in these schools.

Almost every first-century writer condemns the artificiality of the declamations and deplores its results. Old Seneca himself sees its weaknesses quite clearly though he is a great believer in rhetorical education, which he never questions. He does, however, deplore the degeneration of public taste; he knows that his sons will be attracted by some of the slick sayings which he himself condemns, and his running comments on some of the performances he faithfully records are quite devastating. Moreover, he puts in the mouth of Cassius Severus, an excellent speaker in court who did not shine as a declaimer, a thorough condemnation of the whole system as no longer a preparation but a hindrance to speaking in court, and he tells several stories of famous declaimers who were completely stuck before a jury.[1]

We find the same condemnation in Persius, Petronius, Juvenal, Tacitus

---

[1] To Seneca rhetoric is the best general training also for other pursuits: 'facilis ab hac in omnes artes discursus est; instruit etiam quos non sibi exercet' (Controv. 2, Praef. 3). To him eloquence reached its highest point in the days of Cicero, and he gives three possible reasons for its decay: (i) the luxuriousness of contemporary life, (ii) the rewards of eloquence are no longer available – an implied reference to the loss of freedom under the empire, which is somewhat rare at this time, and (iii) the natural law that anything which has reached its highest development must inevitably degenerate (Controv. 1, Praef. 7). This last point is more fully developed by Velleius Paterculus in the short History of Rome which he wrote to commemorate the consulship of his friend Marcus Vinicius in A.D. 30 (I, ch. 16-18). Seneca says to his sons at the end of his second Suasoria (23) that perhaps Arellius Fuscus' exaggeratedly careful style and his broken sentences (fracta compositio) will offend them when they reach his age, but meantime he knows they will delight in these vices of style. Cassius Severus' condemnation of declamations and his reasons for not shining at them will be found in Controv. 3, Praef. 8-15. The most famous story of a declaimer failing in court is told of Albucius in Controv. 7, Praef. 7. Criticism of declamations is also found in the preface to the ninth book of Controversiae.

and Quintilian, but the practice went on. There is something frightening
about an educational method unanimously condemned by all the best
minds in Rome throughout the century, which yet carries on by its own
momentum until it outlives them all. We owe it to Seneca the Elder that
we can have a thorough understanding of what the method was, and we
could have no better guide, for though he was obviously attracted by all
aspects of the rhetorical schools,[1] his comments on various declaimers and
styles are eminently sensible and uniformly interesting.

THE REIGN OF NERO

The early years of Nero, who came to the throne in A.D. 57 produced, as
we saw, four greater writers: Persius, the youthful satirist who died in
A.D. 62 at the age of twenty-eight; Lucan whose epic of the civil wars, the
Pharsalia, glorified the old heroes of the republic at the expense of Caesar;
Petronius whose *Satyricon* was the first picaresque novel in Latin literature
and is extant only in considerable fragments; and the younger Seneca.
Lucan, Petronius and Seneca all were allegedly involved in conspiracy
against Nero and died in A.D. 65 and 66. Lucan does not directly concern
us except as the outstanding example of a potentially great poet spoiled by
an excessive love of rhetoric which often betrayed him into absurdities.
At his best he is rhetorically magnificent and some of his epigrammatic
lines, once read, are never forgotten, like his famous *Victrix causa deis
placuit sed victa Catoni*, or his description of the ineffective Pompey
stat magni nominis umbra.[2] That Lucan shared the feeling that Rome
had degenerated from its earlier glory is obvious, but he made literature,
he did not discuss it.

PERSIUS

From Persius we have a slim book of six satires of which the first exposes
the moral corruption of the times as it affects the kind of welcome his book
may receive. With all the intolerant arrogance of youth he jeers at the
fashionable circles of Rome which may well prefer an inferior poet, and
he draws a scornful picture of a dandified poet giving a public reading of
his work. Poetry, he says bitterly, is only an after dinner relaxation to the
sons of Romulus, and what they want is some pleasant trifles on some
legendary theme. Persius himself would not refuse praise certainly, but he
will not accept the verdict of such a company as the final test of good
poetry. He briefly echoes Horace's picture of the wealthy poet who never

---

[1] See special note on Theodorus of Gadara at end of this chapter.

[2] *Pharsalia* 1, 128 and 135. The epigrammatic force of that seven word line is untranslate-
able. The meaning is 'The victors' cause was pleasing to the gods, the vanquished cause
pleased Cato.' The second phrase plays on Pompeius *Magnus*, 'there he stands, the shadow of
a great name' (the name of Great), i.e. of himself.

will get honest criticism except behind his back. He has none of Horace's urbanity or good-humour, though we should remember that Horace himself only developed those more endearing qualities in middle age and that he could be pretty violent in his twenties, and even obscene, which Persius is not. The younger satirist too deplores that everybody writes with a certain technical perfection but without true poetic feeling so that their admiration of ancient poets like Naevius and Accius only leads them to reproduce their swollen phrases. The debased taste of the day has an eye only for tropes and figures, which even a shipwrecked mariner can produce. What a contrast with the days of Virgil! Satire was appreciated in the times of Lucilius and Horace. It can still be, by those who have read the old comic poets – and anyway Persius does not seek the appreciation of the vulgar.

This last sentiment too is, of course, a Horatian echo, and we note that his reference is to the old comedy only, for certainly his type of satire is much closer to Lucilius than to Horace in spirit, though he also considers that satire should be written in ordinary everyday language, not in that of tragedy or epic.[1]

There is nothing very original in this attack upon contemporary taste on the part of a very young poet who gets his material from books rather than from life. Its chief interest lies in the obvious dislike of some of the results of rhetorical training such as the excessive use of figures, the emphasis on techniques, and the love of striking phrases which we find in all contemporary authors – and to some degree at least in Persius himself.

PETRONIUS

If Persius appears bookish, Petronius is always superbly alive.[2] In that amazing medley of riotous and indecent adventures which make up the *Satyricon* we find several passages bearing on literature. The book as we have it begins with a violent tirade against the practice of declamations which Encolpius addresses to a teacher of rhetoric called Agamemnon. It may be quoted here as a typical denunciation, making, in a more lively manner, most of the criticisms which recur throughout the century:

> Are declaimers pursued by another kind of Furies when they shout: 'These wounds were received on behalf of our public freedom', 'this eye was lost for your sake', 'give me a guide to lead me to my children for these hamstrung knees cannot support my body'? Even these things could be endured if they opened the way for future orators. As

[1] *Satire* V, 1-18.
[2] I am taking for granted that the Petronius mentioned by Tacitus in *Annals* XVI, 18-19 is the author of the *Satyricon*. This is now generally accepted. See Gilbert Bagnani, *Arbiter of Elegance*, Toronto, 1957, and references there.

it is, these inflated subjects and empty-sounding phrases advance them so little that when they get to court they think themselves transported to another world. I think our adolescents become so very stupid at school because they don't hear or see anything related to actual life, but pirates standing ready with chains[1] on the shore, despots issuing edicts ordering sons to cut off their fathers' heads, oracular responses in times of pestilence demanding the sacrifice of three or more virgins, honeyed word-dumplings; every word and deed dipped in syrup and oil. Young people brought up on such a diet no more acquire wisdom than kitchen servants acquire a pleasant perfume. If you'll allow me to say so, you teachers have been the first to destroy eloquence. The stimulation of smooth, empty, ridiculous sound effects has enfeebled and destroyed the body of your speeches. Young men were not confined to declamations when Sophocles and Euripides discovered the words of proper speech, when Pindar and the nine lyrists scrupled to use lines from Homer. Not to go to the poets as my witnesses, certainly neither Plato nor Demosthenes indulged in this sort of exercise. Great and, if I may so put it, modest speech is neither mottled nor turgid, but rises in natural beauty. This windy and enormous verbosity recently invaded Athens from Asia and it blew upon young minds as they rose to great things like an effluvium from a pestilential constellation, while eloquence, its rules corrupted, stood by in silence. Who, since Thucydides and Hypereides, has equalled their fame? Even poetry did not shine with a healthy hue, but all the arts of speech were fed on the same diet and produced nothing capable of lasting to old age. Painting too has come to the same end after the audacity of the Egyptians discovered a short cut to so great an art.

Agamemnon makes no real reply; in fact he agrees in principle. He blames it all on the parents. If you teach the young properly you will be left without pupils, for parents will send them where they get quicker results. It's no good teaching them the right things; they no longer have the patience. The result is that nowadays the young just waste their time at school and learn nothing worthwhile.

Later (83) Encolpius visits a gallery of paintings which contains works of Apelles and other classical painters. He there meets a shabby old man, a

---

[1] *cum catenis*: 'Pirates on the shore waving handcuffs', i.e. waiting for the shipwrecked, as G. Bagnani translates it in *Studies in honour of B. L. Ullman* p. 230, instead of the usual translation 'pirates in chains'. Professor Bagnani also draws my attention to the curiously archaic nature of the passage: not only are all the examples of the good old days Greek classical writers, but the Asiatic style is said to have *recently* (*nuper*) invaded Athens! Since we are dealing with Petronius, this is obviously deliberate, but the intent is obscure. He is probably satirizing the Graecomania of contemporary professors of rhetoric.

poet (which explains his shabbiness, for 'the love of talent never made a man rich') and they discuss the degeneration of taste, all due to the love of money, which has corrupted all the arts, and philosophy as well. It should be added that the poet, before discoursing upon the corruption of the age, tells a story of his relation to a boy-pupil which is certainly not to his credit!

Petronius' work is a *satura*, he passes from prose to verse with the greatest of ease, and it is hard to be sure where he is serious, especially in his poetry. Probably nowhere entirely. No passage is more puzzling, however, than where he has been understood to criticize Lucan, especially for doing away with the divine apparatus in his epic of the civil war. It begins, in prose, as follows (118):

> Poetry has led many astray. For as soon as one has constructed feet into verses and clothed a rather tender meaning in a periodic structure of words, he thinks at once that he has scaled Helicon. Thus those who are trained in the service of the courts have often taken refuge in the quiet pursuit of poetry as in a happier haven; they think that it is easier to construct a poem than a *controversia* embroidered with sparkling little maxims (*sententiolis vibrantibus pictam*). But a more genuine spirit has no liking for such uninspired work[1]; it cannot conceive anything or bring it to birth unless it is steeped in a vast stream of literature. One must avoid, so to speak, all slovenly diction, use expressions far removed from the common people, with the result (as expressed by Horace)[2] 'I hate the vulgar crowd and I avoid it.' Besides this, one should be careful that one's pithy phrases (*sententiae*) do not stand out from the body of one's discourse, but shine as a colouring worked into the cloth itself. Homer is a proof of this, so are the lyric poets, our Roman Virgil and Horace's diligent felicity (*curiosa felicitas*). The others have either not seen the path which leads to poetry, or, if they saw it, have been afraid to take it. Anyone who undertakes a great work on the Civil War will collapse under the burden, unless he is full of literature. It is not a question of describing events in verse, historians do this much better; but the spirit must freely range over byways, interventions by the gods, and swoop over mythical content, so that the poem appears to be the prophesying of a frenzied mind rather than a scrupulously reliable statement of facts before witnesses – as in the following effusion, if it please you, though it still needs final polishing: ...

[1] Reading, with most MSS., *sanitatem* instead of *vanitatem*. The word is here used in contrast to the inspiration of the true poet, it is the σωφροσύνη of Plato in the *Phaedrus* (above, p. 57).
[2] *Odes* III, 1, 1.

The 'effusion' which follows is a poem of two hundred and ninety-six hexameters, which read like the beginning of an epic on Caesar's invasion of Italy. That there is meant to be a reference to Lucan when Petronius refers to epics on the civil wars seems obvious, especially as Lucan was the only Roman epic poet *not* to make use of the usual divine apparatus. There are also many echoes of the *Pharsalia* in the poem. But what else refers to him, and what is the purpose of the poem itself?[1]

The general discussion of poetry in the first part of the passage, quoted above, is not particularly original: too many people write poetry; anyone who can put a few verses together thinks himself a poet; poetry is not merely a pleasant relaxation for tired orators; it requires inspiration and a deep knowledge of great literature; poetic diction is very different from ordinary speech. Most of these ideas can be paralleled in Horace, Cicero and elsewhere.[2] One imagines that the sophisticated courtier of Nero shared Horace's contempt for the mob, even though he could make individual members of it come wonderfully to life in his own work and speak their own language. Brilliant phrases that stand out from the body of a work are certainly a weakness of Lucan's, but so they were of all contemporary work, whether in verse or prose, not excluding Petronius himself, or the poem which follows, and one doubts that he would here have Lucan specifically in mind.[3] We have already seen that Petronius was an adherent of the 'classical' school and are not surprised that he chooses Homer and the Greek lyrists as models, but it is interesting to find Virgil and Horace now recognized as the Roman classics, and the phrase which he coins to describe the poetry of Horace – *curiosa felicitas*, where the adjective implies care or diligence while the noun implies luck or a gift from the gods, i.e. natural talent, is a deservedly famous critical phrase, frequently quoted.

It is with the mention of epics on the civil war that Lucan inevitably comes to our minds. He must have been in Petronius' mind also, for the *Pharsalia* was, as far as we know, the only contemporary poem of the

---

[1] For a full discussion of all the problems raised by this famous passage of Petronius see A. Collignon, *Etude Sur Pétrone* 101-226. See also Florence Th. Baldwin, *The Bellum Civile*.

[2] See Collignon 101-5.

[3] Excessive use of striking and epigrammatic *sententiae* is a vice which developed with the abuse of declamations, and it is not, as such, dealt with by Horace or Cicero, though one thinks of Horace's advice that no part should be elaborated at the expense of the whole (*A.P.* 32-37). Collignon (p. 102) quotes Cicero, *De Orat.* III, 25 (96) that a definite tone should pervade the whole speech, but the following sentence goes on to say that certain ornaments – *quasi verborum et sententiarum flores* – should *not* be scattered throughout the speech. Cicero is of course not referring to *sententiae* in the later technical sense; he means ideas or content as opposed to *verba*, i.e. figures of thought and figures of speech. Parallels for *sententiae* that stand out too much are rarer with later authors. Collignon (p. 105) cites Tacitus, *Dialogus* 21, and one might add Quintilian 8, 5, 25-34.

kind.[1] But when he repeats his general requirement, namely that such a poet must be steeped in great literature, he need not imply that Lucan was not so steeped, which he obviously was. Petronius goes on to make three further points, and they are made in one sentence, i.e. they go together. The epic poet should not be primarily concerned to give the facts, which is the historian's job, but he must be prepared to range over by-ways[2] which are no part of a historical account, he must bring in the gods, and he must be inspired. All this, Petronius repeats, is where he differs from the historian. A poem is a poem, not a history. This is probably intended as a not unfriendly criticism of Lucan but even here, except for the gods, Petronius need not be thinking of him exclusively.

What he seems to imply is that to write an epic on recent or contemporary history is a very difficult task indeed, perhaps that the subject is more suitable for a historian. He does not say that without the usual divine apparatus it will fail, but he expresses the opinion that one should stick to the laws of the genre, including the gods. That, and the other characteristics, the inclusion of *ambages*, for example – i.e. the less direct pressing on with the story but amplification of episodes (one thinks of Dido and the visit to Hades in the *Aeneid*) – and the poetic frenzy generally, remain essential to any epic, whatever its subject.

As for Petronius' poem as a whole, its intention cannot be judged in isolation. Poems of varying length are scattered throughout the work; they are usually short, often echo other poets, and are frequently humorous in intent, just as he often uses a dignified and epic diction at the most un-dignified moments. Sometimes the poems seem to have no other purpose than the author's own amusement, and there does not seem ever to be any intended parody or serious criticism of the authors from whom phrases are borrowed. The nearest parallel to the *Bellum Civile* is a poem of sixty-five *senarii* on the fall of Troy which the same Eumolpus improvises as Encolpius is intently looking at a picture on the subject in a picture gallery (89). This bears much the same relation to the second book of the *Aeneid* as the poem on the civil war bears to the *Pharsalia*. There, certainly, no criticism of Virgil is intended. At the end of it, passers-by throw stones at Eumolpus but he is used to that sort of reception. Yet the poem is not deliberately bad; indeed it is not without merit considered in itself as an exercise in rhetorical poetry, and it seems to have no other purpose. The *Bellum Civile* itself is much longer. It consists of five panels.[3] The

[1] Under Augustus L. Varius Rufus, Cornelius Severus, and Rabirius wrote epics on contemporary history, and we know that the emperor wanted Horace to do so, but we do not know of any epic on recent or contemporary history between their day and Lucan's.

[2] *Ambages* means a detour or digression, and here seems to mean such digressions or side issues as would have no place in a historical account.

[3] Such a division covers the whole poem, except five lines (61-65) immediately after the

first depicts the Romans, having conquered the world, exploiting all its resources to feed their luxury and corruption – a powerful indictment (1-60). Then we have a scene where Pluto rises from the nether world and addresses Fortuna; they contemplate the Roman world and decide to stir up civil war; dread omens follow (67-140). We then see Caesar high up in the Alps addressing his troops and marching forward, overcoming all difficulties (141-208). Then the scene shifts to Rome where all is fear and confusion, and even the great Pompey, in spite of his past glories, takes to flight (209-44). Peace, Faith, Justice and Concord leave the earth while evil spirits, Fury, Treason, Madness among them, rise up from the world below. The gods take sides. Discord rises and calls the peoples and the Roman nobles to war (245-95). There the poem abruptly ends.

Clearly, it conforms to the requirements just enunciated by Petronius himself. No specific historical event is mentioned except that Caesar crossed the Alps. There are plenty of digressions or byways (*ambages*) such as the whole first panel on the luxury of Rome, and the scenes where the gods intervene. In fact little that is found here would find a place in a reliable historical account. The gods fill more than a third of the poem. Moreover, the many echoes, not only of Lucan, but of Virgil, Livy and others,[1] show that the author is 'full of literature'. We may not think that such echoes and reworking of others' phrases and ideas is the best way of showing one's acquaintance with literature, but it was certainly the fashion of the day and a practice taught in the schools where our author was trained, however much he may have disliked them. The diction is poetic, and though there are powerful lines and *sententiae*, they do not quite stand out as they do in other writers of the time, including Lucan. As for poetic genius, it is a competent, in places a striking poem, and Petronius does not claim to be a great poet.

The implied criticism of Lucan remains on this general level. Attempts to find parody, or criticism in detail have not been successful; the whole poem is no more a parody of Lucan than the other poem on the fall of Troy is a parody of Virgil. One imagines Petronius saying: 'My dear Lucan, to write an epic on recent history is almost impossible, and you are not succeeding any better by breaking the rules of the genre. You should keep the divine apparatus and worry a great deal less about what actually happened. Now if I were to attempt so difficult a task, this is how I'd do it. ...' As far as it goes, the poem is serious; it is also highly competent;

first section. These tell how Fortune had raised three generals – Crassus killed in Parthia, Pompey killed by the shores of Egypt and Caesar in Rome – as if the burden of their ashes were too great and the earth had widely separated their deaths. This is no doubt intended as an introductory reference to the triumvirate, but the rhetorical exaggeration is one of the least successful in the whole poem.

[1] All these are carefully studied by Collignon pp. 150-62 and 165-76.

but Petronius cannot be serious for very long, and after less than three hundred lines he gives up. No other hidden meanings, abstruse criticisms or parodies are probably intended. It is just a rather lengthy illustration of what he has just said, no more and no less.

The passages we have discussed are, unfortunately, the only relevant passages on poetry and literature to be found in Petronius as we have him: the attack on declamations, the degenerate state of all the arts, and the reflections on poetry in general which we have just discussed. One wishes there were more, for the author of the *Satyricon* obviously was fully qualified to give us more, had he chosen; indeed he may have done so, since we only have fragments of his fifteenth and sixteenth books. If so, the loss is much to be regretted, for he had a far more mature mind than Persius and a far deeper appreciation of poetry and literature generally than the younger Seneca ever had.

SENECA

Seneca's contribution to criticism is in fact far less than one would expect from the chief Stoic writer of the age. He does not discuss the Stoic theories of poetry or rhetoric. Only once does he discuss style in a general way,[1] and even there he is mainly concerned to prove that a man's style is a reflection of his character. This idea he develops more fully than anyone had done before him, as far as our knowledge goes, and he applies the same idea to society: its virtues or vices also are reflected in the literary fashions of the day. This affects the cultured as well as the people; the difference between them being one of dress rather than of judgement. We should therefore not be surprised if style in one society tends to swollen periods while in another we find broken up, tripping, short sentences.

Maecenas, the friend of Augustus and patron of Horace, is taken as an example of a corrupt style which reflected corruption of the soul and Seneca pursues the parallel in detail.[2] He gives examples of Maecenas' 'drunken style', slack and fitful and involved. Even such praise as is due to his humanity is spoiled by 'the notorious sweetmeats of his most monstrous discourse' (*istis orationis portentosissimae deliciis*). Luxury leads to contempt of anything ordinary, to archaisms, false neologisms, excessive and far-fetched metaphors, untimely abruptness or inappropriate amplification. The fault may lie with the individual or with the times, and the vices that are fashionable are of course most easily forgiven.

No writer however great, Seneca continues, is free from faults which need our indulgence. Moreover, he adds, and here he flies in the face of all 'classical' criticism 'there are no fixed laws of style; the custom of the

<hr/>

[1] *Letter to Lucilius* 114, 1-22.   [2] Ibid. 4-8.

community changes it, and this never remains the same for long'. Some
worship the earliest Roman writers, others avoid anything unusual and
their diction is drab; both are wrong.[1] Then again some seek a jerky and
abrupt word-arrangement, while others go in for musically modulated
composition; exaggerated hyperbata, or slowly ending sentences with
monotonous rhythms, like Cicero.

Seneca then makes the interesting suggestion that it is usually one
dominant personality who leads the stylistic fashion and is followed by
other writers. Sallust for example introduced the fashion of amputated
phrases and obscure brevity. And the imitators inevitably exaggerate
because they deliberately pursue what came naturally to their model.[2] Such
imitation need not then reflect the imitator's character, but it leads to a
desire to attract notice at all costs. Generally, however, there is a direct
relation between character and style and if you look after your character
your style will look after itself.

This general discussion, motivated though it is by a philosophic exhortation, does contain some ideas of interest, particularly that the style
reflects the personality, as stylistic fashions reflect the character of the
community; that great writers are leaders of fashion, that imitation
always exaggerates, and that there are no absolute criteria of style.
Seneca's general advice seems to be a plea for moderation, to avoid extremes, to write naturally, applying to style the Stoic advice to live κατὰ
φύσιν, according to nature.

Elsewhere, Seneca is concerned only with the proper style of philosophical exposition. Everywhere he emphasizes content over form, as one
would expect, and declares his position most clearly and briefly[3] where he
replies to Lucilius' complaint that his letters were not written with enough
care (*minus accurata*). Care, he says, means affectation (*putide loqui*) and he
prefers his letters to be like a conversation (*sermo*); delivery can be left to
the orators. Nevertheless, Seneca does not abjure all embellishment. He
would not want his letters to be dry or jejune (*ieiuna et arida*), philosophy
need not renounce talent. While content is most important, nevertheless
if good writing (*eloquentia*) comes naturally, it should by all means be
used, but not pursued for its own sake. No one seeks out an eloquent
doctor, but if the best doctor happens to be eloquent, there is no harm in
it; his eloquence may even be useful. Or, as he puts it elsewhere,[4] style is
the garb of thought, and if wisdom and elegance can be combined
(*providentia cum elegantia*) the combination is certainly attractive.

Other passages do not add very much. There is a vigorous attack upon
the delivery of a philosopher, Serapio, whom Lucilius had heard.[5] His

[1] Ibid. 13-14.
[3] *Letter* 75, 1-7.
[4] *Letter* 115, 3.
[2] Ibid. 19.
[5] *Letter* 40.

delivery was apparently torrential, which Seneca considers quite unworthy of a philosopher. Seneca wants neither excessive slowness, drop by drop (*stillare*), nor excessive rapidity. While he has delivery mainly in mind, most qualities he mentions inevitably apply to style as well. He seems to want the middle style,[1] but it is probable that he does not have the three-style formula in mind at all, and that his terms are to be taken in a non-technical sense. He is merely pleading for moderation.

On the other hand, Lucilius was disappointed with the style of Papirius Fabianus who seems to have been an old acquaintance of the Seneca family,[2] and Seneca rises to his defence. He insists again that content is what matters, but he cannot accept the criticism that Fabianus' style was too copious, too flowing and unpolished. He admits that it might have been pruned and better constructed, but there is nothing shoddy in his work even if, as a stylist, he is inferior to Cicero, Pollio, or Livy. It seems both unkind and unprofitable to examine this friendly defence in detail in order to point to at least implied contradictions between what he says here and his attack on Serapio. Seneca is more than fair to Fabianus and probably less than fair to Serapio whom he obviously disliked – in any case it is the latter's delivery, but the former's style which he discusses.

A much more interesting question is how far his own practice conforms to this theory. His style is generally regarded as typical of the silver Latin period – with its rhetorical straining after effects, brilliant *sententiae*, paradoxes, antitheses and oxymorons. His tragedies we need not here consider, since he does not anywhere discuss tragic style. Suffice it to say that his style there is definitely rhetorical and belongs with that of Lucan, though avoiding the worst of Lucan's excesses. With Quintilian's harsh verdict before them[3] modern commentators have perhaps tended to be unduly

1 When in this letter (40) Seneca wishes to avoid both extremes he certainly uses terms such as *inopia, exilitas, oratio incomposita* and the like which usually refer to style.

2 *Letter* 100. Papirius Fabianus figures frequently in the pages of Seneca the elder and attained a high reputation as a declaimer in his youth before he turned to philosophy; old Seneca is not as indulgent as his son towards Fabianus' style (*Controv.* 2, *Praef.* 1-3).

3 Quintilian's judgement (10, 1, 125-31) is especially interesting, for Seneca typified for him all that he disliked in the style of the period. Quintilian was writing about thirty years after Seneca's death, and his criticism is a great tribute to Seneca's posthumous popularity.

I have purposely deferred consideration of Seneca under every literary genre because of a widespread but false belief that I both condemn and dislike him. This belief arose because I was trying to recall to more austere standards a style which was depraved and corrupted by every kind of fault. At that time he was almost alone in the hands of our youth. I did not try to ban him altogether but I did not allow him to take precedence over better writers whom he himself was always attacking because he was aware that his own style was different and because he distrusted his capacity to please those to whom these others appealed. Our youth liked him better than they were able to imitate him; indeed they were as inferior to him as he was inferior to the old writers. Would that his imitators had been able to equal him, or at least come close to doing so; but it was only his vices which appealed to them and which everyone tried to reproduce as far as he could. So they

harsh in their judgements. A pointed style was typical of Stoics generally[1] as well as of the silver age in Rome; it was a form of ornamentation that was therefore doubly 'natural' to Seneca. One might say that he conforms to the Stoic virtues in his prose: his diction is 'pure' enough, and he is lucid. As for brevity, it becomes with him a brevity of sentence structure, for no one could suggest that he is brief or concise in dealing with his subject-matter, but then he is a preacher, and brevity is not characteristic of the genre. He tries certainly, as he tells us, to make his letters like conversation; this he considered appropriate – he was probably a lengthy talker, not verbose, but diffuse, as anyone who has read the three books *On Anger* will testify. Stoic ornamentation includes the use of figures, and certainly he uses them to the full. Remembering that he himself admits that every writer is the child of his age, we should certainly not accuse him of deliberate hypocrisy. He was no doubt convinced that his practice squared with his theories. A philosopher will not seek eloquence for its own sake, but if the doctor of souls happens to be a stylist, he will join his wisdom with eloquence and he thought the result would be attractive indeed. We do not find it so, to us the perpetual tinsel brilliance of his epigrams is more monotonous than Cicero's period were to him, but in the final analysis it is the very ordinary level of his wisdom which tires us at least as much as the silver Latin nature of his eloquence. When practised by a literary genius like Tacitus, the most jerky word-arrangement and the most outrageous sequence of *sententiae* may stun us; they never tire us. But Seneca was no genius.

The writers of the Neronian age reflect a feeling of breakdown in Roman society, of decadence from their own golden age. In literature

brought Seneca into disrepute by boasting that they wrote in the same manner. Seneca, however, had other considerable virtues: a ready and broad intelligence, unremitting studiousness, and a great deal of factual knowledge, though as to the last he was sometimes misled by those to whom he had entrusted certain inquiries. He dealt with almost every branch of study, and people read his speeches and his poems, his letters and his dialogues. In philosophy he was lacking in precision, but his attacks on vice were outstanding. His works contain many striking reflections, much that should be read for its ethical content, but his style is for the most part decadent and all the more pernicious in that it abounds in seductive flaws. One might wish that he had followed not his own intelligence but the judgement of others. If he had despised inverted ways of speech and not been so averse to directness in expression, if he had not been in love with everything he wrote, if he had not spoiled the dignity of his subject by those very short, ruptured sentences, he would have won the approval of scholars rather than been adored by adolescents. Even so, he should be read by those who are mature and sufficiently confirmed in a more severe style, if only because he can exercise their judgement of both good and bad style. For there is, as I have said, much in him that is to be commended, much to be admired even, as long as one is careful to select – would that he had done so himself! His natural talents were worthy of higher aims. What he wanted to do, he achieved.

[1] On this point, and for a defence of Seneca's style as conforming to the Stoic virtues see C. N. Smiley, 'Seneca and the Stoic theory of literary style'.

their own Classical writers, within a generation of their death, have begun to have an inhibiting effect, for men despair of rivaling them. This decadence, which contemporary writers do not minimize, but on the contrary seem to exaggerate, they blame in part at least upon the artificial nature of the declamations which have become the chief training in the rhetorical schools. They are very conscious of the stylistic weaknesses of their period: the short, epigrammatic *sententiae*, the short, jerky sentences, the rhetorical exaggerations, which they condemn but cannot escape. They had a great respect for great literature, but the theory of *imitatio* which in a more self-confident age had led to a general emulation of great writers now becomes more exclusively the direct imitation and working-over of particular phrases, images and figures such as we find in Persius and Lucan, and which is deliberately paraded, perhaps with satiric intent, in Petronius. It was a highly self-conscious period, not yet adjusted to empire, romantically looking back, both in politics and in literature, to the last days of the Republic and the early years of Augustus. The first years of Nero were a period of hope, both in politics and literature, but the hope was doomed and the curtain comes down again in the later years of his reign, not to lift till after the murder of Domitian.

NOTE ON
THEODORUS OF GADARA

The two most famous teachers of rhetoric of Augustus' reign were Apollodorus of Pergamum who had taught Augustus himself as a young man, and his younger contemporary Theodorus of Gadara, who taught Tiberius. The rivalry between their schools was intense and rhetoricians continued to call themselves Apollodoreans and Theodoreans through the first and even the second century A.D. One feels that such a lasting rivalry must have been based on important principles but the evidence of Quintilian only refers to technical differences of rhetorical theory and practice and seems to regard many of these as largely a matter of terminology and rigid rules, distinctions without a difference – *quorum diversa apellatio, vis eadem est* (3, 6, 1, where he is discussing some definitions of both rhetoricians).

There is some evidence in the elder Seneca that the followers of Apollodorus were more rigid in the applications of their rules (*Controv.* 10, *Praef.* 15), though in another passage (*Controv.* 2, 1, 36) the rigidity concerns the narrative portion of a speech which Apollodorus always insisted upon while Theodorus allowed it to be omitted under certain circumstances.

A treatise by an unknown author, written at the earliest in the late second century A.D. on the parts of a speech – exordium, narrative, proof and peroration – named after its first modern editor the *Anonymus Seguerianus* – makes frequent references to Apollodorus and Theodorus and the theories of their followers and, *as far as the theory of the parts of a speech is concerned*, fully supports the view that Theodorus was less rigid than Apollodorus and was prepared to omit any one of them at times except the proofs. Also some parts, especially the narrative, could be broken up and interspersed with sections of other parts. Alexander (a second-century rhetorician) is quoted as saying that, *without realizing it* (ἑαυτοὺς λελήθασιν) 'the Apollodoreans' treat rhetoric as if it was an exact science. Finally, whereas Apollodorus excluded appeals to *pathos* in the narrative and the proofs – thus restricting them to the peroration and the exordium, which seems to have been the traditional view, Theodorus also allowed them in the proofs, and some of his followers at least also in the narrative.

The relevance of all this for our purpose is that upon this basis a theory has gradually been built of the rhetorician Theodorus as holding quite un-usual views upon literature in general. In an article 'Die Apollodoreer und die Theodoreer' in *Hermes* 1890 M. Schanz emphasized and amplified this adaptability on the part of Theodorus as applying to all departments of rhetoric and beyond, and maintained that Theodorus recognized expedi-ency as the guiding principle at all times, and calls the Theodoreans 'the Anomalists of rhetoric'.

Building upon this, H. Mutschmann, in his book on Longinus (1913), further extended the application of this principle of Theodorean adapta-bility to all literature. Then, by attributing (quite unjustifiably) all that is said on *pathos* in the *Anonymus Seguerianus* to Theodorus himself, and by giving it the broadest possible (or rather, impossible) interpretation, he declared that Theodorus considered pathos and the irrational, including the imagination, as the supremely important factor in all speaking and writing. This attractive and somewhat startling picture of Theodorus was then elaborated even further by A. Rostagni in his edition *Anonimi del Sublime* (1947). Rostagni embellishes the contrast between the Apollo-doreans as believers in a schematized, scientific, rationalized rhetoric as against the empirical Theodoreans, and Theodorus becomes the apostle of passion as the one most important element in all art, the root of all great-ness in literature.

It is cruel to denounce this pretty picture as fanciful, but the fact is that it is not only completely unsupported by any evidence, but flies in the face of such evidence as we have, especially that of Quintilian, who mentions both rhetoricians frequently, and not very flatteringly, always on techni-calities. I have argued the case much more fully, and examined the evidence summarized at the beginning of this note much more thoroughly in *AJP* 80 (1959) to which I refer the reader who wishes to pursue the matter further. I have there also dealt at length with the equally fanciful theory of both Mutschmann and Rostagni that the author of *On the Sublime* is a younger contemporary, indeed a direct disciple of their Theodorus.

Here I have only given as much as seemed necessary to make clear to the reader why Theodorus has no place, and in my opinion deserves no place, in a chapter on the development of literary theory and criticism in the first century A.D. His place is with Apollodorus in the history of rhetoric in the narrow sense of the term.

CHAPTER XVI

Tacitus

Tacitus' *Dialogue on Orators*[1] is especially interesting to us for two reasons; it is the fullest discussion we possess on the causes of the decadence of *eloquentia*, and it also gives us, and this we do not find elsewhere, the opposite point of view in the person of Marcus Aper, a self-made man from Gaul who had become one of the foremost orators in Rome, and who did not believe that there had been any decadence at all.

The dramatic date of the conversation which Tacitus professes to report is A.D. 74-75, the sixth year of Vespasian's reign, when the historian was about twenty years of age. It takes place in the house of Curiatus Maternus, an orator but also a tragic poet of distinction who has decided to withdraw from the Forum and devote himself to writing poetry. Also present from the beginning is Julius Secundus whom we know from Quintilian[2] as a careful and elegant stylist, contrasted in the *Dialogue* with the bolder and more violent Aper. The fourth speaker, who joins them later, is Vepsanius Messala, the only native Roman of the four, an aristocrat whom we meet also in the *Histories* as a supporter of Vespasian and a historian of the civil war of A.D. 69.[3] When the *Dialogue* was written or published is very uncertain; some date it in the reign of Titus, others in the early years of Domitian, while others again at least defer publication to A.D. 101-2, after the death of Domitian and link it with the consulship of Justus Fabius, to whom it is dedicated, in A.D. 102.[4] It is obvious that it cannot have been published during the more despotic years of Domitian, for the anti-imperial undertones would make publication highly dangerous at that

[1] The *Dialogus* is definitely ascribed to Tacitus by the manuscripts and is now almost unanimously accepted as genuine. The only reason for doubt was the style, which is more flowing and Ciceronian than that of the historian. However, further study of the dialogue has shown it to be more akin to Tacitus in style than at first appears while, on the other hand, a definite development of style can be seen in the historical works themselves. See W. Peterson's and Alfred Gudeman's editions for a full discussion of both genuineness and style.

[2] Quintilian 10, 1, 120 and 10, 3, 12-14. *Dialogus* ch. 2.

[3] *Histories* 3, 9 and 25.

[4] Peterson (xviii) believes it was written in 84-85 and published shortly afterwards, i.e. in the early years of Domitian's reign; Gudeman favours the reign of Titus (A.D. 78-81). In his Loeb translation Peterson accepts either of those dates. More recently, scholars have tended to believe the *Dialogus* was not published till after the death of Domitian, e.g. R. Syme, *Tacitus*, vol. 1, 116, and in *JRS* 47 (1957) 135. See also the Budé edition of Goelzer and Bornecque.

time. Indeed these undertones and the ironic implications seem more pronounced than most commentators have allowed.

The danger of offending the authorities is stressed at the very beginning (ch. 3), for when Aper and Secundus (with the silent young Tacitus in attendance) call upon Maternus, they find him preparing for publication his tragedy *Cato*, of which he had given a reading the previous day, and Secundus expresses the hope that he may tone down those passages which had offended court-circles and were the talk of the town. Maternus assures them he has no intention of doing so, indeed his next play, *Thyestes*, may go even further.

Aper then (chs. 5-10) reproaches Maternus for neglecting his career at the bar. Poetry is all very well for those who have no oratorical ability, but much greater glory is open to Maternus. Aper draws a glowing picture of the rewards of oratory, its usefulness to both the orator and his friends, the delight which an orator finds in the knowledge that his power, wealth, and glory are not the result of patronage but of his own talents. As living examples of such wealth and glory he cites Eprius Marcellus and Vibius Crispus. As for poetry, he continues, it can bring only a limited and ephemeral reputation. Of what use is it? When poets get into trouble they have to come to the orators to get them out of it. Not that Aper has anything against poetry; it is, after all, also a kind of *eloquentia*, if an inferior one. It's all very well for Greeks to write poetry; Romans have better things to do. And Maternus cannot even claim that his poetry will bring security. It is more likely to give offence than his oratory, as his *Cato* proves, without the excuse that he is speaking on behalf of a friend.

This speech is not likely to convince Maternus, but it gives us a vivid picture of the self-made Gaul, proud of the prestige and wealth he has acquired in Rome. However, we should not miss the satiric tone of that picture, for Marcellus and Crispus whom he so much admires were two of the most famous members of that hated class, the *delatores* or public informers.[1] They may be Aper's ideal, but they are unlikely to appeal to the others, or to Tacitus.

Maternus' reply (chs. 11-13) is just that, a reply. It is not in any true sense a 'defence of poetry', for this would introduce an extraneous subject. Maternus is unimpressed by the wealth and glory depicted by Aper, and, on this level, he holds that a poet's prestige is at least as great, citing Virgil as an example. In his own case, it was a recitation of his poetry which broke the power of the buffoon Vatinius under Nero. Crowds of clients, the hurly burly of the forum and the 'bloodstained eloquence of today' hold no attraction for him and he much prefers the solitude of the country-

---

[1] *Histories* 2, 10 and 4, 42-43.

side. And here for a moment (12) we have a positive praise of poetry as 'the primordial eloquence' and a brief expansion of that old commonplace. But the whole speech is essentially an attack on contemporary oratory rather than a defence of poetry, and Maternus is bitingly contemptuous of Aper's idols, Crispus and Marcellus. Are we to envy the fear they inspire or that which they feel? Freedmen have as much power as they. This speech too is excellently in character and one is not surprised that his *Cato* caused umbrage at court.[1]

At this point (ch. 14), Messala arrives. He is delighted to find them engaged in a serious discussion, not occupied with a legal case or practising declamation. He compliments Secundus on his last book and Aper because he has not yet retired from the *controversiae* of the schools but prefers to spend his leisure in the manner of the new and not the old orators. Aper knows well enough that the compliment is ironical, and he twits Messala on his love of the ancients. This brings us to the controversy between 'the ancients' and 'the moderns', a necessary preliminary to a discussion of the reasons for decadence, since it establishes the fact of decadence.

That it is a fact they all agree, except Aper who at once leaps to the defence of his contemporaries, in an extremely interesting speech (chs. 16-24), the more so for us because his point of view is not given full expression in the other extant texts of the period. He first points out that the term 'ancients' is misleading, for the age of Cicero is only a lifetime away. However, this inclusion of Cicero among the ancients is more an *argumentum ad hominem* than a change in the generally accepted notion.

Aper's second point is more interesting: he emphasizes that oratory changes with the times, and that different circumstances require different styles[2]; even among the so-called ancients there were different types of oratory. Cicero too had his detractors, and he quotes from the correspondence of Calvus and Brutus with the great orator.[3] Yet it is clear that to him

---

[1] The speech breathes a certain defiance and at times bitter irony about the imperial system. There is the boast of having broken the power of Vatinius under Nero (we know nothing of the circumstances) and the somewhat arrogant statement, at the end of the same chapter (11): 'So far I have found in righteousness a better preserver of my position than in eloquence' – in view of the fears of his friends and the circumstances of the time.
More bitter is the phrase 'the recent growth of this money-grubbing and bloodstained eloquence born of depraved morals' – *lucrosae huius et sanguinantis eloquentiae usus recens et malis moribus natus* (12). Then the contemptuous reference to Crispus and Marcellus, 'bound to every form of flattery, who never appear slavish enough to the powers that be or free enough to us, no more powerful than (the emperor's) freedmen' – *quod adligati omni adulatione nec imperantibus umquam satis servi videntur nec nobis satis liberi? Quae haec summa eorum potentia est? tantum posse liberti solent* (13); and the reference to the fame of orators being uncertain and pale with fear, *lubricum forum famamque pallentem trepidus experiar*. All these phrases breathe, if not opposition to, at least revulsion from, the imperial regime. No wonder Secundus qualifies the speech to Messala as *audentior*, 'rather daring'.
[2] We have seen the same idea of rhetorical fashions in Seneca, above, pp. 269-70.
[3] Quoted above, pp. 181-2.

GRC K

the changes have been for the better; it was Cassius Severus[1] who saw
what was needed; inordinately long speeches like the Verrine orations
went out of fashion and were no longer effective; the public themselves
became more sophisticated and knew more about both rhetoric and
philosophy. They were no longer satisfied with the rhetorical precepts 'of
those dry as dust textbooks of Hermagoras and Apollodorus', or with
stock sentiments; something new was needed, something quicker and
more striking before judges whose decisions are based on their power and
authority, not on laws and rights.[2] Such judges are impatient and will not
listen for ever.

> Nowadays the judge keeps ahead of the advocate; unless he is coaxed
> and won over[3] by swift-moving argumentation, colourful maxims,
> brilliant careful word-pictures, he turns against you. Even the general
> public who wander in and out have become accustomed to demand
> pleasing embellishments in a speech; they no more tolerate the tire-
> some, old-fashioned ways, than they would endure in the theatre any
> actor who employed the gesturings of Roscius or Ambivius Turpio.

Aper is all in favour of striking, epigrammatic maxims, of commonplaces decked out with poetic grace, which will be everywhere quoted.
Those adornments which the critics of the age unanimously condemned
are to him the glories of contemporary eloquence. The young are quite
right, he thinks, to desire oratorical gems, and they please the judges too.
Old-fashioned eloquence is boring and ridiculous. Look at Calvus' extant
speeches, or most of them anyway. Nobody reads Caesar or Brutus
nowadays.

I come to Cicero (ch. 22), who had the same quarrel with his con-

[1] Ch. 19. It can surely be no accident that the moral character of those orators whom Aper
chooses to praise was notoriously bad. This is true not only of Crispus and Marcellus in his
earlier speech, but also here. Cassius Severus was exiled to Crete by Augustus for libelling
people of repute, under the *lex maiestatis*. See *Annals* I, 72 and 4, 21. He is frequently mentioned
in Quintilian, e.g. 10, 1, 116-17 and Seneca the elder told us that he was a poor declaimer
Controv. 3, *Praef.*

[2] *qui vi et potestate, non iure aut legibus cognoscunt* (19 ad fin.) Gudeman says (note ad loc., p.
216) that Aper cannot mean that judges no longer presided with equity and fairness, and he
must therefore be taken to mean that they were no longer tied down by the *letter* of the law.
But Aper is the kind of person who would have little patience with, or respect for, the
minutiae of the law or for long legal wrangles. He would welcome swift decisions, based on
'authority and power' and consider them a good thing. That, however, does not mean that
Tacitus is not being deliberately ambiguous and ironical. There is a good deal of satiric irony
in his presentation of Aper throughout.

[3] *invitatus et corruptus* (ch. 20): Gudeman keeps *corruptus* here and indeed reads *invitiatus*,
but this rather cuts the ground from under his argument quoted in the last note. *Corruptus* is a
strong word and must mean at least that the judge is influenced to listen to one side, and away
from the path of strict justice. It can mean a good deal more.

temporaries as I have with you. They too admired the ancients, he preferred the eloquence of his day; and it was in taste more than anything else that he surpassed contemporary orators. He was the first to study eloquence, the first to develop a choice of words and to cultivate the arrangement of words (i.e. rhythm); he also attempted to ornament commonplaces and had some pithy maxims especially in those speeches which he composed in his later years towards the end of his life, that is, when he had developed more and learned by practice and experience which was the best style. For his early speeches are not free of old-fashioned blemishes; in them he is slow in his exordia, lengthy in narrative, long-winded in his digressions; his emotions are aroused too slowly and rarely reach boiling point; few of his sentences end rhythmically with a fine finish. There is nothing to quote, nothing to take home with you. As in a primitive building, the walls are strong and lasting, but not sufficiently polished and resplendent. I want the orator, like the rich and reputable head of a family, to live under a roof which not only protects him against wind and rain, but the sight of which also delights his eyes, in a house which is furnished not only with the necessities of life but which also contains gold and gems which he can take in his hand and look at. Certain things should be avoided and left far away, musty and forgotten. No word we use should be covered with rust, nor any sentence have the slow and limp construction of a chronicle. Our orator should avoid coarse and stupid jests, he should vary his word-arrangement and not end his clauses with one and the same rhythm.

I do not wish to ridicule Cicero's 'wheel of Fortune' or his 'Verrine' justice nor that third phrase which takes the place of a maxim in all his speeches, namely *esse videatur* at the end of every other sentence.[1] I mention these unwillingly and omit a greater number; yet these phrases alone are admired and imitated by those who call themselves orators of the old school. I name no names but only indicate a type, you have before your eyes those very people who prefer Lucilius to Horace, Lucretius to Virgil . . . who hate and despise the work of our orators but admire that of Calvus. As they hold forth in their anti-

[1] The 'wheel of Fortune' occurs in *In Pisonem* 22. Aper is not objecting to the metaphor as such, but to its use for a rather poor pun: *in quo cum illum saltatorium orbem versaret, ne tum quidem Fortunae rotam pertimescebat*, i.e. as he was turning in the circle of the dance, he did not even then fear the wheel of fortune, *orbem* and *rotam* being here nearly synonymous. *ius verrinum* is a double pun, 'boar sauce' and 'law of Verres', *Verrine Orations* 2, 1, 121. In this case, however, Cicero disclaims the pun. On the *scurrilitas* of Cicero see Quintilian (6, 3, 1-5) who admits the orator went too far sometimes, and for Ciceronian theory on the subject, above, pp. 187-91. Quintilian 9, 4, 73 for Cicero's use of *esse videatur*, a frequent cadence in the *De Oratore*, but not so very frequent elsewhere, as Gudeman points out (p. 248), at least at the end of a clause.

quated manner before a judge, their audience does not follow them, the people do not hear them, even their client can barely endure them. So gloomy are they and so unsophisticated that they attain the soundness of which they boast not through strength but poverty of speech. Surely doctors do not approve of physical health which results from too much anxiety; not to be ill is not enough, a man should be strong and gay and eager. If all he is praised for is soundness, he is not far from being ill.

This criticism of Cicero would have surprised his contemporary critics, and the orator himself, for he is here praised as the forerunner of silver Latin in some respects – the rhythms, the *sententiae*, the flowery passages – and blamed for his moderation and, of all things, for his insufficient emotionalism. As Maternus will point out, Aper borrows Cicero's critical principles in more than one instance to criticize Cicero himself. This is not misrepresentation but the natural result of a change of taste, and it shows how violent and 'Asiatic' Aper's contemporaries had become. Only with the accusation of *scurrilitas* and rhythmic monotony some of Cicero's contemporary critics might have agreed, but here, one suspects, Aper is using any stick to beat a dog with, for his own contemporaries were not noted for their good taste. The whole speech is a highly vivid, and, one imagines, a very realistic piece of current criticism, again excellently in character.

In his defence of the age of Cicero (chs. 25-26), Messala agrees that different epochs have different styles and indeed that there are different styles within one period, though the differences between Cicero and his own contemporaries are as nothing to those between all of them on the one hand and present day orators on the other. He agrees that pre-Ciceronian eloquence was not fully developed, but he launches into a denunciation of contemporary style. The process of degeneration, to him, evidently began with the empire (26):

> Yet if we have to choose a style, while leaving out of account that most perfect kind of (Ciceronian) eloquence, I would certainly prefer the impetuosity of C. Gracchus and the ripeness of L. Crassus to the curling-pins of Maecenas[1] or the jingles of Gallio. So much better is it to clothe eloquence in a homespun toga than to adorn it with the variegated fineries of a courtesan. The refinements used by the majority of our present day advocates are unworthy of an orator, indeed unworthy of a human being. They reproduce the musical modes of the

[1] We have seen a similar criticism of Maecenas' style in Seneca, *Letters*, 114, 48. See above, p. 268. Gallio was the contemporary and friend of Ovid and of the elder Seneca. He wrote on rhetoric (Quint. 3, 1, 21).

theatre by their unrestrained language, shallow epigrams and the abuse of prose-rhythms. What they should blush to hear said by others most of them actually boast of, as if it brought praise and glory and took the place of talent; they sing and dance their speeches when they deliver them. Hence this foul and absurd but frequent cry: that our orators are said to speak delicately and our actors to dance eloquently.

Aper, Messala continues, named only Cassius Severus from among the moderns. He may indeed be called an orator compared with those who followed him, but he was the first to bring confusion by his contempt for the structure of a speech, by his lack of modesty and his violence, 'he was not a fighter, he was a brawler'. Why did not Aper name those he approved of, for we can trace the decadence from its beginning step by step.

Maternus here interrupts and recalls Messala to the subject he promised to deal with, the reasons for the decadence of oratory which is accepted as a fact by all those present except Aper. The rest of Messala's perform-ance, or what remains of it, is a strong attack on contemporary education: the old Roman virtues have vanished; youth is lazy; teachers are ignorant and parents are indifferent. He elaborates this theme, tracing the vices of education from infancy through the elementary school to the school of rhetoric, and violently attacks the practice of declamation.[1] In strong contrast he praises at length the general education of the orator as preached and practised by Cicero. Thus he gives us one basic reason why *eloquentia* has sunk to the status of the lowest crafts, *una ex sordidissimis artificiis*.

At this point (35) there is a considerable lacuna in the text which must have contained the rest of Messala's speech and presumably also Secundus' contribution to the discussion. When our text resumes, Maternus is speaking[2] and continues to the end. His theme is that great eloquence, in Greece as in Rome, flourished in turbulent times. The great political trials and the indecisions of democracy made the great orators whose influence was as great as their talent. But the price is not worth it; the peace and order of the empire is not conducive to great eloquence, but it is well worth having. Then there is the reorganization of the courts, the limit on

---

[1] In this chapter and throughout the discussion of contemporary education there are a number of expressions which seem to echo Petronius on the same subject. These have been collected by Collignon in his *Etude* pp. 95-99. Tacitus probably had read Petronius and may well have some of these passages in mind. On the other hand, when people discuss a topic of great contemporary interest from the same point of view they naturally express the same sentiments, often in the same words. These echoes seem rather of this kind.

[2] Some commentators, notably Gudeman, have assumed another lacuna somewhere after 40, so that not Maternus, but (presumably) Secundus, speaks 36-40, the sentiments expressed in those chapters being allegedly contrary to those of Maternus, both in 41 and his earlier speech. Most scholars, however, agree with Peterson that Maternus speaks from 36 on. See, in particular, K. von Fritz, in *Rhein. Mus.* 81 (1932), 275-300.

the length of speeches first imposed by Pompey, the fact that the most important cases today are civil cases, or petty cases, before various kinds of magistrates where, with no popular gallery to impress, the orators do not take the same pains, and where things are more efficiently regulated. Good soldiers are trained in wars, great orators in times of civil discord – but neither the one nor the other is worth the price.

There is a good deal of truth in this argument; we know that Tacitus fully realized that the clock could not be turned back to the days of the Republic.[1] The peace which the empire brought was no doubt a blessing, although, in A.D. 75, the late subjects of Caligula and Nero might well have wondered, as might a few years later those of Domitian, especially if they lived in Rome. Certainly the realization that things could never go back does not make Maternus an enthusiastic or an uncritical subject. His last speech must be understood in the light of his earlier attack on 'blood-stained oratory' and of his whole character. Nor should we forget Messala's criticism of contemporary education with which only Aper, one imagines, would disagree. If commentators have thought that Maternus' last speech contradicts his earlier position, it is probably because they have missed the bitter irony of this speech, not only in the nostalgic description of the old orators' life, but also in the allusions to the present day. For the lovers of the ancients, it is far more than eloquence that has been lost, the old Roman way of life and the old Roman virtues have disappeared too, and surely there is irony in words like these (40):

> What we are discussing (i.e. eloquence) is not a thing of ease and quietude which finds joy in righteousness and discretion. That grand and famous eloquence is fostered by licence which fools used to call liberty, it is the companion of sedition; it incites the unbridled mob; it knows neither obedience nor servitude,[2] it is stubborn, reckless and

---

[1] The ambivalence of Tacitus' feelings is seen in many passages. He knows that the rule of one man is now a necessity, but that much has been lost with the republic, e.g. *Histories* 1, 1: 'After the battle of Actium the interests of peace required that all power be concentrated in one man, but the great talents of earlier days (*magna illa ingenia*) disappeared, and truth suffered in many ways. . . .' See also 2, 38.

[2] The MSS. read *sine obsequio, sine servitute*. Gudeman bluntly says: 'The MS. reading "servitute" is absurd', and changes it to *severitate*. Peterson reads *veritate* in his edition, and *reverentia* in his Loeb text, and other suggestions have been made. The difficulty is, of course, that Maternus is supposed to be praising the imperial system. Actually, he is only accepting it. He did not hesitate to call Crispus and Marcellus *servi* (see p. 277, note 1, above). For that matter Tacitus, in *Histories* 4, 8, does not hesitate to make Marcellus himself use *servire* to describe the relation of the senate to the emperor: *se unum esse ex illo senatu qui simul servierit.* This is not the only expression in this speech where Maternus betrays his feelings, whatever his intellectual acceptance of despotic power. There are, I think, traces of the same bitter irony where (36 ad init.) the present settled conditions are compared with the days of Cicero – *mixtis omnibus et moderatore uno carentibus*, as if the rule of one man were the ideal, and that within six years of Nero! Then there is the statement (41) that 'what remains of old forensic activities

proud; it does not exist in well-governed cities. What Spartan, what Cretan orator have we ever heard of, where discipline and laws were most severe? Nor do we know of any eloquence among the Macedonians or the Persians or any race which lived under a strong government.

Maternus the poet, the author of the *Cato*, is certainly not flattering the imperial regime by these comparisons, and we remember that, even for Aper, poetry was a form of *eloquentia*. There were no poets in Sparta or Macedonia either. Nor is this the only passage in the speech where his republican sympathies lead him into bitter irony.

It is often said that Maternus stands for Tacitus in the *Dialogue*, for did Tacitus too not give up a career at the bar to write history, which the ancients considered akin to poetry? This is largely true but it is not the whole truth, some aspect of which is expressed by each speaker. That Tacitus had a great deal of sympathy with Messala's indictment of contemporary education is surely obvious. But Tacitus, unlike Messala, was no mere *laudator temporis acti*. Aper has some truth on his side – and Tacitus saw that truth, else he could not, or would not, have developed his own so characteristic, and characteristically silver Latin style. This does not mean that Aper is not partly satirized, it does account, however, for the brilliance of the satire, as well as the unique, and superbly effective presentation of him as the only critic in our texts who really believes in the greatness of silver Latin style. Irony pervades the whole work; in Maternus the irony is conscious, in Aper it is unconscious, but it is the irony of their creator in both cases.

to our orators is a proof that our state has not yet been made faultless or constituted as one might wish', as if the complete eradication of *eloquentia* was (with all that would imply) devoutly to be wished. Further, can we take completely at face value that 'orators receive less honour and repute *where morals are good* (*inter bonos mores*) and men are prepared to obey their ruler (*in obsequium regentis paratos*)' (40)? Did anyone suggest that morality was flourishing in A.D. 75? Messala certainly did not. Moreover, Maternus continues 'What need is there of long speeches in the Senate when *the best people* (*optimi*) quickly agree? What need of assemblies when decisions are not taken by the inexperienced many but by the wisest man, *sapientissimus et unus*. Why take the responsibility of prosecution when wrong is so rarely done, *cum tam raro et tam parce peccetur*? Why take up an unpopular defence when the clemency of the judge who decides favours the defendants?' There is a bitter irony in this speech of Maternus, as throughout the *Dialogus*, and it is characteristically Tacitean.

CHAPTER XVII

Quintilian

Marcus Fabius Quintilianus was born in Spain about A.D. 35. He was educated in Rome, but he seems to have returned to Spain until he was recalled by the emperor Galba. He soon became famous both as an advocate and as a teacher, and he was appointed to the first imperial Chair of rhetoric by Vespasian. He continued to teach through the reigns of Titus and Domitian, and the latter appointed him tutor to his great-nephews, a post which greatly gratified the professor. He wrote a work on the decay of eloquence, and some extant declamations are attributed to him. Late in life he married a young woman who bore him two sons, but mother and sons died while he was engaged upon his greatest work, the *Institutio Oratoria* or *Education of the Orator*, which has survived.

Quintilian preaches a return to classical or Ciceronian prose, and in this he probably represented a Flavian reaction against the excesses of Nero's reign, but the reaction was but temporary and incomplete.[1] The declamations continued, and so did the stylistic vices which he condemned, notably archaism and an exaggerated care in the choice of words. His immediate influence upon his pupils and contemporaries was no doubt considerable, but the classical revival to which he looked forward did not materialize, and his influence did not last. It is only with the Renaissance that Quintilian came into his own, and then his work dominated rhetoric and education almost as completely as Galen's ruled over the theory and practice of medicine.

The *Institutio* is a fine example of a professorial book. It is a complete survey of the field, eminently clear and sensible, authoritative and definitive. All Roman and Greek theories of rhetoric and education are discussed at length and if Quintilian is not as original as he seems to claim at times, there can be no doubt that he writes out of his own experience as a speaker and teacher, as well as with full knowledge of previous theories. Sometimes he is more than a little dull where he discusses rhetorical theory in con-

---

[1] See G. A. Kennedy in *AJP* 83 (1962), 130-46, and Syme, *Tacitus* 103 and 114-15. Kennedy rather overemphasizes Quintilian's weaknesses, but his article is a useful corrective to the exaggerated praise which is often lavished upon the *Institutio*. Syme (p. 618) notes the curious fact that Quintilian 'mentions Spain only once – and then it is with the curious affectation of not knowing much about a certain local word' (at 1, 5, 57). We find Quintilian's hopes for a classical revival expressed at 1, 1, 122.

siderable detail; of this he is fully aware and indeed apologizes for the dryness of the topics to be dealt with in the central books (3, 1, 2), though even these are lit up now and again by vividly written passages of more general interest.

He takes his 'orator' from infancy to old age, and reviews the whole of Roman education. The first book-and-a-half deal with the elementary stages and general principles many of which are as sound today, and as controversial, as they were eighteen centuries ago. The rest of the second book weighs the various definitions of rhetoric and its different forms. Books three to seven deal with *inventio*, with cases, issues and arguments. It is this part of the work which begins with an apology for the aridity of the subject; it ends it with a fine passage on the folly of thinking that everything can be taught (7, 10, 14):

> Therefore let no one expect to become eloquent through the labours of another. He himself must study through the night, make the effort, grow pale with study, develop his own power, his own habits, his own thinking. These things should not have to be looked for, they should be ready to hand, not as things handed on but as things inborn. We teachers can point the way but each pupil must travel at his own speed. Training has done its job if it has made the plentiful resources of eloquence available; we must each know how to use them for ourselves.

In these central books we find all the familiar formulae[1]: the five aspects of the art of expression: *inventio, dispositio, elocutio, memoria* and *pronuntiatio* (delivery), which makes the basic pattern of the work; the three kinds of rhetoric, forensic, deliberative and epideictic (*laudativa*); the questions and issues which arise in each; the sections of a speech and the function of each section here subordinated to *inventio*; the duties of the orator which are, as in Cicero, to inform, to move and to delight; the need for natural talent, technical knowledge and experience. The formula of types of issues, namely *an sit* (whether the deed was done, i.e. *coniectura*), *quid sit* (e.g. whether it was murder, *definitio*), and *quale sit* (what kind of offence it is, or whether it is tried before the right kind of court, *qualitas*) takes up the first part of the seventh book and is followed by a discussion of points of law and various kinds of ambiguities.

With the eighth book we come to the discussion of style and under this heading comes the formula of the four virtues – latinity, lucidity, ornamentation and appropriateness; each of these is discussed at some length,

[1] For the five aspects of rhetoric see 3, ch. 3; the three kinds of rhetoric at 3, ch. 4; the sections of a speech are the basic structure from the first chapter of book 4 to the beginning of book 6; the duties of the orator are found at 3, 5, 2; the need for talent, training and practice at 3, 5, 1; types of cases are discussed in 7, chapters 2, 3 and 4.

after which come tropes and figures of thought and speech, the latter filling most of the ninth book – about nineteen figures of thought and twenty-eight figures of speech, each discussed individually.

Book ten is the most frequently read because in the first chapter, on what to read, Quintilian gives a survey of Greek and Latin literature with a very brief appraisal of most authors mentioned. After this we find very sensible remarks on *imitatio*, the emulation of great writers, on the process of writing and the proper exercises, on declamations, on *cogitatio* (the need to think about your subject) and on speaking extempore. Appropriateness, memory and delivery are dealt with in the eleventh book; the twelfth deals with the ideal orator: the moral character of the good man skilled in speech, *vir bonus dicendi peritus*, his need of other studies, when he should begin to speak in public and what he will do with himself in old age. Here too is a very interesting discussion of the differences between the Greek and Latin languages and of some of the usual controversies such as Atticism and Asianism, the three styles, and the need for training. The book ends with an exhortation that each man must do his best without despairing (12, 11, 26).

Quintilian's main inspiration is Cicero, whom he reveres, and the chief purpose of his teaching is to redeem *eloquentia* from the excesses of the silver Latin style by a return to the more classical Ciceronian eloquence. He does not hesitate to disagree with the master here and there, or to criticize him on points of detail, but in general he makes the educational and rhetorical theories of Cicero his own: the need for a general as well as a strictly rhetorical education for the orator, the close connexion between eloquence and philosophy, Atticism and Asianism, the three styles, the virtues of style and other traditional formulae – on all these questions Quintilian's views are Ciceronian and we need not, therefore, discuss them at any length. Yet at the same time there are some important differences, implied rather than expressed, between the two men, quite apart from the fact that Quintilian, as a teacher of style, is infinitely more thorough and more patient in dealing with stylistic minutiae.

The first difference is that Cicero was a statesman while Quintilian was a professor who kept himself apart from the politics of the day. The purpose of Cicero's system of education was much broader: he wanted to train men who would be able to deal with the problems of Rome, while Quintilian betrays no interest in those problems. This difference is partly due to their different dates: by the end of the first century A.D. the empire was completely established; the loss of freedom which first-century critics made responsible for the decay of oratory was pretty complete in the last years of Domitian. Yet Tacitus was a contemporary of Quintilian and no one would accuse him of unconcern with public affairs. Quintilian's

Spanish birth may have had something to do with it, though Seneca too belonged to a Spanish family and Lucan was born in Spain. Whatever the reason, the first imperial professor also seems to be the first Roman 'academic' in the modern sense, living in considerable comfort in his ivory tower. The result is not only a lack of real fire in his work, but also a narrowness of view which does affect his conception of both education and rhetoric. One may regret the loss of his book on the causes of the decay of eloquence but the tone would have been, one imagines, very different from that of Tacitus' *Dialogue on Orators*.

Another difference is that Cicero was writing of the art of expression in his own day, and often defending his own practice. Quintilian has nothing but contempt for the excesses of contemporary Latin style; he is definitely hankering after a style which passed away a century before and he seems less aware than Tacitus that you cannot put back the clock. True, Quintilian is no blind traditionalist; he is willing to compromise and to accept certain later fashions up to a point, and he is essentially a moderate. His own style was certainly not Ciceronian, it is neither silver nor gold, but it has been well termed silver-gilt.[1] Nevertheless he does look back rather than forward, and he fails to see, or to point out, what was good in contemporary writing while he is never tired of condemning what was bad. This weakness also makes his work academic and his common sense a trifle lifeless.

Then again, while he pays lip service to the Ciceronian general education it is obvious that he requires much less outside knowledge than Cicero did. His own acquaintance with philosophy was very much less. Cicero too subordinated philosophy to the needs of the orator, but in Quintilian the subordination is much more complete and the knowledge less deep.[2] Where Cicero thinks of the general effect of philosophy upon the mind of the orator, Quintilian is more concerned that his orator should have (or acquire) such knowledge as will enable him to deal with his immediate needs. Both writers use illustrations from all kinds of literature, both advise very wide reading, but, in spite of the literary survey in the tenth book on the one hand, and the definitely rhetorical slant in Cicero on the other, we cannot but feel that the word *orator* itself has, in Quintilian, somewhat narrowed its meaning. Both, however, share the Roman contempt for the rhetorical technicians, and even Quintilian speaks of (1, *Praef.* 24):

those dry textbooks (*nudae artes*) which affect excessive subtlety and

[1] By H. E. Butler in his Loeb edition p. ix.
[2] The need for other subjects of study at 1, ch. 10, philosophy in particular at 12, ch. 2. For Cicero see above, pp. 169-71.

kill whatever is noble in eloquence, drain away the live sap and leave nothing but bare bones. Bare bones are indeed necessary, but they must be bound together by tendons and covered with living flesh.

The first part of the work is perhaps the most interesting of all, and we should note some of his theories of education in passing, for he claims that teachers of rhetoric are wrong to believe elementary education a subject below their dignity. Good latinity should be the main concern from the beginning, so that even nurses and attendants should be chosen with this in mind. We are reminded that educated Romans were at this time bilingual by his advice that boys should be formally instructed in Greek before Latin, and even more when he says that, however, this process should not go on too long 'as is now done in most cases', but that both languages should soon be taught side by side.[1] Early education should be a matter of play, praise and prizes and not be too demanding. Quintilian strongly opposes too rapid methods of teaching to read which in the end cause 'an incredible amount of delay'. Letters must come first, then syllables, then words. He wants children to go to school with their contemporaries rather than be tutored at home, and, while he is against too soft an upbringing which leads to self-indulgence, yet he strongly opposes corporal punishment as debasing (1, 3, 13):

> I do not approve at all of beating a child, though the custom is generally accepted. . . . It is a disgraceful punishment fit only for slaves. It is insulting, as you see at once if you think of it at another age. Moreover, if a pupil's mind is so insensitive that it cannot be corrected by exhortation it will soon be hardened to blows like the worst kind of slaves. There is no need for this kind of correction if the teacher is keen on making the pupils work. . . .

Once the elementary stages of reading and writing are over, the main task of the *grammaticus* is to teach his pupils to use their language correctly, clearly and with some degree of ornamentation. This is done by various exercises and by the study of literature which is essential to the future orator. Correct usage should not be too narrowly interpreted. Quintilian does not endorse Pollio's criticism that Livy was guilty of *patavinitas*,[2] i.e. wrote the Latin of Padua, not Rome. To Quintilian the speech of Italy as a whole is correct Latin. To attain correctness we must take into account analogy, the age of words, the authority of good writers, and usage, this

---

[1] 1, 1, 12-14, and for the playful nature of early education 1, 1, 20; for the dangers of too soft an upbringing 1, 2, 6: *quid non adultus concupiscet qui in purpuris repit*; his objections to corporal punishment at 1, 3, 13-18.

[2] 1, 5, 56, but see p. 295, note 1, below. Correct language 1, ch. 6, with archaism at 1, 6, 39, comedy at 1, 8, 3 and 1, 11, 1-3.

last being the surest guide. Yet all these must be used with discretion, and by his examples Quintilian gives us a good deal of interesting information on Latin usage. Deliberate archaism is to be avoided. At this stage reading must be carefully controlled, both for its linguistic value and its effect on character (I, 8, 6):

> for many Greek poets are rather wanton and there are some passages of Horace which I would not want to explain.

Elegiacs, especially the erotic kind, and crude lampoons had better be avoided. Comedy is useful once the boys have reached a responsible age, for comic actors teach a useful delivery but we must be careful, for repeated imitation becomes second nature. Old Latin poets too should be read (I, 8, 9):

> they are more careful of structure than most modern writers who see only one virtue in all kinds of writing, the use of epigrammatic maxims (*sententiae*). From the old writers we can learn integrity and manliness now that our ways of speech have sunk to all the faults of luxuriousness.

Of other studies necessary at this stage of education he emphasizes two: music and mathematics (*geometria*, which includes arithmetic). About music Quintilian seems on the defensive, he has a long appeal to authority in the matter and then strenuously maintains the usefulness of this study for a good delivery and to appreciate the sound of words. One almost feels he is trying to convince himself. The defence of (elementary) mathematics is of course much easier since the habit of logical deduction is obviously necessary to the pleader. His defence of physical training is very Roman: exercises are necessary to achieve rhythmic stance and gestures in delivery, but there is nothing about the general benefits of physical culture. Sport as such never appealed to the Romans.[1]

Some may feel, Quintilian says, that this is a lot to demand of children but he believes that the young are capable of much, and in any case variety of studies is itself a form of relaxation.[2] The first book ends with a strong condemnation of the mercenary view of education.

The boy then goes to rhetorical school, later than he should because the rhetoricians now seem to think that their job is only to teach declamation and leave the rest to the *grammaticus*. Quintilian has a good deal to say about teacher-pupil relationship, student participation, and methods of teaching. The type of reading recommended at this stage is also interesting: one should never read inferior authors because they are easier, but always

---

[1] For other than rhetorical studies see p. 287, note 2, and gymnastic at I, II, 15.
[2] I, 12, 4.

read the best. From these, however, we may choose those who are most clear and simple: Livy is better than Sallust at this stage, even though the latter is the greater historian. And Cicero of course, and, as Livy put it, whoever is most like Cicero. An excessive admiration for ancient Latin authors is harmful to the young, they are too harsh and meagre; their power can only be appreciated later, when one's own style has been formed. So too some moderns should be read later, but 'our boys must not be captivated by the lascivious ornaments of present-day fashion and tempted by its perverse delights, nor fall in love with this oversweet type of style, the more attractive to childish minds because more congenial to them'.[1] There are good writers still, but the young cannot be trusted to find them without guidance.

And now that his student is prepared for forensic or deliberative themes, Quintilian warns him of the dangers of declamations, as practised in the schools. In itself he admits that 'this most recently invented exercise'[2] is extremely useful, for it includes all kinds of exercises, provided it has some connexion with actual cases (2, 10, 3):

> But the practice has so degenerated through the fault of the teachers that it has become one of the main reasons for the decay of eloquence because of the extravagance and ignorance of the declaimers.

Present themes – magicians, plagues, oracles, cruel stepmothers and the like – have nothing in common with the lawsuits for which they are supposed to train. Such fanciful themes should be forbidden altogether, or at best allowed as an occasional orgy, a kind of blood-letting to get rid of superfluous humours, but as a regular training they are pernicious – histrionic ranting and lunatic ravings. This disables a man for practical oratory (2, 10, 12):

> Therefore declamation, since it is a representation of forensic and deliberative speech, must remain similar to the truth; but since it also has an element of display it may assume a certain lustre.

Contemporary exaggerations are, however, deplorable. This is the same attitude as that of Seneca, Petronius and Tacitus, yet the popularity of declamations continued.

Quintilian reflects that this is part of the general cult of violence: to force what can be opened, to tear what can be untied, to drag what can be led. Hence the current admiration for the natural untrained speaker with his

---

[1] 2, 5, 22.

[2] At 2, 4, 41 however, he says that the practice of fictitious speeches began in the time of Demetrius of Phalerum. Here (2, 10, 1-2) he must therefore be thinking of the extremely artificial kind of declamations which developed in Rome in the first century. See above, pp. 258-61.

passionate, violent delivery. And he adds, giving a curious twist to the
formula of the neighbouring vices, that these appear virtues to the uncultured, that abusive speech is thought to be free, reckless speech considered courageous and slackness mistaken for abundance. Some teachers
of short-cuts to eloquence actually encourage this (2, 12, 8):

> Nevertheless one must admit that instruction (*doctrina*) does take away
> something, as the file takes away from rough surfaces, the grindstone
> from rough edges, and age from wine, but what it takes away is bad,
> and that which the study of letters has polished is less only in this, that
> it is better.

No one should expect from me, Quintilian continues, the kind of absolute
rules which writers of rhetorical textbooks are so fond of. There are no
absolute rules. The most important thing is sound judgement which can
be applied to varying circumstances, so as to achieve what is appropriate,
and what is expedient. 'Rules will help when they point the right road,
not when they keep you in a rut' (2, 13, 16).

In the more technical books, there are a number of passages of general
interest, as when, dealing with the peroration in the sixth book, Quintilian
naturally comes to treat of rousing the audience's emotions. This is to him,
as to Cicero, the supreme task of the orator and in fact our sober professor gets so carried away that he seems to forget his moral inhibitions
and discusses freely how to sweep the judge off his feet by emotional
appeals.[1]

We find here also an interesting passage on *êthos* and *pathos* which
clarifies for us the different senses in which these words, and especially the
confusing *êthos*, seem to have been used apparently since Aristotle.[2]
Pathos is passion, it is violent and temporary, it disturbs and dominates,
while *êthos* refers to the gentler emotions, it is more lasting, it persuades
rather than commands, and induces goodwill. The Roman critics themselves were evidently confused by the word and made no attempt to translate it; even Quintilian is not very sure, though he suggests *mores*, or
rather *morum quaedam proprietas*, 'a certain appropriateness of temper'.
'Love is *pathos*, affection is *êthos*,' and in a peroration the latter can be used
to calm the storm raised by the former. *Ethos*, Quintilian goes on to explain, commends itself by its goodness (which clearly refers to the *character*
of the speaker), its *tone* is mild and courteous, and its chief merit is that it
makes everything seem to follow from the nature of the facts and the
persons concerned (this clearly refers to the lower emotional level, nothing
is forced, everything seems natural). *Ethos* is therefore particularly suited

---

[1] 6, 2, 3-4. The ethos-pathos passage is in the same chapter 8-20.
[2] See above, pp. 86 and 220.

to cases where violence is out of place, as in disputes between friends and relations. It is then linked with irony, for one can often expose a person more effectively, and make him more disliked, by a quiet manner than by displays of violent abuse. Quintilian suggests that certain strong affections like parental love or strong friendship do not belong to either category.

He then mentions another meaning of *éthos* (and this is the original one), namely characterization, when we portray character, be it a peasant, a miser or a coward, and he again emphasizes the importance of the speaker's own character and the impression it leaves on the audience, for the speaker who is thought to be a bad man is in fact a bad speaker. The *éthos* in this sense must, however, be gentle and friendly if it is to be so called. He must speak pleasantly, persuasively and appropriately and will therefore use the middle style. *Pathos* is more like tragedy, *éthos* like comedy.

The passage does not explain how these different meanings of *éthos* came about, but it does clarify what they are. This is only one example out of very many where a passage of the *Institutio* is essential to help us understand the technical vocabulary of rhetoric and criticism. In this case *pathos* presents little difficulty, it means passion or suffering, but the *éthos* of a speech may refer to characterization or to speaking in character, to the character of the speaker himself, to the less exalted emotional tone or the naturalness of his manner. And it is in this last sense that *éthos* was the proper tone of comedy while *pathos* was that of tragedy.

Quintilian further insists with considerable emphasis, that, in order to arouse the emotions of his audience, a speaker must himself feel those emotions, and feel them in the fullest sense. He makes a special point here that he is speaking not from book knowledge but from experience. This is a little surprising, as the same idea is found in Cicero, and indeed can be traced back to Aristotle,[1] but Quintilian does add a fuller explanation of how this is to be achieved, and he is undoubtedly speaking from experience as well. An orator must use the same vivid imagination as the poets to *see* the things he describes as if they were happening before him and identify himself with the client (6, 2, 34):

> When pity is to be aroused we must convince ourselves in our own minds that the things we complain of have happened to ourselves. We must *be* the victims of grievous, undeserved and bitter misfortunes; we must handle the case as our own, and, for the time being, assume the pain of it. We shall then say the things we would have said had we been the victim. I have often seen tragic and comic actors, after they had played a moving role, walk off in tears. Now if the mere acting of another man's script kindles such simulated passion, then surely we

[1] 6, 2, 25-31.

who must think the thoughts and find the words, will be moved as our client is. . . . I have myself often been so moved as not only to weep, but to turn pale with all but genuine sorrow.

Under the same general subject of emotional appeals we find a long discussion of the laughable (*ridiculum*, 4, 3). We seize eagerly upon this, since we have so little on the comic in ancient writers; it is however disappointing and disordered when we compare it to the treatment of the comic in Cicero's *De Oratore*.

It begins well. The difficulty of the subject is underlined by the fact that, of the two greatest orators, Demosthenes was lacking in wit and Cicero, though fully endowed with *urbanitas*, was said to lack restraint. Laughter is compulsive and hard to resist, so completely tied to the particular circumstances that it is very hard to bring under any general rules; indeed the very same joke is successful when spoken by one man and yet falls flat when spoken by another. One cannot teach how to raise a laugh nor learn it; at best the teacher can choose certain themes which give his pupils an opportunity for wit. Yet obviously it can be very useful to raise a laugh, for it relieves the tensions, and often dissolves anger or opposition. As Cicero said,[1] people laugh at a certain ugliness or deformity when pointed out in others, but, Quintilian adds, to point them out in oneself is merely silly. In fact he does not approve of jests at one's own expense. He also makes the point that wit is more successful in repartee than in attack.

He attempts to define and distinguish a number of Latin terms which are applied to different kinds of wit, but he does not relate them, as Cicero did, by significant analysis. He then goes on to general theory and makes the usual distinction between jests of substance (*in rebus*) and verbal wit (*in verbis*).[2] He adds a cross-division: jokes at the expense of others, at one's own expense, and those (like taking a word in a different sense) which do not reflect on either party. Laughter may also be provoked directly by something we do as well as something we say.

Then there is the tone of a joke: it can be frivolous and lively, or insulting, or bitter. But Quintilian is as keen on propriety as Cicero[3]: we should not want to hurt people and we should make it our aim not to lose a friend rather than lose a witticism: the orator's jokes should be gentle, and real misfortune is not a proper butt for ridicule. Besides, the orator should avoid scurrility, uncouth gestures or contorted features – 'let him miss the opportunity for a jest rather than diminish his standing with his audience'.[4] Quintilian would also avoid sarcastic remarks at the expense of classes of people, national, social or professional.

[1] *De Oratore* 2, 236, and above, pp. 187-90.
[3] E.g. *Orator* 88 etc. Above, p. 188.
[2] Cp. *De Oratore* 2, 240-4.
[4] 6, 3, 30.

So far the theory of laughter. The position taken here is in general, as we would expect though with some additions, also that of Cicero. It is in what follows, a long section (36-100) on the sources or *loci* of laughter that there seems no particular order or structure. Quintilian rightly points out that these cannot all be mentioned, for they are as numerous as the sources of maxims, and here too both invention and style are important. He notes that brevity is more pointed, repeats Cicero's differentiation between the consistently humorous or ironical tone of a whole narrative and the brief sally; and also follows him in ranking the spontaneous jest far higher than those 'brought from home'.[1]

Books eight and nine deal, as already mentioned, with style. In introducing the subject, Quintilian emphasizes its difficulty and its importance as all rhetorical training is directed towards it. But he also makes a strong protest against exclusive attention to the words at the expense of the meaning.[2] 'We should be careful about style but concerned with ideas.' A healthy body derives its beauty from its soundness and strength, whereas depilatories and cosmetics deface the body they labour to beautify, 'so too the obviously variegated style of some writers emasculates the very ideas which are thus adorned in expression'.[3] The subject-matter itself will suggest the clearest and best form of expression, and we should not seek out-of-the-way forms and then make the matter fit the words. This spoils our discourse, makes it artificial, and obscures the sense, as exuberant weeds choke the good seed. And Quintilian launches one of his not infrequent attacks on contemporary style (8, *Praef.* 24):

> Our love of words makes us wander all around a topic which can be expressed simply. We repeat what has already been sufficiently stated. What can be said in one word we burden with many. As a rule we think it better to imply something than to say it. No current expression satisfies us while nothing which anyone else might also have said is thought to be good style. We borrow figures of speech and metaphors from the most decadent poets and we consider ourselves a genius if it takes a genius to understand us. Yet Cicero taught us in clear language that the worst fault of style is to shrink from ordinary ways of speech and the usages of common experience. But Cicero, they say, is unpolished and ignorant; we know better when we despise every dictate of nature; we do not look for genuine but for meretricious adornments, as if there were any virtue in words which do not fit the facts. Yet if we are to spend our whole life searching for words which are appropriate, lucid and decorative and arranging them in a fitting manner, then surely the fruit of our studies is lost.

[1] *De Oratore* 2, 230 and *Orator* 89.   [2] 8, *Praef.* 18-22.   [3] Ibid. 20.

And yet you can see most of our speakers hesitate over a single word while they find it, weigh it, and measure it. This would be a detestable habit even if they always did find the right word in the end, for their diffident delay breaks the flow of their speech and quenches the flame of their thought. A pitiful creature is the orator who cannot endure with equanimity the loss of a single word, a very pauper.

When we come to the actual discussion of style, the approach is by way of the four qualities. Latinity has largely been dealt with in the first book. Here he only emphasizes that we should avoid provincial or foreign words,[1] and he tells the story of the old woman in Athens who thought Theophrastus was a foreigner because he used somewhat precious expression and she said his language was too Attic for an Athenian! Lucidity and appropriateness are dealt with at some length; when the most appropriate expression is found, it cannot be bettered, as when Cato said that the remarkable thing about Caesar was that 'he set about destroying the republic (while he was) sober'. Archaism, practised by those who scour old books to find unusual words, is rejected, and so are both prolixity and excessive brevity, both of which make for obscurity (8, 2, 22):

> The first virtue of style, to me, is lucidity, the right words, the right order of words, the conclusion of the period not long delayed. Nothing should be lacking and nothing be superfluous. Then our discourse will be approved by the learned and our meaning clear to the common man.

To speak correctly and clearly, however, is not enough. We must have embellishment (*ornatum*), but art must remain concealed: too lavish a display of flowers and fountains is no indication of good farming, neither is too lavish ornamentation any indication of good style,[2] though epideictic rhetoric may be allowed a freer use of it. Having thus made his general position clear Quintilian goes into considerable detail of vices to avoid and virtues to seek in the use of words and in the arrangement of phrases. He notes that Latin coins new words much less freely than Greek,[3]

---

[1] Quintilian is guilty of contradiction. Here (8, 1, 3) he quotes Asinius Pollio's criticism of Livy as guilty of *patavinitas* (the dialect of Padua) and goes on to say that 'if possible, both all our words and our pronunciation should be those of this city of Rome, so that our discourse should appear to be genuinely Roman, not naturalized'. Yet in 1, 5, 56 where he quotes the same saying of Pollio, he says, on the contrary, that 'I must be allowed to consider whatever is Italian to be Roman'. The difference in his point of view does not look like an oversight, but rather a definite correction, perhaps due to protests from the believers in pure latinity which also in Cicero means the language of the city of Rome. As the *Institutio* was published piecemeal, such a correction in a later part is quite possible, though no attention is drawn to it. Or is it that the language of a provincial should be purer at a higher level of education? Cf. Cicero *De Oratore* 3, 42: *sic in Latino sermone huius est urbis maxime propria (suavitas)*.

[2] 8, 3, 7-9.   [3] 8, 3, 30-31.

and among the virtues lays considerable emphasis on vividness, also on similes and metaphors.

The treatment of *sententiae* is interesting, in view of their prominence in contemporary style. Quintilian notes that in this sense the word is a translation of the Greek γνώμη or maxim, which was fully discussed by Aristotle and Theophrastus as a feature of style, i.e. a general philosophic reflection in a few words. There are traces of the Aristotelian discussion where it is noted that the *sententia* may be a simple statement, though a reason or explanation may be briefly added.[1] Inevitably, the γνῶμαι had been classified by Greek rhetoricians, and Quintilian notes ten different kinds, based on denial, similarity, etc., for they can appear in many guises and most figures; almost any epigram came to be called by this name even if it had no general application.

Quintilian condemns obvious plays on one word, which are little more than puns, and he gives a number of examples from declamations, all in very bad taste. However, he will not follow those who would avoid *sententiae* altogether. True, excessive use of them is merely ridiculous but (8, 5, 34):

> I believe these embellishments to be, as it were, the eyes of eloquence; but I would not want eyes all over the body for then the other parts would lose their function. If necessary, I should prefer the harshness of the ancients to our modern licence. But there is a middle way, just as in dress and food one may have a certain elegance without incurring blame. Let us therefore, if we can, increase the good qualities of our style; let us however first keep it free from faults lest, while we aim to be better than the ancients, we succeed only in being different.

Here as elsewhere, the *via media* is typical of Quintilian's common sense.

What is said about metaphors, which are here also considered one of the main ornaments of good prose, follows orthodox lines. We use them because we must do so where there is no current word to express our thought (a hard man), to express our meaning more graphically (burning with anger), or as an ornament (storms in the assembly). Only for these purposes is a metaphor justifiable. Like Aristotle, Quintilian greatly favours the active metaphor which personifies inanimate things (the flood scorns the bridge), but restraint is necessary: metaphors should not be coarse or in bad taste, they must be appropriate, neither too harsh, too poetic or too far-fetched, for 'a metaphor should either occupy a vacant place or, if it takes the place of another word, it should have more force than the word it displaces' (8, 6, 18).

Many other tropes are treated and illustrated in detail. Quintilian in

---

[1] 8, 5, 4.

each case refers to differences in terminology between rhetoricians and thus gives us a good deal of information about rhetorical theory both earlier and contemporary, as well as a clear definition of every trope. Figures of thought and speech receive the same detailed treatment in the ninth book. These seem to us very numerous, though Quintilian tries to keep the numbers down and has, he says, omitted a great many. He shows that the rhetoricians themselves found it hard to distinguish clearly between figures of thought and figures of speech, tropes and figures, figures and qualities.[1] Here too he preaches moderation, for 'to hunt up figures without reference to the ideas to be expressed is as absurd as to look for a dress or gestures without a body', and when cruelty, envy, pity are in question, 'who will tolerate a man's rage, tears or entreaties expressed in balanced antitheses and rhythms? . . . Where there is a display of art, truth is thought to be absent' (9, 3, 100-2).

The books dealing with style end with a long discussion of *compositio* or word-arrangement. It begins, as so often, with a somewhat stylized passage, this time against those who oppose a study of the subject on the ground that one should speak naturally. This very soon broadens into an attack on those who do not believe in the techniques or art of rhetoric at all. As Quintilian puts it: 'What is most natural is that which is done as perfectly as nature allows.' The excesses of Sotadean or Galliambic rhythms are no argument against the study of rhythm (9, 4, 1-15).

He recognizes the usual three aspects of word-arrangement: the order of the words, the structure of the sentence, and the rhythm,[2] but it is the last of these to which he devotes most attention, and sometimes expresses himself as if it included them all, nor does he keep the three clearly distinguished. He notes (23-32) that the weaker words should come first so as to attain a rising emotional tone, that there is a certain traditional order in certain phrases, e.g. 'men and women' rather than 'women and men', and that, although there are no rules of grammatical order which cannot be broken, the verb should usually come at the end, as the force of the sentence depends on it. Ambiguity should, of course, be avoided.

As to structure, Quintilian recognizes two kinds, the closely construed (*vincta atque contexta*) and the loose or disjointed (*soluta*) in which we recognize the periodic and non-periodic styles of Aristotle. The clash of vowels, especially long vowels, should where possible be avoided, but excessive care to avoid hiatus, as in Isocrates and his school, is unjustified, for, as Cicero remarked, a hiatus may suggest a not unpleasing carelessness of style and preoccupation with content. Clashes of sibilants, however, are displeasing; consecutive words should not begin or end with the same

---

[1] 9,2, 100-107 and the discussion of the difference between tropes and figures at the beginning of 9.   [2] 9, 4, 22.

sounds, too many short words, or too many long ones, in succession are jerky, nor should we have too many clauses with the same rhythm. As for the sentence as a whole, it should rise in intensity.

All this is traditional theory, reminiscent not only of Cicero, to whom Quintilian fully recognizes his debt, but also of Dionysius' work on *Word-Arrangement* and of Demetrius.

The discussion of rhythm[1] does add something to previous writers in that Quintilian specifically attempts to distinguish the rhythms of prose from those of poetry. Prose rhythm is not a closed system of feet; it has no definite limits; it is the relative frequency of long and short syllables which is important, and prose allows much greater freedom in the use of pauses. Though we inevitably analyse all rhythms into feet, we should not, as some tiresome *grammatici* do, reduce a piece of prose to a succession of specific feet. This is not what Cicero meant when he spoke of the rhythmic thunderbolts of Demosthenes,[2] nor is prose subjected to definite rhythmic laws as poetry is. Nevertheless, he adds surprisingly, rhythm is more clearly defined in prose than in the dance or in music.

Words and figures may be chosen for the sake of euphony, provided that the meaning is not interfered with and nothing superfluous is added. Prose rhythm is in fact more difficult to achieve than poetry, precisely because it is more varied and less specific and 'pervades the whole body of discourse'. Rhythm is most obvious and most desirable at the end of a period, and it is for this that declamations mostly earn praise, though the beginning, indeed the whole sentence, deserves attention.

Quintilian's analysis of rhythms and feet is as detailed as those of Cicero and Dionysius. He tells us he is in general agreement with Cicero, except that he rejects feet of more than three syllables. He shows himself more aware that there are subtle differences of length which scansion must ignore as when a syllable is lengthened by position (93). He does not want to go back more than two feet, or three at most, for the final rhythm or *clausula,* and he himself favours the dochmius (◡−−◡−), the spondee preceded by a cretic (−◡−−−), the iambus preceded by a spondee (−−◡−) the molossus, but only if preceded by a short (◡−−−). He mentions other possibilities, but he shares Cicero's dislike of Aristotle's paeon (◡◡◡−). Of all this he gives a large number of examples, mostly taken from Cicero.[3]

As always, however, Quintilian is well aware that one must not overdo things. An orator must not spend all his time measuring syllables! The best rhythmic endings will come spontaneously to a practised stylist. In

[1] 9, 4, 45-146 discusses rhythm.   [2] 9, 4, 55 and Cicero, *Orator* 234.

[3] At 9, 4, 108, in order to save a sentence of Cicero's, *quis non turpe diceret,* Quintilian suggests that we may assume a pause between the last two words. This however, seems a poor suggestion for there is no end to the pauses one may suppose; the only legitimate pause to lengthen a preceding syllable is at the end of a clause.

any case it is not so much a question of particular feet as of the general rhythmic effect, and this effect cannot always be analysed or explained.[1]

The periodic style is naturally the most rhythmical, and this is especially suited to the peroration. History does not require rhythmic clauses so much as a continuous flow, and generally the demonstrative or epideictic requires freer and more relaxed rhythms, while forensic and deliberative must adjust the rhythm to the various themes, for it is not true that particular rhythms are always suitable to the particular sections of a speech. Cicero certainly varied them.

> Sometimes the structure of sentences should be deliberately loose, and much labour is required to avoid being laboured. . . . Nor am I surprised that Latin writers pay more attention to word-arrangement than the Athenians, for Latin is less exact and less graceful, and I would not regard it as a fault if Cicero differs somewhat from Demosthenes in this respect (9, 4, 144-45).

With the ninth book we leave technicalities behind. The last three books deal with more general topics. A pupil who has learned the techniques must now learn to apply them and Quintilian raises the question whether the assured facility and resources which an orator must possess are best developed by reading, writing or speaking.[2] The answer is of course that all three are needed. He condemns the practice of learning lists of synonyms as ridiculous; in any case there are few real synonyms. Real wealth of vocabulary is acquired by wide reading – at first at least only the best authors, both prose and, as Theophrastus recommended, poetry. Quintilian then draws up a reading list of authors, both Greek and Latin, with brief descriptions of each. It is this list which is often proclaimed as a literary history and is the most frequently read. It is of considerable interest since, apart from fragments of Dionysius' *On Imitation*, it is the first such general critical appreciation which we possess. Yet it is by no means the most intrinsically interesting part of Quintilian. The appreciations of Greek authors seem highly traditional, the comments on Latin authors are more fresh and probably more original. Nor should we forget that the whole survey is geared to a specific purpose: the needs of the orator (and writer).

The Greek list is much as we would expect it to be, and all the great names are there, in epic, elegy, lyrics, comedy (Menander might be almost enough by himself), tragedy, history, iambics, oratory and phil-

---

[1] 9, 4, 117: *quaedam vero tradi arte non possunt*. Passages like this show Quintilian well aware of the limitations of theory. So was Dionysius, above, p. 214. An example is given in 119 where *hosce* is said to be far better than *hos*; this, says Quintilian is obviously true, but he cannot say why.

[2] 10, 1, 1: *scribendo plus an legendo an dicendo conferatur*.

osophy, and, inevitably a good many names whom we know only at second or third hand. We may perhaps note that Hesiod is commended for the smoothness of words and structure and as the best writer in the middle style (this too is traditional), that 'Alcaeus, in part of his work, has deservedly been said to possess a golden plectrum; where he attacks the tyrants and makes a great moral contribution, he was terse and magnificently forceful ... but he was wanton and stooped to writing love poetry, though capable of greater things'. The reference to Aristotle's 'sweet style' is always surprising to us, as is Cicero's similar verdict, but then we do not have his more popular dialogues.

Quintilian's Roman list is very revealing and at times deliberately controversial. To appreciate its full significance we need to keep his prejudices clearly in mind. First there is the rhetorical slant; we are concerned with education in rhetoric, and even if, to Quintilian, this means the whole art of self-expression, yet it is the orator he chiefly has in mind. This, however, is patent and does not actually lead him into questionable judgements. Secondly he is quite explicitly concerned to show that, in certain genres at least, the Romans are the equals of the Greeks, and these genres are, for him, oratory, history, elegy and satire, also in epic, with the exception of Homer, for Virgil, though second to Homer, is ahead of all other epic writers; 'he is more careful and more precise, because he had to labour harder, and the uniformity of his achievement may perhaps compensate for the superiority of Homer's intermittent brilliance' (86).[1] As a conscious classicist and admirer of the writers of the golden age, Quintilian is at times less than fair to their predecessors. 'We worship Ennius as we do sacred groves where stand ancient noble trees which inspire us with veneration rather than satisfy our sense of beauty' (88) and even Lucretius, perhaps because of his addiction to old Latin forms, though granted a certain elegance, 'is difficult' (88). To the ancients generally he grants native genius (*ingenium*) but little *ars* (40, cf. 1, 8, 8).

It is probably this same somewhat exaggerated 'classicism' which led Quintilian to his surprising verdict that 'In comedy we are lame indeed' (*in comoedia maxime claudicamus*, 99). It is true that we do not have the Greek originals of the New Comedy and even today too little Menander to appreciate his genius, but Plautus was a great comic writer of the more boisterous type, and Terence's comedies were, and are, much admired.[2] It

[1] 10, 1, 86. Quintilian is presumably thinking of the verbal poetry as such, not of the plan, structure or tone of the epics as a whole. For a discussion of the validity of Quintilian's criticisms, see E. Bolaffi, *La Critica filosofica e Letteraria in Quintiliano*, Brussels (Latomus), 1958

[2] For the opinion of Terence in antiquity see Suetonius' *Life of Terence*, preserved by Donatus, where we learn, for example, that Varro said the beginning of the *Adelphi* was better than the original Menander, that Afranius (fl. late second century B.C.) himself a comic poet, thought him the greatest writer of comedies, quotes high praise from Cicero and

was probably their more primitive accented metres that partly influenced Quintilian to his harsh judgement, for he goes on to say Terence would have been better if he had written in iambic trimeters, and adds: (in comedy) 'We hardly produce a faint shadow of the Greek achievement; the Roman language does not seem to me to allow that charm which only Attic writers possessed; indeed the Greeks did not achieve it in any other dialect.'

Quintilian obviously shared Horace's belief that poetry should instruct as well as delight, and Horace's preference for a moral tale rather than 'melodious trifles' (*nugae canorae*) and we have just seen him deploring that Alcaeus descended to love-poetry. It is this feeling that love-poetry is hardly a full-time occupation which led him to ignore Catullus, except as a writer of iambic lampoons, and to the statement that (96) of Roman lyric poets Horace is almost the only one worth reading 'for he at times rises to the heights and is full of liveliness and grace, varied in his use of figures and full of bold and felicitous phrases' (*verbis felicissime audax*). Few admirers of Horace would go as far as this, at least in comparison with Catullus.

The statement that 'satire is ours entirely' (*satura tota nostra est*) is true only if we understand satire in the narrow sense. Here Roman pride overcomes his classicism for he refuses to endorse Horace's criticisms of Lucilius (93-94), though he gives the palm to Horace in this genre as terser and purer in language. He is also very appreciative of Persius and adds that some now living will achieve a high reputation in the genre. One thinks of Juvenal, but the time of Quintilian's writing is probably too early for such an allusion.

In elegy he briefly mentions Tibullus and Propertius (93) as challenging the Greeks, and puts Ovid below them as more wanton and Gallus (the friend of Virgil) as harsher than either. It is evidently not a genre of much interest to Quintilian (which does not surprise us) and he gives it but the briefest notice. Ovid is also mentioned among the tragedians (98) as the author of a *Medea*, 'which shows, it seems to me, how outstanding he could have been, had he controlled his talent instead of merely indulging it', and among the writers of epic (88): 'Ovid is wanton even in epic, too much in love with his own talent, yet praiseworthy in parts.'

The other two genres in which the Romans are said to equal the Greeks were, as we saw, history and oratory. In the former, Quintilian matches Sallust with Thucydides and Livy with Herodotus. The praise of Sallust for his 'immortal rapidity' and the absence of all unfavourable criticism is

Caesar, whose *dimidiate Menander* was obviously meant as a compliment, though he deplores Terence's lack of force. We also have Varro's statement that Caecilius takes the palm for plot, Terence for characterization, and Plautus for speeches (Aulus Gellius 6, 14, 6).

interesting, for he had often been accused of deliberate archaism and obscurity.[1] The praise of Livy, the chief prose writer among the Augustans, for his 'wonderful charm and his brilliant straightforwardness (*clarissima candor*) in narrative' as well as the eloquence of his speeches, is less surprising.

But it is in oratory above all that the Greeks are equalled by the Romans. And, inevitably, we get the expected comparison of Cicero with Demosthenes, a subject of heated controversy. To Quintilian they are both supreme, though different in style (10, 1, 106):

> Demosthenes is more compact, Cicero more abundant, the former is more closely knit and always fights with the rapier, the latter looser in composition and frequently fights with a broadsword. There is nothing you can omit from the one, nothing you can add to the other. . . . If Cicero had devoted himself entirely to imitating the Greeks, he would have combined the force of Demosthenes with the abundance of Plato and the charm of Isocrates . . . but most of his virtues were drawn from his own nature by the marvellous fertility of his immortal talent. . . . Cicero is not a man's name, it is the name of eloquence.

and a good deal more in this vein. It is perhaps more surprising to find Cicero rivalling Plato in philosophic writing. Yet if we remember that Quintilian is not comparing them as philosophers but as writers on philosophical subjects the comparison is not altogether absurd. Plato is undoubtedly by far the greater writer, but Cicero can handle the dialogue form with considerable skill and force, if with some lack of crispness, and probably no other Roman equalled him in the genre. The last author mentioned is Seneca who to Quintilian is the embodiment of all he dislikes in contemporary style. His criticism, quoted earlier, is devastating.[2]

The list of the main authors to be read is naturally followed by a discussion of *imitatio*. This, in Rome, not only meant emulation of great writers (as it does in Dionysius) but the young orator would choose a patron among his elders, watch and study him in action, and Quintilian approves of this (10, 5, 6). On emulation too he is very sensible; the models are to be studied in depth, mere verbal imitation is bad, for the faults are easy to reproduce; some people think they write like Cicero if they end a clause with *esse videatur*![3] Moreover your model should be congenial to your own talents and you should remember that all styles should be used. The position here explained at greater length, is essentially the same as that of Dionysius.[4]

---

[1] See below, p. 313 and p. 320, note 4. His archaism is noted by Quintilian himself at 8, 3, 29. [2] Above, p. 270, note 3
[3] 10, 2, 18. See also Tacitus, *Dialogus*, above, p. 279.   [4] See p. 212 above

As for practice in writing: 'We do not learn to write well by writing quickly, but to write quickly by writing well. You should be neither too complacent and like everything you write, nor like nothing you write, for too much correcting produces work which is lifeless and covered with scars.'[1] Quintilian strongly disapproves of dictation, for one who dictates is self-conscious, has no time for reflection: 'he lacks both the care of the writer and the impetuosity of the speaker'. Privacy is desirable, but it had better not be too pleasant, for we must learn to concentrate under adverse circumstances, and be able to think on our feet. This is no excuse, however, for relying on inspiration, and we should ponder over our subject as much as we can. Nevertheless the capacity to speak extempore when needed is the crowning achievement of the art of rhetoric.[2]

The treatment of the last quality to be dealt with, namely appropriateness,[3] follows traditional lines; it is linked with the duties of the orator, the purpose of different sections of a speech, the particular case, and the character of the speaker. Boasting, for example, is bad and 'Cicero has been severely criticized for this, although in his speeches he boasted more of his actions than of his eloquence' and Quintilian adds shrewdly that false modesty (*illa iactatio perversa*) is even worse. However, he does add that Cicero should have been more restrained in his poetry!

Memory was much stressed in the rhetorical schools, and speeches were memorized. This had its dangers, as Quintilian points out, for one must adjust to circumstances, but the most interesting part of this chapter (11, 2) is where he discusses systems of mnemonics in use. To us they seem highly elaborate; in fact Quintilian too is of that opinion. He gives some simpler helps; he will not, however, allow his students or his orators to have notes of headings or the like. If the discourse is well constructed, the sequence of subjects should not be difficult. Everyone must exercise his memory throughout life.

The discussion of delivery is even more fascinating, and for the ancients who always *heard* every kind of literature, and expected an author to be able to *speak* what he had written, its importance was by no means restricted to oratory. Even we, in our day of silent reading, still expect a poet to be able to speak his own poetry. It might be well if we expected the same from the writers of prose. Quintilian deals in considerable detail with both voice and gestures and once again he strongly opposes those who believe that all this should come naturally and that there should be no *art* of delivery. On this point he is undoubtedly right, and many an

[1] 10, 4, 3-4.
[2] 10, 7, 1: *Maximus vero studiorum fructus et velut praemium quoddam amplissimum longi laboris ex tempore dicendi facultas* . . . and at 4: *neque hoc ago ut ex tempore dicere malit, sed ut possit.*
[3] *Apte*, discussed in the first chapter of the eleventh book. The reference to Cicero is in sections 23-26.

undergraduate must have wished that his teachers had been trained in it, even if, with Quintilian, we will 'freely admit that natural ability plays the important role'.[1] Every part of the body receives attention: head, eyes, eyebrows, nostrils, lips, neck, shoulders, arms, feet, and above all the hands: 'for while the other parts assist the speaker, the hands, if I may so put it, themselves speak.'[2] Nor does he forget dress. Pliny the elder was apparently quite wrong when he said that Cicero let his toga fall to his heels to hide his varicose veins! The remark occurred in a book which even Quintilian thinks went into excessive detail.[3] Quintilian's remarks on the subject, however, are essential to the understanding of Roman oratory in practice.

The twelfth and last book of the *Institutio Oratoria* describes and advises the now completely trained and practising orator. What kind of a man is he, and how should he behave? In the introduction Quintilian makes his strongest claim to originality: now he is really setting out, he says, on unchartered seas without any precedent to guide him for even Cicero did not venture further but was content to speak only of the style of the perfect orator. There follows an attempt to justify the conception of the orator as *vir bonus dicendi peritus*, a good man skilled in speech, with the emphasis on *bonus*, morally good. If the training of the orator does not train moral character, says Quintilian, we shall have laboured in vain, for in that case 'there is nothing more destructive in public and private affairs than eloquence'. We remember that Cicero had said that 'eloquence without wisdom mostly does great harm, and never does any good'.[4]

The problem is, as we have seen, as old as Isocrates, and Quintilian's is certainly the most thorough and most sincere attempt to solve it. It should be read with sympathy, for in a different form the problem is still with us: our answers are neither more logical nor more convincing, and yet, if we have any faith at all in our own methods of education, we must believe that there *is* a solution, difficult though it is to formulate. Speech, says Quintilian, is nature's greatest gift to man and if excellence in it is but a help to crime it is an unworthy gift indeed: 'I do not say only that the orator must be a good man, but that he will not be an orator unless he is a good man' (12, 1, 3).

In the first place, no man of real intelligence or wisdom will choose the path of evil which renders him continually liable to the punishments of the law and of his own bad conscience, and if evil men are silly enough to make this choice – as even the uneducated agree that they are – they certainly have not the necessary intelligence for a hard course of study in rhetoric. If our own preoccupations and anxieties interfere with our studies,

[1] 11, 3, 12.
[2] For hands 11, 3, 85-107. The quotation is at 85.
[3] 11, 3, 143.
[4] *De Inventione* 1, 1 quoted above, p. 169.

then surely those of evil men will altogether unfit them for serious studies which demand a frugal life. 'You might as well expect a good crop on land choked with weeds and brambles' (12, 1, 7).

Oratory deals with right and wrong, with the just and the unjust. Can an unjust man deal properly with these? Then there is the impression made by the speaker's character; the bad man is bound to betray himself – one does not believe him even when he speaks the truth. A bad man is a poor advocate for any cause.

The subject was obviously a matter of controversy, and perhaps not only Philodemus had objected that Demosthenes and Cicero were great orators, yet that neither of them was of irreproachable character. Quintilian defends the character of both; even if neither of them were perfect either as men or orators. We are now talking in ideal terms; in practice, we must make allowances. The greatest contribution of eloquence is in matters of state before the senate and the people.[1] Honesty is in fact more important than technical skill, even in eloquence, and what is said with honour is well said[2]; that, however, does not negate the fact that, if said with art, it will be better said.

Those are the main arguments,[3] which Quintilian embellishes at some length. What he has in mind is the whole Ciceronian system of education, even if he practised it at a somewhat lower level, and so he once again discusses the relation between philosophy and oratory, where he also follows Cicero with the significant comment (12, 2, 7):

I want the man whom I am educating to acquire Roman wisdom and to show himself a true citizen not in the disputes of the study but in practical experience of public affairs.

and in that sense he must know logic, ethics and natural philosophy. He must be something of an eclectic, not an unquestioning disciple of any school. He must also have knowledge of civil law, and not always rely on outside experts to advise him. He must know history because of the great example it provides. 'As the Greeks excel in moral precepts, the Romans excel in moral examples, which is a better thing' (12, 2, 30).

[1] 12, 1, 26-28: *cum regenda senatus consilia et popularis error ad meliora ducenda.* Quintilian is talking as if he were Cicero, and ignoring that great decisions of state were no longer taken by the people, and precious few by the senate.

[2] 12, 1, 30: *nec quidquam non diserte, quod honeste dicitur,* and the following paragraphs.

[3] Quintilian is also troubled by the fact that the eloquent advocate may have to defend the guilty, and he deals with this point at length (12, 1, 34-45). He does not use the modern argument that even the guilty are entitled to the best legal help, but rather that crimes are sometimes committed from high motives, or reasons of state may require acquittal, for example, of the best general, as when Rutilius voted for Rufinus as consul saying that he would rather be robbed by a Roman than enslaved by an enemy. His other argument, that it will be good practice to know evil more intimately, is not convincing. It should be noted, however, that Quintilian does not relieve the advocate of the moral responsibility.

In a later chapter Quintilian returns to the question of style[1] and recognizes that no one way of speaking is supreme, but then the same can be said of the other arts, a comparison which he pursues at some length in painting and sculpture. He then shows how in the historical development of Roman style we can distinguish three periods, the older and harsher style down to the Gracchi, the middle period of Crassus, and the time when Cicero was supreme; different styles can also be distinguished within each period. He then refers to the Asianism-Atticism controversy, and, like Cicero, denies the Atticists' claim to that title (12, 10, 16-26).

More novel, at least for us, is his comparison of the Greek and Latin languages. He has been ridiculing (as Cicero did) the self-styled Atticists who would only consider the plain style as Attic, and adds that such an opinion is even more absurd in a Roman, in view of the nature of Latin (12, 10, 27):

> Latin eloquence is an apt pupil of the Greek, and very like it in all such matters as invention, arrangement of subject-matter and judgement, but when it comes to style, can hardly start to rival it. The Latin sounds are harsher and we do not possess the two most agreeable Greek letters, one a vowel and one a consonant (phi and upsilon). . . . In their place we have some harsh and disagreeable letters which Greek lacks. . . .

He then goes on to deprecate f and q, deplore endings in m, 'like the mooing of a cow'; Latin accents are also less euphonious, so that it is foolish to expect in Latin the grace of Attic Greek. Hence a Latin writer must be especially careful not to use heavy words for slight subjects (12, 10, 36):

> The less help we get from our language, the more we must strive to accomplish with content. Let our matter be elevated and varied. We must stir all the emotions and illuminate our speech with brilliant metaphors. We cannot be as delicate, let us be stronger; what we lose in subtlety we can gain in weight. They can be more assured in precision, let us outdo them in abundance. Even the lesser lights of Greek literature can reach their own havens. We, for the most part, carry more sail and a stronger breeze must fill our canvas; yet we cannot always ride the high seas, sometimes we must hug the shore. They can easily sail through any shallows; I must find deeper, though not much deeper water where my skiff will not run aground.

[1] In 12, 10, and it should be noted that Quintilian here refers to the formula which divided a book on any art into three sections: the art, the artist, and the product (*ars, artifex, opus*), which he also mentioned in 2, 14, 5 as the best general divisions. This is the formula attributed to Neoptolemus and to which some scholars have tried to make Horace conform in the *Ars Poetica*. See above, pp. 240-1.

It is this lack of delicacy and charm, Quintilian here explains, which is the cause of Roman inferiority in comedy, but it can be compensated by extraneous ornamentation. Some of the older Romans, Scipio, Laelius, Cato, accomplished this, and so did Cicero. It is interesting to find so frank and clear a realization of the peculiar genius of each language; it also explains the fondness of the great Roman orators for the grand style which was, as Quintilian says, more congenial to their language (12, 10, 63).

Cicero remains the best model, as always, but Quintilian is willing to compromise with contemporary trends to the extent of introducing more brilliant epigrams, but not too many: 'let no one push me further' and this last discussion of style ends with another strong condemnation of contemporary vices (12, 10, 73):

> It is a very grave error to believe that popularity and applause are more easily secured by depraved and decadent ways of speech which exult in licence of expression, wanton in childish little epigrams, swell with excessive verbosity in a frenzy of vapid commonplaces, shine with flowery expressions which fade at the least touch, mistake rashness for sublimity, and use every crazy expression to prove their freedom of speech.
>
> I do not deny, nor am I surprised, that these things please many people. Any kind of eloquence at all is pleasant to hear and finds favour, and any kind of speech charms the mind with natural pleasure. Hence those groups of hearers gathered in the forum and by the Old Wall, so that no speaker lacks a ready audience, and when some unusually exquisite phrase is heard by the inexperienced, whatever it is, it excites admiration, and deservedly, if only because they have no hope of doing as well themselves, for to do even this is not easy. But such things vanish and die before their betters, as wool dyed red pleases in the absence of purple ... if you examine these debased expressions more closely as you test dyes with sulphur, they lose their false colour and fade to an unutterably disgusting pallor. They shine in the absence of sunlight as certain small insects become fiery in the dark. Certainly the crowd approves of many bad things, but nobody rejects what is good.

CHAPTER XVIII

After Quintilian

In view of the influence of Quintilian on his younger contemporaries we shall not be surprised to find that the fashionable litterateurs of Rome in the first quarter of the second century A.D., Pliny the younger (an actual pupil), Martial, Suetonius, even the less fashionable Juvenal, adopted the great professor's 'classicism' as their own, though they were neither so severe in their condemnation of modern tendencies, nor so 'classical' in practice. After their day, however, the influence of Quintilian faded before the triumphant archaism of Cornelius Fronto, the teacher of Marcus Aurelius.

PLINY

Pliny the younger, whose letters we possess, was the nephew of that scholarly and prolific Pliny whose *Natural History* is still extant and whose scientific curiosity caused him to die in the eruption of Vesuvius in A.D. 79. His correspondence gives us a lively and vivid picture of the state of letters in Rome in his day.[1] Senator, consul, governor of Bithynia under Trajan, a successful barrister in the centumviral courts, a generous benefactor to his native city of Comum, it is yet literary immortality which he hoped for. He was the friend of Tacitus, who was a few years older, and of Martial. His circle had evidently a great desire for stylistic perfection; they exchanged manuscripts and criticized each other's work continually; Pliny himself explains how he would first discuss his compositions with a few trusted friends, then give a recitation to a larger group who would feel free to make suggestions, and if he was doubtful about these he would again discuss them with a few intimates before publishing the final version.[2] He would do this for his speeches, poems and other compositions, the published version of speeches being considerably altered and enlarged from the spoken version. The subject was, to him and his circle, less important than the style: at one point he considers writing history and actually asks a friend's advice as to what the subject should be.[3]

---

[1] For a full study of the literary habits of this circle, see A. M. Guillemin, *Pline et la vie littéraire de son temps* (Paris, 1929). The author suggests (64) that ancient criticism concentrated on form and technique, much as we do in art criticism today, the subject being of minor importance.

[2] *Ep.* 7, 17 and 8, 21.   [3] *Ep.* 5, 8.

As becomes a pupil of Quintilian, he looks upon Cicero as the supreme model,[1] and, like Cicero himself, takes Demosthenes also as his model. In fact, he once wrote a speech with one by Demosthenes before him.[2] Like his teacher, he deplores the moral decadence[3] of the times and the decay of eloquence, but he is not so burdened with it or so pessimistic as Quintilian. This is no doubt partly due to his more sunny and ingenuous temperament. A man so successful in public affairs, so hopeful of literary immortality, looks forward rather than backward. Better times were ahead and in Pliny we feel the beginning of the more stable period under the great and benevolent emperors of the second century, though he is at pains to show that he was no coward under Domitian.[4] Certainly the despotism of that emperor did not leave its mark on him as it did on Tacitus. Pliny recognized that the historian was a greater literary figure, and we find him supplying Tacitus with information which he hopes will secure mention of himself in the *Histories*.[5]

Pliny's letters are written in a clear-cut, straightforward style; those of the tenth book which contains the correspondence with Trajan from Bithynia are remarkably clear and businesslike, the simple style being the appropriate one for letters. The letters are excellent of their kind; they were intended to be published and therefore are not as intimate or self-revealing as Cicero's; Pliny would even write love-letters to his wife with one eye on possible publication, and he made the selection himself. The letters to the Emperor, it is true, were published after his death, but they are concerned mostly with official business. We also have his *Panegyric* or speech of thanks to the emperor on the occasion of his consulship. There the style is quite different; it is closer to the Ciceronian but Pliny was no master of the Ciceronian period. One may doubt whether he wanted to be so entirely. The sentences are on the whole shorter and less varied, and there is also, inevitably, a fondness for silver Latin *sententiae* and ornamentations; though the subject is unattractive to us, the flattery is nothing like so fulsome as it might have been, and the style is by no means as artificial as in Seneca, for example. Pliny was, after all, trained by Quintilian, and one of his star pupils.

Where we find estimates of his friends' work, usually, though not always, addressed to the writer, they are uniformly kindly and favourable; he knows himself to be indulgent. These judgements of his do not seem to show any particular critical system or criteria. He does, of course, know the difference between the simpler and the more flowery styles – as we saw, he practised both – but his judgements on other people seem to be little more than strings of pleasing epithets, encouraging them to write

---

[1] *Ep.* 1, 54; 4, 8; 7, 4.   [2] *Ep.* 7, 30.   [3] *Ep.* 2, 14.
[4] *Ep.* 7, 33 (see also 7, 19).   [5] *Ep.* 7, 33.

both prose and verse.[1] We do not have his speeches or his poetry. His verse can hardly have been more than competent – was he not one of those busy orators who wrote verse for relaxation to whom Petronius had denied the title of poet? His only *bête noire* was the wealthy informer Regulus who to him is *vir malus dicendi imperitus*, thus reversing the famous definition of Cato.[2]

His truly critical remarks are few, and they mostly reflect current ideas. He admires the Augustans, as a pupil of Quintilian must, but he admires the modern spirit too.[3] He is pleased that it was the simpler passages of his *Panegyricus* that were best received; this, to him, augurs a revival of letters.[4] He knows that to attempt greatness has its dangers, but it is not enough to have no faults; one must take risks, even if one's friends are likely to condemn some passages (of the *Panegyricus*) as bombastic rather than sublime (*tumida, non sublimia*).[5] We find the usual advice as to the best training exercises such as translation, composing answers to well-known speeches, emulating great passages, constant revision, the practice of non-forensic writing such as history and poetry; even light verses, for poetry and history are akin.[6] Brevity is a good thing, but it must not be overdone and even revision can go too far.[7]

There are no original critical ideas in Pliny, but his correspondence is a clear and valuable mirror of his circle of the men of letters of the day. He is a simple and charming person – besides being an obviously able administrator, senator and advocate – and it would be a hard-hearted reader indeed who does not rejoice with him that his books are found in the bookshops of distant Lyons,[8] or that his name is constantly coupled with that of Tacitus as he tells one of his correspondents (9, 23):

... I was never so pleased as in conversation with Cornelius Tacitus lately. He told me that at the recent games he sat next to a Roman knight. After a certain amount of learned conversation the knight asked: 'Are you an Italian or a provincial?' to which Tacitus answered:

---

[1] In *Ep.* 3, 21 he says that Martial's poetry will not be immortal (*non erunt aeterna quae scripsit*), but Martial is dead, and moreover was not quite one of the circle. Perhaps this accounts for the fact that Pliny is even more self-centred than usual, for most of the letter is concerned with Pliny's generosity to the poet – he quotes from a flattering poem (10, 19) about himself. There is also an interesting letter about Silius Italicus (3, 7) which says a good deal about his life, but of his poetry Pliny only says that he wrote with more care than talent: *scribebat carmina maiore cura quam ingenio*. Italicus too had just died.

[2] Regulus was well-known as the informer who had been more active under Nero than Domitian but had attacked several of Pliny's friends. For the witticism quoted see *Ep.* 4, 7, but there is no doubt of his ability. Pliny confesses to missing him after his death 6, 1. See also 1, 5.

[3] 6, 21 ad init.: *sum ego ex, iis, qui mirer antiquos, non tamen, ut quidam, temporum nostrorum ingenia despicio.*

[4] 3, 18.   [5] 9, 26.   [6] 7, 9.   [7] 9, 35.   [8] 9, 11

'You know me from your literary studies.' The other replied: 'Are you Tacitus or Pliny?' I cannot express how delighted I am that our names thus belong to literature rather than to ourselves and that men who would not know us in any other way are familiar with our names through their literary pursuits.

One can imagine a quizzical smile on the lips of Tacitus as he told this anecdote to his ingenuous friend, who could write to a correspondent: 'I enjoyed your letter the more as it was so long, especially as it was all about my writings.'[1]

MARTIAL AND JUVENAL

Martial was a professional writer of light verses such as Pliny wrote for recreation – he calls them epigrams and the vast majority are precisely that, very brief and very pointed, though a number are from ten to thirty lines long. The extant collection in twelve books naturally contains many literary references,[2] but most of them have little significance. Even his reflections on epigrams as a literary genre are occasioned by a particular criticism or some momentary occasion which we can no longer trace. He will tell us at one point that it is a great mistake to look upon epigrams as mere jest and frivolity (*tantum lusus iocosque*), they are just as serious as tragedies on mythical subjects (4, 49), yet he himself frequently calls them jests and frivolity, and adds that they need a dose of impropriety (1, 35). He actually claims to 'spare the individual while denouncing the vice' (10, 33), yet he is a past master at personal invective, often quite ruthless and obscene. Epigram, as he tells us, must 'have wit and gall', that is, have a somewhat bitter point (7, 25), but he reproves those who insist on pungent point and who cannot stomach a poem without it (10, 45). He claims that his poems, even when longer, contain nothing redundant (2, 77), and this certainly is the essence of epigram. However, we should not try to read any theory of the undesirability of mere flawlessness when he says, in answer to the accusation that his work is 'unequal' (*inaequalis*) that the 'equal' books are the bad ones (7, 90), for his meaning probably is simply that no one can be good all the time (7, 81).

These are but random reflections and nothing but the most obvious characteristics of the genre can be extracted from them.

As for his judgements on contemporaries, he is apt to be as flattering and undiscriminating as Pliny, if not for the same reasons. Martial was in need of patrons and says so (8, 55), and presents of money did not come amiss. Thus we have a poem (7, 63) celebrating 'the eternal works of the

---

[1] 9, 20.
[2] These are usefully collected by Keith Preston, in *CP* 15 (1920), 340-52.

immortal Silius (Italicus)', a poor poet but a very wealthy man, and
another which flatters Pliny (10, 19) for which we know he was duly
rewarded.[1]

Martial does, however, take a definite position on some of the critical
questions of the day, where no personal motives influence his opinion.
He strongly opposes those who were still wanting contemporary writers
to model themselves on 'the ancients', who are still the poets of the early
days of the republic. The violence of Martial's criticism of these ancient
poets whom he ridicules[2] seems to indicate that their admirers were still
an influential group. Martial agrees with Messala in Tacitus, for the poets
of the first century – Catullus, Virgil and Horace – are his heroes and his
models; unlike Messala, however, he does not condemn all later literature,
he also considers Lucan and Persius to be great poets.[3] This accords with
his temperament, for it was contemporary life he wrote about, and he is as
irritated as Horace was by those who condemn all contemporary literature
out of hand and always prefer the old to the new.

He also shares with Juvenal the satirist a dislike for those outworn
mythological subjects which were still the current subjects of tragedy and
of a great deal of other poetry. Hence the contempt of both the satirist
and the epigrammatist, not indeed for culture and learning, but for erudite
affectation.[4] Temperamentally, however, the two writers are very different. Juvenal denounces bitterly the vices and luxuries of the day, and it is
in his satires that we find the most uncompromising picture of that moral
degeneration which we have found to concern all the writers of the early
empire. Martial does not denounce but ridicules the vices and foibles of his
contemporaries. Where Juvenal is indignant, Martial laughs, but both
agree in calling upon their contemporaries to abandon worn-out topics
and useless artificial erudition, to look at life around them and to write
about that.

There is another echo of Martial in Juvenal on the shortage of patrons.
The seventh satire expresses a new hope for literature under an emperor
devoted to the Muses, but he is the only one. The wealthy of Rome have
other things to do with their money, and they spend little on poets, who
now have neither the means nor the leisure to write good poetry. Historians fare no better, nor indeed do the orators, and they, poor fellows,
have to keep up a front. As for the teacher of rhetoric, he is as badly off as
the rest – in spite of such fortunate exceptions as Quintilian. The whole
satire implies that it is the decay of culture among the rich that is responsi-

---

[1] See above, p. 310, note 1.

[2] 11, 90; *Accius et quidquid Pacuviusque vomunt.* See also 5, 10; 8, 69.

[3] 1, 61; 4, 29; 8, 56. His special admiration for Catullus should be noted in view of that
poet's neglect by Cicero and Quintilian. See 10, 78.

[4] 4, 49; 10, 21; 8, 3; Juvenal *Sat.* 1, 1-14, 51-54, 162-7.

ble for the decay of 'eloquence' whether in poetry or prose. Here too both
poets seem to be in agreement.

SUETONIUS

Suetonius, whom we know best as the author of the extant *Lives of the
Caesars*, biographies of the Roman emperors from Julius Caesar to
Domitian, also wrote biographies of men famous in the domain of Latin
letters, the *De Viris Illustribus* which is lost, though we have considerable
fragments of those parts of the work which dealt with the *grammatici* and
the rhetoricians, as well as a life of Terence specifically attributed to him
by Donatus, and less certainly, lives of Virgil, Horace, Lucan, Persius, and
other fragments.[1]

In view of this considerable output on various figures in the world of
letters, we might expect some interesting statements of a critical nature,
but we are disappointed. This is due less to the fragmentary nature of the
evidence than to Suetonius' method which is not critical but anecdotal,
just as it is anecdotal rather than historical in the lives of the Caesars. The
result is that, while we may glean from Suetonius some interesting bits of
information, as for example that the dying Virgil ordered that his unfinished *Aeneid* should be burnt, there is no serious critical appreciation of
the poets whose lives he wrote, nor any attempt to describe the theories of
either *grammatici* or rhetors or to fit them into the development of literary
or critical points of view.

A careful study of our fragments[2] shows, however, that Suetonius is in
general agreement with Quintilian's 'classicism', and an even more uncompromising enemy of archaism (which may be accounted for by the
fact that he writes a generation later) and, in common with his contemporaries, more gentle both towards the old Roman writers and towards post-Augustan writers such as Lucan. It is probably his hatred of
archaism which makes him more critical of Sallust[3] than Quintilian was,
but we can only guess at the critical basis of his remarks.

The most interesting critical passage in Suetonius occurs, not in his
literary works but in his life of Augustus and is typical of his general
attitude (ch. 84-89). After stating that Augustus lavished considerable care
upon his style and avoided speaking extempore (though he could do so
when necessary) even in his more important conversations with his wife,
and that the emperor had written works of various kinds, Suetonius
proceeds (ch. 86):

[1] These are printed at the end of J. C. Rolfe's edition of *Suetonius*. For what is known of
Suetonius' life, and possible relation to Tacitus see Syme's *Tacitus* pp. 778-82.

[2] Such as that of G. D'Anna, *Le Idee litterarie di Suetonio*. See also A. Macé, *Essai sur Suétone*.

[3] He speaks three times of the archaism of Sallust: the passage quoted below from the life
of Augustus 86, 3. Cf. *De Gramm.* X and XV.

The style which Augustus cultivated was both fastidious and moderate. He avoided all foolish epigrams (*sententiae*), contrived word-arrangements, and to quote his own phrase, 'the stench of recondite wording'. His main concern was to express his meaning with the utmost clarity. In order to achieve this the more easily and not to confuse or slow down anyone who read or heard him, he did not hesitate to insert prepositions before the names of towns or frequently to repeat conjunctions if their omission, though more graceful, made for obscurity. He showed equal contempt for the affected and the archaic which he considered equally faulty, though different. He occasionally satirized them, especially in the case of his friend Maecenas whose 'perfumed curlyhews', to use his own phrase, he attacked, parodied and ridiculed. He did not spare Tiberius either, who now and then would chase after obsolete and recondite expressions. As for Marcus Antonius, he rebuked him as being out of his mind because he wrote in order to be admired rather than to be understood; then making fun of his bad and erratic judgement in his choice of styles, he added: 'Are you in doubt whether you should emulate Annius Cimber or Veranius Flaccus so that you can use those expressions which Crispus Sallust culled from the *Origins* of Cato? Or are we rather to import into our speech from the Asiatic orators their loquacious and meaningless verbosity?'

Then in a letter which praises the talent of his granddaughter Agrippina he says: 'Yet you must be very careful not to write or speak badly.'

This passage is interesting for the light it throws on Augustus' views on style; it is also relevant to the time when it was written, for Suetonius invokes the authority of the divine Augustus himself against archaism and over-ornamentation, in favour of Quintilian's 'classicism'.

PLUTARCH

The most famous Greek literary figure contemporary with the Roman writers whom we have been discussing is Plutarch, who was born about A.D. 46 and was probably still writing in 127. He spent a good deal of his time in Rome, where he had many friends and a considerable reputation as a lecturer, but most of his writing was done in his native Chaeronea in Boeotia. Apart from the famous *Parallel Lives* of great Greeks and Romans, we also have a large collection of essays, dialogues and letters which go by the name of *Moral Essays*. A number of these have literary titles, but Plutarch was no critic and his contribution to our subject is, in view of his high reputation and later influence, minimal.

The most obviously relevant essay is often referred to as *How to Study*

Poetry, but it is only fair to remember that the full title is *How Youth Should Study Poetry* for it is with the education of the young that Plutarch is here concerned and he approaches poetry entirely from the moral point of view, as he always does. He admits that both style and imaginative power are attractive; the style gives pleasure and imaginative fiction affects the emotions (15 c - 17 d), but these are but the gilding of the moral pill. The content and its effect on character are by far the most important features of poetry, and Plutarch outdoes Plato, from whom he always drew a good deal of his inspiration and philosophy, in his moral attitude. He does, it is true, admit that as poetry is an imitation of life, it must needs contain evil as well as good (17 f - 18 a), but his main concern is that the young shall be so warned and prepared that this will do them no harm. We should draw their attention to the fact that the poets themselves, and especially Homer from whom many of his examples are drawn, frequently express, explicitly or by implication, their disapproval of the unethical conduct or words of their characters (19 a-e). Where this is not the case, we shall draw attention to their better sentiments elsewhere (at the cost, it would seem, of finding a moral where none is intended [27 a-e]) or to the fact that evil is defeated in the end; or we may use the moral sentiments of one poet to minimize an evil impression left by another. In any case, our youth must be trained to discernment; they must not praise everything indiscriminately, but exercise their own judgement, pick out for memorizing what is most useful – even if a maxim has to be altered first to make it morally more palatable (33 c).

Plutarch does not approve of allegorical explanations (19 f) or petty grammatical ingenuity (31 e) to make poetry more morally palatable or conform to either Stoic ideas or grammatical orthodoxy. Provided, however, that our youth will remember the right things, they will see how universal the sayings of the poets are in their application and we must reinforce these with great sayings of philosophers and others which in themselves will help them to realize what they should accept or respect (34 b - 35 f). The approach is uncompromisingly moralistic throughout, but we should note, struggling for expression in spite of it, the notion of poetry as a picture of life reflecting both good and evil. Moreover, Plutarch does admit that there are other approaches, and that, while we are here concerned with the effect on character, others will pay attention to the story itself or to the beauty of the words and their arrangement (30 d).

This, however, he himself never does. The *Lives of the ten Attic orators* may or may not be genuine, but the work concerns itself entirely with historical, and anecdotal, details of biography. In several of these brief 'lives', including those of Demosthenes and Isocrates, there is not a word about style, and in the other cases there is at most one sentence, of a highly conventional kind, as, for example, that Lysias was 'most persuasive and brief', or that Isaeus was like Lysias in euphonious composition and cleverness in dealing with subject-matter 'so that it was hard to tell them apart', that 'he was the first to use rhetorical devices and pay attention to the political style', which Demosthenes imitated. Several of these very brief comments echo what was said by Dionysius of Halicarnassus.[1]

The *Comparison of Aristophanes with Menander* is extant only in epitome but, though it could have been a wonderful subject, our loss is probably not great, for it does little more than reflect the prejudice against the old comedy which, as we saw, seems to have originated in the Lyceum. Coarseness and vulgarity are the chief accusations against Aristophanes as well as excessive and indiscriminate use of antitheses and plays on words, disorderly diction, inattention to writing in character, and so on. That Menander is more careful in all these things is quite true, but there is a complete failure to appreciate the uproarious wit and greatness of Aristophanes. When the author accuses him of frigidity (of all things) and says he was pleasing neither to the many nor the few, he is only betraying the frigidity of his own critical ideas. Plutarch may well have been guilty of such nonsense.

The essay on *Listening to Lectures* is in many ways delightful, but once again Plutarch insists that content is of the first importance and his main concern is that we should benefit from what is said and not pay too much attention to the lecturer's way of saying it, though we may appreciate that too in its place. His statement that beauty is due to many factors which go to make one whole and reaches perfection through symmetry and harmony whereas ugliness will result if even one element is absent or out of place (45 c) was by this time a well worn commonplace. What is much more interesting is his suggestion (45 d-e) that the success of a lecture depends upon a proper *rapport* between lecturer and audience to which each listener has a contribution to make. This principle might have found a wider application, but the essay is concerned with lectures only and we should not subtitle it 'or on reading', as some commentators have done. The whole essay reminds us that at the beginning of the second century A.D. the rhetoric of display had again come into its own.

In the essay *Whether the Athenians were more famous in War or in the Arts* Plutarch follows through the theory of art as imitation or representation of life with relentless logic, for the theme is that deeds are better than

---

[1] He mentions 'Dionysius, Caecilius and their school' as having declared two hundred and thirty-three speeches of Lysias to be genuine out of four hundred and twenty-five (836 b). Caecilius is also mentioned at 832 e as saying that Antiphon was Thucydides' teacher. There seems to be a particularly close correspondence between what is said of Isaeus (839 e-f) and Dionysius' *Isaeus* chs. 2 and 3 as well as about Dinarchus (850 c-e) with Dionysius' *Dinarchus* chs. 5-6.

words. As he put it: 'Without the men of action, there could be no historians' and he goes on to show that though Athens was 'the mother of the arts' which it either discovered or improved, the artists can do no more than represent by words or pictures the deeds of the Athenians, and this is true even of a Thucydides, for all his vivid talent and his capacity to arouse our passions. Altogether language, song, and rhythm can only be seasoning in the presentation of deeds, and though Plutarch makes some room for myth and fiction, it too must be like the truth and is dependent upon it. The deeds of Athens were its glory, and the Spartans were quite right to blame the Athenians for spending so much money on the theatre when they had so many armies to feed, and often kept them on short rations.

Thus we find in Plutarch some ideas which could raise critical problems, but he nowhere develops them or applies them. We are not justified in developing them for him, and trying to find in his works a critical system which is simply not there. As we have seen, he does allow that poetry has three aspects: the content which to him is by far the most important, the style, and the imagination, but the last two are mere seasoning for the first; they are in fact, mere play and of little importance.[1] Throughout his works he has preserved for us a large number of literary, as well as historical, anecdotes,[2] in themselves interesting but not woven into any critical pattern. In discussing *Why the Pythian does not use verse nowadays*, for example, he notes that in the old days history and philosophy too used verse, but nowadays are written in prose so that the change from verse to prose was a general tendency. It is surely an exaggeration to credit him because of this with a historical sense, or to call this 'an illuminating comment on Greek literary history'. We have seen that several of his Roman contemporaries had a far better understanding of the historical process and of 'the influence of contemporary conditions on literature'.[3] Incidentally, Plutarch approves of the change to prose, because 'when history descended from its poetical chariot and walked on foot, it distinguished between myth and truth'.

Plutarch is a great biographer, a superb raconteur and a staunch moralist, but he is no critic and it is at least doubtful whether he ever enjoyed and appreciated literature as such, whether in verse or prose. As he was a Greek, he probably did, and his practice was probably better than his theory. But he hardly admits it, for in theory he was more obstinately utilitarian than any Roman. It would be interesting to know how far his

---

[1] At 348 b (Corinna speaking to Pindar): γλώσσας δὲ καὶ καταχρήσεις καὶ μεταφράσεις καὶ μέλη καὶ ῥυθμοὺς ἡδύσματα τοῖς πράγμασιν ὑποτίθεται (ὁ ποιητής). See also 350 b: ἀλλὰ νὴ Δία παιδία τὰ τῶν ποιητῶν.

[2] Some of these we have quoted earlier. See index under Plutarch.

[3] Seneca for example. See p. 268. The phrases are quoted from Atkins 2, p. 323.

was the typical Greek view of his day, outside Boeotia. Certainly we should not assume without strong evidence that he represents the Greek contemporary point of view.

CHAPTER XIX

Fronto: Triumph of Archaism

The weakness of Quintilian's classicism was, as we have seen, that in all essentials he wanted Latin literature to turn the clock back a century and a half. This concentration upon the past no doubt seemed less artificial in view of the fact that the Greek teachers and critics had successfully advised a return to their own classical centuries and that at this very time – the time of the second sophistic shortly to be discussed – they were writing and speaking Attic Greek with renewed vigour, a language by now much more artificial than the Latin of Cicero. The result, both in Greek and Latin, was an ever widening gap between the language of literature and that of the people, and a deadening contempt on the part of men of letters for the life of their own language.

One last attempt was made to revivify literary Latin by Marcus Cornelius Fronto and his school. Fronto was born in Numidia at the beginning of the second century not long after the death of Quintilian. He was probably of Roman descent and came to Rome in early life where he earned a great reputation both as a teacher and an orator. He went through the usual *cursus honorum*, and became a senator. When Antoninus Pius succeeded Hadrian in 138, he appointed him as tutor in Latin rhetoric to his two adopted sons, Lucius Verus and Marcus Aurelius, and honoured him with the position of *consul suffectus* in 143, the very year when the great Athenian rhetorician Herodes Atticus had been honoured as *consul ordinarius*. Fronto remained on the best of terms with his princely pupils, especially with Marcus, even after the latter had wearied of rhetoric and turned to philosophy. They continued to exchange letters frequently, and it is from the remains of this correspondence, discovered only in 1815, that we must reconstruct the stylistic theories of Fronto, supplemented by his few appearances in the *Noctes Atticae* or *Attic Nights* of Aulus Gellius, a younger contemporary and a Frontonian. This work is an interesting collection of short conversations and essays on points of language and literature. The evidence, such as it is, is therefore contemporary and reliable.

Fronto shared with Quintilian his dislike of silver Latin style, and especially of Seneca; yet from one point of view his own theories can be regarded as a logical continuation and consequence of silver Latin tendencies, going, as it were from emphasis on the brilliant phrase to emphasis on the brilliant word, and they have been regarded as the next stage in the process of decadence. Yet Frontonianism was also a protest against the frozen classicism of Quintilian himself, and to some extent at least represents the irruption of popular forms into literature. Its most obvious feature, how-ever, is a love of the archaic vocabulary of pre-Ciceronian Roman writers. Nevertheless this new eloquence, *elocutio novella* as Fronto himself called it,[1] was intended to be something new, even if novelty was to be secured by means of the very old.[2]

Of course, Fronto did not neglect the other aspects of rhetoric entirely; it still consisted of word-arrangement as well as word choice; lucidity was essential; the arrangement of one's material is as important as Plato re-cognized it to be in the *Phaedrus* (to which Fronto refers) and one must study the taste of one's audience, though without loss of dignity. Restraint is important, one should be able to use the different styles to suit the occasion, and construct one's sentences accordingly.[3] All this, and many other qualities of style, Fronto recognizes and advises, and he is especially interested in the use of figures and similes. Yet every reader of his cor-respondence will recognize that his chief interest is in individual words, and that the words he likes best are the by now archaic language of the early writers of Rome.

Archaism was nothing new. The Romans always looked back nostalgi-cally to the early days of their city, and the simpler virtues of that age remained their ethical ideal, so that archaism in literature was always tinged with ethical feeling. This made the elder Cato the ideal hero of the archaists; he was both a distinguished early prose writer and an uncom-promising model of the traditional virtues, as well as notoriously hostile to Hellenic influence in Rome and to such Hellenists as Scipio in the second century B.C. Sallust was fond of old words and was indeed accused of archaism. Cicero and Horace opposed the uncritical worship of old Roman writers and if archaism is eclipsed in our sources during the Augustan age there is no reason to think that it disappeared. We can trace it in such grammatici as Valerius Probus in the first century A.D. and Quintilian has a good deal to say on the subject.[4] We should also recognize

---

[1] Haines II, p. 80 (146, 15). The references given for the letters are to the pages of C. R. Haines' edition of the correspondence in the Loeb library, and in brackets will be added the page and where needed the line in M. P. J. Van Den Hout's edition.

[2] For a full discussion of Fronto and Aulus Gellius see René Marache, *La critique littéraire de langue latine* and by the same author, *Mots nouveaux et mots archaïques chez Fronton et Aulu-Gelle.* I am much indebted to both books in this chapter. See also Dorothy Brock's *Studies in Fronto and his age.*

[3] For these various factors see respectively Haines 1, 2 (*in verbis eligendis collocandisque*); 52, second letter; 40-42; 118 and 120; (VDH 56; 36, 5-10; 201-2; 17 and 18, 1).

[4] For the archaism of Sallust see above p. 313 and note 3; Quintilian 8, 3, 29; Cicero on

that, while Hellenism made possible the glories of the Latin golden age, it undoubtedly stifled certain aspects of native genius, such as the accentuated metres and the tendency to compound words, and weakened the use of alliteration and assonance so prominent in early Latin writers. From this point of view archaism in the second century A.D., and indeed throughout the history of Roman literature, symbolizes a desire for a native revival. It is not surprising that the desire grew stronger as classicism became more out of date, more frozen and out of touch with linguistic reality.

The archaism of Fronto was peculiar in that it concentrated its attention on single words. Not that Fronto was lacking in caution, moderation and common sense, more so than his disciple Aulus Gellius, but Gellius only exaggerates the tendencies which we find in Fronto himself. The master too discusses, for example, the use of a particular word or a particular simile with Marcus Aurelius,[1] and where he appears in Gellius he is equally involved in the legitimacy of this or that word, e.g. whether *harena* has a plural, whether *praepropter* is a literary or vulgar word, whether Latin is as rich as Greek in words to express colour.[2] To the importance of the right words, and the effectiveness of old words Fronto returns again and again.

> I rejoice above all that you do not snatch at the most obvious word but seek out the best. This is what makes the difference between the great orator and the average, namely that the others are easily satisfied with good words, but the great speaker will not have the good, if a better one exists.[3]
> ... to discern the place for certain words, their weight, rank, age and dignity so that they should not occur in a speech as absurd as a drunken and turbulent banquet ... and when all these words have been investigated, examined, distinguished, then from the whole population of words, if I may so put it, just as when a legion must be levied in time of war we do not merely pick the volunteers but conscript those of the right age who are hiding themselves, so when we need words to defend us we use not only those who volunteer and occur to us of their

archaism *De Oratore* 3, 12, 45; for Horace, above, pp. 242, 253; for Probus, Suetonius *De Grammaticis* 24, and Marache, *La Critique* pp. 62 ff.; for Quintilian on archaism see 1, 6, 39-41; 2, 5, 21; 8, 24-30; 9, 3, 14; on too careful search for words 8, *Praef.* 27. See also the *Dialogus* of Tacitus, above, pp. 277 ff.

[1] Haines 2, 42-44 (92, 14-17). He requires Marcus to give his authority for the use of *obsecrare* in invoking the gods; 2, 108 (152, 8) he objects to the phrase *oculos convenientes*, used it seems by Marcus of himself and Verus as the eyes (of the state) 'in harmony'; cf. 2, 70-72 (142, 14) and *passim*.

[2] *Noctes Atticae* 19, 8; 19, 10; 2, 26 and cf. 19, 13; and 13, 19.

[3] Haines 2, 42 (92, 3).

own accord, but we bring forth those that are in hiding and hunt them out for service.[1]

It is true that Fronto insists the word must not be so obscure as to be unintelligible to one's audience or readers, but he does advise the use of words which they could not hope to use themselves, and which are the result of careful study and a considerable knowledge of old poetry. He advises his imperial pupils to read old writers with this purpose in view. His favourite reading is of authors such as the elder Cato, Sallust, Plautus, Ennius, to some extent Lucretius and Lucilius, and others of the same antiquity. He cannot, of course, ignore Cicero; he grants him many qualities and considered his letters well-nigh perfect, but 'in all his speeches you will find very few words which one could not hope or expect to find there' (*paucissima . . . insperata atque inopinata verba*).[2]

That Fronto does not mention Virgil in the extant letters may be accidental, though it clearly means that he was not among the favourites. There is a discussion by Fronto in Aulus Gellius (that on words of colour)[3] where Virgil is quoted several times, and commended as 'a poet most careful in his use of words'. However, we find that he could have used 'caerulus' rather than 'glaucus', 'but he preferred to use a better-known Greek rather than an unusual Latin word', which is unfavourable criticism, for Fronto condemned Graecisms.[4] He quotes Horace several times and calls him a 'noteworthy poet' (*memorabilis poeta*),[5] but Marcus Aurelius disliked Horace and is certainly never rebuked for it. It is quite clear that Fronto is not partial to the Augustans, and in this connexion his judgement of Augustus' own style stands in remarkable contrast to that of Suetonius[6]:

> After the care of public affairs had been transferred from the magistrates to Caius Caesar and to Augustus, I see in Caesar a power of speech worthy of a general, but in Augustus a *fin de siècle* elegance and consider him endowed with the still unimpaired beauty of the Latin tongue rather than with any abundant eloquence.

And of the following emperors to Vespasian, he goes on to say that one can, as speakers, only be ashamed. This seems a revealing passage; the degeneration of eloquence evidently started with Augustus' reign and went on from there, a rather different picture than we get in first-century writers. Also, Fronto is no kinder than Quintilian to Seneca or to the tinselled eloquence of silver Latin.[7]

---

[1] Haines 2, 52-54 (133-4).   [2] Haines 1, 4-6 (56-58).
[3] *Noct. Att.* 2, 26.   [4] *Noct. Att.* 2, 26.
[5] Haines 1, 122 (19, 11). For Marcus' dislike of him, 1, 138-40 (28, 21-22).
[6] Haines 2, 136-8 (117, 15). Cf. above, p. 314.   [7] Haines 2, 102-4 (149-50).

As for that disorderly eloquence, like a tree bearing mixed fruits, with some pine-nuts from Cato and some soft and feverish little plums from Seneca, in my opinion it should be destroyed root and branch, or, to use the word of Plautus, *exradicitus*. I know the man is full of maxims, indeed he overflows with them; as I see it, his *sententiae* go trotting along, they never reach a full gallop, there is no fight in them, they never strive for grandeur . . .

After comparing Seneca's style with a man who throws his olives up in the air and catches them in his mouth instead of eating them decently, he goes on:

You will say that there are some things in his books which are wisely spoken, and expressed with dignity. True, but then slivers of silver are sometimes found even in sewers. Is that any reason for not cleaning the sewers?

Fronto's main criticism is that of repetition, the same thing said over and over again in different words. He also quotes the first few lines of Lucan's civil war as an example of this weakness.

So he warns Marcus against unnecessary circumlocutions and criticizes an edict of his from this point of view. He dislikes neologisms; old words are better, though they must be refurbished and renewed to justify their usage and what is no longer understood must be avoided.[1] The aim was to enrich the common tongue, which indeed had kept many of these old words in use. It is here that common language and archaism meet. So too the derivations with heavy suffixes. Fronto also advises those very lists of synonyms which Quintilian deprecated.[2]

Fronto's eye always seems fixed on details, on particular words, on the use of a particular figure or simile which he either commends or condemns, and this is equally the case with Aulus Gellius who follows Fronto enthusiastically and applies his principles more freely though without as much discernment.

This is perhaps why, as an attempt to renew Latin eloquence and revivify the Latin language, Fronto's *elocutio novella* failed and only succeeded in adding another kind of ornamentation, another kind of preciousness to the already over-precious style of the period. Nor, in spite of allowing some popular archaic forms,[3] did he do much to bridge the gap between the literary and the living language; on the contrary, the emphasis on erudition only increased it. Not that Fronto failed personally; his reputa-

[1] Haines 2, 114 (154-5).

[2] Haines 2, 76 (144, 22), and cf. Quintilian, 10, 1, 7.

[3] Haines 2, 114 (155): in a corrupt passage one sentence stands out which seems to imply that words used by Accius, Plautus and Sallust were still alive in vulgar Latin, *in ore plebis*.

tion stood very high and we find him in the next two or three centuries frequently ranked as second only to Cicero. But with him rhetoric in the narrow sense triumphs; he has no broad conception of the art of words or of the education of the orator which we have seen in Cicero and which Quintilian sought in vain to perpetuate. Fronto's rhetoric is exclusively that of the schools, even of those rhetorical workshops which Cicero so despised. Declamations continue, and continue to be more artificial than ever, and for all his reputation Fronto did not manage to destroy the 'confused' eloquence he so violently condemned. Neither Quintilian's classicism, nor Fronto's archaism could stop the process of degeneration in a literature more and more detached from the true life of the language.

CHAPTER XX

The Second Sophistic and its Satirist

The second half of the first century saw the development of 'the second Sophistic' which can best be described as the triumph of display oratory mainly in the Greek part of the empire and especially in the province of Asia.[1] The oratory of display – the original epideictic rhetoric – had been the specialty of the old sophists of the fifth and fourth centuries B.C. It never died out, but, as far as our evidence goes, it seemed to go underground at the end of the fourth century. The Eastern Mediterranean and Asia Minor suffered much from the wars of Alexander's successors, the Roman wars of conquest, the exactions of Roman proconsuls under the late Republic, and the Roman civil wars. The reign of Augustus brought peace and better government and by the time of the Flavian emperors the province of Asia was highly prosperous. Its great cities, Ephesus, Pergamum, Smyrna, Antioch and the rest, were wealthy centres of commerce and culture and it is at this time that we witness the resurgence of display oratory, which dominated Greek letters for the next century and a half. Orators had made display speeches at games and international festivals in classical times. No doubt the habit continued but with the coming of great prosperity games and festivals multiplied. Every city had its gymnasia and its games, and also its auditoria where visiting sophists of repute would lecture for substantial remuneration. On official occasions, such as the visit of an important Roman official or even of an emperor, the subject might be an encomium of the city, of the visitor or of Rome, but the most frequent type of subject on other occasions was what the Romans called a *suasoria*, which, as in the schools, meant a speech given in the person of some Greek historical personage, such as Themistocles, Pericles or Demosthenes at a moment of crisis.

Many sophists boasted of their ability to speak impromptu, and the audience would frequently pick some well-worn topic for them to speak on. The sophist would collect his thoughts for a moment and then launch into his speech. The procedure was not unlike that of the Roman declamations as described by Seneca the elder, though it would seem that, as the occasion was more official in the Greek-speaking empire, the audiences were more numerous and more popular, and the performances more

[1] For a discussion of the second Sophistic see A. Boulanger's *Aelius Aristide*.

frequent, so that by the second century any sophist of repute could be sure of a good audience and a good fee in almost any city of Asia.

PHILOSTRATUS

We owe most of our knowledge of the second Sophistic to *The Lives of the Sophists* of Philostratus, written about A.D. 230. He gives us biographical sketches of over fifty sophists from the late first to the early third century.[1] Philostratus has no critical sense and his few critical remarks are all but worthless, but he does give an excellent picture of the prestige, wealth, benefactions and arrogance of the great sophists of that age. 'Sophist' was now a title of great honour, and the sons of the best local families would apprentice themselves to some sophist or teacher of oratory to become sophists themselves and travel all over the empire to lecture. The cities would elect their local sophists to represent them before imperial officials or indeed before the emperor himself. The emperor frequently appointed them state secretaries, consuls or governors of provinces, gave them munificent gifts, and even sometimes endured with surprising meekness displays of proud insolence from these *Graeculi*, as when Polemo of Laodicea, returning home to Smyrna unexpectedly in the middle of the night, turned the proconsul Antoninus, the future emperor, out of his house, or Herodes Atticus insulted Marcus Aurelius himself during a trial before his tribunal.[2] Such incidents could only have happened in the mild reigns of the second-century philhellenic emperors, but it shows the prestige of these rhetoricians, most of whom at one time or another held an imperial chair of rhetoric in Rome, Athens or elsewhere.

It is very difficult to attain any clear idea of the stylistic theories of the period. We can trace several trends, of which Atticism is the most important. This to the Greeks meant to write and orate in the Attic of classical times. To some extent Greek authors had always done this, but Atticism now became more self-conscious and more academic. In its extreme form it led to the precious search for rare old words which we shall see ridiculed by Lucian, and this was clearly a parallel to the contemporary archaism of Fronto, except that it was their golden age which the Greeks imitated.

Then again, like the Roman declaimers, the sophists would strive to startle their audience by brilliant and unusual phrases and rhythms. This led some of them into the kind of extravagances which had been called Asiatic, while Philostratus tells us that others affected a simpler style, so that the perennial antithesis between the simple and the grandiloquent was frequently made. Yet even from these 'simpler' orators Philostratus

---

[1] See W. Cave Wright, *Philostratus and Eunapius* (Loeb Library).
[2] Philostratus *Lives* 1, 25 (534) and 2, 1 (561).

quotes epigrammatic outbursts which would have shocked any upholder of true simplicity. Further confusion arises from the well established tradition that different styles are required by different genres and occasions. It seems, then, an oversimplification to telescope all these trends into one formula of two styles or manners, the archaic-attic-simple on the one hand, and the new, non-Attic, Asiatic on the other.[1] Moreover, not one of these trends is quite the same in Greek as in Latin.

As for the quality of sophistic oratory, the choice phrases quoted by Philostratus as having been received with exstatic admiration even by emperors do not make us feel that these famous professors deserved their reputations. They seem to us, if we can trust our evidence, to have displayed very little genius or originality.

We have the works of three of them: Dio of Prusa, Aelius Aristides and Lucian, but Dio and Lucian abandoned rhetoric in middle age; the former turned to philosophy, the latter to writing satiric dialogues.

DIO OF PRUSA

Dio Cocceianus (A.D. 40-120), nicknamed Chrysostomos (of golden speech) was a contemporary of Pliny and Plutarch, and like them a man of substance, a public man, and benefactor of his native city which for Dio was Prusa in the province of Bithynia.[2] We find him in Rome under Domitian where he seems to have got involved with some of the emperor's enemies and was exiled. He was then about fifty and it was about this time that he was converted to philosophy and became a wandering preacher of Stoic-Cynic morality. Except for the few years of his exile, however, we should not think of him as a mendicant preacher. At the death of Domitian in A.D. 96 his eloquence apparently played some part in securing the loyalty of the Dacian legions for Nerva. He was restored to favour and remained in favour till his death. We meet him, restored to wealth and prestige, in Pliny's correspondence with Trajan from Bithynia. His eighty extant orations fall into two groups, the sophistic and the philosophical; the few which deal with literary matters seem to belong to his earlier, more frivolous period.

This should be kept in mind. The eleventh oration, for example, is an attack on Homer, which applied to the whole story of the Trojan war the test of verisimilitude. Yet Homer is praised by Dio on many other occasions as the greatest of poets, so that this oration is merely a clever sophistic *jeu d'esprit* on the theme that the story of Troy cannot be true,

---

[1] As Norden (*Kunstproza* I, 392 ff.) seems to do. For a discussion of this and similar theories see Boulanger 60-73.

[2] For a full length study of Dio see Hans von Arnim's *Dio von Prusa*. The eighty orations will be found in the Loeb Library edition of J. W. Cohoon (1-31) and H. L. Crosby (32-80).

that the judgement of Paris is as unlikely as his elopement with Helen – they were probably married! As for the Trojan horse, who can believe it? In fact, Troy was probably never taken at all. All this could be very amusing if taken in the right spirit. The same is true of occasional pieces such as that which tries to prove Chryseis to be a shrewd woman who knew just the right time to break with Agamemnon after ten years of living with him, and to get her father to insist on her release (61); or another on whether Nestor had good reason to boast during the quarrel between Agamemnon and Achilles (57). All this was good fun to an audience who knew their Homer. Nor need we take more seriously the theme that Socrates learned his ethics, and some of his techniques, from Homer (55), or the slight piece on Homer himself, with its brief survey of Homeric admirers, and its insistence on Homer's modesty in not naming himself, and on his conception of kinship. The intent may be serious, but at best we have sophistic cleverness put in the service of moral philosophy.

There are, however, three orations that are of considerable interest: the twelfth which compares sculpture with poetry; the eighteenth which advises a friend on how to train for public speaking, and the fifty-second which compares the treatment of the Philoctetes legend by the three Greek tragedians.

In the twelfth oration, delivered at Olympia in A.D. 97, on his return from exile, Dio discusses man's conception of the gods; he distinguishes between the innate idea of godhead common to all men and the acquired conceptions which supplement it. The latter are influenced by the poets and the plastic arts as well as imposed by law. It is in this context that Dio imagines Phidias being called to account for the human shape and other attributes of his famous statue of Zeus, within sight of which Dio was making his speech. In his reply (55) Phidias is first made to emphasize the limitations of the art of sculpture: it cannot represent directly such things as mind and intelligence, but symbolizes them in human shape (συμβόλου δυνάμει) since man stands out in nature by his beauty, dignity and splendour as well as his intelligence. In any case, the sculptor continues, the tradition of anthropomorphism is as old as Homer, and he then compares the two arts. Words in their multitude are a much more fluid medium – there are names for all things abstract or concrete – and Homer even enlarged this medium by his use of all kinds of dialects, his archaisms, neologisms and his metaphors, thus enabling him to express every emotion, every movement, every change in place and time. Sculpture has no such freedom, it must work in a hard substance, lasting yet pliable, it can represent only one moment, one posture of its subject; throughout its slow execution the artist must keep this one model consistently before him whereas the poet can move freely from one aspect of his subject to another, indeed from one subject to another. Moreover, the eye demands a much more precise and clear presentation than the ear which can be charmed by all kinds of vague approximations, and by sound and metre as well. Within the hard limits of his art Phidias claims to have succeeded in representing the supreme god in many of his aspects, as the protector of suppliants, the giver of wealth, the king and ruler, the gentle and kindly father, the austere and dignified upholder of the Commonwealth and the law. Other attributes he could not include: the god of the thunder and lightning, the war-god, and so on.

Metaphors from other arts are frequent in ancient discussions of litera-ture, but this elaborate comparison between poetry and sculpture, to-gether with the notion of each art being limited by the nature of its medium, does not seem to occur elsewhere. We have met the basic idea of what sculpture or painting can and cannot represent in the *Memorabilia* of Socrates,[1] but it is a notion that does not seem to be developed in our texts. Dio was not an original thinker, and he probably reflects ideas that were discussed by others – but we do not happen to have those other discussions.

The eighteenth oration deals with training in public speaking and gives a list of necessary readings. However, before we compare this list with the fuller lists we find in other authors such as Cicero, Dionysius or Quintilian, we should note that Dio deals with a special case: the friend who asks his advice on how to develop a talent for speaking in public is a mature man of established position who has missed a proper education in his youth. This is made clear at the very beginning and Dio also states that he would give quite different advice to a young man (5-6). It is indeed the special purpose of the selection which makes it interesting, and we note that even so, and even at this late date, the models are all Classical, except for one paragraph where he says one should not neglect later authors, and he mentions four Greek orators, all of whom belong to the age of Augustus![2]

The only poets recommended are Menander, Euripides and, of course, Homer. Menander's representation ($\mu i \mu \eta \sigma \iota \varsigma$) of every type of character exceeds in charm and ability that of all the old comic writers, while Euripides' smooth persuasiveness, though it may not completely reach the divine nature and dignity of tragedy, is very useful to a public man; moreover he is clever at fully expressing character and passions, and, having some knowledge of philosophy, he sprinkles his poems with useful maxims at every opportunity. As for Homer, everything is there; it is just a question of what you are able to take from him.

A public man must know history; it will give him a sense of perspective.

---

[1] Above, pp. 37-8.
[2] The names are briefly given without comment in section 7 of the oration, namely Antipater, Theodorus, Plution and Conon.

Herodotus is most enjoyable. Thucydides is mentioned and, of the lesser lights, Theopompus, but Euphorus is unsuitable. Then we come to the orators: everybody knows Demosthenes is the master of his craft and Lysias the pattern of brevity, simplicity and camouflaged cleverness, but Dio advises his friend to read Hypereides and Aeschines because their qualities are simpler and their stylistic elaborations easier to understand.

The Socratics, we find, are indispensable, for no dish is palatable without salt. Some of them, however, are hard reading (Plato?) and Xenophon is selected as the best, indeed as the one indispensable model. From him you can learn almost every kind of public speaking. His ideas are clear and simple, his style smooth, charming and persuasive, and he is everywhere true to life. The *Anabasis* contains something for all occasions and Dio confesses to having been deeply affected on reading it. Time spent on Xenophon will never be wasted. Dio then ends with the advice to dictate rather than write in order to develop readiness, to avoid school exercises but rather to try to reproduce or rebut some actual speech, preferably from Xenophon. This advice too is tempered, no doubt, to fit the particular case.

The reading-list is well adapted to the recipient, and the emphasis everywhere is on authors who are not too difficult, such as Euripides and Menander. Homer and Thucydides needs must be mentioned but are not insisted on; Theopompus, Hyperides and Aeschines are but not Demosthenes or Lysias because these cannot be imitated in a hurry, and, from this point of view, the choice of Xenophon is excellent. Obviously all this advice dates from Dio's sophistic period since the philosophers are not mentioned and he clearly is still a young man. While his own training was no doubt much more exacting, yet it is relevant to note that for the sophists these were the essential authors – the study of them is indeed reflected in Dio's own simple and natural style.

The comparison of the three *Philoctetes* plays of Aeschylus, Sophocles and Euripides in the fifty-second oration is of special interest to literary historians because it gives a good many details of the plots of the plays of Aeschylus and Euripides which are lost. There are also some critical remarks of considerable interest, particularly about plot construction. We find that Euripides was much more careful than Aeschylus to avoid inconsistencies: both have a chorus of Lemnians, Euripides makes his chorus apologize for not having been in touch with Philoctetes during the previous ten years, he even introduces a Lemnian who has visited him before. Similarly, Euripides disguises Odysseus so that he shall not be recognized. Aeschylus simply ignores these details, and Dio approves. 'If poets could avoid everything irrational in tragedy, perhaps it would be reasonable not to ignore (παραπέμψαι) these things either' – but since tragedy often has to assume inconsistencies of time and the like, he thinks Euripides does not gain anything by his careful explanations (7).

Dio's conclusion seems to be that each is excellent in his own way (4): 'The nobility of mind and archaic flavour of Aeschylus, the individuality of his thought and of his language seems suited to tragedy and to the old-time characters of his heroes; there is nothing contrived, rhetorical or humble about them' – his Odysseus is clever and guileful, but not a modern rascal (4-5). On the other hand Euripides' careful attention to detail, in contrast to Aeschylus, 'smacks more of politics and rhetoric and can be very useful to those who read him' (11). He mentions particularly the introductory monologue of Odysseus analysing his own motives and ambitions. Odysseus was evidently accompanied by Diomede, and the arrival of a Trojan embassy gave an excellent opportunity for a set debate. Dio especially commends Euripides' cleverness in handling the plot, his amazing linguistic skill, his clear and realistic dialogue and his lyrics which are both delightful and morally protreptic.

This last may surprise us, especially when we are told later (17) that the lyrics of Sophocles contained less incentive to virtue, but as we do not have Euripides' play we cannot tell what Dio had in mind. 'Sophocles seems to stand between the other two; he has neither the originality of Aeschylus nor the preciseness, cleverness and realism (πολιτικόν) of Euripides, but his poetry is dignified, noble, highly tragic and beautiful in diction, so that it combines pleasure with elevation and stateliness. His handling of the plot is excellent and very persuasive.' Dio then gives details of the Sophoclean plot and remarks on the nobility of Neoptolemus when, after obtaining possession of the bow by deceit at the bidding of Odysseus, he returns it and Philoctetes is only persuaded to go to Troy by the divine intervention of Heracles.

Those three orations contain the main passages of critical interest in Dio. His later work was, as we have seen, of a more philosophical nature. There are other literary references here and there, but they contribute little more. The most interesting of them is probably to be found in the twenty-first oration (11), where he seems to agree with Martial and Juvenal that surely tragedy and literature in general would do well to take contemporary life as their model rather than deal again and again with outworn subjects. However, Dio says, his interlocutor would probably take him more seriously if he, as wise men do, were discoursing on Cyrus and Alcibiades instead of events he can himself remember – 'that's the reason why I do not like the tragedians and do not emulate them'. And yet, he adds, the ancients themselves were ready enough to write on their contemporaries, which people nowadays will not do.

At the time of Dio's death about A.D. 120, the second Sophistic was in full bloom. Some sophists, like Scopelianus of Smyrna and Polemo of Laodicea were known for their passionate eloquence and 'dithyrambic' delivery and would therefore be considered 'Asiatic'. Most of their speeches seem to have been of the *suasoria* type. The two extant orations of Polemo, for example, are speeches by the fathers of Callimachus and Cynegirus, two Athenians who died at Marathon, each father claiming the right to deliver the funeral oration on those who died in that battle because of the heroism of his son. 'Asiatic' though Polemo was, however, he too tries to conform, in a general way, to the requirements of Classical Greek.

HERODES ATTICUS

The fuller and more exact Atticism in this sense, however, is usually associated with Herodes Atticus (c. A.D. 100-75) who was consul in 143 and who was the wealthiest as well as the most famous of the second-century sophists. In his school in Athens his pupils were trained in Attic Greek – by then already ancient Greek – which Herodes tried to revive as the literary language. This worsened the separation of the literary from the living language, and the artificiality of such an attempt to freeze the language of literature to that of its most glorious period is not likely to develop any very original writing. Herodes Atticus was thorough; his pupils really studied the Classics and received a much fuller literary and even philosophic education than was customary. When challenged, they were expected to quote the classical authority for the use of particular words much as a modern student writing Greek prose might be expected to do. At the same time Herodes Atticus was no mere antiquarian searching ancient texts for unusual words. He had a tremendous reputation as a speaker and was therefore attuned to large audiences. He was able to vary his style according to his audience. He was often generous in praise of his contemporaries, notably Polemo. Most of the sophists of the next generation were his pupils.

ARISTIDES

Among these was Aelius Aristides who was born in Mysia about A.D. 117 though he settled in Smyrna.[1] Like all the sophists he travelled a good deal and paid a number of visits to Rome. Fifty-three of his orations are extant, two in fragmentary form. Six of them (47-52) describe the course of a chronic illness and the help he received from the god Asclepius in the form of dreams and prescriptions, his stays in the temple at Pergamum, and other marvels. These 'orations' have made Aelius Aristides the most

[1] For a full study of Aristides see Boulanger and C.A. De Leeuw.

famous valetudinarian in ancient history and are of considerable interest to students of temple medicine and other superstitions in the second century. Among his other works are *suasoriae* of the usual historical type, panegyrics such as his famous oration *On Rome* (26), appeals to the emperor on behalf of Smyrna and the like. Most promising from our point of view are the defence of rhetoric against Plato's attacks in the *Gorgias*, a defence of Militades, Themistocles, Cimon and Pericles against attacks made in the same dialogue (45-46), and some other works on rhetoric (47, 48 and 34). The promise, however, is not fulfilled. Though Aristides writes in good Attic, his thought is confused and completely unoriginal. He states his disagreement with Plato, to him rhetoric is superbly moral and he simply repeats in a particularly muddled and unoriginal way all the old commonplaces on the benefits which rhetoric has brought to mankind. There is nothing new in these orations, nothing that need detain us even briefly. For all his reputation Aelius Aristides was no thinker, nor was he able to arrange his material clearly or convincingly. He is, on the contrary, incredibly diffuse.

LUCIAN

Lucian[1] was a contemporary of Aristides but of a very different stamp. Like Dio of Prusa, he abandoned Sophistic in middle life, but in his case the conversion was not to philosophy but to satire, and he invented what was practically a new genre, the satiric dialogue. He is a far more lively, original and imaginative writer than any of his fellow sophists. Witty, ironic and humorous, he is a satirist of many moods: sometimes as amiable as Horace and seemingly as unconcerned as Petronius, he can also be as bitterly indignant as Juvenal and savage in his attacks upon the pompous and hypocritical personages of the highly civilized but also highly superstitious age of the Antonines.

He was born in Samosata in Syria, and, unlike most sophists, in humble circumstances. His family intended him for his uncle's trade of stonecutter but this was not a success. In *The Dream* he tells how he was dazzled by the promises of Paideia (education) and how she took him in her car travelling east and west, gathering fame and reputation as he went. There is no doubt that he was a famous sophist; one imagines that his wit must have been a relief from the pomposities of his contemporaries even at that stage in his life, but we do not know where or how he acquired his education; he probably exaggerated his parents' poverty, they were not important persons, but they need not have been financially embarrassed.

His later conversion is symbolized in *The Double Indictment*. Justice has

[1] Lucian's works are available in the Loeb Library, edited by A. M. Harmon (Harvard 1913 on). For Lucian as a writer see J. Bompaire, *Lucien Ecrivain*.

come down from heaven to try some outstanding cases in Athens and after some philosophical quarrels have been settled, we find an indictment by Rhetoric against 'the Syrian' whom she is prosecuting for desertion. She took up with him, she tells us, when he was a young barbarian, in preference to many rich and noble suitors, made him a citizen, travelled with him all over the world and made him famous. He has now deserted her for Dialogue; he no longer makes grand speeches in a mighty voice but speaks in short sentences and no longer gets great applause but only an acquiescent smile. The Syrian's defence is interesting. He admits his debt to Rhetoric, but the reason he has left her is that Rhetoric herself has changed for the worse; she is no longer modest in her bearing as she was when she lived with Demosthenes, she now makes up, dresses and does her hair like a courtesan, and the house is always filled with her drunken lovers who have no restraint at all. Anyway, as a man of forty odd, it was only right for him to leave her law cases, indictments against tyrants, encomia of princes, and to keep quiet company with Dialogue in the Academy and the Lyceum.

Acquitted on this charge, the Syrian is now faced with another, from Dialogue himself, who claims also to have been wronged and maltreated by the Syrian who will not respect his dignity, deprives him of the tragic mask and replaces it by the mask of comedy, forces him into the company of Jest, Lampoon and Cynicism and that old dog Menippus, with his loud bark and dreadful grin. The Syrian replies that, when he took him in hand, Dialogue was morose, respected perhaps but disagreeable and un-attractive. He is now washed, smiling and popular and has gained much from Comedy's company. Dialogue is overfond of subtle philosophical problems, questions as to the nature of the gods or of rhetoric, but he has no other complaint, for the Syrian has not deprived him of his Greek mantle or made him a foreigner. The defendant is unanimously acquitted.

In *The Parasite*, a parasite argues that the art of getting free dinners is a true art or *technê*, on the basis of the definition that an art is 'a complex of concepts exercised towards an end which is useful to (human) life' (4). In proving it, he uses many arguments which had been used for centuries to prove that rhetoric was an art or *technê*. Parasitism is 'the science of food and drink, and of what has to be said and done to obtain them, and its end is pleasure' (9). The authority of Homer is invoked and we find that Epicurus stole the 'end' of parasitism and made pleasure the end of happiness.

Lucian was himself an Atticist, and a very successful one, but in *Lexi-phanes* he ridicules the search for unusual words in old authors, and the deliberately precious use of them. Lexiphanes reads an extract from a book of his which is full of such words and this is obviously a parody of some

contemporary writer, who considered himself the pattern of Atticism
(14). Lycinus (= Lucian) then gives him good advice: to read the Classics,
not the lucubrations of recent sophists, to use words to express thought,
not twist the thought in order to bring in some strange word recently
discovered, which is an obvious proof of deliberate archaism and preciosity.
This satire is a useful reminder that there were different kinds of 'Atticism'
and that the generic term, even in its Greek sense, covers very different
practices.

In *The Professor of Rhetoric* Lucian is not attacking the thorough classical
training required by such teachers as Herodes Atticus, the kind of training
he had himself received (from whom we do not know), but the superficial
training of less reputable sophists. As the cynical professor says himself,
there are two ways to rhetoric, a steep and narrow path which means
following in the footsteps of Demosthenes and Plato, imitating those
ancient models, and this takes years of hard work. The other is a much
easier and quicker road. No preliminary instruction is needed; the only
equipment required is ignorance, boldness and shamelessness, and modesty
can be left behind. However, you need a loud voice, dainty clothes, a
singing delivery and a mincing walk, for to be accepted by Rhetoric you
must be very careful of your appearance. You should pick up fifteen or
at most twenty old Attic forms from one source or another, practise these
carefully and scatter them all over any speech you make, for seasoning
($ἥδυσμα$, 16), whether they fit or not. You then collect some strange words
rarely used by ancient writers; have a heap of them ready to hurl at your
audience at any moment. This will ensure their admiration for your
superior education. You can always cover up any barbarism or solecism by
bluffing and quoting some non-existent authority. Do *not* read old books
like that drivelling Isocrates, that unpleasing Demosthenes or frigid Plato;
you can get all you need from a few recent writers and school declamations.
Avoid difficult subjects if you can, but in any case never stop talking and
don't bother about structure. Get your illustrations from distant places;
bring in Marathon, Xerxes, Leonidas on all occasions, together with those
Attic expressions of yours. Sing out your words, sway your hips, bully
your audience if they don't applaud. Always start from the Trojan war or
the Flood. Never write anything down, always improvise, and be sure to
have a *claque* of your friends ready to cover up any hesitation with applause. Boast, make extravagant claims for yourself; sneer at others; come
in late to anyone else's lecture, look and act superior. If you do all this,
your public speaking will be a great success and you can indulge your
every vice in private life.

It seems almost certain from the description of the guide along the easy
road that Lucian has a particular teacher in view, as in the *Lexiphanes*, and

that his readers would recognize him. It is a savage caricature, but of the second Sophistic's lesser practitioners it was probably justified.

Lucian's most important critical work, however, is *How to Write History*; it is also the most serious. He was apparently provoked into writing it by the large number of inferior histories of the Armenian war of A.D. 165 which appeared shortly after it. The first part of the essay exposes, with illustrations, the faults of those historians; the second part sets forth the necessary characteristics of good history. We cannot be sure how far Lucian is original; many of the things here set down can be found in scattered passages in earlier writers,[1] but he certainly objects to the idea that history is, as Quintilian said it was, akin to poetry or a form of epideictic rhetoric.[2] At any rate the discussion is very sound, and for us this is the fullest treatment of the subject since Polybius three centuries before.

The trouble with these modern historians, Lucian tells us, is that they confuse history and encomium; they do not know that a historian's first duty is to tell the truth. The historian cannot, like the poet, allow his imagination free play; if he does, he is writing a kind of prose-poetry, but not history (10). Praise is in place when due, but in moderation. Present historians have two aims: to delight and to benefit their readers, whereas the second should be their only aim, and it is bound up with truth. Delight should be incidental, as a chief aim it destroys truthfulness. Flattery is in any case tiresome to all but the object of it, and often even to him. Besides, to run down the enemy is no flattery to the victor, for it is more glorious to defeat Achilles than Thersites (20).

Then again some of our historians imitate phrases of Thucydides so closely that bits of him are scattered all over their writings; others write like tragic poets; others again have no style at all, they are collecting the materials of history but not writing it. Frigid and irrelevant introductions are followed by wearisome descriptions; they'll even write a whole book on a general's shield (27) or have Probus frighten the enemy with a shout (like Achilles). Excessively poetic words are followed by the most com-

---

[1] Avenarius, in his *Lukians Schrift zur Geschichtschreibung* has painstakingly traced Lucian's ideas to earlier sources in extant texts. In only two cases he can find no earlier authority, namely (i) that the historian needs understanding of affairs (πολιτικὴ σύνεσις) and (ii) that a historian should not conciliate his audience in his proem. If we treated a modern essay, however original, on the writing of history in the same way, we should no doubt achieve the same result. It is the total picture of such an essay which is important.

F. Wehrli, 'Die Geschichtschreibung im Lichte der antiken Theorie', wants to trace the main ideas back to an (unknown) work of Theophrastus on the subject. Avenarius rejects this theory and points out that Cicero (*De Oratore* 2, 62) specifically says that he knows of no special treatise on historiography. Avenarius suggests Lucian may have benefited from a lost work of Plutarch on how to judge true history (πῶς κρίνομεν τὴν ἀληθῆ ἱστορίαν); he does not believe Lucian had any *one* source before him, but rather got his ideas from his teachers in rhetoric.

[2] Quintilian 10, 1, 31.

mon, or a grandiose introduction by a most pedestrian narrative; they have no consistent tone.

Their geography is wrong in fact; and so are the events they narrate. Their fanciful imagination knows no bounds. All is out of proportion: seven lines to describe a battle, and whole pages of irrelevant detail. They profess to have witnessed what they have not seen, and foretell things that do not happen. As for that funeral oration intended to rival Thucydides, which Aphranios is made to speak so passionately that he kills himself at the end, he would have done better to kill his author!

We then come to the positive advice of the second part. Two things are essential for a historian: he must understand public affairs and he must be able to write. The first is a natural gift, the second is the result of practice, hard work, *and a desire to imitate the ancient writers*. Beyond this he must have some experience of military matters. His mind must be free (ἐλεύθερος τὴν γνώμην); neither fear nor hope of favours must prevent him from telling the truth – he is after all not responsible for the misfortunes he records. Upon this primary need of truthfulness and detachment Lucian insists at length and he refers to Thucydides' introduction to his History, his exclusion of the mythical, etc., in contrast to Herodotus (50-55).

As for style, let the historian begin quietly. His diction should be neither *recherché* nor common, but such as the many can understand and the cultured can praise, his first aim always being a clear and lucid presentation of events, using figures which are neither tiresome nor elaborate. His thought may be touched with poetry when he describes great events and his language may rise with their beauty and nobility, but it must never leave the ground altogether. His word-arrangement should be of the intermediate kind without much in the way of rhythms. He should arrange his material very carefully, and evaluate what he himself saw, or follow the most trustworthy reports. When he has gathered all his material he should first write a plain and unadorned account. He can then later add beauty of diction, figures and rhythm (59).

A historian must, like Homer's Zeus, look at both sides with detachment, and only occasionally concentrate attention on an individual, a Brasidas or a Demosthenes. Throughout a battle he must weigh both sides in the balance. His history should reflect what actually happened as in a clear mirror. His material is given, it is what he does with it that matters (63); structure and vividness being here all-important.

The introduction, if any, should aim to secure the attention of the audience and make things easier to understand by a brief discussion of the subject giving reasons and maybe headings, but the aim of the historian's introduction, unlike that of a rhetorician, is *not* to conciliate his audience. The transition to the narrative, and history is of course mainly narrative, should be smooth and easy – as indeed should the narrative itself, it should be well constructed, clear, and consistent. The events have to follow one another quickly but the style should not be hurried, and important events should be sufficiently emphasized. Inevitably, much must be left out, and therefore long descriptions should be omitted, 'lest you should appear to display yourself and forget your history' (65). At times, Lucian admits, descriptions are essential, like that of Epipolae or the harbour of Syracuse in Thucydides, and his long description of the plague is also justified by its importance.

Speeches, if introduced, should be clear, appropriate to the situation and the character who makes them; within those limits the historian may be allowed to display his talent for eloquence. Praise or blame must be relevant, moderate, based on evidence, and short, unlike Theopompus who writes more like an accuser than a historian. A mythical tale may be told, but not to be believed. Generally the historian should look to praise from posterity rather than from his contemporaries, like the Cnidian architect who built the lighthouse at Pharos and prominently displayed the king's name but his own was hidden between the stones.

The great merit of Lucian's essay is that he clearly distinguishes history from rhetoric, whereas Cicero and Dionysius regarded it as one kind of epideictic rhetoric. Lucian establishes it as a separate genre which has its own laws and its own requirements. Polybius had insisted that the historian's first loyalty is to the truth, and Cicero had accepted this, though Dionysius had wavered and brought in moral and patriotic motives which Lucian clearly refuses to recognize. But Lucian, unlike Polybius, also discusses the kind of style appropriate to history, a subject treated only very incidentally by other critics, so that we have in this essay the fullest discussion of historiography as a literary genre from antiquity, and in this regard Lucian's common sense makes a real contribution to literary theory.

HERMOGENES

A younger contemporary of Lucian, Hermogenes of Tarsus, was apparently a child prodigy among the sophists; his fame was so great at the age of fifteen that the emperor Marcus Aurelius made a special journey to hear him declaim and greatly admired his ability to speak extempore. When he grew up, however, his talent suddenly deserted him.[1] We know Hermogenes as the author of a series of textbooks on rhetoric which are still extant; they very soon attained great fame and were not only in general use for centuries but were commented on by other rhetoricians into Byzantine times, and a good many of these commentaries have also sur-

[1] Philostratus, *Lives*, 2, 7.

vived. They are mostly dull reading, but so are the textbooks themselves. Their aim is clearly to teach the pupils to write the Attic of the fourth century, for the models are Demosthenes and Plato. Two of the works, περὶ τῶν στάσεων and περὶ εὑρέσεως deal with the field of *inventio*, and this is largely subordinated to the formula of the sections of a speech, i.e. what arguments to use in the proem, in the narrative, etc. The περὶ ἰδεῶν isolates certain qualities such as clarity, dignity, force, etc., defines them, gives illustrations from Demosthenes who has them all. School exercises (προγυμνάσματα) are also discussed in a separate work. There is hardly a spark of originality either in Hermogenes or his commentators, but his works give one an idea of the kind of training which led to the writing of Attic Greek at the time of the second Sophistic. The great sophists still read their classics, the lesser lights learned from Hermogenes and his like.

CHAPTER XXI

Longinus on Great Writing

It is fitting that we should end our account of the ancient critics with that mysterious masterpiece which is traditionally known as Longinus On The Sublime. Its date and author are uncertain, its traditional title is misleading, its popularity, which was great from the sixteenth to the eighteenth century, mysteriously waned in the nineteenth and has hardly recovered today. Yet is has a good claim to be considered the most enlightening critical document extant from antiquity, even in its present fragmentary state, with about one-third of it lost.[1]

The treatise is preserved in several manuscripts, the oldest of which is dated in the tenth century, and it ascribes the treatise to Dionysius Longinus, who was assumed to be the only Longinus we know, a great teacher and scholar of the third century, whom his contemporaries called a walking library. He was a friend of Porphyry the disciple of Plotinus, and a strong proponent of the classical Greek writers, the most distinguished scholar of his day; his opinions on literature carried great weight. Longinus was also adviser to Zenobia, queen of Palmyra in Asia Minor, was involved with her in a conspiracy against Rome, and was executed by order of the emperor Aurelian in A.D. 273. His name, however, was Cassius, not (as far as we know) Dionysius.

No one paid much attention to this discrepancy – it was not unusual for Greeks to take on a Roman name as well – until it was found early in the nineteenth century that the index of our oldest manuscript noted the author as Dionysius *or* Longinus, and further that one or two other manuscripts had a similar reference. One said the author was unknown. It was then supposed that the author *was* unknown and that some Byzantine scribe assumed that it must be *either* Dionysius of Halicarnassus *or* Longinus and entitled the work accordingly. This, of course, is pure guesswork; one might just as well guess that the mythical Byzantine scribe, faced with

[1] The standard English edition is by Rhys Roberts (1907), to which can now be added that of D. A. Russell (1964). See also that of Rostagni (1947), and my annotated translation (1957). Full bibliographies will be found in these editions. A brief survey of Longinus' influence upon English criticism in Churton Collins' *Studies in Poetry*, and also in S. H. Monk's *The Sublime*. See also J. Brody's *Boileau and Longinus*. Quiller-Couch suggested some reasons for the neglect of Longinus in his *Studies in Literature* pp. 141 ff. For textual difficulties, besides the above editions, see also my notes in *AJP* 78 (1957), 355-74.

an ascription to Dionysius Longinus and knowing only Cassius, put in the
or on his own account. No other probable author has been suggested,
though many improbable have.

It is now fashionable among scholars to date the work in the first
century A.D., and two main arguments support this date: first, that the
treatise is explicitly written in answer to, or at least after reading, a work
of Caecilius of Calacte, the contemporary of Dionysius of Halicarnassus;
second, that the last chapter is on the decay of eloquence which was a
subject much discussed in the first century A.D. This last assertion is indeed
true, as we have seen, but there is no reason to suppose that the decay of
eloquence ceased to be discussed in A.D. 100. It obviously worried Fronto
and Aulius Gellius. That no other discussion of the kind is extant means
nothing. In any case the first-century discussions we possess are Roman;
the subject was much less natural for a Greek. It would, however, be
natural enough for a scholar, who was also a statesman and was involved
in a conspiracy which cost him his life, to discuss the decay of eloquence
and its relation to the loss of freedom. He might even be as ironical as
Tacitus in doing so. It was in any case a commonplace.

As for being dissatisfied with a treatise two hundred years old and
thereby stimulated to write on the same subject, there is nothing very surprising in this, especially for a walking library like Longinus. Caecilius'
works were classics of criticism; Plutarch rebuked him about A.D. 100
for his boldness in writing a comparative study of the styles of Demosthenes
and Cicero; why should Longinus and his friend Terentianus to whom
this treatise is addressed not have read a work of his together a century or
so later? Indeed, it would not be very surprising if a professor of English
literature today wrote to a colleague or a graduate student and began in
the same way: 'When you and I, my dear T., were studying Sydney's
Defence of Poetry together, we felt that he failed to do justice to his subject
and to make the best of his opportunities. . . . You asked me to write
down my thoughts on the subject. Here they are.'

A third argument has been brought up to support the first-century date,
namely that the author of our treatise owed much to Theodorus of
Gadara and was obviously a direct pupil of his. I have disproved this at
length elsewhere, and cannot go into the question here. Suffice it to say
that such a view is, in my opinion, based on a serious misunderstanding
of both Theodorus and our author, and that this whole elaborate theory
seems to be of a type elsewhere not unknown, namely an inverted
pyramid of scholarly conjectures resting upon one point which is a
fallacy.[1]

---

[1] The one point in this case is the use of the imperfect ἐκάλει at 3.5: 'Theodorus used to call
it parenthyrsus', which has led to the suggestion that Longinus was a contemporary of
GRCM

The authorship of Cassius Longinus cannot be proved, and, while it has not been altogether disproved, some doubt is certainly cast upon it by the doubtful ascriptions of certain manuscripts. The first-century date is not only not proved, but in my view improbable. Let us therefore take the work to be of uncertain date and authorship. This, in t hecase of an independent work of genius which does not link up with the theories of any particular period or school is of less importance than usual. We may as well go on calling the author Longinus for the sake of convenience as we turn to the far more important question of subject and content.

First of all, what is it about? The Greek title is περὶ ὕψους; both this noun and the adjective ὑψηλός were used by other critics, by Dionysius in particular, to indicate grandeur of diction and/or word-arrangement, and one is therefore tempted to think that our treatise is on the grand style as contrasted with the plain. This is an error. Longinus is not concerned with particular styles at all, and many of his examples of *hypsos* are not in the grand manner. What he is discussing is 'great writing' in its most general sense, for which he uses a number of other terms as well.[1] He uses these somewhat loosely, as if he had inherited from Plato, along with many other things, a peculiar aversion to a fixed technical vocabulary. The question he tries to answer is: 'What are the characteristics of great writing?', or if we want to preserve the metaphor of height, which is the meaning of *hypsos*, 'How do writers reach the greatest heights?' He is obviously thinking of great passages rather than great books (1, 4):

> Great writing (τὰ ὑπερφυᾶ) does not persuade but takes one out of oneself. . . . Skill of invention, of structure and arrangement are qualities which emerge slowly from the texture of a whole work, not from one or two passages. Greatness, on the other hand, suddenly appears like a thunderbolt, carries everything before it, and reveals the writer's full power in a flash. (1, 4)

This is a description, not a definition. Longinus is too wise to define a thing so intangible; instead, he describes its nature, its different causes and its effect. One proof of it is unanimous recognition.

> Consider that truly great and beautiful writing (καλὰ ὕψη καὶ ἀληθινά) is that which pleases all men at all times. When men of different occupations, lives, interests, generations and tongues all have the same

---

Theodorus. Yet an exactly similar imperfect occurs in Demetrius 76, but no one has deduced from this that Demetrius was a contemporary of the painter Nicias. The notion that the author of our treatise was a direct disciple of Theodorus was built up by M. Schanz in *Hermes* 35 (1890), H. Mutschmann in his *Tendenz, Aufbau und Quellen*, and Rostagni in his edition. See my article in *AJP* 80 (1959), 337-65, and above, pp. 272-4.

[1] For a study of these see *AJP* 78 (1957), 355-60.

opinion on the same subject, then the agreed verdict from such diverse sources attains an authority so strong about the object of its admiration as to be beyond dispute. (7, 4)

Some people, we are told (ch. 2), think that 'great writers are born, not made'. This raises the old problem of the relative importance of art and training (τέχνη) on the one hand and natural talent on the other. Like Horace, Longinus comes to the inevitable conclusion that both are needed. 'Nature supplies the essential element always, but method and training show what is appropriate on each occasion . . . great qualities are too precarious when left to themselves unsteadied and unballasted by knowledge.' Unlike Horace, however, he puts the main emphasis on natural talent.

A lacuna follows, and when the text resumes our author is discussing the vices into which unsuccessful attempts at greatness may fall. There are four of these: (i) turgidity or bombast, which is illustrated from Aeschylus, Gorgias and Xenophon; (ii) puerility, 'an academic notion (σχολαστικὴ νόησις) overelaborated into frigidity'; (iii) *parenthyrsis* or false enthusiasm, a display of empty and inappropriate emotion. 'Like drunkards, such writers are beside themselves but their audience is not'; and (iv) frigidity which here seems to mean frigidity of ideas or imagery. Examples are given under each head. We recognize the theory of neighbouring vices which we met in Demetrius and Horace, but we note that Longinus is thinking of ideas rather than style – and all these faults, he adds, arise from the desire for novel conceits (τὸ περὶ τὰς νοήσεις καινόσπουδον), 'the chief mania of our time' (5).

Longinus now comes to a closer grip with his subject as he warns us that to understand greatness is not easy, that literary judgement is 'the last outgrowth of much experience' and that we must 'beware of the mere outward appearance of greatness which is overlaid with many carelessly fashioned ornaments, and on closer scrutiny proves to be hollow conceit' (7, 1). He then proceeds to the causes of real greatness (8):

There are, one might say, five sources most productive of great writing, and all five presuppose the power of expression in speech as a common basis. First and most important is vigour of mental conception, as we defined it in our work on Xenophon. Second is strong and inspired emotion. Both of these are for the most part innate dispositions, while the others are also a matter of artistic training. They are: the adequate fashioning of figures both of thought and speech; noble diction, which includes both the choice of words and the use of figurative and artistic language; the fifth cause, which embraces all the others, is dignified and distinguished word-arrangement.

Any one of these, it seems, and any combination of them, can lead to great writing, and, as he deals with them in turn, our author gets carried away at times and speaks as if this or that particular aspect of greatness were equal to the whole of it. So that there is some excuse for commentators to be confused. He might, however, reply that greatness is of many different kinds.

Caecilius had apparently neglected to deal with passion or *pathos*, and Longinus reserves it for a special monograph which is unfortunately lost, so that we have only a very short section on it here. On the one hand 'nothing contributes so much to greatness as noble passion in the right place; it breathes the frenzied spirit of its inspiration upon the words and makes them, as it were, prophetic'. On the other hand, while *pathos* is thus an important source of great writing, it is not an essential source for 'there are lowly emotions *such as pity, sorrow and fear* which are not compatible with greatness; moreover, there are great passages devoid of passion'. As an example of the latter he quotes the attempt of the Titans to scale Olympus in the *Odyssey* (11, 315-17).

This is tantalizingly brief. The importance of strong emotion as a source of greatness we can readily understand, but why are pity, sorrow and fear excluded? It seems clear that our author has in mind the emotions felt by the writer or the character in drama rather than those of the audience, and it is probably true that pity, sorrow or fear, each by itself, do not make for a tragic situation or great writing. However, it would have been very interesting to have Longinus' thoughts on the subject.

Greatness without strong emotion he himself explains by saying that 'encomia, ceremonial and display speeches may be great writing but are for the most part devoid of passion'. One doubts, however, whether really great writing of any kind is possible without the writer being emotionally involved, though we should remember that πάθος means passion or at least strong emotion, the less violent emotions being ἦθος, as we have seen.[1]

The next seven chapters (9-15) discuss the first and most important source of greatness, namely vigorous mental power. This of course is an intellectual quality, and here, as indeed in the little he says about passion, Longinus abandons the habit of his contemporaries and predecessors who objectively criticized the product of art and paid very little attention to the mind and qualities of the artist. Not since Plato has our attention been so clearly focused upon him. 'Men whose thoughts and concerns are mean and petty cannot produce anything admirable or worthy of lasting fame. The authors of great works are endowed with great minds, and literary excellence belongs to those of high spirit,' or, as he also puts it more concisely: 'Great writing is the echo of a noble mind' (9, 1-3). He gives as an

---

[1] See above, pp. 291-2.

example of such grandeur of idea the passage in Odysseus' visit to the underworld in the *Odyssey* where Ajax strides away without saying a word, which shows clearly that his subject is not the grand style.

Unfortunately, there is another lacuna at the beginning of this discussion and when the text resumes Longinus is discussing the imagery of the battle of the gods in the *Iliad*, it seems adversely, for he condemns it, unless interpreted allegorically, as 'impious and transgressing the boundaries of good taste' (πρέπον); indeed he says their grandeur is excessive.[1] It looks as if he had been discussing the difference between real greatness and mere grandeur, that mere appearance of greatness against which he had already warned us, and, in contrast, he quotes Homer's picture of Poseidon driving in his chariot over the waves as really satisfactory, and also, from 'the lawgiver of the Jews' the picture of creation in Genesis, as well as the famous prayer of Ajax in the seventeenth book of the *Iliad* that Zeus may lift the fog from the battlefield 'and in the light destroy us if you must'. These last two examples at least are very obviously simple in style if grand in conception.

The quotation from Moses is remarkable, and Longinus is praised for his cosmopolitan spirit both here and in the contrast he draws later between Demosthenes and Cicero, deservedly, for it was a very rare thing for Greek critics to refer to any literature but their own. Yet we must not praise him extravagantly for we know that Caecilius had written a comparison of Cicero and Demosthenes (perhaps in the very treatise which provoked this one) and he was most probably a Jew, so that the Genesis reference may well come from him also.

The rest of the ninth chapter is a digression on Homer (so called by the author himself), fully justified for us by a number of interesting remarks. He has already said in this chapter that 'Homer's stories of wounds, factions, revenge, tears, chains and confused passions among the gods make the men of the Trojan war into gods, and the gods into men' (9, 7). We now find that Longinus believes that Homer wrote the *Odyssey* later than the *Iliad* because the former implies knowledge of the latter, and also because 'the declining passion' of old age is apt to lead great writers to less dramatic narrative and to story-telling (9, 13).

> ... the whole *Iliad*, written at the height of the poet's inspiration, is full of dramatic action, while the *Odyssey* is mostly narrative, which is characteristic of old age. One might compare the Homer of the *Odyssey* to the setting sun: the grandeur remains but not the intensity. The tension is not as great as in those famous lays of the *Iliad*, the great

---

[1] διὰ τὴν ὑπερβολὴν τοῦ μεγέθους, 'excess of grandeur', for one cannot have excess of ὕψος or greatness. Yet the two terms are sometimes used as synonyms by our author.

passages are not sustained without weakening, there is no such out-
pouring of passion and suffering, no such versatility of realism or condensation of imaginative truth. It is like an ocean which has with-
drawn into itself, into the solitude of its own boundaries. Greatness
ebbs and flows as the poet wanders into the realm of the mythical and
the incredible. In saying this I do not forget the storm scenes of the
Odyssey, the adventure with the Cyclops, and other stories. When I
speak of old age, it is the old age of Homer still, but in all these tales
story-telling outweighs action.

This is the most imaginative comparison of the two Homeric epics which
has come down from antiquity; the sequel, where he speaks of πάθος
giving way to ἦθος in old age and compares the *Odyssey* to a comedy of
manners, is more conventional.[1]

The tenth chapter returns to our main theme, mental vigour, and here
Longinus isolates for discussion another quality of great writers, namely
the capacity to select the most vital features or details in a situation and to
combine them into a unified whole. He illustrates this talent by the famous
ode of Sappho which begins: 'Like to the gods he seems to me, the man
who sits gazing on thee. . . .' Catullus imitated it, but the Greek text is
preserved only here. Our author adds an excellent critical paragraph
wherein he points out how the poetess unites contradictory feelings and
phrases into one most vivid description of overwhelming passion. He then
compares a Homeric description of a storm with that of a lesser poet and
shows how one inappropriate phrase can spoil the effect, or, on the other
hand, the use of one eminently appropriate double preposition enhance it
(10, 4-7). It is this combination of insight into the spirit of a whole passage
allied with the perception of significance in the smallest detail which
makes Longinus so acute a critic.

The dwelling upon a particular scene or feeling is, of course, a kind of
amplification or αὔξησις, and by a natural association of ideas Longinus is
led to discuss amplification as such which he calls a quality or virtue,
though it is usually called a figure. He is mainly concerned (11-12, 2) to
point out that amplification as such is merely a quantitative matter which,
if divorced from the kind of selective and harmonizing talent which he has
just described, is quite ineffective. This is presumably what he means by
amplification without added greatness, but the discussion of it is, for us,
interrupted by another lacuna.

When the text emerges again a passionate and fiery orator is being
compared with another writer whose opulence spreads like a sea into wide
open grandeur. The orator is probably Demosthenes and the other may

---

[1] Cf. the statement of Aristotle to the same effect, above, p. 86 and pp. 291-2.

be Plato. At any rate, this is immediately followed by a delightful comparison of Demosthenes with Cicero (12, 4):

> In much the same way, my dear Terentianus, Cicero and Demosthenes differ in their great passages – in so far as a Greek like myself can judge.[1] The greatness of Demosthenes is usually more abrupt; Cicero more abundant. Our man is always violent, swift, strong and forceful; he may be compared to a flash of lightning or a thunderbolt which burns and ravages. Cicero is like an enveloping conflagration which spreads around us and crowds upon us; a vast steady fire which flares up intermittently in this direction and that . . .

but the whole comparison should be read. We then return to Plato and an illustration of his kind of smooth copiousness.

Plato is said to show another path to great writing, by way of *mimêsis*, the emulation of the great. Clearly Longinus uses mimesis in the broadest, not the restricted rhetorical, sense, for he compares it to the inspiration of the Pythian priestess at Delphi (13, 2).

> So from the genius of the ancients exhalations flow, as from the secret clefts, into the minds of those who emulate them, and even those not much given to inspiration become possessed by the greatness of others.

We are strongly advised, when labouring to write well, to ask ourselves 'how Homer would have expressed this, or Plato or Demosthenes, or in history how Thucydides would have made it into a great passage'. More than that, we should wonder what they would have thought of our work. And we should imagine ourselves also writing for posterity.

The last subject treated under the general heading of mental vigour is the power of the imagination or φαντασία and Longinus gives us a fuller discussion of it than any other ancient critic. He makes an interesting distinction between poetic imagination which seeks to enthral, and the oratorical which aims at vivid presentation. His first examples of oratorical imagination are from Euripides, always considered more oratorical and less poetic than his two great fellow-dramatists, while Sophocles is quoted for the best example of poetic imagination. The difference between the two kinds should not be forgotten as when our orators profess to see the Furies. Demosthenes can bring a scene most vividly before his readers' eyes, and Hyperides' saying 'It is not the present speaker who framed this proposal, but the battle of Chaeronea,' is also quoted with approval. The orator's vividly drawn pictures overbear their audience but they must remain within the limits of the probable, and only poetic imagination

---

[1] For this hesitation on the part of a Greek to discuss Latin authors see above, pp. 212-3.

should go beyond probability into the realm of the mythical and the incredible. The boundary between the two may well be blurred at times, as indeed Longinus' illustrations themselves show, but the distinction is a valid one nonetheless.

The first great source of greatness has now been dealt with; the second, πάθος, is, as we saw, reserved for special treatment. The third source was the use of figures of speech and thought. These, as we know, are generally dealt with by ancient critics at considerable length by means of long lists and illustrations. How many figures Longinus dealt with (he says he will take only a few) we do not know, for there is another lacuna at the end of the eighteenth chapter, but his manner of dealing with them is revealing. Not only are his illustrations of individual figures very apt and lively but he introduces the whole subject in the manner of a great teacher. He takes one famous example, the Marathon oath in Demosthenes' *On the Crown*, and analyses it in detail to illustrate his general principle that 'figures naturally reinforce greatness and are supported by it in turn', that the brilliance of the figure and the passion of the speaker can allay suspicion, indeed hide the very fact that an artful figure is being used. This is how he explains the effect of this figure of the oath. The passage is such a perfect example of Longinus' method that it deserves quotation at some length (16, 2)[1]:

> Demosthenes is trying to vindicate his policies. What would have been the natural way of treating his subject? 'You were not wrong, you who took up the fight for the liberty of Greece. You have precedents for this. Neither were they wrong who fought at Marathon, or at Salamis or at Plataea.' But when, like a man suddenly inspired and, as it were, god-possessed, he utters his oath by the heroes of Greece: 'You cannot have been wrong, by those who faced death at Marathon' . . . he seems to deify their ancestors by suggesting that one may invoke those who died such a death, as if they were gods; he recalls to the jury's mind their pride in those who there faced death; he turns what is essentially an argument into a supremely great and passionate passage by the appeal of this strange, extraordinary oath; he impresses his words, like some paean or charm, upon the minds of his hearers who are led by his praise to think with relief that they may take as much pride in their battle against Philip as in the victories of Marathon and

---

[1] *On the Crown* 208: 'It cannot be, it cannot be that you were wrong, men of Athens, in taking up the struggle on behalf of the liberty and salvation of all. No! – by those of your ancestors who faced danger at Marathon, by those who stood in the ranks at Plataea, by those who fought from their ships at Salamis and Artemisium, and many other brave men who lie in our public graves, all of whom the city deemed worthy of the same honour of a public funeral, Aeschines, not only those who were successful and victorious.'

Salamis. In all these ways the orator, by the use of this figure grips his audience and carries them along with him.

He then compares a similar, but somewhat frigid oath in a comedy of Eupolis and continues:

> In Demosthenes, the oath is carefully phrased for men who have suffered a defeat, so that the Athenians should no longer look upon Chaeroneia as a failure. This one figure is at the same time a proof that their action had not been wrong, a precedent, the confirmation of an oath, an encomium, and an exhortation. Then, to counter his opponent's objection: 'The policy you speak of led to defeat, and you swear by victories,' he carefully weighs every word and chooses those not open to the objection: 'Those who faced death at Marathon,' he says, 'those who fought in ships at Artemisium,' 'those who stood in the ranks at Plataea.' He does not use the word 'victorious' anywhere; he avoids any word which would indicate the outcome, since it was successful and the opposite of Chaeroneia. That is why, forestalling his hearers' thought, he immediately adds: 'To all of them, Aeschines, the city gave a public funeral, not only to those who were victorious.'

This is a beautiful piece of criticism which again explains the total effect by a precise analysis of detail, and in every detail it is completely right. He then briefly discusses individual figures. We may note the description of what happens when a Demosthenic asyndeton is rewritten in the manner of Isocrates (21, 2):

> As you expand the passage in this way, and smooth it by adding the connectives, you soon realize that its urgent, rugged passion is falling flat, its sting and its fire have vanished. Just as a runner is deprived of speed when his legs are tied, so passionate emotion resents being fettered by conjunctions and other connectives, its free course is impeded and its catapult-like impetus is lost.

There is also a fascinating description of Demosthenes' use of hyperbaton in his elaborate periods (22, 4):

> The idea from which he started is often left in suspense, and meanwhile he piles up extraneous matter in the middle of his sentence in an ostensibly strange and improbable order; he throws his hearers into a panic lest his whole argument collapse as his realistic vehemence compels them to run that risk with him; then, unexpectedly and after a long interval he comes to the long-awaited conclusion at the end, just at the right moment.

So much for figures. We then come to the choice of words, the third source of great writing, which (30, 1):

> endows our writing, like beautiful statues, with grandeur and beauty, mellowness, weight, strength, power and a certain brightness, thus endowing events with, as it were, a speaking soul . . . beautiful words are in truth the mind's peculiar light.

Unfortunately we come here upon another lacuna. When the text resumes we are in the middle of a sensible discussion of vulgarisms which Longinus allows if they are expressive and appropriate, like the saying of Theopompus that 'Philip had a talent for stomaching the inevitable' (ἀναγκοφαγῆσαι, 31, 1).

Metaphors are, as usual, discussed under diction (32). Here Longinus does not add very much to previous discussions except that he blames Caecilius for restricting the number of metaphors to three in any one passage, and rightly maintains that as long as the emotional tone can carry them there is no specific limit. To prove his point he quotes at length Plato's elaborate description of the creation of the human body in the *Timaeus* (69 c ff.). He then gives examples of bad metaphors from Plato which emboldened Caecilius to try to prove that Lysias is a better writer than Plato.

This leads to an interesting discussion as to which is to be preferred, flawless mediocrity or faulty genius, one of the best passages in the book. Would you rather, Longinus exclaims, be Apollonius than Homer? Eratosthenes than Archilochus? Ion than Sophocles? We may be somewhat surprised to find Apollonius of Rhodes described as flawless, but we will certainly endorse his vigorously expressed preference for the writers of genius, careless as they often are. He takes as his particular examples Hyperides and Demosthenes, and gives a long list of Hyperides' virtues, none of which Demosthenes possessed (34, 3):

> Demosthenes has no sense of character, no easy flow of words; he is not at all smooth, nor good at display. He lacks, for the most part, all the qualities just mentioned. Where he forces himself to utter a jest or witticism, the audience does not laugh with him but at him; when he aims at graceful charm he least achieves it. . . . But no one is awed when reading Hyperides whereas Demosthenes draws upon his noble nature for qualities which are quite perfect . . . and by the fine qualities he does possess he surpasses all men and rises above his deficiencies. He out-thunders and out-shines the orators of all the ages. His hearers can no more resist his successive outbursts of passion and remain unmoved than gaze with open eyes at a falling thunderbolt.

Demosthenes is great in spite of the fact that he lacks many (secondary) qualities. Plato is great in spite of his many faults and mistakes.[1] And Longinus follows this up with a lyrical passage upon the vision of the demi-gods of literature which comes back once more to his first source of great writing, the power to grasp great conceptions (35-36).

> Impeccability escapes all reproach, but greatness is the object of our wonder and admiration. What need to add that each of those great writers redeems all his faults by one successful stroke of greatness ... since the avoidance of error is mostly due to the successful application of the rules of the art while supremacy belongs to genius, it is fitting that art should everywhere give its help to nature. The two together may produce perfection.

The fifth and last source of great writing was the arrangement of words, a subject with which Longinus tells us he has already dealt with in two published works, so that he here deals with it very briefly. He puts most of his emphasis on rhythm, in an almost lyrical passage which extols the music of language as the highest form of music, since it also expresses meaning and therefore appeals to the mind as well as the senses (the following extract in the Greek is one highly elaborated sentence, itself adorned with carefully constructed rhythms, 39, 2):

> Does not the music of the flute stir the emotions of an audience, take them out of themselves, free them with Corybantic frenzy, and by its rhythmic beat compel the hearer to step to its rhythm and identify himself with its tune, even if he be quite unmusical? Yes, in truth it does, and the notes of the lyre, though they carry no meaning, often cast a marvellous spell, as you know, by the variation of sounds, their rapid succession and the mingling of their concords. Yet these are but images and bastard imitations of persuasion and not, as I said, among the nobler pursuits of our human nature. Shall we not then believe that word-arrangement – that music of rational speech which is in man inborn and appeals not only to the ear but to the mind itself – as it sets in motion a variety of words, thoughts, events, and evokes beautiful melodies, all of them born and bred within us, instills the speaker's feelings by the blended variety of its sounds into the heart of those near him and makes those who hear him share his passion? It charms us by the architecture of its phrases as it builds up the music of great passages which casts a spell upon us and, by its sway over our mind,

---

[1] This is clearly the general meaning of the passage, though the text is uncertain. The conjecture ὁ Λύσιας for ἀπουσίας, adopted by all editors, spoils the sense. See *AJP* 78 (1957), 371-4.

ever predisposes us to dignity, honour, greatness and all the qualities it holds within itself.

Longinus then takes a Demosthenic sentence to show that a simple change in the order of words, or even the addition of one syllable by using a lengthened form, completely alters the rhythm and therefore the total effect of the sentence.[1] He then (40) notes how the structure and harmony of a whole sentence or passage must be seen as one unit. Thus it is possible to achieve greatness without using any but the most ordinary words, through a striking word-order, and he gives two quotations from Euripides to show that even those not gifted with poetic genius can achieve greatness.[2] The collocation of sounds alone can do this. Like all the critics, Longinus dislikes short and broken rhythms which result from the excessive use of the pyrrhic ($\cup\cup$), the trochee ($-\cup$) and the double trochee ($-\cup-\cup$); any obvious rhythms easily perceived by the audience must of course be avoided. So must short, rhythmic phrases, which break up the sequence of thought.

One further point is made which belongs to diction rather than word-arrangement, namely that a trivial expression can completely spoil a great passage, and he quotes a passage of Theopompus to prove it.

Then we suddenly come to the last chapter (44) on the reasons for the decay of eloquence. An unnamed philosopher who had recently investigated the question speaks first and gives the lack of freedom as the cause: 'as in the case of the dwarfs we call Pygmies, not only do the cages in which they are kept stunt their growth, but their bonds, I am informed, actually make their bodies shrink, so slavery of every kind, even the best, can be shown to be the cage and common prison house of the soul' (44, 5).

Longinus replies that we are too inclined to blame external circumstances; it is not the peace of the world which destroys great talents, but the love of luxury, the greed for money, and the corruption they bring. 'The love of gold is a disease which shrinks a man, and the love of pleasure is ignoble.' He elaborates and amplifies this theme at considerable length, a rhetorical set piece which many commentators say betrays a deep emotional concern. It may be so, but I cannot but feel that it is magnificent rhetoric, but rather like a declamation on a commonplace topic. In any case, it has no connexion with the rest of the treatise, it says nothing new, and its main importance is that it is often taken to favour a first-century date.

I have, to a large extent, let our author speak for himself because his

---

[1] The sentence is from On the Crown 188: τοῦτο τὸ ψήφισμα τὸν τότε τῇ πόλει περιστάντα κίνδυνον παρελθεῖν ἐποίησεν ὥσπερ νέφος. ('This decree caused the danger which then threatened the city to disappear like a cloud.') Either ὡς νέφος or ὡσπερεὶ νέφος would spoil the rhythm, i.e. $--\cup\triangledown$ would become $-\cup\triangledown$ or $-\cup-\cup\triangledown$.

[2] For this type of criticism of Euripides see p. 95, and Poetics 1453 a 24-30.

meaning is always clear and he expresses it better than I could possibly do. Our treatise needs little explanation of its ideas because Longinus, more than any other ancient critic, speaks a language that the modern reader can understand without intermediary.

The enjoyment to be derived from the treatise *On Great Writing* is, I believe, due mainly to two things: the independence and originality of the author's mind and his own very considerable ability as a writer. He obviously was fully familiar with all the rhetorical formulae of his predecessors but he remains their master, they never master him, as we saw in the way he dealt with the subject of figures. One might say that the first source of greatness, namely vigour and nobility of mind, is essentially the same as the rhetoricians' εὕρεσις or *inventio*, yet great writing as 'the echo of a noble mind' is a very different thing indeed. Even the concept of *mimêsis* or emulation is expressed in a new and more significant manner. At all points where he uses them Longinus puts new flesh on the old formulaic bones, and thus creates something new.

The whole structure of the book, based on the five sources of greatness, is new and original as far as we know, and it is far more alive and significant than any other scheme we know, be it the old parts of a speech, the duties of the orator, or the poem-poetry-poet formula. We have noted too that our author puts far more emphasis on the mind and qualities of the artist than anyone had done since Plato. And the formula of styles has completely disappeared.

Above all, Longinus has a very deep and genuine feeling for great writing and can communicate that feeling but at the same time he has an Aristotelian capacity for precise detail. And it is this combination of mental vigour with real passion and severe intellectual analysis that makes our author a unique phenomenon in the history of ancient criticism.

Epilogue

We have now followed the reflections of ancient writers about literature, both prose and poetry, through nearly a thousand years of literary activity in Greece and Rome, as far as our extant texts make it possible to do so. It is obvious that the most original, challenging and seminal ideas were provided by the philosophers, especially by Plato and Aristotle in the fourth century B.C., and we may now give a brief last word to another philosopher in the third century A.D., then our tale will be told. Plotinus, the founder of Neo-platonism, has unfortunately not given us any consecutive theory of art, so that his ideas on the subject have to be gathered from incidental references of varying importance.[1] Further, where the arts are mentioned, it is either the plastic arts or music which he has in mind, and little or nothing is said about the art of words, though the echoes of Plato's discussions of poetry are so clear that what he says must be taken as applying to it also.[2] Any clear and thought-out theory of art is hard to extract from these almost casual references, but one point in particular is clear and relevant to our purpose, namely Plotinus' attitude to the Platonic-Aristotelian theory of art as imitation.

At certain times, presumably in the earlier essays, he adopts the Platonic theory of imitation in its crudest forms 'art ($\tau\acute{\epsilon}\chi\nu\eta$) comes after nature and imitates it, creating dim and feeble imitations ($\mu\iota\mu\acute{\eta}\mu\alpha\tau\alpha$), playthings of no great value, by using all kinds of devices in the productions of these images'.[3] He repeats the statement elsewhere but qualifies it: 'Those arts which are imitative, painting and sculpture, dancing and the gestures of pantomime, are products of this (physical) world; they have a sensible model, imitate and transpose its visible shapes, movements and symmetries, and one would be wrong to refer them to the intelligible world, except by way of the reason in man. But if the contemplation of the symmetry of living things rises to that of the symmetry of all living things, it is then a part of that faculty which yonder also contemplates the symmetry of all things in the intelligible world.'[4]

Other passages put the products of art on a par with the objects of

---

[1] On this subject see Eugenie De Keyser, *La Signification de l'art dans les Ennéades de Plotin*.

[2] E.g. 6, 4, 10, 12-17 where he points out that a portrait is *not* like an image in water or a mirror, for it continues to exist independently of its model, a clear contradiction of *Republic* 6, 510 e; also 1, 6, 3, 6-16 where he speaks of the form in the mind of the artist; and 5, 8, 1, 32-40, where he is answering 'anyone who despises the arts because they imitate nature. . .'.

[3] 4, 3, 10, 17-19.   [4] 5, 9, 11, 1-8 and the rest of the section.

nature and speak of the Form or of the craft itself in the mind of the artist, point out that a portrait continues to exist independently of its model so that the parallel with images in water, etc.[1] is mistaken, and so we come to the denial of the products of art as mere imitations of things.[2] A stone statue derives its beauty from the form impressed upon it. This form was not in the stone but in the mind of the sculptor, which is possessed of the art. And the beauty of this form in the mind, deriving as it does from the Form in the intelligible, is greater than any beauty in matter:

> If anyone despises the arts, because they create by imitating nature, one should point out to him first that natural objects imitate other (and higher) things. Then one must realize that the arts do not merely imitate what they see but go on back to the reasonable principles (or Forms) from which nature derives. Further, that they add what is lacking, since they possess beauty. Phidias made his statue of Zeus without reference to a visible model, but he grasped what Zeus would be like if he wished to make himself appear before our eyes.

We will not pursue a number of questions which this passage raises for students of Plotinus, the main point of interest to us being that the artist's products now reflect the intelligible directly, and not merely by way of particular objects. The form of the 'real statue' in the artist's mind is itself a reflection or emanation of the true Form in the overall Mind.

This is the only challenge in antiquity to the Platonic theory of art as mere imitation of physical nature, though we have seen that the seeds of this view can be found in certain Platonic passages themselves.[3] Unfortunately, Plotinus does not follow this up, and we have no consistent theory of art from his pen.

With the third century we come to the age of the compilers and commentators. At the beginning of the century we have Philostratus' *Lives of the Sophists* from which we have already quoted and Diogenes Laertius' *Lives of the Philosophers*. These books frequently preserve valuable information for us, in so far as they quote earlier sources, as when Diogenes by good fortune gives us the text of the actual letters of Epicurus, but these authors carry no authority themselves, have no consistent theory or point of view, and suffer equally from 'anecdotage', that is they give us a number of anecdotes from the lives they describe but do not give us a unitary view of these lives or personalities, such as Plutarch and Suetonius, themselves much given to anecdotes, had yet so successfully done in an earlier age. We also have that extraordinary collection of scattered information, gossip and trivialities on matters of all sorts, with special attention to food, wine and courtesans, but not excluding language and literature, the *Deipnosophistae* or *Sophists at Dinner* by Athenaeus. In Latin, the *Saturnalia* of Macrobius (early fourth century) is a banquet of much the same kind. These books cater to a kind of erudite curiosity which takes the place of real learning.

The greatest disappointment, however, are the commentators, Porphyrio on Horace in the third century, Donatus and Servius on Virgil in the fourth. They wrote commentaries on these great authors as schoolbooks, helps to teachers as it were, line by line exegesis of the texts, explanations of linguistic, rhetorical and mythological points, extremely detailed but hardly ever rising to anything that deserves the name of criticism.[1] This throws a great deal of light upon the teaching methods of the *grammatici* in the contemporary schools. The languages they taught, both Greek and Latin, were now dead languages, and this may explain in part the popularity of the Roman grammarians – Charisius, Diomede and their like, also the emphasis on linguistic points, until in the West at least, the *grammatici* became much more numerous than the rhetoricians. But rhetoric too continued to be taught in exactly the same way as before, with the same rules and the same lists of figures. Significantly, on the Latin side, it is the *Ad Herennium* and Cicero's *De Inventione* which become the favourite textbooks, while Cicero's real educational theories, and those of Quintilian, are completely forgotten. Declamations continue in the rhetorical schools with all the vices which we have seen so vigorously denounced by the critics of the first century. It is all very much a closed system, ossified, unchanging and purely rhetorical, more and more divorced, in language, content and interests, from the life of the nations, until we come to the world of Sidonius Apollinaris in the fifth century,[2] a Gaul with an excellent classical education, writing artistic letters and poems in more or less Classical Latin with the barbarian invasions swirling all around him. He did indeed take part in affairs, but his literary pursuits, his imitations of, in this case, the younger Pliny as well as the classical poets, are good examples of what has been called the cult of the antique.

Meanwhile a new kind of literature had grown up, that of the Christian fathers, both Greek and Latin, beginning in the second century with Irenaeus and Clement in Greek and Tertullian in Latin. This literature may be said to culminate in St. Augustine in the fifth century and there we can find new theories of education and of literature and a new attitude, but that is a very different tale and the beginning of a different civilization.

[1] See R. R. Bolgar, *The Classical heritage*, 26-45, especially p. 41 and note p. 396 where he analyses the percentages of notes of different types of Servius' commentary on the second book of the *Aeneid*.

[2] See André Loyen, *Sidoine Apollinaire et l'esprit précieux*, and on this whole subject, H. I. Marrou, *Saint Augustin et la fin de la culture antique*, pp. 1-157.

Bibliography

This bibliography contains only the books and articles referred to in the notes, and a very few others of general interest which may not have been specifically referred to.

S. M. Adams: 'Pindar and the origin of tragedy', *Phoenix* 1955, 170-4.

S. Albertis: 'La définition de la tragédie et la catharsis', *Archives de Philosophie* 21 (1958) 60-75.

R. Altschul: *De Demetrii rhetoris aetate*, Leipzig, 1889.

A. Andrewes: 'The Mytelene debate', *Phoenix* 1962, 64-85.

A. Ardizzoni: Ποίημα, *Richerche sulla teoria del linguaccio poetico nell' antichita*, Bari, 1953.

H. von Arnim: *Leben und Werke des Dio von Prusa*, Berlin 1898.

J. W. H. Atkins: *Literary Criticism in antiquity* 2 vols., Cambridge, 1934, reprinted London, 1952.

C. Augustyniak: *De tribus et quattuor dicendi generibus quid docuerunt antiqui*, Warsaw, 1957.

G. Avenarius: *Lukians Schrift zur Geschichtsschreibung*, Meisenheim/Glan, 1956.

G. Bagnani: *Arbiter of Elegance*, Toronto, 1954.
'Petroniana' in *Studies in honour of Berthold Louis Ullman*, Rome, 1964, vol. 1, 229-39.

G. W. Baker: 'De comicis Graecis litterarum iudiciis' *HSCP* 15 (1904) 121-240.

F. Th. Baldwin: *The Bellum civile of Petronius*, New York, 1911.

E. Barker: *The Politics of Aristotle* (transl.), Oxford, 1946.

K. Barwick: 'Die Gliederung der rhetorischen *TEXNH* und die Horazische Epistula ad Pisones', *Hermes* 57 (1952) 1-62.
Probleme der Stoischen Sprachlehre und Rhetorik, Berlin, 1957.
Martial und die zeitgenössische Rhetorik, Berlin, 1959.

H. Beare: 'Horace, Donatus and the five act law', *Hermathena* 67 (1946) 52-59.

C. Bekker: *Das Spätwerk des Horaz*, Göttingen, 1963.

G. E. Benseler (with F. Blass): *Isocratis opera*, Leipzig (Teubner), 1907.

J. Bernays: *Zwei Abhandlungen über die Aristotelische Theorie des Drama*, Berlin, 1880.

F. Blass: see Benseler.

R. Bolgar: *The Classical heritage and its beneficiaries*, Cambridge, 1954.

J. Bompaire: *Lucien écrivain*, Paris, 1958.

S. F. Bonner: *The literary treatises of Dionysius of Halicarnassus*, Cambridge, 1939.
    Roman Declamations in the late Republic and early Empire, Liverpool, 1949.

H. Bornecque: *Les Déclamations et les Déclamateurs d'après Sénèque le père*, Lille,
    1902.
    Les clausules métriques latines, Lille, 1907.
    Sénèque le rhéteur, Controverses et Suasoires (text and transl.), Paris, 1932, 2 vols.
    (with H. Goelzer): *Tacite: Dialogue des orateurs*, Paris (Budé), 1947.

A. Boulanger: *Aelius Aristide et la sophistique dans la province d'Asie au deuxième
    siècle de notre ère*, Paris, 1923.

C. O. Brink: *Horace on poetry*, Cambridge, 1963.
    'Callimachus and Aristotle', *CQ* 1946, 11-26.
    'Tragic history and Aristotle's school', *Proc. Cambridge Philol. Soc.* 186 (1960)
    14-19.
    'Horace and Varro', *Varron* (Entretiens Hardt IX), Geneva, 1962, 175-206.

M. D. Brock: *Studies in Fronto and his age*, Cambridge, 1911.

J. Brody: *Boileau et Longin*, Geneva, 1958.

S. H. Butcher: *Aristotle's theory of poetry and fine art*, London, 1894 and New York,
    1951.

H. E. Butler: *The Institutio oratoria of Quintilian*, Harvard and London (Loeb), 4
    vols., 1921-2, repr. 1953.

I. Bywater: *Aristotle on the art of poetry*, Oxford, 1909.

H. Caplan: *Rhetorica ad Herennium*, Harvard and London (Loeb), 1954.

P. Cauer: *Grundfragen der Homerkritik*[3], Leipzig, 1921.

J. W. Cohoon (with H. L. Crosby): *Dio Chrysostom*, Harvard and London (Loeb),
    5 vols., 1932-51.

J. Collart: *Varron, Grammairien latin*, Paris, 1954.
    'Analogie et Anomalie', *Varron* (Entretiens Hardt IX), Geneva, 1962, 120-40.

A. Collignon: *Etude sur Pétrone*, Paris, 1892.

Churton Collins: *Studies in poetry and criticism*, London, 1905.

F. H. Colson: 'The analogist and anomalist controversy', *CQ* 13 (1919) 24-36.

Lane Cooper: *An Aristotelian theory of comedy*, New York, 1922.

J. A. Cramer: *Anecdota Graeca Biblioth. regiae Paris*, Oxford, 1839-41.

J. Croissant: *Aristote et les mystères*, Liège and Paris, 1932.

H. L. Crosby: see Cohoon.

H. Dachs: *Die Λύσις ἐκ τοῦ προσώπου*, Erlangen, 1913.

H. Dahlman: *Varro und die hellenistische Sprachtheorie*, Berlin, 1932.
    Varro's Schrift de poematis und die hellenistisch-römische Poetik, Wiesbaden, 1953

J. F. D'Alton: *Roman literary theory and criticism*, London, 1931 and New York,
    1962.

G. D'Anna: *Le Idee litterarie di Suetonio*, Florence, 1954.

E. De Keyser: *La signification de l'art dans les Ennéades de Plotin*, Louvain, 1955.

Ph. De Lacy: 'The Epicurean analysis of language', *AJP* 60 (1939) 65-92.
'Stoic Views of poetry', *AJP* 69 (1948) 241-71.

C. A. De Leeuw: *Aelius Aristides als bron voor de kennis van zyn tyd*, Amsterdam, 1939.

D. De Montmollin: *La Poétique d'Aristote*, Neuchâtel, 1951.

J. D. Denniston: *Euripides Electra*, Oxford, 1939 (repr. 1954).
'Technical terms in Aristophanes', *CQ* 21 (1927) 113-21.

J. De Romilly: *Thucydide et l'impérialisme athénien*, Paris, 1947.
Histoire et raison chez Thucydide, Paris, 1956.

A. Desmouliez: 'Cicéron et les Atticistes', *REL* 30 (1952) 168-85.

H. Diels: *Die Fragmente der Vorsokratiker* 6, Berlin, 1951-2, 3 vols.

J. Wight Duff: *A Literary History of Rome*, London, 1909 etc.

I. Düring: *Aristotle in the ancient literary tradition*, Göteborg, 1957.

J. M. Edmonds: *The Fragments of Attic comedy*, Leiden, 3 vols., 1957-61.

E. Egger: *Essai sur l'histoire de la critique chez les Grecs*, Paris, 1886.

M. Egger: *Denys d' Halicarnasse*, Paris, 1902.

G. F. Else: *Aristotle's Poetics, The Argument*, Harvard, 1957.

P. Faidier: 'La vie littéraire à Rome sous le règne de Néron et le rêve de Sénèque', *Les Etudes Classiques* 1934, 1-16.

G. C. Fiske (with Mary L. Grant): *Cicero's De Oratore and Horace's Ars Poetica*, Madison, 1929.
(with same): 'Cicero's *Orator* and the *Ars Poetica*', *HSCP* 35 (1924) 1-75.

E. Fraenkel: *Horace*, Oxford, 1957.

K. von Fritz: 'Aufbau und Absicht des Dialogus de Oratoribus', *Rhein. Mus.* 81 (1932) 275-300.

G. Funaioli: *Grammaticae Romanae Fragmenta*, Leipzig (Teubner), 1909.

H. Goelzer: see Bornecque.

A. W. Gomme: *A historical commentary on Thucydides*, Oxford, 1956, 3 vols. published.

G. P. Goold: 'A Greek professorial circle in Rome', *TAPA* 92 (1961) 168-92.

M. L. Grant: see Fiske.

W. L. Grant: 'Cicero and the *Tractatus Coislinianus*', *AJP* 49 (1948) 80-86.

N. A. Greenberg: *The Poetic Theory of Philodemus*, Harvard thesis (unpublished), summarized *HSCP* 1957, 146-8.
'Metathesis as an instrument in the criticism of poetry', *TAPA* 89 (1958) 262-70.
'The use of Poiema and Poiesis', *HSCP* 65 (1961) 263-89.

W. Chase Greene: 'Plato's view of poetry', *HSCP* 29 (1918) 1-76.

B. P. Grenfell and A. S. Hunt: *The Hibeh Papyri* (Part I), London, 1906.

A. Grosskinsky: *Das Programm des Thukydides*, Berlin, 1936.

G. M. A. Grube: *Plato's Thought*, London, 1935 and Boston, 1958.

The Drama of Euripides, London, 1941 repr. 1961.

Longinus on Great Writing (transl.), New York, 1957.

Aristotle on Poetry and Style (transl.), New York, 1958.

A Greek Critic, Demetrius On Style, Toronto, 1961.

'Dionysius of Halicarnassus on Thucydides', *Phoenix* 4 (1950) 95-110.

'Theophrastus as a Literary critic', *TAPA* 83 (1952) 172-80.

'Notes on the περὶ ὕψους', *AJP* 78 (1957) 335-74.

'Thrasymachus, Theophrastus and Dionysius of Halicarnassus', *AJP* 73 (1952) 251-67.

'A note on Aristotle's definition of tragedy', *Phoenix* 12 (1958) 26-30.

'Theodorus of Gadara', *AJP* 80 (1959) 337-65.

'The date of Demetrius On Style', *Phoenix* 1964, 294-302

A. Gudeman: *Aristoteles περὶ ποιητικῆς*, Berlin and Leipzig, 1934.

P. Cornelii Taciti Dialogus de Oratoribus, Boston, 1894.

A. M. Guillemin: *Pline et la vie littéraire de son temps*, Paris, 1929.

Le public et la vie littéraire à Rome, Paris, 1927.

'L'imitation dans les littératures antiques', *REL* 2 (1924) 35-57.

La lettre de Cicéron à Lucceius, *REL* 16 (1938) 96 ff.

R. Hackforth: *Plato's Phaedrus*, Cambridge, 1952.

C. R. Haines: *The correspondence of Marcus Cornelius Fronto*, Harvard and London (Loeb), 2 vols., 1919-20 etc.

V. Hall: *A short history of literary criticism*, New York, 1963.

A. M. Harmon: *Lucian*, Harvard and London (Loeb), 7 vols., 1913 etc.

A. Haury: *L'ironie et l'humour chez Cicéron*, Leiden, 1955.

G. L. Hendrickson: 'A pre-Varronian chapter in literary history', *AJP* 19 (1898) 285-311.

'Horace and Lucilius', *Studies in honour of Basil L. Gildersleeve*, Baltimore, 1902.

'The origin and meaning of the ancient characters of style', *AJP* 26 (1905) 248-90.

'The De Analogia of Julius Caesar', *CP* 1 (1906) 97-120.

'Horace, Serm. I, 4', *AJP* 21 (1910) 121-42.

'Horace and Valerius Cato', *CP* 11 (1916) 249-69; also *CP* 12 (1917) 77-92 and 329-50.

'An Epigram of Philodemus and two Latin congeners', *AJP* 39 (1918) 27-41.

'Cicero's correspondence with Brutus and Calvus on oratorical style', *AJP* 47 (1926) 234-58.

Humphrey House: *Aristotle's Poetics*, London, 1956.

H. M. Hubbell: *The influence of Isocrates on Cicero, Dionysius and Aristides*, New Haven, 1913.

The Rhetoric of Philodemus (transl.), New Haven, 1920, in Transactions Connect. Acad. of Arts and Science.

Cicero: De Inventione, De optimo genere oratorum, and Topica, Harvard and London (Loeb), 1949.

'Isocrates and the Epicureans', *CP* 11 (1916) 405-25.

C. N. Jackson: 'Molle atque facetum', *HSCP* 25 (1914) 117-37.

W. Jaeger: *Paideia*, transl. G. Highet, Oxford, vol. 1, 1939; vol. 2, 1943; and vol. 3, 1944.

R. C. Jebb: *The growth and influence of Classical poetry*, London, 1893.
The Attic Orators from Antiphon to Isaeus, London, 1876, 2 vols.

Chr. Jensen: *Philodemus über die Gedichte, fünftes Buch*, Berlin, 1923.
'Herakleides von Pontus bei Philodem und Horaz', *Sitzungsberichte Pruss. Akad.*, 1936, 292-320.

R. Johnson: 'A note on the number of Isocrates' pupils', *AJP* 78 (1957) 297-300.
'Isocrates' methods of teaching', *AJP* 80 (1959) 25-36.

W. P. Johnston: *Greek literary criticism*, Oxford (Chancellor's essay), 1907.

B. Jowett: *Aristotle's Politics* (transl.), Oxford, 1916.

G. Kaibel: *Die Prolegomena περὶ κωμῳδίας*, Berlin, 1898.

H. Keil: *Grammatici Latini*, Leipzig (Teubner), 1855-80.

G. A. Kennedy: *The art of persuasion in Greece*, Princeton, 1963.
'Theophrastus and stylistic distinctions', *HSCP* 1957, 97 ff.
'An estimate of Quintilian', *AJP* 83 (1962) 130-46.

R. G. Kent: *Varro on the Latin language*, Harvard and London (Loeb), 1938, repr. 1951, 2 vols.

Ch. Knapp: 'Molle atque facetum', *AJP* 38 (1917) 194-9.

A. Körte: 'Augusteer bei Philodem', *Rhein. Mus.* 45 (1890) 172-7.
'Charactêr', *Hermes* 64 (1929) 69-86.

H. Koskennieni: 'Studien zur Idee und Phraseologie des griechiscen Briefes bis 400 n. Chr.', *Annales acad. Scient. Fennicae*, Helsinki, 1956.

W. Kroll: 'Rhetorik' in *RE*, suppl. vii, 1039-138, Stuttgart, 1940.
Studien zur Verständnis der römischen Literatur, Stuttgart, 1924.
M. Tullii Ciceronis Orator, Berlin, 1958.

J. Labarbe: *L'Homère de Platon*, Liège, 1949.

K. Lehrs: *De Aristarchi Studiis Homericis*, Leipzig, 1882.

P. Lévêque: *Agathon*, Paris, 1955.

D. Loenen: *Protagoras and the Greek community*, Amsterdam, 1941.

A. Loyen: *Sidoine Apollinaire et l'esprit précieux en Gaulle aux derniers jours de l'Empire*, Paris, 1943.

F. L. Lucas: *Tragedy: serious drama in relation to Aristotle's Poetics*, London, 1957.

A. Macé: *Essai sur Suétone*, Paris, 1900.

A. Ph. McMahon: 'On the second book of Aristotle's *Poetics* and the sources of Theophrastus' definition of tragedy', *HSCP* 28 (1917) 1-46.
'Seven questions on Aristotle's definitions of tragedy and comedy', *HSCP* 40 (1929) 97-202.

R. Marache: *La critique littéraire de langue latine et le développement du goût archaïsant au IIe siècle de notre ère*, Rennes, 1952.
Mots nouveaux et mots archaïques chez Fronton et Aulu-Gelle, Presses Universitaires de France, 1957.

H. I. Marrou: *Histoire de l'éducation dans l'antiquité*, Paris, 1950.
Saint Augustin et la fin de la culture antique, Paris, 1938.

F. Marx: *C. Lucillii Carminum Reliquiae*, Leipzig, 1904.

D. Matthes: 'Hermagoras von Temnos', *Lustrum* 3 (1958) 58-214.
Hermagoras, Fragmenta, Leipzig (Teubner), 1962.

H. J. Mette: *Parateresis, Untersuchungen zur Sprachtheorie des Krates von Pergamum*, Halle, 1952.

A. Michel: *Rhétorique et philosophie chez Cicéron*, Paris, 1960.

S. H. Monk: *The Sublime, a study of critical theories in eighteenth century England*, New York, 1935.

P. Moraux: *Les listes anciennes des ouvrages d'Aristote*, Louvain, 1951.

H. Mutschman: *Tendenz, Aufbau und Quellen der Schrift vom Erhabenen*, Berlin, 1913.

E. Norden: 'Die Composition und Literatursgattung der Horazische Epistula ad Pisones', *Hermes* 40 (1905) 481-528.
Die antike Kunstprosa, 2 vols., Leipzig, 1898, repr. Stuttgart, 1958.

G. Norwood: *Pindar*, Berkeley, 1945.

E. Ofenloch: *Caecilii Calactini Fragmenta*, Leipzig (Teubner), 1907.

W. R. Paton: *The Greek Anthology*, Harvard and London (Loeb), 5 vols., 1916-18.

W. Peterson: *Cornelii Taciti Dialogus de oratoribus*, Oxford, 1893.
Tacitus Dialogus, Harvard and London (Loeb), 1914 etc.

R. Pfeiffer: *Callimachus*, 2 vols., Oxford, 1949 and 1953.

J. A. Philip: 'Mimêsis in the *Sophistes* of Plato', *TAPA* 92 (1961) 453-68.

A. Pickard-Cambridge: *Dithyramb, Tragedy and Comedy*, Oxford, 1962.

L. J. Potts: *Aristotle on the art of Fiction* (transl.), Cambridge, 1953.

K. Preston: 'Martial and formal literary criticism', *CP* 15 (1920) 340-52.

A. Quiller-Couch: *Studies in literature*, Cambridge, 1929.

H. Rabe: *De Theophrasti libris περὶ λέξεως*, Bonn, 1890.
Prolegomenon Sylloge, Leipzig (Teubner), 1931.
Syrianus in Hermogenem Commentaria, Leipzig (Teubner), 2 vols., 1892 and 1893.

H. Rackham: *Rhetorica ad Alexandrum*, Harvard and London (Loeb), 1937, repr. 1957.
Cicero, De Oratore, Harvard and London (Loeb), 1942 etc. 2 vols. (with E. W. Sutton).

L. Radermacher (with H. Usener): *Dionysii Halicarnassi Opuscula*, 2 vols., Leipzig (Teubner), 1909.
Demetrii Phalerei qui dicitur de elocutione libellus, Leipzig, 1901.

J. M. Rist: 'Demetrius the stylist and Artemon the compiler', *Phoenix* 18 (1964) 2-8.

W. Rhys Roberts: *Dionysius of Halicarnassus, The three literary letters*, Cambridge, 1901.

Demetrius On Style, Cambridge, 1902.

Longinus On the Sublime, Cambridge, 1907.

Dionysius On Literary Composition, Cambridge, 1910.

Greek rhetoric and literary criticism, New York, 1928.

'References to Plato in Aristotle's *Rhetoric*', *CP* 19 (1924) 342-6.

'Caecilius of Calacte', *AJP* 18 (1897) 302-12.

A. Roemer: *Aristarch's Athetezen in der Homerkritik*, Leipzig, 1912.

Die Homerexegese Aristarchs in ihren Grundzügen, edited by E. Belzner, Paderborn, 1924.

B. Rogers: *Aristophanes, Frogs*, London, 1923.

J. C. Rolfe: *Suetonius*, Harvard and London (Loeb), 2 vols., 1913-14.

H. J. Rose: *The Eclogues of Virgil*, Berkeley, 1942.

V. Rose: *Aristotelis Fragmenta*, Leipzig (Teubner), 1886.

A. Rostagni: *Scritti Minori*, Turino, 3 vols., 1955.

Anonimi del Sublime, Milan, 1947.

W. J. N. Rudd: 'Had Horace been criticized, a study of Serm. I, 4', *AJP* 76 (1955) 165-75.

'The Poet's defence i and ii, a study of Serm. I, 4', *CQ* 1955, 142-56.

'The names in Horace's Satires', *CQ* N.S. 10 (1960) 161-78.

D. A. Russell: *Longinus On the Sublime*, Oxford, 1964.

W. G. Rutherford: *A chapter in the history of annotation*, London, 1905.

G. Saintsbury: *A History of criticism*, London, 1908.

J. E. Sandys: *A History of Classical scholarship* 3, Cambridge, 1903.

The odes of Pindar, London and New York (Loeb), 1915.

M. Schanz: 'Die Apollodoreer und die Theodoreer', *Hermes* 25 (1890) 36-54.

P. M. Schuhl: *Platon et l'art de son temps*, Paris, 1933.

H. K. Schulte: *Ciceronis Orator*, Frankfurt, 1935.

R. Sealy: 'Dionysius of Halicarnassus and some Demosthenic dates', *REG* 68 (1955) 77-120.

A. Severyns: *Le Cycle épique dans l'école d'Aristarque*, Liège, 1928.

E. E. Sikes: *The Greek view of poetry*, London, 1931.

C. N. Smiley: 'Seneca and the Stoic theory of literary style', *Studies in honour of Ch. Foster Smith*, Madison, 1919.

H. W. Smyth: *Greek Melic Poets*, London, 1900.

F. Solmsen: 'Demetrios περὶ ἑρμηνείας und sein peripatisches Quellenmaterial', *Hermes* 66 (1931) 241-67.

'Drei Rekonstruktionen zur antike Rhetorik und Poetik', *Hermes* 67 (1932) 133-54.

'The origins and methods of Aristotle's Poetics', *CQ* 29 (1935) 192-201.

'Aristotle and Cicero on the orator's playing upon the feelings', *CP* 33 (1938) 390-404.

'The Aristotelian tradition in ancient rhetoric', *AJP* 62 (1941) 35-50 and 169-90.

L. Spengel: *Rhetores Graeci*, Leipzig, 1853-6 - first volume revised and edited by Hammer, Stuttgart, 1928.

W. J. M. Starkie: *The Acharnians of Aristophanes*, London, 1909.

J. Stroux: *De Theophrasti virtutibus dicendi*, Leipzig, 1912.

F. H. Stubbings: see Wace.

S. Sudhaus: *Philodemi volumina rhetorica*, 2 vols. and supplement, Leipzig (Teubner), 1902-6.

E. W. Sutton: see Rackham.

J. Sykutris: Epistolographie, *RE*, Suppl. (1931) 185-220.

R. Syme: *Tacitus*, 2 vols., Oxford, 1958.
'The friend of Tacitus', *JRS* 47 (1957) 131-5.

J. R. M. Tait: *Philodemus' influence on the Latin poets*, Bryn Mawr, 1941.

J. Tate: 'The beginnings of Greek allegory', *CR* 41 (1927) 214-15.
'Plato and allegorical interpretation', *CQ* 23 (1929) 142-54 and *CQ* 24 (1930) 1-10.
'Socrates and the myths', *CQ* 27 (1933) 74-80, and in the same volume his controversy with A. E. Taylor, 158-61.
'On the history of allegorism', *CQ* 28 (1934) 105-14.

G. Thiele: *Hermagoras, ein Beitrag zur Geschichte der Rhetorik*, Strasburg, 1893.

B. L. Ullman: 'History and Tragedy', *TAPA* 73 (1942) 25-57.

H. Usener: see Radermacher.

M. P. J. Van Den Hout: *M. Cornelii Frontonis Epistolae*, Leiden, 1954.

A. J. B. Wace and F. H. Stubbings: *A companion to Homer*, London, 1962.

F. W. Walbank: *A historical commentary on Polybius*, vol. i, Oxford, 1957.
'History and Tragedy', *Historia* 9 (1960) 216-34.

W. P. Wallace: 'Thucydides', *Phoenix* 1964, 251-61.

Chr. Walz: *Rhetores Graeci*, 9 vols. Stuttgart, 1832-6.

E. H. Warmington: *Remains of old Latin*, vol. 3., Harvard and London (Loeb), 1938.

N. Wecklein: 'Uber Zenodot und Aristarch', *Sitzungsber. Bayer. Akad. der Wissenschaft*, 1919.

F. Wehrli: 'Die Geschichtschreibung im Lichte der antiken Theorie', *Festgabe für Ernst Howald*, Zürich, 1947, 54-71.
Demetrius von Phaleron (Die Schule des Aristoteles iv), Basel, 1949.

U. von Wilamowitz: 'Asianismus und Atticismus', *Hermes* 35 (1900) 1-52.

E. P. Wolfer: *Eratosthenes von Kyrene als Mathematiker und Philosoph*, Groningen, 1954.

W. Cave Wright: *Philostratus and Eunapius*, Harvard and London (Loeb), 1952)

P. Wuilleumier: 'La théorie cicéronienne de la prose métrique', *REL* 7 (1929 170-80.

Index of Greek Words

(Numbers in brackets refer to the notes.)

Index of Names

General Index

allegory (*allêgoria*) 55-56, 114, 116, 136(2), 194(6), 315
ambages 206-7
analogy see anomaly
anaphora 112(6)
anomaly 129, 132, 136, 161-2, 182
appropriateness 12, 97, 105, 107, 166, 178, 203, 211, 303, 345
archaism 242, 253, 284, 289, 295, 313, 319-24 *passim*
arrangement of words 97, 112, 217, 224, 297-8, 351
art (rhetoric as an) 50, 59-60, 92, 179, 201-2, 334
    (poetry as an) 152, 252
    (hiding itself) 95
Asianism see Atticism
asyndeton 99, 111-12
Atticism (and Asianism) 122-3, 181, 182-4, 187, 212, 280, 306, 326, 327, 335

brevity 98, 100, 135, 251

catharsis 61, 68-69, 75-76, 90
censorship 51-52 (in Plato); 66 (in Aristotle)
character (the tragic) 79-81
chorus (function of) 89-90, 249
colores 179, 259
comedy (and the comic) 64-65, 73, 114-15, 119, 141-2, 144-9, 187-90, 293-4, 300
contaminatio 155
controversia 257-63 *passim*

decay of eloquence 257-64 *passim*, 275-83 *passim*, 284, 309, 341, 352

declamatio 257-63, 290, 324, 356
decorum see appropriateness
delivery 94, 176-7, 303-4
deus e machina 31(3), 56(4)

eclecticism 144, 168-70
emotions of the artist 14, 56-57, 88-89, 186-7, 243, 248, 292-3, 344
epic 85-87, 248, 265-8
epideictic rhetoric 17, 104, 325
êthos 86, 291-2, 344, 346
etymology 134-5

figures of speech 122, 136(2), 350-1
formulae 137-40, 165
    of five parts of rhetoric 165, 176-7, 247, 285
    of sections of a speech 99, 100, 104-5, 139, 144, 166, 214-15, 273, 285
    of three kinds of rhetoric 17, 93-94, 165, 285
    of three styles 107-8, 111, 138, 166, 179, 180, 223
    of four styles 110, 180, 203
    of poem, poetry and poet 127, 160, 162, 240-1, 306(1)
frigidity 30(1), 96, 105, 111, 114, 343

genres (theory of) 43-44, 129, 178, 248
grammatici 104, 164, 288-9, 356

hamartia 73, 77(2), 79-80, 88, 91
historical development 268, 306, 317
history-writing 11(4), 33-37, 83-84, 156-9, 171(3), 336-8

imitation: of life 7, 24, 30, 37, 51-54, 60(1), 63, 67, 70-71, 195(2), 243, 354